THE RELIGIOUS WORLD

THE RELIGIOUS WORLD

Communities of Faith

second edition

Richard C. Bush
Joseph F. Byrnes
Hyla S. Converse
Kenneth Dollarhide

Azim Nanji
Robert F. Weir
Kyle M. Yates, Jr.
general editor

Oklahoma State University

Macmillan Publishing Company
New York

Collier Macmillan Publishers
London

The front and rear endpaper maps are based on a map reprinted with
permission from *Essentials of Geography and Development,* by Don R. Hoy.
(Copyright © 1980 by Macmillan Publishing Co., Inc.)

The religious data for the rear map was adapted with permission from
Geography: Regions and Concepts, 3rd ed., by Harm J. de Blij. (Copyright © 1981 by John Wiley & Sons, Inc.)

Macmillan Publishing Company
866 Third Avenue, New York, New York 10022

Collier Macmillan Canada, Inc.

Library of Congress Cataloging-in-Publication Data

The Religious world.

  Includes index.
  1. Religions. I. Bush, Richard Clarence, 1923–
BL80.2.R45 1988   291   87–26065
ISBN 0–02–317530–3

Printing: 5 6 7   Year: 9 0 1 2 3 4

Preface to the Second Edition

The acceptance of the first edition of *The Religious World* has been most gratifying. The number of schools using the textbook and the evaluations by those using it have confirmed our original aims and have encouraged us to upgrade and improve the earlier effort.

In this revision, the clearly stated aims of the first edition have been maintained. Our objectives are still the same: to provide a usable text for the majority of college and university students; to make available extra materials in the form of timelines, glossaries, and bibliographies to challenge the more demanding students; and to integrate it all around basic questions most frequently asked. Our use of student evaluations has proved most successful. We have continued to seek student input during the interim between editions, both those who have never before enrolled in an academic course in the subject as well as those majoring or minoring in religious studies.

Many credits are due to a variety of scholars who have assisted in the revision process. Individual authors have sought the help of specialists in their own fields, while more general evaluators have offered suggestions concerning the overall effort. Because many reviewers wished to remain anonymous, it may be better to thank all who have participated, rather than leaving out some who have made valuable recommendations for improvement.

Special appreciation is due to Helen McInnis of Macmillan Publishing Company who has been constant in her demand for excellence. She has been most helpful and understanding in her quest for the best possible revision.

It is our hope that the revised version will increase the interest of those who have supported our effort in the past and will enlist a larger contingent of programs in the future. Our ultimate goal is to make the study of world religions a primary concern in undergraduate programs around the world. Hopefully, this revision will move toward this goal.

Kyle M. Yates, Jr.

Preface to the First Edition

The authors of this book have taught an introductory course on the world's religions for a number of years. Over that span of time, we have used several textbooks and found them all problematic for our students because they fail to address the students' central interests and concerns about religion.

This book is intended to address the actual interests, concerns, and questions that students bring to a course on the world's religions. To that end, we have involved our students at several stages of this book's development. We began by discussing with our students the natural, commonsense questions about the world's religions. We then asked some of them to compare the merits of several possible ways of organizing a book on the world's religions. Later, we class-tested early drafts of the chapters with approximately 500 students enrolled in several sections of our introductory course. The students not only read the chapters, but provided us with written evaluations of the material, the format, and the level of difficulty.

We have organized this book around the questions, introduced in the first chapter, which were raised by our students. We are convinced that, although these questions are neither exclusive nor exhaustive, they are significant questions to ask about any religious tradition and that, when correctly answered, they provide some understanding of the various religions of the world. We have used questions also because we believe in the inherent importance of asking questions. Questions indicate curiosity as often as ignorance, and few of the world's great discoveries or ideas would have occurred if someone had not asked fundamental questions and then set out in a serious attempt to find the right answers.

There are several features to our book not usually found in introductory books on the world's religions. First, unlike the limited perspectives of texts written by individual authors, our book is written by a group of specialists in the major religious traditions. Several members of our group were born in or have lived for significant periods of time in cultures outside of North America and Western Europe, and thus have an understanding of the religions in these cultures based on their own experiences and observations as well as on their academic training in the history of religions.

Second, unlike anthologies containing assorted articles, our book has been written as a textbook with connecting chapters. We have worked with a common format, read and critiqued each other's chapters, and made numerous group decisions about the book's design and the teaching/learning aids to be included in the book.

Third, we have chosen to concentrate on the world's living religions. While the religions of the ancient Near East are fascinating and worthy of serious study, we prefer in this book to introduce students to religious traditions that continue to have adherents and unquestioned significance in the twentieth-century world.

Fourth, our book denotes time periods with B.C.E. and C.E. Rather than designating time periods with B.C. (before Christ) and A.D. (*anno Domini,* "in the year of the Lord"), we think it is preferable to use B.C.E. to indicate time periods *Before the Common Era* of Judaism and Christianity and to use C.E. to designate time periods during the *Common Era* of Judaism and Christianity. Thus the date 587 B.C. is written in our text 586 B.C.E., and the year 1054 A.D. is written 1054 C.E.

Fifth, our book has separate chapters on Native American religions and African religions. Rather than having a chapter on "primitive religions" and thereby suggesting that the native religions of North America and Africa are inferior to the major religions of the world, we prefer to present the beliefs and practices of these traditional religions as worthy of study in their own right.

Sixth, unlike books which attempt to wrap up the past, present, and future of religion in one concluding chapter, our book discusses the past and present situation of particular religions in every chapter, presents an entire chapter on new religions in America, and concludes with a chapter on perennial questions and quests in the religious world. Simply put, we do not claim to have the "last word" in the study of the world's religions; we do hope to raise important questions and describe significant quests worthy of continued reflection long after students have read the final chapter in this book.

In addition to these features, we have included several aids for learning which we hope will be helpful to readers:

- The definition of technical terms the first time they appear in the text.
- Time lines in the longer chapters to pull together major events and dates.
- Numerous pictures, maps, and illustrations to give a visual understanding of each religions.
- Glossaries at the end of each chapter.
- Pronunciation guides in the glossaries for terms that are difficult to pronounce.
- Suggested readings at the end of each chapter.

The maps in the front and back of the book are intended to reflect the current political and religious composition of the world. The map of the world's religions does not indicate the approximate number of adherents in each religion because such figures at best can only be very general estimates: some persons profess more than one faith, religions use varying criteria to determine membership, and some political units refuse to allow membership figures of religions to enter the public domain.

We want to express our appreciation to a number of persons who have helped us along the way. Joanna Dewey, Lionel Arnold, and Joseph Byrnes, our departmental colleagues at Oklahoma State University, have helped us with their suggestions and support. In addition, a number of persons have read portions of the book and made helpful comments, criticisms, and suggestions: Charles Adams, McGill University; Fred Denny, University of Colorado; Kathleen Dugan, University of San Diego; Robert Goldenberg, State University of New York at Stony Brook; N. Q. King, University of California, Santa Cruz; John M. Koller, Rensselaer Polytechnic Institute; Whalen W. Lai, University of California, Davis; Rabbi David Maharam; M. Muinuddin, Council of Muslim Communities of Canada; Robert Monk, McMurry College; Jacob Neddleman, San Francisco State College; Ismail Poonawala, UCLA; Benjamin Ray, University of Virginia; and Rabbi Norbert Rosenthal. Finally, Kenneth J. Scott, our editor at Macmillan, has been helpful to us at many points during the process of producing the book.

Robert F. Weir

Contents

Preface to the Second Edition   v

Preface to the First Edition   vii

1 INTRODUCTION   1
RICHARD C. BUSH

Introductory Statement of Questions   ***2***

*Beginnings   2   Sacred Literature   3   Doctrines   3
Practice   4   Institutions and Organizations   5
Branches, Divisions, and Groups   5   Religion and
Society   6   Goals   6   Religion Today   7*

The Study of Religion: Problems and Approaches   ***8***

*Special Terms   8   Managing the Mass of Data   8
Appreciating the Cultural Context   8   Attempting to
Understand Religious Experience   9   Appreciation and
Criticism   10*

2 NATIVE AMERICAN RELIGIONS   12
KENNETH DOLLARHIDE

Beginnings   ***13***

Beliefs in Supernatural and Natural Powers   ***15***

*A High God   15   Other Spirits and Powers   16
The Sacred Pipe   16*

Rituals and Selected Practices   ***17***

*The Vision Quest   18   Healing Ceremonies   20
Agricultural Ceremonies   21   Ritual Expression and
the Arts   22*

Religion, Moral Conduct, and Society   ***22***

Beliefs and Practices Relating to Death   ***24***

Native American Religions in Contact and Transition   **26**

The Ghost Dance   26   *Peyotism and the Native
American Church*   28

Native American Religion Today   **29**

3   AFRICAN RELIGIONS   32
    Azim Nanji

Beginnings   **33**

A Variety of Beliefs   **35**

The Spiritual Cosmos   35   *The Divine Being*   35   *Lesser
Gods, Ancestor Spirits, and Other Spirits*   36   *Sacred
Spaces, Places, and Symbols*   36   *Concepts of Persons in
Society*   37

Religious Institutions   **38**

Sacred Kings   38   *Prophetic Figures*   40   *Spiritual
Intermediaries*   41

Ritual Expression in African Religions   **42**

Rituals and the Stages of Life   42   *Rituals Accompanying
Hunting, Agricultural, and Pastoral Life*   44
Communication with Ancestors   44   *Ritual Expression and
the Arts*   45

Moral Conduct and Society   **47**

African Religions in Contact and in Transition   **48**

African Islam   48   *African Christianity*   48   *African
Influences in the Americas*   49

African Religions Today   **49**

4   HINDUISM   52
    Hyla S. Converse

Indus Valley Culture   **53**

Beginnings: Vedic Sources, 1500–500 B.C.E.   **55**

*Vedic Religion: The Affirmation of the Value of Human
Existence*   55

Non-Vedic Sources, 500–200 B.C.E.   **63**

*Encounter with Jainism: The Negation of the Value of
Human Existence*   65   *Encounter with Buddhism:
The Negation of the Value of Human Existence*   69

Classical and Medieval Hinduism   **71**

*The Amalgamation of the Vedic World-Affirming and the Non-
Vedic World-Negating Values*   71   *Hinduism as
Participation: The Religious Organization of Life*   71

Hinduism as Withdrawal: The Religious Release from Life 77

The Encounter of Hinduism with Islam 93

The Establishment of Islam in India 93   Relations Between Hindus and Muslims 94   Religious Developments Under Muslim Rule 96

The Sikhs 98

The Modern Encounter of Hinduism with the West 99

Four Modern Hindu Movements 100

Hinduism Today 104

Summary 105

5 BUDDHISM   **113**
Richard C. Bush

Beginnings 114

Background 114   The Founder 114

Sacred Texts 117

From Oral to Written Form 117   Structure and Content of the Texts 117

Early Buddhist Doctrine 119

The Nature of Human Existence 119   The Four Noble Truths and the Noble Eightfold Path 120   Karma and Dependent Origination 121   The Final Goal: Nirvana 122

The Practice of Buddhism 123

Devotional and Ritual Practice 123   The Moral Life 125

Relations Between Monks and the Laity 127

The Order of Monks 127   The Way of Life for the Laity 129

Theravada and Mahayana 130

Basic Teachings of Mahayana Buddhism 132

Primary Sacred Texts 133   Major Mahayana Teachings 134   Mahayana Philosophical Schools 136

Buddhism in China 138

The Initial Problem of Relating to Chinese Culture 138 Buddhist Thought and Life in China 143   Developments in the Monastic Order and Among the Laity 145

Buddhism in Japan 150

Early Developments 150   Doctrine and Practice in the Japanese Buddhist Schools 151   The Japanese Contribution to Buddhism 158

Buddhism in Tibet 159

Buddhism Today   163
    Buddhism Today in Theravada Areas   163   Buddhism
    Today in Mahayana Areas and the West   166

6   RELIGION IN CHINA AND JAPAN   171

Religion in China   171
RICHARD C. BUSH

Beginnings   172
    From Earliest Times, a Focus on Ancestors   172
    The Lord Above and the Concept of Heaven   173
    Earth and Fertility   174   Divination and Other
    Practices   175
The Confucian Approach to Religion in China   177
    The Confucian Literature   177   The Life and Teachings of
    Confucius   178   Mencius the Idealist   179   Orthodox
    Confucian Practice   180
Taoist Patterns of Religion in China   181
    Early Taoist Philosophy   181   The Shift to Religion in Taoist
    Texts   184   Taoist Practices, Groups, and Leaders   186
Folk Religion and Society   189
    Devotion Based on Function   190   Deified Heroes and
    Heroines   190
Chinese Religion and the Modern World   193
    Modern Religio-Political Movements   193   Foreign
    Religions in China   194
Religion in China Today   196

Religion in Japan   197
KENNETH DOLLARHIDE

Beginnings   198
Shinto Mythology and Beliefs   198
Shinto Institutions and Rituals   201
    Shinto Priests   201   Shinto Shrines   201   Shinto
    Festivals   202
Historical Developments in Shinto   202
New Religions in Japan   205
    Tenri-kyo   206   P. L. Kyodan   207   Rissho Kosai
    Kai   207   Soka-Gakkai   207   The Omoto
    Group   208   Ittoen   208
Religion in Japan Today   208

7 JUDAISM 213
Kyle M. Yates, Jr.

Beginnings 213

Ethnic Background 213   Patriarchal Religion 214
Moses and the Exodus from Egypt 214

Early Development 217

Pre-exilic History, 1250–586 B.C.E. 217   Religion and
Culture 219   Exilic and Postexilic Development,
586 B.C.E.–135 C.E. 223

Religious Literature 226

The Hebrew Scriptures 226   The Talmud 228
Additional Literature 229

Doctrines and Confessional Statements 230

Early Confessional Statements 230   Basic Biblical
Concepts 232   Creeds of Medieval and Recent
Judaism 234

The Practice of Judaism 235

Rituals and Worship 235   Festivals and Sacred
Seasons 237   Ethics and Society 241

Divisions and Groups 242

Early Alternative Emphases 242   Groups in Early
Judaism 244   Medieval Movements 245   Modern
Divisions 247

Goals for Believers 250

8 CHRISTIANITY 254
Joseph F. Byrnes

Beginnings 255

The Jewish World 255   The Life and Message of
Jesus 257   New Testament Interpretations of Jesus'
Message 258   Persecution and the Spread of
Christianity 263

Sacred Literature 265

Letters and Gospels 265   Context for the Development
of the New Testament 267   Later Development of
the Canon 269

Practice 269

Weekly and Annual Cycles of Worship 269   Baptism and
Eucharist 270   Liturgical Architecture 272

Doctrine 273

*The Earliest Theologians 273 Teachings of the Councils
of the Church 274 Arianism and the Council of Nicaea
(325) 274 Nestorianism and the Council of Chalcedon
(451) 275 Augustine of Hippo: Divine Grace and Human
Freedom 276*

Institutions and Organization 279

*Original "Gifts" and Subsequent "Orders" 279
Monasticism 280 Development of Papal Authority 281*

Branches, Divisions, and Groups 282

*Earlier Divisions 282 The Two Empires 282
Charlemagne and the Rise and Fall of Western
Christendom 284 The Protestant Reformation 288
Roman Catholic Counter-Reformation 297 The Holy
Orthodox Church 298*

Religion and the Formation of Modern Society 299

*The Enlightenment and Its Renaissance Foundations 299
The Age of Revolution 302 Christian Missions and the
Third World 306*

9 ISLAM   311

Azim Nanji

Beginnings: Arabia Before Islam 312

The Life of Muhammad 313

*The Early Years in Mecca 313 The Years in
Medina 315 The Death and Significance of
Muhammad 316*

The Quran 317

Quranic Teachings: Fundamental Beliefs 319

*Tawhid, the Unity of God 320 Communication from
God 320 Creations of God 321 Ummah:
The Community in Islam 322*

Quranic Teachings: Major Practices 322

*Shahadah, The Profession of Faith 323 Salat, Dhikr, and
Du'a: Acts of Worship 323 Zakat, Purification through
Sharing 325 Ramadan, the Month of Fasting 326
Hajj, The Pilgrimage 326 Other Significant Practices and
Places 329*

Life in the Ummah: Social, Political, and Moral Order 330

*The Shariah 330 The "Model" Muslim City 331
Family Life and Housing in the City 332*

Groups in Islam   333

The Kharijites (Khwarij)   334   The Shia   334
The Sunnis   337   The Muslim Philosophers   339
The Sufis   341

Islam in Contact and in Transition   344

Islam and the Medieval West   344   Islam, Africa, and
Asia   346   The Period of the Great Empires   347
Developments under European Rule and Influence   348
Islam in North America   351

Islam in the Contemporary World   352

10   NEW RELIGIONS IN AMERICA   357
Joseph F. Byrnes

Fundamental Features of the New Religions   357

Religion in America   358

Nineteenth-Century Foundations   358

Church of Jesus Christ of the Latter-Day Saints   358
Church of Christ, Scientist   362   Jehovah's
Witnesses   365

Twentieth-Century Foundations   366

International Society for Krishna Consciousness
(ISKCON)   366   Unification Church   369   Significance
of Twentieth-Century Cults   371

Other American Cultic Traditions   372

11   ENDURING QUESTIONS AND QUESTS   375
Robert F. Weir

Human Questions and Quests   375

Religion and the Question(s) of Meaning   377

A Variety of Perspectives on Religious Meaning   379

Life's Questions and Religious Meaning   379   Religious
Meaning in a Pluralistic Religious World   381

Index   385

List of Illustrations, Maps, and Time Lines

Illustrations

Deer Dance   15

Preparation of Candidate for "Shooting" Ceremony
   in Medewiwin   21

Feather Dance (Comanche)   29

The Mountain of Brightness   34

Granaries and Cliffside Burial Places of the Dogon
   in Mali   37

The Kabaka's Tomb   40

Family Ritual   45

A Chi-Wara Mask   46

Ceremonial Art Figure   46

Traditional Family Homes   49

Indus Valley Stamp-Seal   54

Limestone Figure in Yoga-like Position   55

The Vedic View of the Function of the Ritual   59

The Hindu Organization of Life   72

Shaivite Ascetic Chanting His Prayers   75

Chola Bronze Image of the God Rama   75

Bronze Image of the God Shiva   76

The Bank of the Ganges at Benares   78

Akura Invites Krishna to Mathura   84

Pilgrims at Mathura   86

Shiva-linga   89

Consort of Shiva   90

Portable Deity   104

A Sacred Tank and Temple Complex   105

Temple Entrance at Madurai   107

Stupa at Sarnath   115

Monks Before Images of the Buddha   118

The Shwe Dagon Pagoda in Rangoon   124

Peace and Calm in Bangkok   124

Thai Buddhist Worshipers   125

Thai Spirit House   126

Monks on Daily Begging Rounds   128

Hospitality to Monks   130

Buddhist Cave Sculptures at Lungmen   139

Big Wild Goose Pagoda   140

Calling the Name of Buddha   146

Three Buddhas on a Chinese Altar   147

Kuan Yin Shrine near Hong Kong   148

Chinese Buddha Image   148

Japanese Buddhist Pagoda   151

Japanese Zen Buddhist Garden   156

Longevity, Medicine, and Wisdom Buddha
   Figures   158

Tsongkhapa   160

Yung He Kung Complex   161

Buddhist Temple in Peking   163

Ancestral Tablets   173

The Judgment   175

Pai Yun Taoist Temple   183

New Taoist Temple   184

Worshiping in a Taoist Temple   185

Youth Listen to a Taoist Priest   188

"Bai-bai"-ing in a Folk Religious Temple in
   Taiwan   189

Preparing the God's Palanquin   190

Matsu, the Queen of Heaven   191

The Merging of Chinese Religious Traditions   194
Confucian Temple Restored in China   195
Ise Shrine   202
Izumo Taisha   204
Hatsumode   205
Bronze Statue of Ba'al   219
Stevens' Reconstruction of Solomon's Temple   221
Samaritan Torah Scroll   223
Model of Jerusalem   224
The Western Wall   231
Jewish Torah Crowns and Covers   233
Sukkoth Celebration   236
Seder Dinner   238
Variety of Jewish Candlelabra   239
Blowing of the Shofar   245
Synagogue at Capernaum   246
Yochanan ben Zakai Synagogue   248
Aerial View of Jerusalem   249
Two Pages of a Papyrus New Testament Showing
    Romans II:3–12   266
A 5th Century Baptismal Font   272
Floor Plan of a Typical Christian Basilica   273
Mosaic of Christ, the Pantocrator ("All-Sovereign")
    283
The Cathedral of Chartres   287
Martin Luther Posting His Theses   290
John Calvin Speaking to a Crowd   294
St. Peter's Basilica in Rome   298
Prayer Scene   313
Quranic Calligraphy   318
A Quran School   319
The Great Ummayad Mosque of Damascus   324
Inside a Mosque   325
The Ka'ba   327
A Muslim Cityscape   332
Shia Ritual   335
The Shia Imams   338
Master and Pupil   340
A Sufi Mausoleum   342

A Muslim Monument in Sarajevo, Yugoslavia   345
Islam in China   347
Dar al Islam Complex   351
An Artist's Concept of a Mormon Departure from
    Nauvoo, Illinois in Early Spring, 1846   362
Swami Prabhupada   367
Reverend Sun Myung Moon   370

Maps

Traditional Locations of Native American Tribes   14
Contemporary Locations of Native American Tribes
    in the United States   27
Africa   39
Ancient India 500 B.C.E.   64
Major Hindu Holy Places and Pilgrimage Sites   92
Modern Asia with Historic Buddhist Sites   142
Modern Provinces and Major Cities of China   176
Pilgrimage Sites and Major Modern Cities of
    Japan   199
The World of Early Judaism   218
Important Christian Centers: 6 B.C.E. to the
    Present   259
The World of Islam   312
Major Features of the Pilgrimage   328

Time Lines

Chronological Chart of the Development of Religions
    in India   56
Historical Developments in Buddhism   165
Religion During the Chinese Dynasties   192
Early History of Judaism   215
The Classical Hebrew Prophets   222
Judaism in the Common Era (C.E.)   225
Major Events and Persons in the History of
    Christianity   307
Historical Developments in Islam   343

1

Introduction

In today's highly interdependent world, it has become necessary for an educated person, who wishes to be an informed and responsible citizen, to know something of deeply rooted religious beliefs of the world's peoples. Problems of world hunger, industrialization in the Third World, changing patterns of family life, even war and peace, cannot be faced intelligently without an understanding of the religions that motivate and affect the lives of the people involved. Concerned people who wish to deal with these and other problems will find that the study of the world's religions provides basic information, an appreciation for cultural contexts, and an awareness of personal feelings, all of which are essential for proper awareness and understanding of the changing technological, social, political, and economic environments in our time. There is a great need to include within a liberal arts and humanistic framework the study of religion. Since the academic discipline of religious studies is still a growing one, it is important that a systematic inquiry of the world's religions incorporate fresh insights and methods.

To study religion because of its importance in the modern world is very different from the reasons why many people have studied it in the past. Religious believers, whether they call themselves Buddhists, Hindus, Jews, Christians, or Muslims, study their respective scriptures, teachings, and moral codes because such study is required or expected of those who profess and follow a particular faith, and encourages greater devotion to it. The role of that religion in the world and the ways

it has influenced society may be a topic within the study, but the reason for study is to become a more faithful, devoted, and informed believer. The results of such devotional study may well be considered as data for this book's approach to the world's religions, but our purpose has not been to write a book to be used by religious believers in the study of their own faith.

Rather, this book is written because we believe that the study of religion is essential to the perceptive and wide-ranging understanding of human culture that is the mark of an educated human being. There is little doubt that men and women have had some kind of religious awareness or religious experience and that they have engaged in the practice of what has been called religion for many thousands of years. Pictures that can be seen on cave walls and objects excavated from burial sites in various parts of the world clearly indicate that religious experience has been an integral and vital part of our total human experience through the ages. And anyone who pays any attention to even the briefest summary of the daily news must face the fact that religion is still an important force in the modern world.

If religion is this important, what is it? How do we define this subject we are to study? Natural scientists can state precise definitions of the physics or chemistry they teach. Social scientists are less precise about the limits of their disciplines, but are in considerable agreement about the nature of sociology, political science, and so on. In spite of the many definitions of religion that have been offered, however, there is no consensus among scholars in religious studies on a definition of the subject they study and teach.

Perhaps the major tendency among interpreters of religion is to speak of "the holy" or "the sacred," or to use the phrase "ultimate concern" to suggest the basic character of the religious experience. These terms, in turn, require extensive and rarely satisfying definitions, for they refer to that which transcends ordinary human experience and therefore can hardly be described or communicated in common, everyday language. As a basic definition one may say that religion is a configuration of doctrine and practice related to that which a community regards as sacred or fundamental to its way of life. There is usually a problem of daily life to be dealt with and a goal to be attained, with sacred texts, key personalities, and a community of like-minded persons to help along the way.

We propose, as a helpful method for understanding the world's religions, to put certain questions to each religion to be discussed. In some instances the questions provide a convenient outline for the treatment of the religion. In other instances the questions are presented as a means of summing up at the end of a chapter, which should be helpful to the reader looking back over the material covered.

The questions suggested should not be regarded as a shopping list to be used in checking the supermarket of religions. By approaching our subject through questions, we leave open the possibility that with respect to a particular religion the answer to a question may well be that it does not apply or must be rephrased. As the Buddha, regarded as the founder of the movement that bears his name, said in answer to questions about the existence of an ultimate, eternal soul: "These are questions which lead not to edifying discourse."

In the initial statement of questions that follows, we raise queries about beginnings, sacred texts, doctrines, practices, organization, divisions, relations with society, goals, and the current situation of each religion. Then one or two follow-up questions are suggested, followed by several explanatory paragraphs, as a means of getting further into each question, and in order to give the reader a glimpse of the terrain ahead. Above all we want this approach to be as open-ended as possible: there is considerable flexibility in asking the questions, and the answers can be drawn from the whole inhabited earth.

Introductory Statement of Questions

Beginnings

How did the religion begin? What do scholars know of its origins? What significance do the beginnings have for the community?

With our first set of questions, a fascinating diversity appears. In some religious movements, there is little or no historical information about beginnings, so that the community itself might answer, "We don't know," and in some instances, "It doesn't matter." Archaeologists point to artifacts from an ancient culture that may indicate reliable information or at least provide a hint or two, but precise information about the beginnings of such religions is minimal.

In many situations a core of factual and historical data may be intertwined with myths that tell more about the deeper feelings and values of a people than about historical origins. There are many types of myth, but we are interested here in myth as a story or poem that tells of what happened "in the former days" or "when our fathers walked the land." The events recounted probably cannot be verified, but such myths do not have as their aim what we regard as historical or scientific accuracy. Rather, they are an affirmation of what a people believe about themselves in relation to the cosmos and to supernatural beings. The stories may tell of the creation of the world, of various actions of gods and heroes, how a primeval couple brought forth life, and how life was maintained through such tasks as hunting and fishing. By repeating these myths, ongoing generations can identify themselves and their roles and relate themselves to the world around them and their beginnings. Thus from sacred origins a sacred history emerges, which is the the meaning of *myth,* in contradistinction to *legend,* which is a story about common things and ordinary people without the dominant activities of supernatural beings.

There are certain religious movements for which specific, datable beginnings of the community are extremely important. In Judaism, Christianity, and Islam, for example, the identification of particular events and personalities, the dating of events, and the citing of biographical detail for historic personalities become very significant. Commemorating or remembering an action or word of a key figure at a certain time is central to the total complex of these religions' doctrine and life.

One of the most interesting ways to study a religion is through the lives of its heroes, whether they lived in earlier or later times, or were founder figures or saints. These people, because of their noble deeds, sacrificial living, and devotion to what to them is holy, provide historic and living examples of what their religion means to human beings. What one finds in such lives may differ from what one finds in textbooks, including this book, but their personification of scripture, doctrine, practice, and group involvement is a most valuable resource and stimulus in the quest for religious meaning.

Much has been written, especially in the late nineteenth and earlier twentieth centuries, about the origins of religion—not necessarily the origins or beginnings of particular religions, but the origin of religion in general. These earlier generations of scholars wanted to know how *religion* began. Did human religious experience begin with the worship of one high god, or a totemic symbol, or spirits, or some powerful force? We do not intend to discuss such questions, let alone opt for any one primordial type of religious experience. However interesting it may be to wonder how it all began, such discussion inevitably tends to speculation, which goes considerably beyond our intention of studying particular religions.

Sacred Literature

How important are sacred texts for a given religion? What attitudes are expressed toward this literature? What authority do various sacred texts have in the daily lives of believers?

In Native American, African, and other cultures one may find that very little or nothing at all of the tradition has been recorded in writing. A group may depend on an oral tradition and/or an enactment in ritual for the meaning others may find in sacred texts. The constant repetition of myths and rituals has resulted, however, in a remarkably exact preservation of stories, laws, and rituals.

For each of the major world religions, in contrast, there is an identifiable text, such as the *Quran* for Muslims, or a collection of texts, such as the Buddhist *Tripitaka* ("Three Baskets"), which is held to be sacred and authoritative by that particular community. There may be the claim that the words of the founder himself are to be found in the book, or even that an almighty god has spoken to and through the transmitters or writers. The words of the text are thus to be regarded as divine commands that may not be questioned, and the quoting of a verse may settle all problems in any succeeding age.

In other situations the fact that the words of the text have been handed down from wise men of old may be sufficient to make the book authoritative for the community. A passage in the book may be regarded more as a guide, with the responsibility of making decisions resting on the individual or the community, who may turn to the text for advice or counsel only. The Five Classics of ancient China, with some exceptions, are often treated in this way.

In some religious traditions, sacred literature is ranked in authority or holiness: one book has supreme importance, but it is supplemented by commentaries that spell out in greater detail what may be stated generally or cryptically in the supreme text. Hindu literature, for example, includes *sruti*, "that which is heard," and *smriti*, "that which is remembered," which means that there is greater sanctity for the former, but the latter is no less authoritative for many situations. The *Torah* and the *Talmud* in Judaism, and the *Quran* and the *Sunnah* in Islam, are further examples. When there is a vast body of literature, as in Buddhism, a particular group may devote its whole attention to one book, such as the *Lotus Sutra*, without denigrating other works.

Despite the variety of attitudes to scriptural works, there is a continuing tendency to find in a sacred text or body of sacred literature the primary source for true doctrine, correct ritual, appropriate conduct, and the acceptable ways by which people relate to each other. It is essential, therefore, that a student of the world's religions become familiar with at least some of the more representative passages from the major texts. Most questions are more readily handled if there is some understanding of the sacred literature that is basic to a people's way of life and thought.

Doctrines

What beliefs or doctrines emerge from the sacred literature and other sources? How are these refined and developed in the history of the community?

Many students of religion tend to focus on doctrine, for doctrine is the teaching that a community accepts as true, and therefore expects those entering the community to accept as true. What people believe about the holy, what they claim to be true about the powerful reality to whom or to which they are related, is central to an understanding of the religion. Is there one god, many gods, a divine essence, or no god at all? How individuals expect to grapple with sin and suffering and ignorance, and thus discover and attain a final goal, surely comes from the depth of their lives and touches other lives. One may find doctrines about sacred books, beliefs about a particular personality such as the Buddha or the Christ, a belief about the community itself, and finally a doctrine of "last things" or *eschatology*—doctrines of the end of the world and end times.

Doctrine may be expressed figuratively as in a story about divine beings, or it may be stated categorically in a creed or catechism. It is often expressed simply, as in the Muslim Word of Witness: "There is no God but Allah, and Muhammad is his Prophet." On the other hand, the "doctors" of the Christian church, from which the English word "doctrine" is derived, have sometimes produced volume after volume in an attempt to clarify a single point of doctrine.

One of the most fascinating dimensions of doctrine, or the study of a particular doctrine, is the way the belief of a community is affected by or grows out of historical events, crises, or even happenstance. Historical evidence does not support the stereotype of religious beliefs being the product of ivory-tower musings by tired old men. Not only professional theologians and religious philosophers, but also ordinary human beings, are caught up in the ongoing human struggle out of which emerges the affirmation of what is true and meaningful.

Practice

What practices characterize the religious life? What is the role of ritual and ceremonial? How is the moral life defined and lived?

Our concern here is with what people do in order to express their faith and devotion. One could easily separate ritual practice (worship, prayer, chants, dance) from moral conduct (righteous deeds, acts of duty and charity). However, both involve the realm of action, practice, doing something, and thus, at least in this introduction, the ritual and the moral are kept together, even though it may be necessary in certain contexts to treat them as separate topics.

In any religious movement there are people who can explain little of the doctrine, but faithfully engage in certain rituals that are re-enactments of past events or divine actions. The Lord's Supper in Christianity, investiture with the Sacred Thread in Hinduism, repeating the ninety-nine beautiful names of God in Islam, even meditation on the Void in Buddhism—all vividly portray the depth of meaning of religious experience for believers. Such practices are often a vehicle of inspiration for those within and certainly evoke the interest of people outside the community. Rituals define and enhance community identity; their enactment binds its members together.

One also may say that a religious community's commitment to a moral standard, as exemplified in the lives of certain individuals, is often the most attractive feature of a religion. Usually with a foundation in certain ethical principles or commandments, the moral code proceeds to enunciate what may be done or not done in the family, in earning a livelihood, in rearing children, in marriage and divorce, in death and burial. Hinduism, Jainism, and Buddhism all affirm *ahimsa,* noninjury to any living creature. The Confucian strand in Chinese religion centers on moral obligations within the family, the state, and society. The Shinto religion in Japan, in its traditional orientation, stresses loyalty to the emperor and thus to the state.

A number of scholars have claimed that religion and ethics are best understood as separate categories, which is to contrast, for example, ritual acts and moral duty. To live a righteous life is seen by some as a better way than following prescribed ritual; others feel that, conversely, those who lose themselves in prayer transcend the social activists. In this book, our approach is to see ritual and morality in interaction: worship and prayer, for example, may motivate some persons to live according to higher moral standards. To be sure, an excess of formal rites and ceremonies may motivate others to reject ritual and turn, for example, to social service. Although it may be helpful at some points to treat them separately, we hold that religion and ethics, ritual and moral duty, are intimately related and should be studied together.

Institutions and Organizations

What sort of organizational framework prevails in a religion? What kind of institutions appear and develop? How do individuals relate to such structures?

Because religious experience in many contexts seems to be such an individual thing, especially in great heroes of the faith and in noble mystics who speak of visions of the divine reality, it is easy to ignore the communal participation that prevails. Yet human beings tend to "hang together," to think in terms of community relationships, and, in certain religious contexts at least, to develop organizational and institutional structures through which faith and life are nurtured. In fact, it is clear that human beings need, even require, the sustaining and strengthening power of some kind of an association with their fellow human beings if they are to enjoy a satisfying and meaningful religious life.

Westerners will think immediately of the Jewish synagogue or Christian church, but there are other types of religious organizations in East and West, such as monastic groups, missionary societies, centers for translation and study of sacred texts, agencies that publish and distribute literature, and a host of service and welfare organizations. There are groups, formal and informal, for professional religious leaders and for lay people, and among the laity there are associations for men, women, and youth. In this rather wide spectrum, some institutions and organizations are central and others auxiliary; but all serve to bring people together in structured relationships.

There are other religious groupings that are no different from natural groups such as the family, the village, or the tribe, and even the country or nation as a whole. One scholar has designated the Chinese Confucian tradition as "familism." African and Native American religious traditions are so closely tied up with the tribe that we may speak of Bantu or Navajo religion. And there are persons who maintain that all Japanese, regardless of their turning to Buddhism or secularism, in some sense follow Shinto, the indigenous religion of their land.

Thus people may grow up in a religious community with no thought but that they are a part of it, inheriting its traditions, as it were, with the air they breathe. There are, on the other hand, specific religious groups that one joins by affirming particular beliefs, participating in specified rituals, and undertaking certain responsibilities. Regardless of the pattern, some structure may be discerned that binds people together. This "binding" is actually one of the root meanings of the Latin word *religio,* from which our word *religion* comes.

Branches, Divisions, and Groups

Are there major branches or movements within the religion? On what basis do divisions and groups begin and continue? Are the lines of separation precise or ill-defined?

As human beings differ with respect to politics or the best ways of rearing children, so differences develop with respect to ways of life and doctrine in the religious sphere. Sacred texts are interpreted differently, one point of a doctrine or rite or organizational structure is emphasized to the neglect of some other point, and believers drift into significantly distinct camps. The resulting attitudes toward other groups may at times be sharply differentiated and bitterly antagonistic; at other times people may accept as friends and colleagues those whose convictions are profoundly different.

Some of the world's religions fall into major branches or divisions: Vaishnavite and Shaivite Hinduism; Theravada and Mahayana Buddhism; Orthodox, Reform, and Conservative Judaism; Catholic, Orthodox, and Protestant Christianity; Sunnite and Shi'ite Islam. Then there are subdivisions into what are often called denominations, sects, or schools of thought and practice. If attitudes toward other groups are open and positive, the members tend to seek out and welcome cooperative ventures with other groups, occasionally leading to reunion or union. Those who are convinced that their beliefs and way of life alone are true hesitate to associate in any significant way with another group that might compromise cherished convictions.

Still another variant in the grouping process is the development of "liberal" and "conservative" wings. Such labels are often quite inaccurate and should be avoided, but the student of religion does confront a division in many religious groups between some people who tend to be open to a wide range of new ideas and to changing patterns of life, and others who feel that the values of the past must be conserved at all costs. The result may well be that a "conservative" in one group feels much more at home with a "conservative" in another group than with a "liberal" in his own group, in spite of fundamental differences of belief.

Religion and Society

How is religion related to society as a whole? Is the relationship constant or do variations in the relationship occur? How is social change handled by a religious group?

In more traditional societies it has been noted that belonging to a religious community is almost synonymous with life itself. In such a situation it is very difficult to separate the religious from the social, so that when the student asks a person, "What is your religion?" the reply probably will be, "We have no religion; all this is just our way of life."

When religion and society are closely interrelated, religious sanctions support family life, the world of work, and government, and thus authenticate the existing social order. And it follows in almost any traditional society— Hindu, Muslim, medieval Catholic—that the social order in turn supports religious structures. Change is resisted, and the individual who proposes change is pitted against the inertia that tends to prevail in any society ("We have always done it this way"), and also against the religio-political leadership which sees itself as the preserver of society ("God has commanded us to do it this way").

This traditional blending of religion and society has steadily declined in the West for centuries, with the result that social continuity and stability sometimes have suffered and the benefit of mutual influence has been lost. The "separation of church and state" often has meant a kind of compromise as each works in a separate sphere, but bumps into the other on questions such as prayer in the public schools.

Religion and society have not always consorted together well, either in the past or in modern times. Ancient Taoists, as illustrated by the philosopher Chuang Tzu and those in secret societies, can be considered social rebels against orthodox Confucian society. The history of Christianity is replete with individuals and groups who have regarded the world as evil and left it for a monastery or to build an ideal community, which often involved yet another blending of the religious and the social. Without necessarily regarding the world or society as evil, modern Europe and America in varying degrees have tended to compartmentalize the sacred and the secular. Tension and occasional conflict have thus characterized the relationship of religion and society in both East and West.

Naturally there have been changes across the years in many contexts. Japan is an outstanding example of a society where social and political structures in the past were sanctioned by a blend of Shinto, Confucianism, and Buddhism, but that today impresses many observers as having become highly secularized. As is the case with the secularized societies of the West, however, religion countinues to give meaning to Japanese people's lives in quiet, unobtrusive ways. The formal, structural unity between religion and society may have disappeared, but some continuing mutual influence and tension are inevitable.

Goals

What goals or ends evoke the devotion and hope of religious believers? Do other-worldly or this-worldly goals seem to dominate?

In ancient China the first indication of what may be termed "religious" practice was the placing in human graves of various objects that the dead might need in the afterlife. In many other cultures there has been the recognition of some kind of continuing life beyond the grave, the provision for the needs of those who have gone on, and then, often by inference, the expression of hope that one's own life will continue happily after death. In Hinduism, there is the doctrine of the transmigration of a true, eternal self through a series of existences, the goal being first a higher existence in the next life, but finally a goal of union with the ultimate Self whose nature the individual self shares.

Thus, a happy and peaceful life after death, variously termed *immortality, eternal life,* or *entry into heaven,* is a traditional goal in Christianity and Islam. Believers want, of course, to avoid the opposite, a continuing torment of hellfire where there is punishment for one's sins. Therefore, to win joy in heaven instead of suffering in hell becomes a primary goal. Sometimes this goal of a happy, peaceful existence after death is defined more abstractly, without the vivid imagery of heavens and hells. In the Buddhist texts, for yet another alternative, Gautama the Buddha says that the question of an eternal soul, like that of an absolute divine being, is simply not a good question; he directs attention to what for him is more important: how to handle suffering in this life, with *nirvana,* the ultimate peace or cessation, as a goal.

The goals just discussed may appear to be so remote as to be meaningless. There are other goals that focus definitely on this life, on a better life in a better world, which are increasingly apparent in a number of religions. Stating the goal of the religious life in terms of what can be enjoyed in the family and in common daily life certainly characterizes many of the "New Religions" in Japan. The Social Gospel movement in twentieth-century Protestant Christianity has attempted to involve the church and church leaders in alleviating the working and living conditions of the underprivileged, which stemmed in the early part of the century from a goal of building the kingdom of God on earth. Goals that are oriented toward society thus sometimes tend to replace those distinctly oriented toward the individual. In the contemporary world, a meaningful or authentic existence, self-transformation, and just plain happiness become goals that people seek, whether for their group or for themselves as individuals.

Whereas in recent times there has been a tendency for goals to move from the other-worldly to the this-worldly in a number of religions, there also are examples of secular goals in ancient times. Vedic Indians of almost four thousand years ago asked their gods for long life, many sons, water, herds of cattle, and victory in battle. Buddhists of several East Asian schools of life and thought believe that *nirvana* and *samsara,* being caught up in birth and rebirth, are one.

Religion Today

How does religion fare in the contemporary world? How do religious groups face up to distinctly modern problems?

Those who think of religions as part of the past and therefore as having no relevance for the modern world will be surprised to find that religions have survived in rather vital and meaningful ways. Many young people have left the ways of their ancestors because such ways were out of touch with modern times, but others have been inspired by traditional religions or have been moved to initiate new movements. Whether the young or their elders stay with a religion, start a new one, or cut religious ties altogether is often determined by that religion's response to contemporary issues.

Whatever the reasons, some religions grow and others decline. The number of adherents to Islam is growing, as is the impact of Islam on the contemporary world. Buddhism lost ground in China during the twentieth century, but has won a significant following in the West. Christianity presents another mixed picture: "main-line denominations" appear to be static, while independent, evangelical, and conservative groups are growing in numbers.

The contemporary situation among religions is more complex than a matter of size or growth in numbers. A religion's concern for human suffering, resulting in particular from this century's two world wars and a host of smaller but no less terrible conflicts, is an equally important indicator of that religion's true position in the contemporary world. In the hope of ending war or establishing a just world, people have combined religious and patriotic convictions and gone to war, confident that God must be on their side. Others have been led by religious conviction to become conscientious objectors to war and to protest particular wars. Stands on such issues as the status and rights of women and minorities, drugs and alcohol, vegetarian as opposed to meat diets, prison reform, and social welfare are also measures of a religion's role in the modern world, and people may be attracted to or turned off by the stand taken; this, in turn, also affects growth or decline.

In the organizational sphere, hierarchical structures may give way to more democratic ones, but controversies in some situations have led people to accept the security of having decisions made for them, whether by a charismatic leader or by a powerful council. Tensions and struggles rise and fall between clergy and laity. In the Christian sphere, the ordination of women has been accepted by some churches, rejected by others, and is still the source of division in yet others.

Religions clearly are caught between tradition and change, and the resulting tension affects the interpretation of sacred texts, doctrinal statements, patterns of worship, the moral life, organizational structures, the relation of religion and society, and even the goals toward which the lives of believers are directed. Although the basic picture to be presented of each religion probably will remain constant, the alert student must be prepared for outright change here, a shift of emphasis there, at any time and in any place.

The Study of Religion: Problems and Approaches

The questions set forth in the previous section are suggested as a means of coming to grips with the data, as "handles" for taking hold of the material. We have observed that not all questions apply to every religion to be studied, and that restatement may frequently be appropriate. There are many other questions to be raised, and the raising of such questions is an inherent dimension of the study of religion.

In posing these questions, some picture of the world's religious terrain has emerged. Even as these questions have been raised, certain problems undoubtedly have appeared; and problems, like questions, should be faced squarely.

Special Terms

The first problem for many students is that of terminology. The sheer number of names—names of people, books, places, and concepts—plus the fact that the names come from several strange languages, seems to be almost overwhelming. Terms like *nirvana,* used above, and *tao,* which means "way" in Chinese, are essentially untranslatable, and so it is with other terms from Sanskrit and Pali, Chinese, Japanese, Arabic, Hebrew, Greek, and Latin. We have tried to keep the number of such terms to a minimum, have indicated generally accepted meanings when a word is first used, and have included a glossary at the end of each chapter.

A related problem under terminology is that there are English words that sound alike but have very different meanings, and therefore are worth a second look. *Monastic* and *monistic, ascetic* and *asesthetic,* and *ethic* and *ethnic* are confused frequently, with unfortunate and

sometimes humorous consequences. Students should remember that every discipline has its own lingo: as it is necessary to learn a vocabulary for physics or psychology or business, so it is necessary to develop a minimum working vocabulary for the study of religion. To build up one's own glossary of special or unfamiliar terms, supplementing perhaps the glossaries supplied in this text, would be a most helpful aid to study.

Managing the Mass of Data

A second problem that confronts most students is that the terms are but the gateway to a vast amount of data: texts, doctrines, practices, organizational patterns, significant personalities, and events. The questions suggested are intended to limit the quantity of data by emphasizing basic areas and avoiding unnecessary detail. A question or group of questions also may serve as an organizational device around which to hang bits and pieces of information that relate to doctrine or practice or sacred texts, so that they may be viewed in an overall context. The body of data, although voluminous, is manageable and is a testimony to the richness of the field of study in which we are engaged.

Appreciating the Cultural Context

The context within which a doctrine or practice is viewed presents a more subtle problem than that of terminology or voluminous information. Since it is virtually impossible to find a religion in which *love* is not taught in one way or another, it is easy for some students to conclude that the teaching of love is common to all religions and that all religions can unite on the basis of love. This conclusion ignores the fact that the concept of love as taught in a particular religion is conditioned by the historical background, the personalities of the people who taught and practiced love, the social customs that affect the way people love each other, the ways in which love is depicted in literature and art, and a host of other cultural factors that condition the teaching and practice of love in any religion. Therefore, the cultural context of any doctrine or ritual or organizational pattern must be considered.

In the shaping of the cultural context, the student of

religion is privileged to draw upon the work and findings of scholars in a host of disciplines. Certainly the work of historians is important, particularly those historians who are sensitive to the significance of religion for the personalities and events that shape history. Philosophers are particularly helpful in analyzing and interpreting the ideas of a tradition. This is true of both the philosophers who belong to the tradition and those outside the tradition, whether they are appreciative or critical of it.

Many psychologists are interested in religious experience as a phenomenon of human behavior, and, thus, have produced fascinating studies of religious experience. Sociologists are often concerned with the grouping and organization of religious communities, and with religion as a force in society. Anthropologists have shed light on the role of religion in early or traditional societies: the ways in which religious rites and ceremonies bind a community together, the role of a chief or *shaman* in the life of the people, and what myths say of a tribe's self-understanding and identity. Myths may be approached as literature, as in the discipline of comparative literature, where scholars analyze, interpret, and compare side by side the writings of very different peoples and cultures. The techniques of literary criticism have proved most helpful in the critical study of religious texts, although there are persons in any religion who object to a "critical" study of a text held to be sacred.

The appreciatiion of the arts—painting, sculpture, architecture, music, theatre, dance—is an area of study, in fact of living, that is intimately related to the study and understanding of religion, and, therefore, may be the most important element in the contextual framework of a religion. There are people who have devoted themselves completely to the study of Hindu sculpture or Shinto architecture, with the result that our understanding of Hinduism or Shinto has been advanced profoundly. A work of art is an expression of the artist's feelings, the meaning of which can seldom be expressed adequately by logic or reason. In order to appreciate a painting or a dance movement, it is necessary to identify in a vicarious way with the artist, to try to feel or be sensitive to what the artist feels. The way we identify with a certain character in a play or film is an excellent illustration of the way we may identify with someone involved in a religious experience that we have never had.

Attempting to Understand Religious Experience

As appreciation of the arts is a key element in understanding the context of a religion, so the arts may provide assistance in understanding the major problem in the study of religion. There is something distinctive about religious experience that eludes the kind of study we apply to other disciplines and that can never be understood solely on the basis of factual data alone. Religious experience for most people has been extremely difficult to put into words, for as a total experience it reaches great peaks of emotional intensity and depths of dry tedium, ennobles human personality and then degrades it, becomes intimately personal but never loses its community roots.

A few examples are sufficient for illustration at this point. Muslim and Hindu mystics write beautifully of their visions of the divine, but neither casual reading nor scholarly analysis can communicate what the divine really is. What does it mean to meet God in a burning bush as Moses did, or to say with John Wesley, the eighteenth-century founder of Methodism, "I felt my heart strangely warmed . . ."? In the sixth century B.C.E., a man named Gautama, who was to become the Buddha, left a princely home, spent six years studying and following various teachings and disciplines, and then found enlightenment; but his restrained, almost poetic language hardly describes what enlightenment really means.

In each of these instances the experience can be explained in part by reference to the historical and cultural setting of the age, but the depth of meaning eludes such explanation. The more routine experiences of those whose lives proceed in very ordinary ways, punctuated by visits to a mosque on Friday or a church on Sunday, also are difficult to describe clearly and fully. But in some manner analogous to the way we appreciate a painting or identify with an actor in a play, we can be sensitive to the religious experiences of others, empathize with them, and attempt, at least imaginatively, to sit where they sit and walk in their shoes.

What has been said must in no sense be understood as an effort to sidestep whatever is strange or unusual to us or different from any experience we have ever had. One may be tempted to dismiss other religions as the work of "a bunch of weirdos," or to blur differences by a facile identification, such as "Buddhist meditation is just Christian prayer when you really get down to it." Neither extreme will do. One must attempt to look at all that is brought together in each of the religions to be studied as a distinctive configuration or pattern of doctrine, practice, and grouping that is designated *Hinduism, Buddhism,* or any of the other names that identify the religions to be studied.

It is also tempting to try to explain away whatever seems strange or illogical. According to the Buddhist texts, the Buddha said repeatedly that life is suffering, that pain is a fundamental characteristic of human experience. A person who is happy and basically optimistic about the future may find the Buddha's assertion difficult to understand. "How could he be so pessimistic? Surely he didn't really mean that!" One wonders if our optimistic friend has heard about malnutrition and world hunger, the number of people who go to bed each night without sufficient food and without any prospects for food tomorrow. But regardless of the blinders we may wear with respect to conditions in our own era, we distort and condescend when we try to make a very different view of human existence fit ours, and thus fail to face up to the resounding message that the Buddha or Muhammad or some other religious figure set forth so clearly and distinctively.

Appreciation and Criticism

The problem of bias may well be considered at this point. Many sincere people have studied the religions of the world in order to demonstrate that all religions are inferior to the one they profess to follow. The inadequacies of such an approach, as well as the probable distortions, should be apparent. There are other people who are so enamored of the new ideas and values they find in various religions that they can find nothing of value in their own traditions. That approach clearly has its weaknesses, too. And if this should lead someone to think that having no religion leaves one completely objective to approach the study of religion, then the question must be raised whether someone who has rejected a fundamental component of human life is not the most biased of all.

One who is interested in methodological problems in the study of religion—how scientific or objective can we be; what shall we do with truth claims; can a descriptive approach alone be satisfactory—will find an increasing literature on the subect. A selected few of these volumes are listed in the bibliography that follows, but digging into the study of the religions themselves, pausing occasionally to reflect on questions of method, is our first priority.

Complete freedom from any bias, indeed complete objectivity, in the study of religion may neither be possible nor desirable. What is possible and highly desirable is a working balance of appreciative and critical attitudes. The need to be sensitive to the religious experience of other people by trying to identify with them must be balanced by the corresponding need for times of detachment, when students pull back from what has captivated them and adopt an attitude of critical detachment. We can become so enamored of the religions we study that we are unable to face up to the charlatans who can be found manipulating the faithful in any religious context. We may become so engrossed, on the other hand, in listing the many foibles of a religious leader that we miss the outstanding contribution that he was ultimately able to make. Our approach is to study any religion as a whole, to look at problem areas along with the nobler and more meaningful expressions of religious experience, and, within the limits of our data and our capacities for dealing with it, to see religion as a fundamental dimension of human existence.

SUGGESTED READINGS

BANTON, MICHAEL, ed. *Anthropological Approaches to the Study of Religion*. London: Tavistock Publications, Ltd., 1966.

ELIADE, MIRCEA. *The Quest: History and Meaning in Religion*. Chicago: University of Chicago Press, 1969.

_____. *The Encyclopedia of Religion*. 15 vols. New York: Macmillan, 1987.

GEERTZ, CLIFFORD. "Religion as a Cultural System" in his *The Interpretation of Cultures*. New York, 1973.

KITAGAWA, JOSEPH M., ed. *The History of Religions: Retrospect and Prospect*. New York: Macmillan, 1985.

SMART, NINIAN, *The Phenomenon of Religion*. New York: Seabury Press, 1973. [*See also* Professor Smart's article entitled "The Study and Classification of Religions" in the *Encyclopaedia Britannica*, 15th Edition, Volume 26 of the *Macropaedia*, 1985, 548–568.]

WACH, JOACHIM. *The Comparative Study of Religion*. Edited by Joseph M. Kitagawa. New York: Columbia University Press, 1958.

YINGER, MILTON. *The Scientific Study of Religion*. New York: Macmillan, 1970.

2

Native American Religions

Living all over the North American continent since as early as 40,000 to 20,000 B.C.E., Native Americans have spoken many different languages and developed significantly different ways of life. They have developed advanced agricultural societies such as those of the Hopi and the Pima in the Southwest, and the Algonquin and the Delaware in the Northeast. The Plains tribes, in contrast, have primarily been nomadic hunting societies; prominent among these were the Comanche in the Southwest and the Sioux and the Crow in the northern plains. Each of these societies evolved a different religious tradition, and even tribes living in close proximity to each other often had significantly different beliefs, myths, and ceremonies. These various traditions expressed the particular ways in which Native Americans understood their relationships to each other and to the world in which they lived.

As a consequence of these diverse traditions, Native Americans do not have one completely unified religious system with clearly defined doctrines. Nevertheless, most Native American religions share some common beliefs and practices. Most have beliefs in a Vital Force, Supreme Deity, or High God; and they all have concepts of a sacred person or persons who act as intermediaries between the high god and the tribe. They share common beliefs in the existence of other gods and spirits, they engage in rituals and initiation ceremonies that are believed to have religious significance, and they have long-standing beliefs and practices about dying, death, and bereavement.

Unfortunately, certain aspects of traditional Native American religions are sometimes taken out of context

in films, novels, and television programs. Hollywood film producers, for example, sometimes portray Native Americans as master ecologists, communing with the Great Spirit and dancing or drumming to bring rain. In other instances, Native American rituals are portrayed as exotic or even barbaric, and are highlighted for the apparent purpose of producing thrills or shudders in the viewing audience.

In this chapter, we will discuss the traditional religions which have been practiced by Native Americans in various parts of Canada and the United States. We will trace among these religions both common themes and differences of perspective. As our sources, we will use oral traditions and some of the recorded accounts of religious myths, rituals, and ceremonies made by Native Americans, Christian missionaries, and scholars in several academic disciplines.

It must be remembered, however, that even in the most scholarly study or close observation of a ritual or ceremony by an outsider, much will remain a mystery because of four constraints involved in the study of Native American religions. First, Native American religions are cultural religions, involving the beliefs and practices of particular tribes in particular geographical locations. Persons who do not belong to a particular tribe are thereby restricted in what they can learn about it. Second, Native American religions demand long, involved initiation rites for their own tribal members, and even then many tribal members are never fully initiated into more than one aspect of a particular rite. It is, therefore, almost impossible for a non-Native American ever to be completely initiated into all of the aspects of a tribal religion. Third,

Native American religions are primarily oral traditions. Unlike most of the religions discussed in this book, there is not extensive written material about Native American beliefs and practices because this information has generally been passed on from generation to generation by word of mouth instead of being put in written form. Fourth, many tribes have been virtually annihilated either through intertribal warfare or by European expansion. We thus have practically no information about their religious beliefs and practices.

The descriptions of religious beliefs and practices in this chapter represent diverse tribes and geographical areas. Selected examples come from Eastern woodland tribes, Southeastern tribes, Plains tribes, Southwestern tribes, Northwestern tribes, and Canadian tribes. Particular rituals and traditions are singled out for their value in illustrating common themes or patterns, or occasionally to establish points of contrast among Native American tribes.

Beginnings

Creation myths, or imaginative stories about the beginning of the earth, have traditionally been a common feature of Native American religions. These stories developed as an attempt by Native Americans, as well as persons in a variety of other cultures, to answer certain basic questions about human existence. How did the world begin? Did it simply evolve, or did one or more divine powers cause it to come into existence? How did human beings, other animals, and plants come into existence?

In most of the creation myths of Native Americans, there was no distinct separation made between human beings and animals, trees, or even the earth itself. Only gradually, according to these stories, did humans become masters over the buffaloes, the birds, and all of nature. Because of this concept of a close relationship between humans and the natural world, Native Americans have had a deep and profound respect for the very things they have come to master. Some of the most profoundly religious songs and ceremonies of Native Americans have developed out of this close and mystical relationship. For example, the Osage (Southern Plains) have preserved the following creation story:

Way beyond, a part of the Osage lived in the sky. They desired to know their origin, the source from which they came into existence. They went to the sun. He told them that they were his children. Then they wandered still further and came to the moon. She told them that she gave birth to them, and that the sun was their father. She told them that they must leave their abode and go down to the earth and dwell there. They came to the earth, but found it covered with water. They could not return to the place they had left, so they wept, but no answer came to them from anywhere. They floated about in the air, seeking in every direction for help from some god; but they found none. The animals were with them, and of all these the elk was the finest and most stately, and inspired all the creatures with confidence; so they appealed to the elk for help. He dropped into the water and began to sink—then he called to the winds, and the winds came from all quarters and blew until the water went upward as in a mist.

At first rocks only were exposed, and the people traveled on the rocky places that produced no plants, and there was nothing to eat. Then the water began to go down until the soft earth was exposed. When this happened, the elk in his joy rolled over and over on the soft earth, and all his loose hair clung to the soil. The hair grew, and from them sprang beans, corn, potatoes, and wild turnips, and then all the grasses and trees.[1]

There are several types of creation myths, but among Native American tribes two types of creation stories stand out as the most common. The first type of creation account depicts creation as coming out of chaos; the second type suggests that the world was created as a result of violence between the forces of good and evil.[2]

In the myths in which creation comes out of chaos, the most common form is that of an "earth diver" story in which some animal or primeval man emerges out of water or the inner world, discovers the earth, and brings animals and plants into being out of chaos. The account of the Crow (Northern Plains) is representative of this type of creation story:

In the beginning the earth was covered by water. Old Man Who Did Everything was wandering over the water. He heard voices and found four ducks, two large blue-eyed ducks and two small red-eyed ducks. Old man Who Did Everything asked the ducks to dive under the water in order to discover if anything existed. After the two large ducks failed to discover anything, the two small ducks dived and returned with mud in their bills. Out of this mud Old Man Who Did Everything created the sky, plants, trees, animals, and finally humans. After testing the humans he created, he sent two groups away, and kept the bravest group with him. This group became the Crow people.[3]

Traditional Locations of Native American Tribes

North Alaskan Eskimo
Koyuken
Alaskan Eskimo
Ingalik
Tanana
Taniana
Kutchin
Aleut
Eyak
Tutchone
Teslin
Copper
Kaska
Eskimo
Tlingit
Tahltan
Niska
Slave
Caribou Eskimo
Baffin Island Eskimo
Gitskan
Beaver
Chipewyan
Tsimshian
Sarsi
Labrador Eskimo
Sekani
Blackfoot
Swampy Cree
Bella Bella
Haisla
Blood
Plains Ojibwa
Woods Cree
Mistassni Cree
Naskapi
Nootka
Piegan
Makah
Beothuk
Salish Kootenai
Plains Cree
Ojibwa
Salish
Assiniboin
Algonguin
Huron
Yakima
Nez Perce
Flathead
Ottawa
Abnaki
Arikara
Ojibwa
Penobscot
Klamath
Crow
Hidatsa
Mandan
Menomini
Huron
Pennacook
Modoc
Bannock
Cheyenne
Santee
Sauk
Iroquois
Algonquians
Shastra
Teton
Yankton
Fox
Potawatomi
Tobacco
Yurok
Northern Paiute
Kickapoo
Neutral
Delaware
Pomo
Ponca
Winnebago
Erie
Susquehanna
Nanticoke
Maidu
Shoshoni
Omaha
Iowa
Miami
Powhatan
Costanoan
Yana
Southern Paiute
Ute
Pawnee
Illinois
Tutelo
Salinan
Wintu
Minok
Oto
Missouri
Chumash
Yokuts
Ute
Kansa
Osage
Shawnee
Cherokee
Pamlico
Gabrielino
Navajo
Jicarilla
Kiowa
Catawba
Tuscarora
Mohave
Hopi
Rio Grande
Quapaw
Chickasaw
Yuman
Zuni
Pueblos
Comanche
Wichita
Caddo
Creek
Luiseno
Western Apache
Tonkawa
Natchez
Choctaw
Timulua
Pima
Chiricahua
Mescalero
Atakasa
Lipan
Karankawa
Calusa
Coahuiltec

An example of the second type of myth, in which the earth comes into existence out of violence between two conflicting forces, can be seen in the creation myth of the Seneca (Eastern woodlands). According to this story, the bride of the Sky Chief fell from heaven and landed on the back of a turtle, from which the earth grew. Later, after being impregnated by the wind, the woman gave birth to twins. As they grew up, the twins moved over the earth creating whatever was needed:

One twin made the good things like the sun, moon, stars, vegetables, and fruit. The other twin created all the evil things like flies, gnats, bats, frogs, owls, worms, snakes, and carnivorous monsters. He changed streams so they only ran one way and broke them up with rapids and whirlpools and waterfalls. He caused corn to grow smaller and less tasty, made caves, spread sickness, storms, ice, and death. Although the Good Spirit was not able to correct all the evil his brother did, he was able to change most of it. And this is why we have more good then evil in the world today.[4]

These creation myths were believed to depict actual historical events. Native Americans have usually had a reverent attitude toward nature and have experienced themselves as playing an active part in the continuing growth process of the earth. By telling the creation stories, they believed that they were influencing the universe and the gods and spirits; by repeating the stories, they believed that they were literally keeping the world alive. These creation myths also served the function of establishing a bond between the Creator, humans, and all of nature. Through imaginative language and graphic imagery, the stories helped to explain the world in which a particular tribe lived—by establishing important connections between present and past, between humans and other creatures in nature, and between the world and the spiritual force or forces that brought it into being.

Beliefs in Supernatural and Natural Powers

Native Americans have traditionally believed in a variety of supernatural and natural powers. In an evironment believed to be populated by numerous gods or spirits, many have believed in a high god who exists far up in the sky and keeps in contact with life on earth through

Deer Dance. *This is a Pueblo ceremony at Picuris, New Mexico. The ceremony involves the miming of the hunting of deer, elk, and other large animals. (Courtesy of Donald N. Brown)*

various intermediaries or messengers. They have believed that the earth was their mother, and regarded most events in the natural world as having religious significance. They have also believed that certain persons and objects possess unusual spiritual power.

A High God

The belief in a high god, or creator god, has been a common feature of many Native American religions. Regardless of how distant the high god may be from the daily needs of the people, it has nevertheless been a prominent feature of the belief systems of tribes ranging from the Algonquin in the Northeast to the Paiute along the West Coast. The Seminole (Southeast U.S.), for example, have understood the high god as the one "who makes everybody's breath" and who sends either a human or semidivine intermediary to give assistance to the people.[5]

The ways in which the high god is recognized in rituals and ceremonies have varied from tribe to tribe. In some tribes the high god has been referred to only during certain religious rituals; outside of these rituals, the high god was never mentioned. In other tribes the high god was regarded as a great mystery that could never be fully comprehended. The high god could, however, be pleased or displeased; its aid could be secured by propitiation and ritual action; and it could communicate with human beings through various "messengers" that might be either solicited or unsolicited. It was primarily through these messengers that Native Americans believed that they had contact with the high god.

Other Spirits and Powers

The multitude of spirits and powers found in Native American religions can be illustrated through the beliefs of the Zuñi, a group of the Pueblo, who have been called "one of the most thoroughly religious people of the world."[6] Traditionally, the Zuñi society (Southwest U.S.) has been a theocracy, or a society run by divine guidance, with control vested in a three-member council composed of *shamans;* these shamans have been believed to have special powers given to them from the spiritual world. Because of their abilities to explain unusual events, to communicate with various spirits and powers, and to predict future happenings, these shamans have always been the unquestioned spiritual leaders of the tribe. They have appointed officers to the tribal council with the responsibility of dealing with the secular affairs of the village, the civil law, and the United States government. Then, having delegated these secular matters, the shamans have devoted their time and energy to overseeing the myriad religious societies and ceremonies that characterize life in a Zuñi village.

There are six different religious "orders," or dancing societies, in a typical Zuñi village. The names of the dancing societies are derived from the particular ceremony or set of ceremonies for which the group is responsible, with the result that the societies are known as the sun, the rainmakers, the *kachinas* (spirits under water), the shamans of the *kachinas,* the war gods, and the healing gods.[7] All of the dancing societies as a group are called *kivas,* a name also used to designate the circular chambers under the ground where the dancing ceremonies usually take place. Each of the dancing societies performs in public at least three times each year, and their elaborate preparations are intended to ensure that every color and part of their costumes, every gesture in their dances, and every song they sing is done without mistake. The dancers are young men in the tribe, each one being sponsored by a ceremonial father who has the responsibil-

ity of training the young man in the particular ceremonies of a specific dancing society.

The most famous of these ceremonies is the *kachina* ceremony, a masked dance devoted to the spirits who live under the water. The Zuñi believe that the *kachinas* visit the village once a year, at which time they are impersonated in the dance by a Zuñi man wearing a *kachina* mask and costume. It is believed that when a dancer wears the mask, he becomes the *kachina.* The mask is thus considered to be very sacred, and is burned when the wearer of the mask dies.

There are other ceremonies devoted to other spirits and powers. Some of the ceremonies are performed by shamans in private, for the purpose of healing individual members of the tribe. Other ceremonies are public affairs in which the Zuñi social organization employs diverse methods for dealing with supernatural powers. In addition to the dancing societies, for instance, a Zuñi village also has twelve medicine societies that use their own variations of "secret power" in dealing with gods and spirits. These methods or "powers" include special songs, sand paintings, and the use of herbs and roots.[8]

In their various religious ceremonies, the Zuñi do not humble themselves before the gods or spirits. Instead, they often taunt the spiritual powers. They also believe that, once the specific rituals of a ceremony have been completed, the gods and spirits will grant whatever the shamans have requested. Only when the desired results are not forthcoming do the Zuñi bargain with the gods, using flattery and other methods to appeal to them.

Each god or spirit is believed to have a definite function, domain, and color, and is responsible for protecting all of the people who are members of the Zuñi society. The water serpent, for instance, is the guardian of all sources of water. other deities are responsible for hunts, for the home, and for the medicine societies. And some deities are, in fact, mythical persons who have become cultural heroes known as tricksters. Regarded as being both human and divine, the tricksters are believed to use cunning and daring to teach moral values to members of the tribe.

The Sacred Pipe

Traditionally, one of the universal religious symbols of Native Americans has been the pipe. Indeed, it has been said that "the whole meaning of human existence is bound up with the ritual of the pipe."[9]

As a result, there have been many myths and legends that have explained the origin of the pipe. Some of the stories of Plains and Woodland tribes attempted to explain the origin of the red clay, called *calumet*, which was used to make the pipes; other stories focused more directly on the origin of the pipe itself. The Pawnee, for example, claimed to have received the calumet as a gift directly from the sun.[10] A Sioux legend, in contrast, described how two young men on a hunt came upon a beautiful woman who said that she was on a mission to deliver a gift to their village from the high god. That gift was the pipe, and she explained that the high god wanted them to use the pipe in all of their ceremonies.[11]

The ceremonial pipes were made in various shapes and with very distinct decorations. Some pipes were straight, some were curved, some had the bowl at an angle, and some were made with multiple bowls. The early pipes were often called "cloud-blowers," because in order to draw on them it was necessary to tilt the head back as if one were smoking to the sky.[12] Most pipes were elaborately decorated with figures of animals, birds, and human faces. Horsehair, beads, and feathers were also used as decorative material on the pipes. After Native Americans came into contact with white people, metal pipes were sometimes used.

The Eskimos had very unusual pipes made of bone, ivory, stone, and metal. The stems of the pipes were often made from two pieces of wood, with small plates that could be opened to clean the pipes. The bowls of the pipes were often carved into the shape of arctic animals, such as the seal or whale.

The importance of the pipes can hardly be overemphasized. They were used in all ceremonies, in greeting important guests, in ratifying treaties and contracts, and as passports. One indication of their importance is the statement of marquette, a seventeenth-century Jesuit priest:

there is nothing more mysterious or more remarkable. So much honour is not rendered to the Crowns and sceptres of kings as they render to the calumet [pipe]. It seems to be the god of peace and war, the arbiter of life and death. It is enough to carry it with one and to show it in order to journey with assurance in the midst of enemies, who, in the height of combat, lower their arms when it is displayed. It is for this that the Illinois gave me one to serve as a safeguard among all the nations by whom I must pass in my travel.[13]

Another indication of the importance of the pipe is the fact that the gift of the pipe was traditionally considered the closest tie between two men. The bestower was often called father, and the recipient son. The exchange of the pipe represented an inviolate bond between the two individuals. Thus the pipe was a symbol of sincerity, peace, and brotherhood, and oaths made with it were holy oaths that could not be broken.

Rituals and Selected Practices

Native Americans have observed that in nature, everything sacred comes in fours. Four seasons dictate harvest and hunting patterns, four directions orient the hunter and the warrior, and most animals walk on four feet. Accordingly, many Native American tribes have explained that human life is divided into four cycles: infancy, youth, adulthood, and old age. There have been accompanying rituals and rites of passage through which each individual tribe acknowledged the acceptance of a member into one of these stages.

The first stage, infancy, was initiated immediately after birth, with the particular customs surrounding infancy differing from tribe to tribe. In some tribes (e.g., the Apache and the Comanche), the umbilical cord was taken, dried, placed in a bag, and then hung on the child's cradle. The cradle was incensed at the four corners, and the child was prayed over and blessed by a Native American doctor or medicine man.

In other tribes (e.g., the Papago in the Southwest), a special hut was constructed for a woman who was about to give birth. She remained there, attended by her female relatives, for a period of time whose length depended in part on the gender of her baby: if the baby was a boy, the mother remained in the hut for a month; if the baby was a girl, the mother was expected to resume her normal responsibilities after only two days. During the waiting period, the tribal members believed that the soul entered the baby's body assuring that the birth was neither an accident of nature nor a trick of the gods. At the conclusion of the waiting period, the child was presented to the sun and "given a name of good omen from the dreams of a shaman."[14] After the naming ceremony the child had a place in the tribal community and was taught simple tribal customs, such as respect for elders and the sharing of property.

With the passage into youth, at the age of seven or eight in most tribes, the child was initiated into the tribe. In many tribes this initiation began with a solitary fast in which the child was separated from the tribe for a period of up to ten hours. The time of the fasting was gradually increased until the child went a period of ten days or more without any food, and only a little water was permitted while the child waited for a vision that would determine his or her direction in life. When the vision came, a feast was held in honor of the child, who now had a special place in the community.

The period when a young person entered adulthood was a period of courtship, marriage, career, and acceptance of the responsibilities of being a member of the tribal society. Courtship was traditionally a very complex process. The young woman, except for the times when she attended to her daily tasks, was always chaperoned by her maternal grandmother or by some other older female relative. The young man tried to find her when she was alone, and then attempted to attract her attention. If she was interested in him, she spoke to him for a few moments before returning to her task. Another ploy used by many young men was that of serenading the young woman at night with a flute. Occasionally the young woman would be allowed to step outside her parents' lodge to speak to her suitor, or in some cases to several suitors who were serenading her. Among the Ponca, Omaha, and other Plains tribes, the young woman finally indicated her choice of a mate by "standing in his blanket."

The marriage ceremony itself often consisted of a simple exchange of gifts between the parents of the bride and the groom. This ritual was followed by a feast and dancing. Then the newlyweds moved to their new lodge. Although quite simple, the ceremony was particularly important to the young man because many tribes did not consider a young male a "man" until he was married. Single males were not allowed to participate in many rituals and ceremonies. After marriage, the young man could take part in a number of tribal rituals that had been previously closed to him. For example, after mar-

riage a young hunter could learn additional lessons about hunting, while a young warrior could perfect the skills necessary for him to assume his place of responsibility in the tribe.

The final stage was old age, and the treatment of older adults varied from tribe to tribe. In most tribes they were respected as repositories of sacred knowledge and wisdom that they were to transmit to the next generation, but they were not regarded as persons for whom younger tribal members had unending responsibility. Some tribes developed specific end-of-life rituals. For example, when a man reached old age in the Omaha tribe, he was expected to go out into the prairie, smoke his pipe, and look back over his life to examine the tings that had been important: his first vision quest, his first hunt, his first war party, and his comrades who had died before him. Having finished his pipe, he was expected to empty the ashes on the ground and return to his lodge singing a song that would teach his grandchildren about tribal values and historical events. When he had completed the ritual, he waited patiently to complete the cycle of his life.

Many of the rituals and ceremonies of Native Americans emerged out of the changes they observed taking place in nature and in the human life cycle. Rites having to do with the changes in nature, such as hunting rites and agricultural rites, were aimed at assuring a good hunt or a good crop, and usually involved the entire tribe or clan. Other rites had to do with changes in the lives of individuals. Puberty rites, for example, represented passages of initiation into womanhood or manhood. The rite connected with passage into adulthood was usually characterized by fasting, physical ordeals, and a symbolic transition from death to rebirth as a new adult member of the society. While the age of the participant and the duration of the ordeal varied from tribe to tribe, the essence of the rite was always the same: a quest for a vision, a song, or a dream that would serve to indicate to the youth and the tribe that some divine power would serve as his personal guardian.

The Vision Quest

The vision quest has traditionally been one of the most important ritual practices among most Native American tribes. All important undertakings had first to be received in a vision. Any change in tribal rituals, the conduct of war, hunting practices, songs, or even the giving of names had first to be authorized in a vision. For many tribes, the vision was the source of all things sacred.

The Sioux vision quest is representative of the quests performed by most Plains tribes. For the Sioux, the vision quest is one of the oldest and most important rituals. Traditionally, it has been regarded as serving several purposes: preparing warriors for the warpath, making warriors brave in battle, curing sick relatives, offering thanksgiving to spirits and powers, and asking favors of the high god. The traditional importance of the vision quest is evidenced by a statement of Black Elk, a Sioux medicine man:

> The crying for a vision ritual, like the purification rites of the *Inipi* (steam bath), was used long before the coming of our most sacred pipe. This way of praying is very important, and indeed it is at the center of our religion.[15]

While open to both males and females, the vision quest was traditionally expected of all males. Even if a man had no part in other religious activities, he was expected to perform the vision quest because the quest played a central role in determining his life-style and lifework. It was through the vision experience, or lack of it, that each man received his relative role in the society, his place in hunting parties and war parties, his right to perform certain religious functions, and his overall status among his people.

The direct bearing the vision quest had on an individual's life can be seen in the case of the *Heyoka,* or clown, whose vision was that of the *Wakinyan,* or Thunderbird. This particular vision required the one who had it immediately to begin conducting himself in a manner completely contrary to normal convention: to wash his body in dirt and dry it in water, to wear winter clothing in summer, and to wear summer clothing during the winter months.[16] This person was considered to be the bearer of sacred power; his function and position was thought of as holy. This admittedly extreme form of the vision quest illustrates how influential the vision was in determining an individual's role in the Sioux society.

Before anyone could perform the vision quest, it was first necessary to seek out the assistance of a shaman who would perform the secondary rites connected with the quest and also serve as a spiritual guide. After the shaman had been contacted, the individual preparing for the quest withdrew from other members of the tribe for a short period of fasting, the end of the period being marked by the taking of the *Inipi,* or steam bath. Immediately following the *Inipi,* the young man left camp accompanied by two assistants who prepared the hilltop on which the vision quest would take place. When the site had been prepared, the assistants returned to the tribe. The selection of the site was crucial. Black Elk describes it in the following manner:

> When the assistants arrive they enter the chosen place by walking in a direction always away from their camping circle, and they go directly to the spot which they have chosen to be the center and place all of the equipment there. At this center they first make a hole, in which they place some *kinnikinnik* (Indian tobacco), and then in this hole they set up a long pole with the offerings tied at the top. One of the helpers now goes about ten strides to the west, and in the same manner he sets up a pole here, tying offerings to it. He then goes to the center where he picks up another pole and this he fixes at the north, again returning to the center. In the same manner he sets up poles at the east and south. All this time the other helper has been making a bed of sage at the center, so that when the lamenter is tired he may lie with his head against the center pole, his feet stretching eastward.[17]

The ritual site and the manner in which it was constructed had symbolic meaning. The assistants were symbolically constructing the world. The establishment of the directions was also symbolically applied to the four periods of time (the day, the night, the month or moon, and the year) and the four stages of life (infancy, youth, adulthood, and old age). All of these "fours" were understood as points on a circle, and thus the vision quest site formed a circle.

One of the most important aspects in understanding the vision site was the traditional belief that the four directions and the four times were possible only in reference to the center. This arrangement meant that the world, or universe, depended entirely upon the center; if the center collapsed, the world itself might collapse. The "center," however, was understood neither as some mystical spot nor as a place. Rather, Black Elk states that "Anywhere is the center of the World."[18] Alexander explains the meaning of the "center" in terms of the individual person; wherever the person stands, marks the center point:

The quaternity of the cardinal directions . . . is a mathematical construction, but it is one developed not from chance, but from a reason universal to mankind, and that reason is to be found in the human skeleton itself. Man is upright, erect in his active habit, and he is four-square in his frame, and these two facts give him his image of a physical world circumscribing his bodily life . . . the axial dimension of the universe is thus deduced from the standing position of man.[19]

A world view such as this has two corollaries. First, the entire world is bound together in a kind of dependent unity. Since the directions depend on the center as a defining point, it is also true that the defining point is a defining point only in terms of the directions. Second, individuals are completely responsible for maintaining the cosmos. If the individual should fail in the vision quest, the structure of existence might collapse. Thus, each individual has a responsible role in maintaining the order of the world.

This symbolic centering of the quest site has traditionally extended to many other Sioux practices. The same kind of procedure for laying out the "center" has been used in locating the spot for the altar in the middle of the sweat lodge, for establishing the direction for passing the pipe that binds together participants in smoking rituals, and for most other rites and rituals.

As to the quest itself, a ritual of endurance and prayer follows the centering of the quest site. As Black Elk describes it, the individual involved, known as the lamenter, enters the space enclosed within the circle—the "sacred space"—and goes to the center. He sends a "cry" to Wakan Tanka, the Sioux high god, asking to be heard, to be pitied, to receive a messenger. Then, walking very slowly

he goes to the pole at the west, where he offers up the same prayer, and then returns to the center. In the same manner he goes to the pole at the north, east, and south, always returning to the center each time. The lamenter makes this round over and over very slowly, always returning to the center.[20]

This involved ritual lasts as long as four days, depending upon the length of time vowed by the lamenter. All of this time the lamenter is naked and exposed to the elements, attempting to keep his mind concentrated on the task at hand without the aid of food and water.

This kind of vision quest, while differing in details from tribe to tribe, has been practically universal among Native Americans. It was thought of as the most sacred act that anyone could perform. The importance of the quest, and some of the beliefs connected with it, can be seen in the statement made by Smohalla, a nineteenth-century leader of the Nez Percé (Northwest). When the U.S. government requested that he cease traditional Native American beliefs and practices and "put his people to work," he responded by saying:

My young men shall never work. Men who work cannot dream, and wisdom comes in dreams.

You ask me to plow the ground. Shall I take a knife and tear my mother's breast? Then when I die she will not take me to her bosom to rest.

You ask me to dig for stone. Shall I dig under her skin for bones? Then when I die I cannot enter her body to be born again.

You ask me to cut grass and make hay and sell it, and be rich like white men. But how dare I cut off my mother's hair?

It is a bad law, and my people cannot obey it. I want my people to stay with me here. All the dead men will come to life again. We must wait here in the house of our father and be ready to meet them in the body of our mother.[21]

Healing Ceremonies

Traditionally, the Native American medicine man was more than a doctor. He was a *shaman*, a healer, and an educator all rolled into one person. In addition to knowing "medicine," he was expected to be able to perform religious ceremonies and to communicate with the gods. In the treatment of illnesses he used clairvoyance, spiritualism, demonology, and prophesy, as well as herbs, roots, and other medicines. Thus treatment for disease involved a combination of medicine and religious practices.

All tribes have had curing ceremonies for both physical and mental illnesses. Conducted by the medicine man, or possibly several medicine men, these ceremonies and the medicine used in them have solved many of the medical problems Native Americans have encountered. The Navajo (Southwest U.S.), for example, have traditionally been fearful of the powers of evil and death. As a result of this fear, they developed many ceremonies to deal with these forces of evil. One such ceremony was called the "evil-chasing chant," which was designed to get rid of the evil force that had invaded a sick person's body. They also used other ceremonies and rituals to get rid of diseases caused by evil powers, including sand paintings, which were made on the ground with sand of various colors, corn pollen, powdered flowers, and leaves. Figures were painted with sand to represent the sun, the moon, stars, snakes, and *kachinas,* as well as impressions of various spirits and gods. These "paintings" were designed to put the diseased individual into harmony with the universe. In this manner, the Navajo believed that the evil would be dispelled from the body and the individual would be able to be a productive member of the society again. Because these sand paintings were believed to be sacred, they were destroyed immediately after the ceremony was completed.

In spite of the curative effects of some of these practices, Native American medical knowledge was for many years either ignored by white people or criticized by white doctors who disparaged all use of medicine men, healing ceremonies, and traditional Native American drugs. It was not until the late nineteenth century that white physicians began to realize the value of codeine, even though Native Americans had been using this drug for hundreds of years. Native Americans also used herbs to suppress ovulation, much as modern medical researchers have in recent years used chemicals to develop "the pill." Now, after many years, the contributions of Native American medicine can be seen in the fact that there are over 200 drugs used by Native Americans currently listed in the *Pharmacopeia of the United States.*

Preparation of Candidate for "Shooting" Ceremony in Medewiwin. *This is a Plains Ojibwa initiation ceremony in which a candidate is symbolically shot and resurrected. The photograph was taken on the Waywayseecappo Reserve in Manitoba, Canada.* (Courtesy of James H. Howard)

Agricultural Ceremonies

As indicated by Smohalla's words quoted earlier (page 20), Native Americans have always understood themselves as an active part in the creative processes of mother earth. Through their songs and ceremonies at planting time and harvest time, they believed that it was possible to join the supernatural forces that cause the re-creation of nature and thereby be re-created themselves. The people, as well as the soil, could receive the blessings of the supernatural powers.

Therefore, Native Americans considered agricultural rituals as more than requests for rain and the desire for good crops. The dances, songs, and chants were also used for healing and psychic restoration because the people counted on the earth's power of fertility and the blessings of the gods to produce numerous benefits for them.

The specific rituals used in connection with planting and harvest varied greatly from one tribe to another, and from one region to another. The rituals ranged from the elaborate agricultural ceremonies of the Pueblo to the simple songs sung by the Papago. One of the Papago songs was sung in the evening, after the corn planting was completed. The planter pounded the earth, prayed for rain and a good crop, and sang this simple song:

Blue evening falls,
Blue evening falls,
Near by, in every direction
It sets the corn tassels trembling.[22]

The importance of the agricultural ceremonies was always clear: they were prayers for the very sustenance and welfare of the tribe. Without the corn, beans, and other vegetables, life itself would disappear. These vegetables, the Native Americans thought, were as much gifts of mother earth as were their own lives.

Ritual Expression and the Arts

Native Americans have traditionally expressed their relationship to gods and spirits in a variety of ways, including songs, dances, games, and the visual arts. They have expressed themselves in love songs played on flutes and often sung at night, songs and dances connected with agricultural ceremonies, mourning dances for the dead, and round dances, which still provide entertainment for Native Americans today.

Visual representations of the relationship between Native Americans and their gods and spirits have been widespread and diverse. Some of the visual arts have been used to produce the naturalistic images of seals, whales, and human forms that the Eskimos carved on harpoon heads to guide them to their targets, and in the tattooing of women's faces to ward off evil. Other artistic expressions produced the totem poles of the Nootka and Tlingit tribes along the Pacific coast of Canada; these poles were family crests as well as religious objects, combining artistic representations of family history, animals, and mythological beings to express the unity between all forms of existence. Still other artistic expressions resulted in the geometrical designs and earth tones of Pueblo pottery, and the vivid blues, scarlets, and yellows of Navajo and Zuñi ceremonial costumes; the colors were intended to reflect the stark desert landscape where these people have always lived and the vivid hues of the sun as it rises and sets in the desert sky. Additional uses of geometrical designs and vivid colors developed in paintings, weaving, and craftsmanship with jewelry.

Today, in many of the great museums of the world, the pottery, costumes, textiles, and decorated weapons of Native American tribes have been given a place of honor because of the excellence of the craftsmanship and the striking artistic vision that they embody. It is important to remember, however, that for the Native Americans who made these artistic creations, there was no artifical separation between art and life. Rather, the arts have always nurtured and sustained Native Americans in their daily existence, and have given form to

the coherence of their vision of the physical and spiritual world.

Religion, Moral Conduct, and Society

For most Native Americans, there has been a traditional interrelationship between religious beliefs, moral conduct, and the structures of society. Beginning with religious belief in an orderly universe run by various gods and spirits, Native Americans have concluded that moral conduct should both reflect that orderly system and please the supernatural powers who are in charge of the system. Then, working on the belief that human society is also an orderly, patterned system, they have concluded that the moral conduct of individuals should promote harmonious social relations, with the goals being social equilibrium and community well-being.

In this context the promotion of tribal unity has meant the subordination of individual freedom to social welfare. Even though Plains tribes have tended to grant more individual freedom than woodland or agricultural tribes have, even among Plains tribes the good of the tribe has always been more important than the interests of the individual. In many instances, the promotion of tribal welfare resulted in the prohibiton of certain acts, with some tribes drawing up lists of appropriate and inappropriate activities and developing punishments for community-threatening behavior.

While sharing the same general framework of morality involving supernatural powers and tribal welfare, individual tribes have differed in their understandings of appropriate moral conduct and how best to promote it. The Seminole, for example, developed a way of promoting community well-being through their Green Corn Festival. If a member of the tribe was caught in an antisocial action, that person was brought before the tribal council where it would be determined if he was guilty of the crime for which he was charged. The assumption was that the ''criminal'' was sick, insane, or possessed, because a pattern of socially irresponsible actions could lead to the complete destruction of the tribe. A ritual was performed by a medicine man to exorcise the ''criminal,'' with the hope that the offender would be rehabilitated and the stability of the group ensured. If this ritual failed, the oldest member of the group was sent to execute the criminal—and seldom did the one who was to be executed resist.

The Arapaho and Sioux, as well as many other tribes, understood their camp as a sacred circle or hoop. All who lived within the circle knew that if anyone violated the tribal moral standards, the circle could be destroyed. Out of this understanding of morality came rules of behavior that protected property, guarded against sexual abuses, and specified appropriate behavior toward relatives and other members of the society. The Sioux, for instance, did not tolerate adultery or sexual promiscuity. They also had very specific rules of behavior for a son-in-law and mother-in-law; the two were to communicate only through an intermediary, never directly. As to disciplining tribal members who engaged in immoral behavior, the Arapaho, Sioux, and other Plains tribes developed a severe form of punishment known as shunning. In this practice the offender was thrown out of the tribal circle for a fixed period of time, with the possibility that he could die from hunger because no one would come to his assistance.

The Chippewa ceremonial lodge society (Canada), in contrast to some tribes, put together a set of commandments to govern the conduct of their members. The rules were intended for the Chippewa only and were not to be told to persons outside the society. Included in the rules were prohibitions of lying and fornication. In addition, some of the rules read as follows:

> Respect your lodge; no quarreling may be done there. Whenever visitors come, you must respect them and welcome them. . . . You must get up a feast for the relatives of deceased brothers and sisters of the lodge, and comfort them. The members of the society are as one and should regard each other as equal.[23]

The Eskimos, like many Native American societies, believed that morality tales helped to enforce appropriate behavior. The themes of the stories varied from incest to rape to murder, but they graphically described the punishment and destruction awaiting the individual who went against the tribal ethic. For instance, the Eskimos said that if a person ate caribou and seal meat at the same meal, he had insulted the souls of both the caribou and the seal. The souls of both would retaliate against the entire village, causing everyone to starve. Thus the guilty person was required, according to the story, to do a penance, which generally meant avoiding certain foods and refraining from sexual activity for a specified period of time. Failure to perform the penance would result in banishment from the village, which in turn would usually result in death from freezing or from the attack of some animal.[24]

Probably the most comprehensive system of morality set in a religious context has been that of the Navajo. It begins with a religious world view known as *hózhá*, a concept indicating an ideal cosmological state of affairs in which there is perfect harmony among all powers, persons, and things in the supernatural and natural realms of existence. Connected in a harmonious manner with *hózhá* are believed to be numerous gods and spirits, sometimes referred to as Holy People. These Holy People, a diverse group including such powers as the Sun, Changing Woman (earth), lightning, and whirlwinds, are believed to have created the Navajo, also known as the *diné*, or the Earth Surface People.[25]

For the Navajo, or *diné*, the fundamental purpose of morality traditionally has been that of promoting harmonious social relations, which, in turn, could lead to the realization of the goal of *hózhá*. The basic moral standard intended to lead to this goal has been *k'é*, usually translated as ''moral harmony.'' The Navajo have understood *k'é* to involve the promotion of cooperation and group welfare, and the avoidance of social friction and ''trouble-making actions.'' *K'é* has represented a norm for individuals in society to put aside their divergent interests and live together in a mutually dependent and cooperative manner, as symbolized most clearly for the Navajo in the cooperation necessary to take care of the tribal sheep herd.

In more specific terms, the Navajo have derived moral virtues and traits of character from the norm of *k'é*. Three such virtues and character traits have been particularly important: the virtue of prudence, as indicated by the character traits of independence and self-reliance; the virtue of social control, as indicated by sobriety, truthfulness, and trustworthiness; and the virtue of benevolence, as indicated by generosity, friendliness, and peacefulness. In addition, the Navajo have derived certain ethical principles and moral rules for conduct from the norm of *k'é*. Again, three principles and their applications through moral rules traditionally have been important. First, the Navajo have thought it important to "care for yourself," which has meant prohibitions against gambling, laziness, and the drinking of alcohol. Second, they have thought it important to "avoid and rectify any trouble with others," which has meant prohibitions against fighting, adultery, stealing, lying, and killing. Third, they have thought it important to "help others by treating them as a kinsman," which has traditionally meant a willingness to share with others, including strangers, to the point of self-sacrifice (e.g., by sharing one's food at the risk of personal starvation). By living according to these virtues and principles, the Navajo have believed it possible to achieve the goal of *hózhǫ́*.[26]

Beliefs and Practices Relating to Death

Native Americans have traditionally expressed their attitudes toward death in death songs, stories, and poems that exemplify in a simple manner the attitude they have had toward human existence in the midst of supernatural and natural powers. Because life was often percarious at best, Native Americans developed a deep and profound awareness of the proximity of the next world, where a person might go at any time because of war, famine, or disease.

Two patterns emerge among the many death songs sung by various tribes. One type of song was received in a vision or dream and was to be sung when an individual faced the distinct possibility of death, as at the time of war. An example of this type of song was the song sung by Chief Crazy Horse, a Sioux chief, just before going into battle:

Hoka hey! Follow me
Today is a good day to fight
Today is a good day to die![27]

The second type of song was composed at the very hour of death and was chanted with the dying breath. Songs of this type reflected the gasping for strength in order to face death fearlessly. An example of this type of song was the Warrior song of the Hethushka Society of the Omaha (Central Plains):

I shall vanish and be no more,
But the land over which I now roam
Shall remain
And change not.[28]

Another example of this type of song was a song of the Ojibwa tribe in Canada. The song was composed by a tribal member far from home, and confronting death:

If I die here in a strange land,
If I die in a land not my own,
Nevertheless, the thunder,
The rolling thunder,
Will take me home.
If I die here, the wind,
The wind rushing over the prairie,
The wind will take me home.
The wind and the thunder,
They are the same everywhere,
What does it matter, then,
If I die here in a strange land?[29]

The general Native American belief in another world to come has allowed them to acknowledge and accept their own deaths as the natural outcome of existence. This idea of the inevitability of death appeared in many myths and stories. For instance, in one legend of the Eskimos, who experience darkness for the winter months of the year, there was a parable of the elders debating about whether or not humans should be immortal: " 'Let us do without light,' said one, 'if so we can be without death'; but the other answered, 'No, let us have light and death!' " In another myth of the Eskimos, a creator god showed a leaf to human beings and said: "See this leaf. You are like it. When it falls off the branch and rots there is nothing left of it."[30]

When tribal members died, the disposal of their dead bodies varied from tribe to tribe. Although a few tribes practiced cremation, most tribes either buried the bodies in mother earth or set out the bodies on some type of scaffold. The Paiute and the Shoshone (Southwest U.S.), for example, simply returned dead bodies to the earth. In contrast, the Crow, the Sioux, and other Plains tribes traditionally disposed of dead bodies by constructing a scaffold with four posts and a platform on top. Located in an area known as the "burial ground," each scaffold held a dead body on top, usually dressed in that person's best clothes, and had some of that person's possessions (e.g., a bow, a shield) attached to the posts. The Plains tribes sometimes shot the favorite horse or dog of the deceased, and placed it near the scaffold. An alternative kind of scaffold was used by some Canadian tribes. The Tsawataineuk tribe in British Columbia, for instance, traditionally had family burial trees. Each family disposed of their dead by placing the corpse in a square box, using ropes to hoist the box up in the tree, and then cutting off the limbs under the box so that animals could not reach the dead body.

There have also been mourning ceremonies for the deceased. By having socially acceptable ways to express grief, Native Americans have enabled mourners to work out their grief over a particular period of time and have brought them back into the group as useful, functioning members. The most common mourning ceremony has been the "give away." According to this practice, the death of a family member has meant that surviving family members laid out all of the dead person's possessions, invited friends and relatives to a feast, and then gave away all of the possessions to the people at the feast. In addition to the "give away," some tribes developed their own customs and ceremonies. Among the Omaha, for instance, there has been a funeral custom in which the young men of the tribe made two incisions in their arms, inserted a small willow twig, and then sang songs of mourning for the soul of the departed. Among the Osage, the mourning rite was practiced by an individual who wandered over the plains, wailing and fasting, singing this song:

Behold, I go forth to move around the earth,
Behold, I go forth to move around the earth,
I go forth as the puma that is great in courage.
To move onward I go forth,
I go forth as the puma that is great in courage.
Behold, I go forth to move around the earth.
           Wi'gi-e
O Hon'ga and Wa-zha'zhe,
Verily, I am a person who has made god to be his body,
The god of night,
I have made to be my body,
Therefore I am difficult to be overcome by death.
O Hon'ga and Wa-zha'zhe,
If you also make that god to be your body,

You also shall be free from all causes of death.
Behold, I go forth to move around the earth,
Behold, I go forth to move around the earth,
I go forth as the great black bear that is great in courage.
To move onward I go forth,
I go forth as the great black bear that is great in courage.
Behold, I go forth to move around the earth.[31]

As to the possibility of life beyond death, Native Americans have generally believed that human beings connected as they are with supernatural and natural powers, would continue to exist in some fashion beyond death. The conception of what that continuing existence would be like varied from tribe to tribe. Some tribes believed that the soul (in animals as well as humans) left the body at death, whereas other tribes pictured a kind of parallel existence in which bodies would experience an earth-like existence in some supernatural realm. One of the more graphic conceptions of life after death is presented in an Eskimo poem. The poem, possibly written after the Eskimos came into contact with Christianity, depicts three realms of postmortem existence:

And when we die at last,
we really know very little about what happens then.
But people who dream
have often seen the dead appear to them
just as they were in life.
Therefore we believe life does not end on earth.
We have heard of three places where men go after death:
There is the Land of the Sky, a good place
where there is no sorrow and fear.
There have been wise men who went there
and came back to tell us about it:
They saw people playing ball, happy people
who did nothing but laugh and amuse themselves.
What we see from down here in the form of stars
are the lighted windows of the villages of the dead
in the Land of the Sky.
Then there are other worlds of the dead underground:
Way down deep in a place just like here
except on earth you starve
and down there they live in plenty.
The caribou graze in great herds
and there are endless plains
with juicy berries that are nice to eat.
Down there too, everything
is happiness and fun for the dead.
But there is another place, the Land of the Miserable,
right under the surface of the earth we walk on.
There go all the lazy men who were poor hunters,
and all women who refused to be tattooed,

not caring to suffer a little to become beautiful.
They had no life in them when they lived
so now after death they must squat on their haunches
with hanging heads, bad-tempered and silent,
and live in hunger and idleness
because they wasted their lives.
Only when a butterfly comes flying by
do they lift their heads
(as young birds open pink mouths uselessly after a gnat)
and when they snap at it, a puff of dust
comes out of their dry throats.[32]
Of course it may be
that all I have been telling you is wrong
for you cannot be certain about what you cannot see.
But these are the stories that our people tell.

Native American Religions in Contact and Transition

Native American religions have gone through significant changes over the past four centuries. Contact with Christianity as "the white man's religion," conflict with white settlers and pioneers, defeat by the military forces of the United States, and enforced marches to reservations have all produced inevitable and possibly irremediable changes in the religious beliefs and practices of Native Americans. We will now look at some of the responses to these changes.

As their religions were altered by pressure from white missionaries and government officials, various Native American prophets began to appear. These prophets, also known as "messiahs" or messengers from the high god, urged the people to restore their old way of life. One of the earliest of these prophets was a Tewa name Popé, who originally belonged to the San Juan Pueblo on the Rio Grande. He left his own pueblo, established his headquarters at Taos, and in 1680 led an uprising that expelled the Spanish from the land. Everything Spanish was destroyed, including churches, works of art, homes, tools, and all spanish animals. The Spanish God was declared dead, and the indigenous Hopi religion was restored. In 1692, however, the Spanish returned and brutally put down Popé's revolt.

Another "messianic" revolt occurred in 1752, led by an unknown Delaware who appeared in the Michigan area urging all Native Americans to band together and fight a religious war against the whites. His call was taken up by the Algonquin chief, Pontiac, who formed a confederation of several tribes and attacked the British; he, too, was defeated. Some forty years later the great chief Tecumseh took up the "messianic" battle to restore the old ways. He visited most of the tribes from the headwaters of the Missouri River to as far south as Florida, and formed the greatest alliance that ever existed among Native Americans in North America. He was killed in 1813 in Ontario, Canada, and his efforts ended in failure.

The Ghost Dance

Among the many visionaries, prophets, and dreamers, the most famous was Wovoka, a Paiute from Nevada. During an eclipse of the sun in 1889, Wovoka went into a trance in which the high god spoke to him, telling him that all dead Native Americans would return to the world as young men and all whites would disappear from North America if the people would devote themselves to dancing for periods of up to five days without stopping. This dance, called the Ghost Dance, soon spread rapidly among the Paiute and Shoshonean tribes. Within a short time it spread to the Oklahoma Territory, where the Cheyenne and Arapaho took it up.

As the Ghost Dance move across the Plains, it assumed a violent and anti-white dimension, especially among the Sioux, who believed that the dance would not only bring back the dead and the buffalo, but would cause the total annihilation of the whites. The Sioux believed that white men's bullets could not penetrate their "ghost shirts"—the imaginatively decorated shirts that they wore while performing the Ghost Dance. The dance quickly spread among the Sioux and alarmed whites on and near the reservations in South Dakota. The whites urged the military to stop the dance. In December 1890 the U.S. Seventh Cavalry, with support troops, disarmed a group of Sioux at Wounded Knee, surrounded them, and opened fire, slaughtering unarmed men, women, and children. Shortly afterward the U.S. government ordered the suppression of the Ghost Dance, and it gradually died out.

The death of the Ghost Dance symbolized in many ways the death of the old religions among Native Americans. Never again were there to be strong revivalist move-

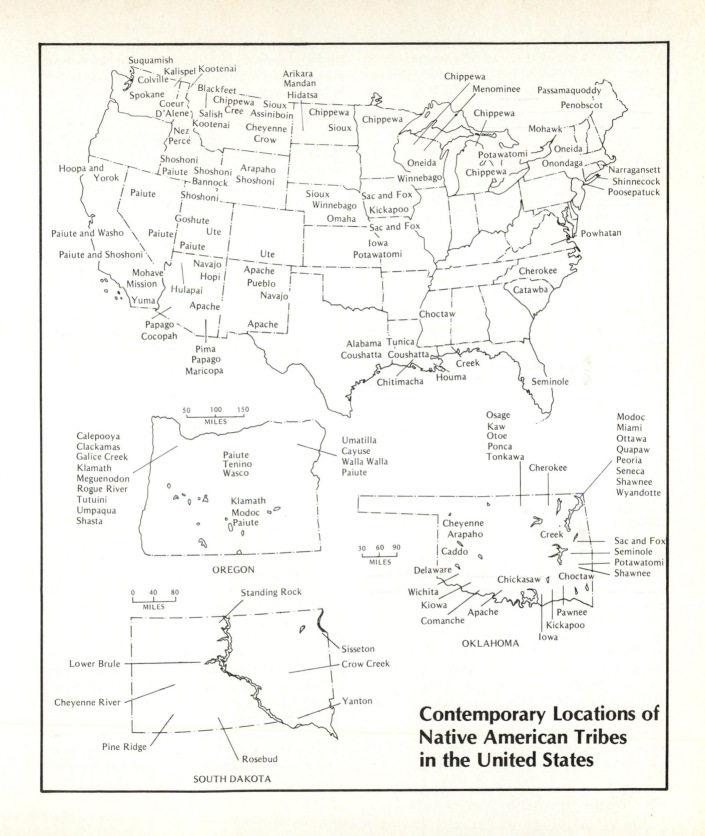

Contemporary Locations of Native American Tribes in the United States

ments among the Native American tribes. Instead, new religions began to appear that brought together certain features of the old tribal religions with the new Christian religion of the whites. One of the results of the attempt to combine Native American religions and Christianity was the Peyote or Native American Church.

Peyotism and the Native American Church

Peyote, a drug derived from the mescaline in the top of small, blue-green cacti that grow in southern Texas and Mexico, produces hallucinogenic effects when taken internally. It has been used by native people in Mexico since pre-Columbian times, and by Native Americans in North America from the eighteenth century to the present. It has often been used in rituals that were not specifically religious in nature: to help tribes locate their enemies, to assist tribal members in finding lost objects, and to foretell the results of proposed tribal ventures.

The ceremonial use of peyote to obtain a religious vision began among the Plains tribes of the Oklahoma Territory toward the end of the nineteenth century. These tribes had been devastated by the collapse of the old ways of life and the suppression of religions, such as the Ghost Dance, that had promised them deliverance from the oppression of the whites. For tribes such as the Kiowa and the Comanche, peyote offered the possibility of a vision for everyone taking part in the peyote ceremony. In later years, many other tribes in the United States and Canada began using the drug. The use of peyote survives today in the rituals of the Native American Church.

Peyotist doctrine includes a belief in a Supreme God, who communicates with humans through such spirits as the Thunderbird. The Thunderbird is believed to carry the people's prayers back to God. Therefore, when the members of a tribe eat peyote, they believe that it enables them to communicate with God and with the spirits of their ancestors, from whom they receive spiritual power, guidance, and healing from illness.

Peyotist ritual usually takes place in a *tipi,* or lodge, around a crescent-shaped earthen altar and a sacred fire. The ceremony begins on a Saturday evening and lasts all night. It is led by a peyote chief who brings a satchel containing the peyote, sometimes called the peyote but-

ton, and the other ritual items: a gourd rattle, which represents the sun or the world; a water drum, made from an iron kettle partially filled with water; a drumstick; a staff; an eagle feather used to ward off evil; an eagle-wing bone whistle; tobacco; cedar incense; sage; and a water bucket. The service includes prayer, singing, the sacramental eating of peyote, water rites, and contemplation. The service concludes with a breakfast on Sunday morning.

Within this general framework of peyotist ritual, there are variations from tribe to tribe. For example, the Mescalero Apache (Southwest U.S.), whose peyote rituals date from 1870, have an involved ceremony that contains all of the basic ingredients of peyotist practice. All persons planning to attend the ceremony are required to purify their bodies by taking a bath at noon on the day the ceremony is to be performed. In the evening they enter the tipi from an eastern direction. Having entered the tipi for the ceremony, the participants do not generally leave until morning; if they have to leave before morning, they are required to take an eagle feather that is kept at the door and return the feather when they return.

The peyote leader, also called a roadman, sits in the west facing the door and holding the gourd rattle and the staff, which is used to ward off evil. After singing a song to the staff, he exchanges the gourd for the drum, but keeps the staff in his left hand throughout the evening. The peyote rests in front of him on an eagle feather or a piece of buckskin; this ceremonial peyote is often called "chief peyote," or "old man peyote." Periodically, the peyote chief consults "old man peyote" to ascertain if anything is amiss in the ceremony, since "evil thoughts or efforts at witchcraft will show on the peyote button."[33] A door-keeper, who keeps out persons who do not belong in the ceremony, and a fire-tender, who keeps the fire going throughout the ceremony, assist the peyote chief.

As to the ceremony itself, the peyote chief first eats some of the peyote, then administers it to novices at the meeting. The peyote is then passed to other participants by the assistants, as the peyote chief prays. Later, beginning at the southeast corner, the drum is passed clockwise as each person sings four songs, either his own ceremonial songs or songs received in a vision. The drum is passed from person to person until everyone has participated in the ritual. At dawn, water is brought in by a woman; morning songs are sung by the peyote chief; and other ceremonies, such as the healing of ill-nesses, may be performed. The leader then picks up "old man peyote," places it in his satchel with the other ritual objects, and the meeting ends.[34]

The peyote cults, as they were known in the early part of this century and are sometimes known today were incorporated into the Native American Church with a federal charter in 1918. There is considerable diversity within the church. Some tribes, for instance, have incor-porated certain features of Christianity into their beliefs and practices: they offer prayers to God in the name of Jesus, accept the teachings of Jesus and many of the New Testament writings as sacred, and use some Chris-tian songs in their services. Some of these Native Ameri-cans find comfort in combining the peyote ceremony with the promise that "when they die, Jesus will be waiting at the gate."[35] These followers of the "way of the peyote" usually accept family responsibilities, sup-port themselves through steady work, and avoid alcohol as signs of their religious convictions.

In 1946, the Supreme Court ruled that the use of peyote by members of the Native American Church was legal. Since that decision, which marked the end of a series of legal battles concerning peyote use, leaders of the Native American Church have been able to obtain the drug from Texas and Mexico, transport it for religious purposes, and use it in their ceremonies without fear of reprisal from white officials.

Feather Dance (Comanche). *This is a Pueblo ceremony at Picuris, New Mexico. The ceremony captures the essence of the Comanche people.* (Courtesy of Donald N. Brown)

Native American Religion Today

There continues to be considerable diversity among Na-tive Americans in terms of religious belief and practice. The Native American Church is growing in membership in both the United States and Canada, especially among young people striving to find their identity and preserve their cultural heritage. Members of at least fifty tribes now belong to this church. Most Native Americans today are at least nominally Christian in that they attend Chris-tian churches and accept Christian doctrines. For many of these persons, however, membership in Christian churches does not necessarily mean the abandonment of the religious traditions that are native to this continent. And for Native American traditionalists, there is an ongo-ing attempt to preserve the rituals and vision quests that predate the introduction of both peyote and Christianity into North America by many hundreds of years.

Throughout the summer months, Native Americans gather at events known as *powwows.* People from one or more tribes drive long distances, if necessary, to be together for a day or a week, to eat together, to greet old friends, and especially to dance together. Some of this dancing is social dancing, or round dancing, and some of it is called "fancy dancing" and has no historical significance. Other dances (e.g., hunting dances, warrior dances) are actually rituals from the past and may last from dusk to dawn.

Powwows play an important role in the lives of many contemporary Native Americans. Winter months are of-ten punctuated by mourning ceremonies for elders of the tribe who have died during the year. But in the warmth of summer, powwows provide an opportunity for new babies to be presented to their relatives and friends, for young girls to put on shawls sewn for them during the winter and join the women in dancing, and for young boys to join the men for the first time in performing dances punctuated by drumming first heard on this continent thousands of years ago. Whatever their immersion in the white world during the week, the Native Americans who participate in the powwows find in them a means of renewing their tribal indentification and keeping alive for their children the beauty and security of the old ways.

For these people, religion is not something that has been kept in a book or nurtured by monks or scholars. Rather, religion is a living force, a dynamic combination of belief and practice that permeates every aspect of their experience. To summarize the religious beliefs and practices of Native Americans is not easy. It is easy, however, to detect in their history and in their rituals the continuous search for a vision that can sustain both individuals and peoples. This combined pursuit of personal and tribal good is, perhaps, what has kept their religious traditions alive during the centuries in which Native Americans have seen alien forces sweep across their lands and violate many of their sacred spaces.

NOTES

1. Francis Laflesche, *The Osage Tribe: The Rite of Vigil*, Thirty-Ninth Annual Report of the Bureau of American Ethnology, Washington (1925), pp. 123–124.
2. Carl Starkoff, *The People of the Center* (New York: Seabury Press, 1974), pp. 37–38.
3. Alice Marriott and Carol K. Rachlin, *Plains Indian Mythology* (New York: Mentor Books, Inc. 1977), pp. 30–34.
4. William E. Coffer, *Spirits of the Sacred Mountain: Creation Stories of the American Indians* (New York: Van Nostrand Reinhold Company, 1978), p. 85.
5. Carl Starkoff, *The People of the Center* p. 27.
6. Peter Farb, *Man's Rise to Civilization as Shown By the Indians of North America* (New York: E. P. Dutton & Co., Inc., 1968), p. 83.
7. Ibid., p. 84.
8. Ibid., p. 84.
9. Hartley B. Alexander, *The World's Rim* (Lincoln: University of Nebraska Press, 1967), p. 4.
10. W. Atkinson, *Indians of the Southwest* (San Antonio: Naylor, 1935), p. 62.
11. James LaPointe, *Legends of the Lakota* (San Francisco: Indian Historical Press, 1976), pp. 23–26.
12. Alice Marriott, *Saynday's People* (Lincoln: University of Nebraska Press, 1947), p. 205.
13. Alexander, *The World's Rim*, pp. 5–6.
14. Ruth Underhill, *Red Man's America* (Chicago: University of Chicago Press, 1971), p. 191.
15. Joseph E. Brown, ed., *The Sacred Pipe: Black Elk's Account of the Seven Rites of the Oglala Sioux* (Norman: University of Oklahoma Press, 1953), p. 45.
16. R. J. Walker, "The Sun Dance and Other Ceremonies of the Oglala Division of the Teton Dakota," *Anthropological Papers of the American Museum of Natural History*, 16 (1917), p. 121.
17. Brown, *The Sacred Pipe*, p. 56.
18. John Neihart, *Black Elk Speaks* Lincoln: University of Nebraska Press, 1961), p. 43.
19. Alexander, *The World's Rim*, p. 10.
20. Brown, *The Sacred Pipe*, pp. 57–58.
21. Herbert J. Spindin, "The Nez Perce Indians," The American Anthropological Association, *Memoirs*, 2, Lancaster (1908), p. 150.
22. Margot Astrov, *American Indian Prose and Poetry* (New York: Capricorn Books, 1962), p. 32.
23. Alexander, *The World's Rim*, p. 213.
24. Harold E. Driver, *Indians of North America* (Chicago: University of Chicago Press, 1961), p. 327.
25. David Little and Sumner B. Twiss, *Comparativer Religious Ethics* (New York and San Francisco: Harper & Row, 1978), pp. 127–128.
26. Ibid., pp. 131–134.
27. LaPointe, *Legends of the Lakota*, p. 160.
28. Alice Fletcher and Francis LaFlesche, *The Omaha Tribe*, Twenty-Seventh Annual Report of the Bureau of American Ethnology, Washington (1911), p. 475.
29. Thomas E. Sanders and Walter W. Peek, eds., *Literature of the American Indian* (Beverly Hills: Glencoe Press, 1976), p. 83.
30. Alexander, *The World's Rim*, pp. 198–199.
31. Francis LaFlesche, *The War Ceremony of the Osage Indians*, One Hundred and First Report of the Bureau of American Ethology, Washington (1939), pp. 123–124.
32. Edward Field, trans., *Songs and Stories of the Netsilik Eskimos*, translated by Edward Field from text collected by Knud Rasmussen, courtesy Education Development Center, Newton, MA. Reprinted from Jerome Rothenberg, ed., *Shaking the Pumpkin* (Garden City, N.Y.: Doubleday & Company, Inc., 1972), pp. 382–383.
33. Weston LaBarre, *The Peyote Cult* (Hamden: The Shoestring Press, 1947), p. 41.
34. Ibid., p. 43.
35. Underhill, *Red Man's America*, p. 139.

GLOSSARY

Calumet the red stone quarried in Minnesota and used to make the Sacred Pipe.

Diné (*dee-nay*) the earth surface people; the name the Navajo call themselves.

Heyoka (*hay-yo-kuh*) the Sioux clown; one who receives the vision of the Thunderbird and becomes a contrary, living his life in an antinatural way. The Heyoka was considered to be the bearer of sacred power and was always thought of as a sacred person.

Hózhǫ a Navajo religious concept indicating the ideal condition when everything is in perfect harmony.

Inipi (*ee-nee-pee*) a steam bath ceremony performed in order to purify oneself before participating in religious ceremonies.

Kachina (*kuh-chi-nuh*) sacred dancers of the Hopi; they are believed to be the spirits of the invisible forces in the world.

K'é (*gay*) a Navajo term meaning moral harmony.

Kinni-kinnik (*kee-nee kee-nik*) native American tobacco.

Kiva (*kee-vuh*) underground ceremonial chamber.

Peyote (*pay-yoh-tay*) a small hallucinogenic cactus used in the ceremonies of the Native American Church.

Powwow gathering of Native Americans to perform the old ceremonies and participate in tribal traditions.

Shaman (*shaa-maan*) a person who functions as an intermediary between human beings and the spirit world.

Wakan Tanka (*waah-kahn-taahn kaah*) the Sioux name for the High God.

Wakinyan (*waah-kin-yaahn*) the Thunderbird described as a great bird who has no shape, no feet, but large talons; is headless but has a great beak; whose voice is the thunder, and whose eye is the lightning.

SUGGESTED READINGS

ALEXANDER, HARTLEY BURR. *The World's Rim: Great Mysteries of the North American Indians*. Lincoln: University of Nebraska Press, 1969.

ASTROV, MARGOT, ed. *American Indian Prose and Poetry, An Anthology*. New York: The John Day Co., Publishers, 1946, 1972.

BAHR, DONALD M. *Pima and Papago Ritual Oratory: A Study of Three Texts*. San Francisco: The Indian Historian Press, 1975.

BLACK ELK (with Joseph E. Brown). *The Sacred Pipe*. Norman: University of Oklahoma Press, 1953.

CATLIN, GEORGE. *O-Kee-Pa: A Religious Ceremony and Other Customs of the Mandans*. Lincoln: University of Nebraska Press, 1976.

COFFER, WILLIAM E. *Spirits of the Sacred Mountain: Creation Stories of the American Indians*. New York: Van Nostrand Reinhold Company, 1978.

DELORIA, VINE, JR. *God is Red*. New York: Grosset & Dunlap, Inc., 1973.

DRIVER, HAROLD E. *Indians of North America*. Chicago: University of Chicago Press, 1961.

DYK, WALTER. *Son of Old Man Hat: A Navaho Autobiography*, Lincoln: University of Nebraska Press, 1967.

LaBARRE, WESTON. *The Peyote Cult*. Hamden: The Shoestring Press, 1947.

La POINTE, JAMES. *Legends of the Lakota*. San Francisco: The Indian Historian Press, 1976.

MARRIOTT, ALICE. *Saynday's People*. Lincoln: University of Nebraska Press, 1947.

MORRISEAU, NORVAL (with Selwyn Dewdney). *Legends of My People: The Great Ojibway*. Toronto: McGraw-Hill Ryerson Ltd., 1965.

RADIN, PAUL. *The Trickster: A Study of American Indian Mythology*. New York: Schocken Books, Inc., 1972.

STARKOFF, CARL. *The People of the Center*. New York: Seabury Press, 1967.

UNDERHILL, RUTH. *Red Man's America*. Chicago: University of Chicago Press, 1971.

———. *Red Man's Religion*. Chicago: University of Chicago Press, 1972.

WATERS, FRANK. *Book of the Hopi*. New York: Ballantine Press, 1963.

3

African Religions

Africa may indeed be the cradle of humanity. Archaeological research has established that human-like creatures lived in East Africa over three million years ago. The roots of history on the African continent are therefore very deep. It is unfortunate that a proper reconstruction of the past, particularly as it applies to Africa south of the Sahara, has only begun recently. Since for that part of Africa few written records were available, it was assumed by early European writers that the history of the continent was insignificant. However, from a combination of sources—archaeological, oral, and written—together with a sympathetic observation of existing African life, we are now learning a great deal about the African past, including the dimension of religious life, that has been an integral feature of the history of Africa's peoples.

The archaeological evidence based on an examination of sites found dating from 30,000 B.C.E., indicates the practice of systematic burials in parts of Africa. Subsequent to this period, there is evidence from a wide variety of rock paintings all over the continent of forms of religious practice. These depict masked figures, serpent-like creatures, and figures that might be interpreted to be fertility symbols, all of which indicate the presence of religious activity. Although this chapter is not concerned with ancient Egyptian religion, it may be pointed out that in the northern part of Africa, religious activity associated with a settled civilization also has ancient roots.

Specific examples of religious artifacts in Africa south of the Sahara during the Iron Age have been excavated that date back approximately 2,000 years. A variety of ritual objects related to divination, and having a continuing history, indicate linkages between this and subsequent periods of religious activity in that area.

With the coming of agriculture and settled life, material culture in Africa increased. Migration in search of better living conditions led to the spread of ideas and material culture over a large part of Africa south of the Sahara, the area that we are most concerned about in this chapter. The evidence about Africa's past, thus includes remains of ritual behaviour, offerings, religious mounuments, burials, and decorative remains such as sculpture, engraving, and painting. Some of the motifs reflected in such remains are widespread and suggest common patterns and continuitites across time and place within Africa. Besides archaeological evidence and anthropological data, there is also linguistic evidence to show common terms and practices present in many African cultures. Though it may not be possible to reconstruct fully all past practices and beliefs, the above examples indicate a remarkably ancient and continuous religious history.

The confluence of African culture with other cultures, such as that of Islam, which penetrated south of the Sahara after the tenth and eleventh centuries C.E. (see Chapter 9), gave rise to several great empires. The best known were those of Mali and Songhay. Smaller kingdoms also flourished in other parts, such as the Kingdoms of Benin in West Africa, Buganda in East Africa, and Zimbabwe in Southern Africa. Long before the discovery of Africa by Europeans from the sixteenth century onwards, Africa had already developed its languages, cultures, political structures, and social institutions. Its societies had adapted from contacts with each other and with other outside cultures. The "Dark Continent," as it was so often erroneously called, already had a long and developed history of civilization.

Indigenous African religions extend today over about two-thirds of the continent. The northern part of Africa is predominantly Muslim, and Islam is widespread also in western and eastern Africa. Christianity has some of its oldest centers in Ethiopia and Egypt in the Coptic rite, and in modern forms has been scattered throughout all parts of Africa south of the Sahara by the activities of Christian missionaries in the nineteenth and twentieth centuries (see Chapter 8). African religions thus coexist today with both Islam and Christianity. Their contact and mutual interaction is a major factor in contemporary African life.

African religions are a mosaic of many self-contained and locally rooted traditions. This makes it difficult to generalize about them or describe them as a single homogeneous or consistent system. Such descriptive terms as "primitive," "pagan," "polytheistic," and "animistic" have been used in the past to describe them. Since these terms have come to sound derogatory or condescending, the term "traditional"—though vague and inadequate—is being used increasingly. It has the merit of emphasizing that these religious traditions have a long history and are rooted in ways of local life that have guided many African societies. The early European visitors to Africa who used some of the negative terms distorted the religious dimension in most African traditional societies because of their own prejudices and preconceptions, and also because they could not perceive that the religious dimension pervaded all aspects of life in those societies.

This chapter is about these African religious traditions, with a focus on common patterns. In view of the diversity of cultures and peoples in Africa, these patterns can only illustrate selected aspects of some religions. A synthesis of the fundamental patterns of belief and their effects on daily life, however, does reveal that religion has governed thought and behavior, and has influenced people's attitudes toward origins, other persons, and the total environment in every society on the African continent.

The groups that are referred to in the chapter represent a variety of socioeconomic groupings. Some are pastoral, like the Masai, while others such as the Gikuyu are agricultural. Some reference is also made to groups for whom hunting was a significant activity in traditional life.

There are four primary sources for the study of African religions: oral tradition, archaeological and linguistic evidence, continuing practice, and the arts and sacred spaces. Few traditions have been recorded in writing, but many of them have been preserved orally by mothers, fathers, priests, and storytellers. Every group has its traditional art, artifacts, and dress. When these are studied in combination with traditional religious practices and ceremonies in many parts of Africa, they provide a firm basis for understanding the role of religion in African life.

Beginnings

Understanding African religions begins with understanding that each group has an awareness of its origins. Each has preserved an account of the creation of human beings, and every creation myth, or story, contains an interpretation of the group's beginnings and explains how the goals of that society are defined. The Gikuyu of Kenya, for example, have preserved the following creation story:

There was wind and rain. And there was also thunder and terrible lightning. The earth and the forest around Kerinyaga shook. The animals of the forest whom the Creator had recently put there were afraid. There was no sunlight. This went on for many days so that the whole land was in darkness. Because the animals could not move, they just sat and moaned with the wind. The plants and trees remained dumb. It was, our elders tell us, all dead except for the thunder, a violence that seemed to strangle life. It was this dark night whose depth you could not measure, not you or I can conceive of its solid blackness, which would not let the sun pierce through it.

But in this darkness, at the foot of Kerinyaga, a tree rose. At first it was a small tree and grew up, finding a way even through the darkness. It wanted to reach the light, and the sun. This tree had Life. It went up, up, sending forth the rich warmth of a blossoming tree—you know a holy tree in the dark night of thunder and moaning. This was Mukuyu, God's tree. Now, you know that at the beginning of things there was only one man (Gikuyu) and one woman (Mumbi). It was under this Mukuyu that He first put them. And immediately the sun rose, and the dark night melted away. The sun shone with the warmth that gave life and activity to all things. The wind and lightning and thunder stopped. The animals stopped wondering and moved. They no longer moaned but gave homage to the Creator and Gikuyu and Mumbi. And the Creator, who is also called Murungu, took Gikuyu and Mumbi from His holy mountain. He took them to the country of ridges near Siriana and there stood them on a big ridge before He finally took them to Mukuruwe wa Gathanga about which you have heard so much. But he had shown them all the land—yes, children, God showed Gikuyu and Mumbi all the land and told them,

> This land I hand over to you. O Man and Woman
> It's yours to rule and till in serenity sacrificing
> Only to me, your God, under my sacred tree. . . .[1]

This dramatic description relates the divine origin of the first human couple, Gikuyu and Mumbi, from whom the group is descended and to whom they owe their name and identity. It establishes, furthermore, a link between the Creator, human beings, and the land that is given to them as a trust, thus affirming the interrelationship that exists between the various levels in creation. The Gikuyu see themselves as part of a divinely rooted whole. Religion is woven into the very fabric of their life and cannot thus be conceived of as a separate human activity.

The Yoruba of Nigeria have a concept of the beginning of time when there existed the heavens above and a watery wasteland below. The host of divinities called *orisha* ruled this domain. The *orisha* Olorun ruled the heavens and Olokun, a female divinity, the wasteland below. One day Olorun delegated Obatala, one of the *orisha,* to create the earth. Obatala was given the shell of a snail, which contained some loose soil, a hen with five toes, and a pigeon. On coming down, he scattered the loose soil, left the pigeon and the hen on it to scratch and spread it about, and then retreated to the heavens.

The Mountain of Brightness. *Mount Kenya or Kere-Nyaga, the mountain of brightness, is believed to be the home of Ngai, Supreme God of the Gikuyu. Ngai chose this location as his official resting place on earth.* (Courtesy of Azim Nanji)

Before long, the soil had covered much of the watery space and solid ground was formed.

In time, Olorun sent a chameleon to inspect the new creation. The chameleon, with his big rolling eyes and capacity to adapt to his new environment, pronounced it fit for habitation. The specific spot where the new creation came into existence was called *Ifé*, the original dwelling place of early humans, and the name given to the sacred city among the Yoruba. Obatala molded the first human forms, male and female, while Olorun breathed life into them. They were then sent to settle the earth and were provided with tools they needed to work and cultivate the land. Soon a society was formed and Obatala became its king. Later he decided to return to the heavens, where his description of the earth caused many *orisha* to descend and live among the people. These *orisha* were instructed by Olorun to be of help and to act as protectors of the human race. According to this story, the making of the earth took four days, while the fifth was reserved for worshiping Olorun.

A third creation story comes from the Dogon people, who live south of the Sahara in cliff villages in Mali. The Dogon possess a remarkable culture of art that expresses their religious beliefs, and they believe that the beginnings of history are intricately linked with the symbolism of water, the source of life in their desert environment.

According to Dogon mythology, the great god Amma and his wife, the earth, first gave birth to a fox, who was single; then she gave birth to twins, whose limbs were like water. The twins were male and female and were called the Great Nommo Couple. Later there were eight more Nommo. They descended to the earth in an ark and became the founders of the human race. Today the Nommo are depicted in Dogon sculpture as figures with raised arms and are symbolized in the sacrifice where they rise into the heavens and fall as rain, rising again in plants and crops, making life possible.

While these creation stories differ about the details involved in the beginning of the earth and the human race, they do have a similar purpose. Each creation story makes real the existing world within which the particular society moves, establishes a link between the divine and the human, and provides a framework in which the identity of the group is defined.

A Variety of Beliefs

In the creation stories, several fundamental concepts appear that are common to many African religions:
1. The concept of a spiritual cosmos or universe with divine beings, sometimes in a hierarchical order.
2. The earth and material life as created.
3. The notion of other gods and lesser spirits.
4. Ancestors.
5. The belief in sacred spaces and places.
6. The concept of persons, male and female, as an integral part of the cosmic scheme.
7. The idea of a society organized around values and traditions drawn from common beginnings and history.

We will now see how these concepts and beliefs function in several African societies.

The Spiritual Cosmos

The key to these concepts is that of a vital force—for which the Polynesian term *mana* has become the best definition. This force or *mana* may originate in a Creative Being, as in the case of the Gikuyu, and underlie all of creation, through which it is dispersed in varying degrees. It is strongest in divine or ancestral beings and in the loci of divine forces, such as sacred places or symbols. It is the essential part of human beings whether they be dead or alive, since death does not indicate an end of the vital force but merely its continuation in another form or on another plane. From a creative Being to other divine intermediaries and symbols, this *mana* reverberates through a hierarchy that includes human beings. Ideally, an equilibrium is maintained at all levels, and human beings are in a position through their ritual and personal or collective behavior to maintain this equilibrium so that the vital force may not be the cause of any harm to others or to oneself. This force may be harnessed so that its positive aspects may benefit all.

The Divine Being

While African religions, for the most part share the concept of a Divine Being, its significance varies from group to group. In some this role is seen as central to the creation and sustenance of the world; in others it may be peripheral and remote. Though represented as a male in most religions, such a being is also depicted as a female in some traditions. However, this Being is seen always as a god of crisis, to be turned to when grave dislocations and catastrophes in life or nature take place. Such Spiritual Beings are believed to have existed from the beginning. This latter idea is expressed in a song attributed to the Pygmies:

> In the beginning was God
> Today is God,
> Tomorrow will be God.
> Who can make an image of God?
> He has no body.
> He is as a word which comes out
> of your mouth
> That word! It is no more,
> It is past and still it lives!
> So is God.[2]

Lesser Gods, Ancestor Spirits, and Other Spirits

Most African people recognize and focus on lesser gods who represent a hierarchy of messengers or links between the spiritual and the material world. Each lesser divinity governs a sphere of life or human activity and may be connected with a natural object or place, such as a rock or river. These beings may derive their power from remoter Beings and are the most immediate link between them and human beings. Although generally beneficient, they can also be dangerous, punishing or damaging human life under certain circumstances.

Ancestor spirits are part of the community. Although they have died and left this world, they are still the "living dead" and linked to this life through their existence as spirits. Those who led exemplary lives now offer protection to the living who were related to them. Also having achieved a high status in worldly life, they continue to enjoy a similar status in the spiritual realm through the veneration of living descendants. Each individual, family or group thus maintains a special relationship with their ancestors, who continue to be an integral part of their lives as well as being a focal point of their identity.

Apart from Divine Beings, lesser gods, and ancestors, the cosmos is also believed to contain other spirits. This underlines the belief among African people that *mana* can rest in all things. Some of these spirits can be evil; their powers can hurt and inflict pain and disease. Among the Akan, for example, there is a belief in an evil power who is seen as the master of all evil actions. Both good and bad spirits inhabit the same localities that human beings do and are, in that sense, a part of the realm occupied by other divinities. Such spirits, when intent on harm and evil, can often possess people and cause disease or madness. Those spirits that play a beneficial role may also possess certain people, through whom they can prophesy or speak to society about the unknown. This world of spirits coexists with the world of material things, representing the two dimensions of a living, dynamic universe central to the beliefs and ways by which most African peoples seek to understand, predict, and bring control to their lives and the world around them.

Sacred Spaces, Places, and Symbols

Since the universe as a whole appears as God's creation, most African religions build their concept of sacred space around natural objects and phenomena. The very pattern of personal and ritual life is linked to the rhythms of nature. If one were to speak of a sacred calendar in African religions, it would be based on the seasons and the cyclical rhythm underlying the movement of the sun, moon, and stars. It is this pattern that guides human life and organizes it around natural symbols and spaces. These act as places of worship, or focal points for human interaction with the divine and the world of spirits. Bodies of water and rivers, for instance, are places where ritual may take place. Places on land, such as caves, hollows, hills, and mountains, are also thought to have a sacred character. Another major category of sacred places involves trees and groves and rocks; in part, these places are considered sacred because they are believed to be dwelling places of the spirits of the ancestors.

Among other symbols that have sacred meaning for some African religions, the most significant are fires, colors, and numbers. The Gikuyu, for example, light a fire on the occasion of the ceremony of purifying the crops; the fire is carried to all regions. Among the Baganda, the number nine has special meaning, and in certain ceremonies, nine vessels or items must be used.

Granaries and Cliffside Burial Places of the Dogon in Mali. (Courtesy of Wouter Van Beek)

Such colors as black or white also have religious meaning for certain groups, so that during ceremonies only animals bearing these colors are offered for sacrifice.

This close regard for nature and its symbols has often been misunderstood by outsiders as reflecting a form of nature worship. Instead, it reflects a deep and abiding affinity with the abstract and the invisible aspects of the universe. Natural objects and places are seen as places of worship and as thresholds to further spiritual understanding of the world.

Concepts of Persons in Society

In the African concept of persons, individuals are seen as rooted in a community. The individual is conscious of self in terms of "I am because we are; and since we are, therefore I am." The essence of being human lies in the perception that persons, as creations of the divine, are an integral part of the cosmos, inextricably bound to its rhythms and patterns. The fulfillment of life lies in relating to all of these—to Creative Beings, the gods, the ancestors, the spirits, to the cosmos, to the earth, and ultimately to all other beings, human and otherwise, who provide the immediate context in which life must be lived.

Each person is believed to be a compound of two elements: the material, inherited from one's parents, and the spiritual, which defines one's personality and character. Among the Ibo, each individual is said to possess a *chi* or personal spirit. Among the Akan, it is believed that the spirit is a gift of the Divine Being.

Some creation stories also depict a past physical relationship between gods and humans. Often it is claimed that the two were close together at the beginning of time. There is the notion, for example, that because the sky was low, the first man and woman had to be careful while cultivating and pounding the grain, so that their hoes and pestles should not touch God, who lived there. Death had not yet entered the world and God had provided enough for them to live on. The woman, however, became greedy and tried to pound more grain than was allotted to them. To do this, she had to use a longer pestle. When she raised it up, she hit the sky and God, being angry, retreated far into the heavens. Since then, people have had to work hard, disease and death have entered their lives, and it is not as easy to reach God.

Among the Akan, the story is told of how the Creator lived on earth in the beginning. An old woman who used to pound yams always kept hitting Him with her pestle until one day He retreated into the sky. The old woman, dismayed at this, called upon her children to gather mortars and pile them up to build a ladder to the sky. Eventually the pile almost reached the sky, but the family fell one short; then the old woman advised the children to take one from the bottom and use it for the top. This caused the whole heap to collapse, killing many people.

The idea of divine–human separation brought about by the movement of God and the heavens as a result of human weakness reflects a realism in these stories about the world and the human condition. As an alternative to this view, the previous closeness between the divine and the human suggests the concept of a middle course—the two existing in complementary worlds that need to be bridged. The linking of the divine and the human is carried out by lesser divinities and ancestral spirits to whom human beings are related by ritual.

The stories also reflect a sense of anguish that arises from the realization that human beings are inevitably overtaken by death. The origin of death is often attributed to some unnatural event or necessity, as in the case of the Dogon story about the Nommo: the ancestor, in the form of a serpent, gained entry into heaven, stole a piece of sun from the Great God, and brought it down to earth. This enabled the people to forge iron for tools used in cultivation. The Nommo, however, had to be sacrificed so that he would rise to the sky and then descend as rain. The story's depiction of the sadness associated with death does not, however, lead to a passive acceptance of the human condition. Rather, religion becomes the means of communication and interrelation

between the realm of the finite and that of the infinite. To be religious is to be aware not only of the distance between the two levels but also of the interdependence and necessary harmony between them.

Religious Institutions

Since the group or community is the context in which individual life is fulfilled, African religion is not just a personal matter, but also a communal one. Within the community certain individuals play several roles, sometimes acting as links or mediators. These may be kings or royal personages whose ancestry is traced back to a founding figure: for example, the former kings of the Baganda of Uganda, and those of the Yoruba. On the other hand, such figures may be individuals whose special qualities or experiences mark them as mediators in the performance of rituals or other significant events, much like the shamans of the Native Americans (see Chapter 2). Among these are the *egwugwu* among the Ibo of Nigeria, whose role it is to embody one of the ancestral spirits of the community. The *egwugwu* form a group and are called upon to deliver justice and resolve problems that affect the Ibo people as a whole. They wear masks to symbolize the ancestral spirit they represent, and a separate house is kept in which they deliberate and make decisions. Among the Gikuyu, too, certain individuals come together to the the highest council of the group. These elders are considered ''holy men'' who have dedicated their lives to the Creator and to the welfare of the community, and all religious ceremonies are in their hands.

Sacred Kings

Africa has had a number of kingdoms in its past history, and a few in the present, in which centralized leadership focused on a king or ruler. The establishment of a royal office reflects the interdependence of political and religious affairs. The rituals involved in the installation of an individual to such a sacred office draw from the heritage of the group and are based on transferring the power (sometimes vital force) inherent in the founding figure to the new ruler. On his installation, the ruler becomes

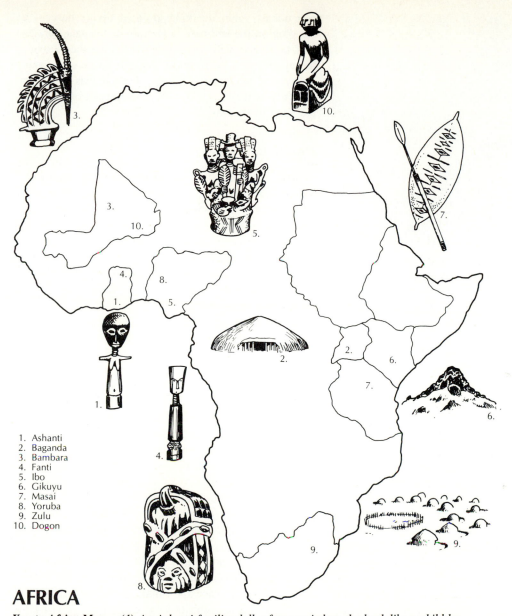

AFRICA

Key to Africa Map. *(1) An Ashanti fertility doll, often carried on the back like a child by women who wanted children and by pregnant women who wished for healthy and beautiful children. (2) The tomb of a Kabaka, former rulers of the Baganda, symbolizing the sacred burial grounds of the dead kings. (3) The chi-wara mask used among the Bambara to symbolize the divinely given gift of agriculture to the people. (4) Like their neighbors the Ashanti, the Fanti also used a type of fertility doll. (5) An Ibo family group making an offering. (6) Mount Kenya, the symbolic home of Ngai, Supreme God among the Gikuyu. (7) The shield and spear associated with the Masai and used for the protection of their cattle. (8) Yoruba helmet-mask. (9) A traditional Zulu village arrangement showing the family huts and an enclosure for the cattle. (10) Dogon mask. (Adapted by permission of Ben Pickard, Pickard Art Galleries, Oklahoma City.)*

1. Ashanti
2. Baganda
3. Bambara
4. Fanti
5. Ibo
6. Gikuyu
7. Masai
8. Yoruba
9. Zulu
10. Dogon

African Religions **39**

The Kabaka's Tomb. *The tomb of the Kabaka outside Kampala, Uganda. The area represents the sacred burial grounds of the traditional rulers of the former Kingdom of Buganda.* (Courtesy of Sara and Amir Jinha)

a mediator between the people and the vital force inherent in the office established by the founder.

The coronation of a new monarch among the Baganda of Uganda, called the *Kabaka,* always followed a set pattern. A period of mourning for the previous king was proclaimed, during which several rituals were performed. The first was a mock battle between the new king and the priests of Baganda. The king, by his "conquest" of the priests, obtained the sacred power necessary to be ruler. This mock combat was a re-enactment of what was believed to be the fight between the original founder of the monarchy and a snake-chief who had ruled the land. Kintu, the founder, established his authority by subjugating the rival forces, and thus every new ruler re-enacted the ritual of conquest before assuming full powers. After the rite of conquest, the new king was required to undergo an additional ritual to prepare him for his duties. He and his queen humbled themselves by crawling to a mound where Kintu had been crowned, and then the chief priest would dress them in their new robes and hand the king a royal spear.

The period of mourning ended after six months with the mummification and burial of the previous ruler. The installation of the new king was completed in additional ceremonies when the king claimed divine descent by standing on the enthronement stool of his ancestors and was presented with the royal spear. He then traveled throughout the land receiving the allegiance of the other leaders and the loyalty of the people. He was now, symbolically as well as politically, the Kabaka of Buganda, the King of the kingdom of the Baganda.

Prophetic Figures

In many African societies, a crucial role has been played by individuals who, at moments of crisis or change, act as a source of inspiration or guidance for the people. Such a figure among the Gikuyu, for instance, would foretell the coming of the British and forewarn the people of the loss of their land. In other instances, prophetic leaders became heads of movements that tried to restore traditional values in the face of invading change. Several such individuals emerged at the time of the European colonization of Africa to resist the invaders' violation of the traditional societies and institutions.

Between 1905 and 1907, for example, under German colonial rule in what is now Tanzania, a major resistance was launched under the leadership of such a prophetic figure. The Maji Maji movement, as it came to be known, was headed by Kinjikitile, who taught that all Africans were one and free, and that those who were ceremonially united by having drunk the water (*maji*) would be aided by the ancestral spirits in their struggle against the Germans. Kinjikitile was accepted as a leader because he was believed to have been inspired by a spirit sent by the Supreme Being, Bokero, and a miraculous account of this experience was recounted to all the followers. People from a wide variety of ethnic groups accepted his leadership and joined in the struggle. Centers of the movement were set up in various locations, where ceremonies took place and rituals involving communication with ancestral spirits were carried out. During the struggle Kinjikitile was seized and hanged by the Germans, but his followers continued the resistance until the Germans finally defeated the movement. One aspect of such prophetic leadership was that it was able to unite the ideas of several African groups and provide a common basis of belief and action during a period of crisis.

Spiritual Intermediaries

A major role in African religious life has been played by intermediaries who are skilled in the understanding and transmission of knowledge about the cosmos and in the use of this knowledge to assist individuals and the group as a whole in critical events. Terms such as *medicine men* and *witchdoctors* have often been used to describe them. Their role, however, has been to act as religious teachers and specialists who preserve and transmit knowledge of each religion, providing a link between the society and the spiritual world. As such, their role is more institutionalized than that of the prophetic figures.

One of the primary activities of such intermediaries is "divination," or the deciphering of messages from the spirit world, that arena of experience not accessible to ordinary human beings. At other times, such figures act as healers and are consulted during sickness or serious injury. They may also be consulted prior to marriage, to determine the sex of an unborn child, before death, and so on. An intermediary may be of either sex and is among the most respected members of the community.

The intermediaries' work as healers provides a good example of the religious dimension of their role. The art of healing in traditional African medicine is based on a perception that illnesses often have a definite socio-cosmological and psychological origin. In order to heal a person, the intermediary therefore has to consult spiritual powers and implore their assistance in driving out the disease. Much of this traditional practice of healing has continued to coexist with modern medicine in African societies today, and continuing efforts are being made to harness the knowledge and experience of these healers to overcome health problems in several African countries. Illustrations of this can be found in Kenya and Nigeria where, with the assistance of international organizations such as WHO (World Health Organization), traditional healing practices are used increasingly in rural areas. Such forms of healing, rooted as they are in traditional religion, are perceived as appropriate means of combating health problems in societies that still maintain a holistic view of persons.

Since intermediaries are the inheritors and preservers of wisdom, they often become part of councils and organi-zations that have the highest status in the community. Among the Gikuyu, members of such a group regularly perform priestly and judicial functions, so that they are depended on for the performance of the most important rituals of the community.

The *babalawo* among the Yoruba are specially trained as diviners, and their art is linked to the god Orumila (or Ifa), the *orisha* of divination. Each fifth day is considered a "day of mysteries" and the *babalawo* consult the oracle using a elaborate series of 256 images, which are then worked out on a board using either sixteen palm nuts or casting a string of eight half-nuts or shells. The results are computed and interpreted and the solution finally offered to the inquirer. Such inquiries are made by people on all important occasions that affect their lives, such as pregnancy, birth, illness, and marriage.

The existence of a vital, mystical force in the universe implies that there are aspects of the unseen that cannot be fully known to all. There is also the possibility that such a force can be used by individuals capable of tapping it to harm other people. In African traditions this has given rise to the existence of figures who have been variously described as "witches," "medicine-men," "sorcerers," and so forth. All of these English terms betray a distortion of the true function of such individuals. The fear of the unknown and of evil is an integral part of religious life, but it is not a part to be merely accepted without any recourse to countermeasures to combat and even defeat such forces. The misuse of spiritual power, as in the case of practicing "witchcraft" among the Gikuyu, demands punishment. The blatant exploitation of spiritual forces for destructive use, though recognized and feared, is regarded in most African traditions as something to be overcome in order to maintain social order and peace.

There are thus a variety of individuals and spiritual forces to whom one can turn to fight the presence of evil and harmful forces. Such individuals perform acts of purification through ritual. Among the Gikuyu, a person is cleansed from evil by the act of "vomiting the sin." After a goat has been slaughtered, the contents of its stomach are mixed with herbs and medicines. An officiating elder using a brush places some of the mixture on the tongue of the offender or evil person, getting him to vomit the mixture on the ground. In this way

holistic – theory that the whole is more important than its individual components

the person becomes cleansed and can re-enter society. On occasion the mixture is also applied to the walls of the person's house, so that the immediate environment in touch with that person may also be purified.

Ritual Expression in African Religions

Rituals and the Stages of Life

African religions recognize several key stages in human life. The major events in life represent the key moments in what is an ongoing transition from birth to death to entry into the community of the ancestral "living dead." These transitional stages are birth, puberty, initiation, marriage, having children, old age, death, and life after death. Because each of these stages constitutes a development and a growth, it is accompanied by ritual acts whose purpose is to direct individuals toward fulfilling appropriate goals in life. The rituals not only prepare individuals for attaining these goals but also inform them of the qualities required by the new stage. Each ritual is therefore an event in both physical and spiritual growth.

Initiation. Among the more elaborate and significant rituals is that accompanying the passage to adulthood. Among the Bambara of Mali, boys are prepared for initiation into manhood by several steps lasting many days. Dressed in white gowns, they are taken to an enclosed sacred grove of thorns some distance from their village. Here they submit to physical and emotional suffering to symbolize not only their transition through a difficult phase of life, but also the struggle involved in making the transition to a new, higher stage of responsibility and knowledge. The fact that the boys are initiated in a group also strengthens the sense of common purpose and solidarity as a basis for their participation as adults in the life of the community.

The grove, set amidst thorn bushes, contains a clearing with a tree at its center, toward which the initiates slowly move. While the thorny grove stands for the testing ground in the initiation ceremony, the tree and the cleared space represent the object of the ceremony and the place where knowledge is to be gained through further initiation. Within the area, they now receive their knowledge. It is conveyed by means of a pole on which 240 objects are represented. These symbolize the sum of Bambara knowledge and experience. Each initiate learns to name the objects and grasp their interrelatedness as well as their symbolic meaning, thus mastering the cultural code of his people. For instance, a spoon is not merely something to eat with, but also a symbol of woman, winter, death, and transmission of knowledge, depending on the context in which it is referred to. The objects are all arranged in opposite and complementary pairs to illustrate the process by which a boy may now go on to understand not only practical and external aspects of things, but also their symbolic and metaphorical meanings. By this understanding he will come to understand the universe of which he is a part and in which he must live and function.

Eventually, the boys crawl out of the grove through a hole in the earth towards the sunlight, marking the end of that stage of initiation. Now they are ready to re-enter the world, equipped with new knowledge and awareness bred by their recent experience. They will be accepted as full participating members of adult society, imbued with the sense of solidarity that comes from a shared ritual experience.

Among the Masai of East Africa, a major collective initiation ceremony precedes the actual recognition of adult status for youths. Traditionally, it is held in a central location once every seven years. The *moran,* or youths, go through ceremonies and rituals where the major emphasis is on preparing them for a life of self-discipline and responsibility as full adults. *Moran* social life is considered by Masai elders to be dominated by a sense of vanity, reflected in the individual's concern for his appearance and self-image. Since their life-style is looked down upon by the adults in the society, the collective initiation ceremony is meant to represent a transition away from a concern for self to a concern for society and from a sense of selfish individuality to a sense of group solidarity and identification. Similar ceremonies also take place among other East African peoples like the Kipsigis, and also involve circumcision at the age of puberty.

Passage into adulthood also involves initiation rituals for females. Among the Gikuyu and Nandi in East Africa, for example, females also go through a series of initiation rites, culminating in clitoridectomy, before they assume the responsibilities of womanhood. The sequence of ritual events begins with a great dance ceremony, involving the participation of the whole community. The dance is accompanied by songs and events that help the initiate prepare for the transition to adult responsibilities and link them with the community as a whole, through whom they learn what these responsibilities are. The candidates are also prepared physically for the circumcision through special meals and a ritual bath.

As the moment of the actual ceremony approaches, the tenor of the song changes from joyful and merry to somber and mournful. This characterizes the sense of sadness that accompanies the loss of childhood innocence and the seriousness of the responsibilities of adult life. After the clitoridectomy, the young women are confined until healing has taken place. They are then adopted as adults by elders in the tribe, marking their rebirth, not as children of their parents, but as children of the whole society. A dance at a later date completes the process. Finally the young women assume adult responsibilities, which include marriage, motherhood, and full participation in all the rituals of adult life.

Besides preparation for adult life and responsibility, initiation becomes a symbol of the endeavor to go beyond oneself. The conquest of both physical and spiritual elements in life marks a passage to knowledge—knowledge that enhances the personality and spirituality of the initiates, giving their life a sense of dignity and purpose.

Death. Just as initiation represents a process in the maturation of an individual, so death is a stage or process that completes life on earth and provides passage to the world of spirits. Death is also accompanied by several rituals. Earlier we have seen how certain stories explain the entry of death into human affairs, emphasizing both its inevitability and its mystery. Death is conceived of as a transition, not as a total end of things. While the material and physical form of an individual is destroyed, the spirit of that individual moves on to join the company of the departed ancestors.

Funeral rites accompany death. Most African peoples bury their dead in graves or in a special hut where the body may be kept for a while before finally being buried in the ground. This practice is particularly common in the case of royalty, as is the case among the Baganda of Uganda.

In the majority of African religions, death is a form of continuation in a spiritual form; hence, the concept of the hereafter involves no heaven or hell as in some other world religions. The individual's soul does not totally depart from relatives and family, since they continue to be in communion with their ancestors. A shrine near the household or village is a reminder of this contact and affinity between the living and the "living dead." An alternative view is held by the Ibo of Nigeria, who believe in reincarnation: certain features of the dead person's soul are believed to return to earthly life in another body.

Birth and Marriage. Birth and marriage are other significant stages in life accompanied by rituals. The Gikuyu perform ceremonies that include the washing and oiling of the child, accompanied by sacrifices and prayers for purification, particularly if the birth has been difficult. The mother and child are also kept in seclusion for a few days; the end of the period is marked by a sacrifice and prayers of thanksgiving to the ancestors and to God. The involvement of the ancestors, God, and ritual acts emphasize the religious nature of birth, making it part of the cycle of experiences that link the child and the parents together in a profoundly religious event.

Marriage has a communal dimension involving the entire extended family, and it is a festive event that is celebrated with much joy and ritual. Marriage brings together man and woman, families, clans, and also the ancestors and the unborn, since it is through the past and the future that the group's identity is remembered and sustained. Marriage is linked to procreation and as such is a duty falling on everyone.

An unmarried person is generally considered abnormal and unfulfilled as a human being in African societies. All the customs and ritual that are related to marriage and procreation reflect an understanding of them as an integral part of the natural rhythm of life. Customs vary from group to group, but much importance is attached to the ritual associated with betrothal, where the families of the couple come together to make arrangements. The exchange of gifts is also an important ritual prior to marriage. The wedding ceremony itself is accompanied by much pomp and ceremony and occasionally by a symbolic event, such as the rite of bathing the couple together to bind and sanctify their new state.

Since marriage is seen in a social and community context, rather than a mere coming together of two individuals, most traditional African societies practice polygamy. In cases of sterility or barrenness, divorce is permitted. All rituals accompanying marriage involve prayers and supplication to Divine Beings and ancestral spirits, and involve the participation of intermediaries.

Rituals Accompanying Hunting, Agricultural, and Pastoral Life

Another important category of ritual in African religions accompanies activities that are important to the daily life of the community, such as hunting or growing food. Since the land and all life on it is conceived of as being interrelated and of common origin, specific rituals are undertaken before life can be taken or food grown and harvested.

The annual hunting festival among the Yoruba of Nigeria focuses on sacrifices offered to Ogun, the patron divinity of hunters. Special ceremonial preparations are made and creatures symbolizing the various types of animals, birds, or other prey are chosen. For example, on an occasion when a dog, a pigeon, and a snail are sacrificed before the shrine of Ogun, the victims are dedicated by the recitation of a special prayer:

Ogun, here are the festival kola-nuts for you from all of us.
Ogun, here is your festival snail from all of us.
Ogun, here is your festival pigeon from all of us.
Ogun, here is your festival dog from all of us.
Spare us so that we can do this again next year.
Ward off death and sickness from us.[3]

Through this act of sacrifice and dedication, the hunters affirm their dependence upon Ogun. Having sought his permission and protection, they can participate in the hunt with the knowledge that their actions will not anger the divinity or violate the laws governing life in their universe.

The Gikuyu, with their great emphasis on land and farming, have several rituals related to the planting and harvesting of crops. In the case of a prolonged drought, an elaborate rain-making ceremony takes place. Specific individuals, representing elders, older women, and young children, and signifying various aspects of attainment

or innocence, are chosen as participants, and a lamb is sacrificed under one of the sacred trees on the chosen day to appease the Creator God (Ngai). The following prayer is recited on this occasion:

Reverend Elder [Ngai] who lives on Kere Nyaga [Mt. Kenya]. You who make mountains tremble and rivers flood; we offer to you this sacrifice that you may bring us rain. People and children are crying; sheep, goats and cattle are crying. We beseech you, with the blood and fat of this lamb which we are going to sacrifice to you. Refined honey and milk we have brought to you. We praise you in the same way as our forefathers used to praise you under the very same tree, and you heard them and brought them rain. We beseech you to accept this, our sacrifice, and bring us rain of prosperity.
Chorus: Peace, we beseech you, Ngai, peace be with us.[4]

After this prayer, a procession goes around the sacred tree seven times, sprinkling milk and honey-beer. During the eighth round, everybody sits down and the lamb is sacrificed, roasted, and eaten by the participants. A final prayer is recited and the party proceeds home, taking some of the sacrificed lamb to be used in a separate planting ceremony. There are other specific ceremonies for planting, purifying, and harvesting the crops.

Among the Ibo, a festival takes place before the harvest is begun to give thanks to Ani, the earth goddess and the source of all fertility. The New Yam Festival, as it is called, is celebrated with great joy, feasting, wrestling matches, and the gathering of all members of the clan. On the last night before the festival, all the old yams are destroyed and all the cooking vessels and utensils cleaned thoroughly to prepare for the new harvest of yams.

Communication with Ancestors

Ancestral spirits, or the "living dead" as they are best characterized, have a special place in African ritual. These are the spirits of departed members of the family (parents being the most important) with whom communication is considered vital, because ancestral spirits are a bridge between the two worlds and still members of the extended human family. They are also considered to be guardians and protectors of family affairs, values, and tradition. Since tradition is the collective experience of the community and the sum of wisdom accumulated over successive generations, ancestors enrich the living

Family Ritual. *An Ibo family group showing husband, wives, and children offering a fowl to Ifijioku, the spirit of the yams.* (Reproduced by Courtesy of the Trustees of the British Museum)

Ritual Expression and the Arts

A vivid aspect of all African religions is the expression of ritual and religious feeling through art, dance, and music. These are part of virtually every ceremony as the media through which devotion, joy, sadness, and even fear are expressed physically and aesthetically by the individual and the community.

The use of art is prominent in rituals where certain persons function as mediators between the two worlds. Such is the case with the *egwugwu* among the Ibo. During ceremonies they wear masks to reflect the identity of the spirit figure they are portraying. In instances where the *egwugwu* meet to resolve a dilemma that affects the community or are seeking to effect justice or redress wrongs, the wearing of masks symbolizes the fact that they represent collectively the spirits of the ancestors, who continue to participate in the affairs of the community, guiding it and ensuring the well-being and continuity of tradition.

Masquerades are also a means of portraying and re-enacting the history of the group. Creation myths are often acted out by individuals wearing masks and symbolizing the forces responsible for creation. The dominant element in such masquerades is the varied use of rhythmic gesture, as the dramatization of the story takes place primarily through the language of dance, accompanied by music. During the performance of such masquerades, the dancers not only re-enact a ritual but also become "possessed" by the spirits whom they are impersonating. The arts and religion become fused on such occasion. Among the Dogon, there exists a society of mask-wearers, who must be initiated into it before they can participate in the dance. The best known of these societies is associated with the Kanaga mask; the members of the society symbolize through dance the "life of the individual beyond death and the life of the community beyond the individual."[5]

Masks can also symbolize the existence of threatening forces, such as those that bring disease or cause harm to come to individuals. Such is the case with the Gelede masks among the Yoruba. The offerings or sacrifices made to Gelede, through the use of masks, are meant to propitiate the divinity Gelede so that a disease may be overcome.

Among the Yoruba, each divinity is identified by giv-

through their experience, which links the two. The living can intuit and divine the will of the ancestors by being in communication with them. This continuous contact between the two worlds is expressed through offerings made to ancestors, especially on occasions of crisis when their help is most needed. The communication with ancestors also represents another type of continuity—that of group identity—which, as in the case of the Gikuyu and the Yoruba creation stories, traces this ancestral link back to divine origins through a hero or divine figure who represents the ideal that each person in the group must constantly strive to attain.

Because of the gradual decline in the use of traditional arts in the context of religious practice, it is not possible to decipher the meaning of many African art forms accurately. The arts are part of the African religious heritage and, where appreciated and understood in that way, go

A Chi-Wara Mask. *A mask used among the Bambara of Mali. It is an antelope headdress used on ceremonial occasions to symbolize the divinely given gift of agriculture to the people.* (Courtesy of Lionel Arnold)

ing it a form. These figures, often expertly carved out of wood, act as family shrines, symbols of the divinity's presence and influence. Associated with each figure is a series of sacrifices, accompanied by dance, song, and instrumental music. Such ancestor figures represented in art are found in many African religions.

Some normally utilitarian objects often acquire symbolic meaning in certain African religions. The stool, both among the Baganda and in the Ashanti kingdom in Nigeria, became a political symbol of the king's authority. The stool became the unifying symbol of the state and was used in major ceremonies.

Ceremonial Art Figure. *A traditional stool among the Luba of Zaire. The wooden figure of the decorated female is often used for ceremonial or ritual purposes.* (Courtesy of Lionel Arnold)

a long way toward illuminating the rich and varied texture of African ritual life.

Moral Conduct and Society

The value of human actions in African religions is based on the effects, negative or positive, that they have on one's life, and the contribution they make to society. Ethical behavior is ultimately that which leads to wisdom, and the possession of wisdom and discipline leads to an individual's being considered a hero or failure in society. Each individual thus strives to be a model, and children acquire and integrate values of the community as part of their daily education, through participation in and observation of ceremonies and festivals. The process of growing up involves the acceptance at each stage of new responsibilities and a more disciplined life.

The primacy of society over the individual is very important to the life of the community, and social order and peace are recognized as the most important goals. Among Africans, the laws, customs, regulations, and rules that govern everyone are believed to have been handed down from earliest times, so that an offense against any of these is a diminishing of both the individual and the society.

Interpersonal relationships are also governed by ethical norms. Among the Gikuyu, for example, young men and women mix freely and even participate in activities that allow for the expression of love and sexual feeling; but, since this is seen as merely a preparation and education for marriage and sex, limits are set beyond which individuals may not go. *Ngweko,* or fondling, thus takes place in a collective and controlled atmosphere, where the limits and possibilities are clearly known and practiced.

Linked to the idea of moral conduct in several African religions are the concepts of individual conscience and evil or wrong-doing. The Akan believe in an inner voice or conscience that guides human action. There are also sayings and proverbs that assert that God hates evil. The Ibo belief in *chi* or personal spirit, referred to earlier, is complemented by the belief that one's *chi* is in one's own hands. Thus, there is an emphasis on individual responsibility in matters of moral and personal behavior.

Evil or wrong-doing, always seen in a social or spiritual context, implies that one has transgressed against society or against ancestors or against gods. In the case of the Gikuyu, we have already noted the use of ritual to purify a person and surroundings from the effects of evil.

Perhaps the best illustration of ethical values and norms are the proverbs and sayings that are so much a part of the ordinary lives of most Africans. The following Yoruba and Akan proverbs illustrate this vividly:

Goodness is the primary nature of God.

You will be punished according to your deeds.

Experience is the lesson learned from mistakes.

It is not mountains, but little acts of wrongdoing that cause our downfall.

The small hand of the child cannot reach the high shelf.
The larger hand of an adult cannot pass through the neck of a calabash.

We are conversing about pumpkins. A woman asks what it is that we are discussing. We say: "this is man's talk." But once we have gathered the fruit, who will split and cook them?

The god who favors a lazy man does not exist. Prosperity lies in one's own hands.

The wisdom of others prevents a leader from being called a fool.

The arrogant pond stands aloof from the river, forgetting the water is common to both.[6]

Vital to the organization of family and society is the organization of space; that is, the arrangement of villages and family dwellings. Because persons and their environment mirror each other, African society organizes space to reflect this reciprocity. The house and the family have a special place at the center of human life, and the community often participates in helping the individual build a dwelling. Since the growth of the family is an important goal, dwellings are built to integrate marital and family units. Where polygamy is prevalent, dwellings are built to accommodate the larger family. Within the family and the family dwelling, the fulfillment of human existence unfolds and is practiced in its highest form. A ruined or disunited family reflects the total failure of those individuals within it to realize their values and, ultimately, can reflect on the failure of the community at large. The sustaining and growth of family life thus remains one of the primary concerns of African religion.

African Religions in Contact and in Transition

One of the great strengths of African religions is their capacity to integrate the social, cultural, and ethical lives of various peoples. In doing this, they have had to adapt as circumstances have altered the physical, social, and economic conditions of life.

Among the most significant contacts that African religions have had, besides those with each other, have been with Islam and with Christianity. Both of these religions are now part of the indigenous scene and have become deeply rooted in Africa. Islam entered Africa in the eighth century C.E. and has since become the dominant religion in North and certain parts of Central, East, and West Africa. Wherever it spread, Islam has left the imprint of its cultural, legal, and social life, so much so that it has been argued that one can speak of Islam as an integral part of African life, in much the same way as one does of indigenous religions.

African Islam

Islam has been a cultural presence in Africa south of the Sahara for more than one thousand years (see Chapter 9). From being the religion of Muslim merchants who had initially come in search of trade, Islam spread among ruling classes, local merchants, and urban centers and finally to rural areas. Over the centuries its language, culture, law, and the arts deeply influenced African ways of life. Several African Muslim empires such as those of Ghana, Mali and Songhay also came to be established during the period. One of the most striking developments in African Islam just before colonial times were the various *jihads,* or holy wars, that occurred in the nineteenth century. Under several charismatic leaders, four such movements broke out in Hausaland in Northern Nigeria, led by Usman dan Fodio; in the neighboring kingdom of Bornu under Muhammad al Kanami; in Niger under Ahmad b Muhammad; and in Senegambia region, led by al-Hajj Umar al-Futi. All of these movements showed religious and political similarities. Their military aspect was accompanied by an idealism that aimed at purifying Islam of such elements as veneration of ancestral spirits and participation in traditional ceremonies that, according to the leaders, were not in keeping with true Islam.

One of the results of the movements was the reform of existing political and social institutions. In addition to strengthening the hold of Muslims over these institutions, the *jihads* also led to greater literacy and awareness of Islam through centers of education that were set up in the areas mentioned. They also led to an increase in solidarity among the various peoples from differing traditions who had converted to Islam and who supported these movements. The long-term effect of the *jihads* was the development of a strong sense of self-identification with Islam that is a continuing part of the Muslim heritage of these areas. While recognizing the necessity of new forms of education, particularly from the West, in recent times the Muslims in Africa have maintained a strong attachment to Muslim education and ways of life.

African Christianity

Where it has ancient roots, in Ethiopia and Egypt, Christianity in its Coptic form has maintained itself and constitutes an integral part of the culture that has developed around it. Much of present Christian growth, however, is the result of European and American missionary activities in the nineteenth and twentieth centuries. Where it was perceived as allied to colonization, Western Christianity often generated conflict and was seen by some African leaders and intellectuals as destroying the African way of life. But the missions also brought a system of education and health services that has survived the negative impact. Traditional forms of Western Christianity have also attracted converts, with the result that the major Christian denominations have established a strong presence in Africa. Another development that has taken place is the emergence of specifically African movements resulting from Christian influence or contact. Such movements, often led by leaders in the prophetic style, have won many adherents because they represent a way of addressing contemporary problems in an African fashion while incorporating features of Christianity with other traditions.

Such transformations of Christian traditions to meet African religious concerns are labeled ''independent African churches'' and form an increasing part of the more pluralistic religious society in Africa. The majority of such independent churches grew up around charismatic leaders. After the establishment of Christian missions among the Zulu in southern Africa, several such movements arose. They were, in part, a reaction by new Zulu Christians to the failure of some of the mission churches to handle effectively the problems created by white settlers' appropriation of Zulu lands, the establishment of a rigid system of color discrimination, and the nationalistic aspirations of the Zulu themselves. One such church, led by Isaiah Shembe (1870–1935), organized its own festivals, rituals, and practices based in large part on Zulu traditional religion. Elements of biblical prophecy were integrated into the teachings, churches were organized, ministers trained, and hymns written to provide for an organized religious life. Shembe's work was eventually carried on by his son, who acted as the new leader of the church. Some Christian groups have viewed these developments as being non-Christian and even ''pagan,'' but for the African independent churches they have provided a vehicle for integrating into their traditional life those biblical elements they consider significant and enriching.

African Influences in the Americas

The fact that several hundred thousand people of African origin were forcibly brought to the Americas as slaves led to a transmission of African influences into American culture. At the religious level such influences often continued in somewhat altered forms among blacks in Latin America and the Caribbean. Some practices associated with beliefs in spirits and healing have played a major role in life in the New World.

Other elements of African culture inspired by the religious dimension that have left their mark in the West are the arts of music and dance in ordinary life, as well as for ritual. So-called ''primitive'' art and symbols also have had an effect in a much broader way on some modern Western artists whose work has become part of the American and Western cultural heritage. The most notable is Picasso, whose works in the early part of the century show a strong influence of African sculpture. Thus, in spite of the inhuman conditions under which the African heritage was brought to the Americas, its

Traditional Family Homes. *A traditional Zulu village setting or* kraal *showing the arrangement of family huts and an enclosure for cattle.* (Courtesy of Zul Khoja)

vitality and sense of continuity has been an important factor in enriching the culture of the Americas.

African Religions Today

The nature and solidarity of African religions have inevitably undergone drastic change in the last century. The modes of production and of daily life, the systems of education and of upbringing, and the patterns of family and social life have undergone erosion. Priorities in the national life of modern African countries do not always include traditional values and ways of life. The mere effort of coping with the pressures of contemporary nation-building and economic survival has tended to reduce the impact of traditional religous life. On the other hand, indigenous religions have acted to provide a unifying element in the face of the fragmentation created by changing circumstances. They have shaped African responses to issues of social and political concern and act as an indigenous source of values and beliefs that influence their contemporary lives. Among these are beliefs that have allowed African groups in the past to create a world of unity and continuity, of harmony between the seen and the unseen. Religious beliefs have also allowed them to cultivate a deep feeling for society, for the landscape, and for the cosmos. Although political conflict and division among various groups and newly established nations have undermined the role of these values and insights, these religions continue to have a sustaining influence at the individual and social levels.

In the words of one of the characters in a modern Nigerian novel, Wole Soyinka's *The Interpreters,* the dead and the past symbolize a "dome of continuity" with the present. The "dome of religion" also provides a bridge that links the past and present, and bridges do not merely lead from here to there: "a bridge also faces backwards."[7]

NOTES

1. Ngugi wa Thiong'o, *Weep Not Child* (London: Heinemann Educational Books, Ltd., 1976), Distributed in the U.S. by Heinemann Educational Books, Inc., Portsmouth, N.H., pp. 23–24.
2. Quoted in John Mbiti, *African Religions and Philosophy* (New York: Anchor Books, 1970), p. 44.
3. Benjamin Ray, *African Religions* (Englewood Cliffs: Prentice-Hall, Inc., 1976), p. 80.
4. Jomo Kenyatta, *Facing Mt. Kenya* (New York: Vintage Books, Inc., 1970), p. 44.
5. Hans Guggenheim, *Dogon World* (New York: The Wunderman Foundation, 1975), p. 30.
6. These proverbs are derived from Isaac Eelano, *Yoruba Proverbs—Their Meaning and Usage* (Ibadan: published by author, 1966) and from Ruth Finnegan, *Oral Literature in Africa* (Oxford: Clarendon Press, 1970).
7. Wole Soyinka, *The Interpreters* (New York: Macmillan Publishing Co., 1970), p. 6.

GLOSSARY

Akan (*aah-kaahn*) a collective name for a family of ethnic groups inhabiting the southern half of Ghana and contiguous areas in the Ivory Coast.

Ani (*aah-nee*) the Earth Goddess and symbol of fertility among the Ibo.

babalawo (*baah-baah-laah-wo*) among the Yoruba, the term used for the specialist in the art of divination.

Baganda (*buh-gaahn-daah*) an African people living in Uganda, who untill modern times possessed a monarchy and a kingdom (Buganda).

Bambara (*buhm-baah-raah*) an African people found primarily in Mali.

Dogon (*doh-gohn*) an African people who have traditionally lived in cliff villages in Mali.

egwugwu (*egg-wu-gwoo*) an intermediary figure among the Ibo, who impersonates one of the ancestral spirits of a village during important ceremonies.

Gikuyu (*gih-koo-yoo*) the name of a people who live in the highlands of Kenya; it is derived from the name of their founding ancestor who is also called Gikuyu.

Ibo (*ee-gboh*) a people found in Eastern Nigeria.

Kabaka (*kuh-baah-kaah*) the title of the king among the Baganda.

Kipsigis a people found in Kenya.

Kere-Nyaga (*kay-ray-nyaah-guh*) also called Kerinyaga, the name for Mt. Kenya, which is considered by the Gikuyu as a creation and resting place of Mogai, (Ngai) or Murungu, the term for God.

Kinjikitile (*kin-jee-kit-ee-leh*) the prophetic figure who led the Maji Maji movement against German occupation of southern Tanzania, 1905–1907.

Kintu (*chin-too*) the founding figure and first king of the Baganda Kingdom.

Maji Maji (*maah-jee maah-jee*) a movement of resistance against German occupation uniting several African peoples in southern Tanzania.

mana a Polynesian term, best translated as "vital force, animating all living things."

Masai (*maah-saahi*) a pastoral people living in Kenya and northern Tanzania.

Mumbi (*moom-bee*) the mother of the Gikuyu people and the wife of its founder.

Nandi (*naahn-dee*) an African people found in West Central Kenya.

Ngai (*ngaai*) or Mogai, the Gikuyu term for God, who first created and divided the universe.

Obatala (*o-baah-tuh-luh*) a Yoruba *orisha* entrusted with the task of shaping the world and the first human beings in it.

Ogun (*o-guhn*) a Yoruba *orisha* associated with hunting and also with iron, and by extension weapons and war.

Olokun (*o-loh-koon*) a female Yoruba *orisha* associated with the waters and the sea.

Olorun (*o-loh-roon*) or Olorun Olodumare, the supreme deity of the sky.

orisha (*oh-ree-shuh*) in Yoruba belief, these are divinities who control the relations between the heavens and the world.

Orunmila (*o-roon-mee-luh*) the *orisha* of divination among the Yoruba.

Yoruba (*yo-roo-buh*) the Yoruba people are found in Nigeria and are probably the largest African group on the continent.

Zulu (*zoo-loo*) an African poeple living in southern Africa.

SUGGESTED READINGS

FERNANDEZ, J. W. *Bwiti, an Ethnography of the Religious Imagination in Africa*. Princeton: Princeton University Press, 1982.

GUGGENHEIM, HANS. *Dogon World*. New York: The Wunderman Foundation, 1975.

HOUNTONDJI, P. *African Philosophy: Myth and Reality*. Bloomington: Indiana University Press, 1983.

IDOWU, E. B. *African Traditional Religion: A Definition*. London: SCM Press, 1973.

KENYATTA, JOMO. *Facing Mt. Kenya*. New York: Vintage Books, 1965.

KING, NOEL Q. *African Cosmos: An Introduction to Religion in Africa*. Belmont: Wadsworth Publishing Company, 1986.

LAWSON, E. T. *Religions of Africa*. New York: Harper & Row, 1984.

LEWIS, I. M., ED. *Islam in Tropical Africa*. 2d. ed. London: International African Institute, 1980.

MACGAFFEY, W. *Religion and Society in Central Africa*. Chicago: University of Chicago Press, 1986.

MBITI, JOHN. *African Religions and Philosophy*. New York: Anchor Books, 1970.

_____. *Concepts of God in Africa*. New York: Praeger Publishers, Inc., 1966.

NGUGI, WA THIONG'O. *Weep Not Child*. London: Heinemann Educational Books Ltd., 1976.

OKOT, P'BITEK. *African Religions in Western Scholarship*. Nairobi: East African Publishing House, 1970.

PARRINDER, GEOFFREY. *Religion in Africa*. London: Penguin Books, 1969.

RANGER, T. O., and I. KIMAMBO, eds. *The Historical Study of African Religion*. Berkeley: University of California Press, 1970.

RAY, BENJAMIN. *African Religions. Englewood Cliffs, N.J.: Prentice-Hall, Inc., 1976*.

SOYINKA, WOLE. *The Interpreters*. New York: Macmillan Publishing Co., 1970.

TURNER, VICTOR. *Revelation and Divination in Ndembu Ritual*. Ithaca, N.Y.: Cornell University Press, 1975.

ZAHN, DOMINIQUE. *The Religion, Spirituality and Thought of Traditional Africa*. Chicago: University of Chicago Press, 1979.

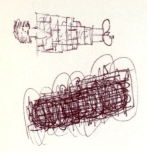

4

Hinduism

आत्मेत्येवोपासीत, अत्र ह्येते सर्व एकं भवन्ति ।

तदेतत्पदनीयमस्य सर्वस्य यदयमात्मा, अनेन ह्येतत्सर्वं वेद ।

यथा ह वै पदेनानुविन्देद्देवम्

*"In all these (individual) things, the (Unmanifest) Atman reveals
Its footprints by which It may be known, just as one follows and
finds (an animal) by its footprints." (Brihadārankyaka Upanishad,
I.4.7)*

In the early morning today, this day, any day, all over India in the homes of pious Hindus the man of the family arose with the dawn, before the sun. He purified himself with water. Repeating sacred verses, he stirred again into flame the coals of the sacred household fire, which is worshiped as the fire-god, Agni. Then facing the east and raising his arms to the rising sun, the god Savitar, he recited the ancient holy verse, "May we attain that excellent glory of Savitar the god. So may he stimulate our prayers. With understanding, earnestly we crave our portion of prosperity from Savitar the god."[1]

This verse has been recited every morning, in this way, without intermission since at least as early as 1500 B.C.E. It is thus part of the longest, unbroken span of ritual practice in the world, one that is nearly 3,500 years old! By the performance of this morning ritual, called the Agnihotra, including the recitation of this verse, the worshiper expects to gain from the sun the gifts of energy and prosperity for himself and his household. It is also believed that by performing the ritual the worshiper gives added vitality to the power of the sun to arise and accomplish its work. This holy verse to the sun appears in a hymn to various gods in an ancient hymn-book called the Rig-Veda. This collection, which contains over one thousand hymns, slowly evolved into its present form by about 1000 B.C.E., with only a few hymns inserted after that time.

The beginnings of the Agnihotra ritual, and of much else in today's Hinduism, carry us far back into the prehistory of the Indian subcontinent. The people who created and used these hymns were the Indo–Aryans. They migrated into India from Central Asia or Iran about 1500 B.C.E. These Indo–Aryans were related by language and religion to other Indo–European peoples, who migrated from Central Asia into Iran, Anatolia, Greece, Italy, and northern Europe between 2000 and 1500 B.C.E.

Recent archaeological and linguistic evidence shows that the *Indo–Aryan culture* established itself in Northwest India and then remained largely isolated from the indigenous cultures to the south and east for nearly a thousand years thereafter. The conquering Indo–Aryans had their own system of belief and practice, which is often called *Brahmanic* or *Vedic* religion. The indigenous cultures, in whose territory Jainism and, later on, Buddhism arose, already had beliefs and practices that differed sharply from those of Vedic religion. Evidence for the existence of these advanced non-Vedic cultures was not available to early scholars, many of whom, therefore, held that Jainism and Buddhism *must have been* developments from Vedic religion. Modern archaeological evidence shows a cultural context for early Jainism that is distinctive and separate from that of early Vedic areas. This new evidence is incorporated in the treatment of Hinduism presented in this chapter.

When Vedic religion finally came into intensive encounter with Jainism and Buddhism between the fifth and second centuries B.C.E., Vedic religion was profoundly modified. *Hinduism* proper emerged from this encounter. Since Hinduism derives from both Vedic and indigenous religions, it will be presented in this chapter by beginning with the separate sources that later mingled. The resulting Hinduism, with its variety and complexity, will then be explored, and, finally, the later developments and the effects of further encounters with other religions and cultures will be examined.

The focus of this chapter is on Hinduism, and therefore only those aspects of Jainism and Buddhism will be considered here that are necessary for the understanding of the development of Hinduism. Similarly, only those aspects of the encounters with Islam and with the West that have to do with Hindu responses and perceptions will be discussed. Buddhism is the subject of Chapter 5 and Islam of Chapter 9.

Indus Valley Culture

The first people whom the Indo–Aryan forebearers of the Hindus encountered as they came into India looking for a land in which to settle were the inhabitants of the cities of the Indus Valley.

Until about 1920 many scholars held that all the battles with the numerous enemies in their "strong forts" described in the hymns of the *Rig-Veda* were mythical encounters with demons and the forces of nature. Some of the references are indeed mythological. But in 1920 the ruin of an impressive, ancient city was discovered near the village of Harappa on an old bed of the Ravi River (see page 64). Soon many other sites of this Indus Valley culture were found and excavated, including the even larger city of Mohenjodaro, which stood on an old bank of the Indus River. Although the lowest levels of Mohenjodaro have not yet been reached, the excavated levels date back to 2700 B.C.E. The people of this culture were Dravidians and were called *Dasas* by the invading Aryans.

It is evident that the Indus Valley culture had begun to deteriorate even before the Aryans migrated into the area around 1500 B.C.E. A vast flood of long duration had also overtaken most of the territory of the Indus Valley people. Thus, when the Aryans pushed into northwest India they encountered the remnants of the dying Indus Valley culture; they fought and won fierce battles with the last defenders of the Indus cities. Many Aryan hymns honoring the war god, Indra, describe such battles, for instance, a battle at Hariyupiya on the Ravi River.

This one great power of thine [Indra] our eyes have witnessed,
   wherewith thou slewest Varashikka's children . . .

At Hariyupiya he smote the vanguard of the Vrichivans,
   and the rear fled in fright.
Three thousand, armed, in quest of fame, together on the
   Yavyavati [Ravi], O much-sought Indra, . . .

Falling before the arrow, like bursting vessels
   went to their destruction.[2]

The Indus Valley culture was highly developed in engineering and technology. It was an urban culture supported by extensive agriculture, made possible partially by irrigation using systems of sluices, diversion dams, and canals. The Indus people built their cities with millions of kiln-baked bricks of standard size and proportion. The cities were remarkable for their skillfully engineered drainage systems. Covered brick drains, which ran along all major streets, received waste and water from private homes. Weights and measures, too, were standardized and highly accurate. The inhabitants of the Indus cities used a fully developed writing system, known to us mainly from the many thousands of small, stone stamping-seals that have been found at all Indus Valley sites.

The seals are exquisitely carved, usually bearing the figure of an animal and some characters of the Indus writing. But with no extended texts from which to work, it has not yet been possible to decipher the writing.

What can be known of the religion of the Indus Valley people is very meager indeed. No written records of a religious nature have survived, and it is very chancy to reconstruct religious beliefs on the basis of artifacts alone. For example, at Columbia University in New York, at the top of imposing steps and in front of a great domed building stands a magnificent marble statue of a woman draped in flowing robes. On the pedestal of the statue is the inscription "Alma Mater." If New York should be buried and all written records lost, and if future archaeologists should dig it up again, it would be easy for them to reconstruct all this as a sacred place where a great mother goddess was worshiped by a coastal people. The domed building would be labeled the temple of the goddess Alma Mater, whose statue stood before its doors. How wrong they would be!

In the Indus Valley cities certain artifacts have been found that appear to have had religious significance, but without written records their exact meaning and use cannot be known. The most astonishing thing about these cities from the standpoint of religion is that there are no large-scale buildings or images whatsoever that were used for religious purposes, such as the great temples and statues from the same period in Egypt and Mesopotamia. This is especially interesting since among the earliest hymns of the invading Aryans scornful references are made to the enemy as a people who have no rituals, "the ancient riteless ones." Now the Aryans, who themselves had elaborate religious rituals, did not build temples either and sharply opposed image worship. Thus, their scorn of the enemy as being "riteless" would have been based on an absence of ritual practice, not on the absence of buildings or images. Yet this observation fits in well with the archaeological material, which provides no evidence for any public ceremonial type of religion in the Indus Valley.

Some of the types of artifacts found in the Indus cities reapppear later in historical times, when their use and meaning can be known. The most important of such objects from the Indus Valley culture are the many stone images of the phallus, the male generative organ, later called the *lingam*. Some of these objects are only a

Indus Valley Stamp-Seal. A 4,000-year-old carved stone seal from Mohenjodaro was used to stamp this plaster impression. This "unicorn" animal appears more frequently on the seals than any other. Characters of the Indus Valley script are seen across the top. The original is approximately 2 by 2 inches. (Courtesy of Hyla Converse)

few inches in size; others are two or three feet high. The workmanship on most of them is of very high quality, indicating the value placed upon them. It is of interest again that in an early hymn of the Aryans the indigenous people are scornfully described as "phallus-worshipers." Along with these have been found stone circles of the type later called the *yoni*, symbol of the female generative organ. In later historical times the *lingam* and *yoni* are connected with the worship of the god Shiva, in whose temples the central image worshiped is the phallus, the *lingam* of Shiva.

Later, Shiva is also represented as the Great *Yogin*, the great meditative ascetic. On a very few of the Indus seals recovered—about five out of many thousands of seals—there is depicted a human figure squatting in a yoga position, surrounded by animals later associated with Shiva. In addition, about five or six limestone figures have been found of men, all in a single pose. They are seated, wearing a robe over the left shoulder that leaves the right shoulder bare. The left hand is on the slightly raised left knee, and the right hand is on the right knee. The seated pose must represent some sort of formalized position, for it is repeated in all of these statues. The position is very similar to later yoga positions of meditation.

A large number of crudely made, baked-clay figurines have been found, both male and female. The greater number are female and in them the sexual characteristics are exaggerated, suggesting that their use might have been related to the desire for fertility. Yet many of them have been found in burial pots, suggesting perhaps some idea of rebirth, but whether in an afterlife or a new existence on earth cannot be known. Female figurines were used later in historical times in fertility rituals.

Probably the most famous carved stone figure from the Indus cities is that of the so-called "priest-king," a small object only about five inches high. The half-closed eyes seem set in meditation. Without any inscription (and even if there were one, it could not yet be

read), it is impossible to tell what the significance of this unique object was for the Indus people. There are also a very few bronze figures—"dancing" girls, a bull, and a few others—all of which are small and may have had a connection with religion.

At Mohenjodaro, and at no other site, an extraordinary rectangular water tank was found.[3] It measured 39 by 23 by 8 feet deep. Wide steps led down to the bottom at each end. The walls and bottom were made of double layers of brick with a layer of bitumen between, making them watertight. Since only one such tank has been found, an identification with later Hindu religious usage of temple tanks cannot be inferred.

Beginnings: Vedic Sources, 1500–500 B.C.E.

Vedic Religion: The Affirmation of the Value of Human Existence

The hymns of the Rig-Veda are our earliest source of knowledge about the Indo–Aryans. Because their religion is known as *Vedic religion,* they are also called *Vedic people.* The earliest part of the Rig-Veda to be collected was the group of hymns in Books II through VII. Books I, VIII, IX, and X were added by stages later.

The encounter of the Indo–Aryans with the Indus Valley culture left little mark on the Indo–Aryan beliefs or way of life. They neither adopted Indus Valley bricks for building, nor pottery styles, nor drainage systems, nor irrigation techniques. They destroyed all these and went their way. Some of the conquered people were absorbed into the Aryan community, but they appear to have been thoroughly "aryanized." The language of the Aryans was Sanskrit, and in this early period of their encounter with the Indus Culture there was a minimal adoption into Vedic Sanskrit of foreign Dravidian words. Since the entry of foreign words into a language is usually a good barometer of foreign cultural influence, this indicates that the inhabitants were Dravidian speakers and that the Aryans had very limited cultural interaction with them.

Some influence did eventually penetrate from the indigenous peoples. By the end of the period when the

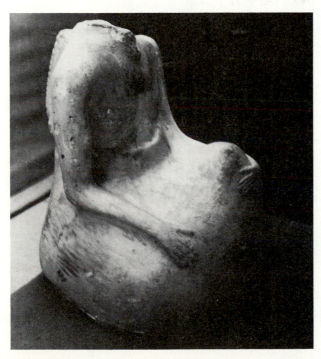

Limestone Figure in Yoga-like Position. *This is one of five or six such figures at the site museum, Mohenjodaro; all of the figures are in this same position. The original is approximately 2½ to 3 feet high.* (Courtesy of Hyla Converse)

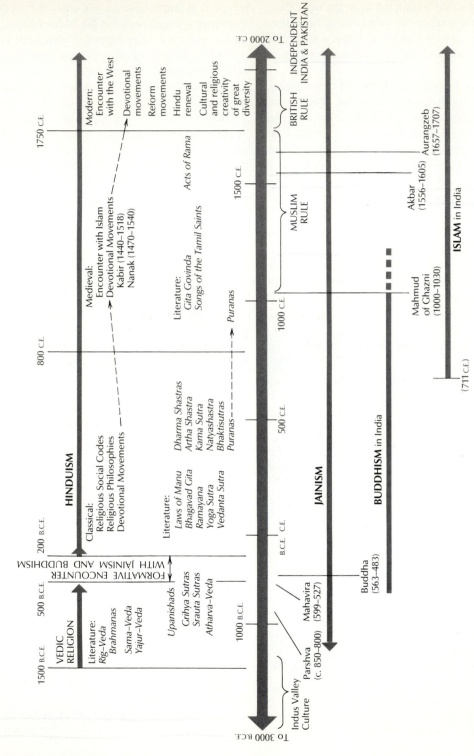

Chronological Chart of the Development of Religions in India

hymns of the Rig-Veda were composed and collected (about 1000 B.C.E.), magic and sorcery, so fiercely condemned in the earliest hymns, had crept into Aryan practice. And in one of the last hymns, in order to claim religious sanction for the new use of sorcery, it is stated that the Vedic god Indra robbed the Dasa enemy of his magic and gave it to the ancient great sages to whom it was believed the Vedic rituals had originally been revealed.

The People. The early Aryans were divided into five major tribes. Within each Aryan tribe there were three class groupings, but they were not rigid. Depending on circumstances, it was possible for a person to move from one group to another. The highest rank was that of the princes and warriors. The society was dominated by the warriors, and the chief prince of the tribe was a warrior who could command the other warriors. Next came the priestly singers, in charge of the sacred ritual traditions and the performance of great public ceremonies. The priests competed hotly with one another to gain the prince's favor, for the privilege of officiating on great occasions was always richly rewarded. The third group, lowest in rank, was called simply "the people." They were the ones who farmed the land and cared for the cattle under the direction of the warrior families. The tribes were divided into clans and the clans into large households. The Aryans were fair-skinned and tawny-bearded, and they held the Dasas in contempt because, among other reasons, they were dark-skinned. The Aryans soon began to speak of themselves as being of the Aryan *varna*, or "color," and they regarded themselves as separate and superior to other peoples.

During the first two hundred years after their arrival, the Indo–Aryans established themselves and settled down in the territory that was to be theirs for the next eight hundred years and that they called *Aryavarta*. This territory included the area of the Five Rivers (*Panj-ab*, "five-rivers"), which are Indus River tributaries, and the area of the Two Rivers (*Do-ab*, "two-rivers"), the Jumna (Yamuna), and the upper Ganges (see page 64). The Aryans settled down quickly and then kept to themselves to an extraordinary degree. Archaeological materials in this area go back to about 1100 B.C.E. The Aryan territory had its own distinctive artifacts and a beautiful Painted Grey Ware pottery. The cultures to the south and east

had a number of distinctive potteries, and most of them also used the Black-and-Red Ware. One of the reasons for the long isolation of the Aryans from their neighbors is indicated in the Vedic texts: it was self-imposed. They were forbidden to go among peoples where the sacred fired, Agni, did not burn and the twice-daily offerings to Agni were not performed. If they did indeed venture into such a land, there were severe penalties to be paid on their return. Thus, the only alternatives envisioned by the Vedic Aryans during this period were self-isolation or conquest.

Vedic Gods, Rituals, and Human Happiness. The Vedic religion was primarily a household religion. Its most widespread and consistent religious practice was the twice-daily ritual with which this chapter opened: in the home at dawn and sunset offerings were made to the gods in the household fire and the sun was worshiped. This *Agnihotra*, as we said, is a ritual that survives to this day. The hymns of the Rig-Veda make it clear that this ritual was carried out by the head of each household (without need of a priest) in the homes of all Aryans, those of the poor and lowly as well as those of priests, warriors, and princes. The hearthfire in each home—the fire that cooked their food, warmed their homes, and dispelled the darkness of night—was worshiped as the god Agni. In some clans the *Agnihotra* ritual was performed at noon as well as at dawn and dusk. Fire was believed to have three forms: the hearthfire (and other fires), the lightning, and the sun. Two of the forms of fire, the hearthfire (Agni) and the sun (Savitar), are worshiped in the *Agnihotra* ritual.

Agni.   A powerful god living in each home was Agni, the hearthfire; no aspect of life, however humble, was beyond his reach or alien to him. Agni had many functions. Along with the sun (Savitar), Agni was worshiped as the source of fertility in man, animals, and the land. Agni was the messenger who went to fetch the other gods and bring them to attend the rituals. Agni was the "mouth of the gods," for the food-offerings and drink-offerings to other gods, as well as to Agni, were placed in the fire, where Agni "ate" (burned) them, thereby passing this food and drink, and its strength, to each god for whom it was designated. In this way Agni could be regarded as both priest of the gods and the household priest of men. Agni also aided in battle by burning up the enemy, and in agriculture by burning forests to clear the land for plowing. He was, in addition, a purifier and powerful force against demons, evil spirits, and magic. And, like the other gods, Agni was a dispenser of all that was desired and expected in Vedic religion: riches, happiness, long life, and many heroic sons. It is not surprising that in the Rig-Veda there are more hymns to Agni than to any other god. The following verses were taken from a few of the earliest hymns to Agni, the god of fire:

He for the Fivefold People's sake [the Aryan five tribes]
    has seated him in every home,
Wise, Youthful, Master of the house.
On all sides may that Agni guard our household folk and
    property;
May he deliver us from woe.

We make you our messenger, you, you the Most Glorious
    One. Bring the gods here to the feast.
O Son of Strength, give to all of us the food that strengthens
    men, give that for which we pray to you.
Rescue from distress whoever sings praise to you at evening
    time and morning time and brings you offerings with
    the rituals you love.

Knower of all that lives, O Agni, may we, both singers of
    praise and chiefs, continue in your keeping.
Lead us to glorious wealth, abundant, excellent. And make
    us rich in hero-sons and their descendants.[4]

Indra. The other god to whom a very large number of the hymns of the Rig-Veda are addressed is Indra. As has been noted already, he was the great warrior god who had led the Aryans to victory and settlement in northern India. With his thunderbolt weapon, he was also the god of storm and rain. He was the great giver of wealth, especially of booty won in battle, of long life, strength, and happiness. When Indra was invoked at special public ceremonies, the ritual of offering the *soma* was performed. Indra was the great *soma* drinker among the gods, although all of them were believed to enjoy it. *Soma* was a drink made from the stems of a plant, whose juices were pressed out and mixed with milk. This drink had an exhilarating effect and invigorated both gods and humans for extraordinary deeds of strength and valor. There are also hymns that warn sharply against the nonritual use of *soma*. Many of the hymns to Indra must have been composed for such great ceremonies, for they refer to the preparation and offering of the *soma*.

The verses below are excerpts from an early hymn to Indra:

Seeking riches, we offer you these gifts of food, which
    will increase your strength like streams of flowing
    water . . .
Strengthened by songs of praise you tore to shreds the Dasa,
    who had believed himself invulnerable . . .

We who add strength to your own splendid vigor, placing
    within your hands the splendid bolt of thunder,
Grown splendid thus with us, may you, O Indra, with Surya
    overcome the Dasa races . . .

Give us the riches that we long for, O most powerful god,
    and many, many noble children.
Give us a friend, O Indra, give us a dwelling place . . .[5]

Other Vedic Gods. Besides Agni and Indra, the Vedic Aryans gave honor and worship to a number of other major gods and many minor ones. Varuna was the great god who was the guardian of Holy Order, or Law. Varuna thus received prayers for rain, or for protection of a ceremony, or to witness a contract. His forgiveness was sought for cheating, gambling, or drunkenness; he was entreated to bring down his wrath on enemies who lied or cheated or injured the worshiper. The means for gaining Varuna's forgiveness, or his retribution on others, was to perform a ritual that would please Varuna and influence him to grant whatever was requested.

Heaven and Earth were regarded as immediate sources of prosperity and were addressed as Father and Mother of all creatures. Savitar, the sun, was worshiped as a source of fertility for man and beast and field. Dawn, the lovely goddess who went before Savitar into the sky each morning, was invoked with some of the most poetic verses in all of the Rig-Veda. Night similarly was a goddess, the twin of Dawn. The rivers also were sometimes worshiped as goddesses, but male deities dominated Vedic religion and society, and the goddesses, while honored, had little influence in the affairs of men. Two of the gods who were to emerge later in Hinduism as powerful and popular gods were of minor importance to Vedic religion. These were Vishnu and Shiva Rudra.

The Vedic gods were vivid and strong-willed. They directed natural forces and historical events. Most of the gods could be counted upon to act in kindly ways toward those who invoked them with the songs and offerings of the Vedic ritual, which the gods dearly desired.

The Vedic gods, when properly invoked, fought for the Vedic Aryan people against the enemy Dasa people. The Vedic gods could bring rain when needed, abundant harvests, increases in cattle, good health, long life, many heroic sons to carry on the family line, and happy homes. The gods coud also give victory, power, and riches. Vedic people thought it was great to be alive! And they fully intended to be rich and happy for as long as they could. Life was a marvelous thing, and they wanted all of it they could get. The gods could make men happy if they themselves were made happy. The primary way to make the gods happy was through the performance of ritual.

Holy Law, Holy Power, and Human Participation.

How did the ritual function? Ritual was understood as the formalized offering of a gift to a god in order to get back from the god the benefits desired. It was not exactly a trading transaction, because there could be no bargaining with a god. But it was clearly and frankly a matter of giving to the god what he wanted, in order to get from him what the performer of the ritual wanted: "I yoke with prayer thine ancient holy power."[6] In the hymns to Agni and Indra on the previous pages, this use of the ritual to "give, in order to get" is clearly evident, as is the practical, material nature of the benefits desired.

The ritual did not function only in this direct, simple fashion, however. It had a cosmic function as well. It affected the whole universe! The universe was governed by Holy Law, and there were three aspects to this Law: (1) the regularities of nature, (2) the ritual regulations, and (3) all civil and criminal laws of Aryan society. All of these were included in what the Vedic Aryan meant by *Holy Law*. Holy Law was the holy structure or order of the universe, dependable and inviolate. This Holy Law might be likened to a great wheel, but the wheel could not turn and the universe could not function without a power that moved it and made it live. This dynamic power that gave energy and strength to all things was the *Holy Power*, Brahman. It operated in ritual actions, circulated in the universe and kept it functioning.

The Ritual and Its Function.

An extraordinary aspect of the Vedic outlook was the belief that this cosmic

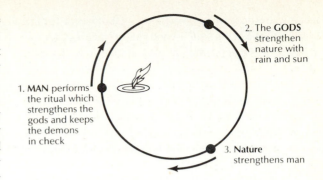

The Vedic View of the Function of the Ritual. *The performance of the Vedic ritual gives strength to the gods and therefore has an indispensable role in regenerating the living power in the universe.*

Holy Power was *strengthened* and *regenerated* in the actions of human worshipers carrying out the ritual. The performance of the *Agnihotra* ritual at dawn strengthened the sun, the god Savitar, and assisted the sun to rise and perform its function in the universe. The only point in the whole universe where this Holy Power was renewed was in the ritual performed by the Vedic worshipers. This gave them a place of key importance in the whole scheme of things. One might think of the ritual as functioning like a power transformer, and of Vedic homes as a network of such transformers, where day by day Vedic worshipers were stepping up the power in cosmic circuits and achieving their own happiness in return.

What would happen if the ritual were not performed? The gods would not die, nature would not cease moving altogether; but they would lose vitality, and human beings would be diminished. One hymn speaks of ancient, forgotten gods to whom rituals were no longer offered and who had, therefore, grown "loose-strung" and lost their alertness and their power to act with vigor. Holy Law and Holy Power thus functioned together in a self-reinforcing, dynamic cycle of interrelated and interdependent parts that formed a whole, and man's ritual action regenerated the power. Man performed the ritual and thereby strengthened the gods, who strengthened nature, which strengthened man, who performed the ritual, and the cycle began again. The gods could also act directly to aid man, as in granting victory in battle.

The ordinary daily *Agnihotra* offerings to the gods

usually consisted of butter oil, flat cakes of various grains, or merely roasted grains, wood, and sometimes fragrant substances. Of the food, a small amount was burned in the fire. The rest was eaten by the people of the household. The great public ceremonies were community feasts, where bread and meat were ritually offered to the gods and then distributed to all the people. One hymn describes the seated people waiting eagerly to bite into the meat.

The preparation and consumption of the *soma* drink mentioned earlier was part of the ritual action that was performed only at the great public ceremonies. The *soma* also was first offered to the gods and then consumed, but by priests and warriors only. The ritual offering of gifts of food and drink to the gods is the central act of the Vedic ritual. The gifts are given in the confident expectation that the gods will reciprocate and give back to the people the gifts that they desire in return.

Other Vedic Beliefs. In the early part of the Vedic period, when the hymns of the earliest collection were composed, the people invoked the gods for many things but never for any sort of life after death. Death was regarded as the end of human existence. The gods were immortal. Man was mortal. The contrast was frequently drawn. The hymns spoke of death as "darkness," as "the pit," as being like sleep. Since this life was their only life, the Vedic people wanted it to be filled full with prosperity and happiness. They sought to achieve the continuity of their family line (the only "immortality" possible) through successive generations of sons and grandsons. By the time, however, that the final book was added to the collection of the Rig-Veda (about 1000 B.C.E.), the Vedic people had come to believe in the possibility of a happy, immortal existence after death with the "gods and fathers" in some sort of heaven.

Entry into this heaven was achieved through good deeds and the performance of the correct rituals, which symbolically "built up" or created for the worshiper his own individual, immortal body. Without the rituals he would have no immortal body. At death, with the help of the proper funeral rituals, the worshiper's good deeds would cling to his immortal body and be carried over with him into "yonder world" as the only form of wealth that he could take along. If one did not perform the proper rituals, one would fail to achieve this heavenly immortality and would simply fall out of existence when one's body died, the physical elements being reabsorbed into nature, as in the earlier belief.

In addition to the Rig-Veda, two other Vedas developed in the early period. The *Sama-Veda* adds very little to our knowledge of Vedic religion. It is the handbook of special chanter-priests, containing those hymns or parts of hymns from the Rig-Veda for which the chanters were responsible during the ceremonies. The *Yajur-Veda* is similarly a handbook for those priests who were responsible for directing any ritual. It contained all the prose formulas that told the worshipers and other priests what to do next during the ritual. It provides a great deal of information on the actual performance of rituals, little of which is found in the Rig-Veda. Long after the end of the Vedic period, a group of ancient materials was raised to the status of a fourth Veda, the *Atharva-Veda*. It contains charms against disease and danger, magical formulas for cursing personal enemies, and philosophical hymns.

Between 1000 B.C.E. and about 700 B.C.E., commentaries and instructions on the rituals began to be composed. They were called *Brahmanas*. To each of the three Vedas were attached its own Brahmanas. They explained why specific rituals or verses were to be used and what benefits were to be expected. They justified details of ritual practice by telling elaborate stories of gods or ancient sages, who, when confronted by some specific need, had performed a ritual in a certain way to get what they desired, and thus humans should perform the ritual in exactly the same way to achieve the same end. The Brahmanas showed a luxurious growth of mythological elements, and consistency between the various myths was of no concern—as indeed, it was not in the Rig-Veda either. In Vedic myths, for instance, various gods were honored for having created the world. What was important was the honor bestowed; a literal account of creation was not intended.

The Brahmanas placed special emphasis on the symbolic meaning of the ritual. It was held that the one who knew this inner symbolic meaning would profit many times more than those who performed the same ritual knowing only its simple traditional meaning. But anxiety developed regarding the lasting effectiveness of the rituals. New rituals began to appear to protect a person from an enemy who might use black magic to steal from him the results of his ritual performances, such as the rewards of his good deeds or his immortal body. Verses were added to the ritual to avert the black magic and turn it back onto the one who tried to use it. In the later Brahmanas there are also verses for bringing about the death of a personal enemy. Thus, the use of magic, so sharply rejected in the early books of the Rig-Veda, came to be sanctioned in these priestly books.

Atman and Brahman, the Ultimate Reality. Another important development took place in the late Vedic period. From about 700 B.C.E., philosophical speculations began to be collected and preserved. Some of these were in the form of dialogues between famous sages of the time and their questioners. These collections were called *Upanishads;* they were strictly limited to a religious elite and were forbidden to be taught to anyone but the teacher's own son or an exceptional pupil. There was one question above all with which the early Upanishads were preoccupied: Is there one single eternal Reality that is the source and essence of the multiform variety of the experienced world? And if there is such an ultimate Reality, they asked, what is It and how might It be known? Such questioning grew logically out of the early Rig-Vedic view that the universe was a unity of interdependent parts—gods, nature, man—functioning in a dynamic order. Even in the earliest collection of the Rig-Veda, a very few hymns point in this direction; and in the final Book X a significant number of philosophical hymns raise such questions as: Where did this world all come from? How did it arise? Could anyone know? Did even the gods know? Various answers were suggested, but it was not until the early Upanishads that these questions were explored in depth.

The answer came from two different directions, but it was the same answer. The first was based on the ancient idea of the Holy Power that circulated in everything and made the universe live and move. This power, the *Brahman*, was now thought to exist independently of the universe, as its source and essence. The Brahman was thus regarded as *transcendent*, but It was also thought of as *immanent;* that is, as being present in everything, everywhere, "right to the tips of the fingernails." The inner essence of each individual thing was thus a part of the Essence of the whole universe.

The second way of thinking about the nature of the ultimate Reality sprang from reflection on the ordinary human perception that it is a person's *self* that organizes, directs, and experiences his own life. From this it was inferred that there must similarly be a Self of the universe, and that this Self was *both transcendent and immanent*. Each individual self was a part of the Great Self of the universe. The term used for the self in both its immanent, individual form and as the transcendent, absolute Reality, was *Atman*. Thus, both Atman and Brahman referred to the same two aspects of reality: the *individual* essence, soul, or self; and the All, the *universal*, Absolute Essence, Soul, Self, the Supreme Reality of the universe, of which the individual self was a part. A brief, poetic statement of this belief appears in the oldest Upanishad, the *Brihadaranyaka Upanishad* and is also printed in Sanskrit at the beginning of this chapter: "The self is the footprint of the All by which It may be tracked."[7]

In the earliest Upanishads, the *Brihadaranyaka* and the *Chandogya,* and especially in the dialogues connected with the names of the two greatest Vedic sages of this period, Yajnavalkya and Uddalaka Aruni, it was the fact of the presence of the Brahman, or Atman, in all things that gave all things in this world a superlative value. One of the finest passages in the Upanishads is the little dialogue between Yajnavalkya and his wife Maitreyi. Yajnavalkya is about to die and wishes to discuss with Maitreyi the provisions he has made for her continued support and that of his other wife Katyayani. But Maitreyi wants to talk about the great issue confronting them and asks, instead, that he teach her about immortality.

Yajnavalkya, pleased with her request, tells her that she was dear to him before, but that she is even dearer now; and then he proceeds to explain that it is the presence of the Atman in all persons and things, as their essence, that makes them dear to us and gives a value to them from beyond themselves. The presence of the Atman, immanent in all existing things, gives each entity its full, individual reality and affirms its value. At death the individual atman ceases to exist as an individual and is merged back into its source, the universal Atman. The universal Atman thus creates the value of the atman, the self, in its individual existence. In this view, as in other positions he takes, Yajnavalkya was reasserting in more philosophical ways the early Vedic belief that life was good, and that it had value. Since after this life there was no other, one should fill this life full of

joy. The fact that each individual life must end cannot negate its reality, beauty, and value. For in its finitude an individual is still an expression of the Infinite, the Absolute, the finite·form of Its presence in the world. Below are excerpts from the dialogue.

"Maitreyi!" said Yajnavalkya, "Listen now. I am about to go forth from this state. Let me make a final settlement for you and Katyayani."

Then Maitreyi said: "If now, sir, this whole earth filled with wealth were mine, would that make me immortal?"

"No," said Yajnavalkya. "Your life would be like the life of the rich. Of immortality, however, there is no hope through wealth."

Then Maitreyi said: "What would I want with it then, if it cannot make me immortal? What you know, sir—please teach me that."

Yajnavalkya replied: "Ah, you are very dear to me, and dear is what you say! Come, sit down. I will explain to you. But while I am explaining, you must try to think carefully of what I say."

Then he said: "Now hear what is true. It is not for love of the husband that a husband is dear (of value, precious), but for love of the Atman a husband is dear.

"Truly, it is not for love of the wife that a wife is dear, but for the love of the Atman a wife is dear . . .

Truly, it is not for love of wealth that wealth is dear, but for the love of the Atman wealth is dear.

"Truly, it is not for love of Brahmanhood . . . Kshatrahood . . . worlds . . . gods . . . spirits . . . not for love of all that all is dear, but for love of the Atman all is dear.

"Truly I say, it is the Atman that should be seen, that should be hearkened to, that should be thought on, that should be pondered, O Maitreyi. Truly, it is by seeing It, by listening to It, by thinking about It, and by understanding the Atman, that this whole world is known. . . . This Atman is everything that is here . . .

"Arising out of these elements, into them also one vanishes away. After death there is no consciousness. This is what I say." Thus spoke Yajnavalkya.[8]

The anxiety about what might happen to a person in some sort of existence after death was intensified by some non-Vedic beliefs that began to be known among the Upanishadic thinkers. In one dialogue a group of priests came to Yajnavalkya and told him that they had heard it said that if in this life a person ate a cow, in the next life the cow would eat him. Yajnavalkya's answer was to dismiss the problem entirely. He folded his arms across his chest and replied, "If the beef is tender, I will eat it." In another dialogue, while on a journey to the east of the Vedic territory, he taught the Atman doctrine to the great King Janaka of Videha as the way of deliverance from the fear that retribution and suffering await one in some sort of existence after this one. Janaka, persuaded to believe in the Atman, was freed from fear, and was so grateful that he offered himself and all of his people to be Yajnavalkya's servants.

Uddalaka Aruni also taught that there was one ultimate Reality that was the source of the existence and value of the whole world, and sometimes he referred to it as Atman and sometimes as Brahman. Whichever term is used, it is clear that the essence or soul of each individual person or thing is a part of, and identical with, the Essence or Soul of the universe. Uddalaka Aruni, in his famous dialogue with his son, used vivid illustrations. He teaches that the Atman invisibly permeates all things, as does salt dissolved in water. The Atman, as the essence of each individual thing, is the unseen source of its vitality, as the invisible essence of the fig seed is the source of the great fig tree. At the end of each example he turns to his son Shvetaketu and declares that he, Shvetaketu, also *is* that Absolute, that Real, that Atman, that All. Below is part of Uddalaka Aruni's dialogue with his son Shvetaketu.

"Bring me a fig from over there," [said Uddalaka Aruni.]
"Here it is, sir."
"Divide it . . . What do you see there?"
"These rather fine seeds, sir."
"Of these, please, divide one. . . . What do you see there?"
"Nothing at all, sir."
Then he said to him: 'Truly, my dear, that finest essence which you cannot even perceive—verily, my dear, from that finest essence this great Nyagrodha [fig] tree thus arises.

"Believe me, my dear," he said, "that which is the finest essence—this whole world has that as its Soul. That is Reality. That is Atman (Soul). That you are, Shvetaketu." . . .

"Of this great tree, my dear, if some one should strike at the root . . . [or] at its top, it would bleed, but still live. Being pervaded by Atman (Soul), it continues to stand, eagerly drinking in moisture and rejoicing.

"If the life leaves one branch of it, then it dries up. . . . If it leaves the whole, the whole dries up. Even so, indeed, my dear, understand." he said.

"Truly, indeed, when life has left it, this body dies. The life does not die.

"That which is the finest essence—this whole world has that as its Soul. That is Reality. That is Atman (Soul). That you are, Shvetaketu."[9]

Uddalaka Aruni, like Yajnavalkya, was also confronted with non-Vedic doctrines regarding the fate of the individual after death. The dialogue dealing most directly with this issue starts out by doubly emphasizing that the doctrine in question, the "Five Fires" doctrine, was never taught to Shvetaketu as part of his rigorous Vedic schooling. Shvetaketu was taunted by some priests because he did not know this doctrine, and went to complain to his father that he had not taught him all the doctrines. His father, one of the most learned and wise of Vedic sages, surprised him by saying that he had never heard of the doctrine either. Uddalaka Aruni then went himself to learn the new teaching; he had to go, not to more learned Brahmins or priests of his own people, but to a king of a neighboring territory to the east of the Vedic Painted Grey Ware area. The king was reluctant to teach him. The doctrine is that of transmigration and karma, the doctrine that the soul passes through an endless series of lives on earth (transmigration), and that the circumstances of each life, up or down the scale of existence in suffering or happiness, are determined directly by one's own actions (karma) in his previous existence. The king taught the doctrine as follows:

Accordingly, those who are of pleasant conduct here—the prospect is, indeed, that they will enter a pleasant womb, either the womb of a Brahmin, or the womb of a Kshatriya, or the womb of a Vaishya. But those who are of stinking conduct here—the prospect is, indeed, that they will enter a stinking womb, either the womb of a dog, or the womb of a swine, or the womb of an outcaste [Chandala].[10]

This doctrine of karma and transmigration appears in the Vedic materials for the first time toward the very end of the thousand years of the Vedic age. It appears as an alien doctrine. It was opposed by Yajnavalkya, one of the two greatest Vedic sages of the time, and unknown to the other, Uddalaka Aruni.

The Upanishads are collections of dialogues, anecdotes, and explanations; and they contain a variety of viewpoints. This was especially true by the time of the middle and late Upanishads, some of which may have been composed and collected as late as 300 B.C.E., after the end of the Vedic period. In some of these later dialogues human life is no longer viewed as the opportunity for the achievement of happiness, but as a life sentence to suffering; existence is no longer looked upon as real, but as illusory; instead of a world-affirming monism some late Upanishads teach a dualism that denies value to the world and karma and transmigration are taken for granted. The older views continued alongside these newer views. It must be emphasized that the Upanishads represented the views of a tiny, elite minority. The Gryha Sutras, the scriptures that explain the household rituals and were the writings closest to the life of the ordinary Vedic people, were composed between 600 and 300 B.C.E.; they do not contain any mention at all of a belief in karma and transmigration. This belief first appears (outside of the Upanishads) in the Laws of Manu (200 B.C.E.–200 C.E.), where it is clumsily inserted into contexts that deny it. But the changes were already in the making in Upanishadic times. What were the influences that brought about these changes?

Non-Vedic Sources, 500–200 B.C.E.

The Vedic age, with its comparative isolation of the Indo–Aryans, came to an end with an intensive encounter with the cultures that lay to the east and south of the Vedic territory. Vedic religion was fundamentally changed by this encounter and emerged from these formative centuries as classical Hinduism. The archaeological evidence for this encounter is the fact that from 500 B.C.E. the Painted Grey Ware pottery (characteristic of the Vedic Aryan territory) began to appear for the first time in the Black-and-Red Ware areas, and vice versa, and also the appearance in both areas of a new pottery, Northern Black Polished Ware. The linguistic evidence is the fact that in this period also, from 500–200 B.C.E., a massive invasion of Dravidian words into Sanskrit occurred unlike anything before or since.[11] This must indicate that for the first time Sanskrit speakers were coming into close social contact with Dravidian speakers. And in this same period, 500–200 B.C.E., important non-Vedic religious ideas began to appear in the Vedic religious writings, at first only among the intellectuals, but eventually to be incorporated fully and taken for granted by all.

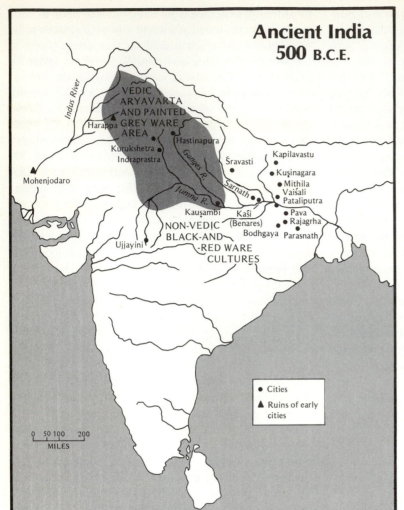

Ancient India 500 B.C.E.

Indus River

VEDIC ARYAVARTA AND PAINTED GREY WARE AREA

Harappa ▲

Hastinapura

Kurukshetra
Indraprastra

Gunges R.

Mohenjodaro ▲

Śravasti •
Kapilavastu •
• Kuṣinagara
Sarnath
• Mithila
Vaiśali •
Jumna R.
Sarnath • Pataliputra

Kauśambi •
Kaśi
(Benares)
• Pava
• Rajagṛha
Bodhgaya Parasnath
NON-VEDIC BLACK-AND- -RED WARE CULTURES

Ujjayini •

● Cities
▲ Ruins of early cities

0 50 100 200
MILES

Vedic and Non-Vedic Cultural Areas About 500 B.C.E. Without exception, all of the original holy places of Jainism and Buddhism lay outside of the traditional Vedic Aryavarta, to the south and east of it. A political unification of the two areas may have provided the conditions necessary for the cultural encounter which took place between 500 and 200 B.C.E.

Without exception *all* of the original holy places of Jainism and Buddhism are to be found in the cultural areas to the east and south of the Painted Grey Ware territory where the Vedic Aryans lived. Jainism was already old and established by the time of the encounter, and Buddhism was to grow up in the midst of it. Jainism and Buddhism were to provide the non-Vedic religious attitudes that would affect the Vedic religion most profoundly.

Fundamental to both Jainism and Buddhism is the belief that all human existence, that is, historical existence on this earth in time and space, is inherently, inevitably characterized by suffering; that all beings are bound on the wheel of an endless series of lives and deaths and rebirths on earth; that each person forges the circumstances of greater or lesser suffering in his next life by his own actions in this life; that a person's only release from suffering is the release from the human condition altogether, and that this release is to be achieved through asceticism or withdrawal.

Such beliefs could hardly stand in sharper contrast to the early Vedic religious outlook! For those who look to geography or climate or differences in social and economic organization as the source of differences in religious values, the Indian experience must raise grave doubt. For the Vedic Aryans and the Jains, with utterly opposing religious views, lived next to each other in bordering territories for eight hundred years, territories in which there was no significant difference of climate or geography. And both cultures included small cities, and the economies of both were based on agriculture, cattle raising, and trade.

Encounter with Jainism: The Negation of the Value of Human Existence

The Jains believed that the universe was never created, nor would it ever cease to exist. It was eternal, but it went through an endless series of alternations, consisting of slow upward development toward perfection, which, when attained, of its own necessity, turned and began a downward deterioration toward utter wickedness and evil. And when this was reached, again a turn would occur and the upward development would start again. (One might think of these alternations as similar to breathing, as perhaps the Jains did, since they practiced breathing disciplines. If one breathes very slowly and evenly, when the lungs are filled there is a sense of exhilaration, power, and well-being. When the lungs are empty there is a sense of weakness, of confusion, and even of disintegration.) Each of these upward or downward swings of the universe was divided into four world ages. The present world age is the final one of a downward movement, and at the lowest level of this age, even the religion of Jainism itself is to be lost entirely. Then the Jain religion will be rediscovered and reintroduced by new saintly leaders called *Tirthankaras* in the course of the next upswing, and lost again at the bottom of the next downswing, and so on.

In each of these enormously long alternations of time, there were always twenty-four Tirthankaras, or saintly teachers. In this world age the twenty-third Tirthankara was a man called Parshva, an ascetic and teacher, who probably lived about 850–800 B.C.E. and is referred to as an historical person in early non-Jain as well as Jain sources. He is represented as one who was a reformer among the Jains, calling for a return to the beliefs and practices of their religious tradition, held to be so ancient that its beginnings reached far back into legendary time.

Parshva was active in Ujjain (which in early historical times continued to be a center for Jainism), as well as in Videha and Magadha.

The twenty-fourth and final Tirthankara of this world age is known by his title, *Mahavira,* the "Great Hero." He too was a wandering ascetic teacher, trying to recall the Jains to the rigorous practice of their ancient faith. He was an older contemporary of the Buddha, and there are a number of sharp, polemic passages in the Buddhist sources directed against him and the faith he held. In the decades before and after about 500 B.C.E., he was teaching in Rajagriha (Magadha), Vaishali (Videha), Kashi (modern Benares), and he died at Pava, north of Rajagriha, which today is the most important place of pilgrimage for Jains (see the map on page 64).

Jiva and Ajiva. The ancient faith and practice to which the Mahavira was trying to recall the Jains of his time may seem to some Western minds difficult to grasp. The Jain view is based on certain primary assumptions about the world and human existence in it. It is important to remember that *if these assumptions are accepted* the rest makes logical sense. The Jains believe that the universe is made up of two sorts of reality: *Jiva* consists of an infinite number of identical spiritual units; *Ajiva* ("non-*Jiva*") consists of matter in all its forms, and the conditions under which matter exists: time, space, movement, rest. Both *Jiva* and *Ajiva* are eternal; they never came into existence, and they will never cease to exist. The whole world is made up of *Jivas* trapped in *Ajiva*. In everything that has finite, material existence there is a *Jiva* in direct contact with *Ajiva;* there are *Jivas* in rocks, rice, cockroaches, mice, human beings, spirits. The key point is that *any contact whatever of the Jiva with Ajiva causes the Jiva to suffer, to hurt.* Thus, the Jains believe that all existence in this world *is* suffering, inevitably. There is no way to reform human society or individuals that could ever stop the suffering. It is built into the very nature of human existence. In every human being is a *Jiva* trapped in *Ajiva,* and the *Jiva* suffers because of its contact with the *Ajiva*. The only way to escape from suffering is for the *Jiva* to escape from the human condition itself, from human existence altogether—for all existence whatever in the world of matter, time, and space chains one to the wheel of suffering.

Transmigration and Karma. Transmigration and *karma* keep the *Jivas* trapped in *Ajiva*. To achieve release from the human condition is not simple. The Jains believe that the *Jiva* suffers through an indefinite number of lives or reincarnations. They believe that every action that a person takes, be it a good action or an evil one, opens up channels of the senses (of sight, hearing, touch, taste, smell) through which an invisible substance, *karma,* filters in and adheres to the *Jiva* within, weighing it down, and determining the conditions of a person's next existence. The consequence of evil actions is a heavy *karma,* which weighs the *Jiva* down and brings it into a new life in circumstances where much suffering has to be endured and many lifetimes will be needed to work back up to where it had been before. The *Jiva* might even be brought down to the animal, insect, plant, or even inanimate world, where eons of time would be required to rise up to the human level again. The consequence of good deeds is a light *karma,* which allows the *Jiva* to rise in its next life to circumstances higher in the scheme of things, where there will be less suffering to be endured. But good deeds can never lead to release.

Withdrawal from Participation. The way to release, instead, is withdrawal from participation in the world. *Karma* is the cause-and-effect mechanism by which all actions bring about their inescapable consequences. *Karma* operates to keep the *Jiva* chained in an unending series of existences in which the *Jiva* suffers, sometimes more, sometimes less. Thus, the way of escape must involve an escape from *karma:* The destruction of old *karma* and the avoidance of new *karma.* For then, at death, with no *karma* to weigh it down, the *Jiva* will float free of all *Ajiva,* free of the human condition, free of all future embodiments. It will rise to the top of the universe to a place or state called *Siddhashila* where the *Jiva,* identical with all other pure *Jivas,* will experience its own pure nature in eternal stillness, isolation, noninvolvement. The Jain scriptures tell us that few have ever attained release. The way to burn up old *karma* is to practice asceticism (voluntary self-deprivation and suffering); the way to avoid new *karma* is to withdraw from all involvement, as much as possible, and to close the channels of the senses and the mind to prevent karmic matter from entering and adhering to the *Jiva.*

The Jain society is dualistic, as is the Jain universe.

On the one hand there are the monks, who practice severe asceticism and strive to make this life their last. The monks practice severe fasting, endure heat and dust without the comfort of clothing or washing, and seek to move about as little as possible. Some famous statues of Jain monks show forest vines twining about their legs, to indicate that they have stood rigidly still for a very long time. On the other hand there are the lay people, who pursue less rigorous practices, striving only to do good deeds and hoping for a better reincarnation the next time.

The activity of the monk in teaching does not produce *karma,* and there is a close relationship between the monks and lay people in Jainism. The monks come into the homes of the lay people, where a number of households may gather to be taught in one place. And the lay people also care for their monks. Since the monks cannot use fire, for this would injure the *Jivas* in the burning wood and thus produce *karma,* the lay people feed their monks and provide what slight shelter they need.

In their effort to attain their highest hope, which is the release of the *Jiva* forever from all involvement in worldly existence, the Jains believe that no spirit or divine being can assist them in any way. They are atheists.* They believe that gods and spirits can influence only the events of the world. The gods cannot assist in achieving release, which has to be achieved by the individual himself, on his own. In fact, the gods cannot even gain their own release until they are reborn as men and undertake the difficult life of the monk. Women are permitted to become nuns, but this cannot lead to release for them. The best for which they can hope is to be reborn the next time as men with the inner strength to be monks.

The logic of this intense desire for release from the human condition leads finally to religious suicide. It is simply the extension of ascetic disciplines, and in the past was indeed highly regarded among the Jains. But it was allowed only for monks, and a monk was not permitted to end his own life until after he had practiced

---

* In the study of religions the term *atheist* simply states a fact— that those to whom it applies do not believe that any divine reality directs the universe or assists in the achievement of the highest religious aims. In the study of religions the term *atheist* implies no negative moral judgment whatever. It is merely descriptive.

asceticism rigorously for at least twelve years. Even then the action must not be one of violence against himself, for any act of violence, even violence against oneself, would produce *karma* that would hold him back from release. The suicide must be accomplished by shutting off one or more of the life support systems—by fasting to death, by walking out into the water until it closed over one, by walking out into the desert until one fell. Both Parshva and Mahavira achieved this kind of holy death, but only after years of austere asceticism and of teaching.

The Ethical Element. In Jainism the ethical element is taken very seriously. It is summarized in the Five Vows that are followed by both lay people and monks. They are: (1) Noninjury (*ahimsa*), (2) Nonlying, (3) Nonstealing, (4) Chastity, and (5) Nongrasping. The first vow, that of Noninjury, reflects the Jain belief that anyone who adds to the suffering of any other *Jiva* will surely bring suffering on himself in his next life. Thus, he should refrain from injury. And since all *Jivas* are, in their pure state, identical, there is no value difference between injuring the *Jiva* in a beetle, or a parrot, or a child, or a man. For this reason, monks and some pious lay people carry feather brooms to dust the path in front of them as they walk, in order to avoid stepping on any small living thing. Some may wear a cloth over the mouth and strain the drinking water through a cloth, to avoid swallowing any small insect accidentally. Jains have also generously endowed hospitals, not only for human beings, but also for animals. In Bombay, for instance, where the rat problem had become critical, the Jains built a "hospice" where the rats could be brought after being captured alive. Here they were segregated by sex so that they could not reproduce, were fed and kept clean, and were allowed to live out their lives. The vow to commit no injury means that Jains have gone into banking, business, trade, and the professions, for they cannot be farmers, fishermen, butchers, or hunters, as all of these occupations require the injuring of *Jivas*. But if someone else has cut the grain, they may use it. They are vegetarians, however, and will not eat meat even though someone else has killed the animal.

It must be emphasized that the motive for adhering to the vow of noninjury is not compassion for those who might be injured, but rather the determination to avoid *karma*. Compassion for anyone is emotional involvement, and the Jains, layman and monk alike, know that it is only by the least involvement and the most detachment possible that one can move toward release. This is made clear in many of the Jain writings, two of which are quoted here.

He who grasps at even a little . . . will never be freed from sorrow . . . The man who cares for his kin and companions is a fool who suffers much.[12]

King Nami of Mithila in Videha became a Jain monk and left his palace. Indra wished to tempt him, and came to him disguised as a brahmin to report that the palace was burning.

"There is fire and storm, your palace is burning!
Good sir! why don't you take care of your harem?"
Nami replied:
"Happy we dwell, happy we live, who call nothing whatever
    our own.
Though Mithila burn, nothing of mine is burned!
When a monk has left his children and wives, and has given
    up worldly actions,
Nothing is pleasant to him, nothing unpleasant.
There is much that is good for the sage, the houseless monk
Set free from all ties, who knows himself to be alone."[13]

This famous Jain story of King Nami makes vividly clear that noninjury is the dispassionate avoidance of aggressive action for the sake of the welfare of one's own soul (*Jiva*). In the context of the basic Jain assumptions about the nature of existence it could be nothing else. *Ahimsa,* noninjury, is not compassionate action. It is not love. *Ahimsa* is what it says it is, *noninjury*.

The vows of nonlying and nonstealing, observed with the same motive of avoiding *karma,* lead to a high level of integrity among the Jains and an enviable reputation. For lay people chastity means the limitation of sexual experience to the marriage relationship; and for monks it means the avoidance of sexual experience altogether. Women, while perceived as lower in rank than men in the scheme of *karma,* are nevertheless respected and well treated. The fifth vow is a general one and its observance leads to the lessening in all actions of any attachment, for *all* attachment, even commitment to a noble cause, produces *karma*.

Sects. The two major sects of Jainism trace their separation to events that occurred about two hundred years after the death of Mahavira. At that time Bhadrabahu, the chief monk among the Jains, foresaw a time of famine ahead, and, to avoid it, led all who would follow, both monks and lay people, to the south of India. South India today still has many areas that are strongly Jain. Some years after the famine had passed, Bhadrabahu returned to the north. He was greatly angered to find that in his absence the practices of the monks had become corrupted: they were now wearing white robes instead of going naked. The practice of nakedness was the refusal to give in to the body's demand for protection and comfort, and Bhadrabahu forcefully opposed the weakness that led the monks to wear clothing. The ones who continued to wear the white robes were called *Shvetambaras* (*Shveta* means "white"). The other monks, who wore nothing, were called "sky-clad," *Digambaras*. The two groups remain separate to this day. *Sky-clad* is a good name for the monks of the older tradition, rather than naked. A few years ago the author was climbing up a long steep trail to visit the cave on the mountain near Rajagriha where the first Buddhist Council is believed to have been held. There is also an ancient Jain holy place on the mountain. At a number of different points on the trail, groups of two and three Digambara monks were encountered. They were indeed "sky-clad." They were not "naked," but clothed in a dignity that was profound and impressive.

Jains today enjoy a high reputation for integrity in business and personal matters. They respect and educate their women. They are generous in many forms of philanthropy. Numerically they are a very small minority in India, and while they consider themselves to be a separate religion, many Hindus regard them as an odd Hindu subcaste. In fact, the Jains have close ties with certain of the subgroups of the Hindu Vaishya caste,[*] intermarrying with them. Jains adopted Vedic rituals for marriages and other family rites, and Hindus permit these exceptional practices to continue. The Jains have also adopted many of the Hindu gods as a means of explaining and influencing worldly events. Jains have built temples where images of their Tirthankaras are venerated in much the same way that Hindus worship before images of their gods. Today the Jain rituals are elaborate, with

[*] See the explanation of the Hindu caste system on page 71 ff.

offerings of flowers, fruit, and other symbolic materials, and the Tirthankaras are praised with chants from holy books. The temples of the Jains are often of impressive size, as at Mt. Abu, and ornamented with skilled craftsmanship in silver, gold, jewels, and marble. In the midst of all this richness, standing or seated, are the images of the Tirthankaras, naked, austere, aloof.

It is evident from this brief account of Jainism that in many ways its early beliefs and practices stood in direct opposition to the Vedic religion existing in the neighboring territory. A tabulation of contrasting beliefs will make this more obvious.

VEDIC RELIGION	JAIN RELIGION
Affirms the value of human existence on this earth.	Negates the value of human existence on this earth.
Asserts that life can be happiness.	Asserts that life is suffering.
Seeks fulfillment of the human condition.	Seeks release from the human condition.
Views this life as one's only life on earth.	Views this life as only one of an unending series of lives on earth.
Advocates ritual participation.	Advocates asceticism and withdrawal.
Is unitary, monistic.	Is dualistic.
Is polytheistic.	Is atheistic.
Considers the ultimate reality to be dynamic, creative.	Considers the ultimate state (of the released *Jiva*) to be static stillness.

The Jain beliefs in an unending series of sorrowful rebirths and in *karma,* which controls the process, are fundamental to the whole Jain religion. These beliefs define the problem of human existence to which Jainism then provides the answer. Without these two beliefs in rebirth and in *karma* the Jain answer would make no sense. Buddhism, too, is based on these two beliefs, and on the assumption that is their context—that life is suffering. But Buddhism explains these differently and offers a modified solution to the problem of suffering, a solution that is bold and daring.

Encounter with Buddhism: The Negation of the Value of Human Existence

Chapter 5 will deal with Buddhism as a whole, but it is important here to look at certain aspects of Buddhist thought that, along with the thought of the Jains, profoundly influenced emerging Hinduism. Buddhism represents a significant reform of Jainism and a rejection of Vedic religion. Like Jainism, the Buddha taught the doctrines of *karma* and rebirth; he believed that the only answer to the problem of life was release from the human condition and that the way to release is through nonattachment. He rejected the harsh asceticism of the Jains for milder forms, however, and proposed a wholly original view of the nature of the human person. He utterly rejected the Vedic ritual religion, with its pursuit of human happiness through full involvement in and enjoyment of the world.

Siddhartha Gautama, whose title is the *Buddha*, the "Enlightened One," is revered by Buddhists as the one who discovered the true facts about human existence. These facts had been there all along (just as the fact that the world is round was there, waiting to be discovered through all the centuries when people wrongly believed that the world was flat). And he is further revered as the one who, having discovered the true facts about human existence, pointed the way to release from human existence, and then himself went that way, leading others. As with Jainism, it is necessary to look at these facts, for they are the basic assumptions that provide the context within which the rest makes sense. The Buddha made these discoveries about life and the world in his great Enlightenment experience. He discovered that life is transitory, sorrowful, and soul-less. These are called the Three Characteristics of Existence, and they are taught again and again in the Buddha's sermons and dialogues, collected in the earliest Buddhist scriptures.

Life is Transitory, Sorrowful, and Soul-less. The Buddha taught that all forms of existence, including human existence and even the constituent elements that combine to form human life, are inherently and inevitably transitory, sorrowful, and soul-less. One of the statements of this view is quoted in Chapter 5 on Buddhism, on page 119. It should be noted that the third characteristic—that there is no immortal, unchanging soul—in effect emphasizes and underlines the first characteristic, that of radical transitoriness, impermanence, or constant change. In Jain belief, the soul was an enduring, permanent reality. The Buddhist assertion that everything, absolutely everything, is transitory means that there can be no enduring reality of any kind; and the third characteristic specifically asserts, so that there can be no mistake, that this transitory, impermanent nature of all existence applies to the spiritual as well as to the material realm. There are no souls.

The word chosen to deny the existence of any eternal soul or permanent self is not the Jain term *Jiva*, but the Vedic term *Atman*, which, it will be recalled, referred equally to the individual soul and to the Absolute, the World Soul. The Buddhist statement and the choice of the term clearly assert that there is no permanence of any kind whatever, neither individual soul nor Absolute unchanging Reality. The only thing that is not transitory is the truth that all is transitory; and that statement concerns the realm of truth, not the realm of reality. All that exists, all that is real, including the self, is subject to the process of cause and effect that makes everything impermanent. The "self" that human beings know in all experience is merely a dynamic process, like a burning candle flame, nothing more.

All existence, thus, is seen as radically transitory—a dynamic, painful process in which there is no permanent, enduring reality whatever, neither soul nor Soul. There is no self, no unchanging personal reality. The only identity that one can have is in the continuity of an individual process. A person is simply the sum of his past at any given moment and the source of his future. The man is not the baby that he was, nor the old man that he will become. Nor are they entirely different persons. His *identity* is to be found in the unbroken continuity of the ever changing process by which the baby becomes the old man and then, through death and rebirth, that same uninterrupted process continues in new circumstances.

The second of the Three Characteristics is that this dynamic process is one whose inherent character is suffering. As with the Jains, the human condition (as well as all the rest of existence) is defined in Buddhism as inevitably suffering, sorrowful. Therefore, the answer to the problem posed by existence cannot be found in the reform or transformation of the individual or society, but only in release from existence itself, by ending the process that gives existence its endless, painful continuity. The process is fueled by *karma,* the inevitable consequences of one's own past action. The Buddhists did not regard *karma* as a substance as the Jains did, but as the energy or fuel that keeps a fire blazing, or as the momentum generated by all one's actions in this life that propels one through death into a new life.

Release from the Human Condition. The Buddhist view of release from the human condition is to be understood in this light. If this process is all there is, then if the process could be stopped, the suffering could be stopped; and there would be nothing remaining, nothing left over. Thus, release from this process of suffering existence must of logical necessity mean what the Buddha said it meant—cessation, extinction, *nirvana* (*nir* meaning "out" and *vana* meaning "blow," as a candle flame that is blown out, extinguished).

The path to release is explained in the Buddha's first sermon after his enlightenment experience. The acceptance of the Buddha's view of reality is the first step. Then come ethical disciplines very similar to those of Jainism. The motivation here, too, is detachment, disinvolvement. One is not to lie or steal—not because this may provide the happiness of a richer relationship with others, but because stealing and lying and all passionate actions tie one into existence much more intensively than abstaining from these actions, that is, nonlying, nonstealing, noninjury.

The final steps on the path to release are techniques for withdrawing from consciousness itself. These techniques were already ancient in the time of the Buddha, and were drawn on by many differing religious groups, including the Jains. The later classical Hindu form of these techniques is the *raja yoga* of Patanjali's *Yoga Sutra,* which will be examined later in this chapter. The general practice held that first the senses must be trained to stop registering sense objects, and then the mind must be trained to eliminate, step by step, all of the content of consciousness. The Buddha used the illustration of the blue flower to teach his method. The monk was to concentrate on the blue flower "until the whole universe was filled with the blue flower," eliminating from his consciousness absolutely everything but the blue flower. Then the form of the flower was to be eliminated, leaving one's whole consciousness, the whole universe, filled only with blueness. Then the monk was to eliminate the blueness. This produces the psychological experience of the cessation of everything connected with human existence. It is the mental elimination of a universe that is regarded as inherently painful.

In Buddhism the experience of this final state on the path is called *samadhi,* and is understood as a foretaste of the final "blowing out," *nirvana,* cessation, extinction. In one of the early dialogues the end of the path is described as follows. In a consciousness that is "invisible, infinite, radiant" all name and form utterly cease. And then "when consciousness has ceased, this all has turned to utter nothingness."[14]

The originality and courage of the Buddha's teachings are impressive. Each man, for himself, must achieve his own release. There are no gods from whom to gain favors. There is no assurance of some happy heaven after death. There is no fate on which to lay the blame. There is no Absolute, no All of which one is a part and from which one derives his value. There are only the inexorable consequences of one's own, self-chosen actions. This world offers no hope. Continuing existence through countless rebirths, all inevitably characterized by suffering, is all that the world can offer. Hope for release lies within each person, on the quality of his determination to achieve equanimity, tranquility, nonresponse to both suffering and joy, through disciplined techniques of detachment. As he follows the Way his character is transformed, for he practices his belief that "the best of virtues is passionlessness" for it leads to "passiveness in pain."[15] The individual alone is master of himself. His destiny is in his own hands.

Buddhism changed in many ways in its long development, in its native India and also in China and Japan and Southeast Asia. The next chapter will explore the varities of Buddhist thought and practice. But both Jainism and this earliest form of Buddhism are important in this examination of Hinduism, because it was out of the encounter of the world-affirming Vedic way of life with the world-negating Jain and Buddhist ways of life and the resulting powerful intellectual ferment that classical Hinduism gradually emerged. The period of the most intense interaction was between 500 and 200 B.C.E.

Classical and Medieval Hinduism

The Amalgamation of the Vedic World-Affirming and the Non-Vedic World-Negating Values

The religious energies of the Vedic people were directed toward embracing this world passionately, participating completely and joyously in all of life. Just as their bodies are the means of the passionate pleasure that lovers find in each other, so the material world was, for Vedic man, the means for achieving his happiness. In this sense he was frankly materialistic (as is his modern Hindu descendant) and found no reason to apologize for his materialistic self-interest. The Jains and Buddhists, on the other hand, directed all their religious energies toward escaping the world, cultivating dispassion, withdrawing completely, and renouncing all joys related to this world. Just as the bodies of lovers entrap them into passionate embraces that lead to further bondage and suffering, said the Jains and Buddhists, so all this material world was the means for achieving only bondage and suffering. The renunciation of this world was the only way to release. They found no reason to apologize for their self-interested abandonment of all worldly interests and responsibilities.

Classical Hinduism was never able to combine these two fundamentally opposing views into a logical synthesis, but it was able to forge them into a viable amalgam. The two elements still remain distinct in the final product. They were combined in two remarkable and different ways. The first way of combining the two attitudes was to offer them as separate options; both the worldly and the ascetic ways were open to all, to be chosen according to one's *karma*, one's situation, one's inclinations, and one's capacity for religious knowledge. The second way, called *karma-yoga*, distinguished between the outer action and the inner attitude toward the action, and offered the ideal of full participation in worldly life while cultivating inner detachment or indifference.

Hinduism is often represented as being immensely complex and confusing. It is complex, but if the historical streams that flowed together to become Hinduism are understood and recognized, the complexity need not be confusing. *Hinduism, drawing on its Vedic origins, is a religious organization of life by castes and stages of life and goals. Hinduism, drawing on the ascetic tradition expressed in Jainism and Buddhism, also provides the option of a religious release from life, through religious disciplines of knowledge, or asceticism, or devotion to a god.*

Hinduism as Participation: The Religious Organization of Life

The aspect of Jainism and Buddhism that decisively shaped the emerging form of classical Hinduism was the belief in *karma* and rebirth—the belief that inescapably one must reap the consequences of one's actions, and that the circumstances of one's next life on earth would be determined by one's own actions in this life. This view is not found anywhere in the Rig-Veda, and when it first appeared in the last writings of the Vedic age, the Upanishads, it was rejected by one of the greatest Vedic sages of the time and unknown by the other. But by five hundred years later, there had been an intensive encounter with the indigenous ascetic religions in which rebirth and *karma* were basic beliefs. Afterwards in the *Dharmashastras,* the Hindu law books on duty and virtue, the belief in *karma* and transmigration was taken for granted and had become part of the basic frame of reference.

Castes. It was the linking of the doctrine of *karma* and transmigration with the three Vedic classes of society, the Aryan *varnas,* (and the addition of a new, fourth one) that caused the fairly fluid social arrangement of Vedic society to crystallize into the Hindu caste system. Hindu caste is not only a fixed ranking system for the social and occupational organization of society. It is at the same time the structure for the cosmic operation of *karma* and transmigration. Each individual is born into

	The "Twice-Born" Aryan Castes			Non-Aryan excluded from "Twice-Born" religion	Excluded even by Shudras
CASTES in order of rank	**BRAHMIN** *Priests* Teachers Advisors to rulers	**KSHATRIYA** *Rulers* Kings, princes, warriors	**VAISHYA** *"The People"* Agriculturalists, Merchants Traders	**SHUDRA** *Servants* of the upper 3 castes Gardeners Musicians Artisans Barbers	**OUTCASTE** Street-sweepers, leather-workers All non-Hindus are excluded also
	Influenced by WORLD-AFFIRMING Vedic views			*Influenced by WORLD-NEGATING Jain and Buddhist views*	
STAGES OF LIFE	**STUDENT** Clothing, subjects, length of schooling differ for each caste	**HOUSEHOLDER** All are obligated to marry and start a household	**RETIRED PERSON** "Forest-dweller" Hermit	**ASCETIC** Not a "stage" Anyone at any time may become an ascetic	
GOALS OF LIFE	**DHARMA** *Virtue* Caste-related duties, both social and ritual, morality	**ARTHA** *Material Success* The attaining of wealth and power	**KAMA** *Pleasure* Aesthetic enjoyment of art, music, sex, dance, poetry, drama	**MOKSHA** *Release* through: Knowledge, Disciplines (yoga), Devotion to gods, Karma-yoga	

The Hindu Organization of Life. *The whole of Hindu society has traditionally been viewed in a religious light. Every caste and every stage of life has had its duties, or* dharma, *and the caste into which a person is born is a direct function of how well or poorly he has fulfilled his* dharma *in his previous life.*

the rank of caste and economic occupation that he has deserved as a result of his deeds in past lives. If he lives pious and virtuous lives through a series of transmigrations he can move up the ladder of castes to the highest one and, from this, finally achieve a permanent place in a heaven with the gods and fathers, or union with the Absolute. Salvation is to be gained by full, dutiful participation in a religiously sanctioned and organized society. Thus, every Hindu is born somewhere in the fixed structure of ranked castes. His position in the structure has been justly determined by his own past deeds, his *karma*. Thus, his first obligation, which is religiously justified and required, is to accept his caste

position and all its obligations, privileges, limitations, or deprivations, and to order his life according to caste laws.

Once born into a caste, one cannot move to another caste, except through death and rebirth in a new earthly life. For serious offenses against caste laws, the leaders of a caste may exile a person permanently from the caste community. This is a very harsh penalty and can result in death, for all economic occupations are strictly allotted to the various castes, and no one may do the work of another caste. No caste group, therefore, will accept into its midst banned members of a different caste.

In each of the four castes there are many subcastes,

called *jatis*.* Members of the same *jatis* feel obligated to help each other out in times of difficulty, thus functioning to provide economic stability for families and society. Most offenses against caste laws, until modern times, were handled directly by the leaders of the *jati* or *jatis* concerned. The castes might be thought of as tribes and the *jatis* as clans. What happened in Hinduism was that the close-knit, face-to-face relationships of Vedic tribal and clan organization, fixed, preserved and sanctioned by the beliefs in *karma* and transmigration, were directly incorporated into the Hindu caste system and were never lost, as they were in most other societies in the development from tribe to empire. The incorporation of a clan-like structure within the castes is undoubtedly one reason for the resiliency and stability of Hindu society through the centuries. Kings, emperors, and raiders might come and go, but they had little effect on the family-*jati*-caste village fabric of Hindu social existence.

Of the four castes, the priestly families, the Brahmins, have traditionally held the highest place in the ranking. In the early Vedic period the Brahmins were only one of a number of types of priests who were needed to carry out the great ceremonies, but over the centuries all priests who dealt with the Holy Power, Brahman, came to be called *Brahmins*. By the end of the Vedic age the priestly class had shifted to the highest social rank. To be a Hindu priest one had to be born into a Brahmin family and then be educated fully in the Vedas, the sacred law books (*Dharmashastras*), the ancient sciences, and all priestly and teaching functions.

The second-ranked caste is that of the Kshatriyas, consisting of kings, nobles, and warriors. The third-ranked caste was in Vedic times simply referred to as "the people," the rest of society. But in Hindu caste terms the third rank, the Vaishyas, refers to agriculturalists, traders, and business people. These three castes were the only classes referred to in the Rig-Veda, except in one instance in a late hymn where mention is made of the fourth group, the Shudras. The Shudras were not only added later to the social scheme, probably drawn from the conquered peoples, but they were also perceived as *different in kind*. Only the first three castes were called the "Aryan *varnas*." Members of the fourth caste, the Shudras, were to be the "servants" of the other three castes. The Shudras were not permitted to participate in any Vedic ritual, nor even to hear the sacred Vedic scriptures recited. Shudras perform their own non-Vedic rituals. Brahmin priests will not officiate at Shudra rites; Shudra priests do so. Boys of the upper three castes, when they commence their studies, go through a ceremony of initiation that symbolizes being "born" into the Aryan community. Thus, the upper three castes are called "twice-born." The Shudras are excluded from both the initiation and the education.

Below the Shudras in the caste ranking, are the outcastes (those outside of caste); their presence is a pollution and they must live strictly segregated from caste society, in huts outside caste villages or towns. They are permitted only those types of occupations that are so filthy or polluting that no caste Hindu could or would engage in them. All non-Hindus are also outcastes, "excluded." And it is believed to be their own fault, for if they had lived a good life in past existences, they would have been born Hindus.

The religious belief that each person has been born into the caste and circumstances he deserves, and that in order to move to a better rank in his next life he must accept his present position fully and carry out all caste duties completely—such a belief provides a powerful moral and religious sanction for keeping things as they are. If people in the lowest caste and among the outcastes suffer because of their position in the structure of society, it is because they have deserved to suffer. They are merely bearing the necessary consequences of their own past actions. The *Laws of Manu* require that for the same crime a Brahmin is to be lightly punished, while a Shudra is to be severely punished. But if a person were to rebel against these discriminations and inequalities of the system, he would only end up in his next incarnation among foul beasts or insects, and then it would take great spans of time and much suffering to work his way back up even to the lowest human rank. It is not surprising that there have never been any rebellions of the lower castes against the upper castes in the history of Hinduism.

---

* Some American scholars today, when writing about Hinduism, use the word *caste* to refer to the many *jatis*, rather than to the four *varnas*. This chapter will follow the traditional usage and refer to the four *varnas* as castes and to the *jatis* as subcastes.

Stages. Besides caste organization, according to the sacred law books, the life of the Hindu is also religiously organized according to life stages. Childhood does not count as a stage. Ritually the first three stages are open only to the upper three castes. The first stage is that of a Student. It begins with the ceremony that brings a boy into full membership in the Aryan community as a "twice-born." Here he is invested with the three-strand Sacred Thread worn by all "twice-born" men over the left shoulder and under the right arm. And he is taught the sacred verse, to be recited in the *Agnihotra* at dawn from then on. He then goes to live in the house of his teacher (*guru*), his spiritual father, to receive his education from him. For Brahmin boys the Student stage begins earliest and lasts longest. For boys of the third caste it is shortest. The boy of each caste wears clothing of a specific cloth (linen, cotton, wool) designated for his caste by the ancient law books; he carries a staff of a designated wood and wears a belt of a designated material, each item identifying him as a member of his caste. Girls are not initiated or formally educated.

After he is through with his schooling, a man enters the next stage, that of Householder. He is obligated to marry and set up a household of his own, where his own sacred fire will burn, where he will perform the daily rituals, and where he will raise his children. The law books list and explain the duties of both husband and wife. Many of the household or seasonal rituals require the wife's participation, but her first obligation is faithfulness to her husband, whom she is to obey and worship as her god. The law books state that a woman must always live under the direction of a man: of her father when she is a child, of her husband when she is a wife, and of her son if she becomes a widow. Without such direction, say the law books, a woman would assuredly fall into wickedness and disgrace. The husband, however, is commanded to provide and care for his wife. He is to make her happy and contented. And the law books warn that the household in which the women are not happy and honored will never prosper. There is no provision for divorce in Hinduism. A man may take a second wife, and he may remarry if his wife dies. The woman may never remarry. The sacred law books regard the Householder stage as the most important, because as a Householder the man is responsible for the support of persons in all the other stages.

The third stage is that of Retirement. The law books state that when a man's face has become wrinkled and his hair has begun to turn grey, and when he has looked on the face of his grandchild, he may turn over the responsibilities of head of household to his son, and he and his wife may retire to a secluded and peaceful place. Here they will perform a much simplified ritual, spend time in contemplation, and live simply off berries, roots, and fruit. Before the law books were written, it was an ancient practice for holy men to seek the seclusion of the forest, either alone or as small communities of hermits, sometimes with their wives. They lived a life of peaceful contemplation in austere simplicity. Thus, this stage, because of its similarity of life-style, was referred to as the hermit or forest-dweller stage, and some retired persons did join these quiet forest hermitages. The wife might prefer to stay with the family and care for her grandchildren. That was perfectly permissible also.

The fourth stage is not a stage. It is that of the Ascetic, the *sannyasin*, who rejects all worldly satisfactions in rigorous disciplines of self-denial. It differs wholly from the first three stages. It offers an alternative option, an altogether different course of life from the first three. First, it is not chronological. One may decide to become an ascetic at any point in one's life. But second, and more important, this option, in that its purpose is to achieve detachment from life, negates the validity of the other three stages, as their purpose is to achieve full, appropriate participation in life during the three major periods of an individual's lifetime. The ascetic's negation of the three worldly stages is not only evident in the purpose of the ascetic option, but also in the rituals used to initiate the individual into his new discipline. These rituals require the symbolic burning of the Vedas, the scriptures of the way of worldly participation; the Sacred Thread, the symbol of the "twice-born's" membership in the Aryan community, is removed and burned; and caste status is rejected—even a Shudra may become an ascetic. So the fourth "stage" is in fact the world-negating, ascetic option, derived historically from the Jain and Buddhist world-view. It is offered as an alternative to the three world-affirming stages, which emphasize participation and derive from the Vedic world-view. Historically there has always been some antagonism between the Brahmin, the repository and symbol of the ritually sanctified participation in life, and the

Shaivite Ascetic Chanting His Prayers. *Asceticism is the fourth stage in the Hindu organization of life, and it is one of the ways of achieving the fourth goal:* moksha, *release. This ascetic can be identified as a follower of Shiva by the trident he carries and the three horizontal white lines across his forehead.* (Courtesy of Hyla Converse)

were preferable to what they had left behind. The reasons for taking up the way of the ascetic wanderer varied, as is to be expected. Drama and story from classical times show us profoundly holy seekers, who were gentle and wise; but they also show fierce holy men, wielders of curses and black magic, and even charlatans and scoundrels. A favorite disguise of spies and seducers was the garb of the holy man, for he could go anywhere and be received by anyone.

Goals. The third aspect of the religious organization of life is that of goals to be achieved. Again the first

Chola Bronze Image of the God Rama. *In Hindu devotion Rama represents, above all, the first of the four goals of life:* dharma, *virtue, the fulfillment of one's obligations in life. Original, Victoria and Albert Museum, London.* (Courtesy of Hyla Converse)

sannyasin, the symbol of the ascetic renunciation of all participation.

By incorporating the ascetic way as a fourth and optional "stage," instead of rejecting it as a contradiction of the Vedic world-view, Hinduism did two things: first, it undercut the challenge and disarmed the threat of Jainism and Buddhism—one could renounce the world, follow the ascetic path, and still remain a Hindu; and second, in a very highly structured society it provided a religious "safety valve," for if the detailed religious obligations of caste and family and stage became too much for him, a man could simply walk away with no guilt and no regrets and become a wandering ascetic. The disciplines of the ascetic's life were difficult, but for some they three goals come straight out of the Vedic world-view, and the fourth is a negation of the validity of these, providing an alternate option.

The first of the goals is *dharma,* or virtue, the fulfillment of general moral requirements, such as honesty, chastity, generosity, and of one's own specific duty (*sva-dharma*), according to caste and stage. This goal applies equally to all and takes precedence over the next two goals. The Hindu law books contain detailed codes for all aspects of *dharma.* The most authoritative and oldest of these law books is the *Laws of Manu.*

The second goal is *artha,* economic and political success. Hinduism is the only religion that imposes the religious obligation to become as rich and powerful as possible. Political power applies especially to the princely and warrior caste. The *Arthashastra* is the most famous

Bronze Image of the God Shiva. *Here Shiva is depicted as Nataraja, "king of the dance." The enjoyment of the dance, dance-drama, music, and the other arts are aspects of the third goal in the Hindu organization of life:* kama, *pleasure. Shiva is the divine patron of the dance and dance-drama.* (Courtesy of Hyla Converse)

treatise on the responsibilities of the king and the means he should use to gain and hold his power, but all the law books also deal with this subject. The command to seek economic success applies especially to the householder stage and refers to all castes.

The third goal is *kama,* which means pleasure, and is not to be confused with *karma.* Hinduism is also one of the few religions that commands the religious person to enjoy life and to seek his own pleasure as part of an overall religious and human fulfillment. *Kama* includes all forms of aesthetic (not to be confused with *ascetic*) enjoyment—painting, sculpture, music, poetry, drama, dance, and sexual pleasures. The *Natyashastra* sets out a philosophy of aesthetic appreciation, especially in relation to music, dance, and drama, and the *Kamasutra* is a handbook on the specifics of erotic pleasures. There are many other classical Hindu books on the various forms of aesthetic enjoyment.

The first three goals are worldly goals leading to full participation in life and the enjoyment and fulfillment of the human condition. They are to be practiced in a harmonious balance, no goal being sought so exclusively as to encroach on the others. In case of a conflict between the demands of *dharma* (duty), and those of *artha* (success) or *kama* (pleasure), the demands of duty are to be followed, but never to the exclusion of success and pleasure.

The fourth goal, like the fourth stage, offers a different option, one that likewise negates the validity of the first three goals. The fourth goal is *moksha,* "release." The goal to be achieved is release from the human condition, rather than the fulfillment of that condition sought in the first three goals.

The first three goals, which express the conviction that life is worthwhile and its fulfillment is desirable, came from the Vedic tradition, of course, whereas the fourth goal, release, which expresses the conviction that the only answer to the problems of human existence is escape, came from the Jain and Buddhist world-view. These two options, affirming the world and negating the world, could never be fully synthesized in Hinduism. They are simply offered side by side. In the next section various forms of the search for release will be examined. It is already evident, however, that the unity of Hinduism is neither doctrinal, nor ethical, nor mythological. It is a practical unity. One is a Hindu if one is born into a caste, if one performs the basic Vedic rituals, and if one acknowledges, even minimally, the authority of the Vedas.

The chart on page 72 summarizes in simplified form the Hindu organization of life.

Hinduism as Withdrawal: The Religious Release from Life

In the previous section the way of *participation* was explored in the Hindu organization of life, which stems largely from Hinduism's Vedic heritage. The other option in Hinduism is the way of *moksha,* withdrawal and release, which stems from the indigenous ascetic heritage of Hinduism. The search for release in Hinduism has taken four major forms, and sometimes these have been combined. The first is the way of knowledge, *jnana,* the search for a living experience of the Truth about life that releases one from bondage to life. This way of knowledge is the way of a variety of religious philosophies of India. The two philosophies that will be considered here are the dualistic Samkhya, and the nondualistic, or monistic, early Vedanta. The second form of search is that of practical disciplines or techniques of withdrawal: *yoga* and asceticism. The third form is the way of devotion, *bhakti,* offered to a god, usually to the gods Vishnu or Shiva, or to their *avatars* (incarnations) or their wives and sons, and, finally, in *karma-yoga* Hinduism offers a way of release that combines participation and withdrawal.

Release Through Knowledge: Samkhya and Vedanta.
Although they are quite different in detail, the Samkyha and Vedanta philosophies both hold that all human existence *appears* to be entrapped in suffering. Both philosophies also hold that this appearance is false. People believe it because they are ignorant of the true human situation. Their ignorance keeps them from escaping what they mistakenly believe to be a prison.

Suppose for a moment that you know nothing about mirages and you are traveling on foot across the Great Salt Plains. When you have left the settlement well behind, you look up and are alarmed to see that not far ahead the road disappears into a vast blue lake out of which rise islands here and there. You turn to look back, and to your horror you see that the water has flowed in

behind you, covering the road back as well. On both sides also the land slopes down and is covered by the water. There you are, trapped on a small rise, with the road under water in both directions and no way to go around. There is nothing to do but stay there. No escape is possible. For many hours you endure the burning sun, the insects, and the threat of a rattler who wishes you out of his territory. At last you decide to go forward and see how deep the water is over the road ahead, and whether the track is visible under it. Perhaps you will be able to make your way through the water, if it is shallow enough. So you walk toward the point where the road disappears into the blue lake. To your astonishment the water seems to keep on receding ahead of you as you advance, leaving the road perfectly dry. As you walk on, you slowly come to realize that all the water out there is an optical illusion, a mirage; you were never trapped at all! Your ignorance of mirages was all that bound you; your ignorance blinded you from seeing your true situation; and your new-found knowledge releases you, by showing you that you had never been bound. In somewhat the same way both Samkhya and Vedanta seek release from the bondage of illusion through the direct *experience* of the true human situation. Ignorance is the problem. Knowledge is the answer, not rituals, not asceticism. This "knowledge," furthermore, is a nonrational, direct experience of *knowing* an ultimate Reality, uncluttered by any ideas or perceptions of the functioning human mind.

Samkhya. Samkhya is a restatement of Jain dualism in Brahmanic terms, with a shift from release through the Jain way of asceticism to release through the Samkhya way of knowledge. Like Jainism, Samkhya is a dualism that seeks to separate pure spirit from all contact with matter. In Samkhya, the units of pure spirit are called *Purusha* (instead of *Jiva*) and the phenomenal world— the world of objects—is *Prakriti* (instead of *Ajiva*). *Prakriti* can exist as pure potentiality, in an unformed state in which its inner elements are inactive and in equilibrium. Simply by coming close to *Prakriti, Purusha* disturbs that equilibrium and the whole complex world develops out of *Prakriti* by stages. *Prakriti* begins the process by responding to *Purusha's* nearness, but *Purusha* has not acted and is not involved.

In regard to human beings, the important point is this: the whole person, with his senses, intelligence, individual personality, and mind, arises out of *Prakriti,* the material reality; and *Purusha,* the spiritual reality, his soul, is not active or involved in any way. It is merely present. The error that causes suffering and bondage, the "mirage," is that the human mind that experiences the world (that thinks, feels, values, acts) has mistakenly believed that *it* is the *Purusha.* But it is not. Samkhya writers use an image of two birds on one tree. One bird is active, hopping about the branches, feeding on the fruit like the active, personal self that is part of *Prakriti;* the other bird sits perfectly still, observing the activity of the first but uninvolved, like *Purusha.*

The truth that sets one free is the knowledge that one's eternal soul (*Purusha*) is not involved in the world in any way. This is not an intellectual knowledge *about* the *Purusha* that it is separate, but the *direct experience* by the *Purusha* itself that it is absolutely separate and distinct from *Prakriti;* it is free, unbound. The path to be taken to gain this knowledge is closely bound up with the goal to be reached. This state is achieved through the mental disciplines of yoga, which block out step by step the ordinary world of experience, until the active individual person ceases to exist in the *Purusha's* "consciousness" and it is aware only of itself. The hope held out to people by this religious philosophy of release is a final state of eternal stillness and isolation of the *Purusha* as pure spirit, identical with all other *Purushas,* utterly untouched by the suffering, pleasures, values, and active purposes of human existence. The human condition thus has as little truth or value as a mirage. The ultimate hope is nearly identical to that held out by Jainism with its similar dualistic system; but the way to the realization of the hope is not through asceticism, (enduring cold and heat and hunger and so on), but through mental and spiritual disciplines, a form of the technique of yoga, which will be considered in the next section.

Vedanta. Vedanta is the second of the ways of release through knowledge. The term *Vedanta* means "end of the Vedas," and the way of knowledge of the Vedanta religious philosophy is based on the final Vedic writings, the Upanishads and their Atman-Brahman monism. A period of 1,500 years separates the Upanishadic dialogues of Yajnavalkya and Uddalaka Aruni from the commentary by Shankara on the *Vedanta Sutra,* a commentary seeking to explain the intent of the Upanishads. That long stretch of time included those formative centuries when the Vedic and non-Vedic streams were fused into Hinduism. The Vedanta philosophy came to dominate all other religious philosophies in India, and the great teacher Shankara has exerted the most far-reaching influence of all Vedantic philosophers, right into the present day.

Shankara himself was an aggressive Shaivite, a worshiper of the god Shiva. He lived about 788–829 C.E. He established an order of monks and a monastery at Bodhgaya, where he took over the Buddhist temple that commemorated the event of the Buddha's enlightenment, walled in the statue of the Buddha, and installed a *lingam* of Shiva for worship. His interest in a monastic order is illustrative of his attitude toward the world. He held that ritual and ascetic disciplines, as well as devotion to a god, could be useful as a means for achieving indifference in the world, which was the necessary precondition for the way of knowledge. The world could be used as a means for discarding the world. In the same way the Buddha had shown that the blue flower could be used for the elimination of the blue flower—and all else—from consciousness. But in early Buddhism the experience of the Truth is the experience of "utter nothingness," while in Vedanta it is the experience of union with the Brahman, the Absolute's inner experience of Itself.

It is important to see clearly the difference between the monism of the early Upanishads, in their Vedic context, and the monism of Shankara, in the non-Vedic context of *karma* and transmigration. Both the Vedic sages Yajnavalkya and Uddalaka Aruni held that the presence of the Supreme Reality, the Brahman, or Atman, in all things gave a superlative value to all things in human experience. The presence of the Atman (or Brahman) was what made a husband and wife dear—of value—to each other; it was the life-giving essence of seeds and trees, the shining source of the reality and value of the world.

By contrast, Shankara, who thought in the context of *karma* and transmigration, held that the Supreme Reality, the Brahman, the unqualified absolute One, is not and cannot be involved in the variety and complexity of the finite world of cause and effect, of time and space and action. He taught that it is a delusion to believe in the reality or value of the world of ordinary experience.

This world is an illusion (*maya*), and to believe that it is real and of value is to remain trapped in the endless suffering of cycles of rebirths and redeaths. Release can be achieved by the experience of the Truth, which is Brahman, the experience that the Brahman is the only reality, that one's soul is not individual and finite but part of the Brahman, and that all finitude (this world, all worlds, all beings) is illusion, false perception, mirage caused by ignorance. The direct knowing of the Brahman, which releases, can be achieved through techniques of meditation.

Shankara held that this world of illusion, while it depended on the Brahman, in no way affected the Brahman. He sometimes called this world the "dream" of the Brahman and sometimes he called it the *lila* of the Brahman. The term *lila* refers to play, to sporting pleasures, and also to stage plays. It may be helpful, therefore, to use the analogy of a dance-drama. The illusion that the drama creates is a "real" illusion. The performance occurs. But the man murdered on the stage goes home after the performance and the murderer is not arrested later by the police. The performance of the drama does not affect the real world, yet it is a real performance. The continuity of the performance depends on the real world (the actors, the audience, the physical setting, and so on). And within the context of the illusion created by the play, the elements of cause and effect, time and space, individuality, and rationality are operative.

It is somewhat in this way that the whole experienced world has a provisional reality, dependent on the Brahman, but it is the reality of an illusion, an illusion replete with *karma*, suffering, and rebirth. Shankara with his Vedanta philosophy points the way to knowledge of the Brahman, and of one's own soul as part of It; and in that knowledge one will recognize that all other experience is an illusion, that one is free and never has been bound by *karma* in suffering and endless rebirths. The achievement of this ultimate state strips the world of all significant value and can be reached only by the renunciation and abandonment of the world. The only reality is the One, the Brahman. All else is ultimately unreal. Thus, the religious experience of the Truth is a state of "knowing" that destroys all subject–object distinctions, rejects human reason, negates all values, invalidates all distinctions between good and evil, obliterates personal individuality, and dissolves the world.

Release Through Techniques of Withdrawal: The Disciplines of Asceticism and Yoga.

Asceticism. Asceticism as a religious technique was apparently already being practiced in India long before the Vedic Aryans first arrived. Some of the hymns in the earliest collection of the Rig-Veda make scornful reference to wandering ascetics. In one of the early Brahmanas there is a passage that asks what is the use of matted hair and hunger, of dust on one's body and nakedness, and self-inflicted suffering? The passage goes on to affirm the Vedic conviction that it is through sons and wealth and ritual that one achieves the best in all worlds. In the *Chandogya Upanishad* there is also a dialogue between Uddalaka Aruni and Shvetaketu in which Uddalaka Aruni tells his son to fast for fifteen days, taking water only. At the end of that time he summons his son and asks him to repeat the Vedas. The son cannot remember them, although he had known them previously. The father tells him to go and eat and then return. Later the son is able to repeat the Vedas. The father explains that wisdom is not to be achieved by fasting, that in order to think clearly, one must have eaten properly. But in Jainism and many other movements that flourished in India between 500–200 B.C.E., asceticism was held to be not only the road to release and eternal bliss, but also the means to gain all sorts of superordinary power, such as the power to curse or bless, or the capacity to defy gravitation, to defy distance, to exist without food, or to live without air. The wandering holy men were thus both feared and revered. All ascetics assumed that asceticism "burns up" old *karma* and avoids new *karma*, thus moving one closer to release.

It has already been noted that the life of *asceticism* was grafted into the Vedic organization of life as the fourth "stage." In Hinduism the householder who walks away into a wandering ascetic life on a holy quest for release is to be revered, even though his action brings great hardship to his family. These very hardships, if borne with patience by family members, could move them up the scale of *karma* in the next incarnation and closer to release. Besides, it is not the fault of the householder who becomes an ascetic that his family suffers thus. It is the result of their own past deeds in other lives, their own *karma* that causes them to suffer, by providing them with precisely these circumstances for their lives. If patiently endured, the hardships suffered by the former family of the ascetic may thus be considered as a form of asceticism, too, even though unchosen.

Yoga. Yoga, the other practical technique of release, is not primarily a form of asceticism, although it has been used by many ascetics. Yoga is a discipline for achieving psychological, mental, and spiritual isolation from ordinary reality. The assumptions about the world and its value that underlie the yoga system are non-Vedic. It was already an old technique around 500 B.C.E. The oldest text about yoga that has survived is the *Yoga Sutra* of Patanjali, which was written in the second century B.C.E. The Sutra itself is in the form of very brief statements, which require the help of commentaries to be understood.

The *Yoga Sutra* starts with the statement that this is a revised text (based on older ones) of yoga and that "Yoga is restraint." This restraint is moral, physical, and mental, leading to a state called *samadhi,* in which all mental activity ceases and with it all consciousness of phenomenal reality. *Yoga* does not mean "union," states the ancient commentator. Its root is a word that means "to contemplate in such a way that all mental states and activities are suppressed." Man's capacity to think, which the Greeks valued so highly—his ability to use reason to examine evidence, to reach valid generalizations, to apply these to extend his knowledge and to test his values—this human capacity *to think* was regarded by these Hindu religious philosophies as, instead, a lower form of consciousness, a capacity only of the *material* self, that must be suppressed and discarded along with all distinctive personal aspects of the individual.

The yoga discipline to achieve the state of *samadhi* is an eightfold path.* The first two steps are preparatory ethical disciplines that should lead to the elimination of desire and the attainment of indifference to pain or pleasure, joy or sorrow. The third and fourth steps are physical disciplines. The last four are psychological or mental disciplines. A summary of these steps, as found in the *Yoga Sutra,* follows:

1. *Restraint, control.* Five moral rules (familiar in Buddhism and Jainism) must be rigorously practiced. These are noninjury, nonlying, nonstealing, chastity, and avoidance of greed. This ethical discipline should lead to inner detachment.

2. *Observance.* The five further ethical disciplines are cleanliness, contentment, austerities (such as fasting, enduring heat or cold, and so on), study, and devotion to the god of one's choice (as a means of gaining detachment).

3. *Posture.* The lotus posture (seated with legs crossed, as in many images of the Buddha) is one of the most common. A posture should be practiced until it is easy and the body ceases to distract one's attention. In this way posture becomes an aid to concentration.

4. *Breath control.* The discipline of breath control enables a person to slow down his breathing, suppress it altogether for a time, or breathe in special rhythms often associated with recited *mantras* or secret phrases. Breath control is used to develop serenity of mind and so to aid in concentration.

5. *Abstraction* of the senses. This is the first of the psychological disciplines. Here the senses are trained not to register the objects of sense perception. The eyes are trained to stare at objects, but not to see them at all. One is to train oneself to "turn off" his sight, hearing, feeling, tasting, smelling. This is to aid him both in detachment and in concentration.

6. *Concentration,* steadying the mind on one thing. One may choose any object—a blue flower, the tip of one's nose, one's navel, the image of a deity. One is to concentrate on this one thing until the mind is completely filled with it, pushing out, excluding, eliminating everything else.

7. *Meditation, dhyana.* This is the state achieved as the end result of concentration (see step 6), when all but the one object has been eliminated from one's consciousness.

8. *Deep meditation,* trance, *samadhi.* Now the one object that filled the consciousness is dissolved, eliminated, suppressed, the final suppression of all consciousness of the phenomenal world. The *Yoga Sutra* speaks in Sankhya terms (although the technique was widely adapted to other systems) and describes this state as the *Purusha* experiencing only itself. This state is the goal sought, a profound isolation from the historical human self and the world of ordinary experience.

The path of yogic discipline represents the withdrawal

* See p. 116 for the Buddhist eightfold path.

...erson so that the outside world in no way ...aches ... This state is consciously chosen and sought by means of disciplines producing serenity and detachment. The yoga discipline is an expression of the conviction that the human person cannot find any enduring and satisfying values, any meaning to his existence in the world of ordinary experience. It seeks escape or release from that world *and from the human self* as it is known in that world.

Yoga has developed many diverse forms, primarily by emphasizing one step of the discipline above the others. The full-fledged yoga of the *Yoga Sutra* is called *raja-yoga*. The yoga that concentrates on the physical disciplines and extends them to promote health is called *hatha-yoga*. There are other varieties. Some ancient authorities describe supernormal powers that can be attained by the practice of yoga, but most of these authorities advise against the use of these powers, since the manipulation of the phenomenal world is against the purpose of yoga and can distract the yogin from his goal. The way of release through knowledge (*jnana*) is often designated as *jnana-yoga*. The way of release through devotion (*bhakti*) is often referred to as *bhakti-yoga*. The way of release through combining full outward action (*karma*) in the world with inner detachment is called *karma-yoga*.

Release Through Devotion. In the yoga discipline of Patanjali, devotion to the god of one's choice was regarded as a helpful means of achieving detachment from the world, but eventually both the god and the world were left behind or transcended in the achievement of *samadhi*. In the great devotional movements that slowly came to dominate popular Hinduism over the centuries, the god became not only the means (through his grace and the believers' devotion, *bhakti*), but also the goal of release. The passionate hope that kept the believer moving on the path was the hope of being united forever with his god, his lord. Whether this goal was envisioned as existence in some sort of heaven in the presence of the god or as being absorbed into the deity in some mystical way, the god to whom devotion was offered was not only present now. He would be there at the end of the road.

The basic frame of reference of all the devotional movements is, as in all Hinduism, the belief in the operation of *karma* in an unending chain of rebirths into suffering, release from which must be a person's highest and most urgent quest. This implies once again the denial that the world can be a place of hope and fulfillment. The devotional movements hold out the way of devotion to a god as the only way to release. The performance of ritual, or asceticism, or meditation, may all be helpful, but without devotion, claim the adherents of these movements, all these other ways are useless. Only devotion and the powerful grace of the god can over rule *karma* and grant release.

The devotional movements developed rapidly between 200 B.C.E. and 400 C.E. They continued to grow and were especially influential in medieval India. These movements produced literature of their own. There were handbooks on how to practice devotion, *Bhakti Sutras*. There were vast bodies of literature called the *Puranas* that detailed the myths and traditions about the activities of a particular god. The devotional movements also drew on already existing literature, such as the two great northern epics, the *Mahabharata* and the *Ramayana,* and the South Indian epic, *Shilappadikaram,* transforming heroes into gods and gathering into the Person of their main deity other gods, persons, and events, like flowers strung on a garland of devotion. They also produced devotional hymns, especially in South India at first, as well as poetry, and dance-dramas of high quality. The courts of kings and emperors, and courtly romances, provided royal and erotic metaphors for devotion. The god to whom one offered devotion was both lord and lover, and the consummate longing of one's life was to remain close to him. In addition to the literature, the Bhakti movements encouraged religious pilgrimage to holy places and produced an enormous growth in temple construction and sculpture for the public worship of the gods. Today these movements represent a major expression of Hindu religious vitality.

What is meant in these movements by the practice of devotion? The *Bhakti Sutras* and the *Puranas* give us particulars. Devotion is an all-absorbing love of god and constant worship of him. When one has achieved this, one "desires nothing else, he grieves not, he hates nothing, he delights not in anything else, he strives for nothing; having realized which, man becomes as if intoxicated, and benumbed; he delights in his own intrinsic bliss . . . Devotion is . . . the suppression of all other preoccupations."[16] Here one can see why *bhakti* is called

The Bank of the Ganges at Benares. *Pilgrims descend stone steps to enter the water of the Ganges River, which is especially holy and efficacious at the sacred city of Benares. By immersing themselves, bathers are cleansed of* karma. (Courtesy of Hyla Converse)

the *yoga of devotion*. One of the most famous of the *Puranas* dedicated to Vishnu is the *Bhagavata Purana*. In it are found the god's instructions on how the devotee is to worship him.

Listening to the Lord's glory, singing of Him, thinking of Him, serving His feet, performing His worship, saluting Him, serving Him, friendship with Him, declaring oneself as His . . . a man could offer unto the Lord devotion of these nine kinds . . . God's images are of eight kinds: stone, wood, metal, plaster, paintings, sand, mind, and precious gem . . .

When I am worshipped in an icon (image), bathing Me and decorating Me are welcome . . . With clothes, sacred thread, jewels, garlands, and fragrant paste, My devotee should decorate My form suitably and with love. With faith, My worshiper should then offer Me water to wash, sandal, flowers, unbroken rice, incense, light, and food of different kinds; also attentions like anointing, massage, holding up of the mirror, etc., and entertainments like song and dance; these special attentions and entertainments may be done on festive days and even daily. . . . One should engage himself in singing of Me, praising Me, dancing with My themes, imitating My exploits and acts [drama], narrating My stories or listening to them.

Whenever and wherever one feels like worshiping Me in images, etc., one should do so. I am however present in oneself and in all beings; for I am the soul of everything.[17]

The devotional movements brought together many strands and provided a focus and a structure of meaning for the immensely complex polytheism of ancient India. The devotional movements swept up into Hinduism many indigenous deities and religious practices. Local gods and goddesses found their place in Hinduism in this way, as did the indigenous practice of image worship and the use of temples as houses for the images, both unknown in Vedic worship. There has always been a certain contempt on the part of the most ancient Brahmin families for temple priests and temple worship of images. Two gods who were only minor deities in the Vedic era became the great gods around whom the devotional movements gravitated in classical and medieval times. They were Vishnu and Shiva. Each was regarded within His own movement as the Supreme Being, and no other god was to be worshiped *as supreme* by his devotees. Other gods are worshiped as lesser gods who acknowledge their dependence on the Supreme Being.

Devotion to Vishnu. Vishnu's devotees are called *Vaishnavas* or *Vaishnavites,* and their religious movement is called *Vaishnavism* (not to be confused with *Vaishya,* which is the third caste). One of Vishnu's major functions is that of Preserver of the world, and the Vaishnavas hold that in the past Vishnu has taken on various physical forms to preserve the world when the need arose, and will do so again. These incarnations of the god Vishnu are called *avatars*. Some of them have occurred in animal form, including a fish, a tortoise, and a boar. One has been a fierce Man-Lion. The structure of such a myth has permitted it to grow and to bring under the umbrella of Vishnu's actions a wide variety of divine heroes, and thus incorporate their followers. Attempts have been made to include the Buddha, and later Muhammad and Jesus, as avatars of Vishnu, and thus to absorb them rather than to fight their challenge. With Buddhism the attempt largely succeeded. The avatars of Vishnu to whom most of Vaishnava devotion is offered are the hero gods Krishna and Rama.

Krishna. The popular worship of Krishna responds to three major aspects of the god, expressed in three periods in his life: as a child, a young cowherd, and a king. According to the ancient myths he was born in a jail, where a wicked enemy had confined his chieftain father and mother, in the town of Mathura on the banks of the Jumma river between present-day Agra and Delhi. Krishna's father, with the help of a loyal herdsman from the other side of the river, was able secretly to exchange the baby Krishna for another infant. Krishna was brought up as the herdsman's son. As a child Krishna is represented as lovable and mischievous, stealing butter from his mother's churn and engaging in other childish pranks. Women desiring sons often worship the child Krishna.

As a young man Krishna made passionate love with the young women of the village, the *gopis,* who loved him devotedly in return. Radha was his favorite, and she was jealous of his attentions to the other *gopis*. The story of the love of Radha and Krishna is vividly told in the medieval poem by Jayadeva, *Gita Govinda,* ''The Song of the Cow-Herd.'' The love of Radha and the *gopis* for Krishna, and his for them, is regarded as the symbol of the love of many souls for God, and of God for many souls. The story of the dalliance of Krishna with the *gopis* is danced out in a festival in the spring each year, the Ras Lila. On that occasion, while the spiritual meaning may be presented, the literal erotic meaning of the story is exuberantly evident. The handsome young god, the passionate lover, playing his flute, has inspired the imagination of painters and poets as well as devotees. The famous medieval princess and poetess Mirabai, for instance, caught in a cruel marriage, poured out her devotion to the god under the symbolism of passionate love.

When Krishna came to full manhood, he fought successfully to regain his throne. Then, as king of the Yadavas, he allied himself with the five Pandu brothers in their struggle against their cousins to regain their rightful sovereignty over the Aryan Kuru tribe. The story of the ''great war'' between the Pandu brothers and their Kuru cousins is told in the longest epic in the world, the *Mahabharata,* the oldest of the Indian epics. Among the five Pandu brothers, the middle one, Arjuna, was Krishna's special friend, and in the epic battle at Kurukshetra, to the north of modern Delhi, Krishna fought beside Arjuna as his chariot-driver. It was in this situation that the famous conversation took place in which Krishna revealed himself as the god Vishnu and taught Arjuna the answers to many religious questions. This dialogue containing the teaching of Krishna is called the *Bhagavad Gita,* "The Lord's Song." Scholars believe that it was composed somewhere between 200 B.C.E. and 200 C.E. and then inserted into the earlier epic material.

The Bhagavad Gita has exerted a far-reaching influence among Vaishnavas from classical times right to the present. Its teachings represent the beliefs of a large segment of Hinduism, and its doctrine of *karma-yoga* fuses the world-affirming and world-negating religious streams that flowed together to create Hinduism. The dilemma in which the hero Arjuna finds himself, as the armies are drawn up for battle, is whether or not to fight. The enemy is his own family, his cousins and uncle and old teachers. He is suddenly repelled by the prospect of killing his own people. To kill one's own family is against all the teachings of Vedic *dharma.* Such action could result in no happiness. Destruction of the family destroys the ancient holy law of the family, produces lawlessness, corrupts the women, results in a mixture of castes, and leads to hell. Arjuna declares that even though he himself is killed, he will not fight, for "it was a great wickedness that we had resolved to commit, in that through greed for the joys of kingship, we undertook to slay our kinfolk."

Akrura Invites Krishna to Mathura. *In this episode from the* Bhagavata Purana *a trap has been laid by the wicked king Kansa. But good triumphs over evil. Krishna's superhuman strength defeats Kansa's plotting. Rajput painting, early sixteenth century.* (Courtesy of the Freer Gallery of Art, Smithsonian Institution, Washington, D.C.)

Arjuna has raised a Vedic problem about right actions and happiness in this world. Krishna replies with a non-Vedic answer that negates the significance of actions (right or wrong) and happiness in this world. Krishna proceeds to explain that the soul that is embodied in any individual is indestructible. It passes through childhood, manhood, old age, death, and into a new body, but is never touched or affected by anything. It is imperishable, indestructible, eternal; pleasure and pain are alike to it. No one can cause the destruction of the imperishable one. The eternal, embodied self is not slain when the body is slain, and it does not slay anyone. The eternal soul in each person merely sheds one body to take on a new one, and the events in which this happens are predetermined by his *karma*. The real person, the soul, remains untouched:

As leaving aside worn-out garments
A man takes other, new ones,
So leaving aside worn-out bodies
To other, new ones goes the embodied (soul).

Swords cut him not,
Fire burns him not,
Water wets him not,
Wind dries him not.[18]

Krishna's advice to Arjuna is clear and unequivocal. "Therefore fight, son of Bharata," and do not mourn—since you *know* that no one kills or is killed in battle. This is the answer of the way of knowledge.

Krishna continues and explains that even within the worldly Vedic context he should fight. He is of the warrior caste and fighting is his particular caste duty, especially in this case, when he is fighting for a just cause. To abandon one's "own duty," *sva-dharma,* can only result in evil. It is better to do one's own duty (*sva-dharma*) poorly than to do another's duty well. Again comes Krishna's advice: Therefore, fight! This is the answer of the way of action, of participation in the world.

Then Krishna explains how the two ways of knowledge and action must be combined with the way of discipline, resulting in the way of *karma-yoga,* which involves full worldly participation outwardly, and inwardly complete indifference to the world. The word *karma* in *karma-yoga* means only "action" or "work," the original meaning of the word, and does not refer here to those fruits

of action that bind one to the wheel of rebirths. The word *yoga* means "restraint." The practice of *karma-yoga* requires that one walk the thin line of tension between action and restraint. One is to act without grasping at the fruits or results of action. Arjuna is to fight and fight to his full capacity, but without emotional response to the situation, without caring about the kingdom he will win or lose. Through the way of discipline, the way of inner nongrasping, one gets rid of the bondage of action. Krishna explains that those who follow the Vedas, who seek happiness and heaven, only get countless rebirths as the consequence of their actions. Freedom from the world is to be achieved by not wanting the world, by abandoning all attachment to it. Arjuna is to concern himself only with the action, not with its consequences:

Discipline is defined as indifference . . .
The disciplined in mental attitude leaves this world behind,
Both good and evil deeds.

Who has no desire towards any thing,
And getting this or that, good or evil,
Neither delights in it nor loathes it,
His mentality is stabilized.

And when he withdraws
His senses from the objects of sense,
As a tortoise (withdraws) his limbs from all sides,
His mentality is stabilized.[19]

The way to achieve this inner indifference, says Krishna, is to offer his discipline of *karma-yoga* to Krishna, who later reveals himself to be Vishnu. Action is necessary, says Krishna, for the world is Vishnu's creation, and so long as one exists in this world, one should go ahead and perform his own *sva-dharma* as a means of maintaining order in the world, but it must be done with indifference:

Therefore unattached ever
Perform action that must be done;
For performing action without attachment
Man attains the highest . . .

Casting on Me all actions . . .
Fight, casting off thy fever.[20]

The only actions that do not result in the bondage of *karma* and rebirth are actions for the purpose of worship.

Pilgrims at Mathura. *Pilgrims prepare to bathe to purify themselves in the holy Jumna River at Mathura, Krishna's birthplace. The bells are struck to attract the deity's attention. Offerings of flowers or lights are set afloat on the river. Across the river is the village where Krishna is believed to have grown up in a foster-home as a cowherd. Pilgrims visit the temples there as well as the many in Mathura.* (Courtesy of Hyla Converse)

Thus, if a man offers all his actions to Krishna as an act of worship, he finds release by the way of devotion.

In the final parts of the Bhagavad Gita, the theme of devotion entirely dominates the teaching. Arjuna beholds a terrifying vision of Krishna as Vishnu, the Supreme One; as the Creator, Preserver, and Destroyer of all; as Time who creates all creatures, sustains them, and swallows them up. The hope is held out that whatever the capacity of a person for knowledge, or discipline, or ritual, or even virtue, if he shows unswerving devotion

to Krishna, then at death he will go to Him, freed from all bondage.

To sum up, the way of release found in the Bhagavad Gita combines the Vedic and the non-Vedic ways of participation and withdrawal in the single path of *karma-yoga,* by distinguishing between outer action and inner attitude. To follow the way of *karma-yoga* means "to embrace the world with dispassion," and to this the Bhagavad Gita adds the theme of *bhakti:* The practice of *karma-yoga* is to be offered to Krishna as worship. The ways of ritual and worldly involvement, of knowledge, of discipline, and of devotion are all combined. This idea of *karma-yoga* has come to dominate the mainstream of Hinduism, even among those who have never heard of the Bhagavad Gita.

Krishna is worshiped all over India, and there are many subsects, such as the Srivaishnavas of South India, with special traditions of their own. Mathura is an important place of pilgrimage where thousands of temples vie for the pilgrims' visits. Steps lead down into the river where the devotees purify themselves by bathing and then offer flowers and lights that are carried away in the sacred stream. Busy bazaars sell lodging and souvenirs to the pilgrims.

As directed in the *Bhakti Sutras,* the images in the temples are bathed and dressed, fed and entertained. Recently in one of the major temples in Mathura an important Vaishnava visitor was denied even a glimpse of the images of Krishna and his consort because the gods were having their afternoon rest and could not be disturbed. Later, in the evening, curtains were again lowered, the temple doors closed, and when the priests had undressed and bathed the images and put them to bed for the night, accomplished musicians played on sitars for an hour or two outside the curtained doors of the inner temple chamber, for the enjoyment of the gods. The whole sequence is repeated daily.

Some of the Bhakti movements rejected image worship centuries ago. Today the intellectual elite among the Vaishnavas, as in the other devotional movements, point out that the worship of god in his image is only one way of worshiping him. Since human beings vary widely in their capacity for understanding, they say, the simpler minds will delight in the concreteness of such image worship, while those with a higher knowledge will understand that the god is not only in his image, but everywhere. Thus, there is no apology for worshiping images even in the most literalistic way—for each worships according to the level of his inclinations and capacity for understanding the Truth. This view is clearly expressed in the last two sentences quoted from the *Bhagavata Purana* on page 83.

Rama. Rama is the second *avatar* of Vishnu who is widely worshiped as a god hero. The oldest account of the life of Rama is told in the second great epic of India, the *Ramayana* by Valmiki. In this earliest telling of the story, dating from about 200 B.C.E., there is no indication that Rama is a divine figure. He was simply a human hero. Rama grew up happily as the eldest of four brothers in the city of Ayodhya, where his father was a just and well-loved king. He was handsome, accomplished, and virtuous. Rama won and married the beautiful Sita, daughter of renowned King Janaka of Videha.

After some years Rama's father decided to retire and turn the kingdom over to Rama, his eldest son and rightful heir. The people were extremely fond of Rama and rejoiced. There was one who did not. The second queen, Kaikeyi, mother of Rama's next younger brother, Bharata, wanted her son to inherit the kingdom instead of Rama. She went to the old king and reminded him of a promise he had once given her that he would grant her anything she desired. She now demanded that the throne be given to Bharata and that Rama be exiled for fourteen years, during which time he must be required to endure the harsh life of a hermit. Without anger or resentment, knowing that his father was bound by his promise, Rama prepared to go into exile. He tried to persuade Sita to stay with his family in Ayodhya, as the life he would have to lead would be filled with hardship. But Sita declared that her place was with her husband and insisted on going with him. Lakshman, the third brother, also accompanied Rama. Soon after they left, the old king died of a broken heart.

The exiles had many adventures and the places where they stayed are today reverently visited by throngs of pilgrims. They settled for a while at Chitrakut in a community of hermits. A major theme developed early in the exile: Rama's struggle against the demons. Demons often tried to harass the holy hermits, seeking to ruin their rituals. Rama on many occasions protected the hermits, killing or driving away the demons. In this way

a symbolic conflict developed, with Rama and the forces of good on one side and the demons and the forces of evil on the other.

After some years Rama, Sita, and Lakshman moved farther south into the Panchavati forest of central India. It was here that a demoness appeared who desired Rama and tried to seduce him. Rama taunted and disfigured her. In rage she went to Ravana, chief of the demons, and he agreed to avenge her. Ravana abducted Sita by trickery and magical powers, and carried her off to his capital on Lanka (Śri Lanka, Ceylon), the large island off the southern tip of India. Sita remained faithful to Rama in spite of the advances of Ravana.

Rama and Lakshman set out to find and rescue Sita, and they were joined by a monkey general named Hanuman and his monkey soldiers. Bears and birds also helped. The monkeys built a causeway across the straits to Lanka. A terrible battle ensued. The monkey, Hanuman, was captured and his tail set on fire. He escaped and with his burning tail set fire to the enemy city. The demons were defeated, Ravana was killed, and Sita was rescued. The fourteen years of exile now being ended, they returned to Ayodhya. Bharata, who had never wanted to be king, and had placed Rama's sandals on the throne during the intervening years to show that he ruled only in his brother's absence, now welcomed Rama back as the rightful king. They all should now have lived happily ever after. But the people began to murmur and to question Sita's purity, since she had spent a year in another man's house. So Sita was required to undergo an ordeal by fire, to prove her purity. She walked into the fire and was not burned by it, showing that she was innocent.

A final chapter was added later. It includes a second murmuring of the people and the demand for a second ordeal. This time Sita had become wearied of it all, and at the ordeal she called on the Earth Mother to take her back to herself to prove her innocence. The earth opened and took Sita into itself. Then the people were sorry for their murmurings. Some years later Rama, who had been a model king, turned the rule over to his sons and departed to a place ten miles up-river from Ayodhya. There he spent twelve years in meditation and ascetic discipline. Finally he walked out into the river, committing religious suicide.

By medieval times people had come to believe that

the human hero Rama was an incarnation of the god Vishnu. Today Rama and Sita are both worshiped all over India as models of virtue (dharma) and symbols of the victory of good over evil. Ayodhya is a place of pilgrimage, and thousands of pilgrims go there each year. It is reported that there are seven thousand temples in Ayodhya, and after visiting Ayodhya for a week, the author does not doubt it. Chitrakut is also a pilgrimage center with many temples. Far to the north in a family-owned temple to Rama and Sita, the author found an elderly Brahmin woman, gentle and kindly, reading and explaining to other women the religious, medieval version of the Rama story by Tulasi Das, after which a *puja* or worship of the images of Rama, Sita, Lakshman, and Hanuman took place. The kindly woman advised the author to be sure to visit Chitrakut, even though the journey is difficult, because "if one prayed sincerely to Sita in Chitrakut, whatever one asked would be granted." She herself had been to both Ayodhya and Chitrakut on pilgrimage a number of times.

Just as in the spring the Ras Lila is danced to honor Krishna, so also in the fall the Ram Lila is celebrated. This is the acting out of the whole of the story of Rama. In North India every village has its Ram Lila grounds, and major cities like Delhi have huge permanent ones. For a period of ten days to two weeks successive segments of the story are acted out each evening, the festivities lasting far into the night. In big cities professional actors play the parts. In villages the local people put on their own show. There are songs and dance and musical instruments and drums and excitement and religious fervor. Many of the Ram Lila grounds, as at Ayodhya, have permanent pavilions on the stage portion of the grounds, the one on the right for Rama's territory and the one on the left for Ravana. At Ayodhya a cable (invisible at night) is strung from high up in the nearby temple tower down to Ravana's palace. Then when the time comes, the temple image of the monkey Hanuman, his tail in flames, slides down the cable, appearing to fly through the night sky. He lands at "Lanka," which is decorated with flammable materials, and the stronghold of the forces of evil goes up in fire. In the language of drama, virtue has triumphed! In one small village, where the threshing is also done on the Ram Lila grounds, there is a brick and plaster image of Ravana. When asked if it was not odd that the image represents Ravana,

not Rama, the headman shrugged and replied, "The god comes and goes. The demon is ever present."

Devotion to Shiva. Shiva is the other major god in devotional Hinduism besides Vishnu. People who give homage to Shiva are called *Shaivas* or *Shaivites* and their religious movement is called *Shaivism.* Since classical times Hindu religious writings have sometimes referred to a triad of gods as summing up the Divine as It functions in the universe. To Brahma is attributed the function of Creation, to Vishnu that of Preservation, to Shiva that of Destruction. But in actual practice this triad is of no significance. As far as is known there are only two temples dedicated to Brahma in all India. And within the devotional movements Vaishnavas attribute all three functions to Vishnu, as was noted in discussion of the Bhagavad Gita; and among Shaivas, Shiva is regarded as the supreme Creator-Destroyer, and also Preserver.

It is probable that the god Shiva was of indigenous origin, and was absorbed into Vedic religion and Hinduism, drawing in other indigenous elements also. In the Rig-Veda he is addressed as Shiva Rudra, *shiva* meaning "kindly, gracious." He was, in fact, a cruel, destructive god, associated with storms and lightning. He is addressed as "kindly" in an effort by the worshiper to induce him to *be* kindly, to turn aside his weapons and to spare the worshiper from the unpredictable and "great wrath of the impetuous One . . ."[21] In the same hymn Rudra is also implored to grant the worshiper fertility and the healing and good health that will promote long life. The request for fertility and long life is made to most of the other gods as well, but none of the others was so much feared, so cruel and unpredictable as Rudra. Thus, from earliest times Shiva Rudra was associated with fertility and death; he was adored and feared as the Creator-Destroyer.

In the Rig-Veda Shiva was never associated with the *lingam,* the representation in stone or precious metal of the phallus, symbol of male fertility. As previously mentioned, the Rig-Veda scornfully denounces the indigenous enemy for being "phallus worshipers," and thousands of representations of the phallus have been found in the ruins of the Indus Valley cities. The connection of the Indus Valley culture with Shaivism cannot be documented, but by the beginning of historical times, in the devotional movement of Shaivism, the *lingam* had already become the primary image for the worship of Shiva. In all Shaivite temples the central place in the holy of holies is occupied by a *lingam*.

Unlike most Vaishnavas, the Shaivas in many places exclude non-Shaivas from the inner sanctum of their temples. One exception is the temple on the campus of the Hindu University in Benares, where anyone may enter, but few do. It is not a living center of devotion. In Ujjain is located one of the seven holiest Shiva-Linga temples in India. The insistence of a wise and highly honored Shaivite teacher in Ujjain made it possible for the author to enter the inner sanctum of this temple. The *lingam* here was about three feet high and ten inches in diameter and was made of solid silver. There were both men and women worshiping the *lingam,* each one murmuring formulas of adoration and request. The *lingam* was worshiped by bathing it in water or milk, by touching it, by placing fragrant ointments on it, by decorating it with flowers, and by giving money offerings to the priests. The *lingam* was set in a *yoni,* the female emblem. Above it hung a golden vessel from which water dripped continuously onto the *lingam,* keeping it moist. The water was collected as it ran off, and this holy water was distributed to devotees as ''medicine'' for fertility, Shiva's ''seed.''

The use of tanks or artificial ponds outside of the temples, with steps going down into them, where the worshiper may purify himself before entering the temple, is a characteristic of both Vaishnavism and Shaivism. At the temple that was visited in Ujjain hundreds more *lingam* images of many types of stone and in many sizes were placed on the terrace that surrounded the tank. *Lingam* images are also worshiped at home altars, and rough-hewn ones may be encountered along mountain trails or village lanes. Most Shaivas carry a *lingam* on them. In some Shaiva communities the groom places a golden *lingam* on a gold chain around his bride's neck, and she never thereafter removes it for any reason.

The *lingam* represents Shiva's creative function. A three-pronged, barbed spear or trident and other weapons are symbols of his destructive function. A Shaiva ascetic may easily be recognized, for he carries the trident. Shiva is also known as Lord of the Dance, and some of the most beautiful cast bronze images in the world are South Indian representations of Shiva dancing. His dance is part of his creative function. In passionate joy he dances out the creation of the world, but as he dances he kills a dwarf beneath his feet. And when he ceases to dance, the world falls into destruction.

In Shiva temple complexes the dance and dance-drama were developed into high art forms, which were used as a means of honoring the god and which eventually became independent of the temple. Originally the dancers, who were trained from childhood, were young women, presented to the temple by their families in infancy and brought up to be *devadasis,* ''servants of the god,'' or they might be daughters of *devadasis.* Besides the dance they were trained in music, poetry, storytelling, and other arts. They were also Shiva's women,

Shiva-linga. *This is a medieval stone carving of a woman clasping a Shiva-linga. The principal image in most Shaivite shrines is the* lingam, *the symbol of divine male creative power. Here, the fertility motif is intensified by a second pillar out of which a plant frond grows and the head of an animal emerges. Original, Allahabad Museum.* (Courtesy of Hyla Converse)

Consort of Shiva. *This is a medieval Chola bronze image of Devi, who represents the female divine creative power in the universe. Original, Victoria and Albert Museum.* (Courtesy of Hyla Converse)

and a man by uniting sexually with a *devadasi* could gain potency from Shiva as well as pleasure. Temple prostitution and the *devadasis* have been outlawed in modern India, but the practice still survives in a few areas.

Shiva is not only the Lord of the Dance, he is also the Great *Yogin*. He not only creates the world in passionate dance; he also negates the world in asceticism, mentally destroying it through the discipline of yoga. This is why the ascetics carry the trident, symbol of destruction. Monastic brotherhoods have found an important place in Shaivism and have taken aggressive action in the spread of Shaivism. Mention has been made of Shankara's transformation of the Buddhist temple at Bodhgaya into a Shiva-Linga shrine. The same kind of thing has taken place at Rameshwaram, "Lord Rama's place," the tip of land from which Rama launched his attack on Lanka to rescue Sita. It used to be a place of Vaishnava pilgrimage. Now the main shrine there is a Shiva-Linga temple, and the myth that justifies it claims that Rama worshiped Shiva on this spot, thus subordinating Vishnu to Shiva.

The Gods in Shiva's Family. Shiva does not have *avatars* like Vishnu. Instead he has a family. His wives represent the various aspects of the female power in the universe, as Shiva represents the male. The Rig-Veda shows no evidence that the Vedic people worshiped powerful goddesses. Occasional hymns honor dawn or the rivers, but the goddesses are not important figures. The devotional movements, and primarily Shaivism, integrated into Hinduism the indigenous religious worship of powerful goddesses. They are addressed as *Devi* ("the goddess") or *Shakti* ("the Power"). Shiva has four wives, of whom Parvati is the beautiful young goddess with whom Shiva makes passionate love. She represents, among other things, the female erotic power in the universe to which the male responds. Umma is the wife and mother. She represents the female power in the universe that conceives, nourishes, and protects. Durga is beautiful and fierce. She rides a white tiger and carries terrible weapons. She is often depicted killing her enemies, cutting off their heads, tearing open their bellies. She is said to represent the female power to avenge wrong, but she is unpredictable, and "wrong" is whoever Durga is against. Kali is a great and powerful goddess capable of terrible destruction. She wears a necklace of human skulls and drinks blood out of a cup made from a skull. She carries fierce weapons, and often holds up a severed head in one hand. She is the goddess of disease. She is the only deity worshiped by upper-caste Hindus to whom blood sacrifices are offered. Bengal has long been a center of Kali worship, and in Calcutta (the name comes from *Kali ghat*) at the most famous temples of Kali, a goat is slaughtered each day and offered to her. She is fierce, fecund, capricious, and terrible. Worship of Kali is largely an attempt to appease her and avert her wrath. On the positive side, she represents for Shaivites the most powerful form of the female forces in the universe, and she is sometimes depicted as overwhelming Shiva himself, standing on his prone, unconscious body.

There are a number of subsects in Shaivism. The Lingayats, for instance, are distinctive because among them no caste differences are recognized, and their women are highly respected and honored. Their name comes from the fact that they always wear a small stone *lingam* in a silver box.

Another sect, that of tantric Shaivism, developed in Bengal in the ninth century and after, in the same region and at the same time as tantric Buddhism. Tantric Shaivism holds that the primal active force in the universe is not male but female, and that she is dark and terrible as well as beautiful and seductive. She is the *Shakti*. A man worships the Shakti in order to master her and thus eliminate her threat. But because he masters her in the sexual embrace, he also surrenders himself to the pleasure that only she can give. Sexual symbolism provides the structure of belief. Tantric Shaivites believe that, as in the sexual act a man may master a woman and reduce her to the instrument of his pleasure and release, so by embracing the dark, enticing, and dangerous power of the Shakti in mastery and surrender he can achieve release from the world. Rather than the way of withdrawal to achieve release, the Tantric Shaivas seek control of the primal power, Shakti, by entering into it, wearing it out, bringing it into submission. They

make use of symbolic designs (*mandalas*) and ritual formulas (*mantras*) to gain control. They practice the secret *yoni parast,* the circle ritual, at special times of the year or month. In this ritual, a woman, who may be the wife or mistress of one of the men participating in the rite, or may have been abducted for the purpose, is placed naked in the center of a circle, decorated with flowers and jewels, worshiped as the goddess Shakti, and then ritually raped by her worshipers. She thereby becomes the instrument of their salvation. In this union of the male and the female powers, the male gains control and neutralizes the power of the female over him. By lust he overcomes lust and is freed from its power; through intense indulgence, not restraint, he exhausts desire by surrendering it to her and achieves control, indifference. Shakti can no longer seduce, entice, or force her will upon him, because male and female have ceased to exist in this mystical oneness that has overcome all duality, all desire.

The worshipers of Shakti practice other rituals, mostly in secret also, including the rituals of the Five Forbidden Things, which are meat, fish, wine, special gestures, promiscuous sexual intercourse, and sometimes the ritual murder of the Shakti at the end of the *yoni parast*. This tradition has also emphasized the use of yoga techniques to seek mastery over the world and even over death, the final symbol of the world. It is the wandering *yogins* of Tantric Shaivism that have been especially known for their magical or supernatural powers, and their great saints are believed to have achieved bodily immortality.

Besides the goddesses, his consorts, Shiva also has two sons who are worshiped. Ganesh is a very popular god. He is fat and smiling and has an elephant's head. He is the god of good fortune and is widely worshiped by Shaivas and also by non-Shaivas. Shiva's other son is mainly worshiped in South India. He has two aspects or is sometimes worshiped as two separate gods. As Kumara, a beautiful and virile youth, he is worshiped by the young maidens who hope for a husband like him. As Karttikeya, he is the war god, both feared and worshiped. The character of Shiva as Creator-Destroyer is thus represented in this son, as well as in his wives.

In the spring Shaivas celebrate the Shivaratri, an all-night ritual festival in honor of the marriage of Shiva and Parvati. In the fall, at the same time as the Ram Lila festival of the Vaishnavas, the Shaivas, especially

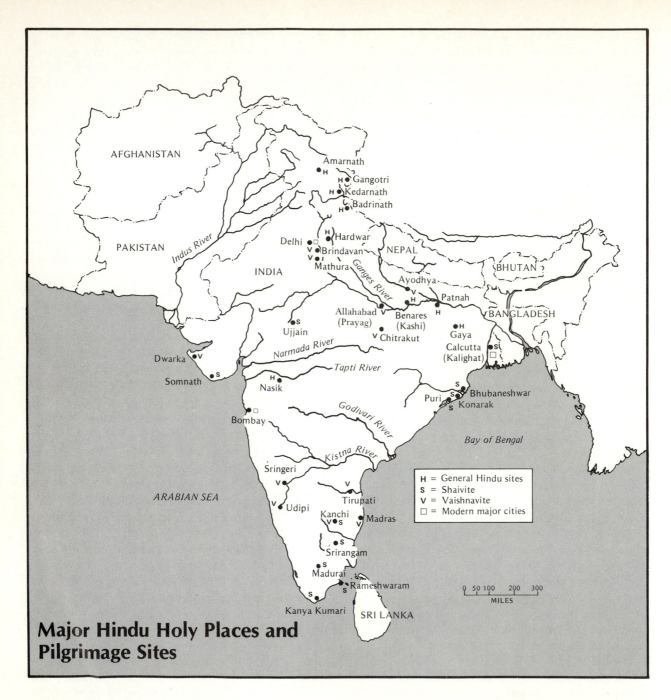

Major Hindu Holy Places and Pilgrimage Sites

Map labels:

AFGHANISTAN

PAKISTAN

INDIA

NEPAL

BHUTAN

BANGLADESH

Amarnath
H Gangotri
H Kedarnath
H Badrinath
H Hardwar
Delhi
V Brindavan
V Mathura
Ayodhya
V Patnah
Allahabad (Prayag)
V Benares (Kashi)
H Chitrakut
Gaya
Calcutta (Kalighat) S
S Ujjain
Dwarka V
Somnath S
H Nasik
Bombay
Puri S
S Bhubaneshwar
S Konarak
Indus River
Ganges River
Narmada River
Tapti River
Godivari River
Kistna River

Bay of Bengal

ARABIAN SEA

Sringeri
V Udipi
V Tirupati
Kanchi V S
V Madras
S Srirangam
S Madurai
S Rameshwaram
S Kanya Kumari

SRI LANKA

H = General Hindu sites
S = Shaivite
V = Vaishnavite
□ = Modern major cities

0 50 100 200 300
MILES

in Bengal, celebrate Durga Puja, in which an image of the goddess is taken out for a parade and then brought to the river for a ceremonial immersion.

Devotion in Hindu Life. In general, in all the devo-

tional movements, taking the god or goddess (images) out of the temple for a parade among the people is a common form of devotional festival. Different localities have their own gods and goddesses, and their own commemorative dates. In many places, such as Puri, Karnack, Kanchi, and Madurai, enormous and elaborate temple chariots have been constructed and are kept for the purpose of conveying the god on these occasions. Worshipers fight for the privilege of pulling on the chariot ropes, and sometimes in a frenzy of devotion throw themselves to their own destruction under the huge wooden wheels.

It is not certain when the cow came to be regarded as sacred and the killing of cows to be banned. Today virtually all groups within Hinduism revere the cow as sacred. Cows are allowed to roam freely, not only in villages and towns, but in large cities. Cow dung and urine are used for purification both ritually and nonritually. Butter oil (from cow's milk) is poured as an offering on the sacred fire.

In concluding this section, it should be said that the original devotional movements, while they sought release from this world, assumed that as long as one was part of this world, one was part of the Hindu religious organization of life, with its castes, stages, and goals. Each had his own *sva-dharma*. The life of the householder or the ascetic, the goal of wealth or devotion, all were integrated into the religious organization of life. Any apparent contradictions in the options offered were explained on the basis of the observation that human beings vary widely in their spiritual capacity for Truth. Yet, whatever the level, all were seeking release from *karma* and transmigration. Devotion tended to be practiced *in addition to* basic rituals and caste rules, although during some of the practices of the devotional movements, such as pilgrimage, caste distinctions were sometimes temporarily set aside.

The Encounter of Hinduism with Islam

In the medieval period Hinduism encountered in Islam another religious system that provided a total way of life. Its assumptions were alien to Hinduism. Hinduism had met alien assumptions before, but it was never able to assimilate and absorb Islamic religious ideas, as it had done with Jainism and Buddhism. Consequently, it was never profoundly influenced by Islam.

The first invaders who swept into India from the north were the Indo–Aryans. They were followed over the centuries by many others: Persians, Greeks, Shungas, Kushans, Huns, and others. Some came and settled, contributing forms and colors to the Indian religious and cultural mosaic. Others appeared swiftly, struck savagely, and rode off with their loot, leaving only the silent ruins of burned and pillaged towns and unburied bones to mark their passage.

Muslims, the adherents of Islam, have been present in India for close to 1,300 years. Chapter 9 will deal fully with the religion of Islam. But it is important for the understanding of modern Hinduism to examine here those aspects of Islam that were dominant in the historical encounter of the two religious communities in India, and the Hindu perception of this encounter and response to it.

The Establishment of Islam in India

The Hindus first learned about Islam from their Muslim conquerors. This is never the best circumstance in which to discover new religious ideas. Yet it was from rulers and warriors that Hindus most frequently experienced Islam, and the Hindu response to Islam stemmed partly from that fact.

The first attempt of Islamic forces to conquer India came in 711–715 C.E., less than one hundred years after the founding of the Islamic community. The Caliph in Damascus, the chief ruler in Islam, whose armies had already swept across Persia, Syria, North Africa, and into Spain, sent a military expedition to conquer Sind, as the start of the conquest of India. Sind is the territory around the mouth of the Indus. Muslim settlements were successfully established and although the military venture was later abandoned, other Muslims continued to immigrate into the area.

The missionary work of the Sufis, Muslim mystics, also started in this early period. The Sufis gathered in communities around saintly teachers who had themselves found the path to a direct experience of God and were prepared to lead others. Gradually Sufi Brotherhoods or Orders were formed, based on the teachings of one leader or another. These Brotherhoods sent out missionaries to many lands, including India.

The second great military venture in the establishment of Islam in India was a series of ten crusades launched by Mahmud of Ghazni between 1000 and 1030 C.E. His religious motivation is recorded by Muslim historians of his own time: "The king (Mahmud), in his zeal to propagate the faith, now marched against the Hindus of Nagarkot, breaking down their idols and levelling their temples."[22] The Muslim historians state that Mahmud made clear his intention to wipe out idolatry and establish Islam. For this reason he picked out for destruction what he had been informed were the holiest and most famous Hindu shrines. Nagarkot was one of these. Another was Thanesar, of which Mahmud had heard that it was "held in the same veneration by idolators, as Mecca by the faithful," and so "in the year A.H.[*] 402 Mahmud resolved on the conquest of Thanesar." A Hindu prince sent a messenger offering Mahmud an enormous ransom, if he would spare the image and temple of the god at Thanesar. A Muslim historian records this exchange. The Hindu prince wrote,

". . . Thanesar is the principal place of worship of the inhabitants of the country. . . . if it is required by the religion of Mahmud to subvert the religion of others, he has already acquitted himself of that duty, in the destruction of the temple at Nagarkot". . . Mahmud replied, "The religion of the faithful inculcates the following tenet: That in proportion as the tenets of the Prophet are diffused, and his followers exert themselves in the subversion of idolatry, so shall be their reward in heaven; that therefore it behooved him (Mahmud), with the assistance of God, to root out the worship of idols from the face of all India. How then should he spare Thanesar?". . . the city was plundered, the idols broken, and the idol Jugsoma was sent to Ghazni to be trodden under foot.[23]

Muslim historians relate that Mahmud also destroyed the temples and idols of Somnath, which he had been informed was the most sacred Hindu shrine of all at that time. A Muslim historian of Mahmud's own time, who saw the idols in Ghazni, writes,

The image was destroyed by Prince Mahmud. . . . He ordered the upper part broken and the remainder to be transported to Ghazni. . . . Part of it has been thrown into the horse yard of the town, together with the Cakrasvamin, an idol of bronze, that had been brought from Thanesar. Another part of the idol from Somnath lies before the door of the mosque of Ghazni, on which people rub their feet to clean them from dirt and wet.[24]

* The letters A.H. stand for *Ann. Hegirae* or "Year of the Hijrah." The Muslim calendar dates from the Prophet Muhammad's *Hijrah* or flight from Mecca to Medina in the year 622 C.E.

After Mahmud came waves of other Muslim invaders, pushing persistently southward until they held most of North India. A new invasion occurred in 1524 that resulted in the establishment of the Mughal dynasty, the greatest of the Muslim dynasties in India. Muslim power was at times extended over most of the Indian subcontinent. Then, in the declining years of the Mughals, when the arduous tasks of ruling no longer appealed to the successors of the great Mughals, Muslim power in India began to ebb away. Hindu and Sikh leaders rebelled and established independent kingdoms that could no longer be controlled. European trading companies, determined to maintain order for the sake of trade, were encroaching more and more in the matter of government. New outsiders then took control of much of India, first under the British East India Company, and then under British colonial rule. The British accorded no preferential status to either Muslim or Hindu. Many Muslims, who were used to superior status and believed that it was God-given, deeply resented this change. The Hindus, who had been oppressed, saw new opportunities, which they were quick to seize, but they also resented having to exchange one alien domination for another.

Relations Between Hindus and Muslims

The nature of the encounter of Hinduism with Islam in India was determined by Hindu religious perceptions of proper relations between themselves and all non-Hindus, as well as by Muslim views of the proper form of any relations between Muslims and all non-Muslims. Alberuni, a Persian Muslim scholar who lived in India during the rule of Mahmud of Ghazni, describes some of the barriers between Hindu and Muslim. He recounts the way in which numerous invasions in the past had made Hindus hate all foreigners:

But then came Islam. The Persian empire perished, and the repugnance of the Hindus against foreigners increased more and more when the Muslims began to make inroads into their country. . . . All these events planted a deeply rooted hatred in their hearts. . . . Mahmud marched into India for a period of thirty years and more. . . . Mahmud utterly ruined the prosperity of the country, and performed there wonderful exploits, by which the Hindus became like atoms of dust scattered in all directions, and like a tale of old in the mouth of the people. Their scattered remains cherish, of course, the most inveterate aversions toward all Muslims. This is the reason too, why Hindu sciences have retired far away from those parts of the country conquered by us, and have fled to places which our hand cannot yet reach, to Kashmir, Benares, and other places. And there the antagonism between them and all foreigners receives more and more nourishment, both from political and religious sources.[25]

Alberuni also recounts the barriers created by Hinduism:

They totally differ from us in religion, as we believe in nothing in which they believe, and *vice versa*. On the whole there is very little disputing about theological topics among themselves; at the utmost, they fight with words, but they will never stake their soul or body or their property on religious controversy. On the contrary, all their fanaticism is directed against those who do not belong to them—against all foreigners. They call them *mleccha, i.e.,* impure, and forbid having any connection with them, be it by intermarriage or any other kind of relationship, or by sitting, eating, and drinking with them, because thereby, they think, they would be polluted. They consider impure anything which touches the fire and water of a foreigner; and no household can exist without these two elements. . . . They are not allowed to receive (in their houses) anybody who does not belong to them, even if he wished it, or has inclined to their religion. This, too, renders any connection with them quite impossible, and constitutes the widest gulf between us and them.[26]

In addition, says Alberuni, there are the "peculiarities of their national character," chief of which is a haughty, vain, stolid self-conceit: "The Hindus believe that there is no country but theirs, no nation like theirs, no kings like theirs, no religion like theirs, no science like theirs."[27] Furthermore, he had found them ungenerous in the extreme in communicating what they knew of science and philosophy not only to foreigners like himself, but also to other Hindus if they were of another caste.

The Sunni Muslim political ideal is a theocracy in which the ruler uses his power to further God's purpose in the world through the implementation of Islamic Law. Islam believes that mankind was created to obey God and that God has revealed in the sacred scriptures, the Quran, exactly how He wishes to be obeyed.

All Muslims, and especially the ruler, are enjoined by the Quran to use all means at their disposal to extend the territory in which God's will is obeyed, which means where Islamic Law is enforced and Islamic faith prac-

ticed. It was in this context that the conquest of India was regarded by Mahmud and others as a holy crusade and the destruction of Hindu temples and idols as a religious duty.

Islamic Law divides non-Muslims into two categories. The first group are called *zimmis;* the term originally applied to Christians and Jews, who share with Islam many of the prophets of the Bible. The second category is that of *kafirs,* idolators and polytheists, with whom Muslim authorities adopted several approaches, depending on area, circumstances, and even the personality of the rulers themselves.

The *zimmis* are to be tolerated, and their life and property protected, as long as they acknowledge the superiority of Islam, show respect to all Muslims, refrain from seeking converts or publicly practicing their faith, and obey other restrictions. If they break any of the restrictions and seek to undermine Muslim authority or Law, their property can be seized and they can be put to death. In addition they are to pay a special tax. Furthermore, the testimony of a non-Muslim is not to be accepted in a Muslim court, if it is brought against a Muslim, although a Muslim's testimony against a non-Muslim is acceptable.

Most Muslim rulers in India, but not all, accorded the Hindus a limited *zimmi* status, because they, like the Jews and Christians, had scriptures. The following account by a Muslim historian who lived at the end of the sixteenth century explains the views of some Muslim legal authorities on the status of Hindus. A Muslim ruler called on a well-known specialist in Muslim law and asked him to explain on what basis it was lawful for him to demand obedience and tribute from Hindus. The Muslim jurist gave this answer:

"It is lawful to exact obedience from all infidels, and they can only be considered obedient who pay the poll-tax and tribute without demur, even should it be obtained by force; for, according to the law of the Prophet, it is written, regarding infidels, 'Tax them to the extent that they can pay, or utterly destroy them.' The learned of the faith have also enjoined the followers of Islam, 'To slay them, or to convert them to the faith'; a maxim conveyed in the words of the Prophet himself. The Imam Hanifa, however, subsequently considers that the poll-tax, or as heavy a tribute imposed upon them as they can bear, may be substituted for death, and he has accordingly forbidden that their blood should be heedlessly spilt. So that it is commanded that the *jizya* [poll-tax] and the *khiraj* [tribute] should be exacted to the uttermost farthing from them, in order that the punishment may approximate as nearly as possible to death.' "28

The above passages represent the attitudes of many of the orthodox religious leaders and officials. Some of the rulers were more liberal. A few were harsher. The Mughal emperor Akbar was an exception to most of the above religiously mandated attitudes and regulations. Early in his reign he announced that he was the ruler of all the people, and that like the sun that shines on Muslim and non-Muslim alike, and like the rain that falls on Believer and Infidel without distinction, so his justice and protection would be extended to all. This was perceived by some Hindus as a policy close to the tradition of the ancient Hindu kings, who supported all religions. But pious orthodox Muslims were outraged. Akbar abolished the special *jizya* tax on non-Muslims. He took Hindu nobles into his court right along with the Muslim nobles, and advanced individuals of both groups to the highest rank, when they earned it. He married Hindu Rajput princesses, and one of them became the mother of his eldest son and successor. He criticized certain Hindu practices, however, and banned the burning alive of Hindu widows on their husbands' funeral pyre.

Akbar was profoundly interested in religious questions. Whenever he was out on a journey or an excursion, if there were some holy hermit in the area, Muslim or Hindu, Akbar would go out of his way to visit the holy man, ask questions, hear his teaching. He was closely in touch with Sufis. He encouraged religious debate, rather than suppressing it as the religious authorities would have preferred. He built a special hall for religious discussion and invited Hindu Brahmins and ascetics, Christians, Jews, and Muslims to come and debate religious issues, with a view to discovering what was best in all religions. But Akbar went so far as to create a religion of his own, a combination of elements from many sources, and he tried to persuade his courtiers to accept it. Some did, some did not.

After Akbar's death, his tolerant attitude toward Hindus was maintained under his son. In the reign of his grandson, however, the famous Shah Jahan who built the Taj Mahal, the orthodox Muslim influence began to reassert itself. In several instances idols were again collected from Hindu homes and temples and publicly desecrated.

It was Shah Jahan's rigidly orthodox son, Aurangzeb, however, who set out to enforce orthodox Islam in his domains. He was determined to root out heresy within Islam. From time to time Muslim heretics were rounded up, sent to Kabul, and traded to Central Asian nomads as slaves in exchange for horses. Aurangzeb was even more harsh on the Hindus. He reinstituted all the restrictive laws against them, and often treated them as *kafirs,* especially when they defended themselves against depredations. Like Mahmud of Ghazni, Aurangzeb destroyed the temples in especially holy Hindu places. He tore down the temple built on the birthplace of Krishna and built a huge mosque on that spot. He did the same to the temple built on the birthplace of Rama, leveling it to build a great mosque there. In Benares, the most famous temple to Shiva was destroyed and a mosque built up. Hundreds of cartloads of images were destroyed.

Religious Developments Under Muslim Rule

In the circumstances described above, Hinduism in its specifically religious aspect was forced to withdraw into itself as far as all public and official life was concerned. Home rituals were less vulnerable than temple ceremony. Orthodox Islam, situated in the midst of Hindu India, remained a rigid entity and had little influence on the character of Hindu religion. What influence there was on Hinduism came from sectarian forms of Islam in India. Certain Muslim subgroups such as Shias and the Sufis provided bridges to Hinduism, for they practiced similar forms of devotion. Among the Hindus the love for Krishna, or another god, was poured out of the heart in songs of devotion, and in dances of joy and self-dedication. Orthodox Islam prohibited singing and dancing as immoral, but the Sufis used hymns as a means of spreading Islam. Many Sufi saints, for instance, composed simple hymns, like folk songs, and went about teaching people to sing about the one God to whom they should give their hearts.

Another bridge between Hinduism and Islam proved to be the attitude of the Sufis toward Islamic Law. The Quran contains detailed regulations for the lives of Muslims and additional regulations were laid down by the

Prophet Muhammad. These laws have been codified and interpreted into a body of religious, political, economic, and social law called the *Shariah*. The performance or nonperformance of the practical duties of the *Shariah* marks the division between the community of Islam and those outside it. In Hinduism the equivalent to the *Shariah* is the system of practical duties of caste, stage, and goal. The devotional movements of both religions taught that all duties, all actions should be transformed by sincerity and devotion into acts of worship. In Indian Sufi writings one often encounters the same sort of ideal that is expressed in the *karma-yoga* of the Bhagavad Gita.

There was one highly significant Hindu religious development that occurred during the period of Muslim dominance. New Hindu devotional movements arose[*] between the twelfth and sixteenth centuries, especially in northern and central India. Although there are differences among them, they have certain characteristics in common. They saw this world as a place of hopeless suffering, of corruption and cruelty, of disappointing and unending labor. Yet joy was possible. It was to be found in the intense, personal relationship between the individual soul and the One Ultimate Being, whatever He may be called. The painful longing of the soul separated from God, and the joy of finding and uniting with Him, were expressed in poetry and song, often using the metaphor of the Lover and the Beloved.

Unlike those of the earlier devotional movements, many of the leaders and followers in these movements came from the Shudra caste. They had been excluded from traditional Hindu ritual experience, as well as from Sanskrit education. It is not surprising, therefore, that many of these movements set little value in rituals, caste, images, and scriptures; that they were anti-Brahmanical; or that they spread their message in song and poetry in the languages of the common people, not in Sanskrit. The distrust of established religion was not limited to Hinduism, but included Islam as well. The direct, inward, mystical union with God made all else irrelevant. Although many of the movements used vivid, concrete images from everyday life and names for God drawn

from the rich Vaishnavite and Shaivite mythology of the past, or even Muslim names for God, it is evident again and again that the God whom they thus sought to describe was indescribable, the Absolute of Vedanta and the Upanishads, now personalized and approachable.

Some of the greatest Hindu devotional poetry came out of these movements. The poets who composed these works seem to have escaped persecution because they remained obscure, or wrote in areas on the fringes of Muslim control, or wrote in periods of turmoil when Muslim control was less effective, or under liberal Muslim rulers. Three of the greatest Hindu devotional poets— Surdas, Tulasidas, and Tukaram—all wrote during the reigns of the most tolerant of all Muslim rulers, Akbar and Jahangir.

Two fifteenth-century leaders, the poet-saint Kabir and Nanak, the founder of the Sikh religion, provide examples of some aspects of the devotional movements. They retained the belief in *karma* and transmigration and a basic Hindu frame of reference, but they rejected both caste and idolatry and stressed belief in one God, although he might be called by many names. Kabir's poetry was widely sung, first around his native Benares, where he worked as a poor weaver. His weaver subcaste was originally Shudra and had been converted to Islam as a group. He himself was inspired by the Vaishnava devotionalism of the wandering saint, Ramananda, and for a time became his disciple. In the following song, Kabir represents God as speaking to him:

O servant, where dost thou seek me?
Lo! I am beside thee.
I am neither in temple nor in mosque: I am neither in Kaaba nor in Kailash:
Neither am I in rites and ceremonies, nor in Yoga and renunciation.
If thou art a true seeker, thou shalt at once see Me: thou shalt meet me in a moment of time.
Kabir says, "O Sadhu! God is the breath of all breath. . . ."[29]

Although Kabir may have been popular within Hinduism in North India, the attempt to join any other name to that of Allah, or to equate Allah with Ram, or to place Hinduism on the same spiritual plane as Islam, was rejected as blasphemy by orthodox Muslims. An incident is reported by Muslim historians in 1499 when Kabir was 59 years old, in a city near Benares where

[*] Religious persecution often does not deter devotional fervor. For instance, the Jewish devotional movement of the Hassidim flourished in the midst of intense persecution of Jews in eastern Europe in the eighteenth century.

he lived. A Brahmim was being taunted by Muslims because of his religion. He replied that "the religions both of the Muslims and Hindus, if acted on with sincerity, are equally acceptable to God." This view is similar to that of Kabir. But the Brahmim was brought before a court of learned Muslim judges. After many arguments "the learned men were of the opinion that unless the infidel, who had maintained the Hindu worship to be equally acceptable to God as that of the true faith, should renounce his error, and adopt the Muslim religion, he ought to suffer death. The Hindu refused to apostatize, and was accordingly executed . . ."[30] Kabir was more fortunate, and his movement and his poetry continue to enrich Hinduism.

The Sikhs

Nanak (1469–1538), a Hindu Vaishnava, came from near Lahore. After an intense religious awakening, he began a life of teaching and wandering that lasted many years until his death. He expressed his religious fervor in poetry and song, and a community of adherents gathered around him. His religious teaching took for granted the Hindu belief in *karma* and transmigration, but like Kabir he rejected Hindu caste and Muslim circumcision because these were marks that separated worshipers of the same God into hostile groups. Nanak opposed the worship of images and was in agreement with Kabir that there was one God only. In his poetry some of the terms used to address God or to describe him come from Islamic forms of prayer and praise. God is "the Creator, the Compassionate, the Self-Existent." But other expressions show clear continuity with the Vedantic tradition that underlay the Hindu devotional movements. God is "the True, the Only Real"; he is known by many names, and *Govind, Hari,* and *Ram* were Vaishnava names that Nanak often used.

His followers referred to Nanak as the *Guru,* the Teacher, a Hindu term. He designated a new Guru to be his successor as leader of his community after his death. There were ten Gurus in all, and since then their sacred scriptures have been regarded as their continuing Guru. The community, referred to as *Sikhs,* was organized like a Sufi Order and like Ismaili communities (see Chapter 9), with strong personal leadership over a network of communities whose loyalty and institutionalized financial support (a sort of taxation) gave stability and continuity to the whole.

Intended by Nanak as a movement to express the unity of all worshipers of the One God, the Sikhs might have remained a quiet stream amid the great rivers of Indian devotion. But Islam influenced the Sikhs in an unintended way. Persecution of the Sikhs galvanized them into a warrior nation, determined to strike back even more fiercely at any who struck at them. Persecution had begun earlier but was seriously intensified under Aurangzeb. Later, in areas where the Sikhs eventually came to power, they took terrible vengeance on their former oppressors. Thus, with the intention of achieving religious unity, the Sikhs, in their fight for survival against Islam, became instead a symbol of religious intransigence and hatred between Muslims and their non-Muslim opponents.

This religious hatred boiled over in 1947 when, at the time independence from Great Britain was achieved in India, Muslim Pakistan separated from India. Over two million people were killed in an orgy of religious fanaticism. Muslims killed Hindus and Sikhs on the Pakistan side of the border, and Hindus and Sikhs killed Muslims on the India side. In Lahore on the Pakistan side, where thirty-five percent of the population had been Hindu and ten percent Sikh, there are now no Hindus and no Sikhs. More recently Sikh perceptions of Hindu dominance in India have led some Sikhs to militancy, and violence has erupted between Sikhs and Hindus. And yet the old ideal of unity persists among many Sikhs in modern India. The author of this chapter, a foreign visitor to Delhi, admired and wished to enter a Sikh shrine. The visitor asked a Sikh who was leaving the shrine whether it was permitted to go inside. The Sikh replied with moving simplicity, "It is God's temple. So it is your temple. Enter."

To sum up, Islam established itself in India where it was largely under the domination of Muslim orthodoxy. In spite of some Shia and Sufi bridges to Hinduism and of attempts such as those of Akbar to establish close relationships with Hindus, the Muslim community never envisioned any other religious alternative except conquest and conversions of Hindus; or, if that were not possible, to remain in the midst of Hindu India as a self-contained community, the vanguard in the continuing struggle of

God against unbelief, of Islam against the infidel. For Muslims as well as for Hindus, assimilation was out of the question.

The influence of Hinduism on Islam has been negligible. Perhaps the hardening of class lines among Muslims might be attributed to caste influence, but in other Muslim countries far from caste influence there have been sharp class distinctions. Perhaps the veneration of the saints could be attributed to the influence of Hindu pilgrimage practices, but Muslim saints are venerated in eastern Iran and Iraq with no help from the Hindus. The influence of Islam on Hinduism was also negligible. It could be claimed that the assertion by the devotional movements that all gods are really the One God, reflects the influence of Islam's radical monotheism, but the character of the assertion clearly points to Upanishadic rather than to Muslim sources.

The encounter of Hinduism with Islam did not stimulate Hindu religious intellectual creativity. The Muslim contribution to Indian culture, in contrast, has been immense in the fields of architecture, crafts, and art. Yet at its religious core, Hinduism was not affected by its encounter with Islam. The Rajput artist was influenced in *how* he painted, but not in *what* he painted. The hostility generated by the Muslim policy of desecration of Hindu images and temples, and of humiliation of non-Muslims still erupts in violence today. It is a bitter legacy and burden for modern India, whose constitution calls for religious toleration and for equality for the large minority of ninety million Muslims in India.

The Modern Encounter of Hinduism with the West

The encounter with the West has elicited a creative ferment within Hinduism comparable to what occurred in the formative years of Hinduism, when Vedic religion encountered Jainism and Buddhism. The result of this encounter is not yet clear, but it is certain that new forms of Hinduism are being forged. A key element is the fact that Western thought itself has been in a state of creative ferment during the period of this encounter. Centuries earlier Vedic religion met the challenge of alien values in Jainism and Buddhism by assimilating, domesticating, and relativizing their threat. In this process Vedic religion itself was profoundly changed, but the Hinduism that it became out-performed Jainism and outlived Buddhism in India. Will Hinduism be able again to assimilate and domesticate alien values, this time Western values, by fusing them into some sort of viable new amalgam? The process is complicated by the fact that India first learned of the West from new conquerors, from the Western colonial power that ruled India.

There are many aspects of Western culture involved in this encounter, such as science, technology, industrial techniques and organization; various political and economic systems from democracy to totalitarianism, from capitalism to Communism; and, of course, the philosophies and religions of the West. Only those attitudes and ideas that have been of interest to Hindus, negatively or positively, will be discussed here.

Hindu religious thinking has been most deeply challenged by modern Western humanism, with its basic assumption that the individual human person as such has value, and that this value stems from the fact of his humanity, not from his social or religious status. From this assumption come others: That individuals have the right to their own lives and to seek their own fulfillment and their own happiness; that society ought to be reformed so that it is brought closer to embodying the value of the individual and his rights, closer to a justice that provides equality before the law; and that it is the responsibility of each person to work to secure justice for all. These ideas are expressed in the French motto, ''Liberty, Equality, Brotherhood,'' and in the assertion on which the United States was founded, that every person has the right to life, liberty, and the pursuit of happiness; that this right cannot be taken away; and that with the right goes the responsibility to seek liberty and justice for all. It is in this sense that Western thinkers have claimed that all men are born equal. The modern West has also held that it is through the free and intransigent use of human reason, of the capacity to think, that the way can be found to establish freedom, justice, and happiness.

Hinduism has traditionally claimed that all men are born unequal. The ''injustices'' of the inequalities of caste and circumstance represent the *hidden justice* of *karma;* thus, they must be accepted, transcended, but not changed. Each person's value and rights depend on the rank and circumstances into which he has been born, and he has been born with precisely *those* rights and values, as reward or punishment for his own actions in past lives. Hindu law is for Hindus. The non-Hindu is outside the system. Western law, like Buddhist axioms, proposes universal principles, applicable to all persons, regardless of religion or status. Western humanistic values are not locked into any one religious system, nor inherently linked to any ethnic group. Although shared with some Western religious groups, they are not limited to them. They represent universally applicable humanistic principles, and they are therefore capable of being appropriated by anyone or any group, even while the Western bearers of these values might be rejected or criticized by means of the very values they hold.

As part of its encounter with the West, Hinduism also encountered Christianity in a new way. Christianity is believed to have existed in India from the first Christian century, and the Mar Thoma church, among other groups in South and Western India, believes that it was founded by the Apostle Thomas. Also at an early time the Syrian Orthodox Church established Christian communities in western India, and Nestorian Christians established themselves in the North. By and large the Hindus appear to have treated the Christians as a non-Hindu caste, isolating themselves from contact with them except in marginal ways. From the twelfth century on, records show that Circassian and Armenian Christians were bought as valued slaves or welcomed as traders and artisans. In the fifteenth century Portuguese traders arrived and settled in Goa on the west coast, and with them came Roman Catholic missionaries. Under Akbar, Catholic priests were invited to court and participated in religious discussions. By treaty arrangement Akbar also permitted the establishment of another Portuguese trading post at the mouth of the Ganges in the east. But under Shah Jahan, because the Portuguese were making converts to Christianity, this trading post was destroyed and ten thousand people killed in a surprise attack. This effectively eliminated Christianity from Bengal at that time.

Modern Christian missionary work in India increased greatly under British colonial rule, which permitted freedom of religion. In spite of conversions to Christianity, the Christian community still represents only a small minority of the Indian population. Yet Christianity has had an important impact on certain currents within Hin-duism. The most important influence has come from the figure of Jesus as a religious and ethical ideal, and from the Christian commitment to unrestricted service expressed in the establishment of schools, colleges, hospitals, agricultural and technical training institutes, and so on, which are open to all, regardless of religious affiliation.

What have been the major forms of the Hindu religious response to these aspects of its encounter with the West? There have been both negative and positive responses, but they have added up to a remarkable rebirth of Hinduism. Four Hindu movements in modern times illustrate major directions that have been taken.

Four Modern Hindu Movements

Humanistic Vedanta: Ram Mohan Roy. Ram Mohan Roy (1772–1833) was a Brahmin from Bengal. Persian and Arabic were the official languages of the Muslim rulers. Ram Mohan Roy studied these and then read widely in the Persian and Arabic literature, as well as in Arabic translations of Greek philosophers. He felt unsatisfied with these studies and turned back to his own tradition, studying Sanskrit and then immersing himself in the Upanishads and the writings of Vedantic philosophers. Still spiritually unsatisfied, he wandered for five years all over India as a holy seeker in quest of spiritual insight. He returned to Bengal where he again took up his studies, acquiring a fluent and polished mastery of English. He was employed by the British East India Company in Calcutta and rose rapidly to high rank. He met Christian missionaries and was impressed by Christian ethics and the ideal of service and reform, but not by traditional Christian theology. He was strongly attracted, however, by Unitarian views.

All of Ram Mohan Roy's education and experience, through which he was confronted with such a variety of answers to life's questions, led him to the conviction that the unprejudiced exercise of human reason should be a sufficient means for open-minded people to examine all sorts of religious claims to see which are consistent with the laws of nature, the sacred traditions, and common sense. He then proceeded to examine the various religious claims, and came to the conclusion that ethical monotheism was the form of religion that was to be chosen above others. He found the Christian ethic superior to all others and summarized it simply as "that law which teaches that man should do unto others as he would be done by." Such an ethic, he said, along with a belief in a Supreme Power superintending the functioning of all things in the universe, would "reconcile us to human nature, and tend to render our existence agreeable to ourselves and profitable to the rest of mankind."[31] Ram Mohan Roy approved the Unitarian view of God and wove it into his own theistic position.

It is interesting to note that Ram Mohan Roy turned back to the springs of his own tradition for the purpose of opposing idolatry, but he reinterpreted these ancient Upanishads in the light of a concern for religious and social reforms based on values newly learned from the West. He found that the Upanishads, on which his views were based, were almost unknown among his fellow Hindus and certainly not followed. So he translated them into two of the regional languages, Bengali and Hindi, and distributed them free of charge. Later he also translated them into English.

While Ram Mohan Roy was eager to show that Hindu culture was in fundamental ways superior to Western culture, he was not afraid to acknowledge the corruptions he saw in Hinduism and courageously attacked evils of many sorts. The widespread ignorance, superstition, and lack of education among his people led him to start a number of schools where Sanskrit, the Vedas, and sacred traditions were taught, and he wrote persuasively to the Governor arguing that the money that the British had allocated for the education of Indians should not be used to start a new Sanskrit school in Calcutta as the British had decided, but that it be used instead for a school that would teach subjects not already available in India: Western mathematics, physical sciences, philosophy, and other useful disciplines necessary for India's advancement.

In order to bring his reforms to a wider public, Ram Mohan Roy established newspapers, published books, and demanded freedom of the press. The Western humanistic basis of his reforms is evident here, for the demand for a free press is based on confidence in human reason and the assumption that only through free inquiry can truth be known or the best alternative be discovered. Through his newspapers he sought reforms in many other areas as well. He campaigned against the widespread practice of the burning of widows alive on the funeral pyres of their husbands; and to get his argument across wrote a dialogue between an advocate of the burning of widows, who gave the traditional reasons why they should be burned, and the opponent, himself, who refuted all the arguments. He also fought against child marriage, ritual rape and ritual murder, and the fatalism that drained away all energies for reform.

Ram Mohan Roy started a religious group based on mutual encouragement both in worship of Brahman and in social reform. It continues to this day and is called the *Brahmo Samaj*. His major interest all his life was to purify Hinduism in order to defend it against itself and against the West. As his best means of immunizing Hinduism against the challenge of Western Christianity, he incorporated certain aspects of Christian ethics into the reinterpretation of his tradition. He took pride in his own tradition, yet showed an openness to learn from the West all that would be helpful in improving the life of his own people. As a result of his efforts he was denounced by many of his own people, and yet he could never be part of Western culture. The position he took was a lonely one, indeed. At the end of his life he went against all Hindu tradition and journeyed outside of India to Britain (one of the first Hindus to do so). Unitarian friends had invited him to come and lecture. He was very well received, but fell ill and died in England in 1833. His work was carried on in India by new generations, who sought in their way to combine the best of Hinduism and Western humanistic values.

Pure Vedic Hinduism: Dayananda Sarasvati. Another sort of answer to the challenge of the West was given by another reformer a little later and in another part of India. Dayananda Sarasvati (1824–1883) lived and worked in Bombay. His answer to the West was to reject it. He sought instead to purify Hinduism in a return to Vedic or Aryan religion; hence the name of the movement he founded, the Arya Samaj. Yet his emphasis was filtered through the critique that Western values brought to bear on Hinduism. Unlike Ram Mohan Roy, Dayananda Sarasvati in going "back to the Vedas" did not emphasize Upanishadic monism and Western-inspired reform. He turned to Vedic ritual and to Vedic social obligations, to *dharma*. Dayananda Sarasvati found that the Vedas were critical of idol worship and that temple worship was not known in Vedic times. So he opposed these. Although classes existed in Vedic times, there was no restriction against inter-caste marriage or social association across caste lines. So among the "Aryan" castes, the upper three, he opposed these restrictive aspects of caste. There was no mention in the Vedas of widow burning, child marriage, the enormously burdensome custom of "bride price," or the dowry system, and so he opposed all of these. He found no prejudice against women and no degradation of them. So he taught respect for women. He found respect for integrity, for worldly activity, and for education; he found great stress laid upon the performance of Vedic rites and the maintaining of a certain separateness from all non-Hindus. He found great self-esteem as a Hindu. And all these things were incorporated into the Arya Samaj.

An additional aspect of the Arya Samaj is the intense and sometimes violent opposition to all non-Hindu elements in India—toward Muslims, Christians, and secular groups such as Communists. The Arya Samaj holds that India is a Hindu country, since the vast majority of the people are Hindu, and therefore the laws of the land should be Hindu laws. If Muslims, Christians, and Communists do not want to live under Hindu laws, say the Arya Samajis, they can leave, and it would be a good thing, too. The Arya Samaj is opposed to the present secular constitution of India. They call instead for *Hinduraj*, "Hindu-rule," and are able to generate a great deal of Hindu emotional response in campaigns against cow slaughter, for the cow is sacred, and Muslims, Christians, and Communists eat beef. The Arya Samaj is militant. If a Communist government should come to power and oppose Hinduism, the Arya Samaj is prepared to fight to defend Hinduism, and has developed a para-military wing for that purpose. In 1975, when the socialist government declared an emergency and suspended all civil rights, many of the leaders of the Arya Samaj were thrown in jail and others went into hiding. The movement continues to be strong. It is not large but has an effective voice.

Mystical Syncretism: Ramakrishna.

Steeped in the Shaivite devotionalism of Bengal, Ramakrishna (1836–1886) experienced frequent ecstatic trances and visions of the goddess Kali, whom he worshiped as the Divine Mother with fervent devotion. He came to believe that all the traditional Hindu devotional movements, whether Shaiva, as in his own most vivid experience, or Vaishnava, were all in fact worshiping the same Divine Being. Later he came to extend this idea to all religions. He preached to those who gathered around him, and eventually his movement reached international audiences. He taught that whatever the forms of their worship, all religions were really worshiping the One Supreme Being. He went on to say that the highest and truest vision of this One Supreme Being was the Divine Mother, the goddess Kali. He defended image worship and most of the traditional forms of Shaivite devotion. He taught people that their own forms, Hindu and non-Hindu, were all paths leading ultimately to the Divine Mother. Since, however, the Shaivite forms of devotion were the clearest in leading to Her, the other forms should eventually be abandoned. Ramakrishna taught that in the highest experience of the Divine, one discards human reason and all rational categories. The ultimate reality is beyond good and evil, beyond rationality. True spirituality is free of materialistic and worldly concerns, whether political, social, economic, or ethical.

A young follower of Ramakrishna, Vivekananda, helped to organize the missionary aspect of the new movement. After a highly successful lecture tour in the West, where Vivekananda explained to eager audiences the superiority of Hindu spirituality over Western materialism, he returned to Calcutta and threw himself into the work of religious education and charitable service to relieve suffering. Education, serving the poor, and international missionary outreach became the threefold emphases of the Ramakrishna Mission.

Spirituality and Politics: Gandhi.

In the first half of the twentieth century the great preoccupation of all Indians, including Hindus, has been the struggle to gain independence from colonial rule, and since 1947, when India became a sovereign state, the absorbing and demanding task has been nation building. There have been many profoundly religious men and women who have devoted their energies to the national struggle. In other eras these energies might have been turned toward the devotional movements or toward philosophy. But in the circumstances of the twentieth century, the *sva-dharma* of many seemed to be that of Arjuna, and they heard in a personal way the advice of Krishna, "Therefore, fight!'' The Bhagavad Gita's ideal of *karma-yoga* seemed to many to have been made for these times, and none exemplified it better or more effectively than Gandhi, in his own way.

Mohandas K. Gandhi (1869–1948) grew up in Gujerat, where Jain influence was strong. He studied in London and became a lawyer. He also read widely in Western literature and was profoundly impressed by the writings of Tolstoy and Ruskin. He went to South Africa, where discrimination against blacks and Asians like himself troubled him deeply. It was at this time that Gandhi read a book called *Self-Help* by an Englishman, Samuel Smiles. The book dealt with Christian ethical issues and called on individuals to take responsibility in their own hands and to act to change unjust situations. Gandhi decided to resist discriminatory laws. He set up a simple community based on Tolstoy's principles, where all legally required discrimination was set aside. He began to use and develop passive (nonviolent) civil disobedience as a technique of political action aimed at reform.

When Gandhi returned to India, he began to work actively for Indian independence. His ability to combine vigorous and decisive political action while maintaining simplicity and spiritual discipline in his own life soon won him a wide following. This was *karma-yoga* again, outer involvement with inner detachment. He developed an idea called ''truth grasping,'' and taught that unless one achieved spiritual integrity and discipline in his own life, one could not win moral victories in the political arena. The self-rule of India for which they struggled, he insisted, had to be matched by an inner ''self-rule.'' He himself led the way. He meditated for a number of hours every day in the early morning darkness, even with the busiest of schedules. He ate sparingly of the simplest food. He dressed with the simplest of clothing that any poor man wore. His house was austerely simple.

Gandhi soon acquired a devoted following that regarded him not only as the astute political leader that he was, but also as a saint—a very effective combination, especially in India. He called on his followers to use nonviolent civil disobedience as a tool in the struggle against the British. He worked with many other nationalist leaders, some of whom disagreed with his condemnation of modern technological and industrial developments and his call to create a simple economic self-sufficiency through the return to cottage crafts. Other leaders, such as Jawaharlal Nehru, a secularized Hindu who became India's first Prime Minister and had a major hand in writing the Constitution, were perhaps greater statesmen, but it was Gandhi who was able to rally a tremendous devotional response from millions and millions of Hindus in the cause of political independence, because his saintly life represented for them a high expression of their best traditional religious values.

A sign of the continuing process of interaction with the west was that Gandhi felt free to incorporate and domesticate whatever he chose from the West; and today, for instance, Hindus in every corner of India sing the hymn ''Abide With Me'' as ''Gandhi's hymn'' with no knowledge of its Western Christian origin. Also, as we have seen, there are movements such as the Arya Samaj that militantly oppose Western or other non-Hindu influence. It was an unbalanced Hindu fanatic of the Arya Samaj who assassinated Gandhi shortly after independence had been won, because he believed that Gandhi was granting too many concessions to Muslims in the cause of Indian unity and thus was betraying Hinduism. Yet many Muslims had believed that Gandhi intended, after independence was won, to force the Muslim minority to live under Hindu laws, and this fear of Hindu religious domination sparked the movement whose aim was to create the separate Muslim state of Pakistan.

Another sign of the interaction with the West is the Indian Constitution itself. The leaders of the independence movement struggled to create a structure that would provide order for their national life and embody the hopes for which they had suffered. The new nation included a large majority of Hindus, a large minority of Muslims, and sizeable other minorities. These leaders could find no basis in the religious traditions of Hinduism on which to build their national life in this new situation. They turned instead to the West and the universal principles of the value of human persons and of the justice due them. These principles in varying forms had already been assimilated as their own by men like Nehru. As a result the new Indian Constitution provides for equality before the law without regard to religion, caste, or sex, forbids such discrimination in public life, and much more. The Constitution is based on the French, British, and American constitutions, and socialist ideas, all adapted to the Indian scene. It stands in clear opposition to the ancient Hindu law books and the Hindu organization

Portable Deity. *The owner of this image wheels it out onto the public road. Worshipers have placed fresh flower garlands both on the image of Shiva and on the lingam. Offerings of money are placed in the container in front of the image and provide a living for the owner, seated at the right.* (Courtesy of Hyla Converse)

of society, but it reflects the opposition to caste that characterized the *bhakti* movements.

Hinduism Today

A few years ago a well-known scholar, just back from India, opened a major presentation on religion in contemporary India with the statement, "In India religious news is bad news." Many liberal democratic Hindu leaders, as well as Indian Socialists and Communists, would agree. Their perspective differs from that of orthodox Hinduism. They are dedicated to creating a new nation, and they would like to mobilize all of the energies of the people in a great effort to eradicate poverty, disease, hunger, and over-population. Often it is religious orthodoxy that opposes them.

The orthodox believe, first, that people deserve what they enjoy or suffer. It is *karma*. They have earned it. Second, the orthodox seek release from all such human problems. And third, they believe that in any case such reformist efforts have little chance to succeed even temporarily, since the world is in one of the time cycles when everything is getting steadily worse.

Modern Hindu liberals regard the hundreds of religious holidays (national, regional, and personal) as "bad news," for many millions of hours are lost to production and the tasks of nation-building. Similarly, absenteeism for the sake of performing pilgrimages is a drain on manpower, and the news that two and a half million pilgrims attended a holy festival for ten days is bad news for the economy. Ascetics who withdraw from society deplete the workforce, and yet must be supported by those who work.

In more direct ways it is bad news when orthodox Hindu groups oppose, often with violence, the exercise by outcastes of constitutionally mandated voting rights, educational rights, and even the right to discard the clothing that had been the public symbol of their ancient oppression. The dowry system is forbidden now by law, and it can be regarded as nothing but bad news when another bride is doused with kerosene and set on fire by her mother-in-law, as reported all too often in the press, because she did not bring a high enough dowry. The orthodox would not approve of such a thing, but neither would they protest effectively, for the ancient Laws of Manu declare that it is only "a minor crime to kill a dog, a Shudra, or a woman." Some orthodox priests still persuade women to burn themselves to death on their husband's funeral fire, although it is now against the law to do so.

The encounter with the West has given rise to sharp tensions within Hinduism, as it struggles out of its past, creating its future, especially in the urban areas. But the vast majority of Hindus live in villages, and religiously they are hardly touched at all by this encounter of Hinduism with the West. They keep to their caste *dharma*. They worship the images in the village temple and in their homes. They say their morning and evening

A Sacred Tank and Temple Complex. *This complex is located at Kanchipuram, in South India. Worshipers bathe in the tank first and then make their offerings in the inner sanctuary. The temple can be identified as Shaivite by the presence of the structure at the right, a dance pavilion, and by the image of Shiva's bull, Nanda, at center.* (Courtesy of Hyla Converse)

prayers. They regard the earth as a mother, and propitiate the demons. They leave food offerings for sacred snakes or trees. They regard cows as sacred and allow them to roam freely and scavenge about. They celebrate Diwali, the festival of lights and good fortune, in the fall and that of Holi, for well-being, in the spring, and other local and sectarian festivals of the village, according to its traditions. They go on pilgrimages to sacred cities, like Benares, and bathe in the sacred rivers. Marriages are arranged for the young, the festive rituals enjoyed, and the debts grumbled over. The dead are burned with the proper rites, and at the dark of the moon the restless spirits of ''fathers'' long gone are honored and appeased. They believe in *karma* and transmigration. They hope for a better life next time around, and they accept in general that sufferings in this life are the result of their own deeds in the last one. But they have common sense as well, and may wield a heavy stick against those who seem to be helping *karma* to pour out more ills upon

their heads than seem inevitably ordained. Religiously, in the villages, nothing much has changed all down the long years, and they do not expect that it will. But in the cities and the towns, from which have always come the energies for change, there is a restlessness, impatience, and violence. This has spawned all kinds of movements; political ones, usually secular, express a yearning for a better life, one that is more joyous, more humane, more just; and religious ones, often led by a *guru,* express a yearning for intense religious experience that will lift the devotee above the plane where injustice and sorrow operate.

Summary

Let us look back again now to the long trail by which Hinduism has come out of the past into the present, and pick out some aspects of the journey.

Beginnings. As we have seen, there is no founder of Hinduism. It began as the Vedic religion of the Aryans who migrated into India about 1500 B.C.E. The Vedic religion was not affected by its encounter with the Indus Valley culture, but in comparative isolation developed its world-affirming, unitary, and then monistic views. The ritual was a primary means of participating in this world, for through it one expected to achieve prosperity and happiness. The encounter of Vedic religion with Jainism and Buddhism profoundly affected Vedic religion. The Jain and Buddhist views were world-negating; they held that life was inherently suffering in endless cycles of *karma* and rebirth, and that one should seek release from it. In the course of a few formative centuries Vedic religion found ways to assimilate a belief in *karma,* rebirth and release, and yet continue to affirm the Vedic values of life in this world. What emerged from this encounter was Hinduism. From medieval times Hinduism was again in close encounter with an alien religion, Islam, but in its religious core Hinduism remained largely unaffected by Islam. In the modern period a new encounter is taking place, between Hinduism and the West. Major effects are already evident, but the final results are still being shaped.

Divisions and Groups. The major groups in Hinduism are those that were discussed in relation to the different ways of release. Seeking release through knowledge, both Samkhya (dualistic) and Vedanta (monistic) philosophies have drawn many followers to their way. Yoga, the discipline of restraint, may be considered to be a group in itself, although other groups have used the techniques of yoga. The Vaishnavas and the Shaivas, devotional movements, are another sort of grouping in Hinduism. Another category that cuts across all these groups is that of the ascetic, the *sannyasin,* who seeks release individually.

The Scriptures or Literature. The basic scriptures, adherence to which is a major sign of Hindu orthodoxy, are the *Vedas.* They include the *Rig-Veda,* and other *Vedas,* the *Brahmanas,* and the *Upanishads.* In dealing with the Hindu organization of life, the way in which Hindu society is to function, the *Dharmashastras,* the sacred law books, are the scriptural authority, among which the major one is the *Manusmriti* (*the Laws of Manu*). The various groups within Hinduism have their own special scriptures. For Samkhya, it is the *Samkhya Karika.* Vedanta goes back to the *Vedanta Sutra,* and many commentaries on it are highly respected also. For Yoga, the major authority is the *Yoga Sutra* of Patanjali. The devotional movements have had a great many scriptural resources, especially the vast body of the *Puranas.* The *Bhagavata Purana* is one important Vaishnava scripture; so also are the *Bhagavad Gita,* the *Ramayana,* and the *Gita Govinda.* The Shaivas have a large number of *Puranas* as well.

Doctrines. We have seen that in Vedic eyes the world was a dynamic whole in which man had a magnificent chance to achieve his happiness. This was expressed in the ritual and its meaning, in the doctrines of Holy Order and Holy Power, and finally in the doctrines of Atman-Brahman. As a result of the encounter with Jainism and Buddhism, this whole dynamic world was transposed into a new context, that of the endless suffering of *karma* and rebirth, and all the worldly happiness that one might achieve was now seen as meager and transitory. The Vedic worldly goals, while preserved in Hinduism in the Hindu organization of castes, stages, and goals, were now no longer regarded as ends in themselves, but as way stations on the path to release. The encounter with Jainism and Buddhism resulted in the crucial shift from the Vedic quest for happiness to the Hindu quest for release; from the Vedic hope for human fulfillment to the Hindu hope for escape from the human condition.

Within the context of *karma* and transmigration, many varieties of doctrine have been operative in Hinduism. Even contradictory differences in doctrine have not been the basis for exclusion from Hinduism, and this has been rationalized under the claim that the widely differing human capacities to know the Truth require a wide variety of expressions of the Truth. In Samkhya is found the dualistic doctrine of *Prakriti* and *Purusha,* in Vedanta the monistic doctrine of Brahman, in Vaishnavism the pluralistic-monistic doctrine of *avatars,* and so on. In the way of discipline (*Yoga*) the final state sought is release, *samadhi,* while the typically Hindu combination, the affirmation of human existence in this world and the flight from it, is found in the doctrine of *karma-yoga.*

In the present situation there is a new atmosphere of intellectual ferment, and Hinduism appears to be exercising its ancient capacity for assimilation. What doctrines will emerge in this process and whether they will provide a new frame of reference is unclear at present.

Institutions, Religion, and Society. Hinduism organizes Hindu society in an elaborate social and economic gridwork, according to castes, stages, and goals. The ascetic lives apart from this structure, although he is part of the scheme. And some who seek release through devotion deny that the rules of the organization need be followed. The possibility of becoming an ascetic provides a "safety valve" in a very tightly organized society. This social organization by castes is the instrument by which *karma* distributes to each the just deserts of his own actions in his past existence, and over the course of many incarnations it provides the pathway to release from all future existences. But there are short-cuts. And these were institutionalized in *ashrams* (retreats) for meditation, which were established by followers of the ways of *knowledge* and of *discipline,* and in a vast array of pilgrimage places, temples, and monastic and devotional brotherhoods created by the followers of the way of *devotion.*

Practices and Goals. As has been noted in the preceding paragraphs on doctrines, the ultimate goal in Hinduism is release. Most people are probably more concerned with a better reincarnation next time around, and some happy couples even pray that they will again be husband and wife. Furthermore, the majority of Hindus accept wholeheartedly the worldly goals of virtue, wealth, and pleasure; and the recognition that, although these goals are valueless in terms of the ultimate scheme of things, this need not deter one from enjoying them now. The goal of asceticism is followed also, both inwardly in the midst of society and outwardly. The wandering holy man on his spiritual quest, sitting in meditation at the source of the Ganges, or inflicting bodily suffering on himself, or smeared with ashes wandering in bazaars or jungle; or groups of hermits living under a tree; or clean and disciplined monks occupied in study—whatever the form, the goal of asceticism has been and still is widely followed in Hinduism.

Among almost all upper-caste, practicing Hindus, the household rituals dating from Vedic times are performed in some way. If these same Hindus are also members of one of the great movements of devotion, they will in addition practice *puja,* the offering of devotion to the image of the god, in their homes and at the temple; and they will, if possible, go on pilgrimage to bathe at sacred places to purify themselves of past *karma* and to offer *puja* to the gods at especially holy shrines.

Caste regulations have been central in Hinduism, although probably never carried out as thoroughly as the law books propose. In the modern situation they are breaking down, both in the face of new ideas about persons and society with which Hinduism is trying to deal, and in the face of industrial and technological changes—it is impossible to maintain the old separations in crowded trains, buses, factories, and business offices. Nevertheless, caste exclusiveness is still firmly entrenched in the social and occupational sectors.

Hinduism Today. Hinduism in the past never grappled with the issue of social justice. The organization of society was religiously sanctioned and inviolable; it included a way for the individual to walk out on it, by becoming an ascetic, if it became too much. But most injustices were simply accepted as being the inevitable personal consequences of one's own past deeds, of *karma,* and thus part of a hidden, cosmic justice. It would have been impious to work to change "unjust" structures of society. Compassion could be expressed in kindness and in almsgiving. One of the most important

Temple Entrance at Madurai. *An ancient carved deity smiles down on a small boy, who waits patiently for worshipers to buy his fragrant fresh flowers, offerings to be placed before the great god in the inner shrine.* (Courtesy of Hyla Converse)

aspects of the present situation is that Hindu leaders, as a result of the encounter with the West, must now deal with the issues of social justice—the structure of society and the plight of the poor, the hungry, and the oppressed—on the basis of a new vision; and, as has been noted, the resources in traditional Hinduism for dealing with the issue of social justice are limited.

Beneath the issue of social justice is, of course, the issue of the nature and value of man and his life in this world, which in turn raises fundamental questions for traditional views of caste and *karma.*

Hinduism has always had an astonishing toughness and resiliency in meeting challenges in the past. In the varieties of its approaches to these contemporary issues, Hinduism is reaching for its own solutions.

NOTES

1. *Rig-Veda*, Book III, Hymn 62, vs. 10–11. From *Hymns of the Rigveda*, trans. by Ralph T. H. Griffith (Benares: E. J. Lazarus and Company, 1896); reprinted in the Chowkhamba Sanskrit Series (Benares, 1963). This famous verse is called either the *Savitri* verse for the god to whom it is addressed, or the *Gayatri* verse for the meter in which the poetry is composed. In all quotations from the *Rig-Veda*, the English of Griffith's translation has been modified to make the reading easier for modern students.
2. *Rig-Veda*, VI.27.4–6.
3. At Lothal, outside the town, a brickwalled "tank" has been excavated. It was connected to the river by a canal and was originally thought to have been a boat dock. This has been disputed and its ancient use is uncertain.
4. *Rig-Veda*, VII.15.1–3; 16.4: II.2.9,12.
5. *Rig-Veda*, II.11.1–2,4,7,12–14, 18–19.
6. *Rig-Veda*, X.13.1.
7. *Brihad-āranyaka Upanishad*, I.4.7, author's translation.
8. *Brihad-āranyaka Upanishad*, II.4.1. From *The Thirteen Principal Upanishads*, trans. by Robert Ernest Hume (London: Oxford University Press, 1921). All further quotations from the *Upanishads* are from Hume's translation, with modifications of the English to simplify the style.
9. *Chāndogya Upanishad*, VI.11–12.
10. *Chāndogya Upanishad*, V.10.7.
11. Burrow, Thomas, *The Sanskrit Language*, London, Faber and Faber, 1955, Revised 1973, pp. 386–387.
12. The *Sūtrakritānga*, I.i.1.2,4. From the *Jaina Sūtras*, trans. by Hermann Jacobi, in the *Sacred Books of the East*, vol. 45 (Oxford: Clarendon Press, 1884–95). For this and the next reference below, a more readable English rendering has been used for the *Sources of the Indian Tradition*, edited by W. T. deBary (New York: Columbia University Press, 1960), pp. 56 and 67, English translator not cited.
13. The *Uttarādyayana*, IX.12–16. *Jaina Sūtras, Ibid*.
14. "Kevaddha Sutta," *Dīgha Nikāya*, XI.67. From *Buddhism in Translation*, trans. by Henry Clarke Warren, vol. 3 in the *Harvard Oriental Series* (Cambridge, Mass.: Harvard University Press, 1896, revised 1922), pp. 312–313.
15. *Dhammapada*, XX. Trans. by Irving Babbitt, New York, Oxford Press, 1936. (Based on trans. by Max Müller, 1870.)
16. Nārada, *Bhakti Sūtra*, 1–22. In deBary, p. 332.
17. Kapila, *Bhāgavata Purāna*, 7.5.24, 11.27.7–51. In deBary, pp. 339–341.
18. *Bhagavad Gītā*, II. 22–23. trans. by Franklin Edgerton, vol. 38 in the *Harvard Oriental Series* (Cambridge, Mass.: Harvard University Press, 1944).
19. *Ibid.*, II.48,50, 57–58.
20. *Ibid.*, III.19,30.
21. *Rig-Veda*, II.33.14.
22. Mahomed Kasim Firishta, *History of the Rise of Mahomedan Power in India*, trans. by John Briggs (London: Longman and Green, 1829); reprint (Lahore: Sang-E-Meel Publications, 1977), vol. I, p. 48.
23. *Ibid.*, pp. 50–52.
24. Al-Biruni, *Alberuni's India*, trans. by Edward C. Sachau (London: Routledge and Kegan Paul, 1888); reprint (Delhi: S. Chand and Co., 1964), vol. II, p. 103.
25. *Ibid.*, vol. I, pp. 21–22.
26. *Ibid.*, p. 19.
27. *Ibid.*, p. 22.
28. Firishta, *Rise of Mahomedan Power*, vol. I, p. 349.
29. Kabir, *Songs of Kabir*, trans. by Rabindranath Tagore (London: Macmillan, 1961), pp. 1, 72.
30. Firishta, *Rise of Mahomedan Power*, vol. I, pp. 576–77.
31. Ram Mohan Roy, *The Precepts of Jesus, The Guide to Peace and Happiness*, pp. xxi–xxiv; quoted in deBary, p. 576.

GLOSSARY

Pronunciation

Sanskrit pronunciation is easily learned, primarily because each Sanskrit letter always stands for the same spoken sound. The pronunciation of key Sanskrit letters is explained below, and for each letter an English equivalent sound is given (in parenthesis) that will be used in the pronunciation guide in the glossary.

The vowels are pronounced as follows:

a as the /a/ in "sofa" (-uh-). (The flat /a/ as in "flat" does not exist in Sanskrit.)
ā as the /a/ in "calm" or "father" (-aah-).

ai as the /ai/ in "aisle" (-y-).
au as the /ow/ in "cow" (-ow-).
e as the /ay/ in "say" (-ay-).
i as the /i/ in "hit" (-i-).
ī as the /i/ in "machine" (-ee-).
o as the /o/ in "go" (-o-).
u as the /u/ in "pull" (-u-).
ū as the /u/ in "rule" (-oo-).
r as the /rry/ in "Harry" (-rri-).

The consonants are pronounced as in English with the following exceptions:

c always as the /ch/ in "child." In this text it has been spelled *ch*.

g always as the /g/ in "go."

ṃ and *ṇ* as the /n/ in "sing."

ph as the /ph/ in "uphill" (two separate sounds). There is no /f/ sound in Sanskrit at all.

s as the /s/ in "sun."

ś and *ṣ* as the /sh/ in "shine." In this text they have been spelled *sh*.

th as the /th/ in "boathouse" (two separate sounds). There is no /th/ sound in Sanskrit like the /th/ sound in English "there" or "thin."

Agni (*uhg-ni*) the Vedic god of fire; fire, the household hearth-fire, ritual fires.

agnihotra (*uhg-ni-ho-truh*) the Vedic morning and evening (and sometimes noon) family ritual in which offerings are made to Agni in the household fire. It is still performed today and is called the *Sandhyā*.

ahimsā (*uh-him-saah*) noninjury.

ajiva (*uh-jee-vuh*) "non-jiva," see **jiva**. Material reality and the conditions under which it exists. With jiva, one of the two eternal realities of Jain dualism.

artha (*uhrt-huh*) material success, wealth and power; one of the three wordly goals to be achieved in Hinduism.

Aryans, Ārya (*aahr-yuh*) the name by which the early Indo–European people who migrated into India referred to themselves. They are also called *Indo–Aryans*.

Āryāvarta (*aahr-yaah-vuhr-tuh*) the heartland of Vedic culture; the area that the Aryans first conquered and settled. Even as late as 1000 C.E., Muslim scholars were told that it comprised the *Punjab* (the land watered by the five tributaries of the Indus River) and the *doab* (the land watered by the upper Ganges River and its tributary, the Jumna). It very largely coincides with the area known to archeologists as the Painted Grey Ware area. See page 64.

ashram, āśrama (*aah-shruhm-uh*) all four Hindu stages of life; more popularly it refers to the retreat or hermitage of a holy teacher or sage.

Ātman (*aaht-muhn*) self, both the individual self or soul and the Self or Soul or Essence of the Universe.

avatar *or* **avatāra** (*uh-vuh-taah-ruh*) an incarnation of a god in human or animal form; most characteristic of **Vishnu,** whose two most famous avatars are **Krishna** and **Rama.**

bhakti (*bhuhk-ti*) devotion to a god; devotional practices.

Brahman (*bruh-muhn*) the holy power that circulates in the universe and makes it live and function (early Vedic meaning); the Ultimate Reality; It is the source of the universe and pervades all things as their Essence. In the *Upanishads* and later, bears the same meaning as **Atman** but is associated with different imagery.

Brāhmaṇas (*braah-muhn-uhs*) Vedic commentaries on the ritual.

Brāhmins (*braah-mins*) the priestly caste, the highest ranked of the four Hindu castes. See **castes** and **varna.**

castes the four major ranked socio-occupational divisions of Hindu society. An individual's caste position is fixed at birth; the only way to change caste is through death and rebirth in a new life. See also **varna.**

Dāsas (*daah-suhs*) people indigenous to India against whom the Aryans fought as they migrated into and settled in Northwest India.

deva, devi (*day-vuh, day-vee*) a god, a goddess.

dharma (*dhuhr-muh*) the true teachings, moral codes, virtue. The first of the four Hindu goals of life.

dharmashastras *or* **dharmaśāstras** (*dhuhr-muh-shaah-struhs*) Hindu law books containing moral, religious, and social codes.

dhyāna (*dhee-aah-nuh*) contemplation, meditation; the next to the final stage in the practice of **yoga.**

Diwāli (*di-vwaah-li*) a modern Hindu autumn festival of lights, good fortune, the new year. The goddess Lakshmi is honored.

Dravidians the principal dark-skinned race inhabiting India when the Aryans invaded, and the major racial strain in South India today. Such languages of South India as Tamil and Telegu have developed from a common Dravidian original language.

Ganesha *or* **Gaṇeśa** (*guh-nay-shuh*) the elephant-headed god of good fortune; son of **Shiva.**

gopi (*go-pee*) a milkmaid, a cowherd's wife or daughter; one of the lovers of **Krishna.**

Gṛhya Sūtras (*grri-yuh soo-truhs*) Hindu texts on domestic rituals and obligations.

guru (*gu-ru*) a holy teacher, a teaching Brāhmin.

Indra (*in-druh*) the Vedic warrior god who led the Aryans to victory and settlement in India. He is also the god of storm; his weapon is the *vajra* or thunderbolt.

Jains (rhymes with "*mines*") adherents of an indigenous religion of India; influential in the development of Hinduism.

jāti (*jaah-ti*) a Hindu subcaste.

jiva (*jee-vuh*) one of the two eternal realities in Jain dualism, thought of as an infinite number of identical spiritual units. All existence is made of jivas trapped in **ajiva;** this entrapment causes the jiva pain.

jnāna (*jnaah-nuh*) knowledge.

kāma (*kaah-muh*) pleasure, desire, one of the four Hindu goals of life. Concept includes dance, poetry, drama, music, and erotic pleasure. Personified, Kāma is the god of love.

karma (*kuhr-muh*) basically, "action"; hence, the results of action; the belief that one's own deeds in this and past lives determine the circumstances in one's present life of happiness or suffering, of caste and sex. Thus, *karma* is the belief that whatever one's present condition, one has earned it by his own past deeds.

karma-yoga (*kuhr-muh-yo-guh*) full outward action and involvement in life along with the cultivation of inner restraint and indifference.

Krishna *or* **Kṛṣṇa** (*krrish-nuh*) a god; an avatar of the god **Vishnu.** His favorite gopi was Radha and later his queen was Rukmini. He is the divine hero of the *Bhagavad Gita*.

kshatriya *or* **kṣatriya** (*kshuh-tri-yuh*) the caste of princes and warriors, the nobility; the caste ranked second in Hinduism. See also **castes** and **varna.**

līlā (*lee-laah*) sport, play, and drama. The Raslila is a spring festival that commemorates the dalliance (līila) of **Krishna** *or* with the gopis by re-enacting it in dramatic form. The Rāmlila is a fall festival when the life story of **Rama** is presented as a drama (lila). In some monistic Hindu philosophies the whole universe is regarded as the lila of the **Brahman.**

liṅga, liṅgam (*ling-guh, ling-guhm*) a representation of the phallus, symbol of the male creative forces in the universe; the emblem of the god **Shiva** and the form in which he is most commonly worshiped.

moksha *or* **mokṣa** (*mo-kshuh*) release, the fourth Hindu goal of life.

prakriti *or* **prakṛti** (*pruh-krri-tee*) primal matter, the active principle in Samkhya, the material world and personality.

pūjā (*poo-jaah*) the actions prescribed for the worship of a god or idol: the offering of food, flowers, adoration, music, lights.

purusha *or* **puruṣa** (*pu-ru-shuh*) primal spirit, the self, the inactive principle in Samkhya dualism; also primal man.

Rāma (*raah-muh*) hero god, one of the most popular **avatars** of **Vishnu.** His wife is **Sita.**

Rig-Veda *or* **Ṛgveda** (*rrig-vay-duh*) the earliest Vedic scripture, a collection of 1,027 hymns to various gods; **Agni** and **Indra** are the most frequently honored.

samādhi (*suh-maah-dhi*) trance; the final stage of the **Yoga** discipline, which is aimed at mental withdrawal from phenomenal reality.

sannyasin (*suhn-yaah-sin*) a Hindu ascetic who must live by the charity of others; the fourth stage of life in Hinduism.

Sanskrit the language of the Vedic Aryans and of classical Hinduism; the basis of most North Indian modern languages.

Savitar (*suh-vi-turh*) the Vedic sun god also called *Surya* (*soo-ree-yuh*).

shakti *or* **śakti** (*shukh-ti*) the wife of a god, especially of **Shiva;** the female active energy principle; in some sects she is regarded as destructive and dangerous as well as beautiful and seductive.

Sītā (*see-taah*) the wife of **Rama** and heroine of the *Ramayana.* See **Rama.**

Shiva *or* **Śiva** (*shi-vuh*) one of the two most important gods in Hinduism. The destroyer-creator; the god of fecundity and death. He has four wives; two, **Kāli** (*kaah-lee*) and **Durgā** (*dur-gaah* are destructive, and two others, **Pārvatī** (*paahr-vuh-tee*) and **Umma** (*oom-aah*) are creative. He is worshiped in the form of his **lingam.**

soma (*so-muh*) an exhilarating drink made from the stems of a certain plant and offered to the gods in specified festive Vedic rituals; personified as a god.

shudra *or* **śūdra** (*shoo-druh*) the lowest of the four Hindu castes, "once-born" only and excluded by the three higher Aryan castes, the "twice-born" castes. Their occupation and station in life is that of servant to the three higher castes.

sva-dharma (*svuh-dhuhr-muh*) "one's own duties and obligations" as determined by caste, stage of life, and goal. In Hinduism it is better to do one's own duty poorly than to do another's duty well.

transmigration the movement of the soul at death from one life to the next. In India the view that human existence is an unending series of earthly lives, with the soul transmigrating from one to the next, has always been linked with the idea of *karma,* and the religious quest has been an effort to find a way of escape from this chain of continuing existences.

Uddālaka Āruni (*ud-daah-luh-kuh aah-ru-ni*) one of the two greatest Vedic sages and teachers of the early *Upanishads.*

Upanishads *or* **Upaniṣads** (*u-puh-ni-shuhds*) the last of the Vedic scriptures; collections of dialogues, stories, and teachings, some of which are philosophical in character.

vaishya *or* **vaiśya** (*vysh-yuh*) the third Hindu caste; merchants, traders, farmers.

varna (*vuhr-nuh*) "color," caste; the three upper castes are called the "*ārya varnas.*" The **Aryans** were fair-skinned people, unlike the dark-skinned indigenous Dravidians. See also **castes.**

Varuṇa (*vuh-ru-nuh*) a Vedic god, the guardian of Holy Order.

Vedas (*vay-duhs*) the most ancient and sacred Hindu scriptures; they include the *Rig-Veda* and the *Sāma-* (*saah-muh*), *Yajur-* (*yuh-jur*) and *Atharvaveda* (*uht-huhr-vuh-vay-duh*), the series of **Brāhmaṇas** and *Āraṇyakas* (*aah-ruhng-yuh-kuhs*), and the many *Upanishads.* They date, with only a few exceptions, to the period between 1500 and 500 B.C.E. The term *Vedic* applies to the scriptures, the people who created and used them, and the period in which they were composed.

Vishnu *or* **Viṣṇu** (*vish-nu*) one of the two greatest gods of Hinduism. His most widely worshiped avatars are **Rāma** and **Krishna.**

Yājnavalkya (*yaah-jnuh-vuhl-kyuh*) one of the two greatest Vedic sages and teachers in the early *Upanishads.*

yogi, yogin (*yo-gee, yo-gin*) a person who practices the discipline of **Yoga.**

yoni (*yo-ni*) a religious image in the form of a circle, symbolizing the human vagina and representing the female creativity of the universe, as the **lingam** represents the male creativity of the universe.

SUGGESTED READINGS

Primary Sources in Translation

AL-BIRUNI. *Alberuni's India.* Translated by Edward C. Sachau. London: Routledge and Kegan Paul, 1888. Reprinted, Delhi: S. Chand and Co., 1964. Two vol. in one.

BADARAYANA. *Vedanta Sutra.* Translated by G. Thibaut. *Sacred Books of the East,* vols. 34, 38, 48. Oxford: Clarendon Press, 1890–1904. Reprinted New York: Dover Publications, 1962. Two vols.

Bhagavad Gita. Translated by Franklin Edgerton. *Harvard Oriental Series,* vol. 38. Cambridge, Mass.: Harvard University Press, 1944. Two vols. Introduction and translation only reprinted, New York: Harper Torch Books, 1964. One vol.

GANDHI, M. K. *Hindu Dharma,* Ahmedabad: Navajivan Publishing House, 1950.

IŚVARA KRISHNA. *The Sankhya-karika of Iśvara Krishna.* Translated by S. S. Suryanarayana Shastri. Madras: University of Madras, 1948.

KAPILA, *Vishnu Purana.* Translated by H. H. Wilson. London: 1840. Five vols. Reprinted, Calcutta: Punthi Pustak, 1961.

LAJPAT RAI, LALA. *The Arya Samaj.* London: Longmans Green, 1915.

The Laws of Manu. Translated by George Bühler. *Sacred Books of the East,* vol. 25. Oxford: Clarendon Press, 1886.

PATANJALI. *The Yoga Sutras of Patanjali.* Translated by Rama Prasada. *Sacred Books of the Hindus,* vol. 4. Allahabad: The Panini Office, 3rd ed., 1924. Translation printed in Radhakrishnan, S., and C. A. Moore, eds. *A Source Book in Indian Philosophy.* Princeton: Princeton University Press, 1957.

RAMAKRISHNA. *The Gospel of Sri Ramakrishna.* Translated by Swami Nikhilananda, New York: Ramakrishna-Vivekananda Center, 1942.

RAMMOHUN ROY. *The English Works of Rammohun Roy.* Edited by K. Nag and D. Burman. Calcutta: Sadharan Brahmo Samaj, 1945–1951. Three vols.

Hymns of the Rigveda. Translated by R. T. H. Griffith, and E. J. Lazarus, 3d ed., 1920–26. Two vols. Reprinted, Benares: Chowkhamba Sanskrit Series, 1963.

The Rig Veda: An Anthology. Translated by Wendy O'Flaherty. New York: Penguin Books, 1981.

TULASIDAS. *The Holy Lake of the Acts of Rama.* Translated by W. D. P. Hill. London: Oxford University Press, 1957.

The Thirteen Principal Upanishads. Translated by R. E. Hume. London: Oxford University Press, 2d ed., rev., 1962.

VAUDEVILLE, CH., *Kabir,* vol. I. Oxford: Clarendon Press, 1974.

VYASA. *The Srimad-Bhagabatam of Krishna Dwaipayana Vyasa* (the *Bhagavata Purana*). Translated by J. M. San-yal. Calcutta: Oriental Publishing Company, 1952–54 (reissue of 1930–34 publication.)

Series of Translations and Anthologies

DE BARY, WM. THEODORE, ed. *Sources of Indian Tradition.* New York: Columbia University Press, 1958.

DIMMIT, CORNELIA, ed., and J. A. B. VAN BUITENEN, trans. *Classical Hindu Mythology: A Reader in the Puranas.* Philadelphia: Temple University Press, 1978.

DIMOCK, EDWARD C., JR., ed. and trans. *Thief of Love: Bengali Tales from Court and Village.* Chicago: University of Chicago Press, 1971.

DUTT, ROMESH C. *The Ramayana and the Mahabharata.* London: J. M. Dent, 1953. Reprint of 1910 publication. [Very greatly condensed.]

EMBREE, AINSLIE T., ed. *The Hindu Tradition.* New York: The Modern Library, 1966.

The Harvard Oriental Series. Cambridge, Mass.: Harvard University Press, 1891–. New volumes are still appearing.

RADHAKRISHNAN, S., and C. A. MOORE, eds. *A Source Book in Indian Philosophy.* Princeton: Princeton University Press, 1957.

Sacred Books of the East. 51 vols. Oxford: Oxford University Press, 1879–1910.

The Sacred Books of the Hindus. Allahabad: The Panini Office, 1924.

Secondary Sources

BASHAM, A. L. *The Wonder That Was India.* London: Hawthorn Books, 1963; New York: Grove Press, Inc., 1959.

BHANDARKAR, RAMAKRISHNA G. *Vaisnavism, Saivism, and Minor Religious Systems.* Varanasi: Indological Book House, 1965. Reprint.

BROCKINGTON, J. L. *The Sacred Thread: Hinduism in Its Continuity and Diversity.* Edinburgh: Edinburgh University Press, 1981.

DANIELOU, ALAIN. *Hindu Polytheism.* New York: Pantheon Books, Inc., 1964.

DIMOCK, EDWARD C., JR. *The Literature of India: An Introduction.* Chicago: University of Chicago Press, 1975.

ELIADE, MIRCEA. *Patanjali and Yoga.* New York: Schocken Books, Inc., 1975.

FARQUHAR, JOHN N. *Modern Religious Movements in India.* Delhi: Munshiram Manoharlal, 1967. Reprint.

GONDA, J. *Vishnuism and Sivaism.* London: University of London, Athlone Press, 1970.

HARPER, E. B., ed. *Contributions to Indian Sociology.* New York: Asia Publishing House, 1967.

HASTINGS, JAMES, ed. *Encyclopedia of Religion and Ethics*. New York: Charles Scribner's Sons, rev. ed., 1955–58.

HAWLEY, JOHN S. *At Play with Krishna: Pilgrimage Dramas from Brindavan*. Princeton: Princeton University Press, 1981.

HEIN, NORVIN. *The Miracle Plays of Mathura*. New Haven: Yale University Press, 1972.

KARVE, IRAWATI. *Hindu Society—An Interpretation*. Copenhagen: G. E. C. Gad Publishers, 1949.

KONOW, SEN and PAUL TUXEN. *Religions of India*. Copenhagen: G. E. C. Gad Publishers, 1949.

MAJUMDAR, RAMESH. *The History and Culture of the Indian People*. Bombay: Bharatiya Vidya Bhavan, and London: George Allen and Unwin, Ltd., 1951–1960. Ten vols.

The New Encyclopedia Britannica, 15th ed. *Marcopaedia,* vol. 8, s.v. "History of Hinduism," Basham, A. L.; "Hindu Mythology," van Buitenen, J. A. B.; "Hindu Sacred Literature," van Buitenen, J. A. B.; "Hindu Mysticism," Dimock, E. C., Jr.

RAWLINSON, H. G. *India: A Short Cultural History*. New York: Praeger Publishers, Inc., 1952.

RENOU, LOUIS. *Hinduism*. New York: Washington Square Press, 1964.

SINGER, MILTON, ed. *Krishna: Myths, Rites, and Attitudes*. Chicago: University of Chicago Press, 1969.

THAPAR, ROMILA. *A History of India*. vol. i. Baltimore: Penguin Books, Inc., 1966.

WALKER, BENJAMIN. *The Hindu World: An Encyclopedic Survey of Hinduism*. New York: Praeger Publishers, Inc., 1968.

ZIMMER, HEINRICH R. *Philosophies of India*. Edited by J. Campbell. New York: Meridian, 1956.

5

Buddhism

बुद्धं सरणं गच्छामि।
धम्मं सरणं गच्छामि।
सङ्घं सरणं गच्छामि॥

Translation of the Pali: "I take my refuge in the Buddha. I take my refuge in the Dhamma. I take my refuge in the Sangha."
(Khuddakapatha 1, 1–3)

The brilliant gold-leafed spire of the Shwe Dagon Pagoda, silhouetted against the deep blue Burmese sky, suggests a pervading sense of peace and calm in the busy city of Rangoon that surrounds it. Around the base of the conical spire, however, there is much activity as the Buddhist faithful come individually or in small groups to place offerings of incense and flowers before the countless Buddha images and shrines. The images and shrines are placed there to gain merit for their donors, and the offerings are presented to gain merit for the living and the dead. A simply-dressed woman places flowers before an image, sits quietly in meditation for a few moments, and then goes her way. The people run the gamut from the fervent to the detached, while still others stand around talking together while they enjoy the beauty of the place.

A thousand miles away a cacophony of sound bursts from a Buddhist temple in the Taiwanese city of Changhua. Monks are chanting, bells are ringing, and there is a steady rhythmic beating on a hollow wooden object painted to resemble a fat red fish. Some of the lay people present seem to be seriously absorbed in the ritual, bowing reverently before an altar dominated by images of three Buddhas who are surrounded by other images, candles, offerings of fruit and flowers, while curls of smoke rise from incense sticks. In contrast to the devout, there are others who are mildly curious, a bit amused, and probably indifferent.

The Buddhist world, where one finds such an incredible variety of experiences, stretches from the southern Asian countries of India, Pakistan, and Sri Lanka to the southeast Asian lands of Burma, Thailand, Laos, Cambodia, Vietnam, Malaysia, Singapore, and Indonesia, then northwest to China, Japan, and Korea, and finally over to Tibet and Central Asia. In some of these countries Buddhism was once a powerful force, but long ago declined; in others it has continued for centuries as a way of faith and life that pervades the total culture. Since World War II, it is no longer unusual to find strong Buddhist communities in the cities of Europe and America. The tremendous variety found across this Buddhist world is astonishing to many observers, but there is much that binds this world together, notably a common origin in the story of a man, his disciples, and the pattern of life and thought that they initiated.

Beginnings

The origins of Buddhism are to be found in the kind of world in which the movement first appeared, the life and teaching of Gautama the Buddha, and early developments in the Buddhist community. The story of these beginnings surely is one of the most fascinating in the history of religions: a background of philosophical and religious ferment, a founder figure whose life commands admiration and awe, doctrines that are both old and new, and a clearly identifiable community of believers.

Background

The rise of Buddhism in the sixth century B.C.E. in India parallels the writing of the Upanishads, those philosophical dialogues (see Chapter 4) that give evidence of individuals who were not content with previous understandings of human existence, and, therefore, sought a deeper truth. At least some people in North India were discussing some of the seminal ideas of the six orthodox philosophies that were to dominate later Hindu thought. The disciplines of yoga were practiced, and the pluralistic theory of a human being formed of several component parts was discussed. There was also a group called the Carvaka materialists, who rejected any idea that could not be perceived by the senses, thus making any notion of ultimate reality such as Brahman-Atman, the doctrine of *karma,* or life after death impossible.

Jainism had already made its appearance by the time of Buddhism (see Chapter 4). Although more ascetic in its orientation than Buddhism, Jainism had a founder, Mahavira, or ''Great Hero,'' whose biography is similar to that of the Buddha. Both Jain and Buddhist doctrines had the flavor of ancient Indian religion, but the substance

was quite different. Jainism and Buddhism were regarded as heterodox by orthodox Vedic priests, who presided over the ritual structure through which people sought to gain a better rebirth in future existences and ultimately to be free of the wheel of *karma* altogether.

Jainism and Buddhism, as has been pointed out in the previous chapter, arose in an area of India outside the Indo–Gangetic plain of northwest India. The two kingdoms of Magadha and Kosala, which figure prominently in the life of the Buddha, were located in northeast India, somewhat east of the area thoroughly pervaded by Hinduism. Furthermore, the Mahavira and the Buddha were from the *kshatriya* or warrior caste, so that both men were not as deeply imbued with Hindu orthodoxy as would have been the case had they been born into families of the Brahmin priesthood. Just as the *Upanishads* grew out of forest dialogues, so the Jain and Buddhist search for and inquiry into truth took place among wandering forest dwellers and ascetics who conversed in the forests, in rest houses provided by the wealthy, or at any point along the road or in the marketplace when they began to talk to each other. It was in this setting that a wanderer appeared whose life and teaching would change radically the religious map of Asia and influence a much wider world in modern times.

The Founder

Early Life. Although it is doubtful that Gautama the Buddha intended to ''found a religion,'' he is regarded as the founder of Buddhism. Whereas there is no one person who may be identified as a founder figure in such religions as Hinduism, other religious movements such as Buddhism can point to a specific person as one whose life and teachings so shaped the movement in its infancy that he or she must be considered the founder.

Gautama, also known as Sakyamuni and Prince Siddhartha, was born into a princely family about 563 B.C.E., and died around 483, having become the leader of a developing community of devoted followers. His father, King Suddhodana, ruled over a small kingdom in what is now Nepal, much as the maharajahs ruled their principalities in modern India. Although the stories of palace luxury seem somewhat exaggerated, there is little reason to doubt that Gautama lived a sheltered life, was married, and had a son. King Suddhodana expected his son to follow him as king, and, therefore, was disturbed by prophecies that his son would withdraw to the forest like many ascetics of that time. The king surrounded the young prince with pleasures and the good things of life, so that the young man might want for nothing and feel no need to seek further.

In spite of all the attention to his every need, and every attempt to keep him away from any distracting stimuli, Gautama one day saw a very old man. He had never before seen such an old person, and had to ask a servant about the white-haired, wrinkled creature. The servant replied that the man was old and that old age came to all human beings. The king ordered further precautions, but later on Gautama saw a sick man, and then a corpse, each provoking his puzzlement, further obvious answers to his questions, and consternation in his father. He had seen the three signs—old age, suffering, and death—that were to become a classic Buddhist description of the human condition. Some accounts of these events record Gautama's seeing a fourth sign, a yellow-robed ascetic. Gautama's question about him was answered: ''He is searching for a way beyond life and death.''

Finding Enlightenment. In spite of his father's extensive efforts to keep him satisfied and happy, when he was twenty-nine Gautama slipped away into the night and took up the life of a wandering seeker in the forest. The stories of his final decision and departure, called ''the Great Renunciation,'' depict a young man with great resolve about what he had to do, but feeling great tenderness toward the sleeping wife and child he left behind. Tradition has it that for about six years he followed various teachers of his time, some of whom certainly were ascetics, and then finally undertook a path of such extreme asceticism that he almost died. He returned to a more moderate way of life, which, however, still involved abstinence from sensual pleasures and focused on intense meditation. This led to enlightenment or *bodhi* while sitting under what is called the Bodhi tree, a *pipal* or fig tree with wide-spreading roots and branches. His words about the experience of enlightenment are found in one of the oldest texts:

I thus knew and thus perceived, my mind was emancipated from the *asava* (canker) of sensual desire, from the *asava* of desire for existence, and from the *asava* of ignorance. And

in me emancipated arose the knowledge of my emancipation. I realized that destroyed is rebirth, the religious life has been led, done is what was to be done, there is nought (for me) beyond this world . . . Ignorance was dispelled, knowledge arose. Darkness was dispelled, light arose.[1]

The significance of the phrase—''in me emancipated arose the knowledge of my emancipation''—must not be overlooked. The man who found freedom in the truth *knew* he was free, *knew* he had found *bodhi,* and hence was the *Buddha,* the enlightened one. Although scholars may question the historical authenticity of some details in the story of the Buddha, this change in a young man's life, authenticated by what happened later, rings true in human experience and is a model for all Buddhists.

Ministry. The story goes on to tell how Mara the Tempter tried to dissuade Gautama. The newly enlight-

Stupa at Sarnath. *One of the holiest shrines of Buddhism is the stupa at Sarnath, the scene of the Buddha's early teaching. The structure is perhaps the simplest, even the plainest, in the Buddhist world; its very simplicity makes it one of the most impressive.* (Courtesy of Richard Bush)

ened Gautama was tempted to remain in the glow of the experience itself and not confuse others who would be unprepared for his new teaching, but he resisted temptation and set forth to tell others about his experience. He first sought out his former teachers, those whom he had followed for a time but whose teaching had not satisfied him. Upaka, the Ajivika ascetic, for example, thought his former pupil's message interesting, but turned away saying, "Would that it might be so, friend." Then Gautama found the five ascetics, his former mentors, at the Deer Park in Sarnath, near modern Varanasi (Benares), and preached to them his first sermon. They became his first followers.

The Deer Park Sermon is primarily an exposition of the Four Noble Truths, the heart of the early Buddhist *dharma* or teaching (Pali, *dhamma*).* Simply put, with further discussion to follow, the Four Noble Truths state:

1. All is suffering.
2. Suffering is caused by desire.
3. To cut off desire is to be rid of suffering.
4. This is accomplished by following the Noble Eightfold Path: right views, right aspiration, right speech, right action, right livelihood, right effort, right mindfulness, and right concentration.

This is not an optimistic, anyone-can-do-it philosophy. On the contrary, it is a terribly realistic view of human existence and a demanding path to follow; yet the Buddha attracted followers from all classes of people. Some were admitted to the rigorous discipline of the *Sangha,* or order of monks; others observed the simpler requirements for lay followers. An order of nuns came into being, approved somewhat hesitantly, it seems, by the Buddha. Ananda and Sariputta became favorite disciples and Devadatta a betrayer. For forty-five years Gautama the Buddha moved about his part of India, "turning the wheel of the law," a simile for presenting his teaching, which is often symbolized as a wheel.

Dialogue appears to have been the primary method of the Buddha's teaching, but discourses also were re-corded, often beginning with a discussion of moral virtues, then moving on to deeper things. His words sound harsh at times, particularly in the face of obtuse questioners, but by patient questioning and careful dialectic he usually won the questioner over to the new truth.

Last Days and Death. The last days and death of the Buddha are poignantly described in a short text called the *Book of the Great Decease* in which each event is artfully embellished with great detail. Gautama was aware that death was near, and when it was hastened by food poisoning, he said that no blame should be cast on the one who prepared the food. There were various reminders of his previous teachings; then the monks were urged:

Be lamps unto yourselves. Be refuges to yourselves. Take yourselves to no external refuge. Hold fast to the Truth as a lamp. Hold fast as a refuge to the Truth.[2]

After a most striking exchange in which no member of the Order expressed any doubt or uncertainty about anything that he had ever said, the Buddha said they would never again be born into a state of suffering and were sure to attain enlightenment.

Then the Exalted One addressed the brethren, and said: "Behold now, brethren, I exhort you, saying: 'Decay is inherent in all component things! Work out your salvation with diligence!' " This was the word of the Tathagata![*3]

He passed through the four stages of rapture and then died. The people wept when they heard of the Buddha's death, and the cremation ceremony was held. After considerable quarreling among his followers, relics were passed out and all peoples did him honor.

The Buddha's Role in Buddhism. Reference has been made in passing to the fact that Buddhist scholars have differed in assessing how much of the traditional story of the Buddha is historical. The accounts were not written down until perhaps two hundred years after his death, but people who do not have written records available have been found to preserve an oral tradition with remarkable accuracy. There is sufficient evidence to assert that

* As will be explained in the section on Buddhist sacred literature, the earliest texts were written in Pali, an Indian language closely related to Sanskrit, but numerous texts also were written in Sanskrit. Since many of the terms used in this chapter and in the chapter on Hinduism are similar and refer to the same idea, the Sanskrit form is used, with the Pali form in parenthesis. Since *Gautama* is widely used as the personal name of the Buddha, the Pali form of *Gotama* has not been used here.

Tathagata means "thus-come," or "one who has achieved complete release or emancipation." It is an honorific term applied to the Buddha.

the bare outline presented here may be regarded as an historical core that is true to the best data we possess. The resulting picture is that of a sensitive, compassionate individual whose analysis of the human predicament gives evidence of a searching, probing mind, and whose proposed remedy or solution is positive and hopeful. He was indeed a remarkable person.

What has been the Buddha's role in the life of the Buddhist community? How have Buddhists past and present looked back to their beginnings and assessed the role of the Buddha? ''Savior'' is hardly an appropriate designation for one who told people to be their own lamps. On the other hand, his life is a model and an example for all those who attempt to work out their own release or liberation. He certainly evokes a noble and dedicated response on the part of those who go to him, along with his doctrine and his order of monks, for refuge. That Jains, and undoubtedly others, called him an ''enticer'' provides non-Buddhist evidence of the way he attracted followers, even from other teachers.

That the Buddha and his teachings have authority is also to be granted, and that his followers have increasingly held him to be above men can hardly be ignored. For example, Caroline Rhys Davids' work, *Gotama the Man,* published in 1928, is reported to have received a cold reception by Buddhist monks in Burma, who regarded ''man'' as a highly inappropriate designation for one honored as ''superior to gods and men.'' Therefore, whether we speak of the teacher in ancient India who attracted monks and lay followers to his way, or note modern Asian devotion before his peaceful, benign image, it is clear that motivation or stimulus toward living the Buddhist life inevitably goes back to the Lord Buddha himself.

Sacred Texts

From Oral to Written Form

There is a basic conviction among Buddhists that the central core of teaching in the Buddhist scriptures reflects the original message of the Buddha himself. There is good reason to believe that what he said to his disciples and to others with whom he conversed was memorized and recited by the monks and thus accurately preserved for about two centuries in oral form. The recital of what he had said was the main business of the early councils, to be discussed below, and has continued to be a major element in Buddhist services to the present day.

The frequent repetition found in these early Buddhist texts undoubtedly was an aid to memorization, just as verses of a song in which only a few words are changed from verse to verse are much easier to remember. Much of this repetition has been omitted from English translations of the scriptures.

In spite of considerable disagreement among Buddhist scholars, texts in the Pali language probably were the earliest to be written down, and are dated about the middle of the third century B.C.E., concurrent with or followed shortly thereafter by Sanskrit versions. Pali is a *prakrit* or dialect of Sanskrit that was spoken in the area where Buddhism arose. It is similar to Sanskrit, as has been and will be noticed in some key words like the following Sanskrit-Pali pairs: *dharma/dhamma, karma/kamma, nirvana/nibbana*. Since these terms were given in Sanskrit transliterations in Chapter 4 on Hinduism, we have continued to use Sanskrit forms with the Pali equivalents in parentheses, for the benefit of those who may go on to collateral readings in which Pali forms are used.

The Sanskrit version of the Buddhist scriptures parallels the Pali version in most important respects, but lacks some of the Pali works and includes additional texts that undoubtedly come from a later time. The literature we will discuss is common to both traditions.

Structure and Content of the Texts

When finally put into writing, the scriptures were inscribed on palm leaf manuscripts that were collected in baskets (*pitaka*). As the collections were standardized, three distinct groups of manuscripts emerged and have been called the Three Baskets (*Tripitaka*) ever since: the Discipline Basket (*Vinaya Pitaka*), the Discourse Basket (*Sutta Pitaka*), and Further or Special Teaching (*Abhidhamma Pitaka*).*

The discipline outlined in the first of these baskets is the discipline to be followed by the Sangha or order of

---

* The names of these collections are regularly referred to in the Pali terminology used here. The Sanskrit forms would be *Sutra* and *Abhidharma*.

monks, and centers in the *pratimoksha* (Pali, *patimokkha*), which means "that which binds" or is obligatory. There are 227 rules that must be followed by the monks; they range in importance from basic moral precepts against taking life or stealing, to rules about the making and distributing of robes. The rules as a whole are summarized in the section on monastic and lay relations that follows.

The *Vinaya*, or Discipline Basket, includes a vast amount of material that represents commentary on the *pratimoksha* and the listing of various examples that illustrate practical applications of the rules. After covering all this material, which amounts to five extensive volumes in English translation, a monk should have little doubt of what is expected of him.

The Discourse Basket is by far the most significant and meaningful to the total Buddhist community and to most students of Buddhism. It is this collection that contains the teaching on doctrinal and ethical matters that concern both monks and lay people. As the word *discourse* suggests, the teaching is presented in the form of a discourse by the Buddha, often as a dialogue in which either his disciples or the people whom he encountered in his journeys raise questions and hear his response.

The Discourse Basket is divided into five sections, the first two of which are grouped on the basis of length: "long" discourses and "middle-length" discourses. The third contains "connected sayings" and the fourth those teachings that involve a "listing." There are passages that tell us much about the life of the Buddha and give insight into the teachings that will be considered when we discuss Buddhist doctrine.

The last part of the Discourse Basket is a collection of miscellaneous short works that are probably more familiar to the average reader than the more systematic presentations in the first four sections. For example, the *Dhammapada*, or "Path of Virtue," is a widely read statement in simple but vivid language of the Buddhist's daily life. The *Suttanipata* is a mixture of poetry and prose and presents important stories from the life of the Buddha and some of his more important teachings. There are also the "Songs of the Elders" and the "Songs of the Sisters," beautiful expressions from monks and nuns, respectively, of what the Buddhist way of life means to them. And there are the *Jataka Tales*, stories of the Buddha's previous births told as fables in which

Monks Before Images of the Buddha. *Thai Buddhist monks, some serious, some in a more jovial mood, are seated before the Buddha depicted in various ways. The image at the left shows the Buddha as the great ascetic; others have him either teaching or meditating.* (Courtesy of Mary Bush)

animals set forth some of the Buddhist virtues; therefore, they have been used in teaching Buddhist children.

The Further or Special Teaching, which comprises the last of the three baskets, the *Abhidhamma Pitaka*, goes far beyond the scope of an introductory treatment of Buddhism. Its first book, for example, is the "Enumeration of Dharmas," an extensive listing of mental processes and elements, sometimes called psychological ethics. The second book is an analysis of the first, and the third goes on to relate the elements to other categories. The work is a systematic reformulation of the Buddha's teaching to clarify doctrinal issues and refute teachings of other schools; it is valuable, therefore, but is more appropriate for advanced study. It is in this Third Basket, incidentally, that major differences between the Pali and

Sanskrit versions of the Buddhist scriptures begin to occur.

Although it would be difficult to maintain that the Third Basket contains the teachings of the Buddha himself, the Discipline Basket and the Discourse Basket may be treated by the student as reliable sources for the Buddha's teaching, as arranged by his followers in the first centuries after his death. This is not to say that the texts are verbatim accounts of his conversations and discourses, or that nothing has been added. But the texts are an authentic reflection of his basic teaching, in many instances rephrased, of course; and the additions represent the honest effort of his followers to explain and elaborate what was remembered, in the spirit of the Buddha who was their Lord.

Early Buddhist Doctrine

When we ask about early Buddhist teaching, certain key doctrines emerge. There is first of all the character of life itself, the nature of being or existence. Then there are the four Noble Truths and the Noble Eightfold Path, which involve what an individual may do about life with all its problems. The goal of *nirvana* and what it means for human beings is another special doctrinal problem for the student of Buddhism.

The Nature of Human Existence

As mentioned briefly in the preceding chapter, the early Buddhist texts unequivocally present a view of life shattering to those who are at ease in their complacency. The Buddha says to his disciples:

"Whether Buddhas arise, O priests, or whether Buddhas do not arise, it remains a fact and the fixed and necessary constitution of being that all its constituents are transitory . . .

[Furthermore] that all its constituents are misery . . .

[And further] that all its elements are lacking in an ego . . .

These facts a Buddha discovers and masters, and when he has discovered and mastered them, he announces, teaches, publishes, proclaims, discloses, minutely explains and makes it clear, that the constituents of being are transitory, full of misery (suffering), and lacking an ego."[4]

Such are the "constituents of being" or "facts of life." It should not surprise anyone to hear that life, first of all, is transitory, impermanent, and changing (all translations of *anicca*), for we know that the human body is changing constantly, and, in fact, goes through a complete change every seven years. We certainly hope that the mind changes with the body, for it would be most unfortunate to hear no new ideas, discover no new ways of doing things, or fail to see that we ourselves are changing. It is a human tendency, however, to think that some great achievement such as "lasting peace" is permanent, that cherished institutions will go on and on, and that great love for another person is eternal. For Buddhists all is impermanent, for life is constantly changing, which leads to misery and suffering, and to the realization that there can be no permanent being.

The second characteristic of human existence, that life is suffering, pain, and misery (all translations of *dukkha*), is also the first of the Four Noble Truths, a later topic of discussion. For Buddhists it is a fact of life that all is suffering, that the nature of existence is pain, sorrow, and misery. Even enjoyment brings suffering. This cycle of birth, sickness, old age, and death means only "grief, lamentation, sorrow, tribulation, and despair," a never-ending refrain that may sound very strange to modern Western students, but is very real to the Buddha and his followers.

It is not hard to understand that the Buddha could have concluded that life is changing and that it involves suffering, whether one agrees with him or not. What is staggering to most people is the third constituent of being, that there is no ego. The Hindu thinkers of his time would probably have agreed that *this* life is changing and does involve suffering at some point at least, but they nevertheless saw some kind of permanent self called *atman* that could move beyond the suffering of this transitory existence. In the Pali Buddhist texts, however, the negative prefix *an-* is placed before the Pali *atta* (*atman*), and the result is the *anatta* doctrine, the third characteristic of human existence, and the point where the Hindu and Buddhist doctrinal systems diverge.

Buddhist and Hindu scholars have debated the question for years: Did the Buddha deny the existence of the *atman* or not? Beneath his refusal to talk about it, is there an underlying belief in an absolute being, personal or impersonal, or does the evidence support his lack of belief in or rejection of such a reality? If one takes seriously his view of existence as transitory and full of suffering, and his idea that belief in anything permanent inevitably leads to attachment to it and therefore to continued suffering, then it is difficult to assert he believed in the existence of the *atman*. If everything is in flux and constantly changing, and if, as we shall see below, everything and every event is dependent on something else, then how is it possible to believe in something like the *atman*?

That early Buddhists did not believe in a permanent self or ego is also consistent with their understanding of a human being as composed of five *skandhas* (Pali, *khandas*), "aggregates" or basic elements of a person: the body (or "name and form"), sensations or feelings, perceptions, predispositions (sometimes translated as "habitual tendencies" or "inclinations"), and consciousness. In several passages the Buddha is presented as saying that no one of these can be identified with a permanent self, that all five together are not the self, and that there is no such self continuing in the absence of the five. It should be observed that there was a school of thought among the early Buddhists that held that the consciousness did survive the death of an individual, an idea that continued in popular belief. Orthodox Buddhists, however, have held that these five elements come together at birth, are dispersed at death, and therefore can be regarded only as convenient names for those basic elements of a human being, all of which are impermanent, involve suffering, and have no ego.

Both instructive and delightful is the story of the monk Malunkyaputta who was determined to know the answers to certain questions: Is the universe finite or infinite, eternal or temporary? Are the soul and body identical or not? Does the saint exist after death or not? Or is it a case of both existing and not existing, or neither of the two options? The Buddha asked Malunkyaputta if answers to these questions were ever promised and if answering the questions was ever made a condition for monks remaining in the order. Malunkyaputta, who had thought of leaving, had to reply in the negative. The Buddha relentlessly pressed home the argument that answers to these questions do not aid a person in living the religious life and do not speak to the perennial problems of old age, death, sorrow, lamentation, misery,

grief, and despair. Therefore, he had never discussed such questions.

"And what, Malunkyaputta, have I elucidated? Misery, . . . I have elucidated; the origin of misery . . . , the cessation of misery . . . And why, Malunkyaputta, have I elucidated this? Because . . . this does profit, has to do with the fundamentals of religion, and tends to aversion, absence of passion, cessation, quiescence, knowledge, supreme wisdom, and Nirvana; therefore have I elucidated it."[5]

The Buddha's appeal to three of the Four Noble Truths is a refusal to engage in Hindu speculation and a return to the mainstream of his thought with its focus on the bedrock human problem of suffering, how to deal with it, and the way to win liberation and release.

The Four Noble Truths and the Noble Eightfold Path

Reference has already been made to the Four Noble Truths in the account of the Buddha's life, and we have seen in the preceding pages that suffering, the second of the constituents of being, parallels the First Noble Truth: namely, that all life is suffering. This is a blanket assertion that life is characterized by suffering from beginning to end, that the moments in which we may taste a little pleasure and feel a bit of happiness quickly fade away. For persons who have ever lived in a society in which the waking hours of all people are consumed by the struggle to survive and stay alive, it is easy to appreciate what the Buddha was talking about. It is quite likely that many of the common people of his time, especially those in the lower castes, lived in extremely grim circumstances, which evoked the compassion of the Buddha, who had been reared in quite different circumstances. The second of the Four Noble Truths proclaims that there is a *cause* for suffering: human misery is rooted in desire, craving, and attachment (all translations of *tanha*). Our craving for self-gratification and for the perpetuation of the self is the origin of misery, for we are ignorant that it leads to rebirth, and that means that the cycle begins all over again. The desire that causes suffering is not only sensual desire or lust; suffering also is caused by desire for rebirth, beautiful things, or a happy life. The Buddhist interpretation of the doctrine of *karma*, and the formula of Dependent Origination, to be discussed shortly, develop further this understanding that every thought, feeling, and action is caused by and rooted in what has gone on before and is going on now.

The third of the Four Noble Truths opens up the possibility of hope in the Buddhist outlook. In all that we have seen up to this point, and in much that follows, Buddhism appears to be life-negating and pessimistic. However, if an end to suffering may be brought about by putting an end to desire or craving, then there is a ray of hope in a bleak and despairing world. By following the way of life that is outlined in the Fourth Noble Truth, craving may be cut out and a disciple freed from the suffering that brings grief and sorrow. If one accepts the first and second Truths, that life is suffering, which is caused by desire, then it is a logical conclusion and a source of hope to know that desire can be cut off and suffering therefore ended.

How does one cut off the craving? The Fourth Noble Truth is a call to follow the Noble Eightfold Path, and the first two steps on the path are *right views or beliefs* and *right aspirations or intentions*. Thus, correct doctrine and the right approach to the path are prerequisites to entering upon it. There is considerable latitude in Buddhist doctrine, but a person may not believe whatever he chooses. It is important, therefore, to know in the beginning the basics of belief and to enter upon the path with the utmost seriousness, determined to be faithful to the end.

The third, fourth, and fifth stages—*right speech, right action,* and *right livelihood*—constitute a middle section applicable to people in all walks of life. The words we speak, the actions in which we engage, and the means by which we earn a living, must all be in accord with the teachings of the Buddha. For example, pretentious speech, disrespectful conduct toward one's elders, and supporting a family by killing living creatures, are wrong speech, action, and livelihood.

The final three stages—*right effort, right mindfulness,* and *right concentration*—lead individuals beyond the common duties and relationships in society through ever higher levels of meditation and trance. Thus, any follower of the Buddha can really attain sufficient self-understanding and level of awareness to cut off any sense of desire or craving and thus bring suffering to an end.

Karma *and Dependent Origination*

The Buddhist understanding of the doctrine of *karma* and of Dependent Origination is an aid in explicating the second and third of the Four Noble Truths, as well as the central problem in Buddhism: if there is no permanent self moving from existence to existence, then how may one speak of transmigration or reincarnation? How may there be rebirth when there is nothing to be reborn, no permanent self to bear the consequences of this life into the next existence?

There are several approaches that may be followed in handling these questions. One very obvious way is to point out that the Buddha does not appear to have given any answer to such questions. Either the questions were not raised or he thought them unimportant, and, therefore, they contributed nothing to living the religious life. As noted above, however, the no-self doctrine stands with "all is suffering" and "all is transient" as an unequivocal foundation for Buddhist teaching.

Another approach is to note that in a number of early Buddhist texts there appear statements about being reborn—*my* past lives, *my* karma affecting *my* next life—and to conclude that some of the early Buddhists continued to follow Hindu beliefs in a permanent self, ignoring the *anatta* doctrine. Such an approach dismisses philosophical speculation because people are not concerned with logical precision.

A third approach is to accept that when the Buddha taught about "no-self" he meant *no*-self, that transmigration of the soul is excess baggage. The five *skandhas* or basic attributes of a person come together at birth and are dispersed at death, leaving no permanent self to continue to another existence; but the deeds done by a person in one existence can cause another person who is a collection of five attributes to come into existence. Through the power of *karma* there is a *causal* relation between the first person and the second, but no relation of identity. As a famous Buddhist simile puts it, when the flame from one burning stick ignites another, a new flame begins to burn, but nothing passes over. Thus, one person's deeds cause another person to come alive, bearing the weight of the earlier person's deeds (*karma*), but nothing like a permanent self passes over.

It may appear that such a view of life could easily

destroy any moral motivation: "For if I will not have to suffer for anything I do in this life, I can do just as I please." Buddhists respond in two ways in order to show that the moral motivation is as powerful in Buddhism as in any other religion. The first response is that for Buddhists, the deed (*karma*) cannot be disassociated from the doer of the deed and his responsibility for it. An evil deed is not as subject to blame as the mind that willed it, so the emphasis must fall on the intent of any action. Buddhist thinkers have continued this emphasis on the will that motivates action, so that intention and motivation are at least as important as the act itself, if not more so. The result is striking: "Buddhism by making the ethical character of an action depend upon the motive and not upon the external performance transformed the doctrine of *karma*. The aim was no longer to attend to external actions, but to the motives that inspire them."[6] Regardless of whether the person willing the action has a permanent soul or not, he or she wills the action and must bear moral responsibility for it.

The second response, which is directed to the problem of no moral responsibility because there is no permanent self to inherit the results in another life, involves an unusual but logical assertion: "I may not have to bear the consequences of my deeds, but someone else in another existence will suffer or benefit because of what I have done. Although I shall not be reborn, I participate in a *continuity of action* (*karma*), so that I am morally obligated to consider how my actions may help or hurt *others* in a future existence." A profound altruism, action for the sake of others, is thus introduced as the framework for Buddhist ethics, resulting in a wide-ranging sense of compassion (*karuna*) for all living creatures, including those yet to be born.

It is important to distinguish between this philosophical understanding of the Buddhist doctrine of rebirth in the light of the *anatta* doctrine and the popular feelings about rebirth in the minds of millions of Buddhist people. Personal conversation with a businessman or homemaker will reveal the notion that a person will be reborn, that the character of that next life will be determined by merit built up in this life. Coupled with such notions, however, is a hesitation to engage in speculation about such topics as a soul or supreme being or life after death. When questioning about such beliefs gets specific, a frequent response is: "We don't really talk much about such matters."

There is still a sense of the continuity of life, of the relatedness of all aspects and events of life, which is set forth in the Formula of Dependent Origination:

On ignorance depends *karma;*
On *karma* depends consciousness;
On consciousness depend name and form;
On name and form depend the six organs of sense;
On the six organs of sense depends contact;
On contact depends sensation;
On sensation depends desire;
On desire depends attachment;
On attachment depends existence;
On existence depends birth;
On birth depend old age and death, sorrow, lamentation, misery, grief, and despair. Thus does this entire aggregation of misery arise.[7]

The process is then reversed for each step: if ignorance ceases, then *karma* ceases, and if *karma* ceases, then consciousness ceases, and so on until with the cessation of birth, old age, sorrow, and so forth, the aggregation of misery is brought to an end. If the series is not broken, then misery continues, for each aspect or phase of life is dependent on another; thus, all aspects and moments of life are bound together, both for the arising and for the cessation of misery. Nothing arises except in dependence on something else. If that something is removed, then the next step, the next arising, cannot take place, thus allowing an individual to proceed toward the goal of release from *samsara,* the process of birth and death and rebirth.

The Final Goal: Nirvana

What may a person expect at the end of the road? What ultimate goal beckons? One who cuts off the desire that causes suffering, who has thus followed the Eightfold Path leading to the higher levels of meditation and concentration, attains *nirvana* (Pali, *nibbana*), which literally means a "snuffing out" of a flame, or cessation. It is not only a Buddhist idea; the thought is expressed in Jain literature and in the great Hindu epic the *Mahabharata,* but it is the ultimate goal of life in Buddhism.

There is a temptation to speak of *nirvana* as a supreme spiritual state of great peace, but it is better to understand it as an experience that eludes description and that leads to complete freedom and deliverance from suffering. The craving, clinging tendency of the human psyche that keeps all creatures bound to *samsara* is extinguished. Since there is no desire to fuel the fires of existence, the burning pain and misery of existence ebbs and goes out. A person who attains *nirvana* is therefore liberated, to what is not stated precisely, but one result is clear: someone else will not be born into a suffering existence, and that brings great joy and peace.

There are intermediate goals, of course, that result from the way monks and lay people follow their respective ethical standards in their homes and in society. As will be noted below, there are models for ascetic monks and nuns, for laymen and laywomen, and for a Buddhist monarch, and the fulfillment of these role models is no mean achievement. In the process of daily life there are opportunities to build up merit through service to others. *Nirvana,* of course, can be attained in this life, resulting in visible peace from which one passes at death into *parinirvana,* the ultimate peace beyond the grave, as did the Buddha who has shown the way. Thus, all other objectives and goals give way to *nirvana,* or *parinirvana,* the fundamental goal for all Buddhists.

This, then, is an attempt to state concisely the key elements in the teaching of the Buddha and of those who have elaborated and developed it through the centuries. There are other doctrines that we will encounter in further study, but this basis remains constant and is a framework for the total picture of doctrine in the Buddhist world.

The Practice of Buddhism

Given the doctrinal structure that has been sketched, we turn to the practice of Buddhism, the activities through which Buddhists express their devotion. Our focus here is on the predominantly Buddhist lands of Sri Lanka (Ceylon), Burma, Thailand (Siam), and Cambodia. Variations in teaching, practice, and organization in East Asia will be considered later in this chapter.

Devotional and Ritual Practice

Buddhist devotion centers first of all in a simple, direct affirmation called the Three Refuges: "I take refuge in the Buddha. I take refuge in the *dharma*. I take refuge in the Sangha." Another way of stating it is: "I go to the Buddha for refuge, I go to . . . ," and so on. We have met the Buddha and have considered the *dharma,* or doctrine, in the preceding sections. The Sangha, or order of monks, will be discussed in the following section.

Taking the Three Refuges is a part of almost every Buddhist activity. "Taking refuge in the Buddha" does not mean for the Buddhist that the Buddha "saves" those who utter these words. The Buddha urged his disciples to work out their own salvation and to be lamps unto themselves. Although popular devotion may slide in the direction of subconscious dependence on the Buddha for help in time of difficulty, the Buddhist way emphasizes the fact that an individual's deeds lead to enlightenment and then on to *nirvana.* Clearly the Buddha is the primary example of how to follow the Way and an inspiration to all those who attempt to follow it. To a lesser extent the monks are an example and an inspiration, and study of the teaching is a great help at every stage; but in the last analysis, the Buddhist way is attained by personal effort and is one's personal responsibility.

The Three Refuges are praised and *sutras* are chanted when monks gather every morning and every evening at the monastery for *puja* (worship or devotion). Burning candles provide light, incense is burned for purification, and flowers and puffed rice provide additional fragrance. Every fortnight, at the new moon and full-moon fast-days called *Uposatha,* the laity assemble at the monastery for *puja,* which includes on those days special readings from the sutras and a lecture on the *dharma* by one of the monks. Laymen may remain at the monastery for the night; women always return home after the service has ended.

There are special *puja* ceremonies, such as Wesak during the full moon of the month of May, when the Buddha's birthday, attainment of enlightenment, and death (entry into *parinirvana*) are all celebrated. Processions move around the lighted monasteries and temples; special programs featuring speeches on the life of the Buddha and on the *dharma* are arranged; and flowers, incense, and candles are everywhere.

The rainy season, which comes in late spring, is a period when monks go on retreat. The first rains are greeted by a celebration in which everyone tries to throw

The Shwe Dagon Pagoda in Rangoon. *The gleaming golden spire of the Shwe Dagon Pagoda is a focal point of Burmese Buddhist devotion. Hundreds of smaller shrines at the base of the spire have been built to bring merit to those seeking a better* karma *to influence their future lives.* (Courtesy of Richard Bush)

water on other people, undoubtedly incorporating pre-Buddhist indigenous rites to welcome the rainy season. Temple images are bathed, special rites are arranged, and processions attract great crowds. There is also a ceremony at the end of the rainy season that looks forward to the end of the rain retreat, when greater movement and activity become possible as they did for the Buddha and his disciples.

Special occasions are not the whole story, however. Daily devotion is much more indicative of the character of Buddhist piety, which is to be experienced everywhere in Buddhist lands, at major shrines and small ones. In Burma, for example, on any day of the week, people pause before a shrine, remove their shoes, bow in reverence, and make offerings of flowers and incense. Merit is derived from these acts of devotion, and even more merit accrues to a person who builds a shrine; therefore, the countryside is dotted with them and the shrines continue to multiply. Unfortunately, many of the shrines

have been allowed to deteriorate because, for many years at least, no merit was understood to be involved in repairing or refurbishing a shrine.

Shrines containing a relic of the Buddha are especially important. Relics are greatly valued and have been since the time when relics of the Buddha were distributed to his disciples after his death. Great temples and monasteries have been built to house a tooth, bone, ashes of the Buddha, or perhaps a piece of wood believed to be from the Bo tree under which he was enlightened. Today most Buddhists who worship before a shrine containing such a relic believe that they receive special merit.

Another feature of Buddhist devotion in Southeast Asia is the presence of spirit worship alongside reverence for the Buddha. These may be spirits of the land, of forces of nature, or of ancestors, and have great power in the ongoing common life of the people. Small spirit houses perched on small posts may be seen in close proximity to Buddhist shrines. In Thailand, the spirit houses are often small models of Buddhist temples (*wats*); but in all the Southeast Asian Buddhist countries the intimate association of devotion to spirits and to the Buddha appears to be no problem to the Buddhist faithful or their leaders.

Peace and Calm in Bangkok. *At many points in the noisy bustling city of Bangkok, Thailand, one may find peace and calm in a Buddhist* wat *or temple. The* wat *itself, the pagoda in the distance, iconography in the foreground—all exhibit a distinctive Thai style.* (Courtesy of Mary Bush)

Meditation. From the early days of Buddhism, meditation has been an important activity for monks and meditation centers for laypersons are popular. *Dhyana* (Pali, *jhana*), the most common word for meditation, is the seventh step on the Noble Eightfold Path, while the sublime state of *samadhi,* for which ''concentration'' is perhaps the best English translation, is the eighth and final step. Concentration definitely includes higher levels of trance, another translation of *dhyana,* so that in a very real sense each includes the other, and *dhyana* and *samadhi* together constitute fulfillment for those who follow the Buddha's path.

One who would develop the discipline of meditation should have a teacher who is a spiritual guide and master to show the way. A clean and quiet place, loose-fitting garments, and a time when one is alert and not likely to fall asleep are important in the meditator's environment, for one who meditates must get rid of all distractions and hindrances. Regular breathing and concentration on some classic object of meditation (not necessarily pleasant) are regarded as essential. After learning to handle the preliminary stages, which may take months or years of disciplined practice, one enters the last stage, made up of four *dhyanas.* The first *dhyana* ''is accomplished by initial thought and discursive thought, is born of aloofness, and is rapturous and joyful.''[8] In the second *dhyana* thought is replaced by concentration, which is transcended in turn by the third, ''equanimity, attentive(ness) and clear consciousness.'' Finally, in the fourth *dhyana* there is ''neither anguish nor joy,'' and one ''is entirely purified by equanimity and mindfulness''; one will remember former lives, and experience complete freedom.[9] From these *dhyanas,* which have form, one may pass to *dhyanas* without form and indescribable, beyond which there is an ultimate trance said by a modern monk to be ''the seeing of things as in truth and reality they are . . . , the true nature of *dharmas* . . . , the insight based on concentration . . . , apprehension of the realities indicated by the symbol.''[10]

This brief description gives an indication of a living tradition with its deep roots in Indian yoga, a form of which was practiced by the Buddha himself under the Bo tree, and which, with numerous variations, is found across the Buddhist world today. Regardless of other practices one may find in southeast or northeast Asian Buddhist countries, meditation is the discipline that unites

Thai Buddhist Worshipers. *Worshipers gather at the rear of a Thai Buddhist* wat *or temple to engage in devotion at a small subsidiary shrine. Old and young, adults and children gather and mingle together.* (Courtesy of Mary Bush)

all followers of the Buddha in a way of life by which life is changed and new insight into the human condition is attained.

The Moral Life

When one inquires about the nature of the Buddhist ethic and how its basic principles are expressed in daily life and conduct, it is clear that *ethical concerns* are uppermost in the teachings of the Buddha. The resulting standards for monks and laypersons are demanding.

The Buddhist ethic is expressed most simply in the Five Precepts, which are the cornerstone of the moral life for both the monastic and lay communities. Buddhists should abstain from: destruction of life, taking what is not given, unchastity, speaking falsely, and drinking ''spirituous, strong, and maddening liquors.'' The third is stated as abstinence from sexual misconduct for laypersons, for whom sexual activity within marriage is, of course, acceptable. Monks are expelled from the order if they break any of the first four precepts, but receive

Thai Spirit House. *The worship or veneration of spirits exists alongside Buddhism in both Thailand and Burma. A spirit house, located in the garden of a private home in Bangkok, is a Buddhist* wat *or temple in miniature, thus exhibiting the blend of devotion to the Buddha and spirits.* (Courtesy of Mary Bush)

less severe punishment for partaking of alcoholic beverages.

The precept against taking life was for the Buddha both a protest against the sacrifices detailed in the Brahmanic literature and a recognition of the worth of any living being, human or animal. To forbid theft—''taking that which is not given''—involves respect for another's rights as well as his property. Sexual misconduct is not allowed because the Buddha thought women should be regarded as a man would regard his mother, sister, or daughter; if such is the case, the sacredness of the home is maintained and its peace realized. A monk, being committed to absolute chastity, is not subject to the sexual distractions that would interfere with the concentration essential to the higher levels of meditation and discipline. Similarly, liquor is forbidden because of its effect on the mind, because it produces sluggishness, and destroys mental alertness and concentration.

The Buddhist concept of *sila,* or morality in general

for monks and the laity, both includes and expands the Five Precepts. *Sila* forbids killing, stealing, and sexual misconduct; expands the precept against false speech to forbid lying, slander, harsh speech, and frivolous chatter; and adds a warning against covetous thoughts, hostile thoughts, and false views. *Sila* also includes such virtues as self-restraint, contentment with daily necessities, perseverence in following the Middle Path, purity, humility, acts of liberality, gratitude, reverence (for Buddha, doctrine, and order), tolerance, and serenity. Benevolence and compassion receive special emphasis and are personified in the Buddha, who chose to stay in the world and teach rather than withdraw. Such compassion must remain detached, however, because attachment to whatever is loved only binds one to the continuing round of existences.[11] Nevertheless, the motivation of service to all creatures is clearly rooted in a powerful sense of compassion, as expressed by the Buddha when he commissioned the monks:

Fare ye forth, brethren, on the mission that is for the good of many, for the happiness of many, to take compassion on the world . . . Beings there are whose eyes are hardly dimmed with dust, perishing because they hear not the Truth.[12]

Thus, the early Buddhist ethic was a Middle Path between extreme asceticism on the one hand and extreme indulgence on the other, just as doctrine attempted to work between extreme metaphysical speculation about absolute being and radical nihilism, which claimed that all is nothingness (*nihilism* comes from Latin *nihil,* meaning ''nothing.'') To the modern observer, Buddhist morality seems to lean toward the ascetic, particularly for the Sangha; compared to much Indian asceticism, though, it appears to be easy going. For the Buddhist community as a whole, it is a path of moderation—a Middle Path of restrained moderation, gentleness, and peace.

Three examples of this ethic of gentleness and peace deserve comment. The first two come from the early texts, suggesting that the Buddha ignored the caste system and was relatively open toward a place for women in the Buddhist community structure. The third is the example of King Ashoka, more than two centuries after the death of the Buddha.

Caste duties were closely associated with the workings of *karma* in Hinduism, and one of the rewards for faithful observance of caste duties was rebirth in a higher caste.

In the Buddha's teaching, by contrast, stealing or adultery was regarded as the same reprehensible immoral act regardless of the caste of the person committing the offense. People who kept the precepts were honored regardless of caste, and men and women were welcomed into the male and female orders from all castes and backgrounds, including a few women who had been courtesans. In two sutras of the *Majjhima Nikaya* the Buddha stated conclusively that morality, not birth, really counts; that being skilled in the *dharma* is the most important thing; and that men from any caste are capable of "taking a back-scratcher and bath powder and going to a river, [and] capable of cleansing themselves of dust and mud."[13] Rather than making a formal protest against caste or attempting a social reform to abolish it, the Buddhists ignored caste restrictions, which thereby became ineffective in Buddhist communities.

Another social advance brought about by Buddhists was a higher place for women. Although women seem to have been regarded as temptresses, there was nothing in the Buddhist texts like the strictures in the *Laws of Manu* that say that a wife is to serve her husband as if he were a god, or that allow a man to divorce his wife immediately if she is disobedient or quarrelsome. Buddhist teaching allowed either husband or wife to divorce the spouse if the spouse were found guilty of adultery or unfaithfulness, although the wife was more vulnerable to divorce in the event that she was not able to bear children. The following text suggests a high degree of mutuality:

> In five ways should a wife . . . be ministered to by her husband: by respect, by courtesy, by faithfulness, by handing over authority to her, by providing her with adornment.
> In these five ways does the wife, ministered to by her husband . . . love him: her duties are well performed, by hospitality to the kin of both, by faithfulness, by watching over the goods he brings, and by skill and industry in discharging all her business.[14]

Although it is clear that the wife was judged primarily on the basis of the work she did in managing the home, a woman appears to have had a place in the home and in society in her own right.

A central theme in Buddhist ethics is that of kingship, or the way a Buddhist king exemplifies in his role as ruler the values cherished in Buddhism. Although a detailed coverage of this is beyond the scope of this text, a model of the Buddhist ruler should be mentioned. Around 260 B.C.E., the very powerful King Ashoka conquered and subsequently ruled all of India except the extreme southern portion. The cost was great in human life, causing the king to reflect with considerable regret on what he had done. Five years later he took refuge in the Buddha, *dharma,* and Sangha, and recorded his new devotion in a series of edicts that tell us much of his understanding of Buddhist doctrine and practice. He announced that he had given up war, which cynics point out he could well afford to do since he controlled India, and proclaimed the Buddhist *dharma* as a way of bringing the people together in peace. He encouraged the holy men of other groups as well as the Buddhists, and threw the weight of his office behind a way of life rooted in the Buddha's Middle Way.

From the middle of the third century B.C.E. until at least the third century C.E., the Buddhist way of life sketched in this section became the predominant religious movement in India. Although that influence faded with the revival of Hinduism, the basic patterns of Buddhist life and thought were confirmed during those centuries, and Buddhism began to reach out to other lands of Asia.

Relations Between Monks and the Laity

The Order of Monks

The Buddha's chief disciples were called *Bhikkus,* or mendicant monks (because of their begging rounds); they became the nucleus of the Sangha or order of monks. These men differed little from other wandering ascetics of the sixth century B.C.E. who had progressed to the third of Hinduism's four chronological stages (*ashramas*), and thus had "left home for homelessness," retiring to the forest and maintaining minimal family ties or none at all. These *samanas,* meaning "recluses," are to be distinguished from the Brahmin priests and seem to have flourished in those areas of India where Jainism and Buddhism arose. They were often to be found in groups who were bound to a particular teacher or leader, followed his doctrines and rules, and acknowledged him as master. Gautama encountered such groups prior to his enlightenment and afterward.

It is likely that the Buddhist Sangha came into being as the Buddha and his disciples, like other such groups, adopted a temporary pattern of retreats during the rainy seasons. During this three-to-four month period the group with their teacher lived in a dwelling provided by a wealthy patron, engaged in more systematic teaching and study, and undoubtedly developed a high degree of cohesiveness and loyalty to the teacher. With time, the Buddhist order became better organized and consequently attained institutional stability.

The *Vinaya Pitaka,* or Discipline Basket of scriptures, which has already been introduced, contained regulations for the monks. The Vinaya took shape in these retreats, and the section containing obligatory rules for the monks (the *pratimoksha*) developed in this context. The rules were read at the Uposatha ceremony, at which time a monk was obligated to confess whether he was guilty of any infractions, and to receive punishment set for that infraction.

The first four precepts of the *pratimoksha* are classed

as *parajika* (defeat) rules because the breaking of them involved expulsion from the order of monks, and therefore "defeat" for a monk:

Whatever monk should indulge in sexual intercourse . . .
Whatever monk should take by means of theft what has not been given to him . . .
Whatever monk should intentionally deprive a human being of life . . . , or should praise the beauty of death, or should incite (anyone) to death, saying, "Hullo there, my man, of what use to you is this evil, difficult life?" . . .
Whatever monk should boast, with reference to himself . . . , though not knowing it fully, saying: "this I know, this I see"; . . . (and should later say) "I said that I know what I do not know, see what I do not see, . . . then he (like all the above) also is one who is defeated, he is not in communion.[15]

These obviously are the first four of the Five Precepts that apply to all monks; the fifth precept against drinking liquor has become rule 51 of the *pratimoksha.* False speech, for the monk, includes pretending to have attained that which has not been attained; this prohibition dealt a telling blow against deceit, hypocrisy, and pretense.

The next thirteen rules, if broken, require a formal meeting of the order, with a month's probation the punishment. These have to do with sexual offenses, having more than adequate dwelling places, stirring up trouble in the order, or bringing disfavor on it. There are two other rules that forbid a monk to take a seat by a woman or to use "wicked words"; these require a meeting, and the punishment is to be determined by the assembled group.

There are thirty rules that require repentance and forfeiture of objects such as robes, sleeping rugs, and begging bowls, if a monk has more of them than he actually needs. Then there are ninety-two rules that require only repentance and have to do with improper speech, inciting division, suggestion of any improper relationship to women, especially *Bhikkhunis* or nuns, and leading anyone else to do wrong.

There are rules which, if broken, need only to be confessed. These have to do with accepting food from a *Bhikkhuni* (nun) who is not a relative or is from a family that is not able to feed a monk. According to another long list of rules, a monk should go about properly clothed, his body under control; with downcast eyes;

Monks on Daily Begging Rounds. *Monks carrying begging bowls on their early morning rounds in Burma will receive food from Buddhist households for their midday meal. The lead monk in this group is actually a Buddhist layman now living in America who returned to his native Burma for a visit. For one week he followed the monastic discipline; he shaved his head, donned the yellow robe, and joined the daily begging rounds.* (Courtesy of Win Myint)

without loud laughter; with little sound; without swaying body, arms, or head; with his arms not akimbo; with his head uncovered, his mind alert. He is to eat what is given without question or without envy of what others have received, and must eat without smacking his lips, stuffing his stomach, or licking his fingers. To do otherwise would evidence the desire that increases suffering. There are other regulations concerning circumstances for the teaching of the *dharma,* and rules for hearing the confessions of the monks and handling the infractions.

Buddhism is highly visible in countries such as Sri Lanka, Burma, and Thailand where monks go on their begging rounds at dawn, pausing before the homes of the Buddhist faithful where rice and other articles of food are placed in their begging bowls. When they return to their monasteries, the food they have received is put together and prepared for their one meal of the day, usually served at noon. From that time until the end of the day the monk is to partake of no solid food.

A Buddhist monk may possess only a few of life's necessities: his begging bowl, an undergarment, two robes, a needle and thread with which to repair his clothing, and a razor for shaving his head and face. Even books are the common property of the monastery, not of individual monks. These limitations on personal property further reinforce a life-style that is rooted completely in simplicity.

The Buddha allowed the creation of a female order, the *Bhikkhunis,* with some reluctance. The major difference in rules for the order of nuns required them to be completely subordinate to the male order and dependent on the male Sangha for protection. It was still the retrained life, with modesty as one of the chief virtues. The *Bhikkhunis* clearly were mocked and scorned by some persons as the monks were scorned, but they were honored and respected by others for their quiet, simple, and ordered life-style.

Both monks and nuns were expected to be models of virtue and piety for lay people. Although laymen and laywomen did not follow the highly developed discipline of monks and nuns, the Sangha was an ever-present reminder of the more disciplined life that one would need to follow in order to attain *nirvana.* A monk always had to remember that his example was a primary factor in the moral life of the laity, as expressed in this pointed reminder:

Should a Bhikku dwell near a certain village or town, leading a life hurtful to the laity, and devoted to evil, (so that) his evil deeds are seen and heard, and the families led astray by him are seen and heard, let that Bhikku be spoken to by the Bhikkus thus: "Your life, Sir, is hurtful to the laity, and evil; your evil deeds, Sir, are seen and heard; and families are seen and heard to be led astray by you. Be so good, Sir, as to depart from this residence; you have dwelt here, Sir, long enough."[16]

The Way of Life for the Laity

The Sangha has traditionally constituted a religious elite, so that the laity looked up to monks as those who knew the truth and followed it. One of the primary duties of the laity was to give gifts to the order, from a few grains of rice dropped in a monk's begging bowl, to gifts of cloth for robes; for the wealthy, the gifts could be the provision of *stupas* and shrines, pagodas and monasteries. Such service to the order was a means of building up merit, which would aid in winning a better life in worlds to come. Laymen studied the scriptures under the guidance of monastic teachers, which contributed to growth in wisdom in this life and a higher existence in the next. We must recognize that we have moved into popular or folk Buddhism, where strict precision of doctrine does not prevail. However the *anatta* doctrine may have been understood by monks and scholars, it did not interfere with many Buddhists assuming that a person will reap in a future life what has been sown in the present.

Although it is possible for a lay person to attain *nirvana* as part of a family in society, it is highly improbable. The lay person normally can only "enter the stream," thus start on the path, and hope later to follow a way of life that will be more conducive to higher attainment. He may thereby surpass a monk who is weak in discipline or spasmodic in his efforts. For that matter, there are very few monks who have "entered the stream" in recent years.

We have noted already that the classic moral standard of the Five Precepts applies to lay persons as well as to monks and that the various virtues apply to both categories, although laymen and laywomen follow the precepts and practice the virtues in terms of life in the home and community. If the layman is a soldier, he undoubtedly will have to kill, and a farmer will have to kill some

Hospitality to Monks. *On special occasions Buddhist families may entertain a group of monks by serving a meal. Such an act of hospitality shows respect to the monks, brings merit to the family, and provides an opportunity for monks to expound the Buddhist teaching.* (Courtesy of Win Myint)

small creatures as he plows his field; but all are obligated to exercise full restraint in any case. More devout Buddhists avoid eating meat and thereby adhere to the precept that forbids taking life. For such people no animal, fish, or fowl may be taken for daily food—their diet is strictly vegetarian.

Parents attempt to rear their children according to the Buddha's teaching and thus bring them into the tradition. It has been customary through the years in Sri Lanka, Burma, and Thailand for boys in early adolescence to enter a monastery, where they have served as novice monks, studied the basics of Buddhism, and, before the appearance of modern schools, also learned to read and write. Today, there is still a ceremony when a child reaches the age of puberty when monks are invited to the home, are greeted by the young boy, and tie a cotton cord around the topknot of his hair. The people present recite the Three Refuges and Five Precepts, and then enjoy entertainment. On the second and third days the monks return to chant sayings of the Buddha, and on the third day the most important guest cuts off the topknot.

It would be a mistake to assume that a distinct monastic order means a separation of monks from the larger Buddhist community. Services rendered by each group to the other result in very close ties, and there are occasions when the two groups participate together. The laity converge on the monastery at Uposatha times, as has been noted, and for that day and evening abstain from sexual relations. They also keep three precepts beyond the standard five: no food after the noon hour; no dancing, singing, music, or other entertainment; and no adorning of the body or sleeping on a high bed.

The relationship between Buddhist monks and the laity is a unique one. Monks clearly are "elders" who receive unflagging respect from laypeople, who regard them as models of the ideal Buddhist life. In central Thailand, for example, the relationship is deepened as monks are invited to a laypeople's homes for special occasions or for meals given to honor the monks. Some of the monks may have connections with families, or a monk's distinguished career may result in an invitation to him and his fellow monks. It is believed that such occasions bring increased merit to the layman and his family.[17]

Our discussion to this point has been concerned entirely with Buddhism in South and Southeast Asia. Although variations may be discerned in the various countries involved, the importance of the Sangha has been constant through the centuries. Laymen and laywomen have assumed vital leadership roles in the twentieth century, but not in opposition to the monks. In spite of occasional tension and power struggles, the Sangha remains the focal point of Buddhist communities, with lay leaders making a particularly relevant contribution in the contemporary world.

Theravada and Mahayana

The two main branches that prevail in the Buddhist world are the Theravada, or "Doctrine of the Elders," the Buddhism found in the southern countries of Asia; and the Mahayana, or "the Great Vehicle," the Buddhism found in the countries of East Asia. The story of how these branches developed is complex, but it should be sketched before we turn to the Mahayana and its presence in China and Japan.

Tradition has it that shortly after the Buddha's death his disciples gathered at Rajagriha to draw together the rules for monks and the teachings the Buddha had given them, probably in response to questions about what he had or had not said. Although there is little concrete historical evidence, such a meeting would have been quite likely and it is reasonable to assume that at least some main points of doctrine and practice would have been discussed. Whether we may speak of collections of scripture—the Vinaya Pitaka and the Sutta Pitaka—at such an early time is a matter of speculation.

One early text tells of another council held at Vesali one hundred years after the death of the Buddha. The monks seem to have been concerned with many points of monastic rules, which evoked considerable dispute. Since the records are hazy, there is little point in trying to attach much significance to the meeting.

Equally questionable are references to a Third Council that, according to tradition, was called by King Ashoka at about 247 B.C.E. in the city of Pataliputra. The accounts speak of it as a "Council of the True Doctrine," and assume the existence of the complete Buddhist scriptures, which would include the Abhidhamma Pitaka, the collection of higher doctrines, in addition to the Vinaya and Sutta Pitakas.

Clearly a great deal of debate took place in these early centuries. There are reports of as many as seventeen or eighteen schools by 200 B.C.E., with their respective teachers interpreting doctrine and practice. The word "schools" is used here for both schools of thought and schools of actual practice or way of life. These schools of thought and life undoubtedly grew out of the ferment that accompanied the growth and spread of the Buddhist movement.

There is fairly good evidence that two distinct groups began to develop during the fourth century B.C.E., following the Second Council. The *Theravadins* (those in the path of the elders) claimed to continue and transmit the teachings of the Buddha and to follow the discipline he instituted. Obviously other groups could hardly accept that claim, and the *Mahasanghikas* (those of the Great Assembly), who also emerged during the second Buddhist century, claimed that the earlier teaching was better preserved in their group. They were more open to new ideas, however, and tended to depict the Buddha as being ultimate, supreme, infinite, and eternal, with appearances at various times and places. The Mahasanghikas had different criteria for entrance to the Sangha, and maintained a comparatively relaxed structure. There were, of course, subgroups within these two major bodies, one of them being a group within the Theravadins that held that there was a personal (*pudgala*) continuation from one existence to another, and were therefore called *Pudgalavadins*.

A third group, or collection of groups, remained fairly close to the Theravadins for a time, but pulled away about 250 B.C.E., probably as a result of decisions at the Third Council. Called *Sarvastivadins* because they maintained that all things exist, they emphasized the perfections of the *bodhisattva,* regarded essentially in those days as a Buddha to come, and made these perfections a model of Buddhist behavior. The Sarvastivadins had rather unusual opinions about space and being, appearing to veer away from the early Buddhist belief that all is becoming. They were opposed by the *Sautrantikas,* a fourth group who interpreted the sutras differently, and even claimed that the Third Basket, the Abhidhamma, should not be treated as scripture.

This brief look at these early schools of thought and life, which can be quite confusing, is intended only to show that differences of opinion did spring up in early Buddhist circles. Each of the main groups mentioned split into various subgroups that eventually died out. The Theravadins took root in Ceylon, now Sri Lanka, which is still considered a Theravada Buddhist country today, while the Mahasanghika proved to be the source of many doctrines later developed in Mahayana Buddhism, which took root in East Asia.

We are now in a position to sketch in broad outline the two main branches of Buddhism that spread across Asia, with increasing numbers of representatives in Europe and North America. These two branches, of course, are the Theravada and the Mahayana. The Buddhism of Tibet, usually designated *Vajrayana* or *Lamaism,* is regarded as a third branch, and will be discussed later.

For many years the two branches were designated *Hinayana* and *Mahayana* by both scholars and casual observers. *Hinayana* means "Little Vehicle" or "Lesser Vehicle," and *Mahayana* means "Great Vehicle." It is immediately apparent that Mahayanists devised the terminology, believing their schools to provide a much greater vehicle for transporting human beings across the sea of sorrow. It was not really until after World War II that the Buddhists who had been designated Hinayana finally were able to register their lack of appreciation for a term they thought both condescending and inaccurate. Therefore, in more recent literature, the term *Theravada* (doctrine or way of the elders) is frequently used in place of *Hinayana*. Although the Theravadins were only one of numerous schools in early Buddhism, it may be conceded that the Theravada tradition does continue the main currents of early Buddhist tradition. The other branch is still designated *Mahayana,* without major objection from those who may not regard it as being "greater."

The Buddhism of Sri Lanka, Burma, Cambodia, and Thailand is Theravada, and that of China, Japan, and Korea is Mahayana. This geographical alignment has led some scholars to designate the former as "Southern" and the latter as "Northern." Since those in the southern countries regard the Pali texts as most authoritative, and those in the northern countries look back to Sanskrit texts, one also finds references to Pali Buddhism and Sanskrit Buddhism.

Reference to the texts leads to the first of several major differences. Both Theravada and Mahayana regard as authoritative scripture the *Tripitaka,* or Three Baskets, but there are differences in the respective versions. The Mahayana add fifty-five large volumes, which include 2,184 texts, and forty-five supplementary volumes. Several of the Mahayana groups focus on a particular scripture, such as the *Lotus Sutra,* with only occasional use of other texts.[18]

Major doctrinal differences are inescapable. Although the early texts speak of three Buddhas prior to Gautama and the future Buddha Maitreya, when Theravada Buddhists speak of the Buddha, they have in mind one Buddha, Gautama. For the Mahayana, however, there are many Buddhas, as when thousands, for example, are brought together in a dramatic assembly in a scene in the *Lotus Sutra.* Certain Buddhas are more important, such as the Buddha Amitabha, Lord of the Pure Land, for those Buddhists who follow the Pure Land School.

In the early texts the future Buddha Maitreya is called a *bodhisattva,* meaning one who had attained enlightenment and is on the way to Nirvana. But this figure of the *bodhisattva* is invested with even greater meaning in the Mahayana, where he or she, having attained en-lightenment (*bodhi*), makes a definite decision to postpone *nirvana* until all creatures have found peace. The Mahayanists contrast this compassionate *bodhisattva* with the figure of the *arhat,* or saint, of Theravada who seems concerned only about his own progress along the path. As we shift from Theravada to Mahayana, *nirvana* is still a goal, but the Mahayanists add other goals: rebirth in the Pure Land of the Buddha Amitabha, or even becoming a Buddha. Theravada speaks of that which is truly real as becoming, a middle way between being and nonbeing. Mahayana metaphysics proclaims "All is Void," the great emptiness, which is a staggering concept until one discovers how liberating it can be.

As with doctrine, so with practice: the differences between Theravada and Mahayana are matters of degree; Mahayanists usually have not rejected Theravada but have seen the Mahayana as a broader and richer tradition. Worship in most Mahayana temples is more active and colorful, and the temples themselves present a bewildering array of objects in contrast with the more austere Theravada.

In terms of organization, the Buddhist clergy are honored by Chinese, Japanese, and Korean laypersons, but the line of separation between clergy and laity is not as obvious as in Theravada countries. Chinese and Japanese Buddhist clergy may be seen in street clothes, and, what is more surprising, a married Buddhist clergy is quite common in Japan and in areas influenced by the Japanese, such as Taiwan. There is evidence of greater lay participation in both the decision-making process and in day-to-day Buddhist life in the Mahayana countries.

Thus, with this brief survey of the differences between these two main branches of Buddhism, we turn from the early Theravada tradition that has continued in the southern Buddhist countries to examine Mahayana thought and life as it began in India and spread to the north and east of the Asian continent.

Basic Teachings of Mahayana Buddhism

By the second century B.C.E. the trends that we now identify as Mahayana had been initiated. From that time until the end of the second century C.E., several of the major texts expressing these trends had begun to appear. These texts, and the monks who followed the new trends and taught the doctrines in the newer texts, brought Mahayana to prominence and were the basis for its spread to East Asia.

Primary Sacred Texts

There are a total of 2,184 Mahayana texts that have canonical status, but we may focus on several that are regarded as primary sources for these teachings and that therefore are especially popular among Buddhists.

Lotus Sutra is an example of a particular scripture that receives special attention from Buddhists in the Mahayana countries. The full name of the sutra is *Lotus Sutra of the Wonderful Law* (Sanskrit, *Saddharma Pundarika Sutra*). It was written in India between the second century B.C.E. and the second century C.E.[19] The lotus flower, a member of the waterlily family, grows in shallow ponds. It became a prominent symbol in Buddhist literature and art because the manner in which its lovely, pale blossoms emerge from the mud and unfold suggests that purity may emerge from the world's suffering and misery. Through poetry and prose *Lotus Sutra* describes a scene of great splendor in which the Buddha proclaims the doctrine to a great host of disciples and bodhisattvas, those who have postponed *nirvana* to help suffering creatures. He speaks of other Buddhas and the way by which all those who are present may become Buddhas, thus going beyond the goal of *nirvana,* which the Buddha had taught earlier because people were not yet ready for this larger truth and way.

The Buddha goes on to tell a story in which those who seek *nirvana* are like a son who left his father's house, wandered about for many years, returned and worked unrecognized as a servant, and finally received his father's wealth when the old man died. The Buddha sends forth a ray of light that illumines countless worlds with a Buddha preaching in each of them. The message, repeated in various stories and poems again and again, is that all beings can and will become Buddhas and thus bless those around them with peace and light.

Sutras of the Perfection of Wisdom (*Prajna-paramita*) contrast worldly truth and absolute truth through a series of paradoxes.[20] The first of these wisdom sutras may

have been written as early as the first century B.C.E., and all of them in one way or another expound the doctrine that everything we know—from what we experience through the senses to our knowledge of Buddhas and bodhisattvas—is completely empty, having no absolute reality.

Among the most popular of the Mahayana texts are those that describe with beautiful imagery the Pure Land of the Buddha Amitabha. Called *Land of Bliss* (*Sukhavati-vyuha*), these sutras relate the vow of the Buddha Amitabha to save all who call upon him in faith by giving them rebirth in his Pure Land or Western Paradise. The sutras date from at least the first century B.C.E.[21]

Acts of the Buddha (*Buddha-carita*) probably was written in the late first or early second century C.E. and is generally attributed to Asvaghosha, an outstanding philosopher monk of the period.[22] In a sense the work is transitional, containing both Theravada and Mahayana ideas. It is a remarkably modern treatment in that the author dwells on the Buddha's innermost feeling in depicting his growing awareness of misery in the world, and his decision to leave the palace and its luxuries to seek enlightenment.

Also attributed to Asvaghosha, but without supporting evidence, is *Awakening of Faith in the Mahayana* (*Mahayana sraddhotpada*), a work also probably written in the first or second century C.E.[23] In it the opposites of absolute/relative, transcendental/phenomenal, emptiness/nonemptiness give way to the One Mind that the unknown author defines as "suchness" or "thusness," the point where these opposites meet and truth is realized. Once again Buddhism is the middle path between extremes.

Descent to the Island of Lanka (*Lankavatara Sutra*), also written in the first few centuries C.E., is of fundamental importance for the Consciousness Only School to be discussed shortly.[24] The author of the work approaches topics such as the void and illusion and the *anatta* or no-self doctrine from a psychological point of view, and arrives at the idea for which the school is known, that there is a "storehouse consciousness" that receives impressions from moments of existence.

A text that has great appeal to laypeople is *Vimalakirti Sutra,* in which the main speaker is the layman whose name is given to the sutra.[25] Although *Vimalakirti* seems to encourage young men to take the vows of a monk, there is a mocking attitude toward the monks, which reflects an increasing self-consciousness among the laity. When the young men say they must respect their parents' wishes and remain householders, the author then indicates that they are to meditate and practice the Buddhist life as laymen.

A laywoman is the central figure in *The Lion's Roar of Queen Srimala*,[26] a text written in the first or second century C.E. This text is earlier than *Lankavatara Sutra*, which quotes *Srimala*, and *Awakening of the Faith*, which draws upon *Srimala*. Queen Srimala grasps the doctrine of the Buddha in short order and soon becomes eloquent in proclaiming it. The doctrine is that the Mahayana includes all other vehicles, and therefore is the one vehicle (*Ekayana*); anyone who realizes the Buddha-nature is able to utter the Lion's roar or proclaim the truth. The idea that any female might be limited in understanding the doctrine, often found in both Theravada and Mahayana, is rejected here in favor of the claim that women can reach the tenth and final stage of the bodhisattva. Queen Srimala herself is very modest and claims that all is due to the Buddha.

Particularly important for the T'ien T'ai school but also widely read in other Mahayana circles, is *Extended Narration of the Buddha's Sport* (*Lalitavistara*), which emphasizes the human element of various events in the Buddha's life. The *Lalitavistara* is undoubtedly a reworking of an earlier Indian work, as is the case with the *Book of the Great Final Nirvana* (*Mahaparinirvana Sutra*), which retells from earlier texts the story of the Buddha's death from a Mahayana point of view.

The list of primary Mahayana texts could be extended to include any number of writings that have had great influence. A few additional writings will be treated in connection with the schools for which they are authoritative. All in all, about twelve to fifteen primary texts, each important for a group or movement within Mahayana Buddhism, are basic to the amazing doctrinal development that we now are to sample.

Major Mahayana Teachings

Recalling a number of distinctive trends in the Mahayana tradition—many Buddhas, the role of the bodhisattva, a wider range of goals for the believer, more active and colorful practice, and greater prominence for the laity—we now turn to a few of the major teachings of the Mahayana, in connection with the philosophical schools that taught these ideas. Various practices and the role of the laity will be treated in connection with particular schools of life and thought as we deal with Buddhism in China and Japan.

Buddhas and Doctrines About Them. In discussing the Lotus Sutra, reference was made to a great assembly of Buddhas and bodhisattvas. One of the most popular of the Buddhas, for the common people at least, does not appear in that book. This Buddha Amitabha, or Buddha of Unlimited Light, is called *A-Mi-T'o-Fo* in Chinese and *Amida Butsu* in Japanese; and has another name that means "unlimited life." He has vowed to save all beings who call on him in faith by causing them to be reborn in his Pure Land of bliss or happiness.

Another Buddha who brings light is the Buddha Vairocana, the one who "shines out," the chief figure of a Mahayana text that bears his name, the *Great Shining Out Sutra* (*Mahavairocana Sutra*). Originally, Vairocana was another name for Gautama, but later came to designate a separate Buddha, at least by the seventh century C.E. The fact that both of these Buddhas are identified with light follows naturally upon the idea that darkness accompanies ignorance and knowledge brings light. In Tibet and in the Shingon school in Japan, Vairocana is regarded as a manifestation of the *dharma-kaya* or body of truth, to be discussed below.

Other Buddhas that should be mentioned are Aksobhya, the "unshakable one"; Ratnasambhava, the "one born of a jewel"; and Vajradhara, the "one who carries the thunderbolt." All of these are heavenly or transcendent Buddhas with remarkable powers, whereas the Buddha Kasyapa, like Gautama, is an earthly Buddha with earthly powers. The existence of these Buddhas leads to the question of whether they share and then express any common or universal Buddhahood. The answer is in the affirmative, and the result is the distinctively Mahayana teaching of the *trikaya,* or "three bodies" of the Buddha, which are experienced in successive levels of meditation.

We meet the historical Buddha or hear any Buddha expound the *dharma* to us through his *nirmana-kaya,* his "created" or "transformed" body. Mahayana Buddhists hold that Gautama was only an appearance of the real Buddha and as such only appeared to be born, grow up, marry, and die. The Buddha appeared as a common mortal only to show that it was possible for an ordinary person to attain enlightenment. Only through the Buddha's *nirmana-kaya* can human beings come to know his teaching and experience enlightenment.

There are transcendent Buddhas, however, who speak in great heavenly assemblies and are visible only through a second body, a *sambhoga-kaya,* meaning "body of bliss." Ordinary human beings do not have the mental or spiritual powers to hear or understand the Buddha in this form, which is visible only to bodhisattvas who have attained great spirituality. Ordinary followers of the Buddha are not deterred by such a concept, however, for prayers and offerings are made to heavenly, transcendent Buddhas, who may well be the only ones who can help the common man or woman.

The third body is the *dharma-kaya,* or "body of truth": the Buddha-reality, the unlimited, eternal source of all possibilities. The *dharma-kaya* is realized only by Buddhas, for all of whom it is the same. There are distinctions or qualifications in the first two bodies, but not in the body of truth, which is devoid of all signs and all qualifications. This means that there is no distinction between subject and object or between mind and matter in the *dharma-kaya,* which is inexpressable and unknowable and realized only by Buddhas.

Thus, the *trikaya* doctrine can appeal to the total Buddhist community, both those who can think only of a powerful being able to grant blessings, and the masses caught up in the miseries and cares of a mundane world. It also appeals to those who are able to envision an ultimate Buddha-nature that remains in the realm of truth that only Buddhas know, a concept fundamental to Mahayana teaching.

The Way of the Bodhisattva. *Bodhi* means "enlightenment" and *sat* means "being" or "having attained" ("being in the state of"); therefore, a *bodhisattva* is one who has attained enlightenment. In Theravada such a person presses on toward the ultimate release of *nirvana,* but in Mahayana the bodhisattva is seen as superior to one who seeks and gains *nirvana.* The reason is that no one, at least no one with a compassionate mind, can ignore the many creatures who are caught up in the misery of human existence, and thus the bodhisattva

is motivated to forego *nirvana* and remain in the world to make his or her merit available to all creatures in need.

In the eyes of Mahayana Buddhists, the bodhisattva therefore is superior to *arhats* and self-enlightened Buddhas because the latter are primarily interested in their own enlightenment and tend to forget others. The *arhat,* in the Mahayana view, seems selfish in comparison to a bodhisattva working for the liberation of all beings and helping all creatures attain Buddhahood. Although able to enter *nirvana,* the bodhisattva refuses in order to be able to point the way to others, which he or she could not do after passing into the ultimate peace.

The bodhisattva motive of compassion and sacrifice for others is the cornerstone of Mahayana ethics, expressed beautifully by a seventh-century C.E. bodhisattva and poet named Shantideva, whose vow is one of the most moving passages in Buddhist literature:

In reward for all this righteousness that I have won by my works I would become a soother of all the sorrows of all creatures. May I be a balm to the sick, their healer and servitor, until sickness come never again; may I quench with rains of food and drink the anguish of hunger and thirst; may I be in the famine of the ages' end their drink and meat; may I become an unfailing store for the poor, and serve them with manifold things for their need. My own being and my pleasures, all my righteousness in the past, present, and future I surrender indifferently, that all creatures may win to their end. The Stillness [*nirvana*] lies in surrender of all things, and my spirit (yearns) for the Stillness; if I must surrender all, it is best to give it for fellow creatures.[27]

Although bodhisattvas listen to the Buddhas, as in the Lotus Sutra, they are not mere assistants. They are both helpers and saviors for all human beings, and thus share the honor with and at times receive more honor than the historical Buddha. Great teachers are also honored by being called bodhisattvas, but are not ranked as high as such great bodhisattvas as Manjusri, the bodhisattva of wisdom; Maitreya, who will be the next human Buddha; and Avalokitesvara, the bodhisattva of compassion—all of whom are ranked with the Buddhas in the devotion of the common people. The last bodhisattva mentioned, known in China as Kuan Yin, reigns supreme in the lives of millions, especially in East Asia.

In keeping with the ever-widening perspective of Mahayana teaching, which does not limit the higher levels of attainment to monks, the bodhisattva path is open to everyone. A larger and larger company of these compassionate beings help any person who may call for assistance, very much as in Hindu *bhakti*. That possibility is cause for hope—not only for loyal and faithful Buddhists, but for all human beings.

The Human Condition and Potential. The Theravada view of human beings as involved in ignorance, misery, and sorrow is retained but softened somewhat in the Mahayana. The store of merit held out by bodhisattvas and the vow of a Buddha Amitabha to save all beings inevitably add a more optimistic note. There is at least some hope in the midst of despair.

The fundamental difference is not limited, however, to the hope of a better future in another realm of existence. Rather, human existence in this world has changed, for some schools of thought and life in the Mahayana at any rate, due to the idea that one does not have to wait for some other realm to experience *nirvana,* but may do so here and now. That life is an endless round of birth and rebirth is a basic conviction of Hindu thought and Buddhist thought, called *samsara. Nirvana,* as we have seen, is the snuffing out of the fires of existence so that one is born no more. In Mahayana teaching, however, one clearly experiences *nirvana* in this life and goes on living, which means living in the world of *samsara.* That might suggest that *nirvana* is submerged in *samsara,* but it really means that *nirvana* transforms *samsara* to the extent that the common life, society, history, and humanity are invested with new value and meaning.

Additional evidence of a new view of humanity and the human potential is the claim in several Mahayana schools that all human beings have the Buddha-nature. In Ch'an or Zen, as the meditation school is called in China and Japan, what one seeks through meditation is to realize the Buddha-nature within, not to attain some state that is external to oneself. If all beings have the Buddha-nature, then there can be no doubt of the inherent value of human nature. It may be clouded over with ignorance or grasping for sensual pleasure or drifting on an ocean of sorrow, but the inherent goodness is there because of the Buddha-nature.

The fact that the Chinese have seen human nature as essentially good, as will be seen in the study of Chinese religion, undoubtedly had tremendous influence on Buddhist thought as it developed in the Chinese context. But there is also evidence that the seeds of these ideas—*nirvana* in *samsara,* and all beings having the Buddha-nature—were present in the beginnings of the Mahayana in ancient India. Buddhism has always had the capacity to preserve tradition and respond to new ideas, whether from within or from outside, a characteristic exhibited more impressively in the teaching of the Mahayana than in the Theravada.

Mahayana Philosophical Schools

Two schools of thought that began in India between the second and fourth centuries C.E. later moved east and took root in China and Japan. Essentially schools of thought, the Void and Consciousness Only School do not have prescribed ritual practices as such, but in both movements meditation on the ideas that all is void or that *dharmas** are known only in the consciousness is integral. The thought of both schools had considerable influence on later Chinese and Japanese schools, which emphasized practice as well as thought or doctrine.

The School of the Void.** Founded by a man named Nagarjuna in the second century C.E., the School of the Void emphasized the Buddha's denial of any theory of absolute existence. With a razor-sharp logic Nagarjuna asserted that being or existence is only relative, that beings have no real or absolute existence, and therefore that all is emptiness, all is Void. The full impact of Nagarjuna's thesis may be seen in the words dedicating his major work to the Buddha, who (Nagarjuna says) proclaimed

. . . The Principle of (universal) relativity,
'Tis like blissful (*nirvana*),
Quiescence of plurality,
There nothing disappears,

* The word *dharma* has been used primarily to mean "law," "doctrine," or "teaching." In Mahayana Buddhism it has the additional meanings of "energies, moments of existence, events"—all of which move in a continuum.
** The School of the Void is called *Madhyamika* or "Middle Path" in Sanskrit. Since there are three primary treatises, the term *San Lun* or "Three Treaties" is used in Chinese, and the same meaning is conveyed by the Japanese term *Sanron.*

Nor anything appears;
Nothing has an end,
Nor is there anything eternal.[28]

He went on to argue that if a thing has a cause, then it does not have self-existence or independent existence. Conversely, that which does exist independently or absolutely does not require a cause, which is impossible since all is subject to causation.

One should note that Nagarjuna rejected both alternatives of the pairs existence/nonexistence, being/nonbeing, eternity/noneternity. Since nonexistence and nonbeing were rejected along with existence and being, Nagarjuna did not advocate annihilation, or say that there are no things at all, or claim that, for example, the teacher and students assembled for a class are not really there. Such *dharmas,* or moments of existence, are real in a temporary, relative sense, but not in an absolute sense. All *dharmas* are empty and all existence is relative because everything, including the world, is caused. Nagarjuna held that nothing is permanent, therefore, everything is in flux. Because *nirvana* is included in this flux, there is no difference between *nirvana* and *samsara,* the process of birth and rebirth.

The conclusion is that all is emptiness, a higher truth that transcends the ordinary or worldly truth, which assumes that this is a real world (in the absolute sense) and that I am real (because of *atman*). Emptiness is the middle path (*Madhyamika*) or middle doctrine that avoids the extremes of absolute existence and nonexistence.

One must always keep in mind that the radical stress of the School of the Void on emptiness has a purpose: only by negating all of the old ideas can the mind be cleared of any and all thoughts that might impede a genuine openness to truth. One may also sense in these thinkers a powerful affirmation that nothing really important in life can be expressed in terms of existence and nonexistence. The stream of life goes on, one moment of temporary existence giving way to another. In this continuing process human beings experience great achievement and failure, great love and hatred. However, nothing that is experienced in the phenomenal world is eternal or absolute; to try to hold on to such fleeting experiences by believing they are absolute and eternal is to be deluded. To realize that all is the Void—a situation of openness in which things are happening, values are emerging, and life is moving on—is wisdom.

The Consciousness Only School.[*] The central tenet of the Consciousness Only School supplies the name: moments of existence, the moments of our lives, are real *only* as they are known in the *consciousness*. The primary texts of this school deny the reality of external objects in the empirical world. By consciousness only are "things" real; therefore, only the consciousness, or higher mind, is real. This higher mind or consciousness is a repository or "consciousness container" (*alayavijnana*), which receives impressions from the stream of experience, the moments of life that pass through it. Although its ideas are difficult to grasp, the Consciousness Only School has been an influential school of thought, and even in modern times has had its loyal adherents. The two brothers Asanga and Vasubandhu with whose writings the school begins were convinced that some spiritual or mental power was real. Unable to accept completely Nagarjuna's thesis that all is Void, they began with the idea of emptiness and posited an idealistic context for a world in which *dharmas* had no absolute existence. That ultimate context, the ideal storehouse, is the consciousness container.

Vasubandhu explains the position of the Consciousness Only School in terms of three transformations (for our purposes we shall reverse the order of his three transformations). His third transformation (our first) is the area of senses in which what we experience through six "consciousnesses"—touch, sight, hearing, smell, taste, and the sense-center consciousness (a kind of coordinating center)—is received and "transformed" at this lowest level of life. Then that which we experience goes through a second transformation called the mind-consciousness, which always distorts the knowing process though ignorance, a false view of the self as real and permanent, self-pride, and self-love. Nevertheless, however clouded, there is the first (our last) and ultimate transformation, the storehouse consciousness, "which brings into fruition all seeds," or the effects of good and evil deeds. Indifferent to associations, it is not affected by ignorance or

---

[*] The Consciousness Only School is termed in Sanskrit *Yogacara,* meaning "way of Yoga" and more descriptively *Vijnanavada,* or "Consciousness Doctrine." The Chinese term is *Wei Shih,* which means Consciousness Only, as does the Japanese term *Hosso.*

memory, except that the "seeds"—the continuing effect of the *dharmas,* or the moments of life—"perfume" the storehouse consciousness and only thus are real because of this momentary contact with the ideal reality. Then the process is reversed: the seeds move out of the storehouse, through the mind with its confusions, and out to experience through the senses these moments of life again. Thus, Vasubandhu says there are three consciousnesses:

> The first is the non-entity of phenomenon,
> The second is the non-entity of self-existence.
> The last is the non-entity of the ultimate existence . . .
> The supreme truth of all *dharmas* (moments of existence)
> Is nothing other than the Truth Norm (suchness).
> It is forever true to its nature,
> Which is the true nature of mind-only (consciousness only).[29]

Like the School of the Void, the Consciousness Only School maintains that all *dharmas* are empty, and goes on to say that at the three levels we have been discussing we are dealing with nonbeing. But at the juncture of being and nonbeing where there is "no-thing," there is the higher consciousness that receives and stores that which is brought into it, and from which life goes out again, until we realize the truth involved and are released to peace and joy.

Buddhism in China

Although Mahayana Buddhism originated in India and was also to be found in Central Asia, China was the first country in which the Mahayana tradition became firmly rooted and developed into a powerful component of the country's culture. Buddhism is extremely weak in China today, due to specific circumstances that will be delineated later, but the record of Buddhist achievement in China is remarkable. Even after sweeping government measures against the movement in the middle of the ninth century C.E., Buddhism demonstrated a tenacious holding power on the one hand, and the capacity to penetrate even the thought of its opponents on the other. This has been the case from the introduction of Buddhism into China to its present uncertain position in that country.

The Initial Problem of Relating to Chinese Culture

Buddhism's Entry into China. The first monks who made the arduous and dangerous journey from India into China discovered a much colder climate and a very different culture than the one they had left behind. The fact that Han Dynasty China (206 B.C.E.–220 C.E.) was one of the great cultural peaks in the history of that country meant that the first Buddhists in China faced a mature civilization that was not too receptive to a new religion. Their practices did not take firm root until about the sixth century C.E., following more than three hundred years of cultural disunity and frequent political chaos.

There are legendary accounts of Buddhism having entered China as early as 221–208 B.C.E. Such stories are dismissed by most scholars today. Tradition has it that the Chinese Emperor Ming Ti, in the year 62 C.E., dreamed of a golden image in the West, which his ministers identified as the Buddha. This led him to send representatives to India requesting Buddhist texts and images; they returned five years later with two Indian teachers, who translated one of the popular sutras into Chinese.

There is a legendary flavor to the story about the emperor's dream and its consequences, but there are more reliable records of vegetarian feasts being held in the first century C.E. in Kiangsu and Shantung provinces. Although they are not identified as Buddhist, it is reasonable to assume that the meatless feasts were an expression of the Buddhist prohibition against taking life. The story suggests that small Buddhist groups were present in China by the end of the first century C.E.

The ancestor cult was a prominent feature of the culture that existed for at least four thousand years before Buddhism was introduced into China. Members of every family, headed by the eldest son, made seasonal offerings to an ancestor as long as there was anyone alive who remembered that person. In contrast, a Chinese who became a Buddhist monk took vows of celibacy, which meant no family, no descendants, and therefore a break in the line of those who could be expected "to keep the ancestral fires lighted," leaving an ancestor uncared for, and therefore a wandering, "hungry ghost." Moreover, Buddhist monks shaved their heads, which, in Chinese eyes, dishonored the bodies received from their parents. There was also a political problem, since monks did not show proper respect for those in authority and were not subject to military service. There were economic problems, since monastic lands were not subject to taxation, the government lost revenue and, in effect, had to support the monks who did not work the lands.

Thus, in spite of devout lay followers, the quite visible monastic leadership provoked a highly negative response from the Chinese. In both life and thought Buddhism seemed other-worldly, particularly to Confucian intellectuals, who were concerned with the world, society, education, and government. And the fact that it was a foreign religion, stemming from people regarded as "barbarians" by the Chinese, provided a major obstacle.

Buddhists were highly resourceful, however, pointing out that a monk could make offerings that would help his father (and others) win a better rebirth. Even having a family member become a monk or nun would bring merit. The Buddhist idea of rebirth supplied a new dimension to the religious life, providing answers to questions about life beyond the grave. And, in spite of objections to celibate monks, there were monks and nuns who lived lives of such noble piety that respect for them and for their movement increased through the years.

Translating Buddhist Texts into Chinese. Since anything associated with foreign barbarians from India handicapped the new movement in China, the translation of Sanskrit texts (most of the texts were in Sanskrit, not Pali) into Chinese was a pressing need. Indian and Central Asian monks were brought to China, sometimes against their will, to work with Chinese monks; and outstanding Chinese monks were sent to India to study Sanskrit and bring back texts.

Indian and Chinese monks who made these travels followed the route established by traders in silks and spices. The highly dangerous route went from Loyang, the ancient capital of China, to the north and west, with the Himalayan mountains to the south and the Gobi desert to the north, and then down into India (or on to the Mediterranean world for the traders). Fierce animals, desperate bandits, and extremes of climate took a heavy toll, but faithful monks accomplished their task and all the texts were finally translated into Chinese.

The translation of Buddhist texts from Sanskrit or Pali into Chinese is nothing less than remarkable when one considers how difficult it was for a Chinese to learn

Buddhist Cave Sculptures at Lungmen. *Magnificent figures of the Buddha were carved out of solid rock in the fifth and sixth centuries* C.E. *Ordered and financed by emperors and other wealthy people to gain merit, the sculptures also express the great devotion and feeling of the artisans.* (Courtesy of Mary Bush)

Sanskrit and an Indian to learn Chinese. The languages are different in every possible way. Over and beyond the obvious differences of vocabulary, structure, and syntax, the Chinese language had never been adapted to the expression of highly theoretical and abstract concepts. The problems might well have been insurmountable had it not been for help from an unexpected quarter, a religio-philosophical movement called Taoism, which will be presented in the following chapter. Buddhist translators and teachers were able to use Taoist concepts

Big Wild Goose Pagoda. *Crowds of Chinese youth gather at the Big Wild Goose Pagoda at Sian, the city that stands on the site of the old capital city of Ch'angan. It was at this place that Hsüan Tsang, famous T'ang Dynasty monk, translated Buddhist sutras he had brought back from India.* (Courtesy of Mary Bush)

and terms in conveying Buddhist ideas, and even employed as assistants Chinese who were Taoists.

In the general discussion of Mahayana Buddhism in the preceding section, reference was made to the School of the Void, first taught in India by Nagarjuna. Terms such as "void" or "emptiness" would have been completely incomprehensible to Chinese listeners, except for the fact that Taoists had spoken several hundred years earlier of the meaning of emptiness, pointing out that an empty bowl was more useful than a full one. Thus, Buddhists used the term *k'ung* out of Taoist literature to translate the Sanskrit term *shunya*, meaning "void" or "empty," and moved ahead. Both Buddhism and Taoism emphasized meditation, for which control of the passions was necessary, and both had an interest in the afterlife and what happened in the long stretch of eternity. In these and several other ways, association with Taoism helped the Buddhists get a hearing, although there were times of considerable rivalry. Both Buddhists and Taoists claimed to have special or supernatural powers, and this led some Chinese to think that Buddhism was some kind of new Taoist sect.

By the end of the second century C.E., the Buddhist monks at Loyang had organized a translation center where hundreds of texts were collected and translated. By the end of the third century, Ch'angan had become the center of Buddhism in China; there monks translated *Sutra of Perfect Wisdom* (*Prajna-paramita*) and *Lotus Sutra of the Wonderful Law,* probably the most famous and widely used Mahayana text.

The story of Buddhism in China can be told through the stories of great monks who did highly creative work in times that became more and more chaotic. In 311 C.E. the Hsiung-nu (Huns) captured Loyang, and five years later took Ch'angan. This did not deter Chinese monks like Taoan (312–395 C.E.), who built a great monastery, worked on rules for the monastic life, translated texts, and specialized in the study of wisdom literature. His disciple, Hui-yuan (334–417 C.E.) founded the White Lotus Society, traditionally regarded as the beginning of the Pure Land School (to be discussed shortly), a very popular movement among the laity. Thus, these two men both strengthened the order of monks in China and also attracted lay followers.

One of the fascinating key personalities in this whole story is Kumarajiva (344–413 C.E.), who was born in Central Asia of a Brahmin father and a Kuchan princess. He studied Theravada Buddhism in Kashmir and later was captured by a Chinese army and remained in their custody for almost twenty years. He was able, however, to have Chinese scholars around him who helped in the translation of texts. He was in Ch'angan by 401 C.E., and there he was made director of a translation bureau set up by the government for the express purpose of translating Buddhist texts into Chinese. Kumarajiva and his assistants translated about three hundred texts, their work greatly enhanced by the master's profound knowledge of the whole range of Buddhist ideas, with which he stretched their minds and thus stimulated a flowering of Buddhism in North China.

Becoming Part of the Chinese World. It is one of the ironies of history that Buddhism began to be really Chinese during an era when non-Chinese peoples frequently held the upper hand in that country. The conquering Hsiung-nu, a central Asian tribe, far from being a threat to the new religion, actually pushed it forward. They accepted Buddhism in part because it was not Chinese and in part because it preached a universal ethic. These new rulers of the early fourth century were concerned about the power of the monks and, in order better to control them, assigned the monks such tasks as managing official charities; building bridges, roads, and watermills; and supervising social service projects.

Slightly before the time of Kumarajiva's great successes, and in a place northwest of Loyang and Ch'angan, another "barbarian" king by the name of Menghsün was an active Buddhist and actually helped to propagate the religion. In his kingdom the northern and southern routes of the silk road came together, which meant that religious and secular travelers passed through in great numbers. To accommodate these travelers, cave temples were dug in the sides of hills at a place called Tunhuang in the middle of the fourth century. Both the temples and the paintings on the cave walls, some of which have been preserved, are masterpieces that enthrall viewers even today.

During the long period of disunity from 220–581 C.E., the strongest and longest dynasty was the Northern Wei (385–534 C.E.), whose emperors were from the To-pa people, a non-Chinese group that may have been of Turkish descent. The dynasty began by accepting Buddhism, but this policy was reversed during the fifth century, when Taoists with political ambitions got the ear of the Emperor Wu and a severe persecution of Buddhism was launched. Not only were young men prevented from entering the Sangha and lay people forbidden to make contributions to the monks, a number of monks were put to death and others forced into hiding. By the middle of the fifth century the tide changed again and Buddhism was back in favor. It was such struggles as these during the Northern Wei Dynasty that tested the mettle of Buddhist leaders and actually resulted in a strengthening of the religion.[30]

After the persecution described above, two of the most impressive achievements of the Buddhist artistic spirit were created at sites in the area ruled by the Northern Wei. Rock sculptures at Yünkang, near the first capital of Tat'ung, were done on a magnificent scale, with the

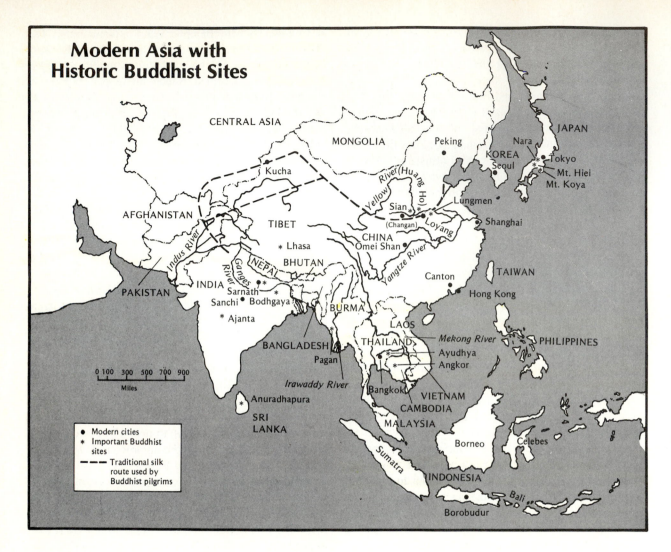

Modern Asia with Historic Buddhist Sites

CENTRAL ASIA

MONGOLIA

Peking

JAPAN

Nara

KOREA

Tokyo

Seoul

Mt. Hiei

Mt. Koya

Kucha

Yellow River (Huang Ho)

Sian

Lungmen

AFGHANISTAN

(Changan)

Loyang

Shanghai

TIBET

CHINA

Lhasa

Omei Shan

Indus River

NEPAL

BHUTAN

Yangtze River

TAIWAN

Ganges River

Canton

PAKISTAN

INDIA

Sarnath

Hong Kong

Sanchi   Bodhgaya

BURMA

Ajanta

LAOS

Mekong River

PHILIPPINES

BANGLADESH

THAILAND

Ayudhya

Pagan

Angkor

Irawaddy River

Bangkok

VIETNAM

0 100 300 500 700 900

CAMBODIA

Miles

Anuradhapura

MALAYSIA

SRI
LANKA

Borneo

Celebes

• Modern cities

* Important Buddhist
  sites

Sumatra

-- Traditional silk
   route used by
   Buddhist pilgrims

INDONESIA

Bali

Borobudur

largest statue of the Buddha rising seventy feet. Images were sculpted in twenty caves, one grouping being a panorama depicting the life of the Buddha. Still more impressive were the Lungmen caves near Loyang, which became the dynastic capital while work on the caves at Yünkang was still going on. It is estimated that from 495–730 C.E. well over 100,000 images were carved in these caves, the work spanning several dynasties.

Especially helpful for understanding Buddhism in China are the inscriptions found throughout both sets of caves. At Yünkang, for example, the Buddhas are requested to grant peace and prosperity to the rulers, who, of course, financed the construction of the caves,

but there are also entreaties for ancestors and teachers and people everywhere who are still caught in the cycles of birth and rebirth. At Lungmen, where the Buddha is depicted in a more spiritual way, and where Maitreya, the Buddha to come, is almost as prominent as Gautama, the inscriptions reveal a pronounced trend toward the Mahayana tradition, with emphasis on the compassion of the bodhisattva and the salvation of all creatures. There is also stress on filial piety in the inscriptions at Lungmen, indicating that Buddhism was taking root in Chinese culture and advocating virtues long cherished by the Chinese.[31]

There were many times during Buddhism's first five

hundred years in China when its future seemed quite uncertain. It is clear that emperors during that period, as well as later rulers down to the present day, have seen in Buddhism and any organized religion a political threat; but it is also clear that Buddhists knew when and how to "lay low," and also how to win their way into court circles and into the imperial family itself. The Mahayana forms of Buddhism were especially suited to cross-culture missionary endeavor, due to their flexibility in doctrine, structure, and prescriptions for day-to-day living. Thus, initial Chinese objections were blunted, the scriptures were translated, Chinese art forms were utilized to blend with Indian and Central Asian forms, and Buddhism slowly became a permanent part of the Chinese cultural milieu.

Buddhist Thought and Life in China

In introducing Mahayana Buddhism, two schools of thought were discussed: Madhyamika, or the School of the Void; and Yogacara, the Consciousness Only School. In spite of their highly theoretical character, both schools had considerable following in China before the ninth century and their influence continues to the present, but neither school was known for distinctive practices except, of course, for meditation. Other schools of thought *and* life, in which doctrine was accompanied by practice, developed in China and won much greater followings among the people. Since even these schools do not flourish in China as they once did, we will only introduce them in this section, and leave fuller discussion for the section on Buddhism in Japan, a country in which several of the schools are very much alive today.

T'ien T'ai. The T'ien T'ai School derives its name from a mountain in Chekiang Province called T'ien T'ai, meaning "Heavenly Terrace," where a man named Chih-i established his new teaching. As a small child, Chih-i was impressed with the truth of the Buddhist doctrine of impermanence when he came upon a library that had been destroyed by soldiers. This experience probably led him to become a monk, after which he studied under a famous teacher in Nanking, and then went on to T'ien T'ai mountain where he established the school. He expressed another deeply Buddhist conviction when he persuaded fishermen at the foot of the mountain to give

up catching and therefore killing fish. He even persuaded the Emperor, who had already turned over tax revenues in the district to Chih-i's work, to ban fishing in the entire area.

Chih-i, who lived from 538–597 C.E., and therefore into the Sui Dynasty that marked the beginning of Buddhism's great era in China, attempted to bring some kind of order into the many variations of Buddhist throught during this period. His first approach was to fit Buddhist teachings into five stages, in such a way that each stage fulfilled and advanced what had gone before. As might be expected, his own T'ien T'ai teaching was the summit and final fulfillment of all that had preceded. Another approach of his was to compare methods of teaching, such as abrupt versus gradual. Then he compared the content of various doctrines, setting up a classification of doctrines in terms of the capacity of different groups to hear and understand: earlier followers could understand the simpler Theravada; the more advanced bodhisattvas could grasp a special doctrine.

Chih-i based his teaching on the Lotus Sutra, in which a great assembly of Buddhas and bodhisattvas proclaim that all creatures will be saved. This doctrine of universal salvation, coupled with a theory that universal truth includes and comprehends all temporary truth, culminates in the ultimate unity of all things. From the truth of temporary existence, and the middle truth that things both exist and do not exist, Chih-i went on to the final truth that all is one, that all moments of existence inhere in a grain of sand, suggesting that all life is caught up in one moment of life. One realizes this through insight resulting from intense concentration, the primary form of practice in the T'ien T'ai School.

Hua Yen. The Hua Yen or "Flower Garland" School, so-called because it is based on the *Flower Garland* (*Hua Yen*) *Sutra*, is so similar to T'ien T'ai that it may be treated quite briefly. Several monks are associated with its beginnings, but Fa Tsang (643–712 C.E.) is regarded as the founder. The son of non-Chinese parents, he was born and reared in Ch'angan and later worked in the translation bureau there. He had a unique opportunity to explain his Hua Yen teaching to the Empress Wu Tse-t'ien, and chose two impressive similes to illustrate the ultimate unity of all things.

Fa Tsang first pointed to the statue of a golden lion

and raised a number of questions about it that we will only summarize. The first question basically is: What are we looking at? Our natural inclination is to say that it is a lion, but we know that it is not really a lion. We are looking at a hunk of gold sculpted to resemble a lion. Since the principle of a lion cannot be seen unless it takes shape and form, the gold with which it takes form is very important. Gold, in turn, must have some guiding principle if it is to take meaningful form. And so the discussion proceeds, Fa Tsang making the point that you cannot have one without the other, that principle and form are completely wrapped up together.

His second illustration for the Empress was actually a demonstration. Fa Tsang placed a Buddha image in the middle of a hall and then placed eight mirrors in an octagonal pattern around the image. The result was not only that the image could be seen in each mirror; in each mirror could be seen the image in every other mirror. To Fa Tsang's satisfaction, and to the delight of the Empress, this clearly demonstrated the interrelatedness of all things, that every moment of reality is present in another. All moments of existence can be found in a grain of dust.

The Hua Yen School also had a theory of the developing stages of Buddhist doctrine, and, as might be expected, Hua Yen teaching was the fulfillment and summation of all the previous stages with their schools. Hua Yen actually went further than T'ien T'ai in relating various phenomena to each other, but the sense of ultimate unity remained essentially the same. The practice of meditation, as in T'ien T'ai, is the way one realizes the ultimate truth.

Pure Land. The name *Ching T'u Tsung* translates into English as the "Pure Land School" and indicates precisely the idea of the school: that there is a Pure Land to which one may be transported at death. The names of many early leaders might be noted, but the stories of three in particular may be mentioned. Tradition regards Hui-yuan as the founder, but the first or founding monk was T'an-luan (476–542 C.E.) who, after a serious illness, had a vision of a heavenly gate that prompted him to seek immortality, first in Taoism, which had several methods that appeared promising. He found satisfaction, however, in what an Indian monk told him of the Buddha Amitabha and proceeded to spread the teach-

ing of faith in Amitabha's vow and the recitation of homage or praise to that Buddha. Another monk, Tao-ch'o (562–645 C.E.), was greatly inspired by T'an-luan's teaching, and emphasized that calling on Amitabha was an easy path that would help people living in an evil age to overcome all evil and be reborn in Amitabha's paradise.

Perhaps the greatest Pure Land master was Shan-tao (613–681 C.E.), who maintained that the Western Paradise was not a dream world, but very real and available to the most ordinary human beings. He did everything possible to promote the teaching and practice of the school: copied and distributed Pure Land sutras, painted pictures of the Paradise, preached to monks and laypeople in the capital of Ch'angan, and encouraged the singing of praises to Amitabha.

The central teaching and practice of the Pure Land School have already been indicated. The Pure Land sutras teach that the Buddha Amitabha (*A-Mi-T'o-Fo* in Chinese), Lord of the Pure Land or Western Paradise, has vowed to save all beings who call upon him with sincere faith and devotion. A person who says sincerely, "*Nan-wu A-Mi-T'o-Fo,*" ("Praise to Amitabha Buddha"), may expect, indeed may be sure, that he or she at death will be reborn immediately in the Pure Land. What is promised is salvation by faith in a Buddha who graciously receives all in a paradise depicted as a beautiful heaven, whose sights and sounds stand in stark contrast to the sorrows and struggles of this life.

Both doctrine and practice are easily grasped and followed and the common people responded to this simple and direct road to salvation. Many so-called intellectuals and highly trained monks were also attracted, along with illiterate peasants, for those who could read the sutras and discuss highly theoretical teachings often grew impatient and longed for such an unashamedly direct and immediate way to truth and peace. Consequently, the Pure Land School has had the largest number of followers in China, virtually from the time of its origin to the present day.

Ch'an—The Meditation School. "Meditation" is an accurate translation of *ch'an* (*zen* in Japanese), and although meditation is the prevailing practice in the Ch'an School, much more is involved than meditation itself. For the outsider looking in, the problem is to determine what this "something more" is, for the Ch'an masters do not explain what is believed or what is going on. Their role is to direct their student-disciples to discover for themselves what Ch'an is all about, and they do this by methods differing from the traditional ones.

A man named Bodhidharma, reputed to have brought Ch'an from India to China around 500 C.E., demonstrated this penchant for the unusual in his audience with the Emperor. Bodhidharma began by saying that he did not know his own name, proceeded to evaluate the Emperor's good deeds as having no particular merit, and, in response to a question about Buddhist *dharma,* said categorically that the *dharma* was empty. He then proceeded to retire to a monastery where he spent nine years meditating with his face to the wall. The report that his legs dropped off, like other elements in the story, might be legendary or might be true!

This strange story does indicate that the concept of emptiness or void is central to Ch'an, as it is to almost every Buddhist school. It is important to "empty the mind," to get rid of all distracting thoughts from past or present, and even to get away from the habit of logical, discursive reasoning. Lines attributed to Bodhidharma suggest the reason for this breaking away:

A special transmission outside the scriptures;
No dependence upon words and letters;
Direct pointing to the [nature] of man;
Seeing into the nature and attainment of Buddhahood.[32]

By going beyond the scriptures (the monks knew them already), a person with a completely clear mind would be able to penetrate reality and understand human nature, including one's own nature, for what it is—the Buddha-nature. This much we can say: Ch'an discipline aims at the discovery of the Buddha-nature within.

The methods used by the Ch'an masters are meant to shock. There are *koans* (riddle-like questions) to solve, such as "Where was your face before you washed it this morning?" and "What is the sound of one hand clapping?" If a student's question is too rational (like "What is the meaning of Buddha-*dharma?*"), the master may answer with a nonsequitur or nonresponsive reply: "It is so windy this morning." And then there are the physical blows, "to knock the sense *out of*" the student. This is the way of "no-mind," of emptiness leading to clarity—and realization of the truth.

The four schools we have introduced have survived in China and have continued with significant strength in Japan. The Chinese group them as follows: T'ien T'ai and Hua Yen for content; Pure Land and Ch'an for practice. One must remember that the lines between them are not sharply drawn, that adherence to one school may not be a lifetime affair, and that a single individual or a family may actually express devotion at more than one temple during one period of time. There have been times when tension or antagonism has prevailed between different schools, but a rather easy-going mutual acceptance has generally prevailed.

Developments in the Monastic Order and Among the Laity

The practice of Buddhism in China has brought monks and laity more closely together than in the Theravada countries. Some Buddhist temples and monasteries were located in rather remote places and therefore visited by lay persons only at times of pilgrimage, whereas others were so situated to serve as convenient hostels for travelers. These were places of continuing contacts between monks and lay persons nonetheless, which was even more the case in local Buddhist temples, even though many of these were located outside a village or town proper. Thus, the fact that monks were somewhat set apart did not result in the Sangha being separated from the laity in a set, formalistic pattern. The Chinese have been more relaxed in this and many other aspects of the practice of Buddhism.

Monastic Life. The Vinaya discipline was eventually brought from India, but the Chinese followed it somewhat less scrupulously. Monks in China did not observe the earlier tradition of going about with begging bowls at the break of day, but have made a ceremonial round each year, at which time they may receive cloth for robes, especially the heavier robes for winter, and other necessities. As is the case in other Buddhist countries, Chinese monks did not work the monastic lands; the farming was done by tenant workers. Certain duties around the monastery were done by apprentice monks, but senior and junior monks spent most of their time in study, conducting services, and meditation.

Each monastery and nunnery was essentially an inde-

Calling the Name of the Buddha. *On Langya Mountain in east central China a monk demonstrates ways to ''call the name of Buddha.'' Other youth as well as children had preceded the young man shown above.* (Courtesy of Mary Bush)

by monks in public places served to educate the masses, and the debates that often ensued had an atmosphere of rivalry and contest that drew large crowds. Monks also won considerable fame as storytellers, having endless material from Buddhist scriptures and legends that they could embellish and develop to delight an audience.

It was at times of personal and family crisis that monks rendered their most noteworthy services. By teaching the doctrine of *karma,* they offered an explanation for what happened beyond the grave that was absent from traditional Chinese thought. Monks were invariably called to chant sutras at rites for the dead, and they conducted memorial services or ''masses for the dead'' at certain intervals following a death. Such rituals were believed to provide easier transport through hell and to help an individual attain a better rebirth. The family of the deceased gave gifts to the monks or to a monastery or temple, and this resulted in more merit for the dead person and for members of his family.

Just as there were many devoted monks who followed the discipline strictly, so there were some others who entered the monastery with less than worthy motives. It was fairly easy for a man with a shaved head and a black or grey robe to escape service in the military or in a forced labor battalion, or to escape the consequences of an alleged or actual crime. The responsibility for examining those who made monastic vows belonged to the abbot of a monastery or to the senior monks. Considerable knowledge of the Buddhist scriptures had to be demonstrated in these examinations, so that candidates who were not serious had to be very clever or had to be lucky enough to encounter an examiner who did not take his task seriously. But the majority of monks and nuns were men and women of great piety, intellect, and devotion. Those who gave the monastery a bad name were definitely a minority and were most apparent in times of crisis and chaos when monastic life may have been the only hope people had.

Throughout this discussion we have made only a few references to nuns, but their discipline and way of life was just as rigorous as that of their male counterparts. Their reasons or motivations for entering the sisterhood were as many and as varied as those of the monks. They also served vegetarian food and ministered to people in difficulty, particularly women who had no place to go or live. One of their most valued contributions was

pendent unit. The abbot who served as head of a particular monastery was elected by the monks around him, and was not responsible to any higher authority. The government had to approve those monasteries that had the power to ordain monks, and thus had to approve the abbot chosen by the monks. Monks known for their scholarship and knowledge of Buddhist texts and doctrine were also highly honored and exercised leadership in the education of younger monks. The abbot assigned monks and lay assistants to their respective duties and generally supervised the total life and operation of the institution. Since a number of monks traveled from monastery to monastery, and laymen also went on pilgrimages from time to time, a monastery was often a very busy place. An atmosphere of peace and serenity seems to have prevailed, however, and these institutions were havens of rest for a wide variety of people.

Monks undoubtedly had contact with the secular world in many important ways. In spite of their remote locations, mountain temples and monasteries provided food and lodging for weary travelers; some monks became specialists in the preparation of vegetarian food and others in the general supervision of such places. Lectures given the establishment of "vegetarian halls" where elderly women who had no family or who were destitute might retire in the closing years of their lives. The women who entered such halls gave their meager savings to the nun in charge and then joined the community on a share-and-share-alike basis, having only the bare essentials of food, clothing, and shelter, and being held together by allegiance to the Buddhist way.

Life Among the Laity. The response of the laity to the monastic communities of monks and nuns in China had been one of appreciation and respect. The laity has traditionally provided generous support for the monastic order, from major gifts by the wealthy of land and buildings, which have provided income for monasteries of great size, to small cash and in-kind gifts from ordinary people. Since such gifts were believed to gain merit for the givers and their families, they were not due entirely to charitable impulses.

The fact that the majority of Chinese lay people were attracted to the Pure Land School with its devotion to the Buddha Amitabha has been noted in a previous section. Equally prominent in lay Buddhist life has been devotion to the Bodhisattva Kuan Yin, whose image came to China from India as a male figure, who was represented in both male and female forms in earlier centuries, and who later was depicted almost universally as female. This gracious Chinese lady's full name is Kuan Shih Yin P'usa (meaning "Hearing World's Cries Bodhisattva"). When the word for praise is prefixed and the word for "world" dropped, the result is a standard temple chant: "*Nanwu Kuan Yin P'usa,*" or "Praise to the Kuan Yin Bodhisattva." She receives the entreaties of women who desire children or easier childbirth, protection for husbands far away, and success for children facing exams or suffering from illness. She thus symbolizes the bodhisattva spirit of compassion and sacrifice for others.

Although some lay Buddhists have not been strictly vegetarian, the more serious among them have regarded "not eating meat" as the mark of a true Buddhist. Special Buddhist celebrations, such as the Buddha's birthday, require vegetarian meals, and traditional Chinese restaurants always included vegetarian dishes.

Lay Buddhist associations became a prominent feature of Buddhist life in China. Although in earlier periods

Three Buddhas on a Chinese Altar. *The typical altar of a Chinese Buddhist temple contains three images, the chief one being in the middle. Other Buddha images are situated in front of the three who form the focal point; still others may be placed elsewhere in the temple.* (Courtesy of Mary Bush)

separate lay organizations for men and women were the pattern, the more recent tendency has been to have one all-inclusive Chinese Buddhist Association (CBA) in most Chinese cities, especially in Hong Kong, Taiwan, and Southeast Asia. The CBA sponsors special events; lectures by outstanding Buddhist scholars and leaders; solicitation of funds for Buddhist schools, orphanages and hospitals; and various services for the poor and disadvantaged.

Participation by women in either a laywoman's organization or in an association of men and women has represented a departure from traditional Chinese cultural patterns. The presence of an order of nuns, though it provoked opposition similar to that provoked by the male order, introduced a new and respected role for women in China, which in turn encouraged more active participation by laywomen. Since this participation brought them out into society more than had been the case, it can be said that Buddhism provided an outlet for women's activity beyond traditional female roles in Chinese society. In the latter part of the seventh century, for example, a woman came to the Chinese throne, which was not sanc-

Kuan Yin Shrine near Hong Kong. *Wandering along a footpath on one of the smaller islands in the Hong Kong group, one finds this small shrine to Kuan Yin. It is only about twelve feet square. Although no village or house is in sight, there are signs of daily use.* (Courtesy of Richard Bush)

tioned according to the Chinese Confucian tradition. Buddhist advisers to Empress Wu found in a sutra the statement of the Buddha to a goddess that she would be reborn as a great monarch; the advisers suggested that the Empress was undoubtedly the reincarnation of the Buddha Maitreya, and therefore her rule was authenticated. Buddhism did not again raise Chinese women to such a high rank, but it has been responsible for advancing the role of women in various ways, particularly in modern times when some of its leaders have been women.

Triumph and Persecution. After five hundred years of uncertainty, Buddhism finally came into its own in China. The developments that have been described in these pages reached their height in the Sui (581–618 C.E.) and T'ang (618–907 C.E.) dynasties. The patterns of thought and life, the schools that formulated and promulgated these patterns, and the monastic order and lay communities had become a part of the Chinese scene. The result was that Sui rulers espoused Buddhism, and early T'ang rulers, though officially Taoist, for the most

Chinese Buddha Image. *A typical Chinese Buddha image radiates an impressive dignity and calm in the Han Shan Temple in Suchou, a beautiful old city in east central China.* (Courtesy of Mary Bush)

part supported and encouraged the religion from India.

Beginning with the emperors of the Sui Dynasty, and continuing into the T'ang, magnificent Buddhist temples and monasteries were erected, largely with imperial patronage. A distinctive architectural style identified with the T'ang emerged in these temples and in other buildings as well, accompanied by a distinctive style in the sculptures placed in the temples. New sculptures were added to the Lungmen caves, mentioned earlier in the chapter. Buddhist festivals held at these temples became extremely colorful and involved vast numbers of the people.

Developments that enhanced Buddhist life emerged during these two dynasties. One of the Sui emperors arranged for groups of monks to go out as missionaries of the *dharma,* and the travels of these missionary monks went beyond China to Korea and Japan. Two great Chinese pilgrims went to India in the seventh century: Hsüan Tsang by the overland silk route from 629–645 C.E., and I-Tsing by the sea route from 671–689 C.E. Both these famous monks brought back texts from India to add to the growing number that were being translated. During the T'ang Dynasty a voluminous catalogue of these translations was issued.

Many of the T'ang emperors supported and encouraged the development and spread of Buddhism. A number of them actually became Buddhist, including the Empress Wu, who did much for Buddhism in return for the authentication of her reign provided by Buddhist monks. Earlier T'ang emperors were extremely tolerant, welcoming to the capital at Ch'angan other religions from afar. Manichaeism, emphasizing the struggle between light and darkness, was brought from Persia. Nestorian Christianity, a movement in the early Eastern Christian tradition, was also in Ch'angan by the seventh century. Neither of these movements survived for more than a hundred years or so, although Christianity was to return in the thirteenth and sixteenth centuries. Islam also entered China at this time, and remains to this day as a religious and cultural minority in that nation, particularly in some of the Autonomous Regions.

The evidence clearly suggests that T'ang Dynasty China was one of the great cosmopolitan empires of any part of the world at any time in history. In spite of its rulers' favorable attitude toward several different religions, the T'ang Dynasty proved to be a watershed for Buddhism. In the eighth century emperors continued to erect magnificent temples, but they also began to issue decrees restricting Buddhism: many monks were ordered back to lay occupations; monastery lands were reduced in size; entrance into the Sangha was restricted; and the remaining monks were prohibited from preaching and selling sacred objects in public. These inhibiting actions were not enforced strictly, but they were a sign of more serious things to come. The vast wealth of Buddhist monasteries, primarily due to gifts from earlier emperors, provoked great envy and resentment by rulers and people, and undoubtedly led to these oppressive measures and to the full-scale persecution to come.

Regardless of the religion favored by any Chinese emperor, the philosophical base for the administration of government in China was set forth by Confucius and his disciples, whom we will discuss in the following chapter. Through the years the Confucian scholar class had looked with disdain on religion, and this attitude intensified from the eighth century onward with a movement called Neo-Confucianism, which stressed the rational side of Confucian teaching. Confucianism old and new was deeply infused with religious thought and practice, as we will see, but the Confucians did not acknowledge their own religiousness, and regarded both Buddhism and Taoism as threats to the imperial order. Buddhism came under attack in the early ninth century in part because it was a foreign religion, and soon afterward it received a telling setback.

In 844 C.E., after decades of Neo-Confucian and Taoist criticism and ridicule, the government acted. Officials confiscated thousands of Buddhist images, many of which were melted down into coins. Almost 5,000 monasteries and some 40,000 temples and shrines were destroyed. By the following year, some 250,000 monks and nuns were forced to become lay persons. Monastic lands were confiscated, which meant much greater tax income for the government. The emperor who instituted the persecution died in 846, and later emperors lightened the burden on the Buddhists, but Buddhism never regained the greatness it had experienced in the seventh and eighth centuries. It must be acknowledged that the religion had already lost some of its earlier vitality, but the persecution clearly meant the end of Buddhist pre-eminence in China.

Buddhism was in its ascendancy in China until at least the middle of the T'ang Dynasty; from that point it entered a period of decline. Since that turning point there have been great monks and lay persons in the Chinese Buddhist community whose achievements have been noteworthy, but a static situation generally has prevailed. Buddhism has continued to influence society, art, and literature in China, and must surely take some satisfaction in the fact that several of the great Neo-Confucians were deeply influenced by Buddhism, despite their vigorous and at times ill-informed attacks against it.

Buddhism in Japan

The sixth to the ninth centuries C.E., the period when Buddhism enjoyed triumph and suffered persecution in China, was precisely the period when it took root and began to be an integral part of life in Japan.

Buddhism was already a thousand years old when it entered Japan, having assimilated influences from the religions of China and from many facets of Chinese culture. The pantheon of Buddhas and bodhisattvas could easily be interpreted to include many of the indigenous Japanese gods who were worshiped in Shinto, an indigenous Japanese religion to be discussed in the following chapter. Buddhism also had an elaborate set of beliefs that dealt with salvation, life after death, and moral conduct, ideas neglected in the older Japanese tradition. The new Buddhist ideas and the practices that accompanied them were readily accepted by the Japanese people.

There were other reasons why Buddhism received a more hospitable reception in Japan than it did in China. After five hundred years in China, Buddhism had developed a magnificent tradition in art and architecture that appealed to Japanese aesthetic tastes. The monks in China and in Korea, through which Buddhism passed on its way to Japan from China, also wore vivid saffron robes and brought beautifully carved statues to adorn the temples where they chanted their sutras. Buddhism, coming as a part of the Chinese culture that was to have such a profound influence on Japan, thus appealed to the Japanese for aesthetic and cultural reasons, as well as in terms of religious beliefs and practices.

Early Developments

The sixth century C.E. was a period of great change all over East Asia. After more than three centuries of disunity, China was united under the Sui Dynasty in 589 C.E.; this unity was continued in the T'ang with a great flowering of religion and culture, as we have seen in the preceding section. During the Sui and the first half of T'ang, Chinese culture in general and Chinese Buddhism in particular had a major impact on East Asia. Chinese culture had already spread to the southern tip of Korea by the fifth century; since the Japanese and Koreans were in contact through travel and trade, Bud-

dhism gradually moved on to Japan. Buddhism was officially introduced into Japan in 552 C.E. when the King of the Korean kingdom of Paekche sent gifts to the Emperor of Japan, including a Buddha image, sacred texts, banners, and several ritual instruments. The message that the Korean king sent with his mission is a candid expression of appreciation for Buddhism:

> This doctrine [Buddhism] is amongst all doctrines the most excellent. But it is hard to explain, and hard to comprehend. . . . This doctrine can create religious merit and retribution without measure and without bound, and so lead on to a full appreciation of the highest wisdom. . . . From distant India it has extended higher to the great Han [China] where there are none who do not receive it with reverence as it is preached to them.[33]

This message and the accompanying works of art greatly impressed the Japanese Court, but the Court was divided into two camps over the question as to whether Buddhas and bodhisattvas were more powerful than the national gods. The debate raged for the first fifty years of Buddhism in Japan, with the new religion favored and then out of favor. Korea sent more gifts, artists, physicians, and missionary monks bearing Buddhist texts. Finally the pro-Buddhist Soga clan defeated the anti-Buddhist clans in 587 C.E. and built a temple at state expense to commemorate the event. The Emperor himself had an asylum, a hospital, and a dispensary built in connection with a temple in 593 C.E., and this act was regarded as the establishment of Buddhism in Japan.

Prince Shotoku (574–622 C.E.), who in 593 became the regent for his aunt, the Empress Suiko, became the key figure in the early flowering of Buddhism. One of his first acts was to proclaim the Three Treasures of the Buddha as his teaching, and the Order of Monks as the foundation of the national faith; this was followed by a Seventeen Article Constitution in which he set forth religious beliefs and moral conduct as the basis of government. Prince Shotoku invited learned monks and scholars from Korea to Japan, and, by establishing direct communications with China, made it possible for Japanese monks to study with Buddhist masters in China and bring back their teachings to Japan. He became an avid student of the Buddhist sutras, wrote commentaries that are studied by scholars to this day, built many temples, and supported the efforts of monks to carry the Buddha's teaching to people throughout the provinces. He is still remembered as a great political leader, and is honored in Japan as her greatest Buddhist saint.

Buddhism's next major advance occurred with the establishment of Japan's first permanent capital in 710 C.E. at Nara. In this new city, which was modeled after the Chinese capital of Ch'angan, a process of Buddhist institutionalization took place. Buddhist rituals were adopted for court ceremonies, and court aristocrats were accommodated along with monks in the magnificent temples built at Nara.

In 752 C.E. the Emperor Shomu founded a national temple at Todaiji, and followed this architectural masterpiece with branch temples at other places in the country. When he abdicated the throne, he bowed before the Buddha image at Todaiji and made his vows as a disciple of the Buddha. Although many emperors supported Buddhism with magnificent gifts and devoutly followed the teaching, the Emperor Shomu was the first and only emperor who officially took refuge in the Buddha, the *dharma*, and the Sangha.

As will be noted in the following chapter, the Japanese emperor is believed to be descended from the Shinto gods, chief of whom is Amaterasu, the Sun Goddess. This explains why, of all the emperors, only Shomu became a Buddhist. Nevertheless, a process began in those early days of Buddhism in Japan that has continued with only minimal interruption through the centuries, namely the accommodation of Buddhism to Shinto and of Shinto to Buddhism. Since the older gods in the Shinto framework were believed to be bodhisattvas and helpers of the Buddha, Buddhist altars were set up in Shinto shrines, or a Buddhist temple and Shinto shrine were placed side by side. In any case Buddhist monks, as well as Shinto priests, were given assignments by the government; most of the time they got along together reasonably well, since (for the most part) Shinto priests handled matters related to daily life while Buddhist monks took care of the rites for the dead.

Doctrine and Practice in the Japanese Buddhist Schools

Chinese Buddhist schools had made their way to Japan by the seventh century C.E. Theravada emphases were to be found in three of the early schools, including one that focused on rules and regulations for monks, and

Japanese Buddhist Pagoda. *The graceful lines of this pagoda in Kyoto, Japan, appear to rise out of the earth like the trees around it. The blending of art forms with nature characterizes both Buddhist and Shinto structures in Japan. (Courtesy of Mary Bush)*

therefore was important for the beginnings of the Sangha in Japan. The philosophical schools of the Void and of Consciousness Only, called *Sanron* and *Hosso* respectively in Japanese, also entered Japan in the seventh century C.E. One should remember that these two were schools of thought only and had not developed cultic practices. The Hua Yen School, discussed briefly in the previous section, was brought to Japan later. The school's name is *Kegon* in Japanese, but the teaching of ultimate unity, encompassing other schools as stages leading up to Hua Yen and claiming that all *dharmas* can be found in a grain of dust, continues what had been taught in China.

Tendai. Gradually the Buddhist schools that involved both doctrine and practice were brought from China to Japan. One of the first was the T'ien T'ai School, discussed in the previous section, which has a similar sounding name, *Tendai*, in Japanese. This school's introduction to Japan was in part a reaction to the politicizing of Buddhism in that country, which accompanied the appointment of Buddhist monks to high political office in

Nara. The daughter of the Emperor Shomu, for example, had appointed a Buddhist monk as her chief minister and would have abdicated the throne in his favor if conservative forces had not interfered. Political power for the monks apparently led to corruption. All of this political involvement provoked a full-scale reaction and resulted in the moving of the capital to Hiei, where the new Emperor Kammu attempted to reform and purify the Buddhist movement. He sent two monks to China in the hope that they might study and bring back texts and new insights for the reform and purification of Buddhism in Japan. Saicho, the first of these monks, returned with the T'ien T'ai teaching, and the Tendai School was soon established in Japan.

Saicho (767–822 C.E.) had actually established a small temple at Mount Hiei six years before the transfer of the capital, and then came to enjoy the patronage of the emperor Kammu, who had sent Saicho to China in 804. At T'ien T'ai, the Heavenly Terrace, Saicho studied the doctrines of universal salvation as taught in the Lotus Sutra and the stages of truth culminating in the teaching he was to adopt. When he returned to Japan he established a monastery on Mount Hiei that became the center for the Tendai School. At this "Center for the Protection of the Nation," novices were required to study and follow monastic disciplines for twelve years so that Japan would be served by moral and devout monks.

Saicho, following Chih-i's classification, understood Buddhist thought as proceeding through five stages. The first stage was Hua Yen, the Chinese School already taught in Japan. Since Hua Yen was understood by few people, the Buddha taught standard Theravada doctrines as a second stage. Then came general Mahayana, the third stage, teaching of the Void as a fourth stage, and Saicho's own school, Tendai, as the fifth stage and culmination.

There were three types or levels of meditation: first, a direct and intensive method of meditation was designed to lead monks directly to a grasp of the ultimate realm of truth; second, a gradual approach to meditation for the laity began with relatively easy practices and then involved such people in more and more difficult exercises; and, third, a combination of the first two, again adapted to the capacity of the people involved. Another example of Saicho's all-inclusiveness was his provision for activities for lay people. The twelve-year program in the mon-

astery for monks was most severe and was enforced strictly, but the laity were encouraged to meditate according to their capacity and to engage in service to their fellow human beings as their station in life allowed. In such ways as these, Saicho hoped to make Tendai a doctrine and a way of life for all people.

Shingon. Saicho did not have the field to himself. The Emperor Kammu died in 806 C.E., which was the same year that another monk returned from China. Kukai had been sent to China for the same reasons as Saicho; but he was a man of different temperament and studied a different doctrine, an esoteric school of thought and practice that came to an end in China by the eighth century C.E., but that flourished in Japan and continues in Japan to the present day. The Chinese used the names *Mi Tsung* ("Esoteric School") or *Chen Yen* ("True Word") for this Buddhist movement; the Japanese accepted the latter idea of the True Word and therefore called the movement *Shingon.*

Kukai (774–835 C.E.) is known for having written a comparative study of Confucianism, Taoism, and Buddhism in which he concluded that Buddhism was superior to the two Chinese systems of thought and practice. With the patronage of Kammu's successor, Kukai established a monastery on Mount Koya and soon was in competition with Saicho. The two men seem to have been very cordial and cooperative at first, with Saicho actually eager to learn any new truth that Kukai might have to teach. However, at one point Kukai sent an arrogant letter to Saicho, asserting that if Saicho wanted to study esoteric Buddhism he would have to come to Mount Koya as a beginning student. Saicho, of course, was deeply hurt and died a bitter man, while Kukai went on to greater things.

Kukai's thought resembled Saicho's to the extent that Kukai also set up a series of stages in the development of insight into the truth, except that Kukai's scheme has ten stages. His beginning stage is one of animal passion with no doctrine at all; it is followed by the teachings of Confucius and Lao Tzu, the Chinese sages, and then by two schools of Indian philosophy. The fourth through the ninth stages are Buddhist schools, ranging from two Theravada movements through Consciousness Only and the Void up to Tendai and Kegon (Chinese Hua Yen). The final stage of course is Shingon.

Central to Shingon is belief in the Buddha Vairocana, the cosmic Buddha of Light. All creatures and things, including other Buddhas, are nothing but manifestations of this universal Buddha who is himself the limitless cosmos. One wonders how anyone could grasp so vast a concept, which is the point at which the esoteric element comes into play. The hiddenness of the Buddha-reality, the mystery that cannot be expressed directly, is revealed through symbols of speech, body, and mind that suggest the hidden mystery, and therefore are called the "Three Great Mysteries."

Remembering that *Shingon* means "True Word," it is not surprising that the most important "mystery" is conveyed by speech. In this instance, speech takes the form of a *mantra,* which is a word or phrase or just a sound that conveys hidden meaning to those whose minds are capable of understanding. The mystery of the body is represented by various finger and hand intertwinings called *mudras,* as when one symbolically indicates meditation by placing the right hand on top of the left hand with the tips of the thumbs touching. The mystery of the mind is expressed in a picture called a *mandala,* which shows the Buddha surrounded by other Buddhas, bodhisattvas, or sacred objects such as a lotus flower. Two very famous *mandalas* in Shingon are the Diamond Mandala, which shows the Buddha Vairocana in the center and expresses the dynamic element of reality, and the Womb Mandala, with a red lotus flower in the center symbolizing the static aspect of reality. It must be emphasized that one must be initiated into Shingon and its ways of thinking before one can understand what the symbols reveal.

Both hand gestures and mystic sounds are employed in a fire ceremony called *goma,* in which an awesome beauty prevails. Another ceremony involves pouring water over the head of an individual as an aid to attaining Buddhahood. With all this attention to symbols, movement, and art forms, Shingon has sparked many developments in Japanese art. Particularly in the areas of painting and sculpture, music, and literature, it is easy to see expressions of Kukai's conviction that anything beautiful expresses the nature of the Buddha.

After the death of Kukai, the Shingon School joined the Tendai School in a period of decline and deterioration. Leaders of both movements became corrupt as the temples became engaged in struggles for power and land-holdings. Monks added military skills to their competence as priests in order to defend their temples and monasteries, but then began to strike back offensively, and Japan was treated to the sorry spectacle of armies of soldier-monks fighting each other and sacking "enemy" temples. The civil government was growing weaker at the same time, so that provincial military forces were summoned as a last resort. The chaos did not come to an end until 1185 C.E., when a new military government was established in the city of Kamakura.

The Pure Land School in Japan. Practices of the popular Pure Land School could be found in Japan as early as the seventh century C.E. Some of the more eclectic Tendai teachers included references to the Western Paradise from time to time, particularly when appealing to the masses. The appeal of the Pure Land School to a wide range of people is based on the same doctrinal base that had been presented to the people of China: the vow of the Buddha Amitabha, called *Amida* in Japan, to give all who call on him in faith the gift of salvation—rebirth in the Pure Land. Several Pure Land leaders in Japan gave this message a powerful expression in preaching, writing, and colorful practice in their temples; but two men in particular, Honen and Shinran, are credited with making Pure Land Buddhism a faith for the remotest villages of Japan.

When Honen (1133–1212 C.E.) was eight years of age, his father was killed by bandits; but as his father lay dying, he begged Honen to become a monk rather than seeking revenge. Thus, an experience that could have made him bitter for life led Honen to enter monastic training in the Shingon tradition at Mount Hiei five years later. He soon became disturbed by the political and religious corruption of his day, including that at Mount Hiei, and was convinced that monastic discipline was not the way. He learned to say *"Namu Amida Butsu,"* which means "Praise to Amida Buddha," and then concluded that the *"Nembutsu"* (a shortened formulation) was superior to all other ways of attaining salvation. Perhaps the chief reason was that everyone was included in Amida's vow:

There shall be no distinction, no regard to male or female, good or bad, exalted or lowly; none shall fail to be in His Land of Purity after having called, with complete desire, on Amida. Just as a bulky boulder may pass over the sea, if loaded on a ship, and accomplish a voyage of myriads of leagues without sinking; so we, though our sin be heavy as stone, are borne on the ship of Amida's primeval vow and cross to the other shore without sinking in the sea of repeated births and deaths.[34]

Honen abandoned all philosophical teachings and the rituals of Shingon and Tendai as useless; all that was needed was saying the *Nembutsu*—"Praise to Amida Buddha"—with sincere faith and simple devotion. Others had taught this, but not with the inspiration and winsomeness of Honen, known as "the bald man with the warm heart." He attracted not only the common people, but also monks and nuns, royalty and nobility alike, attracting so many followers that the leaders in the older Buddhist centers rose in opposition and attacked him in various ways. When his disciples converted two Court ladies to saying the *Nembutsu,* and these women later became nuns, Honen and his followers were charged with seduction; and he and his chief "seducers" were banished. The exile began in 1207 C.E. when Honen was seventy-four. Because the exile seemed to bring more followers to share his faith in Amida, he was allowed to return after four years. He died a year later while reciting the *Nembutsu* and a poem about Amida, whose light, it is said, shines in all directions and whose grace is always available to anyone who calls on his name.

Shinran (1173–1262 C.E.) had become a monk at the age of twenty-eight, but found monastic discipline difficult to follow, and was soon attracted to Honen's teaching. He was one of those in exile with Honen and never ceased to respect the man who had led him to faith in Amida. Shinran apparently said once that he did not really know whether saying the *Nembutsu* led to the Pure Land or to hell, but even if Honen's advice to call upon Amida led him to hell he would have no regrets.

As it happened, Shinran did begin to question the stress that Honen and most of his followers put on saying the *Nembutsu,* and proceeded to the conclusion that even the saying of *"Namu Amida Butsu"* was made possible by the grace of Amida. In fact, Shinran said, the stress on *saying* anything, even the *Nembutsu,* constituted dependence on human action rather than on faith in Amida's grace, or trusting in Self-power rather than Other-power. His disciples later recalled Shinran saying:

Whether sage or fool, whether good or bad, we have simply to give up the idea of estimating our own qualities or of depending upon self. Though entangled in sin and depravity, even in living the life of the most despised outcast, we are embraced by the all-pervading light of grace; indefatigable faith in salvation itself is a manifestation of Buddha's act of embracing us into His grace, because nothing can impede the working of His grace.

Nothing is required except to accept Amida without question. The Nembutsu is neither practice nor virtue to one who practices it. As it is not practiced through one's own will or power, it is no practice; as it is not virtue perfected by one's own will or power, it is no virtue. It solely arises from the Other Power and has nothing to do with Self-Power.[35]

To demonstrate that he was not dependent for salvation on his own actions, such as the keeping of monastic discipline for salvation, Shinran married and had a family. His unprecedented step opened the way for others to follow his example, but his marriage also provoked such outrage from religious and political authorities that he was sent into exile with Honen. As was the case with Honen, exile meant that Shinran came into contact with numerous ordinary people who decided to follow his teaching. He thus became even more convinced that monastic discipline was useless and that faith in Amida was the only way to salvation. Shinran's marriage proved to be a model for increasing numbers of Buddhist monks in Japan, from the Pure Land and other schools, to the extent that a married clergy has become quite common, a point that distinguishes Japanese Buddhism from other countries in the Buddhist world.

As a result of Shinran's radical position, which Honen actually may have advised, two groups began to emerge within the Pure Land movement in Japan. One stems from Honen, stressing the saying of the *Nembutsu* as a sign of faith, and is called *Jodo Shu,* or the "Pure Land School." The other group, deriving from Shinran, emphasizes faith alone, with or without the *Nembutsu,* and is called *Shin Shu,* or the "Faith School." As the closest of friends may have the most intense quarrels, so the two groups have often been vigorous rivals. Nevertheless, cordial relations have generally prevailed, and both groups are now together under the heading of *Jodo Shin Shu,* the "Pure Land Faith School."

Zen—The Meditation School. Like other schools in the Japanese Buddhist framework, Zen had its beginnings as a school in China, where, as we have seen, it was called *Ch'an*. Divisions in the school had already appeared in China and were transmitted to Japan by Eisei (1141–1215 C.E.), who brought the Rinzai sect, and Dogen (1200–1253 C.E.), who introduced the Soto sect.

In our study of Chinese Buddhist schools, we indicated that Ch'an masters attempted to realize the Buddha-nature within by means of striking statements, odd answers to questions, and even physical blows to break down attempts at logical reasoning. Dogen, for example, said he returned from years of study in China empty-handed because he had studied ideas without realizing the truth for himself. A story with the same point is told of Nan-in, a late-nineteenth-century Zen master who received a university professor who had come to ask about Zen. When Nan-in poured a cup of tea for his visitor, he kept pouring until the cup overflowed. The professor pointed out that the cup was overflowing, that there was no more room. Nan-in replied that the professor, like the cup, was full of his own opinions and ideas, and could not understand Zen until he "emptied his cup."

A Zen monastery in Japan is a demanding experience for the clergy for whom it is a way of life, and for the laity who come for a few days or several weeks or months. For those who practice Zen discipline regularly, several hours are spent sitting in meditation every morning. The seated lotus posture, which goes back to ancient Indian yoga, is maintained: legs crossed so that each ankle rests on the opposite thigh, with the body bent slightly forward. Intense concentration is necessary, requiring a functionary to "patrol" those seated in meditation to warn with a noticeable tap on the shoulder those who may be losing their concentration or otherwise be drifting off.

The *Rinzai* sect in particular emphasizes these practices, using *koans* such as "What is the sound of one hand clapping?" *Soto Zen,* in contrast, stresses the idea of realizing the Buddha-nature while "fully functioning" in the normal activities of the day. In spite of such differences, however, both maintain that the ultimate in Zen experience is beyond the power of words to express. Nevertheless, the experience of *satori* (Japanese for "enlightenment") takes place in this life; this in turn makes a difference in the way life continues, whether

in business or manual labor. The distinctive character of *satori* was set forth succinctly by D. T. Suzuki, for many years Japan's most outstanding interpreter of Zen Buddhism for Western readers, when he contrasted *satori* with meditation:

When the mind is so trained as to be able to realize the state of perfect void in which there is not a trace of consciousness left, even the sense of being unconscious having departed, in other words, when all forms of mental activity are swept clean from the field of consciousness which is now like a sky devoid of every speck of cloud, a mere broad expanse of blue, *dhyana* (meditation) is said to have reached its perfection. This may be called ecstasy or trance, but it is not Zen. In Zen there must be a *satori;* there must be a general mental upheaval which destroys the old accumulations of intellectuality and lays down a foundation for a new faith; there must be the awakening of a new sense which will review the old things from an angle of perception entirely and most refreshingly new. In *dhyana* there are none of these things, for it is merely a quieting exercise of the mind. As such it has doubtless its own merits, but Zen ought not to be identified with such *dhyanas.*[36]

The sense of seeing old things or the world in general "from an angle of perception entirely and most refreshingly new" can best be appreciated by noting the ways in which Zen has influenced and penetrated various aspects of Japanese culture. The tea ceremony, in which the very common activities of preparing, serving, and drinking tea are done with quiet simplicity, with special ritual implements, and in a peaceful environment, is a kind of Zen ritual because common things are seen and done in a new light. The Japanese art of flower arranging, in which a single blossom in a simple vase may transcend what is seen in a whole bouquet, is an expression of Zen. The *Noh* drama, short *haiku* poems, portrait painting, and even the code of the *samurai* warrior all illustrate the Zen conviction that beauty or strength of character comes from within. To become aware of that which is within, and to bring it forth in such a way that one looks at life and lives it in a refreshingly new way, is close to the meaning of Zen.

Nichiren Doctrine and Practice. All of the schools of Japanese Buddhism that we have considered to this point had their counterparts in China at one time. With

Japanese Zen Buddhist Garden. *One glance at a Zen Buddhist garden immediately suggests a sense of emptiness. This, in turn, suggests the Void and the experience of "no-mind" that is fundamental to the Zen experience of meditation.* (Courtesy of the Japanese Embassy, San Francisco)

Nichiren Buddhism,* however, a distinctively Japanese school of Buddhism with no counterpart in China enters the scene and therefore deserves special consideration.

Nichiren, a word meaning "Sun Lotus," is the name of the founder and the name of the school based on his teaching. Born in a fisherman's family on the southeast coast of Honshu, Nichiren (1222–1282 C.E.) was sent to a temple at the age of eleven and became a monk at sixteen. He seems to have had doubts about the religion of his time, which probably caused periods of violent illness. He studied Pure Land and Zen without satisfaction, turned to Mount Hiei and Tendai, and left Mount Hiei convinced that the Lotus Sutra and the Tendai School were supreme. Returning to his home temple, he contin-

ued to focus on the Lotus Sutra and at the age of thirty-three proclaimed a new cry of faith, "Homage to the *Lotus Sutra of the Wonderful Law.*"

Convinced that the Lotus Sutra was the final and perfect revelation of the truth, he preached to anyone who would listen. He encountered such opposition, largely owing to his vigorous attacks on other forms of Buddhism, that he moved to Kamakura, the new capital, and became an itinerant preacher. It was a time of chaos heightened by natural disasters, religious strife, and political instability, all of which, Nichiren concluded, was due to the practice of false religion. He singled out Honen as a spirit of hell, claimed that Shingon was the greatest evil threatening the nation, and denounced all Buddhist leaders as traitors and hypocrites. He submitted an essay to the government calling for the suppression of all false religions, the conversion to the unique truth of the Lotus, and the killing of all heretics who resisted. The government was outraged, an angry mob attacked and burned his house, and Nichiren barely escaped. When he returned to Kamakura, the government immediately had him exiled to Izu for two years. When he was allowed to return, more verbal and physical attacks resulted and Nichiren continued to issue inflammatory statements. The arrival of a Mongol envoy demanding tribute in 1268 C.E. seemed to him to confirm his earlier prophecies of a foreign invasion, so that he again petitioned the government to accept his recommendations. The government refused, and Nichiren launched a series of criticisms and again was sent into exile. Released in 1274, he and his disciples settled in a quieter place, Minobu, and there he stayed until his death eight years later.

During his first exile Nichiren came to the clear conviction that Japan was to be the home of true Buddhism and the base for the world-wide propagation of it. On the way to his second period of banishment, he was probably to be executed by the chief of his police escort; but one evening a tremendous light flashed across the sky and most of the guards ran away. Each period of exile, each episode of attacks on him and his attacks on others, only seemed to intensify his conviction that he was chosen for a great mission, that he was a bodhisattva sent to the world in the latter days of the law. After his second exile a seemingly invincible Mongol fleet had to turn back because of a storm, an event that was interpreted as a miraculous sign of his vindication.

---

* Nichiren Buddhism is not to be confused with Nichiren Shoshu, which is a modern movement based on Nichiren's teachings.

He and his followers believed that his sense of mission and his militant approach had been confirmed.

Nichiren's doctrines are based on five principles and three great mysteries. The first of the principles is that the teaching of the Lotus Sutra is the supreme teaching of the Buddha. Secondly, the capacity of individual believers to understand this teaching must be considered. In the third place, the time must be right for preaching the Lotus Sutra, a time that Nichiren saw as *mappo*, the age when the teaching would decline. The fourth principle is that Japan is to be the center from which the Lotus doctrine is to spread around the earth. Finally, the country in which it is preached must be in the *mappo* age, filled with heresy, and yet possess the Lotus Sutra. Japan, for Nichiren, clearly was the place and his time was the *mappo* age.

The first of the three great mysteries is the true object of worship, which reveals that the historical Buddha and the eternal Buddha are one, a central point in Nichiren's doctrine. The second mystery is the recitation of the sacred title of the Lotus Sutra, which as we have noted is "Homage to the *Lotus Sutra of the Wonderful Law*" ("*Namu Myoho Renge Kyo*"). The mere contemplation of truth does not include the social and historical elements that Nichiren regarded as necessary for salvation and that therefore called for the actual saying of the phrase in history and in society. The third mystery is what is called the seat of truth: any time and place where one true follower may be found is by virtue of that follower's presence a time and place where the truth exists.

Further attention should be given to the *mappo* doctrine. Perhaps the most popular version of it, going back to the beginnings of Buddhism, divides time into three ages: a period of a thousand years after the death of the historical Buddha, during which it would be possible to follow his teaching and practice and attain enlightenment; a second period of a thousand years during which there would be no attainment of enlightenment, but only the teaching and practice; and a third period, which might last for 10,000 years and in which there would be retained only the teaching, there being neither practice nor attainment of enlightenment. This third age is the *mappo* age that Nichiren and many who preceded him thought had just begun. The strife and chaos of the eleventh and twelfth centuries C.E. were regarded as signs that the *mappo* age was dawning. Honen, for example, taught that only by relying on Amida Budha could one be saved, whereas Nichiren proclaimed that only by following the Lotus teaching could one be saved during these latter days.

Nichiren practice centers on chanting "*Namu Myoho Renge Kyo*" before an altar holding a copy of the Lotus Sutra on top and flanked by flowers and candles. There may be a statue of Nichiren behind the altar with an image of the historical Buddha behind and above that of Nichiren. A huge *mandala* hangs on the wall behind the images and the altar, providing a colorful and dramatic setting for the worship. The people who assemble follow the rhythm of a drumbeat as they chant the title of the Lotus Sutra, followed by chanting various chapters of the text.

Impressive pilgrimages are made on the anniversary of Nichiren's birthday (October 12) to Minobu (near Tokyo), where he died. The seeking of converts through outdoor preaching, a traditional practice of the Nichiren movement, has now given way to sermons and lectures in meeting halls throughout Japan. This kind of outreach extends far beyond Japan, with a noticeable presence in India and Nepal as well as in the United States.

From the earliest times to the present, Nichiren's disciples have pursued their objectives forcefully and enthusiastically. At various times they have not hesitated to attack other Buddhist groups, as well as the Japanese government, based on Nichiren's conviction that Japan must commit herself to true Buddhism and abandon what he thought were false forms of the faith. This kind of attitude—that there is only one true way and all others are false—has generated one sectarian division after another, a phenomenon in Nichiren Buddhism and in other religious movements in many parts of the world. The identification of this one true faith with Japan as the country whose political institutions would be at the service of the Buddha would seem to imply an identification of religion and the state, but in Nichiren's lifetime and in the movement he founded, the focus on Japan has not meant government favor. The opposite has been the case: the Japanese government at various times has been highly suspicious of Nichiren Buddhism and on occasion has employed repressive measures against it. At such times the followers of Nichiren have had to remember the master's words that enlightenment is experienced

Longevity, Medicine, and Wisdom Buddha Figures. *The figures on the main altar of the Yung He Kung Tibetan Buddhist temple in Peking are the Longevity Buddha, the Medicine Buddha, and the Wisdom Buddha.* (Purchased from Yung He Kung temple shop)

not in some future lifetime or heavenly Pure Land, but on the dirty earth with all of its problems.

The Japanese Contribution to Buddhism

With the rise of Nichiren Buddhism and the various subgroups it has spawned, the basic patterns of Buddhist doctrine and practice in Japan can be seen in relationship to each other. No major schools of any significance emerged after the eventful thirteenth century C.E. when

Nichiren arose to proclaim that Japan was living in the Latter Days of the Law. Although some sectarian rivalry continued, the prevailing tendency has been for Buddhist groups to coexist with attitudes of mutual acceptance of each other and of the indigenous faith of Shinto, whose shrines existed side by side with Buddhist temples. The Tokugawa Shogunate (1600–1868), when Japan was under the control of a military lord or *shogun*, was a time of strict government oversight of all religious activity, but Buddhist life continued nonetheless. And Buddhism has been the soil from which many "new religions" have sprung in the late nineteenth and early twentieth centuries, as we will see in the following chapter.

Japan is the place where one may see most clearly that Buddhism has gradually turned almost 180 degrees from its character at the time of its birth 2,500 years ago. The focus has shifted from an exclusive community of monks to that of a totally inclusive community of monks and laity, and, in fact, to the acceptance of a married clergy. Consequently, the concept of the religious life has changed from a life that can be more effectively lived in a monastery to one that has significance in the common life. Goals have changed from what must be seen as otherworldly to goals that can be attained in this life. Buddhists in Japan have entered actively into society, in fact, they have attempted to reshape it by pioneering in social service programs. And while there has been no lack of outstanding Buddhist thinkers and saints in any Buddhist nation, Japan surely must be singled out for an amazing company of gifted and devoted individuals: Prince Shotoku, Saicho, Kukai, Honen, Shinran, Nichiren, and a host of others. Building on the work of their Indian and Chinese forebears, but alert to challenges and opportunities in Japan, their lives and teachings have been responsible for a living Buddhism that continues tradition but has effected striking changes that are still taking place.

Buddhism in Tibet

The form of Buddhism that dominates the religious life of Tibet has been known by many names: *Vajrayana,* the Diamond Vehicle or the "unbreakable"; *Lamaism,* the religion of the lamas, as the monks in Tibet are called; and *Tantrayana,* the vehicle that emphasizes a method for body, speech, and mind. *Tantrayana* is the most significant term, for it indicates the continuity of the earlier tantric traditions of Hinduism and Buddhism in India with the basic character of Buddhism in Tibet. Because of this continuity, Tibetan Buddhism is often classed under the Mahayana; because of very real differences, it may be seen as a third vehicle, distinct from both Theravada and Mahayana.

Although there is an extensive tantric literature, those who follow the tantric way claim that the methods can be learned only from a teacher. The teacher not only communicates the meaning of the texts, but also engages the student in such a way that the student is awakened to that within him that can become the basis of a vital mystical experience. The word *tantra* means "to weave" and thus suggests action or "getting one's act together." Actions of body, speech, and mind are unique, but complement each other. Among tantric "actions," the meditation or lotus posture, going back to early Buddhism and further back to Indian yoga, is well known to us. There are *mudras,* hand positions, and ritual dances. Speech involves the saying of *mantras,* sacred phrases or even single syllables, as well as the reciting of spells and singing of hymns. These liturgies bring about an emotional release that opens up for a person a state of ecstatic bliss that transcends all knowing and acting. The ultimate tantric "action" is mind control, as the devotee, by a process of concentration in which both that which is terrible and that which is lovely have been faced and overcome, rises to the heights of the void. Bodily postures associated with the last process, that of resisting that which is appealing in its loveliness, have brought considerable notoriety to the Tantrayana, because pictures of Buddhas in sexual union with female bodhisattvas have led monks to seek union with female counterparts. Reformers have had to condemn such practices, and leaders of the movement past and present have maintained that *yab-yum,* the "father-mother" act, is intended to symbolize the union of wisdom and compassion in the one who has attained the highest spiritual levels and is not to be followed literally.

Buddhism entered Tibet in the middle of the seventh century C.E. at a time when Bonism, the indigenous worship of various aspects of nature, had declined in power. Srongtsan-Gampo, the ruler of Tibet at that time, married a princess from Nepal and then later a woman of the Chinese court, both of whom were Buddhists. He sent groups of young men to India to study, but all of the first group died because of the heat. Thonmi, a member of the second group, survived and returned with sacred texts. He became the teacher of the King, and thus had the opportunity to influence the monarch with the teachings of the Buddha. King Srongtsan made re-

Tsongkhapa. *Lamas chant before a huge statue of Tsongkhapa, reformer of Buddhism in Tibet in the fourteenth century C.E. The statue is situated in the Hall of the Prayer Wheel, part of the Yung He Kung or Lama temple in Peking.* (Purchased at Yung He Kung temple shop)

forms in government according to Buddhist principles, prohibiting hunting and killing of animals for sport, and made Buddhism the religion of Tibet.

The early centuries of Buddhism in Tibet, as in China and Japan, were characterized by gradual growth. There were years of struggle with the native Bon religion during the eighth century, with leaders of the local religion claiming that the Tibetan gods were angered by the presence of foreigners teaching an alien religion. Buddhists countered by installing local Tibetan deities as guardians to Buddhas and bodhisattvas and by including indigenous rituals in those imported from India. Both actions strengthened the tantric pattern of Buddhism in Tibet.

This synthesizing of Buddhist and Tibetan piety was the work of two men, Santarakshita and Padmasambhava, who were part of the tantric movement in Buddhism. Padmasambhava in particular was known for having at his command powers by which he could control various spirits. He proceeded to communicate his higher wisdom and advanced powers to an inner circle of monks, who initiated what is known as the Old Translation or Old Tantric School. In addition to Tantric practice, the two leaders also instilled in their followers the philosophy of the Consciousness Only School (discussed on pages (137–138).

The early centuries were also a time when Buddhist sutras were translated from Sanskrit into Tibetan. The basic *Tripitaka* or Three Baskets comprises the first section of the Tibetan canon called the *Kagyur,* which includes, as well, several of the more important tantric writings.

Yung He Kung Complex. *Roof lines of temples in the Yung He Kung complex in Peking appear to intersect and blend against the sky.* (Courtesy of Mary Bush)

The second section, called the *Tangyur,* is a collection of commentaries on sutras and *tantras* by Indian and Tibetan scholars. Then there is a collection of Mahayana literature such as the sutras of the wisdom schools and the School of the Void, the *Bodhicharyavatara,* and so on. Finally there is what might be called a miscellaneous collection of writings by Tibetan scholars, further tantric writings, guides to meditation, and classical stories. *The Great Stages of Enlightenment,* written by the fourteenth-century reformer Tsongkhapa, is an example of the kind of text read and studied in Tibet.

The first of the great reformers was Atisha, who went from India to Tibet in the middle of the eleventh century. In his writing and in his speaking as he traveled about the country, Atisha attempted to set forth a simple and basic statement of the meaning of doctrine and the boundaries of practice. Atisha was brought to Tibet because a wide variety of Buddhist and non-Buddhist teachers had been spreading questionable doctrines and practices,

such as engaging in sexual intercourse with women in connection with tantric rites. Sexual symbolism, he said, was intended only to illustrate how one who had attained the higher stages of the Buddha's path was truly free. It was by seeing Theravada, Mahayana, and Tantrayana as a series of stages, each valid in its own way, that Atisha systematized Buddhist doctrine.

A monk named Marpa had studied under Atisha at Nalanda and in a sense continued his master's work in Tibet. Marpa and his disciples founded the School of the Successive Order (*Kagyupa*), which encouraged his followers to move quickly beyond Theravada and Mahayana texts to tantric practice, which, they were told, would result in physical attainments such as lightness of the body, a bright complexion and long life, and feelings of inexpressible joy.

Much more famous in the annals of Tibetan Buddhism than Marpa is his disciple Milarepa, who was alleged to have caused the death by black magic of almost forty people, including several relatives, after a family dispute. Fearing what this would do to his *karma,* as well he might, he turned for spiritual counsel to Marpa, who required several years of discipline and self-denial from Milarepa before even beginning to instruct him. Milarepa ultimately became a brilliant student and proceeded to become a powerful teacher and promoter of the Buddhist faith.

None of the preceding leaders can compare with Tsongkhapa, the scholar, teacher, and reformer of the fourteenth century. In his early youth Tsongkhapa began wrestling with the ideas in the texts of various schools of Buddhism, plus astrology and medicine, but concentrated on the Madhyamika or School of the Void philosophy of Nagarjuna. Standing in the tradition of the earlier reformer, Atisha, he asserted that those *tantras* with sexual symbolism were not to be taken literally, and insisted on thoroughgoing morality and control of the mind as prerequisites for tantric practice. The result of his activity was the establishment of the Gelukpa school, a continuation with some revision of a school founded by Atisha.

A number of schools of life and thought have appeared through the centuries, but three have managed to survive in some strength. The Old Translation School of Santarakshita and Padmasambhava continues what may be called the classic tantric tradition in Tibet. It also continues the ideas of the Consciousness Only School and emphasizes in particular the widely known *Tibetan Book of the Dead.* The Gelukpa School stems from the work of Atisha and Tsongkhapa, emphasizes the latter's *The Great Stages of Enlightenment,* and stresses moral standards and control of the mind as a prerequisite to engaging in tantric doctrine and practice.

The Kagyupa School, growing out of the work of Marpa and Milarepa, tends more than the two previous schools toward activity in the world, such as building temples and maintaining religious institutions. Followers seem to move rapidly beyond sacred texts and monastic discipline in order to gain higher powers, but moral teachings and service are still stressed. The Kagyupa School has split into a number of sectarian divisions, one of which calls for monks at an advanced stage to be enclosed for life in a cell with only a small opening through which food can be passed.

In spite of influence of the Consciousness Only School

at various points, practically all of the Tibetan Buddhist schools draw upon Nagarjuna's teaching of the Void. It must also be noted that each of the schools believes that those who follow its teaching and practice will realize a self-transcending experience that amounts to becoming a divine being.

Regardless of the school to which monks may belong, they are respected and honored as members of the highest social class. Their course of study is long and arduous, calling for fifteen to twenty years' study of texts and commentaries as well as study and training in ritual and tantric materials. One component of monastic training has become an outstanding feature of Buddhist life in Tibet, namely the demonstration of knowledge and skill in debate with one's peers. Frequent debates are held in the monasteries, with occasional public debates that attract great crowds.

As important as debating skill, if not more so, is the realization of the Four Purities. The first of these is the purity of the earth, which means the realization that the world and thought and activity are all empty or "Void." The second is more personal, as one realizes that the body can be transformed into deity, speech can become a mantra, and mind has immeasurable potential. The third purity involves the dissolving of ritual objects and instruments into the void and are emanated into space. Finally, fulfilling the bodhisattva motif, from the deified self is sent forth "an infinite quantity of light which spreads out through space and alleviates the sufferings of living beings," which in turn are transformed as "the mystic reabsorbs the light into himself."[37]

Monks or *lamas* of the highest order are regarded as incarnations of bodhisattvas who have postponed *nirvana* in order to help suffering beings. Great care is exercised in the selection of these incarnate lamas; this is heightened and intensified in the selection of a Dalai Lama, as he is both a spiritual and temporal ruler and is regarded as the incarnation of the Bodhisattva Avalokitesvara (Kuan Yin). Special rites and ceremonies, including a visit by high officials to the chief oracle of Tibet, must be conducted before a young boy is selected for the post. The boy chosen is then trained for many years before taking office as the ruler of Tibet. He is assisted by the Panchen Lama, who is intended to be a spiritual ruler, but who has at times been involved in political tensions.

Buddhist Temple in Peking. *The Buddhist temple about the waves symbolizes the way the Buddha* dharma *transports one over the sea of life, a part of the rich art and sculpture of the Yung He Kung or Lama Temple in Peking.* (Courtesy of Mary Bush)

The lives of the laity are built around the practice of religion. Some type of religious devotion accompanies every important action, whether related to the family, business, agriculture, or the coming and going of daily life. The recitation of the *mantra, Om Manipadme Om* ("Hail to the Jewel in the Lotus"), can be heard repeatedly while prayer wheels turn. A prayer wheel is a cylinder that spins around the end of a stick. They may range in size from a small one only a few inches long that can be held in the hand to large ones several feet high that are placed in the ground around a monastery. Written

prayers are placed in the cylinder, which is then spun round and round, sending the prayers to Buddhas, bodhisattvas, and guardian deities. Such cultic acts improve the *karma* of laypeople and bring about purification, but as with almost everything in the Tibetan Buddhist world, the end is always an experience that transcends the common life and brings union with the Buddha realm.

Through the centuries Buddhist monasteries in Tibet attained and exercised great economic power. The centrality of the monasteries in the total life of the country is due even more to their religious or spiritual role. The laity depended on the monks for all kinds of spiritual assistance and lay gifts to the monasteries strengthened the institution. The fact that pre-Buddhist festivals and rites came under the supervision of the monks is but another factor in the all-encompassing power of Buddhism in Tibet.

The Tibetans, almost all of whom are Buddhists, probably number only about five million, including those living in various parts of China and the hundred thousand or so who have migrated to India and to the West. Thus, in terms of numbers Tibetan Buddhism is only an insignificant minority in the Buddhist world, but in terms of its distinctive life-style, which is receiving increasing attention from scholars and other interested observers, Tibetan Buddhism is a significant religious movement in today's world. As the People's Republic of China, which has established political control over Tibet, provides greater freedom for various religous groups, one may hope for greater opportunities to study and relate to a way of life and thought that only a few outside observers have kown and interpreted.

Buddhism Today

Buddhism Today in Theravada Areas

From the early days of Buddhism in India to the Theravada Buddhist countries of today, the Buddhist way of life has provided the unifying force for community life in all its ramifications. In the three major Theravada countries—Sri Lanka, Burma, and Thailand—an overarching Buddhist cosmology supported the monarchy through the centuries; it continues to do so in Thailand, where Buddhist and also Brahmin rituals still are enacted in the courts of the ruling monarch. In all three countries

Buddhism has adjusted to the indigenous worship of spirits, such as worship at *nats* in Burma, with the result that there is no conflict between the spirit houses along the roadside and the Buddhist temples that dot the landscape.

During the last few centuries European colonial powers appeared in Asia, exerting cultural influence throughout the continent and political control over certain countries in particular. The Portuguese and the Dutch appeared first and established control and created difficulty for the Sangha in Sri Lanka. The British replaced the Dutch in Sri Lanka and established control over Burma. The French occupied the Buddhist countries of Laos, Cambodia, and Vietnam. Only Thailand of the predominantly Buddhist countries of South and Southeast Asia remained free of colonial domination. China, Japan, and Korea, whose Buddhists were Mahayanist in character, did not come under Western political control, although China was humiliated by the Western powers during the nineteenth century and Korea was occupied by Japan for several decades prior to World War II.

The occupation of Sri Lanka and Burma by Britain meant that Western commercial interests, Christian missionaries, and European and American educational institutions had access to these Buddhist nations in ways that otherwise would have been impossible. The British colonial government certainly did not operate in association with the Buddhist Sangha, and thus the influence that the monks had exercised previously through the kings was all but nullified. Christian missionaries and their converts, in contrast, were favored and encouraged in many instances by the colonial government, at least in the eyes of local people. Attending English and American schools, where English was taught and often became the language of instruction, was "the thing to do"; this meant that many young people adopted Western ways of living and were isolated from their own culture with its Buddhist orientation. Although it is easy to oversimplify what happened during the colonial period, there is no question that Buddhist leaders regarded British rule as an intrusion upon their way of life, an attack upon their traditional religious beliefs and practices, and a hindrance to authentic cultural development.

During World War II, when Japanese forces occupied Burma and the states of Indo–China (as well as several other countries in Asia), the British and French had to withdraw. Anticolonial sentiment, which had been building up during the 1920s and 1930s, was heightened to the extent that when European colonial governments returned after the war, it was only a matter of time before they again were on their way out. As Sri Lankans and Burmese assumed the reins of government, a Buddhist presence was again felt in political life. Being a good citizen was equated with being a good Buddhist, and thus a nationalist spirit and an activist Buddhism came together in the renewed nations of Asia.

This association of nationalism and Buddhism has been quite prominent, for example, in contemporary Burma. U Nu, prime minister of Burma during the 1950s, regarded Buddhism as an essential element in the socialist state he headed. He was a vigorous advocate of meditation, and strongly encouraged government officials and workers to stop for a few moments each day at one of the meditation centers he was instrumental in establishing. U Nu also encouraged Buddhist education and the strengthening of the Sangha, and in return received continuing support from Buddhist monks and laity. His successor, General Ne Win, though a Buddhist, reversed the trend of close cooperation between religion and government, but Buddhism continues as the sustaining force in Burmese society.

Another facet of what has been called a contemporary Buddhist renaissance is the attempt to present Buddhism as highly compatible with modern science and democracy. Traditional Buddhist cosmology postulated a world view of endless *kalpas,* or long periods of time. This view accords well with the scientific world-view that the universe is billions of years old. Buddhists believe their analysis of human beings, the human mind in particular, to be closely related to modern psychological studies. Buddhists have offered the discussion of ethical problems in the Buddhist texts as a model for parliamentary discussions in modern democracies. And they have presented the Buddha's compassion for all living beings as fundamental to the achievement of world peace. As the world surveyed the destruction and loss of life brought by World War II, Buddhist leaders said, in effect: "Give Buddhism a chance. Follow the Middle Path to world peace."

This stress on Buddhism as a religion with a scientific approach and a message of peace was often repeated in the Sixth World Buddhist Council, held near Rangoon

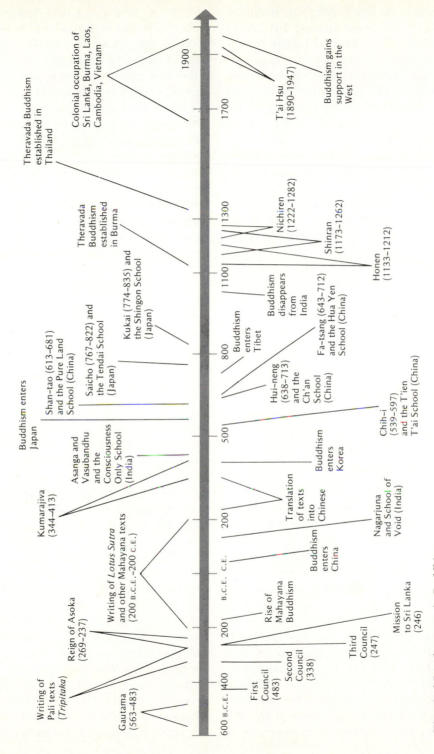

Historical Developments in Buddhism.

Gautama
(563–483)

Writing of
Pali texts
(*Tripitaka*)

First
Council
(483)

600 B.C.E. 400

Reign of Asoka
(269–237)

Second
Council
(338)

Third Council
(247)

Mission
to Sri Lanka
(246)

200

Rise of
Mahayana
Buddhism

Writing of *Lotus Sutra*
and other Mahayana texts
(200 B.C.E.–200 C.E.)

B.C.E.   C.E.

Buddhism
enters China

200

Kumarajiva
(344–413)

Nagarjuna
and School of
Void (India)

Translation
of texts
into
Chinese

Asanga and
Vasubandhu
and the
Consciousness
Only School
(India)

500

Buddhism
enters
Korea

Buddhism enters
Japan

Chih-i
(539–597)
and the T'ien
T'ai School (China)

Hui-neng
(638–713)
and the Ch'an
School
(China)

800

Buddhism
enters Tibet

Shan-tao (613–681)
and the Pure Land
School (China)

Saicho (767–822) and
the Tendai School
(Japan)

Kukai (774–835) and
the Shingon School
(Japan)

Fa-tsang (643–712)
and the Hua Yen
School (China)

Buddhism
disappears
from
India

1100

Theravada
Buddhism
established
in Burma

Honen
(1133–1212)

Shinran
(1173–1262)

Nichiren
(1222–1282)

1300

Theravada Buddhism
established in Thailand

Colonial occupation of
Sri Lanka, Burma, Laos,
Cambodia, Vietnam

1700

1900

T'ai Hsu
(1890–1947)

Buddhism gains
support in the
West

in 1954–1956. The Burmese hosts, along with Buddhists from other Theravada countries, planned and carried through the conference, which attracted Buddhists from all over the world and was the highlight of twentieth-century Buddhism. Texts were studied and recited, as according to tradition had been done at the Third Council held under King Ashoka in the third century B.C.E., with which the Sixth Council was compared. Educational and social concerns were also emphasized, as was the importance of teaching Buddhist doctrine to a world that had been torn by war and yearned for peace. Buddhists came from all over the world to participate in council sessions, which were held in a great hall constructed to look from the outside like a cave. The World Peace Pagoda stood nearby as a testimony to the Buddhist hope for a peaceful world.

Theravada Buddhists have also given leadership to the formation and ongoing life of the World Fellowship of Buddhists, which has met approximately every two years since 1950 as a World Buddhist Conference (as distinct from the 1954–56 World Buddhist Council). Formally organized in 1952, the new organization has attempted to promote closer relations between Theravadins and Mahayanists, teaching of the *dharma* in East and West, improvement of education, discussion of social issues, and overall development of Buddhism in the contemporary world.

Buddhism Today in Mahayana Areas and the West

Although trends in modern Theravada countries are sufficiently similar to allow discussion of them in a group, the situation in the Mahayana world is quite different. Without question the most outstanding expressions of Mahayana thought and life today are to be found in Japan. The major schools are still active there, several Buddhist universities are well known, and the religious life is practiced in temples and homes. Although the increasing secularization of Japan has been a difficult challenge to all religious groups, Buddhist leaders have responded to that challenge by showing, even more effectively than in the Theravada countries, that Buddhism is highly compatible with modern science; that its leaders and people can play a role in modern political life; and that meditation, as practiced in Zen and in other schools

as well, can be a source of insight and meaning in the press of a rapidly changing and complex world.

China, once the home of the Mahayana tradition from which it spread to Korea and Japan, was the scene of a Buddhist reform movement in the first third of this century, which was interrupted by the Japanese invasion of China in 1937 and the eight years of war that followed. The founder and leader of the movement was a Buddhist abbot by the name of T'ai Hsü (1890–1947), who was distressed with the low state to which the Sangha had sunk: poorly trained and undisciplined monks, few capable leaders, and a low reputation among the laity. T'ai Hsü lectured all over China and in other countries as well, wrote articles and books, drew up ambitious plans for the education of clergy and laity, and even outlined the reorganization and revival of Buddhism in China and the world. He had just reactivated the reform movement and won full acceptance of his leadership when he died in 1947. The Communist victory two years later meant the end of his reform movement in China, although his disciples have continued a number of activities in his name in Taiwan, where there has been something of a Buddhist revival in recent years.

The policy of the People's Republic of China with respect to Buddhists and other religious groups has been to bring them under the supervision and "protection" of the government. A Chinese Buddhist Association was set up in 1953, replacing an earlier organization with the same name, and a periodical, *Modern Buddhism,* was published, all under the authority and guidance of the government's Religious Affairs Bureau. Although a few Buddhists openly opposed government pressures, the majority seem to have supported the government, with increasing emphasis on productive labor and decreasing stress on traditional Buddhist activities. Lands still owned by the monasteries were confiscated by the government, and monks and nuns left monastery and cloister to work in factories and fields. Some temples were refurbished by the Communist government as outstanding examples of historical cultural monuments, which suggested that Buddhism was a thing of the past, not the present. With the Cultural Revolution of 1966, all Buddhist temples were closed; and there was no visible evidence of Buddhist activity anywhere in China. The reopening of a few temples in the early 1970s meant that visitors could see a few monks reciting sutras, and by the early 1980s the laity could be seen in the temples.

Our study of Buddhism can best be concluded by observing that Buddhism in the twentieth century has become a world religion in the full sense of the word. Although there have been Buddhists at various times who were not Asians, Buddhism has traditionally been essentially an Asian religion. At the present time, however, Buddhist groups and temples can be found in almost every major city of Europe and North America. Events during and after World War II brought many Americans to Japan, where they saw Buddhism at first hand, Zen in particular having a great appeal for many of them. Bangkok became an international center at approximately the same time, so that many Westerners became acquainted with the Theravada Buddhism of Thailand.

Currently Asian Buddhists have reached out to the West from Japan and Southeast Asia, and have won the allegiance of Americans and Europeans in significant numbers. Buddhist meditation centers have become common, and universities such as the Dharma Realm University in California have been established. Innumerable books and pamphlets, in which American or European converts proclaim Buddhist teachings and values, are now available.

The Buddha who spoke in the accents of ancient India, whose Middle Path spread at various times to every nook and corner of Asia, is now a focal point for religious devotion throughout the modern world. He is a "world-honored one" in fact as well as in the deepest feelings of his disciples.

NOTES

1. *The Middle Length Sayings* (*Majjhima Nikaya*), trans. by I. B. Horner (London: Luzac and Company, 1954), p. 249.
2. *The Dialogues of the Buddha* (*Digha Nikaya*), trans. by T. W. Rhys Davids (London: Oxford University Press, 1899–1921), vol. II, p. 100.
3. *Digha Nikaya*, vol. II, pp. 155–156.
4. S. Radhkrishnan and C. A. Moore, eds., *A Sourcebook in Indian Philosophy* (Princeton: Princeton University Press, 1957), pp. 273–274.
5. H. C. Warren, trans., *Buddhism in Translation* (Cambridge: Harvard University Press, 1947), p. 22.
6. E. J. Thomas, *History of Buddhist Thought* (London: Kegan Paul, 1933), p. 117.
7. From Radhakrishnan and Moore, *A Sourcebook in Indian Philosophy*, p. 278. *Karma* is substituted for *kamma*.
8. *Majjhima Nikaya*, vol. I, pp. 271–280.
9. *Ibid*.
10. Sangarakshita, *A Survey of Buddhism* (Bangalore: Indian Institute of World Culture, 1957), p. 172.
11. S. Tachibana, *The Ethics of Buddhism* (London: Oxford University Press, 1926), pp. 101–267. This work is still the most comprehensive and systematic treatment of Buddhist ethics.
12. *Majjhima Nikaya*, vol. II, p. 106.
13. *Ibid.*, pp. 147–157; 177–184.
14. *Digha Nikaya* (Long Discourses), vol. II, p. 190.
15. *The Book of the Discipline* (*Vinaya Pitaka*), trans. by I. B. Horner (London: Oxford University Press, 1938), vol. I, pp. 38, 72, 125–158.
16. T. W. Rhys Davids and Herman Oldenberg, eds. and trans., *Vinaya Texts*, vol. 13 of *Sacred Books of the East* (London: Oxford University Press, 1881), p. 13.
17. Jane Bunnag, *Buddhist Monk, Buddhist Layman* (Cambridge: Cambridge University Press, 1973), pp. 19–82.
18. Richard H. Robinson, *The Buddhist Religion* (Belmont, Calif.: Dickenson Publishing Co., 1970), pp. 125–128, has a list of the Pali, Chinese, and Tibetan scriptures.
19. Several scholars have translated the *Lotus Sutra* into English: H. Kerns, trans., *Saddharma Pundarika* (London: Oxford University Press, 1884); W. E. Soothill, trans., *The Lotus of the Wonderful Law* (London: Oxford University Press, 1930); Bunno Kato, trans., *Myoho-Renge-Kyo. The Sutra of the Lotus Flower on the Wonderful Law* (Tokyo: Kosei Publishing Co., 1971); Leon Hurvitz, trans., *Scripture of the Lotus Blossom of the Fine Dharma* (New York: Columbia University Press, 1976).
20. Volume 49 of the *Sacred Books of the East, Buddhist Mahayana Texts* (London: Oxford University Press, 1894), contains short versions of the *Prajna-Paramita* or *Wisdom Sutras*, translated by Max Müller. Better translations may be found in Edward Conze, trans., *Buddhist Wisdom Books* (London: George Allen and Unwin, Ltd., 1958); and in the same translator's *The Perfection of Wisdom* (Berkeley: Four Seasons Foundation, 1973).
21. The Longer and Shorter *Sukhavati Vyuha*, or *Land of Bliss* is included in *Buddhist Mahayana Texts* (see footnote 20).
22. The *Buddha Carita, Acts of the Buddha*, translated by E. B. Cowell, is also in *Buddhist Mahayana Texts*.
23. Yoshito S. Hakeda, trans. *The Awakening of Faith, Attributed to Asvagosha*. (New York: Columbia University Press, 1967).
24. D. T. Suzuki, trans., *The Lankavatara Sutra* (London: G. Routledge and Sons, 1932).
25. The best translation is Idumi Hokei, "Vimalakirti's Dis-

course on Emancipation,'' published serially in *Eastern Buddhist*, II, III, IV. See also Charles Luk (Lu K'uanyu), trans., *The Vimalakirti Nirdesa Sutra* (Berkeley: Shambala, 1972); A. F. Thurman, trans., *The Holy Teaching of Vimalakirti* (University Park, Pennsylvania: University of Pennsylvania Press, 1976).

26. Alex and Hideko Wayman, trans., *The Lion's Roar of Queen Srimala* (New York: Columbia University Press, 1974).

27. Following L. D. Barnett's abridged English translation of the *Bodhicharyavatara* (''Thought of the Descent of Bodhi''), published under the title of *The Path of Light* (London: Wisdom of the East Series, 1909, 1947), p. 45.

28. Th. Stcherbatsky, trans., *The Conception of Buddhist Nirvana* (Leningrad: Academy of Sciences, 1927), p. 69. Several works by Nagarjuna are translated in Frederick J. Streng, *Emptiness: A Study in Religious Meaning* (Nashville: Abingdon Press, 1967).

29. Vasubandhu's *Trimsika*, from passages translated by Ch'an Wing-tsit for Radhakrishnan and Moore, eds., *Sourcebook in Indian Philosophy*, p. 337.

30. The preceding account is based on the story of this period in Kenneth Ch'en's *Buddhism in China* (Princeton: Princeton University Press, 1964), pp. 145–152.

31. Ch'en, *Buddhism in China*, pp. 165–179.

32. D. T. Suzuki, *Essays in Zen Buddhism* (London: Luzac and Co., 1927), First Series, p. 163. In the third line ''nature'' has been substituted for ''soul'' because the idea of a soul in Buddhism is highly questionable.

33. *Nihongi, The Chronicles of Japan from the Earliest Times to 697* A.D., trans. by W. G. Aston (Rutland, Vt., and Tokyo: Charles E. Tuttle Co., 1972), pp. 10–12.

34. Quoted in M. Anesaki, *History of Japanese Religion* (London: Kegan Paul, 1930), p. 183.

35. *Shinshu Seiten, The Holy Scriptures of Shinshu* (Honolulu: The Hongpa Hongwanji Mission of Hawaii, 1955), p. 267.

36. Suzuki, *Essays in Zen Buddhism,* First Series, p. 246.

37. Giuseppe Tucci, *The Religions of Tibet* (Berkeley: University of California Press, 1980), p. 54.

GLOSSARY

The following terms recur frequently in the study of Buddhism, whether in this chapter or in further study that the student may do. Some Sanskrit terms used in Buddhism are listed in the glossary for the chapter on Hinduism (see pp. 108 ff.) and have not been repeated here if there is no essential change in meaning. The guide to pronunciation in that glossary applies also to Sanskrit terms in this list.

ālaya vijnāna (*aah-laah-yuh vij-naah-nuh*) the storehouse consciousness or consciousness container, a teaching of the Consciousness Only School.

Amitābha Buddha (*aah-mee-taah-buh*) a Buddha who is the lord of the Pure Land or Western Paradise, the home at death for those who have had faith in his vow to save them. **A-mi-t'o-fo** in Chinese, **Amida Butsu** in Japanese.

anātta (*uhn-aaht-tuh*) ''no self,'' that is, no permanent or absolute immortal self such as the *ātman* of Hindu thought, thus the Sanskrit form *anātman*.

anicca (*uh-nee-chuh*) impermanence, change, tranformation; a characteristic of life.

arhat (*aarh-huht*) one who is following various disciplines leading to enlightenment. Usually a monk in the Theravada tradition.

bhikkhu (*bhik-koo*) monks who follow the discipline of the Sangha.

bhikkhuni (*bhik-koo-nee*) nuns who follow the discipline of the female order.

bodhi (*boh-dhee*) enlightenment.

bodhisattva (*boh-dhee-suh-tvuh*) one who has attained enlightenment but postpones **nirvana** in order to aid suffering creatures.

dharma (*dhur-muh*) (Pali *dhamma*) teaching, law, duty, morality, as in Hinduism; but also, in several Mahayana schools, moments of existence, energies, states in a continuum.

dhyāna (*dhee-yaah-nuh*) (Pali *jhana*) refers specifically to the next to last stage in Buddhist meditation, as in yoga; also refers to four levels of trance beyond the eight stages and to meditation in general.

dukkha (*dhu-kuh*) suffering, pain, misery; basic nature of existence.

karuna (*kuh-roo-nuh*) an attitude of compassion found in Buddhas and bodhisattvas, which is to be emulated by Buddhist people.

koan (*ko-ahn*) a riddle-like statement or question used in the practice of Ch'an or Zen to destroy logic or reason in the student.

Kuan Yin (*guahn-yin*) a **bodhisattva** whose full name in Chinese is Kuan Shih Yin P'u Sa, or ''Hearing World's Cries Bodhisattva.'' *Shih* is pronounced /shr/. Her name is Kwannon Bosatsu in Japanese.

Maitreya (*my-tray-yuh*) the Buddha to come, called Milei-fo in Chinese.

mandala (*muhn-duh-luh*) a picture with an orderly arrangement of symbols, used as an object of meditation. Pronounced *mandara* in Japanese.

mantra (*muhn-truh*) a phrase, word, or syllable with mystic meaning or power.

mappo (*mop-poh*) the doctrine that people are living in the last days and that a new age is about to dawn, especially emphasized in Nichiren Buddhism.

mudrā (*mu-drah*)   a position or gesture with the hand(s) that conveys hidden meaning.

Nanwu A-mi-t'o-f'o (*nahn-woo ah-mee-toh-fowh*)   Chinese phrase meaning "Praise to Amitabha Buddha."

Namu Amida Butsu (*nah-moo-ah-mee-dah-boots*)   the Japanese equivalent of the previous phrase, often shortened to Nembutsu.

Nan-wu Kuan Yin P'u Sa (*nahn-woo-guahn-yin poo sah*)   Chinese phrase meaning "Praise to Kuan Yin Bodhisattva."

Namu Kwannon Bosatsu (*nah-moo-kah-nohn Boh-sahts*)   the Japanese equivalent of the previous phrase.

Namu Myoho Renge-kyo (*nah-moo myoh-hoh reng-geh-kyoh*)   Japanese phrase meaning "Homage to the *Lotus Sutra of the Wonderful Law*," used in Nichiren Buddhism.

nirvāna (*nir-vaah-nuh*)   the "snuffing out" of the fires of life, which brings release from rebirth and a sublime calm and peace.

parājika (*puh-ruh-jee-kuh*)   basic core of rules in the monastic discipline, which if broken cause "defeat."

parinirvāna (*puh-ri-nir-vaah-nuh*)   the ultimate peace that comes after death.

prakrit (*pray-krit*)   a term referring to ancient Indian languages, such as Pali, which are related to Sanskrit but not the same language.

puja (*poo-juh*)   an act of worship or devotion to deities, as in Hinduism, and to Buddhas and bodhisattvas in Buddhism.

Sākyamuni (*shaah-kyuh-mun-nee*)   a name of the original, historical Buddha, which means "wise one of the Sakya (clan)." Commonly used in China (*Shr-jya-moo-nee*) and Japan instead of Gautama to designate this Buddha.

samādhi (*suh-maah-dhi*)   indescribable highest level of meditation, leading to trance.

samana (*suh-muh-nuh*)   general term used for wandering, celibate recluses, one group of which were followers of the Buddha.

samsāra (*suhm-saah-ruh*)   literally *migration*, thus suggesting the process or cycles of rebirth; generally refers to the world of suffering, death, and rebirth.

sangha (*suhng-huh*)   the order of monks who follow the Buddha's discipline.

satori (*sah-toh-ree*)   the ultimate experience in Zen, in which there is a total transformation of the individual, who then sees everything from a new perspective.

śīla (*shee-luh*)   basic moral code forbidding theft, adultery, taking life, false speech, and drinking alcoholic beverages.

skandhās (*skuhn-daahs*)   the aggregates or constituent elements in personality, which are five in number: body (name and form), feelings or sensations, perceptions, habitual tendencies or inclinations, and consciousness.

stūpa (*stoo-puh*)   a shrine, often conical in shape, in which relics of the Buddha are housed.

śūnya (*shoon-yaah*)   empty of any absolute reality, thus emptiness or *sunyata*.

sūtra (*soo-truh*)   a written text regarded as sacred or normative by followers of a religion.

tantra (*tuhn-truh*)   literally, to weave; a movement within Buddhism emphasizing symbolic rites that involve gestures, postures, breathing, special sounds and formulas, all communicated by teacher to disciple. Tantrayana is one of the names given to Buddhism in Tibet, where this movement was strongest before the recent conquest by China.

trikāya (*trih-kaah-yuh*)   the three bodies of the Buddha: *nirmanakaya*, transformation or visible body; *sambhogakaya*, the body of bliss; and *dharmakaya*, body of truth.

tripitaka (*trih-pih-tuh-kuh*)   the three baskets of Buddhist sacred texts: *Vinaya Pitaka*, Discipline Basket (for monks); *Sutta Pitaka*, Discourse Basket; and *Abhidhamma Pitaka*, Basket of Further or Special Teaching.

uposatha (*oo-poh-suh-thuh*)   fortnightly meetings at the monastery that bring laymen and monks together.

vajra (*vuhj-ruh*)   diamond, therefore suggesting brilliance, a term associated with Buddhist wisdom literature. *Vajracchedika Sutra* is the *Diamond Cutter Sutra*, a Zen text. *Vajrayana* is the third vehicle, or Esoteric Buddhism. See also **tantra.**

yab-yum   the "father-mother" act as depicted in Tantric Buddhism.

SUGGESTED READINGS

Listed under Primary Sources in English translation are those works that contain key texts or passages from the Buddhist scriptures. The listing of Secondary Sources includes a representative sampling of works in English that undergraduate students may find interesting and helpful for collateral reading and further study. Many of the volumes in the list of secondary sources contain extensive bibliographies, which the student is urged to consult.

Primary Sources in Translation

CONZE, EDWARD, trans. *Buddhist Wisdom Books,* containing *The Diamond Sutra* and *The Heart Sutra.* London: George Allen and Unwin, Ltd., 1958.

———, trans. *The Perfection of Wisdom in Eight Thousand Lines and Its Verse Summary.* Berkeley: Four Seasons Foundation, 1973.

DeBary, William Theodore, ed. *The Buddhist Tradition in India, China, and Japan*. New York: The Modern Library, 1969.

Evans-Wentz, W. Y., ed. *The Tibetan Book of the Dead*. Translated by Lama Kazi Dawa-Samdup. New York: Oxford University Press, 1960.

———, ed. *Tibetan Yoga and Secret Doctrines*. Translated by Lama Kazi Dawa-Samdup. New York: Oxford University Press, 1967.

Hamilton, Clarence H., ed. *Selections from Buddhist Literature*. Indianapolis: Bobbs-Merrill, 1952.

Hurvitz, Leon, trans. *Scripture of the Lotus Blossom of the Fine Dharma*. New York: Columbia University Press, 1976.

Kato, Bunno, trans. *Myoho-Renge-Kyo. The Sutra of the Lotus Flower of the Wonderful Law*. Tokyo: Kosei Publishing Co., 1971.

Luk, Charles (Lu K'uan-yu), trans. *The Vimalakirti Nirdesa Sutra*. Berkeley: Shambala, 1972.

Muller, F. Max, ed. and trans. *Buddhist Mahayana Sutras. Sacred Books of the East*, Vol. 49. London: Oxford University Press, 1894, 1927.

Soothill, W. E., trans. *The Lotus of the Wonderful Law*. London: Oxford University Press, 1930.

Suzuki, D. T., trans. *The Lankavatara Sutra*. London: G. Routledge and Sons, 1932.

Warren, Henry Clark, ed. *Buddhism in Translation*. Cambridge: Harvard University Press, 1947.

Wayman, Alex and Hideko. *The Lion's Roar of Queen Srimala*. New York: Columbia University Press, 1974.

Secondary Sources

Anesaki, Masaharu. *Nichiren, The Buddhist Prophet*. Cambridge: Harvard University Press, 1916.

Aung, Maung Htin. *Folk Elements in Burmese Buddhism*. London: Oxford University Press, 1962.

Bunnag, Jane. *Buddhist Monk, Buddhist Layman: A Study of Urban Monastic Organization in Central Thailand*. Cambridge: Cambridge University Press, 1963.

Chang, Garma C. C. *The Buddhist Teaching of Totality*. University Park, PA: Pennsylvania State University Press, 1971.

Chatterjee, A. K. *The Yogacara Idealism*. Benares: Benares Hindu University Press, 1962.

Ch'en, K. S. *Buddhism in China: A Historical Survey*. Princeton: Princeton University Press, 1964.

———. *The Chinese Transformation of Buddhism*. Princeton: Princeton University Press, 1973.

Conze, Edward. *Buddhism: Its Essence and Development*. 2d ed. New York: Harper Torchbook, 1959.

———. *Buddhist Meditation*. 2d ed. London: George Allen and Unwin, 1956.

Dayal, Har. *The Bodhisattva Doctrine in Buddhist Sanskrit Literature*. London: Kegan Paul, 1932.

Denwood, Philip, and Piatigorsky, Alexander, eds. *Buddhist Studies: Ancient and Modern*. London: Curzon Press, 1983.

Dumoulin, Heinrich and Maraldo, John C., eds. *Buddhism in the Modern World*. New York: Macmillan Publishing Co., 1976.

Eliot, Charles. *Japanese Buddhism*. New York: Barnes & Noble Books, 1959.

Getty, Alice. *The Gods of Northern Buddhism*. Tokyo: Charles E. Tuttle Co., 1962.

Gombrich, Richard. *Precept and Practice: Traditional Buddhism in the Rural Highlands of Ceylon*. London: Oxford University Press, 1971.

Kapleau, Phillip. *The Three Pillars of Zen*. Boston: Beacon Press, 1967.

Morgan, Kenneth W., ed. *The Path of the Buddha: Buddhism Interpreted by Buddhists*. New York: The Ronald Press Company, 1956.

Murti, T. R. V. *The Central Philosophy of Buddhism: A Study of the Madhyamika System*. London: George Allen and Unwin, Ltd., 1955.

Robinson, Richard H., and Johnson, Willard L. *The Buddhist Religion: A Historical Introduction*. Belmont: Wadsworth, 1977.

Stcherbatsky, Theodoro. *The Central Conception of Buddhism*. London: Royal Asiatic Society, 1923. Reprinted Calcutta: Susil Gupta, 1956.

Streng, Frederick J. *Emptiness: A Study in Religious Meaning*. Nashville: Abingdon Press, 1967.

Suzuki, Daisetz Teitaro. *Essays in Zen Buddhism*. 3 vols. London: Rider, 1949–1953.

Takakausu, Junjiro. *The Essentials of Buddhist Philosophy*. Honolulu: University of Hawaii Press, 1947.

Thomas, Edward Joseph. *The History of Buddhist Thought*. London: Routledge and Kegan Paul, 1933.

———. *The Life of the Buddha as Legend and History*. London: Routledge and Kegan Paul, 1927.

Tucci, Guiseppe. *The Religions of Tibet*. Berkeley: University of California Press, 1980.

Welch, Holmes. *Buddhism under Mao*. Cambridge: Harvard University Press, 1972.

———. *The Buddhist Revival in China*. Cambridge: Harvard University Press, 1968.

———. *The Practice of Chinese Buddhism*. Cambridge: Harvard University Press, 1967.

Wright, Arthur F. *Buddhism in Chinese History*. Stanford: Stanford University Press, 1959.

Zurcher, Erik. *The Buddhist Conquest of China*. Leiden: Brill, 1959.

6

Religion in China and Japan

明乎郊社之禮，禘嘗之義，治國其如示諸掌乎．

Translation of the Chinese: "If one understands the meaning of sacrifices to Heaven and Earth, and the significance of various sacrifices to ancestors, governing a kingdom would be as easy as looking at the palm." (Doctrine of the Mean XIX, 6B)

There are several reasons for studying religion in China and religion in Japan in the same chapter. In the previous chapter we noted that Mahayana Buddhism has traditionally been a major religion in both countries, and that several important Buddhist schools of life and thought are essentially the same in both countries. Chinese language and culture had a profound influence during the formative years of the cultural development of Japan, and many Chinese characters are still used in written Japanese. Although each of the two countries has its own distinctive cultural identity, it is clear that there is a historic and continuing affinity between them. We turn first to religion in China.

Religion in China

When one asks how religion began in China, the best possible answer is that religion emerged as the Chinese people became aware of themselves and their families in relation to the forces of nature they had to face. There are no written records from the earliest stages of this awareness, and no reference to any great event or personality to mark a specific beginning.

Nevertheless, there is some evidence that indicates people believed in ultimate realities that had power to affect their lives, and that the ancient Chinese engaged in certain practices in order to change or influence these powerful realities. Both belief and practice were related closely to society, rulers in authority, and, in particular, the family. The resulting way, called *tao* in Chinese, is a total way of life involving family relationships, the ruler and his people, literature, art, and music, and every other aspect of human existence. Many educated Chinese do not acknowledge that the Chinese have a religion; but when we examine all that is meant by *tao*, which is a total philosophy and way of life, we begin to discern that it includes profoundly religious dimensions, and that it unquestionably functions as a religion in the daily lives of people.

Beginnings

From Earliest Times, a Focus on Ancestors

The first of the powerful realities to which the Chinese appear to have devoted themselves from the earliest times to the present is their ancestors. Archaeological remains from the Shang Dynasty (c. 1750–1027 B.C.E.) reveal a concern for the dead that parallels similar concerns in many ancient cultures. Objects that the dead might need in the afterlife have been found in excavated grave sites, indicating that the living provided in the grave what they thought would be needed in the world beyond.

The great attention given to the deceased from royal or wealthy families has meant that those graves or vaults were better equipped to survive the ravages of time and weather. Dead monarchs were provided with weapons and other articles to use, and the sacrificed bodies of wives, concubines, servants, and soldiers to serve them. Later rulers were repelled by the idea of sacrificing living human beings to care for a king who had died, and thus were buried instead with thousands of life-sized

terra cotta soldiers in battle array.* Such elaborate preparations for the life beyond represent a major exception to normal burial practices, even though later emperors were buried in magnificent splendor. A few graves of the common people have been discovered; these contain only an ordinary vessel or a knife.

Later writings and practices suggest a twofold purpose for the ancestor cult. First, a family wants its ancestors to continue a happy life beyond the grave and then in turn to bless the family they have left behind. The *Book of Songs* says:

All around the fragrance is diffused. Complete and brilliant is the sacrificial service; grandly come our ancestors. They will reward their descendants with great blessing, long life, years without end.[1]

The second purpose is that of satisfying the relative who has died, so that he or she will not need to return to bother the family again. There are good and evil spirits in the Chinese world-view: ancestors who receive proper burial and appropriate offerings are regarded as beneficent spirits; those who are not cared for become ghosts. The latter are capable of causing harm to the family and to others if not satisfied by the rites done for them. In order to pacify spirits who are hungry for food and attention because they have unfilial descendants, some Chinese still celebrate in early autumn the "Festival of the Hungry Ghosts," when they make offerings to satisfy unhappy spirits from any family and thus ward off potential danger from them.

Offerings at funerals and at graves today reflect the modern scene and the needs of modern people. Paper houses, cars, and money are burned at funeral services to symbolize the good life that the living hope the dead will enjoy. These practices are based on a belief that the spirits of the dead are still close at hand, a concern for the well-being of the ancestors, and a conviction that the living and the dead form one community, which is sustained and hallowed by ancestral rites.

Devotion to the ancestors, both in times past and in the present, is expressed not only at funeral services, but in offerings that are made to them at all important anniversaries. Their past good deeds, love for the family, and service to community and country are extolled. Re-

* Excavations in the People's Republic of China have uncovered such a burial for the first Emperor of China who died in 210 B.C.E.

Ancestral Tablets. *Ancestral tablets carrying the name of the deceased, an honorific statement, and in a few instances a photograph, may be found in ancestral shrines or in a wide variety of temples. Here the tablets are placed in a side shrine of a Chinese Buddhist temple.* (Courtesy of Mary Bush)

ports of family happenings—births, marriages, deaths, great achievements, and disasters—are all included in the rituals, over which the father of the family presides.

Therefore, when we seek to discover the origins of religion in China, or what survives of that way of life today, we must clearly look to ancestors and to a devotion to them characterized by a loyalty much like the loving obedience they received when they were alive.

The Lord Above and the Concept of Heaven

The second ancient, powerful reality is the royal ancestor who was seen as supreme over all other ancestors, just as the ruler is supreme over his people. The name of the first imperial dynasty was Shang. Thus, the Chinese people confronted Shang Ti, the Lord Above, who was also called Lord of the Shangs.* This Lord was not the only god or spirit, but certainly the leading one, personified as a powerful ruler like his earthly counterpart. He was believed to send rain upon the land and victory in battle, and to grant good harvests and countless other blessings.

The Shang Dynasty was overthrown in the eleventh century B.C.E. and the Chou rulers came to the throne, utilizing much from the previous dynasty. A transforma-

* Two Chinese characters pronounced ''shang'' are used here. The name of the deity is Shang (''above'') Ti (''lord'').

tion took place in the understanding of Shang Ti, and the somewhat personal Lord Above was replaced by the concept of *T'ien* ("Heaven"). *T'ien* can mean simply the sky above, or it can mean Nature in a general sense. There is a note of fate about it, but there is strong ethical content as well. Clearly *T'ien* refers to a supreme power that governs the world and the affairs of human beings in a broad, impersonal sense.[2] *T'ien* is ever-present, sees and hears all, loves virtue and rewards it, and punishes evil. The *Book of Songs* extols "the ordinances of Heaven, how deep and unremitting," and cites examples of kings who kept the ordinances of Heaven. On the other hand, a king without virtue causes the following:

O unpitying great Heaven, there is no end to the disorder! With every month it continues to grow, so that the people have no repose. I am as if intoxicated with the grief of my heart. Who holds the ordering of the kingdom? He (the king) attends not himself to the government, and the result is toil and pain to the people.[3]

Whereas all the common people made offerings to their ancestors, only the ruler and his ministers approached *T'ien* or Heaven, sacrificing a bullock and a ram at the winter solstice to plead for the continuation of Heaven's mandate. It was believed that the ruler reigned by *T'ien Ming,* the "mandate of Heaven." If the ruler was judged to be virtuous and the kingdom prospered, it was clear that he retained the mandate. If there were crop failures, losses in war, or natural catastrophes, it was equally clear that he had lost the mandate and revolt was justified.

Earth and Fertility

As with ancestors and Heaven, there is no reliable evidence as to precisely when and how the worship of Earth, the third ancient supreme reality, assumed a major role in the religion of the Chinese. The cult of *she chi,* the gods of Earth and Grain, was taking shape as early as the beginning of the Chou Dynasty in the eleventh century B.C.E. It also seems reasonable that an agricultural people, concerned about the fertility of the soil and good crops, would find it natural to revere the land.

At least by the time of the Chou Dynasty, there was a mound of earth at the edge of each village where local officials made their offerings to *she chi* in order to gain fertility of the soil and to increase human fertility. A receptacle of grain was placed in the marital bedroom to ensure offspring. Officials were sworn into office before the mound of earth, and offerings were made there in the hope of blessings in many areas of life. Gradually the gods of earth and grain coalesced into the worship of the Earth God, *T'u Ti Kung,* who was associated with community responsibility and civic virtue in addition to fertility. The birthday of *T'u Ti Kung* became the basis for tremendous celebrations, resulting in a strong sense of community identity, just as the ancestor cult gave unity to the family and the rites of *T'ien* or Heaven gave a sense of imperial identity and sanction.

Sun and rain fall down from Heaven, are received by the Earth, which nurtures the seeds, and the crops emerge. This continuing interaction leads to a fundamental view of the operation of the universe and all of life based on the concept of *yang* and *yin* as two complementary forces: *yang* is above, bright, assertive, and masculine; *yin* is below, dim, receptive, and feminine. As long as the two forces are in balance they complement one another. Actually there is a little bit of *yang* in the *yin* force and a bit of *yin* in the *yang* force, which helps to maintain the balance. The pairing of these qualities should not suggest that *yang* is good or superior and *yin* is less than good or inferior. Lightness and darkness are both necessary; and, although women were subject to men in traditional Chinese society, both male and female roles were seen as necessary and important to the harmonious and meaningful functioning of society. Rather than conceiving ultimate reality as an absolute being, associated with Heaven, the interaction of Heaven and Earth in a process of constant change becomes the true reality on which all else depends.

Our exploration of the beginnings of religion in China has shown us the primary objects of belief, three powerful realities that people experienced as having a profound effect on their existence. This structure of belief, including ancestors, Heaven and Earth, the last two involved in an underlying polarity of complementary forces, *yang* and *yin,* is really the doctrinal basis for Chinese religion as it continues in modern times. The Imperial sacrifices or offerings to Heaven ceased with the fall of the Empire in 1911, but Nationalist Chinese political leaders in the middle decades of the twentieth century still claimed to have the mandate of Heaven and therefore to deserve the loyalty of the people. The *yang–yin* dialectic can still be discerned as a philosophical foundation, and devotion to ancestors and to the Earth God continues in many parts of the Chinese world today.

Divination and Other Practices

The patterns and methods of devotion related to the doctrinal structure also constitute a distinctive mainstream of religious practice. Whether one makes offerings to ancestors, or to a host of gods like T'u Ti Kung, or to Buddhas and bodhisattvas, or to Taoist gods or immortals, the pattern is basically the same: grain, fruit, candles, or incense sticks are held with both hands about a foot in front of the bowed (or bowing) head; the hands move up and down rhythmically, then finally place the offering on the temple altar or the smoking incense sticks in the urn near the altar. It is with this great dignity and ceremony that emperors and great officials have traditionally made their offerings to Heaven and Earth; the common people usually display less formality as they approach their ancestors and the popular deities they revere.

Divination, the effort to divine or foresee the will of gods or spirits, plays an important part in practices of devotion. In ancient times diviners placed a short metal rod in a fire, with the shoulderbone or shinbone of an animal on top of the rod. Heat conducted up through the rod caused the bone to crack; the crack was then interpreted by the diviner to see whether a proposed action—business, marriage, war—would work out well or not, or whether the time for such action was appropriate. Divination by oracle bones disappeared long ago, but the use of divining blocks has not. Two thin wooden blocks, six to eight inches long, shaped something like a boomerang and having rough and smooth sides, are thrown on the floor before the temple altar. Two rough sides up means that the action should not be pursued; one smooth and one rough side up means the action will do well; two smooth sides up means "the deity is laughing" and the blocks should be thrown on the floor again.

The use of the *Book of Changes (I Ching)* is another form of divination from the past that is still in use today. The book is based on sixty-four numbered hexagrams or figures of six lines each. By a set procedure of sorting yarrow stalks or tossing coins, a person obtains the number of one of the sixty-four hexagrams in this book. Each hexagram is associated with a judgment, an image, and a brief statement corresponding to each of the unbroken "nine" lines and broken "six" lines that make up each six-line figure. For example, if the stalks or coins result in hexagram number 12, entitled "Standstill" or "Stagnation," the following statements are read, plus a commentary that is not included here.

THE JUDGMENT: *Standstill*. Evil people do not further the perseverance of the superior man. The great departs, the small approaches.

THE IMAGE: Heaven and earth do not unite: the image of *Standstill*. Thus the superior man falls back upon his inner worth in order to escape the difficulties. He does not permit himself to be honored with revenue.

The meaning of each line is explained in the following list. (Note that the first or beginning line is the bottom line.)

Six at the beginning means: When ribbon grass is pulled up, the sod comes with it. Each according to his kind. Perseverance brings good fortune and success.
Six in the second place means: They bear and endure; this means good fortune for inferior people. The standstill . . . helps the great man attain success.
Six in the third place means: They bear shame.
Nine in the fourth place means: He who acts at the command of the highest remains without blame. Those of like mind partake of blessing.
Nine in the fifth place means: Standstill is giving way. Good fortune for the great man. "What if it should fail, what if it should fail?" In this way he ties it to a cluster of mulberry shoots.
Nine at the top means: The standstill comes to an end. First standstill, then good fortune.[4]

Since the upper trigram means Heaven and the lower trigram means Earth, Heaven is pulling away from Earth and everything is at a standstill. By way of contrast, hexagram 11, showing Earth above Heaven, bears the judgment of "Peace" because the two are working toward each other. Description of a *change*, which in hexagram 11 is from a discouraging situation to a hopeful

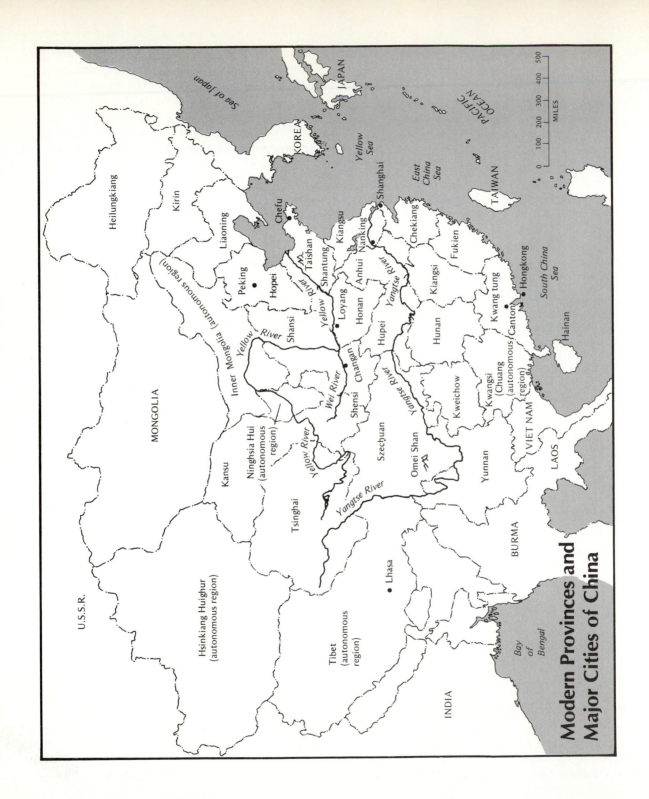

Modern Provinces and Major Cities of China

one, is typical of the book as a whole. One must always be cautious, however, as in line five above, and perseverance is a constant refrain. The reference in the same line to mulberry shoots expresses a hope for the future, based on the fact that a mulberry tree cut to the roots will send forth very strong shoots.

These practices of divination are concrete expressions of the philosophy of change that we have seen in the interaction of the forces of *yang* and *yin*. By correctly interpreting the hexagrams according to the *I Ching*, it was (and still is) believed that one could predict, measure, and relate to the course of events and make decisions about them, and thus participate in the interaction of heaven and earth. As Richard Wilhelm, one of the translators of the *I Ching*, puts it:

Everything that happens on earth is only a reproduction, as it were, of an event in a world beyond our sense perception; as regards its occurence in time, it is later than the suprasensible event. The holy men and sages . . . have access to these ideas through direct intuition and are therefore able to intervene decisively in events in the world. Thus man is linked with heaven, the suprasensible world of ideas, and with earth, the material world of visible things, to form with these a trinity of the primal powers.[5]

The Confucian Approach to Religion in China

It has long been customary to speak of the "Three Religions of China"—Confucianism, Taoism, and Buddhism—and then to argue whether Confucianism is a religion. It is more accurate to see these three movements as three "ways of handling" the complexity of belief and practice that had emerged by the first centuries of the Chou Dynasty. Both Confucian and Taoist philosophers were then part of an incredible ferment of ideas that saw the origin of the phrase: "Let a hundred flowers blossom, a hundred schools of thought contend." By the time of Confucius, the middle of the sixth century B.C.E., Taoist ideas (discussed on page 182) were already circulating, and both philosophies may be seen as responses to the problems of how to govern and provide some kind of social order during a time of increasing political and economic chaos.

It is helpful in understanding the Chinese religious

scene to look upon the three ancient sacrifices as the mainstream of Chinese religion, and to see Confucianism, Taoism, and Buddhism as three powerful currents in the mainstream, mixing with it and with each other. There are other currents that flow into the mainstream, which also "handle" the inherited traditions in still different ways, but the pattern of mixing and mingling is continuous.

The Confucian Literature

The Five Classics are regarded as the fountainhead of Confucian literature in spite of the fact that they were written before the time of Confucius. We have already referred to the *I Ching* or *Book of Changes*, a book of divination, and have quoted from the *Shih Ching* or *Book of Songs*, which is a collection of poems about the common life, romance, and war, along with special selections used in rites and ceremonies. Also related to the ancient ceremonial cult is the *Li Chi* or *Record of Rites*, which contains invaluable material helpful for understanding the ceremonies. The *Shu Ching* or *Book of History*, and the *Ch'un Ch'iu* or *Annals of Spring and Autumn* can be described as chronicles of ancient times, the latter being an account of the period 722–481 B.C.E. and the former an account of the period preceding that. The interpreters of the events and personalities of those ancient times expressed a view of life that is profoundly ethical. They viewed history as the unfolding of a purpose or destiny that affects the lives of all human beings and places grave responsibilities on leaders in particular.

Except for the *Ch'un Ch'iu* or *Annals of Spring and Autumn*, all of these books were written or compiled in some form by about the eighth century B.C.E. They were grouped together as the Five Classics, have been regarded as the primary source of ancient wisdom, and are still treasured today, at least by traditionally oriented Chinese. There are references to a sixth classic, a *Book of Music* that has disappeared, probably during a government-sponsored burning of Confucian books in 221 B.C.E. that only a few ancient works survived. It should be noted that all of these classics, except the *Book of Changes*, are interpreted by the Chinese as literature or history, although religious feelings and ideas surface again and again in their pages. The *Book of Changes*, which was treated in our discussion of religious practice, has been used for over 2,500 years to divine insights from an unseen world in order to provide guidance for life in this world, and is therefore central to religion in China.

In addition to the Five Classics, there is a collection known as the Four Books. Written during the fifth and fourth centuries B.C.E., the latter texts are an important part of the Confucian tradition. The Four Books are *Lun Yü* or the *Analects, Chung Yung,* or the *Doctrine of the Mean, Ta Hsüeh* or the *Great Learning,* and *Meng Tzu,* or the *Book of Mencius.* The first of these, the *Analects,* is considered to be a faithful rendering of what Confucius said to his disciples and is basic to understanding his life and thought.

The Life and Teachings of Confucius

Confucius is a latinization of K'ung Fu Tzu, ''Honored Philosopher K'ung,'' who was born in 551 B.C.E. in the province of Lu (modern Shantung). His father died when he was about three, and his mother reared Confucius in a state close to poverty; he was married by family arrangement at the age of nineteen. Although not much is known about his marriage except that he had one son, we do know something of his career in public office: he was supervisor of grain stores and later of public lands, then prime minister of the state of Lu about 501 B.C.E. Confucius resigned the latter post when his ruler neglected affairs of state and ignored his counsels, and set out in 497 B.C.E. as a wandering teacher with a band of disciples. Returning to his native state, he spent the last three years of his life there in teaching and literary studies and died in 479 B.C.E. He is supposed to have been a man of reserved simplicity, respectful toward officials and mourners, and a lover of music and ritual. He nevertheless spoke candidly about issues that people raised and is said to have been rather stubborn: ''Is he [Confucius] not the one who knows that he cannot succeed and keeps on trying to do so?''[6]

The Five Classics were the lifelong object of Confucius' study, for he believed that the wisdom of the past should be preserved and followed in the present. He claimed no originality for himself, but saw himself as a transmitter of past values to the present; and he tried to convince people that following those values would result in a good society, a good government, and a good life for human beings—in reality a vision of the future, rooted and authenticated in the past.

Hsiao, filial piety, both obedience to elders while they were alive and veneration of their spirits after they were gone, was a constant emphasis in Confucius' teaching, even to the point of saying that a son should not report his father's theft of a sheep to the authorities. The performance of rites for ancestors was a fundamental dimension of *li,* propriety, the proper way of carrying out rites for ancestors and the whole range of ceremonial acts for the state and the community. Confucius once exclaimed: ''I love the rite, I love the ceremony,''[7] but this should not be interpreted as slavish devotion to form. He also stressed the meaning for those involved: ''In ceremonials, it is better to be simple than lavish; and in the rites of mourning, heartfelt distress is better than observance of detail.''[8] To be engaged in the rites with reverence and dignity, to worship the spirits ''as if they were present,'' was to relate to the ultimate powers that affected human existence, to be a part of the cosmos. Therefore, rites and ceremonies, the way of propriety, brought to human beings a total view of life and the world, which led to and stimulated moral conduct.

Confucius proceeded in this context to elevate the ethical dimensions of the traditional culture, and he can be credited with deepening the Chinese understanding of them. He insisted on righteousness (*i,* pronounced ''yee'') in human relationships, and thought it was essential for a government official who wanted the confidence of the people. Governmental regulations, laws, and punishments may be necessary, but the righteous ruler will stimulate righteousness in the people. Confucius stressed *chung,* loyalty, as another necessity in human relationships, but tempered it with *shu,* reciprocity, giving and receiving, the idea of a Golden Rule. The combination of loyalty and reciprocity brought about humanity or humanness (*jen,* pronounced ''ren''), which brings about benevolence among human beings. Confucius added: ''The firm of spirit, the resolute in character, the simple in manner, and the slow of speech are not far from humanity. . . . It [jen] is to love your fellow man.''[9]

For a person to live a moral life according to these principles would result in his becoming a ''princely man'' or ''superior man'' (*chün jen*), one who develops his character by engaging in rites and ceremonies, and lives a life of moral virtue. Education, which means the study of the Five Classics with a teacher, is the method whereby a person develops moral character and learns how to carry out the ceremonies. The Confucian hope that everything "will work out all right" if this life-style is followed, is set forth in the book called *The Great Learning,* formerly attributed to Confucius but now believed to have been written about two centuries later. In it Confucius is presented as saying:

To gather in the same places where our fathers before us have gathered; to perform the same ceremonies which they before us have performed; to play the same music which they before us have played; to pay respect to those whom they honored; to love those who were dear to them—in fact, to serve those now dead as if they were living, and now departed as if they were still with us: this is the highest achievement of true filial piety.

The performance of sacrifices to Heaven and Earth is meant for the service of God. The performance of ceremonies in the ancestral temple is meant for the worship of ancestors. If one only understood the meaning of the sacrifices to Heaven and Earth, and the significance of the services in ancestral worship in summer and autumn, it would be as easy to govern a nation as to point a finger at the palm.[10]

There is an unmistakably religious feeling about these lines, as there is about Confucius' own words about ritual and ceremony. The Analects state that Confucius offered sacrifices as if the spirits were present, which has often been interpreted as meaning that he didn't believe in them but acted as if they were present. It seems much more likely that spirits were so real to him that he thought they were indeed present. When asked about prayer, he replied, "My prayer has been for a long time." Faced with the illness of a disciple, he exclaimed, "Heaven is destroying me!"[11]

A common judgment of Chinese and Western interpreters alike is that Confucius was interested only in ethics, both personal and social, and had no interest in the transcendent. Asked about spirits and about life beyond the grave, he said, "When still unable to do your duty to men, how can you do your duty to the spirits? . . . Not yet understanding life, how can you understand death?"[12] Certainly he devoted himself to what he believed were the practical and demanding problems of human beings, society, and government. Yet this was done within the context of a religious frame of reference that included Heaven, Earth, and ancestral spirits. In

part because he had a healthy respect for such powerful realities, he expressed himself conclusively: "To devote oneself earnestly to one's duty to humanity, and, while respecting the spirits, to keep them at a distance, may be called wisdom."[13]

The Great Learning and the Doctrine of the Mean were made the second and third of the Four Books because they were thought to have been written by Confucius. They have continued to hold a place of moral authority in Chinese culture, because the teaching in them is essentially Confucian in content even though Confucius did not write them.

Mencius the Idealist

Mencius (371 B.C.E.–c.289 B.C.E.) was considered to be Confucius' greatest disciple. The Book of Mencius records his conversation with a ruler in which Mencius holds that righteousness is more important than life, and that the ruler had a distinct obligation to be sensitive to the needs of his people. Mencius thus introduced into the Confucian system of thought a profound note of compassion as he spoke of "the mind which cannot bear to see the suffering of others." Because of this mind, one is impelled to rush and save "the child about to fall into the well,"[14] a phrase Confucians have since repeated again and again.

Mencius is best known for his theory of the original and essential goodness of human nature, which suggests that any Confucian religiousness is the development of the natural goodness that a human being receives at birth. Mencius based his theory of humanity's inherent goodness on an analysis of human beings, in which he finds that all of us have innate feelings of respect, shame, right and wrong, and sympathy. If that is the case, Mencius goes on to say, then the feeling of respect leads to propriety, the feeling of shame to righteousness (we are ashamed if we do wrong), the feeling of right and wrong to wisdom, and the feeling of sympathy to humanness. The third of these values, *chih,* wisdom, was also discussed by Confucius, but is raised by Mencius to be one of four that he considered normative.

Mencius' argument may sound naive to some today, as it probably did to some of his contemporaries, but he believed strongly that human beings are inherently good because they are born with feelings that lead directly to that goodness. With a reasonable amount of parental guidance and education in the classic Confucian virtues, human beings would develop naturally the potential goodness with which they were born. It was a natural and logical conclusion for Mencius that a good society would result. Just as the ruler's virtue worked down through the ranks of officialdom to the village and the family, so the individuals in the family and the village who developed their inherent goodness into lives of virtue became an important part of a social hierarchy reaching up to the ruler and all levels of government. Thus, Mencius laid the conceptual foundation for the way Confucian moral philosophy was to penetrate the Chinese political system.

Mencius' idealism cannot be fully appreciated unless he is compared with another philosopher, Hsün Tzu, who lived shortly after Mencius and who maintained stoutly that human nature is originally evil and therefore has to be restrained. Education was as important to Hsün Tzu as it was to Mencius, but the purpose of education for Hsün Tzu was to restrain evil impulses; he also recommended police power to control those who did not respond to education. He further held that spirits did not really exist and therefore rites and ceremonies had only a subjective value. This realism, though not specifically Confucian, did have a profound influence on Chinese political philosophy. The idealism of Mencius was the official philosophy, but a more realistic policy could be adopted when needed.

Orthodox Confucian Practice

Confucius, Mencius, and their contemporaries became the models for scholars, teachers, and government officials for more than 2,000 years. To quote Confucius and Mencius was to say the last word on any subject. Not only was there a deeply religious tone to much that they said, the practices that stemmed from their teachings also had a profoundly religious character.

Confucius' great love for the rites and ceremonies that he inherited has been noted above. The fact that he blessed and encouraged the ancient rituals has led most scholars to speak of them as "Confucian rituals." They indeed became a part of what has been called "the state cult of Confucius"[15] as early as the second

century B.C.E. and were celebrated with only rare interruptions until the establishment of the Chinese Republic in 1911.

During the Early or Former Han Dynasty (206 B.C.E.– 9 C.E.) rituals that had been performed for centuries were structured systematically to bring Heaven, Earth, and human beings into majestic harmony. At the apex were the sacrifices to Heaven, over which the emperor presided, as had the kings of the Chou Dynasty; but there were also sacrifices to Earth, the ancestors of the imperial family, and the gods of the soil and grain. These ceremonies, "imperial" in the fullest sense of the word, were grand and glorious in every way.

The next level of sacrifices involved the emperor to a lesser extent and focused on Shen Nung, the god of agriculture and the patron deity of silkworms, the sun and moon, various rulers, and great men. The lowest level included gods of mountains and rivers, fire, medicine, literature, and, probably most important, the city gods. The emperor's role in this third group was slight; in fact, the diffusion of the cult, with local officials throughout the Empire in charge, was a major factor in bringing about national harmony. Local magistrates had definite responsibilities in arranging and officiating at the temple sacrifices of any of the deities or spirits mentioned above.

Regardless of the degree to which the emperor was involved, the imperial sacrifices were believed to bring a sense of universal splendor to the whole country. The gods of Earth and Grain who were worshiped throughout the land touched the lives of people at the very core of their existence, especially as they gathered at shrines of the Earth God, T'u Ti Kung.

Ch'eng Huang, the City God, may well have been just as important as the Earth God to many people, because he was the guardian of civic virtue and morality. As the local magistrate presided over the daily business of the community, so the City God presided over local spiritual affairs, at times revealing to a magistrate how to handle difficult cases.

Not only did the teaching and practice attributed to Confucius pervade all that went on in both the grand and humble sacrifices, there were also temples dedicated to Confucius himself, officially called "temples of culture or literature" but built in his honor nonetheless. It is necessary to distinguish here between the honor, veneration, and respect that were offered to Confucius in these temples, and the actual worship of him, which was not. Yet such devotion to the greatest of all Chinese sages formed a part of the state cult of traditional China.

It is ironic that official worship of Confucius actually was instituted in 1906 in a last desperate effort to save the fading Ch'ing Dynasty. The great civilization based on Confucian teaching was crumbling before the onslaught of change and this last gesture had little effect. Confucian values continued to surface in the twentieth century, but the all-embracing state cult was dead.

Such was the state cult of Confucian China. The imperial power expanded the scope of this official cult on various occasions as it approved the worship of local gods and deities who exemplified Confucian virtues or who performed great deeds for the benefit of people or the country. (Two of these cults will be discussed briefly in the section on folk religion later in this chapter.) Thus, the government was able to gain the support of local cults, and at the same time keep them within the framework of orthodoxy and maintain a close watch on the lives of the people. Much that is genuinely Confucian, of course, was not a part of the state cult; ancestor rites, for example, continued as the mainstream of Chinese religious devotion, absorbing the major concern of noble and common families alike.

Taoist Patterns of Religion in China

Early Taoism (pronounced "Dowism") can almost be described as a counterculture to the orthodox, refined morality of the Confucians and their sacrifices to Heaven, Earth, and ancestors. Traditionally, the official structure of belief and practice in China has been Confucian to the core, but a number of the great emperors had Taoist leanings, and Taoist ideas have permeated Chinese culture as a whole. Although Taoism has always been classified as heterodox, like Buddhism, which came from India, the practice of Taoism has been permitted. Neither Taoism nor Buddhism was regarded as orthodox, but they were legal, with the exception of certain secret societies that had a Taoist and/or Buddhist flavor and revolted against the state.

Early Taoist Philosophy

The Tao Te Ching. Taoist ideas undoubtedly were circulating in China during the time the Confucian classics were being written and collected. The first book expressing Taoist ideas, however, was probably written between the sixth and fourth centuries B.C.E. It is entitled *Tao Te Ching,* which may be translated literally as "The Book of the Way and Its Virtue." *Te* is translated as "power" in Arthur Waley's translation,[16] which is one of the best, and also carries the idea of how one attains *tao,* which does mean "way" in the sense of a path or road, but which also carries the idea of truth, way of life, or the basic nature of the world process.

Not only is the date of the Tao Te Ching uncertain, but there also is little precise information about the author. Tradition has held that the book represents the sayings of an old philosopher named Lao Tzu, which were given to a gatekeeper as Lao Tzu departed for the West, meaning the land of the dead. This lack of information about the author, except for a few hazy references, may be intentional, for whoever wrote the book advises against seeking fame or praise for one's achievements. There is also the possibility that the ideas of several people are included in the work, and therefore the person who collected various passages and wove them together felt it best to preserve the anonymity of all who had a part in it.

There is no definition of *tao* in the *Tao Te Ching,* no attempt at systematic discussion of what the term might mean. The book begins with the discouraging statement that the *tao* that can be named (or discussed or defined) is not the *tao.* There are words about the interaction of being and nonbeing, and about *tao* as invisible, inaudible, and subtle. There also are a few barbs ridiculing the Confucian virtues of filial piety, righteousness, wisdom, and humanity, suggesting that when people talk about such virtues as the Confucians do, it can only mean that the virtues have been lost.

There are several fascinating similes that suggest or hint at the meaning of *tao:* an empty bowl that can be used, a valley and the female that receive all things, water that seeks the lowest level, an infant that acts spontaneously, and uncarved wood in its state of simplicity. The first part of the sixteenth stanza, referring to emptiness, is a kind of short summary or synthesis:

Push far enough towards the Void,
Hold fast enough to Quietness,
And of the ten thousand things none but can be worked on
    by you.
I have beheld them, whither they go back.
See, all things howsoever they flourish.
Return to the root from which they grew.
This return to the root is called Quietness;
Quietness is called submission to Fate;
What has submitted to Fate has become part of the always-
    so.[17]

Returning to the root suggests the characteristic Taoist approach to life, and the method for discovering and attaining *tao*. This method is *wu-wei*, literally "nonaction," but in actuality a life force that moves through a person and that can be appropriated naturally and effortlessly. "Nonstriving" is a better translation of *wu-wei*, for a person who acts in this way flows with the tide, utilizes his or her natural abilities, and adjusts to existing circumstances. Stanza 63 puts it briefly and succinctly:

It acts without action, does without doing, finds flavor in
    what is flavorless,
Can make the small great and the few many,
'Requites injuries with good deeds,
Deals with the hard while it is still easy,
With the great while it is still small.
. . . .
Therefore the Sage knows too how to make the easy difficult,
    and by doing so avoid all difficulties![18]

Wu-wei is expressed by the athlete who runs or throws effortlessly and naturally, and by the worker who "lets the tool do the work," each person fulfilling his or her basic potential without straining or pulling.

It is quite possible that this little book, with its scorn of Confucian morals and its gentle advocacy of a more natural, yielding way of life, was an attempt to state an alternative approach to social organization and government. There is a plea against oppression of the people, which is also to be found in Mencius, and against threatening them with death.[19] There is a plea for absolute simplicity in a small country with few people who do not use the utensils that are present in great number.[20] The ruler is advised not "to do many things," to place himself below the people in order to be above them, and to follow in order to lead.[21]

Chuang Tzu. Chuang Tzu, a man who lived during the fourth century B.C.E., picked up and developed further the ideas in the Tao Te Ching. Chuang Chou, who came to be called Chuang Tzu, at some point declined the offer of a fine government position by asking if a sacred tortoise that had been encased in a box for several hundred years would not prefer to be wagging its tail in the mud along the river bank. When the government emissaries who invited him to take the position said that the tortoise would certainly prefer the natural environment, Chuang Tzu said: "I too would rather sit here and wag my tail in the mud."[22]

The book *Chuang Tzu* is an amazing combination of mystery, questioning, whimsical humor, and flights of fancy. The writer is struck by the sound of the human voice and asks if it is any different from the cackling of chickens. Dreams also are puzzling, and Chuang Tzu wonders whether waking or dreaming is real. After dreaming he was a butterfly, he awakes in a pleasant state and muses: "I do not know whether it was Chou dreaming that he was a butterfly or the butterfly dreaming that it was Chou."[23] Is there a distinction or is all life a dream? The answer suggests a recurring theme in Chuang Tzu's thought, the transformation that characterizes waking and dreaming, the world of nature, and life and death.

It is quite possible that Chuang Tzu draws upon the concept of interacting *yang* and *yin,* along with ideas from the I Ching, as he identifies *tao* with the process of transformation and change that goes on and on. He would insist with the writer of the Tao Te Ching that *tao* cannot be described, that it is an all-pervading unity that includes large and small, ugly and beautiful, generosity and deceit.

That ultimate unity includes human beings, especially those who are open to it, who with emptiness are ready to receive all things and relate to the process without striving or artificiality. Once again the flash of humor: "The duck's legs are short, but if we try to lengthen them, the duck will feel pain. The crane's legs are long, but if we try to cut off a portion of them, the crane will feel grief."[24] The point about not trying to change nature is set forth magnificently in Chuang Tzu's sum-

Pai Yun Taoist Temple. *The autumn sun shines brightly on the peaceful entry to the Pai Yun Taoist Temple in Peking. In spite of people moving to and fro, the grounds and small temples within also convey a sense of peace and serenity.* (Courtesy of Mary Bush)

mary statement: "The universe and I exist together, and all things and I are one. . . . Let us not proceed. Let us let things take their own course."[25] He looks back to a "pure man of old" as a model, but what he sees is very different from what Confucius saw:

The pure man of old knew neither to love life nor to hate death. He did not rejoice in birth, nor did he resist death. Without any concern he came and without any concern he went, that was all. He did not forget his beginning nor seek his end. He accepted (his body) with pleasure, and forgetting (life and death), he returned to (the natural state). He did not violate Tao with his mind, and he did not assist Nature with man. This is what is meant by a pure man.[26]

This attitude toward death, not resisting it but accepting it, is perhaps the ultimate test of accepting the transforma-

tion of things as *tao*. With a fine sense of the incongruous, Chuang Tzu tells stories of men who are about to die. Since one man's organs are on top of his body, cheeks level with navel, shoulders above head, hair pointing to the sky, Chuang Tzu says, in a masterpiece of understatement, "The *yin* and *yang* in him were out of order. . . ." But the man's mind is at ease and he exclaims:

Suppose my right arm is transformed into a sling. With it I should look for a dove to roast. Suppose my buttocks were transformed into wheels and my spirit into a horse. I should mount them. What need do I have for a chariot?[27]

Another man is about to die, and his wife and children naturally gather about weeping. Chuang Tzu speaks through the man's friend and says: "Don't disturb the transformation that is about to take place."[28]

New Taoist Temple. *A rather grand Taoist temple was erected in southern Taiwan in 1960, at a time when the local economy was not flourishing. Although an hour's drive from the city of Tainan, the temple has attracted a number of worshipers, some casual, some very serious.* (Richard Bush)

Such words at such a time may sound insensitive to some, but not to Chuang Tzu. When his own wife died, a friend came to call and found the widowed husband sitting on the ground, singing and drumming on a bowl. The friend was shocked and asked how Chuang Tzu could behave in such a way after the death of one so dear. Chuang Tzu replied:

When she died, how could I help being affected? But . . . I realize that originally she had no life; and not only no life, she had no form; not only no form, she had no material force (*ch'i*). In the limbo of existence and non-existence, there was transformation and the material force was evolved. The material force was transformed to be form, form was transformed to become life, and now birth has transformed to become death. This is like the rotation of the four seasons, spring, summer, fall, and winter. Now she lies asleep in the great house (the universe). For me to go about weeping and wailing would be to show my ignorance of destiny. Therefore I desist.[29]

There are certain tendencies toward the fanciful in Chuang Tzu that surface later in Taoist religion. We

can read of river and mountain immortals that point to the later "eight immortals," and of the Yellow Emperor who could rise up into the clouds, thus blazing a trail for the Taoist adepts who performed great feats of levitation. And there is a reference to a person who lived for centuries, a model for later Taoists who devoted themselves to practices intended to bring about equally long lives.

The mystical philosophy of the *Tao Te Ching* and the *Chuang Tzu* book may be seen as radically different from the popular religion that bears the name Taoist, or the philosophical and the religious Taoism may be regarded as two sides of the same coin. Regardless of what mature scholars and beginning students may conclude in this debate, it is necessary to recognize the deeply religious attitudes expressed in the work of Lao Tzu and Chuang Tzu, their awareness of a transcendent reality beyond "the dusty world"—not a god figure, to be sure, but a process of change and transformation that affects human existence profoundly. Human beings adjust to it and relate to it by thought and action that does not depend on striving. The result is a sense of peace and tranquillity that transcends description, but is known clearly by those who experience it.

The Shift to Religion in Taoist Texts

When we survey the vast body of Taoist literature, we find a shift from philosophical to religious concerns. The 1,120 volumes of the *Tao Tsang,* or *Storehouse of Tao,* were not published in their entirety until the Ming Dynasty (1368–1644). The collection begins with three basic sections, each of which presents the teachings of a different order or sect within the Taoist fold. Each of these three sections includes materials dealing with basic doctrines, charms for commanding spirits, esoteric secrets, spiritual charts and maps, lists and names of spirits, vows and rules for initiates, liturgies of renewal and burial, collections of magical rites, cures, blessings and incantations, biographies of famous Taoists, hymns and melodies, and documents, memorials, and rescripts. In addition to the three basic sections, the *Tao Tsang* includes four supplements that contain the teachings of other sects and miscellaneous materials. Very few of these volumes have been translated into Western languages; but, as a result of publication efforts in recent

Worshiping in a Taoist Temple. *Two high school students and an old man are praying or meditating in a Taoist temple in southern Taiwan. The students may be concerned about exams; the man may be seeking guidance in a business deal or concerned with marital problems.* (Courtesy of Richard Bush)

decades, scholars are now at work on these texts and translations have begun to appear.

As examples of this extensive literature, a few Taoist texts may be mentioned in order to have a glimpse of the religious or popular Taoism that began to spread during the Former Han Dynasty (206 B.C.E.–9 C.E.) and then attracted much attention in the Latter Han (25–220 C.E.). One such book is the *Ts'an T'ung Ch'i,* which describes alchemical processes in which lead, mercury, and gold are melted into potions that are supposed to give exceedingly long life, even immortality to those who take them. Discussions on control of the breath are included, and words and phrases from the Tao Te Ching may be found throughout, for Wei Po-yang, the author, was trying to harmonize various teachings in order to indicate how a person could become a *hsien,*

an immortal, immune to fire, water, and all danger.

The most famous of these popular Taoist works is the *Pao P'u Tzu* (*Philosopher Embracing Simplicity*), which was written in the early fourth century C.E. by Ko Hung, who lived from about 253–333. He, too, wrote at length on alchemy, but also included a lot of Confucian moral teaching that he used to sanction the elaborate system of merit he developed. Good deeds would increase one's life; bad deeds would make it shorter. The whole aim, of course, is to be an immortal, and alchemy, certain sexual practices, and diets contribute to that end, the alchemic elixirs most of all. Ko Hung says in the *Pao P'u Tzu* that all the books he had read

consider reconverted cinnabar and gold fluid to be the most important. Thus these two things represent the acme of the way to immortality. . . . The transformations of the two substances (mercury and gold) are the more wonderful the more they are heated. Yellow gold does not disintegrate even after having been smelted a hundred times. . . . If these two medicines are eaten, they will strengthen our bodies and therefore enable us not to grow old nor to die.[30]

Yet another fourth century C.E. work, entitled *Yellow Canon Court,* presents meditation as a process of internal alchemical refinement. One who meditates seeks an inner vision combining thought, word, and deed, which after a long process leads to a body and life impervious to death. The book picks up an ancient Taoist theme of chaos (*hun-tun*), which is not seen in a negative sense, "but rather a vision concerning the true order of cosmic and human life, . . . [that] reality is a fluid fusion of chaos and cosmos."[31]

In the three books just discussed, and in others we have not considered, we can observe the main trends in popular or religious Taoism. The major concern in this kind of Taoism is with gaining superhuman powers, such as immortality, by engaging in exercises that seem to run counter to *wu-wei,* the nonstriving advised in the *Tao Te Ching;* seeking such powers is contrary to being merely a part of the process of change as Chuang Tzu saw it. There are references in Chuang Tzu's work, however, to "pure men of old" who could climb to great heights, or who could not be burned by fire or drowned in water. Chuang Tzu also spoke of "immortals" of rivers and mountains, of the universe as a great furnace, and of wonderful islands to be visited. Regardless of what he may have meant, later Taoists found in his book the incentive to see if such things could really be true, and a new, popular, religious Taoism emerged.

Taoist Practices, Groups, and Leaders

To inquire about ways in which popular Taoism was practiced, the organization of groups, and the individuals who led these groups, is to enter a world that seems strange and mysterious. However different popular or religious Taoism may be from the philosophical and mystical Taoism of earlier times, both belong to the Taoist framework and bear the same name.[32] Confucians might not agree with Taoist philosophy, but they could only be shocked by the practitioners of Taoist religion.

Some practices in these popular Taoist movements seem to have involved a passion for immortality of the physical body on earth. Others appear to have been directed toward what is called immortality of the soul or the inner person. As previously mentioned, two early pieces of Taoist popular literature illustrate the attempts to gain immortality by the practice of alchemy. Through melting metals such as gold and cinnabar (mercuric sulphide), and drinking the mixture obtained in the process, individuals hoped to become immortal. However, anything more than a tiny amount has the opposite effect. Thus, after a number of people died, a tiny "pill of immortality" composed of the resolidified metal was taken.

Other practices also proved fatal. There were persons who thought that by jumping into a fire one might ascend to heaven like a flame, a practice that was soon abandoned. It is possible that some died from starvation because dietary recommendations called for eating lighter food such as flowers and vegetables without any of the heavier grains that would weigh one down. Breathing exercises were believed to prolong life, especially if one breathed the morning mist in springtime or the *yin* clouds in autumn. The combined practices of breathing, dietetics, and alchemy were utilized in what was called the Interior Gods Hygiene School because such practices would encourage the 36,000 gods within the body who are trying to sustain life.

Expeditions were sent out to look for the Islands of the Blessed, where magical plants with rejuvenating powers were believed to grow. Some adepts engaged in gymnastic exercises, coupled with the breathing regimens mentioned above. Others engaged in sexual practices that involved union with a female partner without releasing any semen. And there were still others who merely sat or lay in the sun, not to get suntans and look better, but to absorb the sun's health-giving rays and live longer.

The Interior Gods Hygiene School included groups who followed one or more of the practices outlined here. A very different group called *Ch'ing T'an,* the School of Pure Conversation, appeared during the third and fourth centuries C.E. A more intellectual group than those previously discussed and those to be treated below, the Pure Conversation group discussed philosophy, wrote poetry, made music, and engaged in quiet meditation. Although the tendency in these groups was for the members to turn their backs on anything resembling worldly advantage, some of these "pure ones" seem to have had a genuine concern for society and even entered government service. Others drank great amounts of wine and engaged in unconventional social behavior to the extent that they were shunned by polite society.

The most striking Taoist groups were those that developed in the second century C.E. under the leadership of the Chang family. In Szechuan Province in west China, Chang Tao-ling claimed to have concluded a universal treaty with all demons and spirits and thus to have gained control over them. He had charms that could protect people from demons and even exorcise evil spirits. He called himself a *T'ien Shih* or Celestial Master, the name by which the sect is known. He passed his power and authority on to his son Chang Heng and his grandson Chang Lu, the succession constituting a beginning of what has been called a Taoist papacy. The group was also called *Wu Tou Mi Tao,* which means "Five Pecks of Rice *Tao,*" the five pecks or bushels being the amount believers were to contribute to the leaders of the movement.

Another movement sprang up in the eastern provinces, notably Kiangsi, led by Chang Chiao (no relation to the Chang Tao-ling family) who had a revelation while still a young man that in 184 C.E., after ten years of political and natural catastrophes, an age of Great Peace would be inaugurated. Chang Chiao told the people of his time that the misfortunes of that era were due to human sin, so that all were to confess their sins and drink sanctified water. They would then be immune to any danger; death in battle would indicate that they had insufficient faith or had not confessed all their sins. People gave up their belongings to be distributed among the poor, built roads and bridges by voluntary labor, and developed a powerful mass movement. Government forces finally attacked and Chang Chiao was killed in 184 C.E., the year the Great Peace was to have dawned, but various elements of the Great Peace movement continued.

Military force has been necessary at many points in Chinese history to deal with Taoist and quasi-Taoist secret societies that have specialized in combat techniques along with less harmful rituals. The fact that such groups met in secret, used code language, and often were opposed to authority meant that government suspicions were continually aroused. The societies were also charged with harboring criminals and fomenting rebellion, so that police and military forces were sent against them at various times. Obviously much of the suspicion was unjustified and the governments certainly overreacted. It also must be recognized that the severity of government controls and pressures, especially in times of disaster or chaos, provoked the most innocent of secret societies to revolutionary activity.

Many of the Taoist groups that have appeared in succeeding centuries have been led by men with unusual gifts or strengths and the ability to attract followers by their dynamic personalities. The Taoist priest is often this kind of charismatic individual, a continuation of the shamans* of ancient China, men and women who were believed to communicate with spirits and transmit messages from them to ordinary human beings. The *Tao Shih,* meaning literally a "*tao* professional," was in ancient times a specialist in alchemy, and today is one who knows the rituals for the great festivals and for exorcising demons from buildings and from people. The community still regards him as a charismatic individual whose "gifts" enable him to be a medium between the spirit world and human beings.

Although Taoist rituals are not limited to Taoist temples, the temples are quite colorful places where one may observe very lively activity. Three images usually grace the main altar, as is also the case in Buddhist temples in China. In the Han Dynasty the *tao* was personified and deified as the "Celestial Venerable of Mysterious Origin," or the "Pure August One," and later received the name of the Jade Emperor (*Yü Huang*), by which he is known today. He is flanked on the altars by the "August Ruler of the Tao" on one side and by the "August Old Ruler" on the other. The latter figure is regarded as an incarnation of Lao Tzu and is depicted as a white-haired old man. Substitutions may be made for the two-side figures in this Taoist trinity, but not for the Jade Emperor, who is constant and rules over all.

Taoism, however, is more than ritual, meditation, and alchemy. There is a moral element, particularly in terms of an altruism that focuses on the good of others. According to a second century C.E. text, the *Tai-ping Jung,*

---

* The shaman or "medium" is found in many cultures, and is a man or woman who has gifts for handling the spirit world and the capacity to be possessed by spirits and to communicate with them. The role of the shaman was first discussed in Chapter 2.

Youth Listen to a Taoist Priest.   *An elderly Taoist priest talks to two young men about the way the* Tao *is related to modern life. The three stand before one of the small halls of the Pai Yun Taoist Temple in Peking, where other such conversations were taking place.* (Courtesy of Mary Bush)

those who receive the *tao* should pass it on to others, those who have the good things of life should share with those in need. This is part of an all-encompassing Central Harmony.[33] Taoist monasteries, where *Tao Shih* gathered from all over China in former years, have had strict rules of admission and communal life. The previous record of behavior, belief, and health of each new arrival was checked thoroughly, and admission was denied if there was anything irregular or undocumented. A precise

etiquette and protocol was followed for the new member, who was then assigned to the most menial tasks as he began his residence. Sponsorship by a senior *Tao Shih* was required, as well as the sponsorship of some wealthy person to pay expenses.

The daily schedule in a monastery included periods of work and worship. Scriptures were chanted and lectures on the scriptures were a major part of the day's activities. Study sessions included the Confucian Five

"Bai-bai"-ing in a Folk Religious Temple in Taiwan. *A female devotee is kneeling before an altar table behind which is an image of the deity. In the background is the temple shop, where articles needed for worship* (bai-bai) *may be purchased.* (Courtesy of Richard Bush)

were milder punishments for laziness, neglect of duties, or the failure to get up in the morning. A Taoist monk was not allowed to marry, but a *Tao Shih* or priest might marry and have a family.

Both philosophical and religious Taoism have found it possible to blend into the total cultural scene in China. The *Tao Shih* appears occasionally in Chinese fiction, sometimes providing a sense of mystery, sometimes using his powers to aid or hinder a figure in the story. Most important of all is the influence that Taoist philosophy has had on Chinese painting. Whenever we see a painting in which trees and mountains blend softly into the mist, and there is no horizon, only infinity, then we can be sure that the painter has been influenced by Taoism. So it is with poets, Confucian scholars, and the common people—the *tao* pervades all.

Folk Religion and Society

We may well ask how people in China have managed to handle the incredible diversity of doctrine and practice around them. We may also wonder how any unity or harmony, highly valued as these are by the Chinese, is at all possible, given the diversity that we have already seen and that is still to be discussed.

A highly visible cult has continued from ancient times to the present as the mainstream of Chinese religion. Confucians stressed offerings to ancestors, as well as the sacrifices to Heaven and to Earth, and offerings to the Earth God continue to the present day. The triad of Taoist deities, with the Jade Emperor in the center, reigns supreme in Taoist temples. Buddhas and bodhisattvas brought from India and enshrined in Buddhist temples, mountain shrines, and magnificent caves, are still present. Rather than the traditional "three religions of China," however, it is much more accurate to speak of a basic, continuing tradition with three approaches to it, three identifiable patterns of belief and practice with supporting scriptures and institutional expressions. Although Taoists have gently ridiculed Confucians, and Confucians have acknowledged little value in Taoism and Buddhism, and Buddhists have looked condescendingly on Confucians and Taoists, the three movements do complement each

Classics and Four Books, as well as specifically Taoist texts. Meals in the monastery were very simple and usually vegetarian. Appreciation for the life-style in a Taoist monastery has been expressed with great feeling by a Japanese scholar who stayed in the White Cloud Monastery in Peking for an extended period during World War II when Japanese forces controlled much of China. On one occasion he realized that he was the only person in the monastery who had an electric light burning.

I then realized that in the monastic world the scale of values was reversed, that little significance was attached to artificial, so-called cultural activities. [Rather than gathering scraps of knowledge] . . . it is better to be embraced in the vastness of nature, to melt into it. Then there is no wasted resistance to life, no useless conflagration. When one's breathing is in harmony with nature, one becomes identical with its very life-flow. The life of the *tao-shih* at the White Cloud Monastery was the perfect expression of this natural identity. I was suddenly overcome by a sense of hollowness, of humility and sadness at the sharp realization that not only was my body that of an alien but my heart as well. I doused the lamp.[34]

Taoist monastic rules were quite comprehensive and were similar in character to those for Buddhist monks. A Taoist monk could be expelled for immorality, destruction of property, and mishandling of funds, and there

Preparing the God's Palanquin. *Men of a Taiwanese town prepare a palanquin in which eight men will carry the image of a deity or a Buddha around the streets. Whether this is done on the birthday of the deity or on some other special occasion, it is important to pass every house.* (Courtesy of Richard Bush)

other in striking ways, and indeed have learned to live together.

Devotion Based on Function

What has been described thus far is only the beginning of diversity. Most Chinese cities and towns enshrine a City God who guards community virtue and watches over civic undertakings. Fulfilling much the same function in the home is the Kitchen God, who is dispatched to heaven on New Year's Eve to report the family's behavior during the past year (after being plied with wine to dull his memory of less than praiseworthy happenings). Goddesses such as Nai-nai and Niang-niang (names of endearment for grandmotherly figures) are approached by women who wish to bear a child, or to pray for easier childbirth or family harmony. The Bodhisattva Kuan Yin fulfills the same functions. There are also gods of roads and highways, of war and community protection, of heaven and hell. In addition to the Earth God, farmers invoke Shen Nung, who is heralded as the creator of agriculture. Yao Wang's name means literally "the Medicine King," and he is assisted by a host of healing deities. Moreover, each trade has its patron deity, such as Lu Pan for the carpenters.

Obviously the Chinese can handle this widespread diversity by making offerings in the temple of a god who is supposed to give the particular aid that a family needs at that moment, such as healing for a sick relative, success in a business deal, or leniency from the law. It is quite appropriate to seek one god's blessings on one day and the aid of another deity the following day. The need of the moment suggests the choice of a deity; the gods whose services are not needed are usually neither dishonored nor rejected.

In some situations, however, attention given to the temple of one god may mean the decline of another god. The question is whether a god or goddess is found to be effective or not. If prayer has been offered to Kuan Yin for a male heir and only females are born to the family, the mother might turn to Nai-nai or Niang-niang. If a son is born, she tells other women and allegiance begins to shift. There are also special times and ceremonies when the power of a god may be restored, a "recharging" of the deity with wonder-working power. If a god is effective, his temple is kept in good repair and frequently redecorated; if his power wanes, his temple will be neglected and fall into disrepair.

Deified Heroes and Heroines

The picture is further elaborated by another contribution to diversity: the deification of heroes and heroines, men and women who are regarded as models of virtuous conduct and honored for deeds of great benefit to the people. The origin of devotion to such heroes is "generally marked by two inseparable elements: a public crisis and a hero."[35] The crisis might be war, famine, plague, imminent crop failure, or natural disaster; in such cases offerings are made to gods, Buddhas, and spirits as people intercede for help. When there is no relief, someone may remember the great virtue and prowess of a powerful person of the past, such as Kuan Yü, who tried unsuccessfully to restore the Han Dynasty early in the third century C.E. A shrine is then erected to the hero and offerings are made, or an older cult and shrine to that particular deified hero is quickly revived after years of neglect. Basic to the cult of deified heroes and its revival is a powerful faith:

Through the magical prowess of his soul, the deified hero was able to enter into the common people's daily life and into their memory by receiving their worship and listening to their prayers of mundane affairs—requests for an heir, for cure of sickness, for financial prosperity, for safety on a dangerous trip, for success in work. Occasional realization of success in any of these requests enhanced the fame of the hero as an efficacious god.[36]

This highly dramatic position of the hero as god stems from the development of a body of mythological lore handed down from generation to generation, usually as a part of regular rituals.

Were it not for the enhancement of heroes by myths that grow and develop through the years, even the moral virtues they possessed might soon be forgotten. The heroes are "loyal and righteous," "generous in charity," "devoted in service," and therefore a continuing inspiration to the people. Many of the temples were originally established by government decree and the people were ordered by the government to pay homage to the heroes thus enshrined, precisely because such devotion appeared to deepen civic values. Elaborate ceremonies impressed these ancient virtues on the minds of the people, for such rituals were institutionalized in community life and people from all levels of the community took part. Nevertheless, it was easy to forget past values as the generations rolled on and the temple's upkeep was neglected, so that a dream of the old general or of a woman who had given generous gifts to the poor was needed to awaken memory and devotion.

Kuan Yü, who as a deity is called Kuan Kung, seems to have survived as a personifier of virtues as well as one who continues to perform mighty acts for the benefit of the people. Devotion to him is based on much more than his having been a mighty warrior and therefore a "god of war":

He was worshiped by merchants as a god of wealth and of fidelity in business contracts, by common people as a curer of disease, by soldiers as their patron god, and by many local communities as the chief protective deity against calamities and destruction. For many social organizations, such as fraternities and secret societies, he was the overseer of fraternal ties and a blessing spirit for their cause of mutual interest and justice.[37]

Kuan Kung is the best example of the great hero of the past who embodies the values of a political order that controls from above, and who also appears to meet the needs of common people below.

Matsu, the Queen of Heaven. *The female deity who is worshiped all along the east coast of China and the west coast of Taiwan presides in her temple, with a minor deity at the left. A simple offering of oranges has been placed on the altar; a box for money offerings is placed in front of the altar.* (Courtesy of Mary Bush)

On the southeast coast of China in past years, and now all along the western coast of Taiwan, Kuan Kung is rivaled by a female deity known as Matsu, *T'ien Hou*, Queen of Heaven. There are several versions of her story, but the most popular begins with Matsu as a daughter of a family that lived along the Fukien coast. Many fishermen from the village were at sea in their boats when a fierce storm hit the area. Knowing they could not find their way home, the teenage Matsu set fire to her home, providing a beacon to lead them to safety. The stories depict her coming out of the clouds to give help and supplying herbs she had gathered to save people's lives in a plague; they also maintain that Chinese ambassadors to Korea received her help, for which the Emperor himself honored her. Her devotion to others

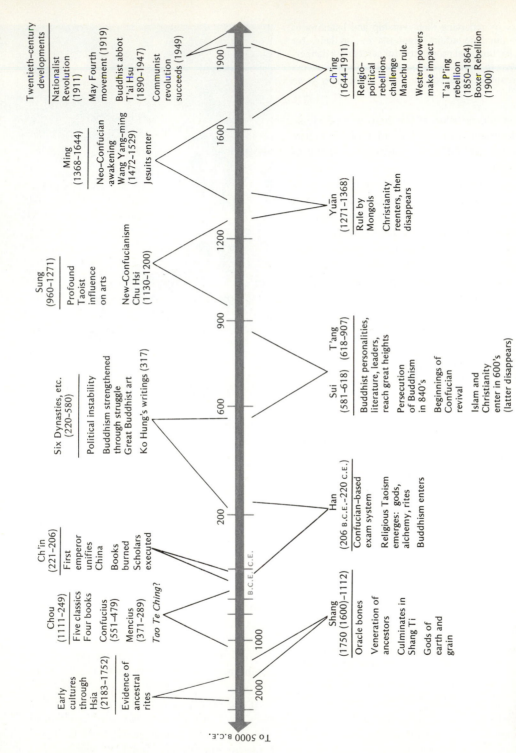

Early
cultures
through
Hsia
(2183–1752)

Evidence of
ancestral
rites

Chou
(1111–249)

Five classics
Four books

Confucius
(551–479)

Mencius
(371–289)

Tao Te Ching?

Ch'in
(221–206)

First
emperor
unifies
China

Books
burned

Scholars
executed

Six Dynasties, etc.
(220–580)

Political instability

Buddhism strengthened
through struggle

Great Buddhist art

Ko Hung's writings (317)

Sung
(960–1271)

Profound
Taoist
influence
on arts

New-Confucianism
Chu Hsi
(1130–1200)

Ming
(1368–1644)

Neo-Confucian
awakening

Wang Yang-ming
(1472–1529)

Jesuits enter

Twentieth-century
developments

Nationalist
Revolution
(1911)

May Fourth
movement (1919)

Buddhist abbot
T'ai Hsu
(1890–1947)

Communist
revolution
succeeds (1949)

Shang
(1750 (1600)–1112)

Oracle bones

Veneration of
ancestors

Culminates in
Shang Ti

Gods of
earth and
grain

Han
(206 B.C.E.–220 C.E.)

Confucian-based
exam system

Religious Taoism
emerges: gods,
alchemy, rites

Buddhism enters

Sui   T'ang
(581–618) (618–907)

Buddhist personalities,
literature, leaders,
reach great heights

Persecution
of Buddhism
in 840's

Beginnings of
Confucian
revival

Islam and
Christianity
enter in 600's
(latter disappears)

Yuán
(1271–1368)

Rule by
Mongols

Christianity
reenters, then
disappears

Ch'ing
(1644–1911)

Religio-
political
rebellions
challenge
Manchu rule

Western powers
make impact

T'ai P'ing
rebellion
(1850–1864)

Boxer Rebellion
(1900)

B.C.E. | C.E.

To 5000 B.C.E.

2000

1000

200

600

900

1200

1600

1900

Religion During the Chinese Dynasties.

is highlighted by the claim that she refused an arranged marriage in order to help persons in need.

The celebration of Matsu's birthday in Taiwan is a tumultuous event, as pilgrims come from all over the island to the central temple at Peikang, bringing their own Matsu images to be recharged with power at the central shrine. Parades in her honor sometimes stall traffic for hours, and her temples are filled with devotees whose sincerity cannot be doubted. She is depicted as a dour, impassive old lady, but devotion in her name is warm and enthusiastic. When asked why he had brought his daughter to a Matsu temple, a young father responded: "Every so often I feel in my heart that I want to worship Matsu. That is why I come."

Thus there are no deep divisions in the Chinese religious scene. One may speak of Confucianism, Taoism, and Buddhism as the main branches of a tree, and think of the many local cults as smaller branches. The image of several currents side by side in a mainstream is even more appropriate. Buddhism has its schools of life and thought, as discussed in Chapter 5. Taoist groupings have been treated in connection with Taoist belief and practice. Confucian virtues and rites are ever present, bolstering the family, society, and government. In all this diversity there is little that appears exclusive, in the sense of "Ours is the only way." The tendency is rather toward coexistence, mutual acceptance, and the blending of all these currents. One feature, however, remains constant: the cult of the ancestors has always been and continues to be the mainstream. The result, most of the time, is a sense of give-and-take, a relaxed harmony in religious groupings accompanying and echoing the harmony in society, families, and human beings.

Chinese Religion and the Modern World

As we come to inquire about the role of religion in modern China, and to ask about the effect of Western ideas and culture on Chinese religion, it becomes more and more difficult to give clear-cut answers. Many complex factors must be grasped in order to understand any aspect of Chinese life during the last two centuries, and religion is no exception.

Modern Religio-Political Movements

During the first century and a half of the Ch'ing Dynasty (1644–1911), a series of powerful rulers maintained a strong sense of continuity; the power of the Manchus, a people who had come from lands north of China to conquer the Chinese and establish the dynasty, seemed to be unassailable. Various religio-political groups, such as were mentioned in our discussion of Taoism, nevertheless were active in various parts of China, and were by no means limited to the Taoist context. From the end of the eighteenth century to the collapse of the empire in 1911, a wide spectrum of Taoist and other groups emerged from relative secrecy to carry out a series of rebellions that disturbed increasingly large sections of the country and ultimately weakened the Ch'ing Dynasty.

The first of these modern rebellions centered in the White Lotus societies, Buddhist groups that can definitely be traced to the twelfth century C.E., and perhaps to a time seven or eight centuries earlier.[38] The followers worshiped the Buddha Amitabha, as in Pure Land Buddhism, but thought of him as a Buddha of Light. The White Lotus sects also emphasized Maitreya Buddha, whom they believed to be waiting in the Tuśita heaven for the proper time to come and bring a paradise on earth. This kind of teaching appealed to the disadvantaged, whose economic lot was pitiful, and to men who occupied a somewhat higher position in society, but who were "losers" for one reason or another and were inclined to blame the Ch'ing government for their misfortunes.

A most unusual doctrinal dimension of the White Lotus groups was that of belief in and worship of an Unborn Old Mother, which originated in Chinese folk religion with possible Taoist origins. Popular scriptures proclaimed that Wu Sheng Lao Mu, also translated as Eternal Venerable Mother, thought continually of her children, wept over their condition, and longed to bring them to her eternal home. Devotion to her involved a variety of practices: meditation on her name and on other sayings, faith healing, and recitals of chants and formulas believed to bring good fortune and protection from evil. Men and women met together, and women were counted among the leaders of some of these groups.

After a false start in 1786, a major White Lotus Rebellion broke out in 1796 and gained great success in border areas for a couple of years. The great Ch'ien Lung Em-

The Merging of Chinese Religious Traditions. *The small shrine at the edge of a farmer's field houses an image of the Earth God, while on the tree to the left is a banner proclaiming "Praise to Buddha Amitabha." A current of indigenous Chinese religion thus stands side by side in Taiwan with the basic affirmation of Pure Land Buddhism that has come from India.* (Courtesy of Mary Bush)

peror of the Ch'ing Dynasty had just stepped down and government forces were weak. Only after 1802 did government forces become effective, and in 1805 they finally managed to defeat the rebels; the loss of life was finally estimated at about 300,000 people, including a number of women on the rebel side.

Although the White Lotus Rebellion was put down, the basic spirit and idea lived on. Soon another group of the poor and disgruntled, still basically within the White Lotus framework, began to take shape. Convinced that they were living in a time of great distress and that several Buddhas had come into the world without effecting any change, they placed their hope in the Buddha Maitreya and his inauguration of a new age. This generation of Maitreya followers, like their predecessors, were able to interpret certain cryptic passages in popular scriptures to suggest that the time of Maitreya's coming was imminent. Their leaders stressed an eight-syllable

mantra, which they recited or chanted in praise and honor of the Eternal Mother figure: "True Emptiness [is the] Original Home of the Unborn Venerable Mother." Another version, also eight characters in Chinese, substituted "father-mother" for "venerable mother." Since the eight Chinese characters were called eight "trigrams," the name for the next revolt became the Eight Trigrams Rebellion.[39] The rebellion originated with a man named Lin Ch'ing who, though he had failed at everything else, joined a revived White Lotus group in 1806 and soon became a teacher capable of winning the allegiance of others. He also began mapping a strategy for a rebellion with other leaders of the sect and training a fighting force. The group was able to maintain a high degree of secrecy until they managed to capture several villages and towns, ending with an assault on the Imperial City in Peking in 1813. However, this movement, with its strange mixture of Chinese religious and cultural phenomena, collapsed and its leaders were executed.

Foreign Religions in China

Before mentioning two additional rebellions of the nineteenth century, it is necessary to discuss two other religions, Islam and Christianity, both of which entered China in the seventh century C.E. Strict Islamic monotheism, Muslim prohibitions against the eating of pork, and other requirements have meant that Islam has traditionally won a following primarily among minority peoples on the frontiers of China, not among ethnic Chinese. Nevertheless, Islam is reported to have had about forty million followers in China by the middle of the twentieth century.

Nestorian Christians, representatives of Eastern Christendom, were present for about a century during the early T'ang Dynasty, and then disappeared. Catholic Christians who entered in the Yuan Dynasty survived for the same amount of time, but it was not until Jesuit missionaries arrived in the late sixteenth century that Christianity began to take root in China. The Jesuits made several interesting efforts to relate Christianity to Chinese tradition, as in allowing veneration of ancestors as a civil ceremony, but these were ended by papal order. It was not until the nineteenth century that Catholics and Protestants began to have any noticeable follow-

Confucian Temple Restored in China. *The impressive Confucian temple in Nanking (Nanjing) has been restored at government expense. Completed in February of 1986, the community celebrated its reopening with great pride.* (Courtesy of Mary Bush)

ing among the Chinese. By the middle of the twentieth century, the total Christian community numbered only about four million, less than one percent of the population. Christianity was associated with the Western powers that had forced humiliating treaties on China, and most Chinese regarded as foreign the whole gamut of Christian worship, life, and thought.

One prominent exception to the generally negative Chinese reaction to Christianity was the fascinating movement of the mid-nineteenth century called the Heavenly Kingdom of Great Peace (*T'ai P'ing T'ien Kuo,* or *T'ai P'ing,* "Great Peace," for short). Its leader, Hung Hsiu-ch'uan, had a month's study with a Baptist missionary from America and thus gained a smattering

of Christianity with which he fused traditional Chinese teachings to form the basis for the new movement. For example, the fifth commandment of the Decalogue, requiring the honoring of father and mother, was expanded to an extensive statement on filial piety. The trinity included God the Father and Jesus the Great Elder Brother, but the third person of the trinity was the Great Younger Brother, Hung himself.

Hung had a driving passion to stamp out demons, which he believed had flourished since the appearance of Taoism and Buddhism, and which he associated with the imperial court. He sought followers who would contribute all their personal possessions to a common treasury, receive thoroughgoing training in his doctrines, and be willing to fight for the cause. Discipline was strictly followed, especially in the early days of the movement.

By the late 1840s, the T'ai P'ing organization had attained considerable strength. Although the imperial army beat off a T'ai P'ing attack in 1850, Hung's forces proceeded to occupy and control several provinces in central China. The political organization deteriorated, however, and Hung began to give less attention to his duties and spend more time with his wives. The imperial army finally launched a decisive campaign in 1864, in the face of which Hung committed suicide. Thus, another religio-political rebellion of the nineteenth century, in this case influenced somewhat from the West, came to an end.

In the late nineteenth and early twentieth centuries, many efforts were made to preserve Chinese tradition, particularly as expressed in Confucianism. The Self Strengthening Movement of the late nineteenth century advocated using Western technology for national defense, but holding on to Confucian tradition for the substance of life. At the end of that century K'ang Yu-wei (1858–1927) tried unsuccessfully to inaugurate political, social, and educational reforms based on Western models, while still holding on to the compassion taught by Mencius and later Confucians. The Boxer Rebellion of 1900, irrational and fanatical as it may seem to outsiders, was an intense effort by Chinese traditionalists to wipe out every vestige of foreign influence.

The Nationalist Revolution of 1911 swept out the Ch'ing Dynasty and resulted more than a decade later in a Republic of China. The most dynamic force during this time of great change was the New Culture Movement of the 1920s and 1930s. It originated with the May Fourth Movement of 1919, in which students protested the way Chinese diplomats had made concessions to European countries at the Versailles Peace Conference. This early generation of "militant students" carried banners proclaiming, "Down with the Old Curiosity Shop of Confucius!" and called themselves "Mr. Science" and "Mr. Democracy," clearly identifying themselves with the new ideas from the West that one of their leaders, Peking University Professor Hu Shih, was advocating. The Confucian spirit was revived again in the New Life Movement of the early 1930s, in which Chiang K'ai-shek, then President of China, set forth Confucian virtues such as propriety, righteousness, integrity, and a sense of shame as the foundation for his country.

Religion in China Today

A hundred years of continual change in China came to a tumultuous climax at the midpoint of the twentieth century. Eight years of war with Japan, with the disorder, suffering, and death that accompany war, came to an end in 1945. Civil war between the Nationalist forces led by Chiang K'ai-shek and the Communist armies led by Mao Tse-tung followed within a year, ending with the Communist victory in 1949. About two million Chinese who supported the Nationalist cause moved to Taiwan, across the Taiwan Straits from the southeast coast of China, while the Communist leaders set about one of the most thoroughgoing social revolutions in human history. We must now attempt to summarize a few recent developments in the religious traditions that have been traced in the preceding pages.

Several refugee scholars who left their homeland in the face of the Communist revolution issued a "Manifesto to the World in Behalf of Chinese Culture" in 1958. These men, who belonged to the Neo-Confucian school of philosophy, asserted that there is a profound spiritual element in Chinese culture, and that this spiritual element has a transcendent quality that is necessary if "harmony is to prevail between Heaven and Earth and man as described in the ancient classics."[40] The writers agreed that the Chinese people are very practical, but they also feel that sensitivity to that which goes beyond the everyday world is needed to protect and preserve practical life. Younger Chinese scholars in various parts of Asia and the West have begun to acknowledge the transcendent element in Confucian thought, which is quite a change from the young intellectuals earlier in this century.

Perhaps the most outstanding Chinese religious leader of the twentieth century was a Buddhist abbot by the name of T'ai Hsü (1890–1947), who was mentioned in our discussion of Chinese Buddhism in the previous chapter. A second reference to him is justified here because he responded to the challenge of the West by adopting certain ideas from Europe and America if he found them helpful or useful in his own Buddhist tradition. His disciples on Taiwan carry on his reform emphasis and continue to publish the magazine he founded, *Hai Ch'ao* (*Sound of the Tide*).

Lively Taoist activity also may be found on Taiwan. Professor K. Schipper has discovered that an authentic line of succession in the Taoist priesthood has been preserved and that ancient rituals are faithfully enacted.[41] Taoist festivals still draw tremendous crowds of people, to the extent that government suspicions are aroused, as with Taoists of old.

The most obvious religious activity on Taiwan falls under the category of folk religion. We have referred earlier in this chapter to the birthday celebrations for Matsu, the deified heroine of fishermen and their families. Birthdays of other gods and goddesses are celebrated with equal fervor, new temples are being constructed, and old and new temples are often centers of community political activity in Taiwan where various strands of Chinese religious life can be observed in full flower at the present time.

In the early years of the People's Republic of China, various religious groups were tolerated and formed into national religious organizations under the supervision of the government's Bureau of Religious Affairs. The Constitution provided for "freedom of religious belief," but by specifying "belief," all actual activity or practice could be prohibited. The number of temples, mosques, and churches was severely limited during the Anti-Rightist and Great Leap Forward movements of 1957–1958 and succeeding years. The most devastating period for religious groups was that of the Great Proletarian Cultural Revolution from 1966 to the mid-1970s when, among nine hundred million people, there was no observable practice of religion except in two Muslim mosques that were open for diplomats from Muslim countries. A Catholic and a Protestant church were finally opened for foreigners in early 1972, Chinese began to attend in 1979, and then various religious edifices were opened in a few places later that year and in following years.

Many observers of the People's Republic of China have been impressed with the way Communism in that country provides a religious dimension to the lives of many of the people. Marxist ideology in general and the thought of Mao Tse-tung in particular have been expounded as absolute truth, the only valid understanding of human existence. The dialectic of history according

to Marxism, and Mao's teaching on opposing forces in unending contradiction, may be seen as a new and more aggressive version of the *yin–yang* process from traditional Chinese thought. Mao Tse-tung, who led the Communist movement in China from the 1920s until his death in 1976, appeared during the late 1960s to have been deified by his more devoted followers, and became the source of inspiration and the object of devotion in songs and rituals with a strongly religious character. Mao was called "our great helmsman" and "the red sun in the hearts of people throughout the world." He was praised for "unlimited wisdom, courage, and strength" and for "always being with us." A poem expressed such sentiments with sweeping superlatives:

Stars are bright in the sky;
Each of them bows to the Polaris.
Though the Polaris is brightest,
It is not as bright as Chairman Mao,
And there is only the star of Chairman Mao in my heart.
Stars are bright in the sky,
As I stand on the bridge and look in the direction of Peking.
There I see the Gate of Heavenly Peace,
And Chairman Mao is our great savior.
Chairman Mao is our great savior.[42]

Although scholars have not reached agreement as to whether Chinese Communism or "Maoism" may properly be called a religion, it is clear that this movement has functioned as a religion in the lives of many Chinese.

The future of religion in the Chinese world is uncertain. Nevertheless, despite periods of upheaval and chaos, Chinese culture has shown remarkable powers of survival, and there is no questioning the close and pervading relationship of religion to the daily lives of Chinese people. As long as any group or pattern of religious life seems vital to the ongoing concerns of the people, one may expect the mainstream of Chinese religion and the major currents within it, particularly folk religion, to be a major factor in Chinese life.

Religion in Japan

Japan existed as an isolated island nation for about five hundred years, and was not unified under any single national leadership before the second century C.E. At the first mention of Japan in Chinese documents, in 57

C.E., the nation consisted of about one hundred scattered tribal communities; as late as 265 C.E., Japan was still divided into forty separate communities. The religion of that period probably took the form of nature worship, combined with clan and ancestor worship that differed from place to place.

The influence of Chinese Confucian and Buddhist culture on Japan, beginning about the third century C.E., was overwhelming. Confucianism gave the Japanese an ethical, moral, and legal code that greatly influenced the structure of the government. Buddhism contributed to the development of the religious and aesthetic spirit. The Japanese people assimilated these new ideas and reshaped them into uniquely Japanese expressions. This trend marked the development of Japanese art, architecture, language, and law. Most certainly, such assimilation characterized the development of Japanese religion following the introduction of Chinese Buddhism in the sixth century and the development of Shinto and other Japanese faiths from that time to the present day. Japanese Buddhism was discussed in Chapter 5. The indigenous religions of Japan will be discussed in this chapter.

Beginnings

Shinto is the indigenous faith of Japan. One of the basic beliefs in Shinto is the idea that all gods or spirits, all people, and nature itself were born from the same parents. Because of this, all things, both those that can be seen and those unseen, have a divine nature. The practical result of this belief is that a Japanese person may call himself Buddhist, Christian, or an adherent of one of the other 375 religious groups found in Japan today—and still understand himself to be Shinto as well.

Unlike most of the religions discussed in this book, Shinto has no historical founder, no sacred scriptures, and no strict dogma. All Japanese people are Shinto by the fact of their birth, and the religion is basically a mixture of the various attitudes and ideas that have become essential to the way the Japanese people live and view the universe. Shinto is, as Sokyo Ono says,

both a personal faith in the kami and a communal way of life according to the mind of the kami, which emerged in the

course of centuries as various ethnic and cultural influences, both indigenous and foreign, were fused and the country attained unity under the Imperial family.[43]

The term *Shinto* is made up of two Chinese characters *shen* and *tao*, meaning "gods" or "spirits" and "way" or "path," respectively. Thus, Shinto means "The Way of the Gods." The indigenous Japanese pronunciation of Shinto is *Kami no michi* or "The Way of the Kami." The *kami* includes all things that are seen as capable of growth and regeneration, and includes natural phenomena such as the sun, moon, rivers, trees, mountains, some animals, and ancestral spirits. The ancestral spirits include the Imperial Ancestors, family ancestors, nobles, clan leaders, and national heroes, as well as all persons who have given their lives to Japan for noble causes.

Shinto Mythology and Beliefs

Early Japanese myths describe how the *kami* came into existence, how the land of Japan was formed, and how a special relationship began between the *kami* and the people. In order to understand these myths, it is necessary to have some understanding of the beginnings of the Japanese people, and how the myths came to be put into written form.

Most scholars agree that the Japanese people originally came from Northeast Asia, the South Pacific, and South China, and that these people brought with them their myths and legends, religious practices, and rituals. The early Japanese myths are therefore not indigenous to Japan, but came from a variety of places and countries. These early people of Japan settled in various places; the myths were only gradually fused, under Imperial direction, to form an integrated whole that has come down to the present day.

The early myths were recorded in the *Kojiki*, or *The Records of Ancient Matters*, written in 712 C.E.; and the *Nihon-shoki* or *Nihongi*, *The Chronicles of Japan From the Earliest Times to 697 C.E.*, written in 720 C.E. These documents are the two earliest records of Japanese history, written well after Japan had become unified under an Emperor. During the time in which the *Kojiki* and *Nihongi* were written, Confucianism was the "state" religion of Japan, and Buddhism was spread-

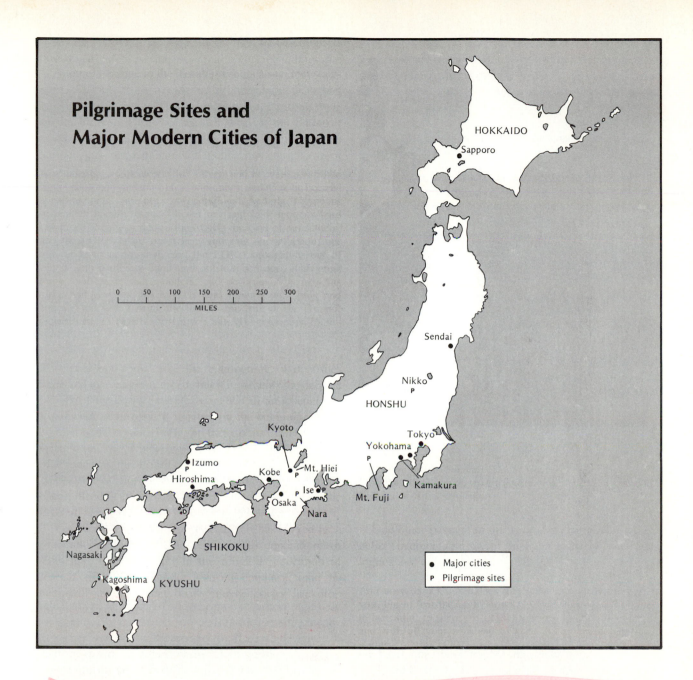

Pilgrimage Sites and Major Modern Cities of Japan

HOKKAIDO

Sapporo

0 50 100 150 200 250 300

MILES

Sendai

Nikko
P

HONSHU

Kyoto

Izumo
P

Hiroshima

Kobe

Mt. Hiei

Tokyo

Yokohama
P

Kamakura

Ise
P

Mt. Fuji

Osaka

Nara

Nagasaki

SHIKOKU

Kagoshima

KYUSHU

● Major cities
P Pilgrimage sites

ing across the country. Since both of these books were written under Imperial order, it is certain that they reflect the point of view of the aristocrats of Japan. By this late date the Chinese Classics were also well known, and these two records reflect considerable Chinese influence.

The *Kojiki* and *Nihongi* begin with a myth, or divine history, which tells about the creation of Japan. In the beginning, according to the myth, there was only chaos. Out of this chaos an egg appeared, and from this egg heaven and earth came into existence, followed by various gods and other divine beings. Finally the two primordial beings—Izanagi (He Who Invites) and Izanami (She Who Invites)—came into creation, and from these two beings, the land of Japan and its people were derived. As to the creation of the land of Japan, the *Nihongi* says:

> Izanagi and Izanami stood on the floating bridge of Heaven, and held council together, saying: "Is there not a country beneath?"
> Thereupon they thrust down the jewel-spear of Heaven and groping about therewith found the ocean. The brine which dripped from the point of the spear coagulated and became an island which received the name of Ono-goro-jima.[44]

Izanagi and Izanami then descended the spear and, walking around it, met, realized their sexuality, and gave birth to the islands of Japan, the natural environment, and various *kami*. With the birth of the *kami* of fire, Izanami's sex organs were burned and she died. Izanagi killed the fire *kami* and proceeded to bury his sister-spouse, who descended to the Kingdom of Death. Izanagi followed her to the Kingdom of Death and asked her to return to continue her creative work. The *Nihongi* continues:

> Thereafter, Izanagi went after Izanami, and entered the land of Yomi. When he reached her they conversed together, and Izanami said: "My Lord and husband, why is thy coming so late? I have already eaten of the cooking-furnace of Yomi . . . I pray thee, do not thou look on me." Izanagi did not give ear to her, but secretly took his many-toothed comb, and breaking off its end tooth, made of it a torch, and looked at her. Putrifying matter had gushed up, and maggots swarmed . . . Izanagi was greatly shaken and said, "Nay! I have come unawares to a hideous and polluted land." So he speedily ran away back again.[45]

After returning from the land of Death, Izanagi felt the need to purify himself. As he washed in a stream, he gave birth to various *kami*. From his left eye he gave birth to Amaterasu, the Sun Goddess; from his right eye came Tsuku-yomi, the Moon God; and from his nose he gave birth to Susano(w)o, the God of the Seas.

The supreme deity in Shinto is Amaterasu. She, as the Sun Goddess, represents light, life, and the bright forces of the world; and from her sprang forth the Imperial family. Her brother, Susano(w)o, who represents the dark forces, is depicted as having a violent disposition and always tormenting the Sun Goddess. Once Amaterasu became so enraged at Susano(w)o that she withdrew into a heavenly cave—and immediately the world was plunged into darkness. The heavenly *kami* became upset, but finally induced her to come out of the cave—and light returned to the world. The method of inducement, according to the story, was relatively simple. The *kami* brought birds, jewels, and a mirror; hung them all on an evergreen tree; and then began dancing, singing, and enjoying themselves. Amaterasu heard the noise and said:

> Since I have shut myself up in the rock-cave, there ought surely to be continual night in the Central Land of Fertile Reed Plains—How then can Ama no Uzume be so jolly? So with her august hand, she opened for a narrow space the rock-door and peeped out. The Tajikara forthwith took Amaterasu by the hand, and led her out.[46]

Susano(w)o was finally expelled from Heaven and banished to the province of Izumo in western Honshu. He married a princess, killed an eight-headed dragon, and presented the Sun Goddess with the sword he had used to kill the dragon. This sword became one of the symbols of the Emperor of Japan.

Amaterasu eventually pacified the land and sent her grandson Ninigi to rule over the land. He was given, as symbols of his authority, the mirror and string of jewels used to entice the Sun Goddess out of the cave, and the sword that was presented to the Sun Goddess by Susano(w)o as a symbol of peace between them. These three items—the mirror, jewels, and sword—came to be known as the three divine treasures, the symbols of the divine power of the Emperor of Japan. Many *kami* were sent to accompany Ninigi on his mission. After negotiating with the Ruler of the Land, Ninigi and the other *kami* eventually gained control of the land. Much later, Ninigi's great grandson, Emperor Jimmu, became the first human ruler of Japan. Thus, the idea that the Emperor of Japan is the direct descendant of the Sun Goddess is deeply rooted in the mythology of Japan. According to Japanese tradition, this event happened in 660 B.C.E., although there is no historical evidence to support this date.

The various myths found in the *Nihongi* and *Kojiki* serve several purposes. They give some clues regarding beliefs and customs in ancient Japan and provide the Japanese people with models to follow and traditional practices to continue. For all of the basic human experiences—birth, marriage, the planting of crops, the constructing of buildings, death—people can find counterparts in the myths. There are also important themes in the myths that, down to the modern period, help shape Japanese society. To cite but two examples, the heavenly myth enriches religious devotion and the imperial theme in the myths serves as the foundation of the Japanese state.

These political and religious themes are incorporated in the mythological story of the establishment of Amaterasu's Shrine at Ise. According to the *Nihongi,* the Sun Goddess ordered the shrine to be constructed and in it were placed the Three Treasures: the mirror, the jewels, and the sword. Since its construction in approximately 260 C.E., the shrine has always been associated with the Imperial house. Known as the Grand Imperial Shrine, it is the most sacred shrine in Japan.

Shinto Institutions and Rituals

According to the Shinto myths, the *kami* are without number, for the simple reason that human minds cannot conceive of how many *kami* there actually are. Symbolic of the infinite number of *kami* is the occasional claim that Japan is the land of eight million deities. And, as a matter of fact, there are thousands of religious shrines in Japan dedicated to innumerable deities. Connected with the shrines are numerous Shinto priests and festivals.

Shinto Priests

The shrines are served by priests whose primary function is to perform the rituals at the shrine and thereby ensure good relations between the world of the *kami* and the human world. Originally the priesthood was an hereditary position, but this practice was abolished in 1868 and all priests became civil servants. After World War II the priests became private citizens employed by a particular shrine.

A Shinto priest receives his training in one of three ways. He attends Kokugakuin University in Tokyo, or he goes to a seminary, or he simply gets the necessary training from another Shinto priest. Given the simplicity of Shinto ritual, there is no need for a long, elaborate period of training for the priesthood.

Many of the larger shrines in Japan employ priests on a full-time basis. However, because priests usually have families to support, those serving the smaller shrines are often engaged in other work when not performing specific ceremonies and duties at the shrine. Thus, many priests are teachers, office workers, or government officials who function only part-time as priests.

The wives of many Shinto priests were left in charge of local shrines during World War II while their husbands were in military service. Since many of these priests did not return from battle, some of the widows simply continued to function as priests in their husbands' absence. As a result today there are provisions for women, as well as for men, to become regular shrine priests.

Shinto Shrines

The approach to a typical large Shinto shrine is spectacular. The shrine is reached through an avenue of large cedar trees that form an impressive, natural approach to the shrine itself. The end of this approach is marked by the *torii,* the special ritual gate constructed of two upright pillars and two horizontal beams; often there is more than one *torii* marking the entrance to the shrine. These *torii* are the most common symbol of Shinto, and no Shinto shrine is complete without this simple but graceful symbol. The *torii* serves the purpose of separating the mundane world from the sacred world.

Beyond the *torii,* there is a pathway leading to the shrine. Around this pathway there are usually several walls or fences, and within the inner fence stands the shrine itself. Depending upon the size of the shrine, there is often a garden and a rest house for the worshipers who come to the shrine for festivals.

Shinto ritual is extremely simple and unpretentious. Before approaching the shrine, a worshiper purifies himself at a basin provided for that purpose. The hands are washed and the mouth is rinsed with water. These rituals reflect one of the essential aspects of Shinto, namely a love of purity and cleanliness and an abhorrence for anything that pollutes. Above the shrine are twisted straw ropes stretched horizontally, and from these ropes hang white strips of paper, which are symbols of the purity and sacredness of the shrine.

Ise Shrine. *The most important Shinto shrine in Japan, dedicated to Amaterasu, the Sun Goddess. Along with the priests at the shrine, there is a princess of the imperial family who is a priestess who serves the Sun Goddess at Ise.* (Courtesy of Japan National Tourist Organization)

Behind the oratory is the main shrine, called *honden,* which is the most sacred structure in the compound. It usually consists of two rooms: an inner room and an outer room. The inner room contains the divine spirit, usually represented by a mirror; this room is usually kept closed to the public because of its sacredness. The outer room contains the sacred strips of paper; this room is often open to the public.

Shinto Festivals

There are many festivals celebrated in Japan, ranging from local festivals celebrating particular events to national festivals such as the New Year's celebration when millions of people visit the Meiji Shrine, located in the precinct of the Imperial Palace in Tokyo, and other shrines in Japan. During these festivals the worshipers offer food to the various deities, the priests recite formal prayers called *norito,* and sacred dances are performed by both male and female dancers. The atmosphere is both sacred and festive.

Characteristic of all shrine festivals is the procession of the portable shrines, which are carried by young men who snake through the streets with the shrines on their shoulders, swaying through a crowd of spectators. The procession of the shrines plays an extremely important role in any festival, for it is the means of seeking protection of the deity against evil, especially natural evils such as storms, fire, or pestilence. It is through such festivals that the deity is brought into close contact with the people at a time when the people are under the influence of both the deity and the shrine.

After the ritual of washing the hands and rinsing the mouth, the worshiper goes before the shrine to pray. At the front of the oratory (chamber for prayer) there is often a bell with a rope hanging from it, which is pulled to attract the attention of the deity enshrined in the main shrine. The ringing of the bell is followed by clapping the hands twice. The worshiper then bows and stands and offers a silent prayer. If the worshiper desires to have the services of a priest, a request is made and the worshiper is taken to a room where the desired service is performed by a priest. These priestly services are usually rites of purification.

Historical Developments in Shinto

It is sometimes said in Japan that one is born Shinto and dies Buddhist. This is a popular expression of the intimate link that has existed between Shinto and Buddhism since Chinese Buddhism made its initial impact in Japan in the sixth century C.E. Before that time, Shinto expressed itself in what Genchi Kato calls Nature Worship: a diverse collection of folk beliefs, ancestor worship, totemism, and primitive polytheism.[47]

Since the arrival of Buddhism in Japan, Shinto has

gone through three significant historical periods; each will be mentioned briefly, then discussed at greater length. During the sixth century C.E., as a result of the contact between Shinto and Buddhism, several Buddhist ideas and practices influenced Shinto: the Buddhist doctrine of an afterlife, the discipline of the Buddhist monks, the Buddhist code of ethics, elaborate Buddhist rituals, and Buddhist art all became part of Shinto teaching and practice. By the seventh century C.E., when Buddhism became the state religion of Japan, Shinto represented a blend of Buddhist and indigenous Japanese ideas and practices.

A thousand years later, the process of assimilation came to an end. The history of Shinto between 1600 and 1800 is a record of how it separated from Buddhism and assumed the status of the official Japanese religion, with priests, shrines, and rituals of its own, existing alongside those of the Buddhist faith.

Still later, Shinto changed again as a result of World War II. It lost its status as the official religion of Japan in much the same way that the Emperor lost his divine status. To understand the influence of Shinto in Japan today, it is necessary to look at what has happened to the faith in the rapidly changing Japan of the period since 1945.

We now turn to some of the details behind these historical developments. Since there are no written records about Shinto prior to the arrival of Buddhism in Japan, it is impossible to know exactly what early Shinto was or how it was practiced by the Japanese people. Even the name *Shinto* did not exist at this early period. It is clear, however, that there was in Japan some form of nature worship stressing the unity between humans, nature, and spirits. There is little doubt that ancestor worship was also a part of this indigenous religion. Because of their isolation, the early Japanese were apparently tolerant of all religions and creeds, and were ready to welcome any teaching that would enrich their lives and culture.

As indicated above, when Chinese Buddhism entered Japan it brought many new ideas and doctrines, most of which the Japanese people readily accepted as valuable additions to their culture. In addition, images were installed in many Shinto shrines for the first time; many of the Shinto shrines were renamed; giving them Buddhist names; and the *kami* were worshiped according to Buddhist rites. Buddhist temples were established in the pre-cincts of the Shinto shrines, and, finally, even the *kami* were thought of as incarnations of Buddhist deities.

Taoism and Confucianism also had an impact upon Shinto during this period. Because of the influence of all three Chinese religious traditions, Shinto priests arrived at a compromise formula for the people:

For moral conduct, people rely on the Confucian codes. The domain of inner problems is left over to Shinto and Buddhism. In other words, Confucianism works for ethics, and Shinto and Buddhism for religion.[48]

Over the course of several centuries, however, Buddhism became active in matters of both religion and politics. Buddhist monks began to dispossess Shinto priests in the shrines, eventually making them totally subordinate. By the eighteenth century, there arose a protest movement against the power of the Buddhist monks, and a renewed interest in Shinto. A "National Learning School" of Shinto thinking was established that attempted to purge Buddhist teachings from Shinto doctrines. Although this school spread among Japanese intellectuals, it was not until 1868 and the establishment of the Meiji Government that the Emperor ordered the complete separation of Shinto and Buddhism with the following statement:

There is no Shinto Shrine, ever so small, in which the title of its *kami* has not been designated ever since the middle ages by a Buddhist term, . . . Each of those Shrines shall, as soon as possible, submit a notice containing the detailed history of the Shrine.

Any Shrine where the annual festival is attended by an Imperial Messenger which possesses any letter, tablet, etc., written by a member of the Imperial Family shall also give notice of it, after which they will receive official instructions.

Any Shrine which regards a Buddhist statue or statues as its deity shall change it immediately. Moreover, any Shrine which has a Buddhist image hung in front of it or is equipped with a Buddhist gong, bell or other instrument, or which has adoped some Buddhist theory, etc., shall abandon it as soon as possible.[49]

In May 1868, all Buddhist monks who were living in Shinto shrines were ordered to return to the secular life or be reordained as Shinto priests. They were also ordered to let their hair grow as a sign that they rejected Buddhism. Moreover, members of the Imperial family and court nobles were expressly forbidden to become Buddhist monks.

Izumo Taisha. *The grand Shrine of Izumo. This is the oldest center of Shinto worship in Japan and is second in importance only to the shrine at Ise.* (Courtesy of Japan National Tourist Organization)

Over the next several years, many Buddhist temples were destroyed, statues broken, and books burned. Other temples were converted into Shinto shrines, and many monks were forced to become Shinto priests. In response to a growing public reaction against these extreme measures taken by Shinto officials, the government of Japan issued a decree in 1873 that gave both Buddhism and Shinto equal protection under the law.

With a change in the Japanese Constitution in 1889, Shinto priests actually became government officials, and received a salary just as other civil servants did. This dual status gradually led to a degeneration of the religious work of the Shinto priests, with the result that many Japanese once again became interested in Buddhism or joined various new Shinto sects that were beginning to spring up all over Japan.

The separation between Shinto and Buddhism, with Shinto as the "official" religion of the State, remained until the defeat of Japan in World War II in 1945. With the Allied occupation of Japan, Shinto suffered a drastic blow. The Allied Commander maintained that Shinto had served the war-making purposes of the Japanese military leaders; Shinto was therefore separated from the government of Japan. A directive was issued that stated in part that "the sponsorship, support, perpetuation, control and dissemination of Shinto by the Japanese national, prefectural, and local governments, or by public officials, subordinates, and employees acting in their official capacity are prohibited and will cease immediately."[50] On January 1, 1946, the Emperor issued the famous statement officially renouncing his divinity, saying:

We stand by the people and we wish always to share with them in their moments of joys and sorrows. The ties between us and our people have always stood upon mutual trust and affection. They do not depend upon mere legends and myths. They are not predicated on the false assumption that the Emperor is divine and that the Japanese people are superior to other races and fated to rule the world. . . .[51]

Yet the Emperor remains a powerful symbol of Japanese values and beliefs. Ise has remained the Emperor's Shrine, and on special occasions the Emperor performs Shinto rites as a Shinto priest.

In 1946, the Association of Shinto Shrines was founded. All Shinto shrines were invited to affiliate with the association, and over 80,000 shrines did so. It is administered by a board of councillors, made up of prefectural organizations, who elect an administrative secretary who is responsible for major policy decisions. On the local level, shrines are managed by local priests and a committee of lay worshipers. Closely related to the Association is Kokugakuin University, the only Shinto university in Japan.

In Japan today, the home of a typical Shinto follower may have a shrine, called a *kamidana,* or "godshelf," along with a Buddhist altar. Many religious believers in Japan celebrate both Shinto and Buddhist feast-days and holidays, and live comfortably within this dual tradition. Buddhist monks may participate in Shinto shrine festivals, while Shinto priests may well be found at a Buddhist temple. This freedom and flexibility in religious practice is due to the lack of rigid dogma in Shinto: no commandments prevent Shinto followers from practicing a religion practically identical to that of their forefathers, in a country dramatically different from the Japan of even fifty, not to mention 1,500 years ago.

Hatsumode. *These women are making a special visit to a Shinto shrine on the first day of the New Year. The purpose of the visit is to pray for divine protection, health, and happiness throughout the year. (Courtesy of Japan National Tourist Organization)*

New Religions in Japan

A tolerance of ambiguity and a willingness to adopt old forms to new needs and constraints characterizes much of Japanese life. It also provides much of the fascination the country has for scholars of religion, as well as for persons interested in cross-cultural studies of all kinds.

This flexibility in Japanese religious life has led to a virtual explosion of new religions in recent Japanese history. In general terms, these "new" Japanese religions have emerged as a response to modernity. The industrial revolution, the breakup of social class structures, and the subtle and ongoing changes in the status of women have required religious beliefs and organizations that can give energy to the new working class and that can be made readily available to them as a source of support in confusing circumstances.

The loss of the Emperor's divine status after World War II and the agony of Japan's first defeat left the people devastated and in need of accessible religious teachings. The traditional orientation of Buddhist thought was of little comfort, and families in which everyone was working had little time for the study of difficult Buddhist doctrine. For the laboring classes, the old Buddhist practices, while part of their heritage, seemed in need of reform. As in industry and education, the emphasis in religion was on modernization.

Shinto suffered during this time because of its traditional connection with ancestor worship and the no longer divine Emperor. For a Japan wiping the slate clean and rushing headlong into the twentieth century, a religion founded in nature worship may also have seemed out-of-date.

Another religious alternative was Christianity, and thousands of Japanese did convert to Christianity. This religion, however, was a foreigner's religion, and in the post-1945 period it was distinctly the religion of the occupiers of the land. Nevertheless, the same openness that had characterized the earlier coexistence and weaving together of Shinto and Buddhist ideas and practices allowed the Japanese to incorporate distinctly Christian teachings into many of their own developing new religions.

There are now hundreds of different religious sects in Japan. Although it is obviously impossible to list and describe all of the new religions, they can be roughly grouped into three different categories: those that claim to have been primarily influenced by Shinto; those that have been primarily influenced by Buddhism; and those that have been influenced by a mixture of Shinto, Buddhist, and Christian ideas and practices. The religions in this third group are sometimes referred to as *Spiritualist religions*.

There are several features that most of these new religions have in common. The founder of the new sect usually has a revelation in which some deity appears and gives the founder a new doctrine and a mission to propagate this new faith among the people. Many of these groups are highly syncretistic; that is, they take doctrines and practices from various religious traditions and mix them together indiscriminately. In addition, many of the new religions practice faith healing.

In this section we will look at two religions that are primarily Shinto in orientation. We will then briefly discuss two religions that are fundamentally influenced by Buddhism. And, finally, we will highlight several of the so-called Spiritualist groups.

Tenri-kyo

One of the largest of the new religions is Tenri-kyo (Heavenly Reason Sect), a founder religion largely influenced by Shinto. In terms of doctrine, Tenri-kyo teaches that God is the Parent who has promised a joyful life to believers. This joyful life is to be experienced in this world rather than in a spiritual world in the Heaven beyond. The only way to salvation for humans is mental growth: the mind should be developed until it approaches the mind of God the Parent.

Salvation, according to this religion, is thus rooted in the processes of the mind; it comes about by developing the mind-consciousness of the individual. This salvation achieved through mind development is claimed to have two aspects: it is spiritual in the sense that it transcends all temporality and, at the same time, temporal in that it is a state of natural happiness in this world. Thus, in a song chanted in Tenri meetings both morning and evening and written by the foundress, a woman called Miki Nakayama (1798–1887), a "most mysterious salvation" is promised: "painless childbirth, and freedom from smallpox." The foundress also discloses the root of disease when the song says, "Suffering is rooted in your own mind." And, in the final stanza of the song, happy people are pictured doing holy work, and are referred to as the "complete working team."[52]

This song of the faithful focuses them on modern understandings of preventive medicine, freedom for women, and the social benefits of working together. It also encourages them to be open to the benefits brought about in a changing world. No wonder, then, that in the shrine room of the Sanctuary in Tenri City, in a room where Miki Nakayama is still believed to reside, meals are prepared for her daily, a hot bath is drawn for her every morning, and a television set stands ready to bring her the latest benefits of the modern age. This incorporation of the promise of new technology into the religion is believed by the faithful to be as important to the foundress as the perpetual adoration of the priests, who alternate in giving their devotions in front of her door.[53]

The reasons for the popularity of Miki Nakayama and the religion she founded are clear. Quite simply, a religious leader who can make modern life less confusing, find benefits in the structure of modern civilization, and encourage individuals to develop their minds clearly has great appeal for many Japanese people and a growing number of North Americans.

P. L. Kyodan

Another of the new religions strongly influenced by Shinto is the P. L. Kyodan, or Perfect Liberty Association, which emphasizes the concept of art as self-expression. For the follower of this sect, the purpose of life is to create art, and to be engaged in that creative expression is to be happy. Humans are conceived of as social beings, and there is no idea of individuals or art apart from society. The major belief of this sect is that world peace can be achieved only after so many people have become artists in their own lives that such evils as hatred and strife will cease to exist.[54]

Rissho Kosai Kai

As some of the new religions have been strongly influenced by Shinto, others have stemmed primarily from Buddhist beginnings. It cannot be overemphasized, however, how much most of these new religions incorporate with little stress ideas and practices from a variety of religious sources: Shinto, Buddhist, Confucianism, and Christian.

Most of the new religions focus on the practical concerns of the average citizen. Even those religions developing out of a Buddhist background, with its ancient teaching that all life is suffering, have taken a positive focus in the modern world. They offer comfort to workers who are living in a time of rapid change, even going so far in some cases as to promise higher wages and a better standard of living to the faithful. In this manner, these religions serve to blunt the impact of the West on Japanese culture.

One of these new religions, the Rissho Kosai Kai,

or Society for the Establishment of Righteousness and Friendly Intercourse, exemplifies the group of religions stemming from the Buddhist tradition. Founded in 1938, it did not develop a large following until after 1945. Today it claims to have over two million followers.

This sect carries forward a practice from the Tokugawa period (1571–1817) of registering entire families for membership, including the names of deceased parents. Thus, the link to the ancestor that has always been important in Japan is held intact in this religion. In addition, the sect brings from Nichiren Buddhism the emphasis upon the Lotus Sutra as the sacred text and the practice of chanting the title of the sutra to express gratitude and faith.

The Nichiren belief that salvation can be achieved in this world is interwoven with the social goals of efficiency and happiness. For the attainment of these goals, and for relief from the numerous irritations of daily life, followers of this sect participate in counseling sessions in which they learn that the responsibility for their happiness is their own. In addition, simple nostrums or remedies and problem-solving techniques are applied to the concerns of the home and the workplace, with the idea that reason and faith must be combined to produce happiness.

Soka-Gakkai

In marked contrast to this religion of adjustment is the Soka-Gakkai, or Value Creating Society, which also claims Nichiren as its founder. Although this sect was founded in 1930 by Tsunesaburo Makiguchi, a school teacher from Hokkaido, it did not meet with very much success until after World War II under the leadership of Josei Toda (1900–1958) and, later, Daisaku Ikeda. Soka-Gakkai now claims over ten million followers in Japan.

In terms of doctrine and practice, Soka-Gakkai takes its major teachings from Makiguchi's essay *On Values* and the traditional doctrines of Nichiren Shoshu. Makiguchi's essay is particularly noteworthy because of its emphasis on the practical aspects of religious belief; for him, concrete ''benefits'' of religious devotion are much more important than some abstract notion of ''truth'' that has little meaning for ordinary people. As a result of this emphasis, Soka-Gakkai has involved itself in social and political movements for years, first by intervening on behalf of coal miners in Hokkaido in 1957 and later by electing several members to the Japanese Diet (Parliament) in every Japanese election since 1962. In addition, through its Department of Education it has donated thousands of books to schools throughout Japan, and it has opened its own schools, including Soka University. Soka-Gokkai is not officially connected with Nichiren Shoshu in Japan or elsewhere, even though there are similarities in doctrine and sometimes Nichiren Shoshu monks officiate at Soka-Gakkai temple functions.

Through its organizational scheme and radical method of gaining converts—by means of *shakubuku,* or "break and subdue"—Soka-Gakkai aims at nothing less than purifying all of Japan. In recent years this organization, composed of lay persons, has moved beyond Japan and can now be found in North America, Europe, Korea, and many other countries where it is winning converts and becoming involved in various kinds of political and social activity.

The Omoto Group

The devastation produced by World War II in Japan was followed by the emergence of numerous new religions and the re-establishment of other religions that had languished in the decades before the war. These religions, both new and old, provided a focus of devotion for the faithful and were not reluctant to suggest directions for the future. Like Soka-Gakkai, many of the so-called "founder religions" made world peace a major concern of their teachings.[55] The variety of religious thought and action that has always characterized Japanese religious life meant that many and diverse paths to peace were suggested.

The founders of these new faiths were all charismatic leaders who could communicate their ideas effectively. They also had ready access to the mass media to carry their ideas about salvation and concerns for social action directly to the people. Elements of traditional Christianity existed in some of these founder religions, alongside ideas taken from Shinto and Buddhism. Thus, here too old ideas and new technological methods were woven skillfully together.

A collection of new religions called the Omoto group actually originated in the nineteenth century, but flourished in the period between the world wars and especially after World War II. The ideas of these sects, particularly the idea of world peace after the war, still live in Japan and still attract the young. One of the teachers of the Omoto sect organized a nationwide campaign in the 1950s to stop the testing of atomic bombs in the Pacific. The struggle to bring about world peace is carried forward today by Omoto leaders who point to the special role that Japan has in reminding the world of the potential horrors of atomic war.

Ittoen

Concern for social action is found in most of the new religions of Japan, whether that action focuses on mundane matters of daily life or major concerns such as global peace. Because of the emphasis upon social action, the doctrinal differences among the new religions is often regarded as being not terribly important. The religion called Ittoen is indicative of the toleration Japanese people have for many religious beliefs and organizational forms, and for the general acceptance of the necessary ambiguities in the national religious scene.

The worshiper who follows Ittoen literally worships before three altars: one representing the essence of Christianity, one symbolizing the essence of Buddhism, and one being dedicated to what this sect calls the Light. In a service repeated every day, the faithful are reminded that the founder of this sect, Tenko-san, believed and taught "not only in God, Buddha or Confucius but in the essence of each, and that all is within the gate of the One and Only Light."[56]

Religion in Japan Today

As we have seen, new religions were on the rise in Japan in the late nineteenth and early twentieth centuries as a response to the industrial revolution and the breakup of the old class structures. New religions during that period were characterized by interests in modern healing practices, job safety, the promotion of efficiency, and the realization of happiness.

The moral and spiritual gulf that opened in postwar

Japan, and the subsequent loss of faith in traditional, mainstream religions, allowed room for the proliferation of scores of new religions launched by strong founders, often rural women. These optimistic faiths, with their emphasis on mental discipline and the power of such simple practices as daily chanting, appealed mainly to peasants and workers. Other sects also arose, however, that made appeals to the intelligentsia. For example, some of the new religious sects established outstanding collections of foreign literature in religious universities, while others promoted the value of traditional Japanese art in the life of the nation.

With the customary Japanese talent for assimilation and the accomodation of new ideas, these new religions have managed to retain a Shinto world-view while directly incorporating Buddhist and Christian teachings. These religions have sought to have impact through social action—intervening, for example, in behalf of the fledgling trade union movement, and supporting the quest for world peace. At the same time, they have emphasized the spiritual side of a nation that could otherwise have been eclipsed in the race to compete with Western industry and business, a race that has literally transformed the face of modern Japan.

Although much has been made of the genius of Japanese industry, it may be that the real lesson Japan can teach the West lies in its willingness and ability to tolerate disparate ideas and beliefs without resort to unduly oppressive or restrictive measures. Secure in the value of traditional teachings and beliefs, Japan in the history of its contact with China and the West has extracted what it has found to be most valuable. New faiths have found their relevance for their followers neither through a slavish devotion to the past nor by a faddish devotion to the present. Rather, they have confronted the cultural upheaval in modern Japan by recognizing the pain involved in the loss of an old identity, and by offering spiritual renewal for the forging of a new national consciousness. In so doing, the new religions of Japan have accepted the challenge of modernity. How they will survive and in what form is something we cannot know; that they will survive seems both likely and hopeful.

NOTES

Religion in China

1. *The Book of Songs,* in *Sacred Books of the East,* trans. by James Legge (Oxford: Clarendon Press, 1899), vol. III, p. 370.
2. Fung Yu-lan, *A History of Chinese Philosophy* (Princeton: Princeton University Press, 1952), vol. I, p. 31.
3. Legge, *Sacred Books of the East,* p. 353.
4. *The I Ching or Book of Changes,* trans. by Richard Wilhelm and Cary F. Baynes (New York: Bollingen Books, 1950), pp. 54–57.
5. *Ibid.,* p. xxxvii.
6. Analects XIV:41. Unless otherwise noted, quotations from the Confucian *Analects* and the *Book of Mencius* are from Ch'an Wing-tsit, ed. and trans., *A Sourcebook in Chinese Philosophy* (Princeton: Princeton University Press, 1963).
7. *Ibid.,* III:17.
8. *Ibid.,* III:4.
9. *Ibid.,* XIII:27; XII:22.
10. *The Wisdom of Confucius,* trans. by Lin Yutang (New York: Random House, 1938), p. 115.
11. *Analects* VII:34; XI:8.
12. *Ibid.,* XI:11.
13. *Ibid.,* XI:11; VI:20.
14. *Book of Mencius* 2A:6.
15. John K. Shryock, *The Origin and Development of the State Cult of Confucius* (New York and London: The Century Co., 1932).
16. Arthur Waley, *The Way and Its Power, A Study of the Tao Te Ching and Its Place in Chinese Thought* (New York: Grove Press, n.d.).
17. *Tao Te Ching,* 16. In Waley, p. 162.
18. *Tao Te Ching,* 63. In Waley, p. 219.
19. *Tao Te Ching,* 72, 74. In Waley, pp. 232, 234.
20. *Tao Te Ching,* 80. In Waley, p. 241.
21. *Tao Te Ching,* 75,66. In Waley, pp. 235, 224.
22. Quoted in Theodore de Bary, ed., *Sources of the Chinese Tradition* (New York: Columbia University Press, 1960), I, p. 77.
23. De Bary, p. 73.
24. Quoted from Ch'an Wing-tsit, *A Sourcebook in Chinese Philosophy* (cf. no. 6 above), p. 189.
25. Ch'an, p. 186.
26. *Ibid.,* p. 192.
27. *Ibid.,* p. 197.
28. *Ibid.,* p. 197.
29. *Ibid.,* p. 209.
30. Quoted in DeBary, p. 261.
31. N. J. Girardo, *Myth and Meaning in Early Taoism* (Berkeley: University of California Press, 1974), p. 308.

32. Michael Strickmann argues that the term ''Taoist'' should apply only to the Celestial Master sect that stems from Chang Tao-ling, a severe limitation of the term that we are not prepared to accept. See his article ''On the Alchemy of T'ao Hung-ching'' in Holmes Welch and Anna Seidel, eds., *Facets of Taoism* (New Haven: Yale University Press, 1979), especially pp. 164–167.

33. Chunj-Yuan Chang, *Creativity in Taoism* (New York: Harper & Row, 1963), pp. 67–73, 81, 86.

34. Yoshitoyo Yoshioka, ''Taoist Monastic Life,'' in Welch and Seidel, *Facets of Taoism*, p. 243. The entire article is a splendid summary of the life of Taoist monks.

35. C. K. Yang, *Religion in Chinese Society* (Berkeley: University of California Press, 1961), p. 167.

36. *Ibid.*, p. 166.

37. *Ibid.*, p. 159.

38. For the history, beliefs, and practices of the White Lotus groups, see Daniel Overmeyer, *Folk Buddhist Religion* (Cambridge: Harvard University Press, 1976).

39. An extensive account of this rebellion may be found in Susan Naquin, *Millenarian Rebellion in China* (Cambridge: Harvard University Press, 1970).

40. ''Manifesto to the World in Behalf of Chinese Culture,'' trans. by Robert P. Kramers, in *Quarterly Notes on Christianity and Chinese Religion*, II (May, 1958), pp. 1–25.

41. K. Schipper, unpublished manuscript.

42. Poem by Ts'ai Yung-hsiang in *Jen-min Jih-pao* (*People's Daily*), December 1, 1966. Translated in *Current Background*, 814 (January 24, 1967), p. 6.

Religion in Japan

43. Sokyo Ono, *Shinto the Kami Way* (Rutland and Tokyo: Charles E. Tuttle, 1962), p. 3.

44. *Nihongi, The Chronicles of Japan from the Earliest Times to 697 A.D.,* trans. by W. G. Aston (Rutland, Vt., and Tokyo: Charles E. Tuttle C., 1972), pp. 10–12.

45. *Nihongi*, p. 24.

46. *Nihongi*, p. 45.

47. Genchi Kato, as found in S. G. Champion, *Eleven Religions and Their Proverbial Lore* (New York: E. P. Dutton, 1945), p. 225.

48. Jean Herbert, *Shinto The Fountainhead of Japan* (New York: Stein and Day, 1967), p. 225.

49. *Ibid.*, p. 49.

50. *Ibid.*, p. 53.

51. Floyd Ross, *Shinto: The Way of Japan* (Boston: Beacon Press, 1965), p. 155.

52. Harry Thomsen, *The New Religions of Japan* (Rutland and Tokyo: Charles E. Tuttle, 1963), pp. 43, 47, 48.

53. *Ibid.*, p. 37.

54. *Ibid.*, p. 196.

55. *Ibid.*, p. 127.

56. *Ibid.*, p. 227.

G L O S S A R Y

Chinese Terms

No system of transliteration or romantization is adequate to convey in English spelling the sound of Chinese words. Therefore, we have in this listing provided first the traditional Wade-Giles spelling that has been in use for almost a century, secondly the *pin-yin* system devised and adopted by the People's Republic of China, and then, thirdly, a close approximation of the sounds in English that follows the form used in other glossaries in this book.

Ch'eng Huang *or* **Cheng Huang** (*chuhng hwahng*)   the City God.

chih *or* **jy** (*juhr*)   the Confucian virtue of knowledge or wisdom.

chun jen *or* **jiun ren** (*jyun ren*)   a princely man, superior man, therefore person of virtue.

chung *or* **jong** (*joong*)   the Confucian virtue of loyalty.

hsiao *or* **shiau** (*syiaow*)   the Confucian virtue of filial piety, including devotion to living elders of the family, particularly the father, and veneration of ancestors.

hsien *or* **shian** (*syen*)   immortals or fairies in Taoist religion.

i (*yee*)   the Confucian virtue of righteousness or uprightness.

I Ching *or* **I Jing** (*ee jing*)   the Book of Changes, used for divination.

jen, ren (*ren*)   man in the generic sense, human being, person; also the Confucian virtue of humanness, being human, humanity.

li (*lee*)   the Confucian virtue of propriety, rites, or ceremony. Another term pronounced the same way refers to the Neo-Confucian idea of a principle in all things.

Matsu *or* **Matzu** (*madzuh*)   popular name for the Queen of Heaven, a goddess worshiped by people who live close to the sea in Taiwan or on the southeast coast of China.

Shang Ti *or* **Shang Di** (*shahng dee*)   the Lord Above, ancestor of the royal family in ancient times, worshiped as a supreme deity.

she chi *or* **she ji** (*shuh jee*)   gods of earth and grain.

shu (*shoo*)   the Confucian virtue of reciprocity.

T'ai P'ing T'ien Kuo *or* **Tai Ping Tian Guo** (*tai ping tyan gwouh*)   the Great Peace Heavenly Kingdom, a religio-political-economic movement of the middle of the nineteenth century.

tao *or* **dau** (*dow*)   the way, truth, way of life, essentially indefinable.

Tao Te Ching *or* **Dau De Jing** (*dow duh jing*)   title of the basic Taoist text, usually translated "*The Book of the Way and Its Virtue* (or *Power*)."

tao shih *or* **dau shr** (*dow shuhr*)   a Taoist priest or professional who knows the rituals and methods of attaining such Taoist goals as long life or imperviousness to pain, and can perform feats of magic.

te *or* **de** (*duh*)   general term for virtue, involving the method for attainment of virtue, truth, or power.

T'ien *or* **tian** (*tyan*)   heaven in the sense of ultimate reality or power, prominent in Chinese thought from the Chou dynasty onward.

T'ien Hou *or* **Tien Hou** (*tyan hoh*)   Queen of Heaven, goddess of folk religion in coastal areas, often called Matsu.

T'ien Ming *or* **Tian Ming** (*tyen ming*)   mandate of Heaven, which sanctioned the ruling house, but could be withdrawn.

T'u Ti Kung *or* **Tu Di Gong** (*too dee goong*)   the Earth God.

wu-wei *or* **u-uei** (*woo-way*)   literally "nonaction," but refers to "nonstriving," a using of one's natural capacity without pushing or straining.

yang-yin *or* **iang-in** (*yahng-yin*)   interacting forces of light/dark, assertive/responsive, male/female.

Yu Huang *or* **iu huang** (*yoo-hwahng*)   the Jade Emperor, chief deity in popular, religious Taoism.

Japanese Terms

Amaterasu (*ah-mah-te-raah-soo*)   the name of the Sun Goddess. The most important deity in Shintō.

Honden (*hohn-den*)   the most sacred structure in a Shintō Shrine.

Ittoen (*ee-toh-en*)   one of the new religions in Japan.

Izanagi (*ee-zah-nah-gee*)   the male primordial being in Japanese mythology.

Izanami (*ee-zah-nah-mee*)   the female primordial being in Japanese mythology.

Jimmu (*jee-muh*)   the first human emperor of Japan.

kami (*kah-mue*)   gods or spirits.

Kamidana (*kah-mee-dah-nah*)   literally, a god shelf. A small household shrine found in most Japanese homes.

Miki Nakayama (*mee-kee nah-kah-yah-mah*)   The foundress of Tenri Kyō.

Ninigi (*nee-nee-gee*)   the grandson of the Sun Goddess, who was sent to pacify the land.

norito (*noh-ri-toh*)   a formal prayer said by Shinto priests.

Omoto (*oh-moh-toh*)   one of the new religions in Japan.

Risshō-Kōsai-Kai (*ree-shohh-kohh-sy*)   one of the new religions in Japan.

shakubuku (*sah-koo-boo-koo*)   aggressive method of seeking converts used in Sōka-Gakkai.

Sōka-Gakkai (*sohh-kah-gah-ky*)   one of the new religions in Japan.

Tenri-kyō (*ten-ree-kyohh*)   one of the new religions in Japan.

torii (*tohh-ree*)   the gate leading to a Shintō Shrine.

SUGGESTED READINGS

Only a few of the more readily available texts and collections of texts have been listed under primary sources in translation. Older translations of the standard Confucian texts may be found in the *Sacred Books of the East,* a series that also includes two volumes of the texts of Taoism (see note 1, p. 208). Many of these texts have been translated into more readable English by Burton Watson and published by Columbia University Press. For the beginning student the collections by Thompson and by DeBary are highly recommended. For secondary sources a sampling of available books, ranging from survey to fairly specialized scholarly works, is presented.

China: Primary Sources in Translation

CHAN, WING-TSIT, ed. *A Source Book in Chinese Philosophy.* Princeton: Princeton University Press, 1963.

DE BARY, W. T., ed. *Sources of Chinese Tradition.* New York: Columbia University Press, 1960.

THOMPSON, LAURENCE G. *The Chinese Way in Religion.* Belmont, Calif.: Dickenson Pub. Co., Inc., 1973.

WALEY, ARTHUR. *The Way and Its Power: A Study of the Tao Te Ching and Its Place in Chinese Thought.* New York: Grove Press, n.d.

WARE, JAMES R. *Alchemy, Medicine, Religion in the China of* A.D. *320.* Cambridge: The M.I.T. Press, 1966.

WILHELM, RICHARD, AND BAYNES, CARY, F., trans. *The I Ching or Book of Changes.* New York: Bollingen Books, 1950.

China: Secondary Sources

BUSH, RICHARD C., JR. *Religion in Communist China.* Nashville and New York: Abingdon Press, 1970.

CHAN, WING-TSIT. *Religious Trends in Modern China.* New York: Columbia University Press, 1953.

GIRARDOT, NORMAN J. *Myth and Meaning in Early Taoism.* Berkeley: University of California Press, 1974.

GROOT, J. J. M. DE. *The Religious System of China.* Leiden: E. J. Brill, 1892–1910, 6 vols.

———. *Sectarianism and Religious Persecution in China.* Leiden: E. J. Brill, 1901, 2 vols.

HSU, FRANCIS L. K. *Under the Ancestors' Shadow.* New York: Doubleday & Company, Inc., 1967.

JORDAN, DAVID, K. *Gods, Ghosts, and Ancestors: The Folk Religion of a Taiwanese Village*. Berkeley, Los Angeles, and London: University of California Press, 1972.

MacINNIS, DONALD E. *Religious Policy and Practice in Communist China*. New York: Macmillan; London: Collier-Macmillan Ltd., 1972.

NAQUIN, SUSAN. *Millenarian Rebellion in China; The Eight Trigrams Uprising of 1813*. New Haven: Yale University Press, 1976.

OVERMYER, DANIEL L. *Folk Buddhist Religion. Dissenting Sects in Late Traditional China*. Cambridge: Harvard University Press, 1976.

———. *Religions of China*. New York: Harper & Row, 1986.

SASO, MICHAEL R. *Taoism and the Rite of Cosmic Renewal*. Pullman: Washington State University Press, 1972.

———. *The Teachings of Taoist Master Chuang*. New Haven: Yale University Press, 1978.

SHRYOCK, JOHN K. *The Origin and Development of the State Cult of Confucius*. New York and London: The Century Co., 1931.

SMITH, D. HOWARD. *Chinese Religions*. New York: Holt, Rinehart and Winston, 1968.

THOMPSON, LAURENCE G. *Chinese Religion: An Introduction*. 3d ed. Belmont, Calif.: Wadsworth, 1979.

TU WEI-MING. *Confucian Thought: Selfhood as Creative Transformation*. Albany: State University of New York Press, 1985.

WELCH, HOLMES. *The Parting of the Way*. London: Methuen & Co., Ltd.; Boston: Beacon Press, 1957.

———, AND SEIDEL, ANNA, eds. *Facets of Taoism*. New Haven: Yale University Press, 1979.

YANG, C. K. *Religion in Chinese Society*. Berkeley: University of California Press, 1961.

Japan: Primary Sources in Translation

ASTON, W. G., trans. *Nihongi, The Chronicles of Japan from the Earliest Times to 697 A.D.* Rutland, Vt. and Tokyo: Charles E. Tuttle Co., 1972.

PHILIPPI, DONALD, L., trans. *Kojiki*. Princeton, N.J.: Princeton University Press, and Tokyo: University of Tokyo Press, 1968.

Japan: Secondary Sources

ANESAKI, MASAHARU. *History of Japanese Religion*. Tokyo and Rutland, Vt.: Charles E. Tuttle Co., 1964.

EARHART, H. BRYAN. *Japanese Religion: Unity and Diversity*. Encino, Calif.: Dickenson Publications, 1974.

HERBERT, JEAN. *Shinto: The Fountainhead of Japan*. New York: Stein and Day, 1967.

HORI, ICHIRO. *Folk Religion in Japan*. Chicago: University of Chicago Press, 1968.

ONO, SOKYO. *Shinto: The Kami Way*. Tokyo and Rutland, Vt.: Charles E. Tuttle Co., 1962.

ROSS, FLOYD. *Shinto: The Way of Japan*. Boston: Beacon Press, 1965.

THOMSEN, HARRY. *The New Religions of Japan*. Tokyo and Rutland, Vt.: Charles E. Tuttle Co., 1963.

7

Judaism

שְׁמַע יִשְׂרָאֵל יְהוָה אֱלֹהֵינוּ יְהוָה ׀ אֶחָד׃

Translation of the Hebrew: "Hear O Israel, the LORD our God, the LORD is one." (Deuteronomy 6:4)

Judaism appears to be easy to define: it is the religion practiced by Jews past and present. However, this leads into two problems far more complicated. First, there is little agreement on a precise definition of who should be properly called *Jews*. For some, a Jew is such by virtue of ethnic affinity or "belonging to a people." For others, being a Jew is equated with religious practice or "belonging to a religion." The Supreme Court in Israel has ruled in favor of the former, while the Parliament of the same country has voted in terms of the latter.

Second, what about Jews who accept only a secular form of Jewish culture? There are many persons who are Jews by birth but are not religious believers in terms of Judaism, and even in Israel there are groups that claim connection with Judaism without adhering to the basic laws in Judaism. There are likewise Jewish converts who practice the faith but cannot claim Jewish birth; there are also Jews who practice other religions. Obviously there must be some ambiguity in the term *Jew* to cover this variety of situations. How then did religion and ethnic origin become bound together? What are the origins of this religious movement?

Beginnings

Ethnic Background

Historically, Judaism has always placed great emphasis on ethnic origins and racial solidarity, with Abraham as the "Father of the Faithful" occupying a primary place as the progenitor of the race. He is, however, never viewed as the first man but as the father of a new people. He is described in the ancient genealogies as descended through many generations from Adam and Eve, who are pictured as the parents of the human race. Abraham's deep sense of divine call and guidance accounts for his break with his cultural heritage and his journey to a new land. His experience is traditionally described in the first book of the *Hebrew Scriptures*:

Now the Lord said to Abram, "Go from your country and your kindred and your father's house to the land that I will show you. And I will bless you, and make your name great, so that you will be a blessing. I will bless those who bless you, and him who curses you I will curse; and by you all the families of the earth will bless themselves." (Genesis 12: 1–3)

213

Such was the religious turning point that evolved over many centuries into the developed form of religion we call Judaism, the term "Judaism" actually being coined by Greek-speaking Jews about 1,500 years after Abraham to distinguish their religious system from that of Hellenism. The growth process was extremely long because many factors and groups were involved.

Abraham (ca. 1800 or 1600 B.C.E.) became the first of a series of patriarchs who preceded the actual founding of the religion by Moses. His name was changed from *Abram* ("Exalted Father") to *Abraham* ("Father of a Multitude"), signifying for later generations the broadening of his responsibility from the father of a family to the father of a people. The story of Isaac's birth when Abraham and Sarah were at an advanced age further heightened the uniqueness of the line of these patriarchs. Isaac's son, Jacob, whose name was changed from *Jacob* ("Supplanter") to *Israel* ("Prince of God"), rounded out the triad of patriarchal greats and prepared for the founding of the people known as the *Israelites*. The twelve sons of Jacob (or Israel) became the nucleus for this people, although there were many groups of unrelated people who would join with the basic nucleus.

Patriarchal Religion

The religion of these patriarchs is important for our understanding of the Jewish tradition. Abraham was seemingly instrumental in breaking with the older polytheistic pattern of worshiping many gods to seek emphasis upon one God. The general Semitic word for God was *'El*, which designated the high god in any given pantheon of gods. This was the title by which God was worshiped by the patriarchs, although various compound names were used, such as *'El Shaddai* ("God of the Mountain"), *'El Elyon* ("God, Most High God"), *'El Roi* ("God Who Sees"), *'El Bethel* ("God of the House of God"), and *'El Olam* ("God of Eternity"). These descriptive phrases using *'El* were important in singling out special attributes, but also had application to specific holy places. The most important title was *'El Shaddai,* which probably embodied the name of the personal god of Abraham's family. It has often been translated as "God Almighty," which relates well to the majesty and strength of the mountain as well as signifying the strength of Abraham's commitment. Later generations referred to *'El Shaddai*

as the God of Abraham, Isaac, and Jacob or the God of the Fathers.

Among the patriarchs there was a strong sense of tribal solidarity in which *'El Shaddai* was intimately involved. He was the one who called out Abraham and continued to lead all the patriarchs. He was further associated with Abraham in a covenant relationship (described in Genesis 15:17–21) that bound the patriarch and deity in solemn agreement. This was the forerunner of subsequent covenant ceremonies in the development of Judaism.

Another term from the patriarchal period was important. Abraham was designated as a *Hebrew* after leaving Mesopotamia and entering Canaan. Originally, this term referred to the patriarchs as rootless or displaced people and probably was equivalent to the terms *Habiru* or *'Apiru* found in ancient documents of the Near East during the second millenium B.C.E. As indicated above, the Hebrew people came to be known as *Israelites* and later as *Jews,* but the term *Hebrew* has been kept alive as the name of their language.

The patriarchal period ended with a long period of sojourn in Egypt that, according to various sources, may have lasted 215 or 430 years. While not oppressed during the early years, the Israelites came to have a slave status after the memory of their outstanding leader, Joseph, faded. This paved the way for much suffering and the need for another great leader. The accompanying timeline will help to clarify these historical relationships.

Moses and the Exodus from Egypt

During the fourteenth century B.C.E., such a leader, Moses, emerged and became the founder of the religious system now known as Judasim. Many dramatic stories were included in the Hebrew Scriptures about his birth, his years of training in the royal household of Egypt, his exile in the land of Midian, and his attempt to secure release for his people. After several attempts, he was successful in persuading the Pharaoh to allow his people to journey into the wilderness for the purpose of sacrificing to God. The Exodus or flight from Egypt took place about 1290 B.C.E. and truly marked a new era for the Israelites. Future Jewish writers were to regard it as the crucial event of their history and the hub of their faith.

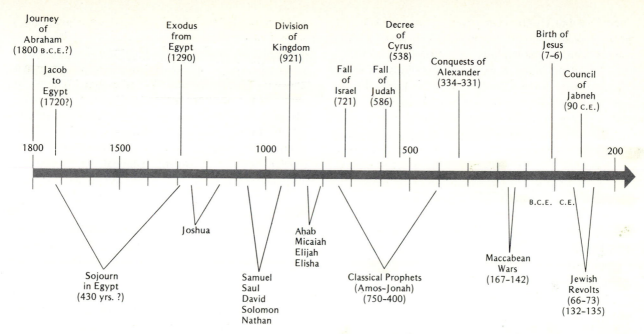

Journey of Abraham (1800 B.C.E.?) • Jacob to Egypt (1720?) • Exodus from Egypt (1290) • Division of Kingdom (921) • Fall of Israel (721) • Fall of Judah (586) • Decree of Cyrus (538) • Conquests of Alexander (334–331) • Birth of Jesus (7–6) • Council of Jabneh (90 C.E.)

1800 | 1500 | 1000 | 500 | 200

B.C.E. C.E.

Joshua | Sojourn in Egypt (430 yrs. ?) | Samuel Saul David Solomon Nathan | Ahab Micaiah Elijah Elisha | Classical Prophets (Amos–Jonah) (750–400) | Maccabean Wars (167–142) | Jewish Revolts (66–73) (132–135)

Early History of Judaism.

The Exodus from Egypt involved the crossing of the "Reed Sea." This has improperly been translated as the "Red Sea," but the original Hebrew describes this crossing through a body of water characterized as abounding in reeds. The location was probably north of the Red Sea in the area now covered by the Suez Canal.

After crossing the Reed Sea, the people assembled at Mount Sinai and did not return to Egypt. The location of this sacred mountain is not certain; the most likely site is that which still bears the name *Jebal Musa* (Arabic for "Mountain of Moses") in the southern part of the Sinai Peninsula. Here the foundation of their faith was established.

Events at Mount Sinai. The two dominant events at Mount Sinai concerned the giving of the Law and the establishing of the Covenant. The former concerned the stipulations of obligations under the latter. These obligations were necessary to the understanding and keeping of the covenant or "contract" between the God of the Jews and his people; the covenant itself was inseparably linked to the *Torah*, the five books of the Law in the Hebrew Scriptures.

The Torah is not homogeneous but developed from the needs of many generations of people in Israel. The individual laws contained in the Torah are of two types. First, many commandments are phrased in a conditional form. *If* or *when* something occurs, *then* a certain punishment shall be carried out. This is well illustrated by the teachings in the book of Exodus: "If a man steals an ox or a sheep, and kills it or sells it, he shall pay five oxen for an ox, and four sheep for a sheep" (Exodus 22:1). It is obvious that the legal consequences are conditioned by the circumstances. This type of law is quite common in the ancient law codes of the Near East, especially the well-known Code of Hammurabi.

The second type of law, called absolute or apodictic, is unconditional and is set forth in terse phrases. "You shall not oppress a stranger" (Exodus 23:9) establishes a rule for life, one with no "ifs, ands, or buts." Although the first type of law has frequent parallels in ancient literature, the second type has few parallels. This absolute pattern appears to be more characteristic of Israelite demands upon the covenant people.

The best example of absolute law is seen in the Ten Commandments, or *Decalogue,* which represents a vital part of the Mosaic tradition at Sinai. These are known in the Hebrew text as the "Ten Words" and originally

Judaism **215**

stood in a fairly abbreviated form. Certain commandments maintain this terse brevity: "You shall not kill; you shall not commit adultery; you shall not steal" (Exodus 20:13–15). Commentary and explanations have been added to these original injunctions. The total effect of these commandments is most forceful, touching upon many areas of life and most of life's basic relationships.

It is interesting to note that the Decalogue found in Exodus 20:1–17, coming from one tradition, is paralleled by a similar version in Deuteronomy 5:6–21, coming from a second tradition. Another Decalogue, originating in a third tradition, is found in Exodus 34:10–26 and is ritual in nature as compared with the highly ethical content of the other Decalogues. All three of these lists of commandments are linked with the experiences at Mount Sinai and with the founder, Moses. These three traditions, plus a fourth, will be discussed later in the section on religious literature.

The other important event at Sinai concerned the establishment of the covenant between God and the people of Israel. This was in reality a moral agreement between the two parties that emphasized a close or intimate relationship. Basic to the agreement was the idea of faithfulness on the part of both parties. A lack of faithfulness on either side would make the covenant null and void.

The story of Moses receiving the Ten Commandments on Mount Sinai is followed immediately by the introduction to the covenant ceremony:

Moses came and told the people all the words of the Lord and all the ordinances; and all the people answered with one voice, and said, "All the words which the Lord has spoken we will do." (Exodus 24:3)

This was the act of ratifying the covenant by the people. Hereby they were accepting the terms of the covenant and agreeing to the obligations of the Law.

The ceremony continued with acts making the covenant effective. The older traditions present two versions of this concluding ceremony. According to Exodus 24:1–2 and 9–11, the ceremony involved a sacred meal on top of the mountain with at least seventy-four leaders of Israel participating. According to the other tradition in Exodus 24:3–8, the covenant ceremony was concluded with the entire population witnessing a sacrificial rite. These represent two types of ritual in antiquity for sealing covenant obligations—the communal meal shared by a

special group and the offering of sacrifice in the presence of all the people. There was now a strong bond between God and his people conditioned by vows of faithfulness and predicated on the basis of covenant obligations couched in legal tones of laws and ordinances.

Mosaic Religion. This period in Israel's history is basic to all that follows in Judaism. Moses stands as founder of a major religion and Sinai represents the source of water for a mighty stream. Although the stream may widen and deepen, it will never rise higher than the source, the Exodus and the experiences at Sinai.

Moses' religious experience had its beginning before the Exodus in the episode of the burning bush. Although the account was written in poetic language, the experience clearly had a dramatic effect on Moses. He first came to understand that God had concern for the suffering and oppression of Moses' people and intended to do something about it. This stood in sharp contrast to the seemingly capricious nature of most of the gods of antiquity. Second, Moses realized that he must know the name of the One appearing to him, or the people of Israel would not accept his leadership. A name was more important to people long ago than it is to persons in the modern world because the name signified and described the very character of the person or god addressed. It further was believed that special power and vitality resided in the name. Of course, Moses could have spoken of "The God of the Fathers" or used such titles as *'El* or an alternative term, *'Elohim,* which was used with basically the same meaning as *'El.* However, such a break with the past and the prospect of a new beginning demanded a new revelation of the character of the One who was willing to deliver and guide this slave people.

The following passage presents the answer to Moses' question about the name of "The God of the Fathers":

God [*'Elohim*] said to Moses, "I AM WHO I AM," [*'Ehyeh 'asher'ehyeh*]. And he said, "Say this to the people of Israel, I AM [*'Ehyeh*] has sent me to you." God [*'Elohim*] also said to Moses, "Say this to the people of Israel, 'The LORD [*Yahweh*] the God of your father, the God of Abraham, the God of Isaac, and the God of Jacob, has sent me to you,' this is my name forever, and thus I am to be remembered throughout all generations." (Exodus 3:14–15)

It is obvious from this passage that there is a definite continuity with the faith of the patriarchs; the new name in no way applies to a new god. However, the exact meaning of the new nomenclature is less certain. The phrase "I am who I am" may also be translated "I will be who I will be" or more probably "I cause to be what I cause to be." The first person verb 'ehyeh then becomes a third person verbal form Yahweh, meaning "He who causes to be." This is the name by which successive generations would know the God who appeared to Moses.

Yet, it is not quite as simple as it may appear. The name Yahweh was long written in the Hebrew without the vowels as YHWH, and before Judaism was fully developed the name was no longer pronounced at all by faithful worshipers. Another word, 'Adonai (Lord), was substituted in oral use while the vowels of 'Adonai were combined with the consonants YHWH in written form. The end result is some confusion as to spelling, meaning, and origin of the term. In fact, the preceding passage comes from an earlier tradition, while a later tradition suggests:

And God ['Elohim] said to Moses, "I am the LORD [Yahweh]. I appeared to Abraham, to Isaac, and to Jacob, as God Almighty ['El Shaddai], but by my name the LORD [Yahweh] I did not make myself known to them." (Exodus 6:2–3)

This appears to clarify the origin of the name as coming through Moses. However, another tradition traces the use of the term back to the grandson of Adam, Enosh: "At that time, men began to call upon the name of the LORD [Yahweh]" (Genesis 4:26). The Hebrew Scriptures therefore contain at least two traditions concerning the point of the origin of the sacred name.

Beyond the name, there is certainty in regard to the pattern of the Mosaic faith. First, it is clear that there was only one God, Yahweh, to be linked to the covenant and the law. While it is not possible to force a theoretical monotheism on Moses, in which he would argue that no other gods existed, he was emphatic that Yahweh was to have complete claim on Israel's allegiance. The first commandment in the Decalogue states the principle, "You shall have no other gods before [or beside] me" (Exodus 20:3). Second, there can be no doubt about Moses' sense of Yahweh's providential leadership over his people. The crossing of the Reed Sea, the victories in battle, and repeated wonders and signs all picture Yahweh as guiding his people from Egypt to the Promised Land. All of these events led to Israel's understanding that Yahweh was inseparably linked with their entire historical process and intimately concerned with Israel's well-being.

The Importance of Moses. A further statement needs to be made about Moses. In spite of all kinds of adversity and disaffection of the people he led, he had amazing success as a leader. He took a mixed multitude of slaves who had lived for many generations in a country alien to their heritage, and molded them into a people. Although there was a nucleus of kindred tribes, many other displaced peoples joined the Israelites in the Exodus from Egypt. There were times of great murmuring against Moses' leadership, desires to return to the seeming security of Egypt, and obstacles in the form of enemy forces. Although Moses cannot be held up as the paragon of patience and gentleness, he was capable of holding this diverse group together long enough to create a bond that has lasted more than 3,000 years. He was able to organize the beginnings of the priesthood, plan a system of worship, and provide for his people a pattern of religious faith and a pattern of ethical relationships that have endured to the present day. It is no wonder that future generations assigned to Moses many features of Judaism that actually took centuries to develop into practice. His leadership qualities made him a magnet to draw the Torah together.

Early Development

Religions differ in the nature of their development. Some develop rapidly as a result of dominant characteristics of their founders and immediate interpretation by disciples. Other religions, due to rival faiths or divergent emphases, require greater time for formative development. The latter is the case with Judaism, which was shaped during a period of over 1,000 years. What factors influenced the development of Judaism? How were these factors brought into a harmony that would produce a unified religious tradition?

Pre-exilic History, 1250–586 B.C.E.

Upon leaving Mount Sinai, the tribes of Israel considered an immediate entry into Canaan but ended up wandering for a long period, approximately a generation. After many trials and much murmuring, they moved to a position for the conquest of the land of Canaan, long regarded by their ancestors as "the Promised Land." On the eve of the invasion, Moses turned over his authority to a younger leader, Joshua. After many campaigns, a foothold was secured by the capture of key sites in Canaan (roughly the territory occupied by Israel and Jordan today). Since the land was not fully conquered, additional conquests were made during the next two hundred years as the native population was subjugated and assimilated.

This period proved to be a time of further trials as enemies to the north, east, and south mounted frequent attacks against the new inhabitants of Canaan.

Some stability was achieved by the establishment of a monarchy with Saul, a young military hero, as king. He was followed by David, destined to be viewed as an ideal king by future generations, and by Solomon, who gained a reputation for greatness as a man of wisdom. However, his wisdom was transitory, with the result that the kingdom split apart soon after his death. The next two hundred years witnessed one kingdom in the

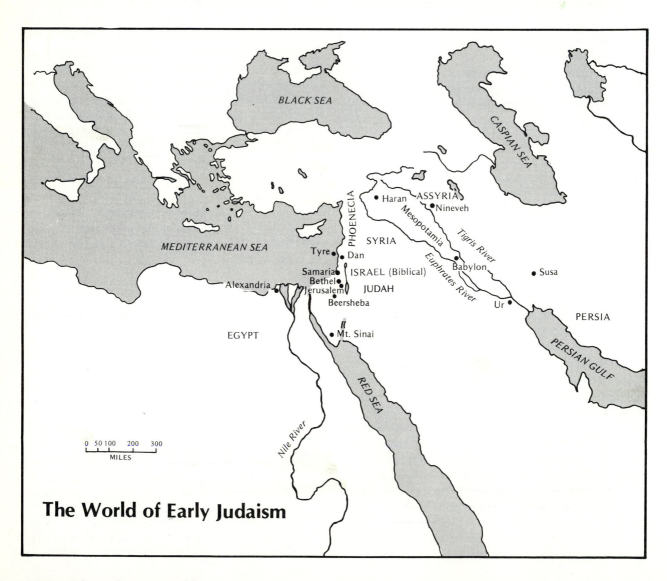

The World of Early Judaism

north and another in the south. The northern kingdom, known by the name of Israel, was conquered by the Assyrians in 721 B.C.E. The southern kingdom, called Judah, was able to survive until 586 B.C.E., only to fall to the Babylonians. People of both kingdoms were carried into exile in the territories of the respective powers. For each, the years that followed were known as the Exile. This was a time of consolidation and renewal in which the faith of Judaism was shaped. Although the full format was not to be realized until the years following the return to Canaan, the basic foundations were established before and during the periods of exile.

Religion and Culture

From the time of Israel's entrance into Canaan until the end of the exile, there was an ideological struggle going on with rival cultures. This was especially evident in the early years of the conquest and settlement of Canaan, as the Israelites changed from wandering herdsmen to a settled agricultural society. Many of the tribal groups living in the land were absorbed into Israel's society. Since Israel's culture was often crude in comparison with the more sophisticated ways of life of the neighbors long settled in the area, there was a srong temptation placed on Israel to absorb all the features of the dominant culture of the Canaanites and to forsake the desert style of simplicity. The Israelites did adopt many features of this native culture in terms of arts and crafts, architecture, city planning, poetic structure, and rituals—but the greatest danger for the Mosaic faith lay in terms of religious thought and practice.

Canaanite Religion. The Canaanite religion centered in nature, strongly emphasizing fertility. The chief god was *'El,* already encountered in the discussion of the religion of the early Hebrew patriarchs. He was the progenitor of about seventy divine offsprings who made up the pantheon of gods. Most important among these offsprings was Ba'al, the god of storms, and 'Anath (also known as Ashtoreth and Astarte), who was goddess of love, war, and fertility. The mythology associated with Ba'al and 'Anath is very extensive and elaborate. Much of the mythology centered on sex and fertility, and this carried over into the worship and rituals of the religion. Sacred prostitution, both male and female, was

Bronze Statue of Ba'al. This 6¼ inch figurine was discovered in the Late Bronze Age remains at Shechem in 1964. It represents one of the Canaanite deities, probably Ba'al. (Photo by Lee C. Ellenberger; reproduced by permission of Joint Expedition to Shechem)

common in daily rituals as well as in the prolonged festivals. The mating of the rain-vegetation god with the fertility goddess was apparently acted out in repeated rituals, and participation was required if a person hoped for fertility of the soil or fertility in the family.

Opposition to these practices was frequently referred to in the Hebrew Scriptures. A direct prohibition was spelled out in the book of Deuteronomy in the seventh century B.C.E.:

There shall be no cult prostitute of the daughters of Israel, neither shall there be a cult prostitute of the sons of Israel.

You shall not bring the hire of a harlot, or the wages of the dog [i.e., Sodomite] into the house of the Lord your God in payment for any vow; for both of these are an abomination to the Lord your God. (Deuteronomy 23:17–18)

In spite of these laws, the struggle persisted and caused much syncretism or blending of Ba'al and Yahweh worship on the popular level.

This fusion of different religions reached the higher official levels numerous times. For example, Ba'alism was introduced into the kingdom of Israel by the rather infamous Jezebel, wife of King Ahab. The same thing happened on a much larger scale when Manasseh, King of Judah, introduced Assyrian astral cults, consultation with the dead, and even child sacrifice. The ideological conflicts and temptations continued until the time of the Babylonian exile, when the battle was finally won and monotheism prevailed.

The Temple of Solomon. Of much importance in pre-exilic religious development is the building of the Temple at Jerusalem by Solomon. This temple had been a dream of his father, David, who was responsible for the planning and securing of the site to be used. The actual building of the Temple consumed the time and energy of Solomon from the fourth to the eleventh year of his reign. He was assisted by Hiram, King of Tyre, and Hiram's skilled workmen from Phoenicia, who were responsible for cutting and transporting the lumber, cutting and shaping the stone, and casting the bronze objects.

The Temple was a long building of stone, open on one of its shorter sides. It stood in a large courtyard on a platform, ten steps above the level of the courtyard. On either side of the entrance were two freestanding columns cast from bronze that reached a height of about 37½ feet. Although their purpose is not known for certain, many scholars consider them to have been fire basins used for the burning of incense. Entrance was through huge cypress doors that led into the main part of the structure. Like most of the sanctuaries excavated in the region, this Temple had three basic chambers. The first, the Vestibule, was about 15 by 30 feet and was adorned by double doors of carved cypress inlaid with gold, leading into the main chamber. This main chamber, called the Holy Place, was 60 by 30 feet by 45 feet high. The walls were paneled with cedar, and huge cedar beams were used in the roof. The walls were carved with palm trees, flowers, and hybrid animals known as *Cherubim*. Inside this main sanctuary were the seven-branched golden candlesticks, the table for sacred unleavened bread, and a small altar. The third chamber was a perfect cube (30 by 30 by 30 feet) and was known as the Holy of Holies. It was approached by a flight of steps leading to another double door. Inside were two large cherubim that acted as guardians of the most sacred area. They were made of olive wood decorated with gold leaf. Beneath them was the Ark of the Covenant, a sacred box containing religious objects and serving as God's earthly throne.

Outside in the courtyard were two important structures used in the system of worship. The first was the Altar of Burnt Offering, built like a Babylonian ziggurat or temple tower. It was made of stone with a base 30 feet square and a height of 15 feet. The top was reached by a flight of steps on one side. The other structure, called the Bronze Sea, was a huge bronze bowl resting on the backs of twelve bronze oxen, three pointing to each cardinal point of the compass. This bowl, which held more than 10,000 gallons of water, was used for ritual washings.

The Temple was designed as a royal chapel rather than as a place of assembly for the people. Only the priests were allowed inside the Temple, while the Holy of Holies was apparently entered only by the High Priest and then only on one of the High Holy Days, the Day of Atonement. The people gathered outside, around the Altar of Burnt Offering. Elaborate rituals were designed for the priests within and the congregation on the outside.

The Temple thus became the focus of religious attention for many generations. Solomon's Temple lasted with renovation and some modification from about 950 B.C.E. until its destruction in 586 B.C.E. It was rebuilt about 515 B.C.E., lasting until 19 B.C.E. when a new temple was begun by Herod the Great. This third temple structure was not completed until shortly before it was destroyed in 70 C.E. at the hands of the Roman Tenth Legion. Since that time, Judaism has shifted its focus of religious attention to other patterns, including the well-known synagogue.

The Prophetic Movement. Also of great significance was the work of the prophets of Israel, key figures who left an indelible mark on the nation. The movement

Stevens' Reconstruction of Solomon's Temple. *This is an artist's drawing (assisted by W. F. Albright and G. E. Wright) of the Temple built by King Solomon at Jerusalem. The building was a royal chapel of the tenth century* B.C.E. (Reproduced by permission of the American Schools of Oriental Research)

began as early as 1050 B.C.E. under another outstanding leader, Samuel. Bands of ecstatic prophets began to appear who exhibited a highly charged kind of enthusiasm. The story is told about King Saul being directed by Samuel to join one of these prophetic bands. Samuel said:

you will meet a band of prophets coming down from the high place with the harp, tambourine, flute, and lyre before them, prophesying. Then the spirit of the LORD will come mightily upon you, and you shall prophesy with them and be turned into another man. (I Samuel 10:5b–6)

From these bands of prophets, individuals began to act independently from the group. Many began to speak more and more as a voice of conscience, pointing out evils in society and calling for reform. Finally, about 750 B.C.E., messages began to be recorded in written form, sometimes by the prophets themselves, sometimes by scribes, and on other occasions by disciples of the prophets. There were still bands of professional prophets connected with shrines or royal thrones, but the ones

who most influenced their period were the classical or writing prophets. Between 750 and 400 B.C.E., a total of twelve prophets left a heritage in brief books connected with their utterances. Another three left a heritage that developed into longer prophetic works. While a roll call of the prophets would be beyond the scope of our study here, the accompanying timeline will give a historical context to these creative individuals.

A few quotations may present some of the dominant themes developed by the prophets. Amos (750 B.C.E.) was probably the first of the writing prophets, the one who set the pattern and example for the rest. Demanding social justice in all phases of life, he called to the people:

Seek the LORD and live . . .
Hate evil and love good,
   and establish justice in the gate.
   (Amos 5:6, 5:15)

Hosea (745 B.C.E.) continued the call for reform, adding an element of compassion and love not generally found in the words of Amos:

When Israel was a child, I loved him,
  and out of Egypt, I called my son.
The more I called them,
  the more they went from me . . .
Return, O Israel, to the LORD your God,
  for you have stumbled because of your
  iniquity.
    (Hosea 11:1–2a; 14:1)

Isaiah (742–698 B.C.E.) recognized the doom that was coming, but kept on pleading for a change of direction while also injecting a strong element of hope. He said:

The ox knows its owner,
  and the ass its master's crib;
But Israel does not know,
  my people does not understand . . .
Come now, let us reason together,
  says my LORD:
Though your sins be like scarlet
  they shall be white as snow;
Though they are red like crimson,
  they shall become like wool.
    (Isaiah 1:3; 1:18)

Micah (724–701 B.C.E.) described the moral corruption of his day in terms much like Amos, pictured the concern of God in language reminiscent of Hosea, quoted the same passage as Isaiah in terms of future hope (cf. Micah 4:1–4 with Isaiah 2:2–4), and summed up the teaching of all three by saying:

He has showed you, O man, what is good;
  and what does the LORD require of you
But to do justice, to love kindness,
  and to walk humbly with your God.
    (Micah 6:8)

Jeremiah (626–580 B.C.E.) also spoke of God's judgment upon the nation, but added an important note of personal responsibility, saying:

In those days they shall no longer say:
  "The fathers have eaten sour grapes, and
  the children's teeth are set on edge."
But every one shall die for his own sins;
  each man who eats sour grapes, his teeth are
  set on edge.
    (Jeremiah 31:29)

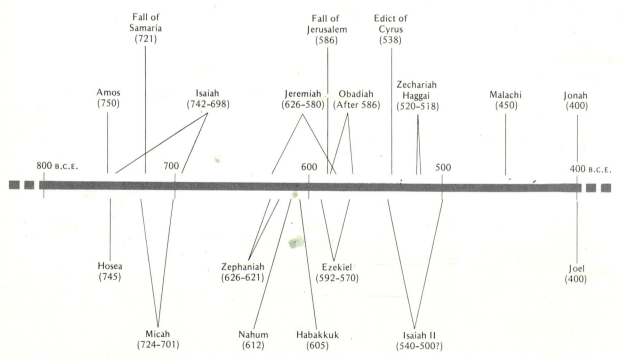

The Classical Hebrew Prophets.

It would be hard to overestimate the impact of the pre-exilic prophets on Israel's religious life. They collectively acted as a voice of conscience for kings, priests, and professional prophets. Few of them were revolutionaries; all were conscientious reformers. Abraham Heschel has stated well the depth of sensitivity inherent in these prophets:

Indeed, the sort of crimes and even the amount of delinquency that fill the prophets of Israel with dismay do not go beyond that which we regard as normal, as typical ingredients of social dynamics. To us a single act of injustice—cheating in business, exploitation of the poor—is slight; to the prophets, a disaster. To us injustice is injurious to the welfare of the people; to the prophets it is a death blow to existence; to us, an episode; to them, a catastrophe, a threat to the world.[1]

Exilic and Postexilic Development, 586 B.C.E.–135 C.E.

The pre-exilic prophets continually pointed toward a coming exile. Amos and Hosea saw it coming at the hands of the mighty Assyrians; and thus it did come for the northern kingdom, Israel. The prophets of the southern kingdom later realized that the Babylonians would swallow up their nation, Judah; and so they did. While the northern kingdom was crushed beneath the Assyrians and then the Babylonians for more than 180 years, the southern kingdom was spared until the Babylonians under Nebuchadnezzar conquered Jerusalem in 586 B.C.E. From this point until the return of some Judeans to Jerusalem under the Persians was a period of forty-nine years.

This proved to be a time of consolidation and development for the people of Judah. Surely it was a time of sorrow and frustration, in that they were separated from Jerusalem and left without the Temple that had been a major focus of their religion. However, they adjusted well to the new environment and began the final shaping of a complete religious system, one not as dependent upon the Temple complex. Their meetings in homes for study and worship served as the beginnings for a synagogue system, which was to become the norm in Judaism. Their gathering and editing of past traditions received new impetus as various groups contributed to the effort.

The Exile in Babylonia came to a sudden end soon after Cyrus, the ruler of the Persian Empire, marched

Samaritan Torah Scroll. *This scroll is zealously guarded by the Samaritan priests at Nablus, who are pictured above. The Samaritan community traces its heritage to ancient Israel prior to the fifth-century B.C.E. split of the two groups. (Courtesy of Kyle Yates)*

into Babylon almost unopposed in 539 B.C.E. The Neo-Babylonian Empire had lasted less than seventy-five years and slipped forever into oblivion. The Persians under Cyrus proved to be among the most enlightened rulers of antiquity. They gathered together the peoples carried captive by the Assyrians and Babylonians over the previous two hundred years and sent them back to their homelands, even assisting them in the rebuilding of their cities and shrines. Cyrus recorded in his famous proclamation, The Cyrus Cylinder, the following account of the events:

When I entered Babylon as a friend and (when) I established the seat of the government in the palace of the ruler under jubilation and rejoicing, Marduk, the great lord, [induced] the magnanimous inhabitants of Babylon [to love me] and I was daily endeavoring to worship him. My numerous troops walked around in Babylon in peace. . . . I strove for peace in Babylon and in all (other) sacred cities. . . . I returned to (these) sacred cities on the other side of the Tigris, the sanctuaries of which have been ruins for a long time, the images

Model of Jerusalem. *This large-scale model of Jerusalem vividly depicts the city just prior to its destruction in 70 C.E. It was designed by leading Israeli archaeologists and stands on the grounds of the Holy Land Hotel in Jerusalem.* (Courtesy of Kyle Yates)

which (used) to live therein and established for them permanent sanctuaries. I (also) gathered all their (former) inhabitants and returned (to them) their habitations.[2]

Although the Jews were not given full autonomy in government upon their return, they were provided a measure of freedom greater than they had known for more than two generations. It was a time of new beginning, a new era, a new exodus. The enthusiasm of the situation was caught by an anonymous prophet (often called Deutero-Isaiah) about 540 B.C.E. He exclaimed:

> Comfort, comfort my people, says your God.
> Speak tenderly to Jerusalem, and cry to her
> that her warfare (i.e. time of service) is
> ended, that her iniquity is pardoned,
> that she has received from the Lord's hand
> double for all her sins. A voice cries:
> "In the wilderness prepare the way of the LORD,
> make straight in the desert a highway for our God."
>   (Isaiah 40:1–3)

Returning to their homeland in the territory around Jerusalem, the Jews were forced to struggle for their existence. Rival groups had filled the vacuum created by the exile. It was not until more than twenty years later that the Temple was rebuilt, and then in a manner that caused old men to cry over its comparison with the Temple first built by Solomon. It was still later, at least seventy years later, that the walls of Jerusalem were rebuilt under the direction of a new Persian governor by the name of Nehemiah. The restoration was slow in coming about and did not in any way meet the expectations of those first returning under Cyrus.

Persian control ended with the coming of Alexander the Great in 333 B.C.E. as he swept down through the land of Canaan and moved into Egypt. After Alexander's defeat of the Persians, his march into the borders of India, and his subsequent death at Babylon, his newly-created empire was divided among three of his generals. The homeland of the Jews was first assigned to Ptolemy

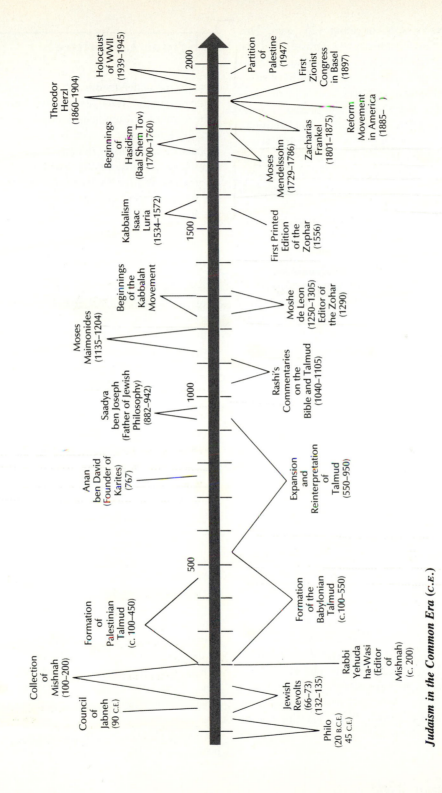

Judaism in the Common Era (C.E.)

Collection of Mishnah (100–200)

Council of Jabneh (90 C.E.)

Formation of Palestinian Talmud (c. 100–450)

Philo (20 B.C.E. 45 C.E.)

Jewish Revolts (66–73) (132–135)

Rabbi Yehuda ha-Wasi (Editor of Mishnah) (c. 200)

Formation of the Babylonian Talmud (c.100–550)

Anan ben David (Founder of Karites) (767)

Saadya ben Joseph (Father of Jewish Philosophy) (882–942)

Expansion and Reinterpretation of Talmud (550–950)

Moses Maimonides (1135–1204)

Beginnings of the Kabbalah Movement

Rashi's Commentaries on the Bible and Talmud (1040–1105)

Moshe de Leon (1250–1305) Editor of the Zohar (1290)

Kabbalism Isaac Luria (1534–1572)

First Printed Edition of the Zophar (1556)

Theodor Herzl (1860–1904)

Holocaust of WWII (1939–1945)

Beginnings of Hasidism (Baal Shem Tov) (1700–1760)

Partition of Palestine (1947)

First Zionist Congress in Basel (1897)

Moses Mendelssohn (1729–1786)

Zacharias Frankel (1801–1875)

Reform Movement in America (1885–)

500

1000

1500

2000

of Egypt and his successors for about 125 years. This was a time when Greek culture was stressed but the Jewish traditions were allowed to exist without serious challenge. About 198 B.C.E., however, the political situation changed. The Seleucids of Syria, also heirs of Alexander, gained control over the area and placed pressure on the Jews to conform to Greek culture and religion. The ferment of resistance came to a head in 168 B.C.E. when Antiochus IV Epiphanes placed extreme restraints upon the practice of Judaism. He prohibited circumcision, banned possession of copies of the Torah, and demanded worship of the Greek gods.

The actions of Antiochus IV led a pious group under a priest named Mattathias and his five sons to band together to oppose the Syrian Greeks. The Macabean wars (named after one of the sons of Mattathias, Judas Maccabeus) resulted in religious freedom in 161 B.C.E., and the struggle continued until political freedom was won as well in 142 B.C.E. Yet freedom was not to last even one hundred years: the Romans moved into Palestine under Pompey in 63 B.C.E. Jewish autonomy was not to be realized again for many centuries, until the creation of the state of Israel in 1948 C.E.

After several years of crisis and intrigue, Herod the Great gained control of most of the territory once ruled by David and Solomon. At his death, the territory was divided among his three sons. This division, as well as many other factors and factions, led to two Jewish revolts that insured the dispersion of Jews to many parts of the world. The dispersion had actually been going on for centuries on a voluntary basis; now it became final. The revolt of 66–73 C.E. was caused by unrest under Roman domination and resulted in the destruction of the temple of Herod in 70 C.E. This brought to an end the sacrificial and ritual system as practiced at Jerusalem. Clearly this was the end of an era that had begun with David and Solomon about one thousand years before. Never since 70 C.E. has a major segment of Judaism practiced sacrifice. Another abortive revolt took place in the next century, as Jewish revolutionaries attempted to throw off the Roman domination. The struggle in 132–135 C.E. ended with Jerusalem being rebuilt as a Roman city called Aelia Capitolina, with the Jews being formally banned from their Holy City. The timeline on the previous page will help put these events into proper perspective.

Religious Literature

Basic to the understanding of any religion is an analysis of the question, "What literature is believed by the group to be of religious significance?" Although oral traditions kept alive for years or centuries may point to important aspects of a religion, among literate peoples the most significant features finally find their way into written documents. Written traditions of this sort also make possible more detailed critical analysis of the intention of the authors.

The Hebrew Scriptures

Among the many and varied writings of a religious nature in Judaism, one body of literature has special status—the *Hebrew Scriptures*. While other works are studied with great zeal by many Jewish scholars, the Hebrew Scriptures have maintained a unique authority. This sense of special authority grows out of the claims of revelation from God and inspiration by God. The concept of *revelation* requires a belief that God has disclosed truth, and that that truth has been committed to mankind through the books of Scripture. *Inspiration* refers to the process whereby the writers or speakers are aided by God in understanding and communicating the message. Both of these concepts combine to form a basis for authority and authenticity of the collection of sacred books.

Nature and Growth. The Scriptures are clearly of a composite nature, divisible into twenty-four separate writings in the Hebrew edition. These writings display a wide diversity in approaches and in literary forms employed. Some books are primarily of a historical nature; others emphasize legal and ritualistic aspects; others have a prophetic tone; still others are poetic or devotional. Although much of the material is concerned with stories of the past and hope for the future, the major emphasis is upon the needs of the contemporary situation at the time of writing of the separate books. The writing of these works covered approximately one thousand years, involving scores of authors, compilers, and editors. Persons who contributed to the process came from many backgrounds and varied greatly in their education and perspectives. Few books were written as a completed unit; rather, most of them appear to have been gathered over a long period of time.

Even before the Scriptures were put into written form, there was a long period of development and growth. There was a preliterary stage in which the traditions were carried in oral form. Brief units such as speeches, songs, genealogies, sagas, prayers, proverbs, and prophetic sayings were passed on from generation to generation. Next there was an early literary stage in which small codes of law, collections of prophetic oracles, groupings of songs, collections of proverbs, and historical accounts took shape. It was from these small literary units that many of the independent books evolved.

Modern scholarship has raised many questions about the traditions associated with the authorship of many of the books. Chief among these questions is: How much of the text originated with Moses and how much did he personally write down? It is possible by critical analysis of the books of the Torah (Genesis, Exodus, Leviticus, Numbers, and Deuteronomy) to distinguish at least four major sources of tradition. These are designated by the letters *J, E, D,* and *P* for convenience and represent strands or sources from various periods: *J* from about 950, *E* from about 850, *D* from about 700, and *P* from about 500 (all B.C.E.). This analysis suggests that the material was not put into definitive form by Moses; successive generations continued to respond to the leadership of God in a dynamic, not a static, manner. Although much of the material relates best to a later historical setting, it is still possible to see Moses as the one laying the foundation for the Torah.

The separate books were then gathered into three larger collections or divisions. First was the *Torah* (or Law), which contained five books and which has always held a place of pre-eminence over the other divisions as the most direct revelation of God. Constant devotion to the Torah has been one of the strongest unifying factors in the history of Judaism. The second division was called the *Nebi'im* (or the Prophets), embracing four historical books called the Former Prophets and four prophetic books called the Latter Prophets. The Former Prophets included the books of Joshua, Judges, Samuel, and Kings, covering Hebrew history during a period of approximately 700 years. The Latter Prophets involved the three prophets Isaiah, Jeremiah, and Ezekiel, as well as so-called minor prophets (Hosea, Joel, Amos, Obadiah, Jonah, Micah, Nahum, Habakkuk, Zephaniah, Haggai, Zechariah, and Malachi). While this last group is called "The Twelve," it is actually counted as the fourth prophetic book. The third division was described as the *Kethubim* (or Writings), including eleven books of a more widely diverse nature. This group included Psalms, Proverbs, Job, Song of Songs, Ruth, Lamentations, Ecclesiastes (*Koheleth*), Esther, Daniel, Ezra-Nehemiah and Chronicles.

Although a great deal of diversity is evident, there is also a dynamic unity present, making the Hebrew Scriptures a living and dynamic compilation of books (see Table 7–1). The Hebrew concept of history gives a linear dimension that unifies the material. This is coupled with the ongoing sense of revelation by the God who is constantly concerned about revealing himself and his will. The deep sense of election of the Jewish people as a chosen people forms the third essential element of this unity. Thus, history, revelation, and response by a chosen people link together the many diverse components of the various books.

Canonization. The unique authority of the total collection is best illustrated by the process called *canonization.* The word *canon* refers to a rule or standard by which a collection of writings was authorized as sacred scripture. The process was one of gradual acceptance as the Law was probably closed by 400 B.C.E., the Prophets by 200 B.C.E., and the Writings during the first century C.E. The principle at work was the meeting of the needs of the people rather than official selection. The Council of Jabneh (or Jamnia), which apparently met about 90 C.E., was composed of Jewish scholars who discussed the usefulness of books already accepted while questioning the legitimacy of certain other books. These scholars were motivated by a desire to establish bounds for scripture in a time of real confusion. The Greek version of the Hebrew sacred books, called the *Septuagint,* included a number of writings not acceptable to the Jewish scholars of Palestine. Early Christian writings were appearing as a challenge to the older works of Judaism. Out of this council meeting and subsequent discussions, a standard listing or canon of Jewish scripture evolved.

The Hebrew Scriptures have become a common ground for the major religions of the West. They provide the

TABLE 7–1. *Summary of Hebrew Scripture*

	Hebrew Title	Meaning	English Title
Torah	Bereshith	"in the beginning"	Genesis
	Shemoth	"names"	Exodus
	Wayiqra	"and he called"	Leviticus
	Bemidbar	"in the wilderness"	Numbers
	Debarim	"words"	Deuteronomy
Prophets	Yehoshua	"Joshua"	Joshua
	Shofetim	"judges"	Judges
	Shemuel	"Samuel"	I and II Samuel
	Melakim	"Kings"	I and II Kings
	Yeshayahu	"Isaiah"	Isaiah
	Yirmeyahu	"Jeremiah"	Jeremiah
	Yehezqel	"Ezekiel"	Ezekiel
	Tere Asar	"the twelve"	The Minor Prophets
Writings	Tehillim	"praises"	Psalms
	Iyyob	"Job"	Job
	Mishle	"Proverbs"	Proverbs
	Ruth	"Ruth"	Ruth
	Shir Hashirim	"song of songs"	Song of Solomon
	Koheleth	"Preacher"	Ecclesiastes
	Ekah	"how"	Lamentations
	Ester	"Esther"	Esther
	Daniel	"Daniel"	Daniel
	Ezra-Nehemyah	"Ezra-Nehemiah"	Ezra and Nehemiah
	Dibre Hayamin	"chronicles"	I and II Chronicles

best source of history for the development of Judaism, the historical background for Christianity, and essential earlier teaching preparing for the introduction of Islam. They are filled with understanding of problems faced by persons long ago and answers that are still considered applicable to persons in the modern world. Certainly, the material in the Hebrew Scriptures presents a connected story of ancient life. The longings and aspirations of a people, their ethical teachings, directions for life, foundations for actions, and insights for understanding are all presented in historical context for application to any time period and any cultural situation.

The Talmud

Although the canonical scriptures have always had a primary place in Judaism, the *Talmud* has also had an influential place, in that proper interpretation of the Scripture is most frequently learned from the teaching of the Talmud. This work was produced by Jewish sages who lived in Palestine and Babylonia during the first seven centuries C.E. It is a compilation of law and interpretation that extends the Scripture into new areas of awareness and opens up discussion on subjects of interest to any age. The method of argument and mode of inquiry have created an enduring and abiding interest on the part of lay people as well as scholars. The open-ended nature of the discussion prepares the way for the consideration of concerns quite remote from those of the rabbis who originally put the material together.

There are two basic traditions, both beginning with the same material, called the Palestinian Mishnah. Although tradition asserts that the material was systematized by Rabbi Akiba about 100 C.E., this document was edited by Rabbi Yehuda ha-Nasi during the late second century C.E. It contained the oral laws thought to date back to teachings revealed to Moses but not previously put into written form. Closely linked with the Mishnah was the Tosefta, which signified additional or supplemental teaching, much of which came from the same rabbinic authorities. This oral law then became two traditions, the Palestinian Talmud and the Babylonian Talmud. The former was completed in the fifth century C.E., while the latter was finished about one hundred years later. Each Talmud was made up of *Mishnah* ("oral law" in the Hebrew language) plus *Gemara* ("study" or "commentary" in the Aramaic language) with a blending of *Tosefta* ("additional law" in Aramaic). Table 7–2 shows a more detailed breakdown.

Although much of the Talmud is concerned primarily with legal precepts as commentary on the Mishnah, it also contains many intriguing glimpses into Jewish life. Parables, maxims, anecdotes, and biographical sketches are interspersed throughout the material. Practical suggestions concern the raising of children, the process of education, moral values, and many areas of daily endeavor. The admonition, "Give every man the benefit of the doubt," has become a contemporary maxim. Of great wisdom is the teaching, "Do not threaten a child. Either punish him or forgive him."

The two Talmuds thus have much in common beginning with the basic Palestinian Mishnah. The Palestinian version of the Talmud, however, is only one-third the length of the Babylonian version. The Babylonian version is not only greater in length but more powerful, challenging, and interesting than the Palestinian Talmud, which tends to be dominated by antiquarian stories and concerns. For a diligent student of Judaism, whether lay person or rabbi, the Talmud is designed not to be read casually but to be studied intently. For many of the faithful, it becomes a lifelong endeavor.

Additional Literature

During the postexilic period, a vast body of religious literature was written by Jews that did not find its way into the canon of Scripture. Some books were written in Hebrew, some in Greek, and some in Aramaic, the latter being the spoken language in Palestine after the Babylonian Exile. Since one principle followed by the leaders in the Council of Jabneh (or Jamnia) was that a book must have been originally written in Hebrew or Aramaic, many of these books were not seriously considered. They were important, however, to Jews of certain areas and certain sects before and after the beginning of the common era.

TABLE 7–2. *Summary of Rabbinic Writings*

Writings	Sections	Dates	Contents
MIDRASH	Halakah	100 B.C.E.–300 C.E.	*Legal* material as commentary on the Torah.
	Haggadah	100 B.C.E.–300 C.E.	*Narrative* material as commentary on the entire Hebrew Scriptures.
TALMUD	Mishnah	100–200 C.E.	Collection of *oral law* not included in the Torah.
	Palestinian Gemara	200–450 C.E.	Commentary on the Mishnah; coupled with the Mishnah as the Palestinian Talmud.
	Babylonian Gemara	200–550 C.E.	Commentary on the Mishnah; coupled with the Mishnah as the Babylonian Talmud.
TOSEFTA		100–300 C.E.	Additional or supplementary material not included in the Mishnah.

Mention has already been made of the translation of Jewish sacred literature into Greek in the collection known as the Septuagint. This effort began about 275 B.C.E. under Ptolemy II, King of Egypt, and continued until about 100 B.C.E. His purpose was to build a great library in Alexandria, Egypt, which would include the wisdom of the known world. Many Jewish books included at this date for translation were not accepted later at the Council of Jabneh. The Talmud refers to these works as *Sefarim Hitzonim* (Outside Books) and other sources call them *Apocrypha* (Hidden Away). While they did not find their way into the Jewish Canon, these works were carried over into the early Christian canon and are still found in the Bibles of Roman Catholicism and Eastern Orthodoxy. The Protestant reformers, in contrast, reverted to the Hebrew canon and refused to include these books as scripture.

Many of the "Outside Books" resemble the books of the canon, while others are regarded as of much less religious value. Some are cast as historical novels (Tobit and Judith); some are folktales (Susannah and the Elders, Bel and the Dragon); some are wisdom writings (Ecclesiasticus or Ben Sira and the Wisdom of Solomon); some describe the Jewish revolt against the Syrian Greeks (I and II Maccabees); others are of a more miscellaneous nature (III and IV Maccabees, I and II Ezra, Baruch, Prayer of Manasseh, Additions to Esther, and the Son of the Three Children).

Another collection of noncanonical Jewish writings turned up in the manuscripts of the Dead Sea Discoveries. These manuscripts were found beginning in 1947 near the northwest corner of the Dead Sea, at a Jewish monastery called Qumran. All of the canonical books except Esther were found in at least partial form, as well as many other works that come from the first century B.C.E. and first century C.E. These works are of great assistance in reconstructing the Judaism of this period. Yet none of these noncanonical works has been of great significance to later Judaism, since Rabbi Akiba warned in the Talmud (Sanhedrin 10:1) that anyone who reads the so-called "Outside Books" has no share in the world to come.

Hundreds of other works could be added to the list of books in the religious literature of the Jews since the days of Talmud. Some of these will be mentioned where appropriate in the discussions that follow.

Doctrines and Confessional Statements

Of great significance in any religion is the pattern of doctrines that shape the beliefs and practices. What beliefs, doctrines, and dogmas emerge from the sacred literature of Judaism? How are these refined by the history of the community and affected by the divisions and sects that have developed? How do these doctrines fit into a system of belief and issue in creeds or produce systematic theology? Let it be said by way of introduction that Judaism is strong in the expression of doctrinal concepts but weak in formulating systems of belief that must be accepted in full. While there are a few creeds or formal statements of belief, they have limited authority and do not function as statements of dogma even though they may be a part of ritual.

Early Confessional Statements

The earliest statements of faith were set forth in brief form in the Torah of ancient Israel. The first is called the *Shema* (after its opening Hebrew word) and serves as the heart of both morning and evening prayers in Judaism:

Hear, O Israel: The LORD our God is One; and you shall love the LORD your God with all your heart, and with all your soul, and with all your might. And these words which I command you this day shall be upon your heart; and you shall teach them diligently to your children, and shall talk of them when you sit in your house, and when you walk by the way, and when you lie down, and when you rise. And you shall bind them as a sign upon your hand, and they shall be as frontlets between your eyes. And you shall write them on the doorposts of your house and on your gates. (Deuteronomy 6:4–9)

These words have been further coupled with passages in Deuteronomy 11:13–21 and Numbers 15:37–41 as the most basic part of the liturgy for worship. However, the opening line has been the key statement of belief for all Judaism. It contains only six Hebrew words and embodies two central truths, the Oneness of God and the loyalty of Israel. Terse, pointed, and emphatic, it asserts: "Hear O-Israel, Yahweh our-God, Yahweh

One!'' It says more about Judaism than many complete books.

Another passage in the Torah presents a succinct statement of Israel's faith, a response by a worshiper in ancient Israel when he brought his offerings of the first fruits of the harvest. Part of it is still used in the Passover ritual today:

A wandering Aramean was my father; and he went down into Egypt and sojourned there, few in number; and there he became a nation, great, mighty, and populous. And the Egyptians treated us harshly, and afflicted us, and laid upon us hard bondage. Then we cried to the LORD the God of our fathers, and the LORD heard our voice, and saw our affliction, our toil, and our oppression; and the LORD brought us out of Egypt with a mighty hand and outstretched arm, with great terror, with signs and wonders; and he brought us into this place and gave us this land, a land flowing with milk and honey. And now I bring the first of the fruit of the ground, which thou, O LORD, hast given me. (Deuteronomy 26:5b–10a)

This may not sound like the cataloguing of doctrines expected in a religious creed, but it represents the deepest beliefs of the early Israelites couched in an inseparable framework of history. It touches on the beginnings with Abraham, the sojourn in Egypt, the exodus from Egyptian oppression, the wanderings in Sinai, and the conquests of Canaan as the Promised Land. At the center of the confession of faith is the understanding that Yahweh hears, heeds, enables, and provides for Israel in the time of greatest need.

Yet another passage from the Torah has served as a foundational statement of belief for all generations of Jews and as a vital part in the religious education of Jewish children. It contains a strong emphasis upon the historical situation that forms the necessary backdrop for the actual beliefs:

When your son asks you in time to come, "What is the meaning of the testimonies and the statutes and the ordinances which the LORD your God has commanded you?" then you shall say to your son, "We were Pharaoh's slaves in Egypt, and the LORD brought us out from there, that he might bring us in and give us the land which he swore to give to our fathers. And the LORD commanded us to do all these statutes, to fear the LORD our God, for our own good always, that he might preserve us alive, as at this day." (Deuteronomy 6:20–24)

The Western Wall. *A typical crowd of Jewish worshipers at the Western Wall (also known as the Wailing Wall) in Jerusalem on the Sabbath. The Mosque of Omar is in the background.* (Reproduced by permission of the Consulate General of Israel, Houston)

One other passage in the Torah sets forth a structured belief statement reinforcing the requirements of the Decalogues and codes of laws:

And now, Israel, what does the LORD your God require of you, but to fear the LORD your God, to walk in all his ways, to love him, to serve the LORD your God with all your heart and with all your soul and to keep the commandments and statutes of the LORD, which I command you this day for your good? (Deuteronomy 10:12–13)

Note the action quality demanded throughout this terse statement of belief. There is a positive approach to the life to be lived under God, devoid of detailed prohibitions. Herein is the prophetic ideal concerning the essentials of faith within the covenant. Note once again the positive appeal to action rather than to static concepts. Many other passages could be singled out as examples of concise belief statements, but these will demonstrate Israel's early attempt to summarize the fundamental patterns of doctrine in action and in historical remembrance.

Basic Biblical Concepts

The Nature of God. The most basic doctrinal consideration for Judaism involves the person of God and his active concern for the world. As the *Shema* emphasizes, the Oneness of God has been an unchanging foundation of the faith since the time of the Babylonian exile. Although Abraham and his family came out of a background in *polytheism* (belief in many gods), the principle of *monolatry* (worship of one God) began with Abraham and became the Hebrew ideal. It has already been mentioned that the later Israelites were guilty of apostasy in relation to Ba'al and other gods. However, this problem was overcome during the Babylonian exile and the principle of *monotheism* (belief in one god only) became the hallmark of Judaism. Actually the earlier history of Israel is the history of monotheism's struggle for absolute acceptance. Once this had happened, Judaism was ready to face the world.

God is also pictured in unequivocal terms as the Creator of all that exists in the world, as well as above and below the world. The Hebrew Scriptures celebrate the event of creation in both prose and poetic passages. The most famous description of creation is found in the first chapter of Genesis, a passage probably to be dated about 500 B.C.E. from priestly sources (the *P* tradition). The opening statement establishes the setting and the mood, saying: "In the beginning, God created the Heavens and the Earth" (Genesis 1:1). The continuing description, divided into six days of creative activity followed by the seventh day of rest, has become a literary classic throughout Western civilization. The account clearly implies that God exists from the beginning, is omnipotent with power to create and develop all things, and is in control of the entire process. This creation narrative stands in sharp contrast to the creation documents of Mesopotamia, where the gods are in constant conflict until one god finally wins out. There are obvious parallels between the Jewish and Babylonian accounts, but the monotheistic position presents a distinct contrast to the Babylonian polytheism. The Hebrew description presents God evidencing a clear purpose, order, and supremacy. This position has continued into present-day Judaism, altered only by added interpretation and elaboration.

God, however, is presented as more than One who is also creator. He is both a personal God who is concerned with human needs and a spiritual Being who must be distinguished from material and physical existence. During biblical times, God was described in terms of human-like traits (anthropomorphisms) and human-like emotions (anthropopathisms). Yet, at the same time there was the effort to present God as pure spirit. The result is a constant tension in biblical Judaism between regarding God as just another person and seeing God as only an ethereal spirit. The Decalogue carefully spells out the danger of making any graven image, thus eliminating the danger that God may be limited in time and space. Being a personal god, God is available to meet the needs of mankind; as spirit, God transcends mankind and cannot be boxed in by human ingenuity.

The Nature of Mankind. Although God is the subject of revelation and the object of worship, there are other subjects of concern in Judaism. Mankind, male and female, is pictured in an exalted state in the creation account of Genesis. There is clearly the idea of superiority over other forms of creation and the concept of dominion over other creatures. This involves the rulership of God over the created order. The added emphasis upon being created in the "Image of God" (Genesis 1:26–27, 5:1–3, 9:6) asserts the inherent dignity of mankind. This is further amplified by Psalm 8, where mankind is pictured as little lower than the divine. The net result is an exalted view of mankind seldom found in any ancient literature.

Individuals are also viewed as unified psychophysical organisms in Judaism. While other groups have sometimes separated life into body/soul/spirit or just body/soul, Judaism has generally held to the unified nature of mankind. The Jewish mind has almost always conceived of human beings as animated bodies rather than incarnated souls. Hebrew psychology emphasizes the unitary nature of human life rather than compartmentalizing life. A man or a woman *becomes* a living soul, rather than *having* a soul. Death comes when God takes back the divine breath that has animated the flesh. The "living soul" then ceases to exist. Such a position stands

Jewish Torah Crowns and Covers. *These are located in "David's Tomb" on Mt. Zion in Jerusalem.* (Reproduced by permission of the Consulate General of Israel, Houston)

in sharp contrast to the transmigration of the soul in Hinduism, the rebirth process in Buddhism, and the body–soul dualism sometimes found in later Christianity.

In Jewish thought, humanity is thus seen as the crown of creation, the appointed overseer of nature, and the closest thing to divinity on earth. Yet, there is another side to the equation: mankind is given responsibility for caring for all of creation. The maxim "Privilege brings Responsibility" is most applicable. Mankind is charged: "Be fruitful and multiply and fill up the earth and subdue it" (Genesis 1:28). While the admonition may seem to relate only to the population explosion,

the charge involves the proper preservation and conservation of all earth, which is entrusted to mankind. The basis of modern ecological endeavors is inherent in the relation of mankind to creation.

Israel in History. The elements of God, humanity, and history are inseparable. The Jews have always seen God as the Lord of history, whether explicitly stated or implicitly accepted. Mankind is also included in the ongoing process called history.

The Israelites lived for many generations in a life-or-death struggle with the nature-oriented religions of the Babylonians, Egyptians, Canaanites, Assyrians, Persians, Greeks, and Romans. These religious systems placed their emphasis on natural objects and often on fertility symbols. Sin was the disturbance of the cosmic state and linked to the status quo. There was no personal election or any role to play in history. In contrast, the religion of Israel, which became Judaism, was dynamic, active, and revolutionary in terms of Near Eastern thought. Israelite worship centered on the God of history, who was viewed as active in the entire process from creation to the end of time. While other religions of the area engaged in rites of sympathetic magic during religious festivals, Judaism long based its emphasis on historical memory and on commemoration of divine assistance. For many peoples, history was primarily for the glorification of rulers. For Jews, the emphasis has always been on the glory of what God has done for his people. G. Ernest Wright expressed this unique outlook as he said: "The Israelite eye was thus trained to take human events seriously, because in them was to be learned more clearly than anywhere else what God willed and what he was about."[3]

The Jews saw history as the arena in which God acted and Israel responded. Theology to the Israelites was not a system of ideas but faith in action. The writer of Israel's earliest history (the *J* writer of the tenth century B.C.E.) was therefore not primarily concerned to show how old the Israelites were, but how long God had been dealing with the historical process that led to the choosing of Abraham as heir of a special promise. There has always been in Judaism an emphatic demand that history be interpreted from the standpoint of God. Past, present, and future all have a vital connection with God's purpose for Israel and for the world. Israel has never seen itself as just another of many nations but as God's Chosen People, first among nations in the divine concern and affection. Although interpreted in various ways in later periods, this concept of divine election has given the Jews a special sense of obligation and responsibility.

Creeds of Medieval and Recent Judaism

Outstanding among the creedal statements within Judaism is the summary of doctrine by Moses Maimonides (1135–1204). While analyzing the 613 basic commandments recognized in Judaism, he realized the need for a definitive list of primary beliefs for the medieval Jewish adherent. Several versions of his doctrinal summary have been passed down to modern times. The following is a summary of his basic statements:

1. God is the author and guide of everything that has been and will be created.
2. God is Unity, there is none like unto His Unity and He alone is our God.
3. God is not a body and He has no form whatsoever.
4. God is the first and the last.
5. We must pray to God alone and to no one else.
6. All the words of the prophets are true.
7. Moses is the chief of all prophets whose prophecy is true.
8. The Torah that we possess is the same that was given to Moses.
9. The Torah will never be changed and there will never be any other law of God.
10. God discerns the hearts of all men, knows all their thoughts and deeds.
11. God rewards those who keep His commandments and punishes those who transgress them.
12. Messiah, though he tarry, will come.
13. There will be resurrection of the dead.[4]

These creedal affirmations have been carried over into the Prayerbook in a more authoritarian form with the prefix "I believe . . ." as an introduction to each statement. This practice does not, however, establish these affirmations as fixed dogmas, in spite of their use in many synagogues and temples.

Other persons have expressed the essence of Judaism, sometimes in even more concise terms than Maimonides. Moses Mendelssohn, who was so influential in establishing a base for later Reform Judaism, reduced the essential doctrines to three: (1) the existence of God, (2) providence, and (3) the immortality of the soul. Samuel David Luzzatto (1800–1865) carried the process one step further by affirming that the one essential dogma of Judaism is the belief in the divine origin of the Torah.

Many efforts have thus been made to reduce Judaism to its essence, but no genuine consensus has been achieved. The threefold division into Reform/Conservative/Orthodox forms of Judaism has rendered this process of consensus impossible in the present status of Judaism.

The Practice of Judaism

Most of the preceding discussion has been of necessity either historical or theoretical in nature. Such a foundation is essential in order to understand how the religion has developed to this point in time. Now, the questions of actual practice of the faith are an important part of this chapter. What practices characterize the religious life? What rituals, festivals, and special days mark out the Jewish year? How are these eventful days to be interpreted? How is the moral life defined, lived, and related to contemporary issues? These and many other questions are involved in a discussion of Judaism as it has been practiced and is practiced today.

Rituals and Worship

The actual rituals of the faith have changed with the needs and aspirations of different ages. The pattern of sacrifice and offerings in ancient Israel was clearly set out in the Torah. Many ritual laws established the procedure for priests and people at the Temple in Jerusalem. However, it is now known that there were other shrines and temples during the pre-exilic period that probably used rituals not specifically set forth in the Torah. The shrines at Dan and Bethel in the northern kingdom, as well as those Amos mentioned at Gilgal and Beersheba, are examples of rival sanctuaries.

The exact procedures for sacrifices and offerings at the Temple were recorded in the books of Exodus and Leviticus. There were burnt offerings emphasizing praise and consecration, peace offerings stressing communion with God, sin offerings related to forgiveness of sin, and guilt offerings releasing a person from the penalty of sin. All of these were animal sacrifices and/or offerings. Other presentations include vegetable, drink, and incense offerings as well as special offerings in the form of first fruits of the harvest, firstlings of the flock, tithes, and taxes. An elaborate system was developed with specific requirements as to the ritual to be used in each case. At the heart of the entire sacrificial system was a deep need to express inner realities in an external manner. The act of sacrifice was the act of demonstrating a sense of dependency on God.

This elaborate system was operative as long as the Temple stood. With the destruction of the Temple by the Romans, however, a change took place. An alternative had already developed in the form of the synagogue, and the emphasis changed from sacrifice to prayer and study of the Torah. As indicated, this was not an abrupt change since the synagogue had its roots in the study and praise at homes during the Exile, 600 years earlier. In fact, synagogues were found in all parts of Palestine and in other areas where the Jews had been dispersed long before 70 C.E. While the loss of the Temple was a great sorrow to leaders of Judaism, especially to the Sadducees, the way was prepared for an alternative that would better meet the needs of Jews about to be scattered to all parts of the Roman Empire. Any community could establish a synagogue if ten Jewish men of good report could be gathered together. It was not necessary to have a hereditary priest, only a person who could serve as teacher for the group.

Ritual in the synagogue has always been kept simple. Basically the synagogue (or temple in Reform Judaism) is a place of assembly for the people where God may be met in worship and study. Although the pattern for services varies from Orthodox to Conservative to Reform traditions, the basics are still the same. The primary concern is worship. As Samuel S. Cohen has aptly stated: "While religion is much more than worship, it is nothing without worship."[5] Emphasis is placed on prayer, chants, reading of the Torah and other Scriptures, and participation by the congregation. The Torah Scroll, housed in its special shrine, is the major object of focus. An important part of the liturgy concerns the removal, reading, and replacement of the scroll. Another concern is education: the synagogue has always served as a house of study as well as a house of prayer. The exposition of the Torah during services is supplemented by classes for children and adults.

There are several differences in the services of the three movements. Orthodox synagogues continue the use of the ancient Hebrew language as well as the separation of men and women. The liturgy is also much more traditional. In Reform temples, there is less Hebrew used with more emphasis on the sermon and more innovation employed in the form of dance and modern music. Conservative synagogues vary greatly but usually find a middle ground between the old and new.

Sukkoth Celebration. *An Orthodox Jewish Family involved in Sukkoth celebration in Jerusalem.*
(Reproduced by permission of the Consulate General of Israel, Houston)

As significant as the synagogue has been for more than 2,000 years, worship of God really begins and ends with the family. Sabbath services and most festivals begin with observances in the close unity of the family, move to the synagogue or temple, and then continue within the life of the family.

The dietary laws are also a form of continual family devotion to God. The emphasis here is placed on training in holiness in the context of the home. The dietary regulations (*kashruth* or fitness) are too involved for detailed analysis in this study; however, some general aspects should be noted. Certain animals are regarded as basically unclean and therefore prohibited:

1. Quadrupeds that do not chew the cud and have a split hoof.
2. Carnivorous birds.
3. Winged insects.
4. Aquatic animals lacking fins and scales.
5. Small creeping animals.

All animals are unclean if killed by beast or bird of prey, if they died of themselves, or if they were improperly slaughtered. Both the fat of certain animals and all blood are prohibited. Furthermore, there are special restrictions regarding the eating of meat and milk products, stemming back to the admonition in the Torah: "you shall not boil a kid in its mother's milk" (Exodus 23:19; Exodus 34:26; Deuteronomy 14:21). This restriction was applied to any mixture of meat and milk in rabbinic teaching. While these dietary laws have come under question in modern Judaism and many variations exist today, there can be no doubt that they have strengthened Judaism during centuries of adversity and persecution and have helped maintain the religious character of the home.

Festivals and Sacred Seasons

Basic to the religious calendar in Judaism is the weekly observance of the Sabbath from sunset on Friday until sunset on Saturday. This event commemorates the creation of the world and the human race but even more specifically the "rest" of God at the conclusion of the process. The intended purpose in the life of the believer is clearly related to the rest of body and mind as well as to concentration upon the Creator. Extensive preparations are made in advance in the form of cooking, cleaning the house, bathing, and putting on fresh garments. The mother lights the Sabbath candles shortly before sunset and recites a special benediction; she may add another prayer for the children. Next the father recites a blessing (*Kiddush*) over the wine and for the Sabbath, after which each person drinks the wine. Following a ceremonial washing of the hands, the father recites another blessing over the Sabbath bread, after which the bread is eaten. The meal that follows often involves the singing of Sabbath songs. Two more meals on Saturday are equally ceremonial, with the last meal completed just before sunset. The final act (*Havdallah*) involves a ceremony in which blessings are pronounced over the lighting of a twisted candle, the drinking of another cup of wine, and the smelling of spices. Interspersed with these observances in the home are the synagogue or temple services on Friday night and Saturday morning that link the family to the community of believers and provide opportunity for corporate worship with the group.

Other services and festivals are of a more seasonal nature. They are thought to give rhythm and stability to the Jewish year. While several of the festivals have ancient roots in agricultural rites, they are now very closely linked with the chief events of Jewish history and provide a means of commemoration of these events in terms of either solemn or joyful expression. It should be noted that the lunar calendar is still in use for religious festivals, and thus the corresponding dates in the Western calendar vary from year to year. Adjustment to the solar calendar must be made to keep the festivals in the proper season of the year. This is accomplished by adding a "leap month" to the normal twelve-month year seven times in a cycle of nineteen years. The Jewish calendar begins in the fall during the month of Tishri (September–October) with the New Year celebrations. An alternate liturgical calendar begins in the month of Nisan (March–April).

The most significant festivals fall in two seasons of the year, fall and spring, with two minor festivals during the winter months (see Table 7–3). The three fall festivals occur in rapid succession during a twenty-five-day period. The season begins with Rosh Hashanah (Head of the Year), continues with ten days of spiritual examination leading to Yom Kippur (Day of Atonement), and continues five days later with Sukkoth (Feast of Booths), which lasts another nine days. Rosh Hashanah and Yom Kippur are known as the "High Holy Days." Each of these festivals is significant in itself, but the cumulative effect is also important.

Rosh Hashanah, the Jewish New Year, is characterized by the blowing of the ancient *shofar* or ram's horn. It is also described in Talmudic sources as the Day of Judgment, when the books of heaven are opened and the deeds of each person are recorded for the past year. It serves as a fitting prelude to the penitential season of ten days in which each person engages in re-examination of faith, self-examination, and prayers for forgiveness. This is also a time for restitution to one's neighbors when apologies or compensation can be made for previous wrongs. The High Holy Days come to a climax with Yom Kippur, which is the holiest day of the year. Emphasis is placed on confession of sin, solemn fasting, meditation, and prayer, and all of these elements are performed with great intensity. The desired result is clearly a pardon for one's sins based upon the mercy of God, not on the merit of the individual. After a period of five days, Sukkoth (Feast of Booths) lasts for eight days (nine days outside Israel) and serves as a joyful

TABLE 7–3. *The Jewish Calendar*

Hebrew Month	Western Equivalent		Special Days
Tishri	September–October	1	Rosh Hashanah *or* New Year
		10	Yom Kippur *or* Day of Atonement
		15–23	Sukkoth *or* Feast of Booths
Marchesvan	October–November		
Kislev	November–December	25	Hanukkah *or* Dedication of Lights
Tebet	December–January		
Shebat	January–February		
Adar	February–March	13–14	Purim *or* Feast of Lots
Adar-Sheni	Intercalary Month		
Nisan	March–April	14	Pesach *or* Passover
Iyyar	April–May	5	Israel Independence Day
Sivan	May–June	6	Shavuoth *or* Pentecost
Tammuz	June–July		
Ab	July–August	9	Tishah B'av *or* Destruction of Temple
Elul	August–September		

Seder Dinner. *This picture of a grandfather and his grandson shows the basic ingredients of the passover meal. The ritual and the food items evoke remembrance of the exodus from Egypt. (Reproduced by permission of the Consulate General of Israel, Houston)*

time after the rigorous period of self-examination. It represents both an agricultural or harvest festival and a commemoration of the forty years of wandering in the wilderness by the Israelites under Moses. Ideally, each family builds its own hut or booth with branches over the roof. In this the family eats meals and spends as much time as possible together. Services are held at the synagogue or temple each day during the festival, with an emphasis on palm branches and other twigs reminiscent of the booths in the wilderness.

The festivals in the spring open with Pesach (Passover), which focuses attention back upon the Exodus from Egypt. The historical aspects are now dominant, but the roots go back to an older agricultural festival. The original version of the passover story is found in Exodus 12:5–13. Here it is told that each family killed a male lamb without blemish, placing the blood on the doorposts and lintel of the house. The houses so marked were not touched by the death angel and the inhabitants were spared.

One of the most memorable aspects of the Passover festival is the *seder* ("order"), a meal filled with great symbolism and remembrance. The house is carefully cleaned and the food prepared in advance; in many homes special dishes used only for Passover are brought out.

מנורות שבת

Variety of Jewish Candlelabra. (Reproduced by permission of the Consulate General of Israel, Houston)

Unleavened bread (*matzoth*) is used throughout the festival. The food includes unleavened bread, unseasoned horseradish, chopped apples mixed with nuts and cinnamon and wine, shankbone of a lamb, roasted egg, vegetables (parsley and radish), salt water, and wine. There are four cups of wine, two before the meal and two afterwards. A special glass of wine is also left for Elijah, the prophet, in case he should arrive. The outside door is also opened at one point in the ceremony to give him easy entrance. The service follows the order of the *Haggadah* (Story of the Passover) and involves all the family and guests present. Each of the foods mentioned has a point of reference with the Exodus from Egypt.

The story is retold in words, prayers, songs, and by questions asked by the youngest child at the table. In the midst of the service, the family eats an elaborate meal, which consists of traditional dishes normally used only at Passover. The meal closes with the wish and prayer, "Next year in Jerusalem." While this ceremony is primarily a family festival, services are also held at the synagogue or temple.

The Passover festival is not complete within itself but is closely linked with Shavuoth (Feast of Weeks or Pentecost), although the two festivals are forty-nine days apart. The period between is known as Sefirah (Counting) because of the admonition found in the Torah:

And you shall count from the morrow after the Sabbath, from the day that you brought the sheaf of the wave offering; seven full weeks shall they be, counting fifty days to the morrow after the seventh sabbath; then you shall present a cereal offering of new grain to the LORD. (Leviticus 23:15–16)

It is again obvious that both festivals were orginally associated with spring agricultural rites. However, just as the Passover festival became increasingly linked with the Exodus and less with grain festivals, so the emphasis of the Feast of Weeks shifted to the anniversary of the giving of the Torah to Moses on Mt. Sinai. Services are held in the synagogue or temple where the focus of attention is centered upon the reading of the Ten Commandments. The Book of Ruth in the Hebrew Scriptures is also used in the services because of the harvest theme woven into its love story. The original connection with agriculture is kept alive with a profusion of plants and flowers used as decoration in the home as well as in the synagogue or temple.

Two other festivals are highlighted during the winter months, neither of which is based on Mosaic tradition. Hanukkah (Feast of Dedication) is celebrated for eight days during the month of December. It is historic in emphasis, linked to the victory over the Syrian Greeks during the Maccabean struggles. According to Jewish legend, there was only one small cruse of oil pure enough to use in the rededication of the Temple. Tradition describes how it lasted miraculously eight days rather than one day as expected. This event is commemorated by the lighting of candles, one more each day for eight days, and for this reason Hanukkah has also come to be known as the "Feast of Lights."

The other winter festival is known as Purim (Feast of Lots) and takes place in late February or early March. It memorializes the story of Esther, who helped save her people in the city of Susa during the Persian period (fifth century B.C.E.). The reference to lots relates to the casting of lots by the Prime Minister, Haman, in order to set the date for the wholesale slaughter of the Jews. Thanks to Esther, the tables were turned and Haman was hanged from his own gallows. The story symbolizes heroic resistance to persecution and has been used to encourage persons under any kind of persecution. The Book of Esther from the Hebrew Scriptures is read during the ceremony in the synagogue or temple. Because of the joyful nature of the occasion, children are encouraged to hiss, clap, stamp their feet, or use noise-makers wherever the name of Haman is mentioned. All the major Jewish festivals and their dates are shown in Table 7–4.

There are several other minor festivals and fast days that round out the Jewish calendar. The previously mentioned ceremonies demonstrate the drama and symbols that are a vital part of Judaism. However, one other type of ceremony should be mentioned—the rites of passage for Jewish boys and sometimes Jewish girls. Boys have two meaningful rites that indicate their inclusion in Judaism: (1) circumcision, which is performed at the age of eight days either in the home or in a hospital; and (2) *Bar Mitzvah* (Son of the Commandment), which is performed as soon as possible after the thirteenth birthday (usually on a Sabbath). The circumcision is accomplished by a trained layman, usually noted for his piety, while the boy is held by his godfather. The father then recites a blessing and formally confers upon him his name. The Bar Mitzvah signifies the boy's entry into

TABLE 7–4. *Major Jewish Festivals*

Hebrew Name	Date	English Equivalent	Commemoration
Rosh Hashanah	Tishri 1 (or 1–2)	New Year	Creation, judgment, and beginning of New Year
Yom Kippur	Tishri 10	Day of Atonement	Confession, prayer, and dedication
Sukkoth	Tishri 15–23 (or 24)	Feast of Booths	Wandering in the wilderness
Hanukkah	Kislev 25–Tebet 4	Feast of Dedication	Rededication of Temple in 165 B.C.E.
Purim	Adar 13–14	Feast of Lots	Deliverance of Jews by Esther
Pesach	Nisan 14	Passover	Deliverance and exodus from Egypt
Shavuoth	Sivan 6–7	Pentecost	Harvest and giving of the Torah

religious responsibility and is the occasion for the boy to read from the Scriptures in a public service, usually in the synagogue. In the Reform tradition and in some Conservative congregations, a similar procedure is followed for girls. Instead of circumcision, there are prayers of dedication and blessings in her behalf. A parallel service, *Bas Mitzvah* (Daughter of the Commandment), is provided for the girl embarking upon religious responsibility.

Ethics and Society

Attention has repeatedly been called to the importance of the Torah in the life of Judaism. The term was originally applied to the *Pentateuch* or first five books of the Hebrew Scripture. However, the term has increasingly been made more general until it often applies to the teaching of all Jewish texts or to the totality of the teaching of God within Judaism. References to the Torah in the previous pages have been based upon the original meaning. It is now necessary to shift to the broader meaning, because Jewish ethics have continually expanded the horizon of law, statute, and commandment. Only in the modern era has this direction been altered with the rise of the Reform and Conservative movements. It is now estimated that about one hundred of the precepts of Judaism are practiced by observant Jews today, compared with 613 precepts in the original Torah and in the Talmud; many of the original commands related to the sacrificial cult, which is no longer operative.

The principles of Jewish ethics were first set forth in the Ten Commandments, expanded in the law codes of the Torah of Hebrew Scripture, critiqued by the Hebrew prophets, further expanded in the oral law of the Mishnah, interpreted and analyzed in the Gemara and the Midrash, reinterpreted in philosophical or mystical terms in medieval times, rationally examined during the Enlightenment, and finally re-examined by all three major divisions of Judaism in the modern era. Many changes have taken place in Jewish ethics over this period of time. Among the more obvious discarded principles and practices are *lex talionis* (an eye for an eye), justification for slavery, the practice of polygamy, and the inferior status of women. Nevertheless, in spite of four thousand years of reinterpretation, there are also many emphases that have been maintained since biblical times.

Probably the most striking statement of ethical position in Western religion is found in the Decalogue, already discussed but not quoted in this chapter. The following is a brief reconstruction of an early form of this doctrinal and ethical summary:

God spoke all these words:

1. I am the LORD your God.
2. You shall have no other gods before Me.
3. You shall not take the name of the LORD your God in vain.
4. Remember the Sabbath day to keep it holy.
5. Honor your father and your mother.
6. You shall not commit murder.
7. You shall not commit adultery.
8. You shall not steal.
9. You shall not bear false witness against your neighbor.
10. You shall not covet anything that belongs to your neighbor.*

While the first four commandments are concerned with doctrinal and ritual matters, the last six are clearly ethical. Yet even the first four touch upon ethical requirements in terms of Jewish patterns of thought. In Judaism, past or present, religion and morality are blended in an indissoluble unity. Correct moral conduct is constantly interpreted in the light of the nature of God, since God alone is the example of everything that is good and proper.

Mention has been made of the ethical emphases that have remained basically constant since the biblical period. The following may serve as examples of these basic emphases:

1. *Justice and Righteousness.* These two concepts were certainly implied in the Decalogue but were clarified and applied by the eighth-century B.C.E. prophets of Israel. God became the example of each concept for Amos and thereby the image of how each individual should respond. Amos placed both concepts in parallel as he said: "Let justice roll down like waters, and righteousness like an everflowing stream" (Amos 5:24). Nevertheless, he and other prophets seem to make a distinction, as Abraham Heschel points out: "However, it seems that justice is a mode of action, righteousness a quality of the person."[6] In later Judaism, the two concepts are seen as complementary, and both are essential for the

---

* Note the differences in the order of the Commandments in the Protestant and Catholic lists.

moral well-being of mankind and society. One does what is just toward others because one is right within oneself.

2. *Sanctity of Life*. The sixth commandment establishes a base for regarding all life as vitally important. The usual translation, "Thou shalt not kill," is better translated as in the previously listed reconstruction, "You shall not commit murder." The verb used normally applies to premeditated murder, but frequently is used in regard to involuntary manslaughter as well. Although caution must be exercised in interpreting the commandment absolutely in either way, this commandment has served as a guidepost in Judaism to show respect for all forms of life. The sanctity of life is especially important in relation to humanity, since human beings are regarded as having special nobility of character, being created in the image of God. Life is thus viewed as the unique gift of God, which should not be taken away except by God. The presence of capital punishment in the Torah does not negate the principle but modifies it so that the covenant community can act for God.

3. *Liberation from Bondage and Persecution*. The Hebrew faith was born in the days immediately following the bondage in Egypt. The cry for freedom from persecution—"Let my people go!"—has been sounded over and over again in the history of the Jewish people, in Assyria, Babylonia, Palestine, Spain, Portugal, Italy, France, England, Germany, Poland, and the Soviet Union. This theme has kept alive a desire for freedom and a concern for the weak and oppressed. In Jewish law, the ransoming of captives was a sacred obligation of the community, placed above that of feeding and clothing the poor. During the Middle Ages, large numbers of Jews were kidnapped and held for ransom; it was the duty of the community to redeem the victims by paying the ransom. This obligation even applied to those taken captive for debts that were owed.

4. *Social Responsibility*. A basic maxim in Judaism is: "Love for God is incomplete without love for one's fellow man." The maxim applies to reverence for parents, which is placed just below love for God. It also involves respect for the aged, care for widows and orphans, and aid to the poor. In Jewish thought, expressions of concern for those less fortunate are not a matter of philanthropic giving but an act of justice. The poor person's right to food, clothing, and shelter becomes in Judaism a legal claim against the more fortunate. This

is clearly legislated in the Torah in the instruction to tithe to the poor and in the requirement that a corner of each field be left for gleaning by the poor. The Talmud continues this legislation, specifying means for the collection of food and money for the poor. Maimonides demonstrates the importance of this in medieval society by devoting ten chapters to gifts for the poor in his work, *Mishneh Torah* (*A Copy of the Law*). In the modern era, this sense of social responsibility is still evident in the United Jewish Appeal and the activity of B'nai B'rith, both of which have supported causes beyond the bounds of Judaism itself.

Divisions and Groups

No religion has maintained a monolithic structure without significant divisions, sects, or divergent movements. Even a cursory glance at the history of Judaism shows how various separate emphases led to differing sects. These were followed by rival movements, which finally issued in the modern divisions of today. Yet it is amazing how little fragmentation has taken place in Judaism, considering the nearly 4,000 years since Abraham.

Early Alternative Emphases

Some division appeared as early as the story of Moses at Mount Sinai. While Moses was on the mountain, the people pressured the brother of Moses, Aaron, into assisting them in building a golden calf as an object of worship. The experiment was shortlived, however, because of Moses' reaction when he returned. The effort was not a new approach but rather a return to the pattern of worship known among certain of the tribes in the mixed multitude that left Egypt together. This rival concept lay dormant for many generations but was not completely forgotten even though the faith of Moses in Yahweh became dominant. The struggle with Ba'alism kept alive the fertility image always associated with the bull or the bull calf. In reality, the Mosaic faith was greatly influenced and modified by Ba'alism for many centuries.

Following the division of the kingdom immediately after Solomon's death, a major split occurred. The northern kingdom (Israel) adopted the calf image once again, setting up one image at Bethel near the border with Judah and another at Dan adjacent to the border with Syria. This was viewed as apostasy by the southern kingdom (Judah). However, it should be remembered that the Temple at Jerusalem in Judah had images of cherubim within. The apparent justification for these hybrid animal figures in apposition to images of real bull calves was undoubtedly the fact that these were not real animals but displayed a combination of animal-bird-human features. Thus, they could be viewed as escaping the commandment against graven images or likenesses to anything above, on, or below the earth. Regardless of the justification by each group, the religious rivalry continued for at least two hundred years.

Another division in emphasis can be seen in the separate and often rival functions of priests, prophets, and sages. Although it is impossible to distinguish all the chronological details, the functions of each group are quite evident and an overall chronological construction is possible. While there are overlapping features in their work, it becomes apparent that each group made a significant contribution to the development of Judaism.

Priests. First in historical longevity and visibility were the priests, with each individual priest known as a *Kohen*. In the pre-Mosaic period, this function was performed by the patriarch or head of the family. Under Moses' system of organization, his tribe, known as Levi, assumed sacred responsibility. This applied especially to his brother, Aaron, who was designated as the High Priest. The office, as well as the general priesthood, became a matter of heredity with all priests coming from the tribe of Levi and the leadership from the descendants of Aaron. Although politics often entered into the picture, with one or another part of the tribe gaining the ascendancy, the hereditary control gave great stability and long tradition to the movement.

The priests performed basic duties that seem to have increased in terms of responsibility and power with the passing years. They served as the keepers of various sanctuaries, with special emphasis upon the sacred vessels associated with worship; they were responsible for delivering the sacred oracles, with primary concern for the casting of lots as to the will of Yahweh; they were assigned the task of safeguarding the sacred tradition in terms of teaching moral precepts to the people; and

they acted as the leaders in worship and sacrifice. There were others who had various responsibilities in music and in the preparation of the sacrifices, but the priests bore the primary responsibility.

Prophets. Second in terms of longevity and influence were the prophets, with individual prophets being referred to as *Nabi'*. Not established as an official order by Moses, the prophets however followed the example of Moses as a charismatic figure who served as a spokesman for Yahweh. The prophetic movement originated as bands of prophets who had ecstatic experiences based upon highly emotional group encounters. The ancient descriptions refer to music, wine, dancing, and contagious emotionalism, producing rather extreme behavior. At the same time there were seers whose task was the divining or predicting of the future. Out of both these movements came a group of quite individual and independent prophets who acted as spokesmen for Yahweh, voices of conscience for kings and leaders, and reformers of society. While some prophets acted in a revolutionary manner, their major task was to call the people back to moral responsibility and the kings back to the leadership of Yahweh. They based their message upon the authority of God ("Thus saith the LORD") and expressed a sense of divine compulsion to convey that message. There was almost always a note of urgency in the appeals of the prophets as they spoke primarily to their contemporary situations. Although they sometimes looked to the future for understanding, it was usually to illuminate the needs of the present.

The relationship between priest and prophet was not always amicable, although basically complementary. The antagonism was evident in the encounter of Amos with Amaziah, the chief priest at Bethel. Amos recorded his conflict with Amaziah (Amos 7:10–17), telling how the chief priest reported his activity to the king and describing his subsequent condemnation of Amaziah. This element of conflict was further accentuated by Hosea, who also decried the example of the professional prophets of his day. The antagonism continued in postexilic times, as evidenced by Malachi's statement:

For the lips of a priest should guard knowledge and men should seek instruction from his mouth for he is a messenger of the Lord of Hosts. But you have caused many to stumble by your instruction; you have corrupted the covenant of Levi, says the Lord of Hosts, and so I make you despised and as you have not kept my ways but have shown partiality in your instruction . . . (Malachi 2:7–8)

Sages. A third group, known as the *sages* or *wise men,* performed a distinctly different function with their ongoing search for wisdom. Two different emphases were present: one focused attention on practical wisdom in the form of admonitions for daily life, and the other dealt with speculative issues about life. Most of the sages were older teachers of young men, preparing them to take their place in life with clear knowledge of the wisdom of experience. Their emphasis was not upon the ritual concerns of the priests nor on the ethical and theological concerns of the prophets. Rather, their teaching was directed toward successful living under God in very concrete and practical terms.

The wisdom movement that produced the sages began shortly after the prophetic movement (ca. 1000 B.C.E.) but outlasted it. Sages appear to have been a part of the royal court of David and Solomon. In fact, Solomon, who was noted for his wisdom in the early days of his reign, became the patron of the movement and caused much of the material to be gathered around his name. Many if not all of the kings had advisors who were either sages or professional prophets. Later, after the exile in Babylonia, wise teachers apparently stood quite apart from official life. There were no kings under the Persians, and the priests were dominant. The sages, however, continued to have great prestige as teachers of young people from the leading families.

Groups in Early Judaism

During the Maccabean wars with the Seleucid Greeks, which ended in the brief period of freedom for the Jews of Palestine in 142 B.C.E., forces were set in motion that resulted in several rival movements. The most important groups to arise within the next few generations were the Pharisees, the Sadducees, and the Essenes. Each had characteristic emphases that were opposed or rejected by the other groups.

The Pharisees. The Pharisees represented the People's Party, a basic lay movement with strong grassroot support. They were separatists, concerned with ritual purity, but not true conservatives in that their emphasis on the twofold law (Torah plus oral tradition) placed them outside strict Mosaic interpretation of revelation, although they claimed the oral law was also Mosaic. Differing schools of teaching came into existence under leaders such as Shammai, Hillel, and Gamaliel, because the oral law was considered more flexible than the unchangeable Torah.

The Sadducees. The Sadducees represented the Priestly Party, composed mostly of wealthy aristocrats. Their strength lay in close connection with Temple life and the control of the *Sanhedrin,* the seventy-one member court that met in Jerusalem with jurisdiction over all religious matters. The Sadducees were the true conservatives in that they accepted only the Torah without the added oral law accepted by the Pharisees. They also rejected the doctrines concerning resurrection, future life, angels, demons, and providence that were strongly set forth by the Pharisees.

The Essenes. The Essenes represented the Monastic Party, with special emphasis on ascetic withdrawal from the world. The Qumran site, located at the north end of the Dead Sea, was one of the main centers for the group, although there is evidence of cell groups in other parts of Palestine, especially in Galilee. The movement was a cooperative brotherhood with strict discipline and priestly participation. Special attention was given to intense study of scripture, ritual purification, and messianic hope. Their studies produced extensive literary activity, both in the copying of existing manuscripts and the producing of sectarian material. Since 1947, thousands of manuscript fragments and some virtually complete documents have added greatly to the understanding of this monastic community overlooking the Dead Sea. The community came to a sudden end in the spring of 68 C.E., when the Roman Tenth Legion moved down the Jordan valley on its way to besiege Jerusalem.

The Zealots. Another group during this period was the Zealots, who came into being as a revolutionary movement against the Romans. Although many of the Zealots had strong religious enthusiasm, the movement was based more upon nationalism and deep hatred for the Romans. The members were a mixed group, ranging from simple desperadoes to fanatical patriots. Their ac-

Blowing of the Shofar. *Part of the Passover Pilgrimage in Jerusalem.* (Reproduced by permission of the Consulate General of Israel, Houston)

tions precipitated the wars with Rome in 66–70 and 132–135 C.E. While they dreamed of achieving the success of the Maccabean freedom fighters several centuries before, they were not as successful in the fight against Rome.

Medieval Movements

For several centuries Jews had been moving out into the provinces of the Roman Empire. Changing circumstances produced a variety of approaches within Judaism. The orthodoxy of the Talmud and rabbis was challenged or altered by the Karaites, several philosophical movements, Kabbalah, and Hasidism.

Reference has been made previously to the development of the Palestinian and Babylonian Talmuds, which represent the best of early Jewish interpretation of the Torah. The process began with the gathering of the oral law and the editing of the Mishnah by Rabbi Yehuda ha-Nasi at the end of the second century C.E. From that point, various interpreters took over the task of expounding the Mishnah during the next three hundred years. The result was the production of the two Talmuds. This was not, however, the end of the process. Expansion and reinterpretation of the Talmud took place from the

Synagogue at Capernaum. *This synagogue is one of the best examples of a basilical building in Galilee, probably dating from the third or fourth century C.E. Shown here are the aisle, benches along the western wall, and the major chamber on the right.* (Courtesy of Kyle Yates)

the Jewish faith and produced an allegorical interpretation of the Torah. Nine centuries later a Jewish philosopher from Egypt became the head of the Rabbinic academy in Babylon. Embracing some of the thought of Plato and Philo, Saadya ben Joseph was closer to the Jewish orthodoxy of his day. He vigorously opposed the individualistic movement of Karaism while attempting to bridge the gap between reason and revelation. He emphasized personal immortality, bodily resurrection, and freedom of human will.

As Saadya had applied Platonic thought to Judaism, two centuries later Moses Maimonides (1135–1204) seriously applied the teachings of Aristotle to the Jewish heritage. He placed great emphasis on intellectual knowledge of God and viewed the Hebrew prophets as recipients of this knowledge, a situation that could recur at any time when persons become receptive. He was concerned about ethics and commandments but reinterpreted these in terms of rational principles. Saadya is often called the "father of Jewish philosophy," but Maimonides is generally described as the "greatest philosopher in the Jewish tradition." His brief creed of Judaism was presented earlier.

Kabbalah. Another significant development in medieval Jewish life came in a type of esoteric teaching known as *Kabbalah,* the term signifying "reception" or "oral transmission." The emphasis in the thirteenth century was placed on special mystical teachings that were viewed as passed down in oral form. These teachings concerned hidden or unintelligible doctrines that could be properly understood only by those with insight into the secret wisdom. Using symbolic language, the teachers presented a pattern of life that emphasized inner contemplation and a mild form of asceticism. The major literary work, the *Zohar,* was probably composed by Rabbi Moshe de Leon during the thirteenth century. It offers a commentary on the Torah with a thoroughgoing mystical interpretation: God is the "Infinite One" with ten basic qualities emanating as powers reaching into the physical world; the glory or presence of God needs once again to be joined with The Infinite in order to restore the harmony of the universe; this fusion can be accomplished by mystical union between the worshiper and God, and by keeping the Torah and living a moral life.

The leading teacher of Kabbalism was Isaac Luria

sixth century to the end of the tenth century as a continuation of the earlier concern of the Pharisees in the oral law and its application. The resulting emphasis came to be known as *talmudic* or *rabbinic Judaism.*

During the eighth century, a rival movement was founded by Anan ben David of Baghdad, whose followers were called *Karaites.* The group may be regarded as a direct successor to the Sadducees and strongly opposed to talmudic Judaism. The principle of individual interpretation of the Torah became the hallmark of the group and led the Karaite writers to reject the talmudic authority and frequently attack the rabbinic methods of interpretation. They have continued as a group of dissenters to this day, although they were almost wiped out in World War II. Several thousand still exist as a part of the Israeli community.

Philosophy became an important part of Jewish life during the medieval period. Previously, the development of Jewish philosophical thought had been emphasized by Philo of Alexandria during the first century of the common era. He had applied the teaching of Plato to

(1534–1572), whose parents migrated to Palestine in 1492 after being expelled from Spain. Crucial to his interpretation of Kabbalism was the doctrine of reincarnation, in which a person could increase in standing before God through a series of existences. The end result could be union with God, although it was also possible for individuals to return as animals or plants if their lives warranted this negative evaluation. While this doctrine did not correspond to the biblical view of man as a psychophysical whole, it did provide for a mystical search for perfect union with God and the experiential possibility of such a union. The movement brought strong reaction from other leaders of the medieval community but nevertheless provided a new experiential dimension to Judaism.

Hasidism. Another movement in Judaism arose in the eighteenth century; it was located in Eastern Europe and was called *Hasidism*. This movement embodied a strong type of pietism in which the adherents were called *Hasidim* (Pious Ones), a term that had been used many centuries before during the struggle for freedom against the Syrian Greeks. Emphasis was once again placed on purity and devotion to the Torah. This time, however, there was a close tie to the mystical teachings of Kabbalism rather than to a guerrilla war for independence. The ideal came to be the perfectly righteous man (*Zaddik*) who alone could achieve union with the divine and therefore guide other believers even better than the Torah or a rabbi. The Zaddik was thus a type of holy man who could perform miracles and aid ordinary persons to seek union with God. The approach used to accomplish this goal was a type of loving humility based upon a form of self-negation. The result was a movement that combined a simple understanding of the esoteric faith of Kabbalism with an extreme emphasis on the importance of the Zaddik.

Modern Divisions

Contemporary divisions in Judaism (Reform, Conservative, and Orthodox) have their origin in the directions taken by Jews during the Enlightenment, the great flowering of rationalism in Europe in the eighteenth century, also called the Age of Reason. In fact, Isidore Epstein has summarized the impact of the Enlightenment on Judaism in this way:

All modern movements in Judaism stem directly or indirectly from the Enlightenment—the movement which characterized the general atmosphere of the eighteenth century and represented the efforts of Western mankind to apply the rule of reason to all phases of human life.[7]

There can be no doubt that Judaism was entering a new day, a new era, a new exodus from the ghettos. During the Middle Ages, Jews had been forced to live in special quarters of major cities in Italy, Spain, Germany, and Poland. The area was often walled off from the rest of the city and, since 1516, called a *ghetto*. While a new beginning for Judaism was now possible, the process was to be painful and fraught with divisions.

The greatest voice in the application of the principles of the Enlightenment was Moses Mendelssohn (1729–1786). His basic position was best expressed in this emphatic statement: "I recognize no external verities except those which cannot only be conceived but also be established and verified by human reason."[8] Although Mendelssohn remained a thoroughgoing exponent of rationalism, he also was committed to demonstrating the harmony between Judaism and the rationalistic approach of his day. His translation of the Torah into German and his commentary work on the Hebrew Scriptures related Judaism to the culture of the West.

The efforts of Mendelssohn and his followers brought reaction from both conservative and reformist elements. Some groups began to model synagogue services after German Protestant groups. They introduced instrumental music, allowed men and women to sit together, used the vernacular rather than Hebrew, ignored the regulations concerning head cover and shawls, and even switched the day of worship to Sunday. Other groups, represented by Rabbi Moses Sofer of Pressburg (1762–1839), forbade the reading of Mendelssohn's works or any secular education. These groups opposed all forms of modernity. Yet another group represented by Zacharias Frankel (1801–1875) accepted the need for modernization while still holding firmly to the essentials of the teachings of the past. Thus, the stage was set for the establishment of major modern divisions within Judaism.

The Reform Movement. The Reform Movement, growing out of the mood of the Enlightenment, was

Yochanan ben Zakai Synagogue. *This Orthodox synagogue is located in the old city of Jerusalem. It exemplifies a typical pattern of medieval Jewish architecture still alive in many parts of the world.* (Reproduced by permission of the Consulate General of Israel, Houston)

further accelerated by the principle of religious toleration accorded to the Jews by the French National Assembly in 1791. The ghetto walls also collapsed in Holland in 1796, in Italy in 1798, and in Germany in 1812, as full citizen rights were given to Jewish subjects. The first Jewish Reform Temple was built at Seesen, Brunswick,* in 1810; others followed in rapid order in other sections of Germany. The traditionalists were dubbed as "Orthodox," a name that was emphasized by Samson Raphael Hirsch (1808–1888) who established a school of Neo-Orthodoxy that has basically continued to this day in Orthodox synagogues. The Reform Movement made gains until the Breslau** Conference in 1846 when the controversy over whether to worship on Saturday or Sunday brought a stalemate.

* Now in the Federal Republic of Germany.
** Now Wroclaw in Poland.

The leadership of the Reform Movement then shifted to the United States, where there was very little organized resistance. An important statement of principles was formulated by the American Reform Movement in 1885 as the "Pittsburgh Platform." These principles included: (1) rejection of strict adherence to Mosaic and talmudic legislation, (2) establishment of Sunday services, and (3) repudiation of Jewish nationalism. Another statement seven years later made circumcision unnecessary for proselytes.

The Conservative Movement. The radical nature of these principles brought many protests and caused the Conservative Movement to evolve under the leadership of Sabato Morais (1823–1901) and Solomon Schechter (1830–1915). Following the lead of Zechariah Frankel's positive-historical school in Germany, the Conservative Movement took a position halfway between Orthodoxy and Reform. While modifying and liberalizing some aspects of worship and practice, there was a strong commitment to the rabbinic tradition, with some adaptation to modern needs. The Conservative Movement has consequently refused to lay down strong principles of agreement or disagreement with either Orthodoxy or Reform.

The absence of definite dogmas has led to the Reconstructionist approach within the Conservative Movement. Inspired by Mordecai Kaplan, who was its leading spokesman for more than 50 years beginning in 1922, this approach has placed great emphasis on Jewish culture in which religion is only one part. It has been characterized as "Conservatism without religious affirmations." Rejected are beliefs in the supernatural, the divine origin of the Torah, messianism, and the resurrection of the dead.

Zionism. One other movement, Zionism, has had great effect upon the history of the formation of the nation of Israel. The roots of Zionism reach back to the destruction of the Temple in 70 C.E. and the final defeat of the Jews at the end of Second Jewish Revolt in 135 C.E. The capture of Jerusalem by the Muslims in 640 C.E. added to the longing of the Jews to return. The Christian Crusades also destroyed Jews from England, across France and Germany, all the way to Palestine. Almost the entire Jewish population of Jerusalem was destroyed by the Crusaders in 1099. However, it was the persecution of Jews during medieval times, and their forced withdrawal into ghettos all over Europe, that was the immediate cause of the Zionist movement to re-establish a Jewish homeland. The demand of Christians that Jews accept Christianity was a major effort of the Inquisition, the interrogating arm of the Counter-Reformation effort of the Roman Catholic Church. In 1478 the church sought to punish the insincere converts who still practiced Judaism secretly. Thousands of Jews were burned alive and the property of others was confiscated. A decree to expel all non-Christians, put forth by Ferdinand and Isabella of Spain in 1492, resulted in the departure of 150,000 Jews in four months. A similar edict was issued in Portugal in 1497. Displaced Jews moved from place to place seeking a permanent home, forced to live in ghettos in most areas where they settled.

It was Theodor Herzl (1860–1904) who emphasized that the only hope for Jews lay in the form of a national

Aerial View of Jerusalem. The letters in the photograph indicate the locations of (A) the Garden of Gethsemane and Church of All Nations; (B) the Temple Mount where the temples of Solomon, Zerubbabel, and Herod stood and where the mosques of Omar and Al Aksa now stand; (C) the Western Wall, which serves as a focus for Jewish pilgrimage and prayer; (D) the extensive excavations in the reconstructed Jewish Quarter of the old city (under N. Avigad). (Reproduced by permission of the Consulate General of Israel, Houston)

home in Palestine. The first Zionist Congress, meeting in Basel in 1897, articulated these hopes. Twenty years later, the British government endorsed the concept in the Balfour Declaration that "viewed with favor the establishment of a national home for the Jewish people in Palestine." The issue was debated by many leaders during the years between the two World Wars—and then the Holocaust during World War II appeared to render imperative the need for a Jewish homeland. The merciless extermination of six million Jews by the Nazi powers reduced the total Jewish population of the world by fully one-third as men, women, and children were tortured, starved, machine-gunned, or gassed in a wholesale slaughter never before known to mankind. This slaughter increased the solidarity of the Jewish people around the world and made them more aware of the need for a national homeland.

As that war ended, the memory of the Holocaust and the realization that thousands of homeless Jews remained in concentration camps in Germany made an impact upon many world leaders. When the British announced their intention to end their mandate control of Palestine, the United Nations voted in November of 1947 to partition the area into Jewish and Arab sectors. Almost at the moment of the British departure, a National Council meeting in Tel Aviv proclaimed the establishment of the state of Israel on May 14, 1948. During the intervening decades, there has been a mixture of war and unofficial peace. The issues at stake are far from settled, although the dreams of the early leaders have been fulfilled in many ways.

Goals for Believers

By way of conclusion, we ask: What goals motivate Jews toward religious behavior? What does the adherent to Judaism hope to gain by being a part of the faith? In what ways are these goals other-wordly or this-worldly? These questions are vital to the understanding of any faith, to empathy with the believers, and to an assessment by the believer of the worth of the religious effort.

The most basic goal for a Jewish person is "life in covenant with God." Many people who do not frequent the synagogue or temple and do not keep carefully the dietary laws regard themselves as a part of the covenant. Such a man has his sons circumcised and confirmed in the covenant through the ceremony of *Bar Mitzvah,* and his daughters confirmed through *Bas Mitzvah.* Originally, recognition of the covenant meant strict adherence to the Torah responsibilities. These are interpreted today in many ways and with various degrees of strictness. However, the common feature is the heritage of being a part of the ongoing life of Judaism bound up in the covenant relation with God.

A second goal can best be described as "life according to the Torah." As indicated previously, the breadth of meaning for the term *Torah* may vary as well as the degree of strict adherence. Yet, the way of the Torah is the direction for all of life for the devout within Judaism. The search for understanding of the Torah becomes a dominant drive for the Jew in terms of the meaning of life as such, as well as in the quest for religious meaning. Samuel S. Cohen suggests:

Perhaps nowhere except among the Brahmans of India has study of sacred literature been accorded so high a place as in Judaism. Touching and illuminating every phase of life, the Torah has welded religion and life into an indissoluble union. It not only presents a road map of life but makes the pursuit of its directions the very condition of blessedness.[9]

Judaism has always stressed the attainment of knowledge, not only for pragmatic ends, but as a goal to be achieved for its own sake.

A third goal relates to "life in the future." While hope for the future played an important part in biblical, talmudic, and medieval Judaism, in modern Judaism it occupies a subordinate place. The concepts of Messiah, messianic age, life after death, bodily ressurection, heaven, and hell are no longer primary concerns. This is especially true of the Reform and Conservative traditions, although Orthodoxy accepts many of these concepts. Many contemporary writers interpret the biblical and talmudic references concerning immortality (living on in an afterlife) or resurrection (raising of the body at a future time) as metaphors for the revival of the nation Israel. They likewise apply hope of the messianic age to the creation of the state of Israel. Even the concept of the Day of Judgment has been reduced to a series of days representing each Yom Kippur (Day of Atonement). Yet for many Jews today, especially those in Orthodox tradition, these concepts represent a third goal in the religious life. Many from the Reform tradition accept some idea of life after death while rejecting or questioning the concepts of heaven, hell, or bodily resurrection. The idea of future retribution for the wicked necessitates some conception of immortality. The fact that the "world to come" and "life eternal" are mentioned in the Union Prayer Book of Reform Judaism keeps the concept before the people. These ideas are further reinforced by the creed of Maimonides, found in expanded form in the prayerbooks of many congregations, which affirms in the last two statements:

I firmly believe in the coming of Messiah; and although he may tarry, I daily wait for his coming. I firmly believe that there will be a revival of the dead at a time which will please the Creator; blessed and exalted be his name forever and ever.[10]

It becomes apparent, even in this brief survey, that the emphasis in Judaism is on a life to be lived here and now under God. It is further a life guided by the Torah of God and fulfilled in the covenant community. Many rituals, ceremonies, festivals, and fasts are designed to strengthen commitment and praise God. The ultimate goal is that of Atonement with God (restoration of fellowship between God and man), whether viewed as accomplished only on Yom Kippur or also in a life to come.

NOTES

1. Abraham Heschel, *The Prophets* (New York: Harper & Row, 1962), p. 4.
2. James Pritchard, *The Ancient Near East* (Princeton, N.J.: Princeton University Press, 1958), pp. 207–208.
3. G. Ernest Wright, *God Who Acts* (London: SCM Press, 1952), p. 44.
4. Moses Maimonides, *Commentary on the Mishnah,* Sanhedrin 10:1, as paraphrased in Abraham M. Heller, *The Vocabulary of Jewish Life,* rev. ed. (New York: Hebrew Publishing Company, 1967), pp. 191–192.
5. Samuel S. Cohen, *Judaism, A Way of Life* (New York: Schocken Books, Inc., 1948), p. 315.
6. Heschel, p. 201.
7. Isidore Epstein, *Judaism* (Harmonsworth, England: Penguin Books, 1956), p. 287.
8. Moses Mendelssohn, *Jerusalem and Other Writings* (New York: Schocken Books, Inc., 1969), p. 98.
9. Cohen, pp. 238–239.
10. Philip Birnbaum, *Encyclopedia of Jewish Concepts* (New York: Sanhedrin Press, rev. ed. 1975), p. 51.

GLOSSARY

'Adonai (*á-doh-nái*) Hebrew name applied to God, meaning "Lord"; vowels used with *YHWH;* substitute pronunciation for **Yahweh.**

Ba'al (*baáh-uhl*) storm god of the ancient Canaanites, linked with fertility and nature.

Bar Mitzvah confirmation ceremony for boys at age thirteen, meaning "Son of the Commandment."

Bas Mitzvah corresponding confirmation ceremony for girls (Reform and Conservative traditions), meaning "Daughter of the Commandment."

Canon standard collection of books in Hebrew Scripture, traditionally approved by Council of Jabneh in 90 C.E.

Conservative Movement recent division in Judaism attempting to reach a middle ground between Orthodox and Reform positions.

Covenant agreement between God and Israel, based upon promise of faithfulness on part of both parties.

Cyrus Persian ruler who captured Babylon in 539 B.C.E. and permitted Jews to return to Jerusalem.

Decalogue Ten Commandments given to Moses (Exodus 20:1–17). Cf. Deuteronomy 5:6–21, Exodus 34:10–26.

'El (*ale*) general Semitic name for God, used primarily by the Patriarchs.

'Elohim (*Eh-lo-heém*) another Semitic name for God, used extensively by Israelites; also generic word for divinity.

Essenes ascetic Jewish sect in second and first century B.C.E. and first century C.E.; probably active in monastic life at Qumran near the Dead Sea.

Exile period of Jewish captivity in Babylonia, beginning with fall of Jerusalem in 586 B.C.E. and ending with return to Jerusalem in 537 B.C.E.

Exodus deliverance of Israelites from Egypt under Moses about 1290 B.C.E.

Gemara (*guh-maáh-ruh*) Aramaic commentary on the Mishnah or oral law, part of Babylonia and Palestinian Talmud.

Ḥanukkah (*ḥaáh-noo-kúh*) Feast of Dedication (also Feast of Lights); eight-day festival in November/December, commemorating victory of Jews over Syrian Greeks in 161 B.C.E.

Hasidism mystical movement in Eastern Europe, composed of the Hasidim who were the "Pious Ones."

Hebrew early name for Israelites, used primarily during patriarchal period; also name for language of ancient and modern Jews.

Israel new name given to Jacob, grandson of Abraham; name of tribes also known as Israelites; name of Northern Kingdom after Solomon's death; name of modern state in the Near East.

Jehovah name for God coined in sixteenth century C.E.; combination of **Yahweh** and **'Adonai.**

Judah name of son of Jacob; tribe of Israelites; name of Southern Kingdom after death of Solomon.

Kabbalah (*kab-báah-luh*) medieval mystical movement based on older traditions.

Karaite member of a Jewish sect originating in the eighth century C.E. that rejected Rabbinic Judaism and placed emphasis on Scripture alone.

Kethubim   the third division of Hebrew Scriptures called "The Writings," composed of poetic and wisdom books.

Maccabean Revolt   revolt of Jewish freedom fighters against Syrian Greeks between 167 B.C.E. and 142 B.C.E.

Maimonides   greatest of medieval Jewish philosophers (1135–1204 C.E.).

Mendelssohn   leading Jewish rationalist during period of the Enlightenment (1729–1786 C.E.).

Messiah   the "Anointed One" expected as Redeemer of Israel and the world.

Midrash   expositions of biblical texts to bring out legal precepts or ethical principles.

Mishnah   earliest compilation of oral law by Yehuda ha-Nasi during late second century C.E.

Moses   leader of Israelites during and after the Exodus in thirteenth century B.C.E.; founder of Mosaic faith that developed into Judaism.

Nabi'   prophetic spokesman for God, serving as one of the reformers in Israel from the eighth to fifth centuries B.C.E.

Nebi'im (*néh-bih-eém*)   gregarious and ecstatic prophetic group developing during the days of Samuel, Saul, and David.

Orthodox Movement   modern designation for strict traditional Judaism.

Pentateuch   first five books of the Hebrew Scriptures; also known as Law of Moses and the **Torah.**

Pesach (*péh-saakh*)   Spring festival known as Passover, connected with Exodus from Egypt by the Israelites under Moses.

Pharisees   people's party in Hellenistic and Roman Judaism, emphasizing oral law, resurrection, and ceremonial purity; control of synagogues.

Purim (*poo-reém*)   late winter festival associated with the Book of Esther and symbolizing heroic resistance to persecution.

Rabbi   a teacher or spiritual leader of a Jewish congregation.

Reconstructionism   recent movement founded by Mordecai Kaplan that emphasizes Judaism as civilization and denies reality of a personal or supernatural God.

Reform Movement   a movement growing out of the Enlightenment in Europe attempting to relate Judaism to modern society.

Rosh Hashanah (*rosh-haah-shaáh-nuh*)   Jewish New Year, celebrated in September or October; meaning "Head of the Year;" also called the Day of Judgment.

Sabbath   seventh day of the week, observed as a day of rest and sanctification with important rituals in home and synagogue.

Sadducees   conservative religious party in Hellenistic and Roman Judaism that rejected oral law and resurrection.

Sanhedrin   Supreme Council in Hellenistic and Roman Judaism, composed of seventy-one rabbinical scholars meeting in Jerusalem.

Seder (*séh-der*)   family meal in Passover ceremony, involving special foods with symbolic meanings.

Shabuoth (*shaah-voó-ohth*)   Feast of Weeks, also known as Pentecost, commemorating the giving of the **Torah** at Mt. Sinai.

Shema (*shéh-muh*)   opening word of basic prayers recited morning and evening by Jews; basic statement of faith in Judaism (Cf. Deuteronomy 6:4–9).

Sukkoth (*sook-ohth*)   Feast of Booths, a fall festival emphasizing the wandering in the wilderness following the **Exodus.**

Temple   three successive sanctuaries at Jerusalem built under Solomon, Zerubbabel, and Herod; name applied to synagogue in Reform Judaism.

Torah   first five books in Hebrew Scripture, the **Pentateuch;** all major Jewish texts; the totality of God's teachings in Judaism.

Yahweh (*yaáh-way*)   probably original pronunciation of special covenant name for God revealed to Moses; later written *YHWH* but pronounced as 'Adonai.

Yom Kippur (*yóhm-ki-poór*)   Day of Atonement observed in the fall as a day of confession, fast, and prayer for forgiveness.

Zionism   modern movement first led by Theodor Herzl to gain a homeland for the Jews in Palestine.

SUGGESTED READINGS

Primary Sources in Translation

EPSTEIN, ISIDORE, ed. *The Babylonian Talmud.* 18 vols. London: The Soncino Press, 1948.

GASTOR, THEODOR H., trans. *The Dead Sea Scriptures in English Translation.* Rev. ed. New York: Doubleday & Company, Inc., 1964.

GLATZER, NAHUM N., ed. *Hammer On The Rock: A Midrash Reader.* New York: Schocken Books, Inc., 1962.

The Holy Bible, Revised Standard Version. New York: Thomas Nelson, Inc., 1946, 1952.

The Holy Scriptures According to the Masoretic Text. Philadelphia: Jewish Publication Society, 1955.

LEVIANT, CURT. *Masterpieces of Hebrew Literature.* New York: KTAV Publishing House, 1969.

LIPMAN, EUGENE J., trans. *The Mishnah, Oral Teachings of Judaism.* New York: W. W. Norton & Company, Inc., 1970.

MILLGRAM, ABRAHAM E. *An Anthology of Medieval Hebrew Literature.* London: Abelard-Schuman, 1961.

MONTEFIORE, C. G., and HERBERT LOEWE. *A Rabbinic Anthology.* Rev. ed. New York: Schocken Books, Inc., 1974.

PRITCHARD, JAMES, ed., *The Ancient Near East*. Princeton, N.J.: Princeton University Press, 1958.

Secondary Sources

ALBRIGHT, W. F. *Archaelogy and the Religion of Israel*. 3d ed. Baltimore: Johns Hopkins Press, 1957.

ANDERSON, BERNHARD W. *Understanding the Old Testament*. 3d ed. Englewood Cliffs, N.J.: Prentice-Hall, Inc., 1975.

BAECK, LEO. *The Essence of Judaism*. Rev. ed. New York: Schocken Books, Inc., 1961.

BAMBERGER, BERNARD J. *The Search for Jewish Theology*. Rev. ed. New York: Behrman House, 1978.

_____. *The Story of Judaism*. 3d ed. New York: Schocken Books, Inc., 1970.

BIRNBAUM, PHILLIP. *Encyclopedia of Jewish Concepts*. Rev. ed. New York: Sanhedrin Press, 1975.

BLUMENTHAL, DAVID R. *Understanding Jewish Mysticism*. New York: KTAV Publishing House, 1978.

BRIGHT, JOHN. *History of Israel*. Philadelphia: Westminster Press, 1959.

BUBER, MARTIN. *The Prophetic Faith*. New York: Harper & Row, 1949.

CRONBACH, ABRAHAM. *Judaism for Today*. New York: Bookman and Associates, 1954.

EPSTEIN, ISIDORE. *Judaism*. Harmonsworth, England: Penguin Books, 1956.

HARSHBARGER, LUTHER H., and JOHN A. MOURANT. *Judaism and Christianity*. Boston: Allyn and Bacon, 1968.

HESCHEL, ABRAHAM. *The Prophets*. New York: Harper & Row, 1962.

LACHS, SAMUEL T., and SAUL P. WACHS. *Judaism*. Niles, Ill.: Argus, 1979.

NEUSNER, JACOB. *Invitation to the Talmud*. New York: Harper & Row, 1973.

SACHAR, ABRAM L. *A History of the Jews*. 5th ed. New York: Alfred A. Knopf, Inc., 1967.

SACHAR, HOWARD. *Diaspora: An Inquiry into the Contemporary Jewish World*. New York: Harper & Row, 1986.

SANDMEL, SAMUEL. *We Jews and Jesus*. Rev. ed. New York: Oxford University Press, 1973.

SCHWARZ, LEO W., ed. *Great Ages and Ideas of the Jewish People*. New York: Random House, Inc., 1956.

SELTZER, ROBERT M. *Jewish People—Jewish Thought*. New York: Macmillan, 1980.

deVAUX, ROLAND. *Ancient Israel, Its Life and Institutions*. New York: McGraw-Hill Book Company, 1961.

8

Christianity

παρέδωκα γὰρ ὑμῖν ἐν πρώτοις, ὃ καὶ παρέλαβον,
ὅτι Χριστὸς ἀπέθανεν ὑπὲρ τῶν ἁμαρτιῶν ἡμῶν
κατὰ τὰς γραφάς, καὶ ὅτι ἐτάφη, καὶ ὅτι ἐγήγερται
τῇ ἡμέρᾳ τῇ τρίτῃ κατὰ τὰς γραφάς, καὶ ὅτι ὤφθη
Κηφᾷ, εἶτα τοῖς δώδεκα·

Translation of the Greek: "For I delivered to you as of first importance what I also received, that Christ died for our sins in accordance with the scriptures, that he was buried, that he was raised on the third day in accordance with the scriptures, and that he appeared to Cephas, then to the twelve." (I Corinthians 15:3–5)

On December 25, 1886, a young atheistic intellectual who would later become a world-renowned author, playwright, and French ambassador to the United States—Paul Claudel—went to the Paris cathedral of Notre-Dame to attend the Christmas day service. He was in the cathedral, not to worship, but to stir up poetic emotion that he thought would help him with his writing. As the choir performed a canticle taken from the Gospel of Luke, wherein Mary, the mother of Christ, praises God for choosing her to conceive the divine child in her womb, a sudden conversion took place. Claudel described it this way:

At that moment happened the event that has dominated my whole life. In a moment my heart was touched and I believed. I suddenly had an overwhelming feeling of the innocence, the eternal childhood of God, an unspeakable revelation.[1]

Claudel believed then that God existed and had communicated His meaning in Christ, and by the time the choir began the singing of the Christmas carol *Adeste Fideles* he knew he was a Christian.

Such a dramatic embrace of Christianity was not a unique event in Christian history. Augustine of Hippo, a bishop in North Africa in the first third of the fifth century, described how this awareness came upon him as he found himself "weeping in the bitter contrition" of his heart over his inability to control his evil impulses and make sense of an evil world.

Suddenly a voice reached my ears from a nearby house . . . : "Take it and read it. Take it and read it." . . . So I went eagerly back to the place where Alypius [his friend] was sitting, since it was there that I had left the book of the Apostle [Epistles of Paul] when I rose to my feet. I snatched up the book, opened it, and read in silence the passage on which my eyes first fell: . . . "Put ye on the Lord Jesus Christ, and make not provision for the appetites of the flesh." I had no wish to read further, there was no need to. For as soon as I had reached the end of this sentence it was as though my heart was filled with a light of confidence and all the shadows of my doubt were swept away.[2]

Augustine was himself inspired in his new awareness by a quotation from Paul of Tarsus, whose own faith in Christ came in a flash of sudden awareness. Paul's writings constitute more than half of the New Testament and center on the necessity of a profound acceptance of the presence, power, and love of God as revealed in the personality of Jesus Christ.

The Jesus that these converts believed to be both human and divine was born in Palestine, probably around the year 6 B.C.E. He preached a message of salvation that was founded on the Jewish scriptures and traditions, but which bore the imprint of his own mind and emotions, personality and experience. Jesus believed that he possessed a unique relationship with a fathering God, whose kingdom he was to proclaim by requiring a radical behavior change. He taught that only when individual people and all the kingdoms of the earth together have attained the highest possible level of love of one another, and of God, can the transformation of the world into the Kingdom of God take place. And he said that one cannot know the hour when this will take place.

Christians believe that acceptance of Christ's teachings means sharing in his suffering and death and resurrection. This sharing is accomplished in a way that is both spiritual and physical: in prayer and contemplation, and in day-to-day life. They believe, then, that what Christ was and is, every person must become in his or her own way: children of God, united to God.

Christianity began with the life and preaching of Jesus of Nazareth, but Christianity has a history: practices, doctrines, organizational structures, and the development of different approaches across the centuries are all part of it. This history is told in the pages that follow, according to theme and in a general chronological order. "Beginnings" is the story of Jesus of Nazareth and the early Christian Church through the period of persecutions. In the "Sacred Literature" section we double back to consider the history of the actual writing of the New Testament. Then we move on in "Practice" to study the development of Christian styles of worship through a time period well beyond the early persecutions. The "Doctrine" section picks up Christian history at the point when Christian teachings become more complex, and proceeds through the end of Augustine's career. "Institutions and Organization" is a study of the establishment of the basic Church organization—from the beginning up through the end of the Roman Empire. "Branches, Divisions, and Groups" is the longest section of all. It continues the discussion of institutions and organization while dealing with the separate development of the Eastern Orthodox, Roman Catholic, Protestant, and other traditions. The chapter concludes with "Religion and the Formation of Modern Society." Each section deals with a separate issue and moves forward in history beyond the preceding section.

Beginnings

The Jewish World

By the time of the birth of Jesus of Nazareth the Jewish Kingdom had been a political pawn of Rome for half a century. Since the Jews had been ruled by Greek dynasties from the time of Alexander the Great, there were three ways of life, language, and religion interacting at the same time: Jewish, Greek (we use the adjective *Hellenistic* to indicate the cultural composite that resulted from Greek rule in the Near East), and Roman.

Jesus' teachings were based on Judaism, but they were then transmitted by followers whose writing bore the influence of Hellenistic culture, and whose lives were circumscribed by Roman politics. Since Jesus himself was born and spent his early years in Galilee, he would have been little influenced by the Hellenistic culture and the complications of political life in Jerusalem, although he would have been told stories of the anti-Roman rebel movement that centered around the city of Caesarea, the Roman provincial capital. Because he brought his preaching to Jerusalem and was executed there, the political power of Rome was eventually significant in his ministry—and in his death.

Jerusalem was the crossroads of purely Jewish politics as well as the Jewish political reaction to other peoples. It was the seat of highest authority and its temple was the goal of all great festival pilgrimages. In Jerusalem met the Sanhedrin, foremost legal and spiritual authority for Jews throughout the land and all over the world. The Sanhedrin also was the chief Jewish political agency under the Romans and was in charge of finance for the eleven geographical subdivisions into which the Romans had divided the land. Furthermore, it was the first communal court of justice in the province of Jerusalem and the highest Jewish court of law in Judea.

The family of kings, part Hellenistic and part Jewish, which ruled as clients of Rome from 37 B.C.E. onwards, represented the worst features of all three cultures. King Herod was nominally a Jew, but was actually a foreigner and a member of a subjected Hellenistic dynasty that never had any love for the Jews. He was just accommodating enough to secure himself from major rebellion, but he was in no way trusted by the Jews. In 20 B.C.E. Herod began the rebuilding of the temple on a scale more grandiose than either the First or Second Temples; the work took forty-six years. The life-style of his court was Hellenistic, including game hunting, gymnastics, musical performances, dramatic spectacles, and chariot races. Foreigners from many lands came to the court to take part in the contests, present their written works, and simply carry out their official functions as ambassadors, messengers, or bodyguards. Herod saw himself as a reconciler: by rebuilding the temple he reinforced the old priestly class of the Sadducees but he stayed on good terms with the Pharisees; he tried to bring the Jewish and Hellenistic peoples of his kingdom together, and at the same time genuinely honor the Roman authorities by such gestures as the placing of Roman emblems over the gateway to the Temple and the construction of Greco-Roman baths, colonnades, fountains, and even temples. But in his thirty-three years as ruler he sharpened the mistrust of the Jews toward non-Jews, and sank into such depths of personal corruption and cruelty—committing atrocity after atrocity even against members of his own family—that most who knew of him could not help but hold him in contempt. The imaginations of members of Jewish reform movements were inflamed by the image of a cosmic war of the forces of good against the forces of evil. One important belief was that final freedom would be gained through a warrior Messiah from the House of David.

Rebellion was almost continuous. When Jesus was a young boy there was an uprising against Archelaus, Herod's son, who called in the Roman army, which then proceeded to destroy Caesarea and to execute two thousand Jews. Unintimidated, the radical Zealot party insisted that only when the Jewish people were independent of foreign rule could they worship God as they desired. Eventually they antagonized the Romans to massive sup-

pression in 66 C.E. and destruction of Jerusalem itself in 70 C.E. In this violent era, four influential groups affected the explosive combination of religion and politics that was the setting of Jesus' life and preaching.

The more conservative Jews were the Sadducees, drawn from the wealthier levels of society and representing the Jewish nationalist sentiment. A priestly party, they provided the succession of high priests for the temple from a time not long after the Maccabean revolt in the mid-second century B.C.E. In their religious attitudes they were conservative, and while they hated the rule of the Herods, they cooperated with the Romans for the sake of stability of peace. But they lacked popular support. The Pharisees, on the contrary, represented the masses of Palestinian Jewish people. Their origins are somewhat obscure, but it is clear that observance and understanding of the Law, *Torah,* was the goal of human existence. They commented upon, analyzed, and interpreted every element of the law, applying it to every possible contingency in life. Originally they were considered liberals—because by offering varied interpretations of the law they renounced a fundamentalist application of it. By Jesus' day they had developed such an intricate commentary on the law that instead of providing guidance they caused confusion. Associated with the Pharisees in the popular imagination, the Scribes were moralists, lawyers, and teachers combined; they were learned in both secular and religious lore, and enjoyed enormous intellectual prestige.

The Essenes, not mentioned at all in the Bible, were an organized community that lived a separated life in a monastic desert setting. They expected the imminent end of the present world and were consequently concerned about membership in the future kingdom. In their religious literature a leading role is given to a Teacher of Righteousness who, with his followers, will prepare for the final battle between the Sons of Light and the Sons of Darkness by separating himself from the evils of society. Some of these ideas were taken over or at least shared by Christians. Finally, there were the Herodians, who were to exercise little influence on the development of Christianity, but who constituted a powerful element of Jewish society. They did not disdain to take on a number of Hellenistic ways, and came to be considered irreligious because of their preoccupation with the refinements of worldly learning and pleasures. Thus, the Sadducees, Pharisees and Scribes, Essenes, and Herodians together constitute a summary of Jewish goals and life-styles. Obviously, they could only respond in different ways to the preaching of Jesus.

The Life and Message of Jesus

Most historians agree that the Gospels do not present a biography of Christ in the modern sense of the word "biography." However, by using methods we shall discuss in the next section, biblical scholars have been able to reconstruct the historically verifiable elements of the life and message of Jesus.

Jesus' Life. The beginning of Jesus' ministry was in some way linked to the preaching and mission of John the Baptist, and Jesus was baptized by John. A key theme in Jesus' own preaching was the Kingdom of God as both a present and future kingdom, a kingdom of this world and of another world. His preaching was supported by his effectiveness as an exorcist and healer; he was able to help those who believed themselves to be possessed by demons.

Some responded to Jesus' message by forming a unified group around him, which was made up of both men and women and had a notable diversity of previous background. A central feature of the life of this group was the sharing of a common meal in which they celebrated the meaning of the presence of the Kingdom and their relationship to it. Elements of Jesus' preaching and of the behavior of his followers caused the formation of a deep-seated opposition among Jewish leaders, which came to a climax during a Passover celebration at Jerusalem where Jesus was arrested. He was tried by the Jewish authorities on a charge of blasphemy and by the Roman authorities on a charge of sedition, and then he was crucified. An inner group, specially formed by him from among his followers, believed God had raised Jesus and that they were empowered to speak in his name.

Jesus' Message. By close study of linguistic style and literary characteristics, biblical scholars have tried to isolate those passages in the New Testament where they believe we can come closest to the words of the historical Jesus. Beginning with the passages on the Kingdom of God, scholars then proceed to isolate those themes that are fundamental to Jesus' preaching. They encompass the passages on the Fatherhood of God and radical moral behavior.

Proclamation of the Kingdom of God. Scholars generally agree that four sayings reported by the evangelists are close to direct quotes:

The time is fulfilled, and the kingdom of God is at hand. (Mark 1:15a)

But if it is by the finger of God that I cast out demons, then the kingdom of God has come upon you. (Luke 11:20)

The kingdom of God is not coming with signs to be observed; nor will they say, "Lo, here it is!" or "There!" for behold, the kingdom of God is in the midst of you. (Luke 17:20–21)

From the days of John the Baptist until now the kingdom of Heaven has suffered violence, and the men of violence plunder it. (Matt. 11:12)

Jesus proclaimed here that God acts as King, and that He visits and redeems his people. The pair of apparent contradictions—that the Kingdom was here and yet to come, that it belonged to this world and to another—was resolved by Jesus in the course of his preaching ministry. The Kingdom is present in the acceptance of God's presence in life and society and in the suffering—even in the violence—that must be undergone to reshape one's existence. On the other hand, no concrete moment in life, or specific person, group, or set of events is so perfectly representative of the Kingdom that onlookers can say, "Lo, here it is!" (Luke 17:20–21). The perfection of the Kingdom must always be thought of as yet to come. But this notion of "yet to come" leads to another apparent contradiction, because Jesus dissociated himself from any suggestion that events or figures in future *time* could be unequivocally labelled as belonging to the kingdom. It would appear that Jesus promised his followers a future that would be a fulfillment of the experience of the presence of God and His Kingdom, but that it would be beyond the range of events or figures that they could expect on the basis of their experience in *this* world.

Fatherhood of God. Jesus addressed God as Father in a special way and taught others to do so. In the New Testament he is quoted as referring to "the Father," "your Father," and "my Father." But it was the last that conveys best the type of intimacy with God that he preached. "The Father" was a time-honored scriptural way of referring to God. Jesus said "your Father" when speaking to his disciples; he seems never to have spoken of God as Father to others except in parables and metaphors, and never does he suggest the words "your Father" in these cases. He taught the disciples that God shows himself to be a Father by His forgiveness, by tenderness and care, and by assuring salvation. Fatherly goodness will be revealed in totality at the end of time. When Jesus himself addressed God in his prayers, he used the words "my Father" with all the resonances that this form of address has in the semitic language that Jesus spoke, Aramaic. In Aramaic the word is *Abba,* a form of address expressing respect, familiarity, and obedience. On occasion Jesus distinguished "my Father" from "your Father," claiming for himself a special relationship with God; his use of *abba* expressed his belief that he possessed such a revelation of divine knowledge that he could speak with complete authority.

It is obvious that when Jesus commended "Abba" to his disciples as a form of address to God he was sharing what he took to be his own prerogatives with them. The giving of the Lord's Prayer to the disciples authorized them to say "Abba" just as Jesus did. He may have forbidden them to use the word in ordinary speech, because he wanted them to reserve it for God. With the at once dignified and childlike "*Abba, dear Father,*" the early Church took over the central element of Jesus' faith in God.

Radical Moral Behavior. Among the most radical sayings are the following:

Leave the dead to bury their own dead. (Luke 9:60a)

If anyone strikes you on the right cheek, turn to him the other also; and if any one would sue you and take your coat, let him have your cloak as well; and if anyone forces you to go one mile, go with him two miles. (Matt. 5:39b–41)

It is obvious that these sayings do not challenge a person to radical behavior so much as to radical questioning. A literal adherence to these requirements would be in some cases absurd or irresponsible or at least unproductive. The dead cannot bury the dead, of course, and so the meaning of the passage must be understood from the context. Giving away the coat or going the extra mile in every case would be fine if one did not have other obligations to self, family, and friends. And there are times when such acts would not even serve the needs of the persons who would demand such things. To submit to the violence of others might deepen those others in their violence, to give away time or goods would not in itself accomplish anything in particular and might well cause a people to renege on their basic obligations to family or friends. Yet, when people radically question themselves, they may well find themselves called to radical behavior.

A number of other sayings are admonitions to concrete behavior that require a reversal of basic human tendencies:

Whoever would save his life will lose it. (Mark 8:35)

How hard it will be for those who have riches to enter the kingdom of God. (Mark 10:23b)

But many that are first will be last, and the last first. (Mark 10:31)

Every one who exalts himself will be humbled, and he who humbles himself will be exalted. (Luke 14:11)

Such sayings give what will be the state of things in an ideal world, and so cause their hearers to bring judgment upon the present. However, by taking these sayings to heart, one can do more than radically rethink one's existence. One can begin to radically change one's behavior.

Finally, everyone is warned that conflict will be the result of such behavior change. With the exorcisms of Jesus, the death of John the Baptist, and the possible fate of Jesus and his disciples in the background, followers are told: "No one can enter a strong man's house and plunder his goods, unless he first binds the strong man; then indeed he may plunder his house" (Mark 3:27). Existence is essentially an area of conflict by means of which the Kingdom of God becomes a matter of human existence.

New Testament Interpretations of Jesus' Message

Christianity spread rapidly from Jerusalem and other parts of Palestine into the Hellenistic Near East, North Africa, Greece itself, and on to Rome within about twenty years. It developed in its own way in all these areas, with the greatest change occurring at the time of the destruction of Jerusalem and the Temple by the Romans

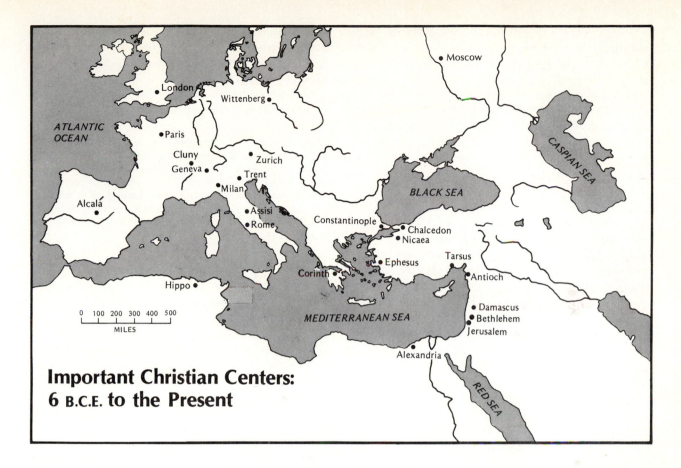

Important Christian Centers: 6 B.C.E. to the Present

in 70 C.E. By the end of the first century, the basic New Testament teachings of Christianity as we now know them had been formulated. Generally, New Testament Christianity went through the following phases.

Jerusalem Church. The earliest Christians in Jerusalem believed in and practiced the Judaism of their ancestors, differing from their fellow Jews only in that Jesus had been the Messiah raised up from death into heaven by God. They attended the temple regularly, and obeyed the Jewish laws on such matters as circumcision, diet, the Sabbath rest, and so on. They believed, of course, that Jesus had perfected the interpretation of the Law of God, and therefore they collected stories of Jesus' own interpretations of the law. Since they believed that Jesus was risen from the dead, and that his spirit was among them, they at times created illustrative stories as well. It is clear that the early Jerusalem Christianity

was looked upon with tolerance by the Jews themselves because it was left unmolested when other Christians—who came from other areas of Palestine and the Near East and had then settled in Jerusalem—were driven out of Jerusalem by persecution.

Palestinian Christian Phase. Other Palestinian Christians were less concerned with emphasis on Jesus as interpreter of the Law and put more emphasis on his proclamation of the Kingdom. They continued the proclamation of Jesus' message in the form of the sayings of Jesus, because they believed that the spirit of Jesus was inspiring prophets in their midst. The references to the work of the Spirit and the warnings against false prophets represent this phase of developement. Palestinian Christianity might be called a charismatic and apocalyptic movement, then, proclaiming Jesus as Messiah, even as they felt animated by his presence, and were awaiting his coming with full power. The collections of stories that nourished these beliefs began to be shaped into the earliest forms of what we now call the *gospels*.

Hellenistic Jewish Mission Phase. The greater part of the New Testament as we now know it does not come as much from Palestinian Judiasm as it does from Hellenistic culture. From the beginning of its days in Jerusalem, the Christian community included Greek-speaking Jews among its members, and it was they who brought Christianity into the Hellenistic world. They understood the Greek world, they were mission-minded, and some were philosophically sophisticated. Those who actively promoted Christian teachings moved out to other Greek-speaking Jews, to the gentiles who were closely involved with the Greek-speaking Jewish communities, and ultimately to all the Greek-speaking world. The author of the Acts of the Apostles was a member of this movement and reports speeches that must be typical samples of the movement's preaching in the synagogues and on the street corners of the Hellenistic cities. For these Christians "Messiah" became "Christ"—Greek for "anointed one"—but more importantly, the role of Jesus was expressed by the use of the terms "Son of God" or "Lord." In the Hellenistic world, the term "Son of God" was a more apt term to indicate that Jesus possessed divine qualities. And "Lord" was the most common term of honor and respect used for gods, emperors, kings, and men of substantial power. The basic act of faith became the affirmation, "Jesus is Lord."

Gentile Christianity. When Christianity was accepted and lived by those who had been gentiles all their lives, there were further elaborations of the basic teachings. Because of the so-called mystery religions with their emphasis on the cult of a dying and rising hero and on immortality and security for members of the cults, gentile Christians thought more naturally in terms of a redeemer figure who descends to the earth from a heavenly sphere, accomplishes the redemption of those on earth, and then returns to the higher sphere. It was believed that the disciples shared in the triumph of Jesus as divine Man, and they expected to overcome in their lives and deaths what Jesus overcame in his life and death. Thus, they would enter into glory with him. They thought of their own triumph more in terms of immortality of the soul than of resurrection of the body, and so, too, there was less emphasis on the coming of the Christ in the power of his resurrected body and more emphasis on his dwelling in eternal glory. These beliefs are expressed in brief hymns, not composed by Paul, but quoted in some of his letters, or in letters attributed to him.

Who is the image of the invisible God, first born of all creation, For in him was created everything in heavens and on earth, Everything was created through him and unto him. Who is the beginning, the first born of the dead. For in him all the fullness was pleased to dwell, And through him to reconcile everything unto himself, And he is before everything and everything is united in him. And he is the head of the body (the church). (Col. 1:15–20)

Writings of Paul and of John. The foregoing "phases" must not be understood to be mutually exclusive or rigidly chronological. Soon enough, one could find in any given Christian community the conservatism of the Jerusalem church, the charismatic and apocalyptic qualities of Palestinian Christianity, or the emphases and concerns of the Hellenistic Jewish Mission or of the Gentile Christian churches. But there are two collections of writings that were so distinct in their structures and theologies that they must be singled out: the letters of Paul, who was the outstanding personality of the Hellenistic Jewish Mission, and John's writings (attributed to him, but more accurately called the "Johannine tradition"), the most theologically and literarily refined writings of the New Testament.

Paul. Coming from the thoroughly Hellenized town of Tarsus, Paul knew Greek and his letters show that he wrote it well. Some traces of Greek philosophical rhetoric also show in his writings indicating that he probably had at least some Greek education. His birthdate is unknown, but it probably occurred in the first decade C.E. He came from Jewish parents, however, and his references to receiving his training at the feet of Rabbi Gamaliel (Acts 22, 3) suggest that he was preparing to be a rabbi himself. There are three accounts of Paul's conversion to Christianity in the Acts of the Apostles, and he himself gives a brief account of it in his letter to the Christians living in Galatia. Although the accounts in Acts vary somewhat as to whether his companions heard a voice or not, and whether they remained speechless or fell to the ground, they all agree on the basic dialogue between the fallen and blinded Paul: "Saul, Saul, why do you persecute me?—"Who are you, Lord?"—"I am Jesus (of Nazareth) whom you are persecuting" (Acts 9:5; 22:7–9; 26:14–16). This revelation of Jesus to Paul on the road to Damascus dominated every movement and thought for the rest of Paul's life. He wrote that God had been pleased to reveal His Son to him, so that he might preach the Good News of him to the Gentiles. Cured of his blindness in Damascus, he remained there for some years, before several visits to Jerusalem and the beginning of his Missions wherein he preached in Asia Minor and Greece.

One of the major questions to be settled in the first part of Paul's missionary career concerned the obligation of gentile converts to follow the laws of Judaism. At an important meeting in Jerusalem Paul and Barnabas met with the whole Jerusalem church, and Paul opposed a number of leading Pharisee converts (Paul himself had been a Pharisee). Paul insisted that Christians should not be obligated to follow Jewish laws. Although his viewpoint won the day there were still to be occasions when some of the Jerusalem Christians would refuse to eat with gentiles, even shaming Peter himself into avoiding meals with gentiles; Paul had to persist in opposing the imposition of Jewish law. During the second period of his career, Paul established major Christian communities at Thessalonica and Corinth. During the third period he made Ephesus the center of his missionary activity, and wrote major letters to Christians living at Philippi and Corinth. In his final years, Paul was made a prisoner because of a disturbance created by his return to Jerusalem and presence in the temple, and was sent to Rome because of his own request that he be tried as a Roman citizen. While under house arrest he wrote his letters to Philemon and to the Christians living at Colossae and Ephesus. Paul's arrival at Rome and his free and open style of preaching form a climax to his career; he died several years later under conditions that we learn about only from the writings of the later historian Eusebius. According to Eusebius' generally accepted account, Paul was beheaded under the persecution of Nero and was buried just outside of Rome.

Salvation in Christ. Although Paul wrote most of his epistles before the gospels were set down, he did not concern himself with the stories about the sayings of Jesus, the Galilean rabbi. Rather, he was concerned with the saving effects of the passion, death, and resurrection of Jesus, the Christ, events that transcend historical data. Salvation was a dynamic force present in Christ and transferred to those who give assent to Christ. Christians were to allow Christ's personality to take over their own personalities and so be transformed in accordance with the plan of God, which existed from all eternity.

Christ himself was the pre-existent Son of God, who was to be addressed by the title "Kyrios" ("Lord"), which was the title attributed to God Himself in the Greek translation of the Hebrew bible that was used in the Hellenistic Jewish communities. Use of this title was Paul's way of expressing faith in the divinity of Christ. Predominately a functional title indicating Christ's dominion over human beings and his influence in their lives, it also suggests an equality of Christ with the Father. The titles "Father" and "Son" suggest subordination, but "Kyrios" ascribes to both God and Jesus a dominion over creation and a right to the adoration of all peoples. In Philippians Paul applies what Isaiah said of God to Christ: "To me every knee shall bow, every tongue shall swear" (2:10). For Paul, "salvation," the saving effects of Christ's passion, death, and resurrection are reconciliation of human beings with God, the expiation of sins, redemptive liberation, and justification. Taking the idea of "justification" from the law courts, Paul understood human beings to be acquitted from the evil imputed to them. The Christian is not simply declared upright, but is actually constituted as such. Having studied the Law at great length, Paul despaired of keeping it, of becoming upright by following it. Only by opening oneself up to faith in Christ could one be justified, that is, saved.

Faith. The human being shares in the divine existence and justice by faith. In other words, people can appropriate to themselves the effects of Christ's passion, death, and resurrection by a faith. This faith begins by a hearing of the preaching of Christ and ends by submission to it. It is not just an intellectual assent to some formula or proposition, but it is a vital commitment engaging the whole personality to Christ. Paul believed that this profound engagement of the human personality brought with it the obligation to psychologically conform to the new Christ-reality within. He taught that faith was the gift of God, but somehow left open the notion that humans were free in their response to God's initiative, that they could reject God's initiative.

Baptism, the immersion of the body into water, the ritual existing from the beginning of Christianity, was the effective sign of the Christian's unification with Christ.

> Through baptism we have been buried with him in death, so that just as he was raised from the dead through the Father's glory, we too may live a new life. For if we have grown into union with him by undergoing a death like his, of course we shall do so by being raised to life like him. (Rom. 6:4–5)

This is not an isolated, individualistic experience, because through baptism a special union with all Christians is formed. Persons attain salvation by identifying with a saving community; by becoming part of the body of Christ. Paul's basic conversion experience involved the realization that the Christians he was going to persecute in Damascus were somehow identified with Christ: the voice had said to him, "I am Jesus, whom you are persecuting." And in his later writings he, or one of his disciples, returned to the idea that "there is only one body and one Spirit, just as there is only one hope in the calling you have received: one Lord, one faith, one baptism, one God and Father of all" (Eph. 4:4).

Ethics. According to Paul, the new life in Christ that Christians live does not take away their obligations to behave according to certain norms that are derived from the new life. Christian freedom is opposed to "loose" living. Usually, the latter part of Paul's epistles are filled with detailed instructions for the Christian's ethical conduct. He lists the virtues and vices that should or should not characterize the Christian way of life. These lists can be compared with similar enumerations of virtues and vices found in the works of both Greek philosophers and Jewish teachers. Similar to these lists, and related to them, are Paul's exhortations to the members of each household to perform their duties. Here Paul addresses himself to husbands and wives, parents and children, and masters and slaves, all within the framework of the society in which he lived.

Gospel of John. Although the gospel has behind it the common Christianity of the first century, there is no book, either in the Bible or out of it, that is similar to the Gospel of John. It differs from the other gospels in that readers who have no background in Judaism would be able to understand it. It describes the events of Christ's life, presents his preaching, and in general introduces the community history—all of which are integral to the other gospels—yet the language used to interpret the life of Christ is different from that used in other biblical writings. This suggests that John the evangelist had a non-Christian public to which he wished to appeal.

From its beginning the Gospel of John provides a full explanation of who Jesus is in terms that would be recognized by those informed enough to know something of the philosophies and religious symbols of Hellenistic society. As a leading scholar has put it, "the gospel could be read intelligently by a person who started with no knowledge of Christianity beyond the minimum that a reasonably well-informed member of the public with interest in religion might be supposed to have by the close of the first century, and Christian ideas are instilled step by step until the whole mystery can be divulged."[3] Therefore, the gospel was probably addressed to a wide public made up of devout and thinking people in a varied and cosmopolitan city such as Hellenistic Ephesus under Roman rule. Compared with the Gospel of Mark, which begins with a description of Jesus' baptism by John the Baptist that assumes most readers are already familiar with both men and the event, the Gospel of John begins with a prologue that introduces the eternal Word and "a man sent from God whose name was John [the Baptist]." First it is said that the Word incarnate is a human person, and then one learns that his name is Jesus, the Christ.

Little is known about John—the author of the gospel is identified with the "disciple whom Jesus loved," but he is not named. Tradition has identified this beloved disciple with John, the son of Zebedee, one of the inner group of disciples given special mention in Mark's gospel. Although we cannot reject these traditions, scholars have noted that there are several distinct "hands" in the "Johannine" writings, especially if one takes into consideration the so-called Epistles of John. (The "John of Patmos," who authored the book of Revelation, is almost certainly not to be identified with John, the beloved disciple, or John, the author of the gospel, even if these latter two should be the same person—which is not a certainty either.) Rather, the Gospel of John, the most intellectual and literary of the New Testament biblical writings, must be seen as the work of a group of Christians, with one personality predominating. But if the individuality and personality of the author are not clear, the individuality and personality of the gospel are strikingly clear.

Leading Ideas. John emphasizes the *eternal life* that one can obtain from the knowledge of Christ and of the God who sent him. He agrees with other Christian authors that the believer will enter into eternal life at the general resurrection, but for him this is of less importance than the fact that the believer already enjoys eternal life, from knowing Christ—his meaning and his message. Accordingly, *knowledge of God* is developed as a basic theme. *Truth* is the eternal reality, all that is permanent in God's world beyond Himself. *Faith* is seeing, a form of vision that brings one into the glory of God. In this *Union with God* one is possessed by love that exists in this world and in the next. *Light, Glory*, and *Judgment* are labels for the elements of one's life in union with God, the three words giving the type of perception, beauty, and discrimination that belong to the Christian in God. *Spirit* is the evangelist's primary way of defining divinity, whereas *Messiah, Son of Man, Son of God*, and, of course *Logos*—or *Word*—are the titles that highlight the various elements of Jesus' reality, and would have powerful connotations for those who knew the mystery religions and philosophies of the Hellenistic world as well as for Jews and for Christians.

Passion-Narrative. In his presentation of the passion (that is, the suffering), death, and resurrection of Jesus, John the evangelist brings together all that he said earlier in the gospel and dramatically presents the meaning of Jesus and Jesus' mission. All the "signs" of Jesus' mission that are displayed earlier in the gospel are brought together in this one great sign, his life-giving death. The sign of the wine of Cana (when Jesus changed water into wine), the sign of the temple (which is the Body of Christ destroyed to be raised again), the signs of the life-giving word (at Cana and Bethesda), the sign of Bread (the flesh of the Son of Man given for the life of the world), the sign of the pool of Siloam (the light of truth that both saves and judges), the sign of Lazarus (life victorious over death), and the sign of the King of Israel (cheered on his entry to Jerusalem to die) are brought together in this ultimate sign of life-giving death. For John the evangelist, as for no other Christian biblical author, the totally self-sacrificing death of Christ was,

essentially, his resurrection. No higher exaltation, no higher glory can be conceived, he says, that that which Christ attained in his self-sacrifice. The death in time and space is really an event on a spiritual plane. The later resurrection appearances are anticlimactic in that they concretize in time and space what has already happened on a spiritual plane.

Persecution and the Spread of Christianity

By strong and sometimes dramatic preaching, teaching, and varieties of apparent wonderworking, adherents were gained for the new religious way, Christianity, and these people were called "Christians," or "Nazarenes," or "Followers of the 'Way.'" Rather quickly Christians gained a reputation with the central authorities as a troublesome group. Although they had Jewish origins, they did not get along with the Jews (by the year 85 there were condemnatory references to them in some synagogue liturgies), and in general seemed to be a mysterious group; their meetings were suspect and they were thought to be political separatists. The Roman authorities did not show the same tolerance toward Christians that they extended to Jews—apart from periods of Jewish uprising in Palestine and Jerusalem itself, of course.

The story of the spread of Christianity in the Roman Empire, then, is a story of enthusiasm, hostility, persecution, and final triumph. After the enthusiastic work of the first preachers, teachers, and healers, hostility quickly developed between the regular run of Roman citizens, who felt that Christian converts were intolerant of other religions and felt themselves superior, and the Christians, usually themselves Roman citizens, who felt that the others had rejected the truth. By studying the persecutions we can see how and on what terms Christianity developed in the Roman world, and understand the human circumstances that caused the elaboration of the biblical teachings into new interpretations.

The persecution of *Nero* (37–68 C.E.) is the best known, and was, in fact, the earliest of the persecutions. On the night of June 18, 64, a great fire broke out in the center of Rome. Even though Nero had rushed to the city from his palace several miles away, organized a fight against the fire, and housed some of the homeless in his palace gardens, he was suspected of having set the fire because of his earlier cruel and bizarre behavior. Stories were told that he had even ordered the city burned to gain inspiration for the composition of a great epic poem. Although details are scarce, it seems that Nero placed blame on the small Christian minority to turn suspicion from himself. He then proceeded to arrange tortures and executions of Christians for the amusement of the local populace. We use the term "local" because there is no evidence that the Neronian persecution extended beyond the city of Rome itself, but it was the first arbitrary and wholesale persecution of the social subgroup known as Christians, and was well remembered because of the refinements of its cruelty.

In this persecution and across the persecutions of Domitian, Marcus Aurelius, and Septimius Severus, martyrdom came to be held in great esteem and some Christians actively sought it out. A leading historian of early Christianity says,

Behind their action lies the whole theology of martyrdom in the early Church. They were seeking by their death to attain to the closest possible imitation of Christ's passion and death. This was the heart of their attitude. . . . There is no evidence that the Christians regarded their quarrel specifically with the authorities, let alone with the Roman Empire. Their witness was against the "world" (which, of course, was represented for the time being by the pagan Roman Empire), but they saw their acts in eschatological and not political terms. The Devil was their enemy; the Paraclete was their Advocate whose verdict on the word would be the same as that of Jesus had been on the Pharisees (John 16:8–11).[4]

The last persecution before the Roman Empire became Christian was called "the Great Persecution," and took place under Diocletian (245–313 C.E.) who had set himself to the reorganization of defense, the type of currency, taxation, and price levels. Diocletian had no difficulties with Christians early on, and, in fact, his wife and one of his daughters were Christians. Difficulties probably first appeared in the ranks of the army, when Diocletian allowed himself to be convinced that the Christians, who by now were quite numerous in the ranks of the army, were a danger to military morale. Some Christian soldiers and officers had already been executed for trying to leave the army because of their ambivalence about military activity; others who had refused to join were also executed. Soon afterwards, Diocletian refused to allow Christians to occupy positions of authority, and ordered Christian buildings and books to be destroyed. When fire broke out in the imperial palace Christians were blamed for trying to seek revenge, and so were rounded up and ordered to offer sacrifice to the gods. And again, throughout the Empire, churches and sacred books were burned, and Christians were executed in great numbers.

Even with the death of Diocletian, persecution continued until the after a complicated series of military campaigns involving four major authority figures at last brought to the throne an emperor who gave Christians their freedom, and, at length, became one himself: Constantine. Some persecutions involved very few executions, but Christian communities were always thrown into disarray. On occasion, vast numbers lapsed from their faith, and many denied having been Christians. For generations Church authorities were not sure how those who had lapsed should be treated. Since so many clergy had lapsed also, some began to doubt the validity of services presided over by these clergy.

The question not answered by any history of the persecutions is this: How did those who were Christians get to be Christians in the first place? It certainly happened that the bravery and hope for future happiness demonstrated by some of the martyrs inspired others to join the religion that could so strengthen and reward people, but there had to be a number of motives, spiritual and otherwise, for joining the new religion. Feats of healing and the driving out of demons were impressive to average people, not as inclined to prayer as the leaders whose letters and treatises we can read today.

A certain number of nonbiblical documents that have come down to us from Christian circles of those days put emphasis on competitive wonderworking. In these stories the Christian preacher would effect healings and exorcisms that were greater than those accomplished by priests of the Roman religion or other sectarians. Or they would counteract the efforts of the non-Christian wonderworker in obvious competitions. The spiritual-minded Christian leaders themselves would boast of the authority over demons possessed by those who spoke in the name of Jesus. Jesus' own defeat of demons would be highlighted in the preaching. It seems clear that conversions to Christianity in great numbers at the same time were more often brought about by wondrous works and exorcisms than because of some realization in the depths of the human heart. The more profound type of conversion would take place in an interpersonal type of situation where the principal elements of the Christian faith could be conveyed with some rationality and beauty. That many came to Christianity because of the wonder-working is not a blot on the Christian historical record: this was the only means of communicating that would be understood by the common people, and was the only way to compete with the wonderworking rabbis of Judaism and the regular run of mystical magicians of Asia Minor.

Since Christian teachings—and all others—were preached most often to the uneducated, unsophisticated, wanderers, and workers who at best were artisans, the means of attraction and presentation had to be geared to the audience. That the audiences did not always arrive finally at a grasp of the profundity and subtlety of the message has been a problem for Christian preachers from Paul on.

Sacred Literature

Letters and Gospels

Of the specifically Christian books of the Bible, the New Testament, all the books save one are attributed to an author. We find "The Gospel of Matthew," "The First Letter of Paul to the Thessalonians," and so on; the only exception is "The Letter to the Hebrews." The suggestion is that these books were written by relatives of Jesus or those closely associated with him, and by Paul and those associated with him. Modern New Testament scholars are mainly of the opinion that, with the exception of some of the Letters of Paul, the books were the work of anonymous authors, and that the attribution to given names was a matter of traditions and loyalty. Instead of speaking of Matthew, scholars speak of a "Matthean tradition" or a "Lukan tradition." We have already approached this issue in referring to the "Johannine tradition," and it should be added that some of the later letters attributed to Paul are best referred to as of the "Pauline tradition." For believing Christians this view of authorship presents no problem because no one is denying that these writings were taken to be inspired (regardless of author) in the earliest Christian Church.

The majority of New Testament scholars believes that the gospels were not written by eyewitnesses of the ministry of Jesus. They were written in the period between 70 and 100, forty years or so after the crucifixion, and were circulated anonymously. Of the thirteen letters associated with Paul's name, about seven were attributed to him, and the others were written by his pupils and followers. Even some of these, along with writings ascribed to Peter, James, and Jude, were probably written much later—sometime between 90 and 140—by Christian pastors who had their own ideas of what constituted the major topics of their preaching missions. The following breakdown has been offered by a leading scripture scholar.

50–60 Paul writes 1 Thessalonians, Galatians; 1 Corinthians, and the collection of letters that is now 2 Corinthians; (the collection of letters that is now) Philippians; Philemon; and Romans—probably in that order, although we cannot be sure of the place in the order of the individual elements in 2 Corinthians and Philippians.

70–90 Pupils and followers of Paul write the deutero-Pauline letters: 2 Thessalonians, Colossians, and Ephesians. Unknown Christians write what we now know as the Gospels of Matthew, Mark, and Luke, and the Acts of the Apostles.

80–100 The Gospel and Letters of John are produced most probably not by one individual, but by men who are members of a tightly-knit group. . . .

90–100 A church leader named John writes the book of Revelation while in exile on the island of Patmos.

90–140 Leaders in various churches produce texts representing a more authoritarian church structure: the Pastorals, 1 and 2 Peter, James, and Jude.[5]

"The Synoptic Problem." Matthew, Mark, and Luke are usually called the *Synoptic Gospels* (from the Greek *synoptikos,* which means "seeing the whole together"), because they tell the same story in very similar ways, and if we set them side by side it is obvious that there is some kind of literary relation among them. In some

Two Pages of a Papyrus New Testament Showing Romans 11:3–12. *These pages come from a collection called the Chester Beatty papyri, taking their name from the museum in Dublin where they are kept. They are among the earliest New Testament pages we possess—from around the year 200.* (Religious News Service Photo)

sections of the gospels it is obvious that all three gospels are related to one another, and in other sections it is obvious that Matthew and Luke are related to each other but not to the gospel of Mark. This interrelatedness can be shown from the passages on the Baptism of Jesus. A pattern is clear here: Mark and Matthew can agree against Luke, and Mark and Luke can agree against Matthew, but Matthew and Luke do not agree against Mark. In Mark and Matthew Jesus came from Galilee, but this is not mentioned in Luke. In Mark and Luke the Spirit simply descends like a dove (in addition, it alights on Jesus in Matthew). In Mark and Luke, the voice from heaven says, "You are my beloved Son, with you I am well pleased," but the quote is given in Matthew as "This is my beloved Son, with whom I am well pleased." This type of verbal interrelatedness, where Mark is the common base for the wording, is followed throughout the gospels. And the same situation prevails when we look at the order of events. Mark's order is always followed.

Matt. 3:13–17	*Mark 1:9–11*	*Luke 3:21–22*
Then Jesus came from Galilee to the Jordan to John, to be baptized by him. John would have prevented him, saying, "I need to be baptized by you, and do you come to me?" But Jesus answered him, "Let it be so now; for thus it is fitting for us to fulfill all righteousness." Then he consented.	In those days Jesus came from Nazareth of Galilee	Now when all the people were baptized
And when Jesus was baptized, he went up immediately from the water, and behold, the heavens were opened	and was baptized by John in the Jordan. And when he came up out of the water, immediately he saw the heavens opened	and when Jesus also had been baptized and was praying, the heaven was opened,
and he saw the Spirit of God descending like a dove and alighting on him; and lo, a voice from heaven, saying, "This is my beloved Son, with whom I am well pleased."	and the Spirit descending upon him like a dove; and a voice came from heaven, "Thou art my beloved Son; with thee I am well pleased."	and the Holy Spirit descended upon him in bodily form, as a dove, and a voice came from heaven, "Thou art my beloved son; with thee I am well pleased."

Another striking verbal pattern occurs in the gospels in that Matthew and Luke closely resemble one another in some passages that are not found in Mark. The first occurrence of this is in the preaching of John the Baptist.

Matt. 3:7–10	*Luke 3:7–9*
But when he say many of the Pharisees and Sadducees coming for baptism, he said to them, "You brood of vipers! Who warned you to flee from the wrath to come? Bear fruit that befits repentance, and do not presume to say to yourselves, 'We have Abraham as our father'; for I tell you, God is able from these stones to raise up children to Abraham. Even now the ax is laid to the root of the trees; every tree therefore that does not bear good fruit is cut down and thrown into the fire."	He said therefore to the multitudes that came out to be baptized by him, "You brood of vipers! Who warned you to flee from the wrath to come? Bear fruits that befit repentance, and do not begin to say to yourselves, 'We have Abraham as our father'; for I tell you, God is able from these stones to raise up children to Abraham. Even now the ax is laid to the root of the trees; every tree therefore that does not bear good fruit is cut down and thrown into the fire."

The frequent appearance of such parallel passages, virtually always teaching material (such as the teaching of John the Baptist in the above passages), in Matthew and Luke has led biblical scholars to assume that these two gospels have a source in common besides Mark. No such document has been found, but biblical scholars assume its existence and for convenience's sake call it "Q" (for the German *Quelle,* or "source"). Since Matthew and Luke have much in them that is unique—e.g., selections from the Sermon on the Mount in Matthew—we can best show the interrelatedness of the synoptic gospels by way of the accompanying diagram.[6]

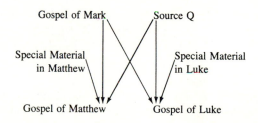

Context for the Development of the New Testament

The New Testament grew up in a context of religious battles lost and won. First there was a subgroup of Palestinian Christians who resisted all reference to a new religion of Christianity, believing that Jesus' principal purpose was the reform of Judaism. This group, called the *Ebionites,* became separated both from Judaism as well as from Christianity, because whatever emphasis they did put on Jesus was unacceptable to mainline Jews. The Ebionites regarded Matthew as the only valid gospel and insisted on the use of Hebrew in their writings and services. Thus, from the beginning we have considerable differences of opinion among Christian groups as to the list of writings that were to be considered inspired. And almost from the beginning there were attempts to compose a formal list of books. The formal list of scriptural writings has always been called the *Canon* of the biblical writings, from the Greek word, "kanon," meaning "rule." The Canon contained the rule of faith.

The first attempt to put together a biblical Canon was made by a preacher named Marcion (d. ca. 160). But Marcion went to the opposite extreme from the Ebionites by rejecting the entire Jewish Bible (the writings involved here are called the Old Testament by Christians and are accepted in their entirety). Marcion had a negative influence on the formation of a Canon. Born and raised a Christian, Marcion became convinced that because the world was evil, its creator must be either evil or ignorant. He came to believe that the God and Father of Jesus is not the same as Jehovah, the God of the Old Testament. This meant that the Jewish scriptures were inspired by an ignorant, evil, arbitrary god, and were, consequently, to be rejected. He even rejected some of the Christian writings that were said to come too much under Jewish influence, accepting only the epistles of Paul and the Gospel of Luke. Marcion's viewpoint gained a large number of adherents, but the majority of the Christian leaders and people rejected him, and by doing so the Christian Church made another advance in forming a Canon of scriptures and in fashioning its own organizational identity.

The term *gnosticism* is used for a wide range of groups that differed among themselves (Marcion's group was a subdivision of the gnostics), but who agreed that special mystical knowledge was required in order to commit oneself to the true faith. The word *gnosticism* is derived from the Greek "gnosis," meaning "knowledge," and so properly indicates the orientation of these groups. This special knowledge was to the Gnostics the secret key to salvation, which was their main concern. A human

being is really a spirit that is imprisoned in a body, and the body is an evil guide.

The Gnostic's final goal is to escape from the body and the material world. A spiritual messenger of some sort must come to do the liberating, to awaken spirits from their sleep in matter, and bring them the secret knowledge necessary for salvation. Since there are evil spheres of existence above this earth, the liberated spirits must still break through each one of these spheres using the knowledge brought by the heavenly messenger. Gnostics who were or became Christians (the group was not an outgrowth of Christianity but had its own existence) applied all these ideas to Christ, and put their own special interpretation on the relationship of Christ to earth, heaven, and God. They did not believe that Christ had a human body, or at least that his apparent body was composed of spiritual matter.

As far as their morality was concerned, Gnostics varied in their beliefs. Some felt that the body, being evil, should be controlled by severe self-discipline; others, that the body should be left to its own devices, being a lost cause. Accordingly, Gnostics could go to the opposed extremes of severe self-discipline and libertinism, and often these extremes would gain local Christian groups a bad reputation. Since some individual Gnostic groups had their own books in which they said the true teaching of Jesus was contained, the Church at large was forced to respond to these groups the same way it responded to Marcion. The mainline Church sought to show that its doctrines were not based on the supposed witness of a single teacher or gospel, but on a consensus derived from the whole apostolic tradition. Against the secret traditions of the Gnostics, the major Christian groups had recourse to a Canon and a full range of apostolic and gospel teachings.

Although the challenge of Gnosticism was strongest throughout the second century, another individual challenge to the fuller, developing list of New Testament books came from a preacher who had been a pagan priest until his conversion to Christianity in the middle of this century. Montanus believed that he and two other women had received a special influx of the power of the Holy Spirit, both to prophesy and inaugurate a new age. This new age was to be characterized by a more refined and demanding moral life, just as Christ's Sermon on the Mount was more refined and demanding than the Old Law. The promotion of such ideas, of course, diminished the significance of the New Testament. Since the conviction of the Church was that the new era had begun with Christ, the idea that Christ's activity should be superceded and that the gospels should be only a transitory stage in sacred history was completely inadmissible. To be sure, the rigorism of the Montanists attracted more than one Christian thinker, scandalized by the behavior of many Christians between the time of the apostles and the arrival of Montanus on the scene. But rigorous Christians of later centuries had the advantage of a full established Canon of scripture and a theological tradition when they gave themselves over to cultivating a sense of the presence of the Spirit. These things Montanus did not have, though, like Marcion and the other Gnostics, he contributed in a negative way to the establishment of the Canon by his denial of scriptural authority.

Later Development of the Canon

Lists were gradually drawn up because of Marcion, who diminished the list of acceptable inspired books, and the Gnostics, who generally added to the list of inspired books. Oddly enough, it was a follower of Montanus, the brilliant Christian intellectual Tertullian (ca. 160–ca. 220), who first used the term *New Testament* as distinct from the *Old Testament*. The most famous list of New Testament books that we have from the early centuries dates from the end of the second century and makes negative references to Marcion. It established the existence of the four gospels that are accepted by Christians today, and listed the Acts of the Apostles, thirteen letters attributed to Paul, and other epistles; but it included two apocalypses, the Book of Revelation and the apocalypse of Peter.

In the third century, the Christian philosopher Origen listed all the books that we know of today, but said that some were disputed. One of the principal disputes centered around the Book of Revelation, which never achieved full status in the Syrian churches.

The most important event in the history of the New Testament Canon, however, occurred in the fourth century, when the spiritually powerful bishop of Alexandria, Athanasius, circulated in 367 a formal letter to all the churches under his charge. He unequivocally listed the books of the New Testament as they are accepted today. When the biblical scholar Jerome made the so-called latin vulgate translation of the Bible, both the Old and New Testaments, he followed Athanasius' list of inspired New Testament books. Since Jerome's translation became the standard bible of Western Christianity, the Canon of Athanasius became the norm.

Practice

Weekly and Annual Cycles of Worship

Christians shared with Jews the notion that certain rituals were signs of God's presence and action. Following Christ's example they repeated these rituals, with the added remembrance that Christ had sanctified the ritual for their use. As God was present in Christ, so God-in-Christ was present in the ritual. Based upon their own developing traditions, Christians sorted out and highlighted some of the Jewish traditions. They considered circumcision to have passed away with the Old Law, but they kept the ritual of baptism, which had been an important part of the ceremonies of conversion to Judaism. The use of bread and wine in its Jewish Passover-meal setting was at the center of a commemoration of Christ's actions at the Last Supper and his death on the cross. Even in St. Paul's day, Christians would meet for worship on Sunday in commemoration of the Lord's resurrection, and this association of Sunday with the resurrection led to the annual celebration of Easter on the Sunday following the date of the Jewish Passover, which was the fourteenth day of the Jewish month Nisan. For other yearly commemorations, days of Jewish origin that had Christian associations were adapted, Pentecost being the most important example. By the fourth century Christians were celebrating a special day for the Ascension and the Nativity of Jesus. And like the Jews Christians kept certain days for fasting, but whereas the Jewish days for fasting were Mondays and Thursdays, the Christians would fast on Wednesdays and Fridays. In some early Christian documents there are warnings that fast days must be free of evil acts and desires. Gradually, a much longer period of fasting before Easter developed in conjunction with the preparation of those to be baptized in a special Easter ceremony. And by the fourth and fifth centuries there were dramatic ceremonies developed for the Sunday, Thursday, and Friday before Easter; these days are called Palm Sunday, Holy Thursday, and Good Friday.

The feast of Christmas began to be celebrated during the fourth century. Although Christ's birthdate is unknown, December 25 and January 6 were chosen to combat various pagan feasts of the Winter Solstice. Different elements of the story of Jesus' birth and mission were emphasized in Roman and in Egyptian (and Near Eastern) Christianity: actual birth, adoration by magi, and even the much later event of Christ's Baptism in the Jordan. By the end of the next century the Churches had developed a period of preparation for Christmas, which was called "Advent"—the Latin *"Adventus Domini"* meant "Coming of the Lord."

In time, separate celebrations of events in the life of the Virgin Mary as well as special commemorations of the martyrs and other outstanding Christians came to be celebrated. By the Middle Ages a full calendar of celebrations was drawn up, and even Sundays and other days of the week were given specific names—e.g., the Sixth Sunday after Pentecost, Thursday after the third week after Epiphany. This whole ensemble of celebrations has come to be called the *Church Year*.

Baptism and Eucharist

Among the earliest descriptions (ca. 155) we have of the baptismal ceremonies and their conjunction with Eucharist (ritual commemoration of Jesus' last supper with his disciples shortly before his death) is that of Justin Martyr (ca. 100–ca. 165). Justin chose to reveal the faith and practice of the Christians of his experience to those who wanted to know about it, either because they were attracted or they had heard malicious rumors. The last seven chapters of his *First Apology* contain two descriptions of Christian worship: the first is an account of Eucharist preceded by baptism, and the other, an account of Eurcharist preceded by a scripture-reading service. The scripture-reading service with its accompanying prayers had passed into Christian use from the Jewish synagogue where it had consisted in readings

from the Law and the prophets, a sermon, and prayers. Justin also reported readings from "the memoirs of the apostles." Probably, in imitation of the synagogue service, there was also the singing of psalms. Then a bishop or presbyter would deliver a discourse in which he would comment on the meanings of the scripture readings, perhaps presiding from a special chair, as did those teaching in the synagogue. When the sermon was finished, all arose for the common prayers and then passed to the Eucharist, which began with a kiss or embrace called the "Kiss of Peace." Then, said Justin, "bread and a cup of water mingled with wine are presented to the president of the brethren," who then proceeded to offer the great Eucharistic prayer—in spontaneous fashion, but following certain patterns. From his writing, it is clear that Justin conceived of the Eucharist as a recalling of Christ's passion, in fact, of all of Christ's life. The bread and wine were eaten in remembrance that Christ, "being incarnate by God's Word, took on flesh and blood and suffered for the salvation of humankind." He also took it to be a "sacrifice" unto God, a Communion fellowship, and a thanksgiving for creation, providence, and the gift of God in Christ.

The association of Baptism with Eucharist, in Justin's report and in other early documents, is a clear indication of the communal nature of both baptism and the Eucharist. One is initiated into a community of believers who share in Christ's life as it were, and then is brought to eucharist as the first and basic act of the community that one has joined.

A more detailed description of Baptism—in Africa around the year 200—is found in the writings of Tertullian. After a preparatory fast the ceremony began with an act of renunciation of the devil and his works, followed by a declaration of faith, which probably took the form of the repeated answer, "I believe," to three questions about the fundamental meaning of Father, Son, and Holy Spirit. After each answer, the candidate was dipped or immersed in water, and after coming up from the font, the candidate was anointed with oil and hands were laid on him or her with a prayer beseeching the gift of the Spirit. In other ceremonies that have come down to us we see that the number of anointings and their position in relationship to the washing with water varied. In one of the Syrian liturgies, the anointing came before the washing with water. Because of the variety possible, the questions of the relationship of the anointing to the water-ceremony, meaning of the more solemn anointing (connected with the conferring of the Holy Spirit), and the official who was supposed to administer, came to be widely debated. Eventually, a separate ceremony called "Confirmation" evolved in Christian communities, with its administration reserved to a bishop. Even when separate, however, it was considered part of or a completion of the baptismal initiation.

The initiation ceremony with three anointings, and our first full text of the Eucharist was set down in the *Apostolic Tradition* of Hippolytus (ca. 170–236). The central prayer of the Eucharist that is given in Hippolytus contains the basic themes of all Eucharistic prayers before and since, themes that reach back to the essential blessing prayers (for the synagogue service and the sabbath meals) of the late Jewish biblical period. The prayer that is recited by the one presiding reads as follows:

To him [the bishop, the one presiding] then the deacons shall bring the offering, and he, laying his hand upon it, with all the presbytery, shall say as the thanksgiving:

> The Lord be with you.
> And all shall say
> *And with your spirit.*
> Lift up your hearts.
> *We lift them up unto the Lord.*
> Let us give thanks to the Lord.
> *It is meet and right.*

And then he shall proceed immediately:

We give you thanks, O God, through your beloved Servant Jesus Christ, whom at the end of time you sent to us as Saviour and Redeemer and the Messenger of your counsel. Who is your Word, inseparable from you; through whom you did make all things and in whom you are well pleased. Whom you did send from heaven into the womb of the Virgin, and who, dwelling within her, was made flesh, and was manifested as your Son, being born of the Holy Spirit and the Virgin. Who, fulfilling your will, and winning for himself a holy people, spread out his hands when he came to suffer, that by his death he might set free those who believed in you. Who, when he was betrayed to his willing death, that he might bring to nought death, and break the bonds of the devil, and tread hell under foot, and give light to the righteous, and set up a boundary post, and manifest his resurrection, taking bread and giving thanks to you said: Take, eat: This is my body, which is broken for you. And likewise also the cup, saying: This is my blood, which is shed for you. As often as you perform this, perform my memorial.

Having in memory, therefore, his death and resurrection,

we offer to you the bread and the cup, yielding you thanks, because you have counted us worthy to stand before you and to minister to you.

And we pray you that you would send your Holy Spirit upon the offerings of your holy church; that you, gathering them into one, would grant to all your saints who partake to be filled with the Holy Spirit, that their faith may be confirmed in truth, that we may praise and glorify you. Through your Servant Jesus Christ, through whom be to you glory and honour, with the Holy Spirit in the holy church, both now and always and world without end. Amen.[7]

In common with Jewish prayers (which, of course, did not apply the notions of redemption and salvation of a whole people to the specific actions of Christ, but to God alone) and with later Christian Eucharistic prayers, there is a thanksgiving for creation and redemption. Then there is the formal remembrance of the saving activity of God accomplished by means of Christ's actions: his death and the Last Supper, which indicated the saving and sacrificial meaning of that death. A whole people is to be saved and gathered into God's kingdom at the end of time by Christ's death ("winning for himself a holy people") and by the coming of the Holy Spirit ("would grant to all your saints who partake to be filled with the Holy Spirit"). Emphasis is on God's saving presence in Christ and Christ's saving presence in the Eucharistic gathering and in the offerings. Later controversies about the exact nature of Christ's presence in the bread and wine, and of the exact moment of consecration (either "This is my body . . . blood" or "send the Holy Spirit upon the offerings") are not foreshadowed here. God is thanked by the presider and congregation making memory of His saving action in Christ, and in that memorial the congregation is once again to enjoy the presence of Christ.

Ultimately, the early initiation and eucharistic liturgies were to reach full expression and balance in the liturgies used in the fourth century in Jerusalem. The classic text from this period, *The Mystagogic Catecheses* of St. Cyril of Jerusalem (ca. 315–386), gives the full details of this rich and balanced set of prayers and gestures.

Bishop Cyril tells how the candidates used to assemble in the vestibule of the baptistry, face west and with hands stretched out make a formal renunciation of Satan. Then turning to the east, they solemnly professed their faith in the Trinity and in the One Baptism of Repentance. Passing into the inner chamber they next took off their

A 5th Century Baptismal Font. *This font was excavated near a Byzantine monastery at Khirbet Khudriya, twelve miles north of Jerusalem. A candidate for baptism would kneel in the font while water was poured over his or her head—a combination of immersion and pouring.* (Courtesy of Kyle Yates)

clothes and were anointed with exorcized oil. They were then led by the hand, one by one, to the font, where after again making a formal profession of their faith, they were immersed in the blessed baptismal water to symbolize the Christ's three days in the tomb. This was followed by a post-Baptismal anointing with chrism (a specially prepared and blessed oil) and the putting on of white garments. Then the newly baptized—called *neophytes* after the greek words for "newly enlightened"— carry lighted candles from the baptistery to the church proper for the celebration of the Eucharist. Cyril's text is evidence of an early elaboration of ceremony and a new sense of the awesomeness of the rite. In this document we have the earliest evidence of the symbolic washing of the celebrant's hands and the use of the Lord's Prayer at the conclusion of the Eucharistic prayer (something that by the early fifth century was found in most liturgies). Cyril also gave elaborate instructions to prevent any careless dropping of bread or wine at communion. He repeatedly mentioned the solemn invocation of the Spirit by which the bread and wine become Christ's body and blood; he spoke also of the "fearful" presence upon the holy Table. The attitude of fear and trembling was even more pronounced in the rituals and writings that came out of Caesarea, Antioch, and, later, Constantinople. Before the end of the fourth century in the those

"Eastern" regions (the Eastern Roman Empire) where there were Christian communities, it was thought necessary to screen off the holy Table by curtains. And when the great church of Holy Wisdom was built in Constantinople there was not only an elaborate curtain before the canopied altar, embroidered in gold with a figure of Christ blessing the people and holding the gospel book in his left hand, but also a screen with three doors on which were figures of angels and prophets and the monograms of Justinian and Theodora—greatest of the Byzantine Christian rulers—over the central door. This screen eventually became a necessary feature of Eastern churches, where the doors were used for ceremonial "entrances" at the reading of the Gospel and the Offertory.

Liturgical Architecture

The style of liturgies changed with the Christianization of the Roman Empire that began with the reign of Constantine in 312. Differing cultural values came to be reflected in ceremonial, vessels and vestments, art and architecture. Until Constantine's time, Christian worship had been relatively simple. At first, Christians gathered for worship in their own homes. At times they even gathered in cemeteries such as the Roman catacombs (seldom used for secret worship because the authorities well knew that they were Christian cemeteries). By the third century there were structures set aside for worship. The oldest church that still exists is in the little Syrian town of Dura-Europos, and the building dates from about 250. After Constantine's conversion, Christian worship began to be influenced by imperial ceremonial. Incense, which was used as a sign of respect for the emperor, began to be used as a sign of respect for God. Presbyters (priests, ministers) presiding at the ceremonies began to dress in special and richer garments. Services were begun with a processional, choirs were developed, and eventually the people began to have a less active part to play in the liturgies.

During the second century it had become customary to commemorate the anniversary of a martyr's death by celebrating communion where the martyr had been buried, and before long churches were built in those places. But the reverence for the bones of the martyr became so important that they were transferred to churches that could not be built near the place of burial. Eventually these bodily relics were said to have miraculous powers, and a search began to find the bodily remains of New Testament saints. But the churches built in the time of Constantine and his successors contrasted with the simplicity of churches such as that of Dura-Europos. Constantine's mother, Helena, constructed the Church of the Nativity in Bethlehem and another church on the Mount of Olives, presumably the scene of Christ's agonized prayers before the beginning of his suffering and death.

The great churches were modeled in shape after the huge Roman law buildings, called *basilicas,* and eventually came to be built somewhat differently in Rome and Constantinople, with a greater richness and a more profound aura of mystery. In general, Christian basilicas had three principal sections: the atrium, the naves, and the sanctuary. At the center of the atrium was a fountain where people could perform their ritual washings; at the end of the atrium were the doors leading into the naves. The taller and wider nave was in the center and was separated from the lateral naves by rows of columns. At the end of the main nave and near the sanctuary was a special fenced-in section reserved for the choir, and on each of the two sides there was a pulpit, which was used for the reading and exposition of Scripture as well as for the leader of song. The sanctuary was at the end of the nave, and was somewhat wider than the nave, giving the building the shape of a cross or T. In the middle of the sanctuary was the altar where the bread and wine were placed for the celebration of Communion. The back wall of the sanctuary with its ceiling was in a half-dome shape called the apse. Against the back wall of the apse were the benches for the presiding clergy with, in the center, a bishop's chair called in Latin a *cathedra,* and from which was derived the later term *cathedral,* the church from which the bishop presided.

The lavishness of ceremonial and building during and after the reign of the emperor Constantine was sign of a new role for Christianity in the Western and Eastern Roman Empires. The problem of working out the spiritual meaning of this role and dealing with a wide range of Christian experiences and interpretations led to a clash of minds and a clash of personalities that marked the elaboration of Christian teachings in the centuries to follow.

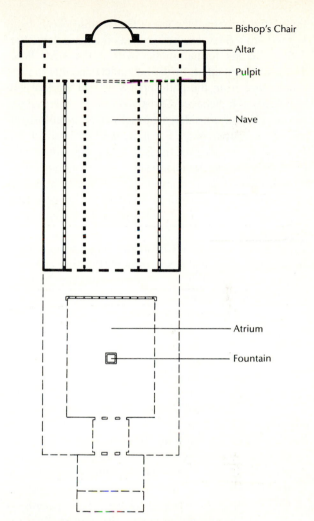

Floor Plan of a Typical Christian Basilica.

Doctrine

The Earliest Theologians

Some Christian leaders were so put off by Gnosticism with its complex and unreal speculations that they wished to avoid philosophy altogether. The severe Tertullian was quite contemptuous of anyone who would try to understand or interpret Christianity from a background of Stoic or Platonic or Aristotelian philosophy. Already, by the middle of the second century, however, Justin the Martyr promoted the use of Greek philosophy. Justin began with a Stoic teacher, passed on to an Aristotelian, and ended his formal studies with a Platonist. When Justin was converted, he did not understand this to mean a departure from the philosophies he had worked with previously. He believed Christianity to be "the true philosophy," and considered himself to be a philosopher presenting Christianity. For him, the transcendent God of Plato was the God of the Bible. The superior insights of Plato were the foundation of his own notion of the divine Logos or Reason, by means of which he attempted to show how the Father deals with inferior created order. In effect, the Logos was the Son of God, incarnate as Jesus of Nazareth.

Although Justin gave Christianity a rich way of teaching the meaning of the Son through Platonic concepts, and although Justin is the most important theologian of the second century, his Logos theology became a source of contention for Christian leaders for centuries to come. In some ways the great controversies that followed the liberation of the Church by Constantine were all a matter of disagreement over the meaning of Christ, the Logos. Many believed, by way of reaction to Justin, that either the Father and Christ were the same or that Christ was a man. The notion of Trinity, of three persons in one God, had not been clearly developed, nor had anyone presented the idea that Christ had two natures, the nature of God and the nature of man, inhering in one divine Person. All of this was to develop during and after the reign of Constantine. In the meantime, the challenge of Justin's theology was met by the simple teaching of a group, called the *Monarchians,* that Father, Son, and Holy Spirit are modes of the same existing being. This would mean to some that the Father suffered on the cross; others said that the Father and the Logos were two distinct persons.

Years later, a similar but more expanded Christian philosophy was produced by the great Christian thinker, Origen. Origen believed that there was an ordered hierarchy in the universe, which he explained in great detail, and that ultimately everyone and everything was capable of redemption. He believed that the Bible could be interpreted in many senses, of which the literal sense was by no means the most important. From Justin to Origen we can see the development of a simple organized presentation of Christian doctrine with some philosophical so-

phistication to a massive, complex set of interpretations that covers every aspect of Christian belief and life. Justin attempted to present the Christianity of his era to society around him and to the higher authorities. He answered the objections raised against Christians by non-Christians, pointed out various ways in which Christians were cultured and productive members of society, and claimed that Christians had the same spiritual background as Jews and that they were no more secret or perverse than the officially tolerated Jews.

Teachings of the Councils of the Church

Almost two hundred years after the death of Christ, the discussions of his relationship to the Father and of the meaning of his own personality could not be settled by an appeal to the Bible (because the Canon had not yet been finally determined) or to an individual teacher such as Justin or Origen (because the issues were too complex). People agonized over the meaning of Christ's relationship to the Father because their prayer life and fundamental beliefs about the meaning of life were at issue. And they wondered about the presence of divinity and humanity in the person of Christ because they wanted to know how to commit themselves to that person.

Arianism and the Council of Nicaea (325)

In the city of Alexandria in Egypt there was a popular and handsome preacher, a priest by the name of Arius (ca. 250–ca. 336). Arius preached that the Logos did not exist from all eternity with the Father. He said that the Logos, the Word, was not God, but the first of all creatures. He did not deny that the Word existed before the incarnation, because he believed that before anything else, the Word was created by God. But to make the Word divine would be to have two Gods. When Arius was condemned by the bishop of Alexandria, he did not accept the judgment, but appealed to the people of the city and to a number of prominent bishops, who had been fellow students with him years before. It is said that people marched in the streets shouting the formulas of Arius, so when the bishops who had known him earlier came to his defense, the emperor Constantine decided to gather a great council of all the Christian bishops in the empire to resolve the issue. Although the bishops met in an atmosphere of triumph—they were impressed by their numbers—the problem of Arianism was not easily resolved. Arius' champion in the Council meetings, the bishop Eusebius of Nicomedia (d. ca. 342), believed that a simple presentation of Arius's ideas was all that was necessary to resolve the problem. But there was a small, determined group of bishops who were convinced that Arianism was a serious threat to the Christian faith. First, the majority of the bishops had little interest in the debate, but when he gave his explanation, Eusebius of Nicomedia was amazed at the angry reaction of many of the bishops. Somehow the clarity of the notion that the Word or Son of God was no more than a creature so stirred the assembly that some shouted, "You lie!" "Blasphemy!" "Heresy!" Quite convinced that they had to condemn Arianism in the most unambiguous way possible, they found that the simple quotation of biblical passages was not enough. Instead they decided to work out a creed that would express orthodoxy—the true faith of the Church—and exclude the teaching of Arius. The formula they produced is called the *Nicene Creed* (best known to Christians in a more elaborate version worked out in the sixty odd years following the council). The following version was recorded by the historian Eusebius of Caesarea:

We believe in one God, the father Almighty, maker of all things visible and invisible.

And in one Lord Jesus Christ the Son of God, the only-begotten of the Father, that is, from the substance of the Father, God of God, light of light, true God of true God, begotten, not made, of one substance [*homoousios*] with the Father, through whom all things were made, both in heaven and on earth, who for us humans and for our salvation descended and became incarnate, becoming human, suffered and rose again on the third day, ascended to the heavens, and will come to judge the living and the dead.

And in the Holy Spirit.

But those who say that there was when He was not and that before being begotten He was not, or that He came from that which is not, or that the Son of God is of a different substance [*hypostasis*] or essence [*ousia*], or that He is created, or mutable, these the Catholic Church anathematizes.[8]

The bishop's principle concern was to reject the notion that the Logos was a creature; hence, the phrases "God of God," "light of light," "true God of true God." Most anti-Arian is the phrase "begotten, not made." But the term *homoousios*, "*of one substance* with the Father," which was meant to be a term of permanent clarity, did not work well because it could also be interpreted to imply that there was no distinction between Father and Son, and thereby lead back to the old Monarchian problem. The work of Nicaea would have to be taken up again by the great Athanasius, because Eusebius of Nicomedia appealed to Constantine himself (the emperor's summer palace was at Nicomedia) and convinced him that the Arians were treated too harshly. Arius was recalled from exile, and Constantine ordered the bishops of Constantinople to revoke his excommunication.

The absolute and unbending little man, Athanasius (ca. 296–373), who succeeded Arius' original opponent as bishop of Alexandria, was not by nature contentious. He preferred to spend his time (and in later years even went into hiding) with the desert monks who had trained him as a youth. When he reluctantly agreed to become the bishop of Alexandria, the Arian faction was waiting for him. Rumors began to circulate that he dabbled in magic and was an ecclesiastical tyrant. When it became obvious that both Constantine and his sons were more or less embracing Arian Christianity, Athanasius escaped to Rome where he convinced the Pope and the Roman clergy that the formula of Nicaea was the right beginning and simply needed clarification. Although Athanasius lived to be an old man in spite of his years of strife and persecution, he did not live to see the ratification of the Nicene formulas at the second great universal gathering of church leaders at Constantinople in 381. Constantinople confirmed Nicaea and added a formula to clarify the relationship of the Holy Spirit to the Father and the Son.

Nestorianism and the Council of Chalcedon (451)

Although the meaning of the Trinity—a point of contention in the fourth century—was always to defy perfect formulation, the fundamental question of Christology, how divinity and humanity are united in Jesus Christ, was at the center of Christian argument and discussion during the fifth century. There were in the Eastern Empire two different approaches, casually called the "Alexandrine" because the major proponents of this position were from Alexandria, and the "Antiochene" because the major proponents were from Antioch. For the Alexandrine group, the importance of Jesus as teacher of divine truth was such that his divinity had to be absolutely asserted even if no good way could be found to safeguard the meaning of his humanity. The Antiochene group believed that for Jesus to be the savior of humanity he had to be fully human; although God dwelt in him, it should not be understood in such a way as to take away from his humanity. Both groups agreed that Jesus was both divine and human, but when they were finished defending their respective positions they had produced some unfortunate ideas: the Alexandrines, that Jesus' humanity was more a matter of appearance than anything else; the Antiochenes, that Jesus' humanity and divinity should be completely separated (only his humanity suffered, only his divinity worked miracles, and so on).

The arguments came to a head when Nestorius (d. ca. 451), a clergyman of the Antiochene persuasion, became the patriarch of Constantinople. Nestorius said that in Jesus there were two "natures" and two "persons," one human and one divine. While it was not altogether clear what Nestorius meant by "nature" and "person," the Alexandrines joined forces and engineered the assembly of the third major Church Council at Ephesus in 431, only about three years after Nestorius had become patriarch of Constantinople. Although Nestorius' ideas were declared heretical, his supporters continued promoting them.

The problem continued on until 451, when the fourth great Church Council was convoked at Chalcedon. Those gathered in Council proceeded to sort out the differences of the preceding generation of churchmen. To describe the union of the humanity and divinity in Christ they made use of Tertullian's formula of two centuries earlier: that in Christ there are two natures in one person—Christ's human nature and his divine nature inhere in his one divine person. This definition soon became standard throughout Western Christianity, but there were always some in the East who rejected it and separated themselves from the majority of Christians, thus becoming the first of the long-lasting schisms (official separations) in the history of Christianity. Some in Syria and Persia insisted on the divine–human distinction even in the person of Jesus, and were eventually to be called "Nestorians." Others embraced the opposite view, rejecting the very notion of two natures, and were called *Monophysites*, from the Greek *monos*, "one," and

physis, "nature." Although the Nestorians can be found in only a few villages of Kurdistan, the Christian churches of Egypt, Ethiopia, and certain parts of Syria are today principally Monophysite.

Augustine of Hippo: Divine Grace and Human Freedom

There is no more important Christian intellectual or Church leader in the first ten centuries of the Christian tradition than Augustine (354–430). He was born in North Africa, far from the controversies that had led to the Council of Chalcedon. His education was in Italy and his language was Latin. Previous major controversies were carried out in Greek and resolved in Greek. But with Augustine and one of his mentors, the bishop of Milan, Ambrose, Latin became an instrument of sophisticated theological expression. And it was Augustine's way of interpreting the Christian tradition that became a standard in Western Christianity. When, much later, Western Christians divided into Protestant and Catholic, both groups looked to Augustine as their basic teacher. While Augustine's teachings covered every area of Christian thought and life, his ideas on the meaning of divine grace and human freedom were at the center of all Christian discussions of this major issue—"How can there be freedom when God is all-powerful and knows everything, past, present, and future?" He resolved a major controversy about freedom in his own day, and it was a controversy as important as the controversies dealt with at Nicaea, Constantinople, Ephesus, and Chalcedon. But to understand how Augustine formulated his views on sin, freedom, and God's power, we must look at his life experiences.

Life and Training. Augustine was born of a Christian mother and a pagan father in Tegaste, North Africa (within the boundaries of present-day Tunisia), in the decadent and weak years of the Western Roman Empire. A prodigious student from the beginning, he received his education in rhetoric in several African cities and then went to Rome for further training. For a few years he took up life with a small community of scholars in the north of Italy, and then he encountered the influential Ambrose. While his intellectual formation was going on, Augustine was attracted to two systems of thought,

Manichaeism and Neo-Platonism. Manichaeism, besides being a system of thought, was also a religion, a combination of Christianity and an ancient Persian religion, Zoroastrianism. Neo-Platonism was, as the name implies, a redoing of the philosophy of Plato, with emphasis on the more cosmic and even "religious" aspects of Plato's thought. Both schools of thought contributed to the formation of Augustine's ideas, though he felt that he had rejected the religions and moved beyond the philosophical system.

Manichaeism proposed that there were two great principles, good and evil. While evil was not quite equal to good, nor in any way an alternate to good, the Manichaeans believed that evil so controlled the world that the spark of goodness within a person could only be preserved and liberated from the body by great self-control and discipline. They believed there was a great gap between the realm of the material body and the realm of spirit. In effect, then, evil was represented by a divine power almost as strong as the good God. While Augustine rejected this notion of a separate power of evil even before he became a Christian, he always had a keen sense of the presence of evil and the power of evil in life. In fact, it was a long time before he could comprehend how the presence of evil in nature and in human beings was compatible with the presence of God. He could only resolve this by turning to Neo-Platonism.

At the center of Neo-Platonist thought is the notion that the good exists at the highest level of existence and that throughout the cosmos everything that is, is a greater or lesser copy of the good. The goal of everyone and everything is to ascend toward the good. Human beings in particular are meant to enter into the deepest parts of their minds and find a way of ascending in thought and meditation to the meaning of highest good and to the very good itself. Evil, then, can simply be seen as an absence of good or the inappropriate presence of something from a lower level of existence on a higher level of existence. For example, animal sexuality is inappropriate on the higher level of human existence, and the behavior of children is inappropriate in adults. The problem came for Augustine when he realized that the lower behaviors, the evil that he found in his own life, could not be eliminated simply by an act of the will.

The youth, adolescence, and early manhood of Augustine embraced a number of experiences, involving stealing and sexual license, that he was later to recall as partly or totally evil. As a young man, he wanted to gain complete control of his sexual energies, because he wanted to be a free, purely intellectual person. Augustine had a series of mistresses and fell deeply in love with one of them, having a child by her. In the last years before his conversion to Christianity, he came to believe that there might be moral reasons for leading a well controlled sexual life, whether married or not. The intensity of his conversion—recounted at the beginning of this chapter—was the result of the dead end he had reached in his own intellectual and personal fight against ignorance and evil.

Writings. In addition to the famous description of the development of his own life and thought, the *Confessions*, Augustine wrote voluminously. Two of his major treatises were entitled *City of God* and *On the Trinity*. The *City of God* was a long and complex discussion of the meaning of the presence of good and evil in human society relative to the perfection of heaven. He dealt with such problems as the obvious presence of good in a secular state and the presence of evil in the Church. In *On the Trinity,* Augustine developed at length a discussion of why the Holy Spirit should be understood to proceed from the Father *and* the Son (a formula that was to serve as a basic point of contention between Eastern and Western Christianity many centuries later). To describe the relationship of the members of the Trinity to one another he used metaphors taken from philosophical explanations of the structure of the human spiritual personality and the nature of love. He fancifully but effectively said that the members of the Trinity could be recognized by "footprints" found in the souls of humans.

Augustine also wrote at great length to oppose what he took to be two influential and dangerous heresies of his day, *Donatism* (a term derived from the name of the priest who promoted the ideas in Augustine's day) and *Pelagianism*. The Donatist Church had gained a great following among Christian rigorists in North Africa; they were the spiritual descendents of those associated with Cyprian of Carthage, who a generation or two earlier had rejected all those who had renounced or even hidden their Christianity during the times of persecution. By Augustine's day, these people had separated themselves from the regular community of Christians because of their concern for the purity of life and religious viewpoints of all who would administer the sacraments and lead in prayer. The notion was that a bishop or priest who was in sin would block completely the effectiveness of any ceremony over which he presided or of the prayers that he led. Just as the bishops and priests who had renounced their faith during the persecutions had become spiritually useless, so did all sinful bishops and priests. But Augustine realized that such a view would destroy the notion of Church, because no one could be certain that a Baptism or Eucharist or ordination was "real." He argued that the official prayer ceremonies—the sacraments—of the Church had their own efficacy based on God's power, apart from the destructive influences of whatever evil personalities that might be present or preside. His opposition to the powerful Donatists on this and other issues brought Augustine into great and at times dangerous conflict as a bishop fighting for orthodoxy. But his arguments against Pelagianism, the view of free will promoted by the British monk Pelagius, were to prove even more important in determining the later theology of the Christian Church.

Grace and Free Will. It is impossible to logically demonstrate how God can know and control everything and leave His creatures free and uncontrolled at the same time. Augustine insisted on order, logic, and the "hard saying" that God determines everything. He was not ready to accept the illogical attempts of Pelagius to teach that human beings could at times be *independent* of God's jurisdiction. Pelagius was a strict man, disturbed by the moral laxity of Rome, but also disturbed by a Manichaean pessimism about the human being's ability to do good. Some of the phrases of Augustine that were repeated in his presence undermined moral responsibility, he felt. Worse still, it seemed to him that Augustine and others who promoted the notion that original sin was transmitted across the generations of human life might cause people to believe that the souls of children were derived from their parents. For Augustine, the key to the problem was to teach clearly the meaning of God's *grace,* a word for God's love and power infused into human hearts by the presence of God's Holy Spirit. It reaches into every part of the human personality, and is not, as Pelagius had thought,

a vague matter of teaching and example. By Adam's sin human nature had not been destroyed, but it had been seriously damaged and needed to be restored by divine grace, lost in the Fall but later restored by Christ. Grace was more than human nature, more than free will, more than the forgiveness of sins and the commandments—grace was the divinely given power to avoid and conquer sin. Free will would only serve in the production of sin, because people would have to know the law before choosing, and even after knowing the law people could not delight in it or love it enough to bother with it unless God's grace was present. Grace preceded and followed the human being's life of love; and it was this life of love that Augustine called free will—not exactly free will in our modern sense. He said:

> By the law is the knowledge of sin, by faith the acquisition of grace against sin, by grace the healing of the soul from the fault of sin, by the health of the soul the freedom of the will, by free will the love of righteousness, by love of righteousness the accomplishment of the law.[9]

Augustine had to face the fact that if God did everything, He necessarily knew about and caused the final salvation and damnation of all humankind, which is to say he *predestined* people to heaven or to hell. Augustine quite simply admitted that this was the way things were, but he introduced other considerations that might be thought to "soften" this "hard" saying. Recognizing that the whole apparatus of Church and sacraments would be rendered superfluous if the final destiny of every person was foreordained, Augustine insisted on prayer and especially on participation in the official prayers of the Church. (Recall, too, that he defended against the Donatists the notion that the sacraments were effective whether or not the presiding bishop or priest was sinful.) The proper way to show concern for perfection was by a commitment to grace as it was mediated through the church and its sacraments. Since piety and a well-lived life were signs of predestination, Augustine encouraged self-perfecting which, he believed, could be accomplished by prayer and sacrifice. "If you are not predestined, make yourself predestined," he said. However, he did not flinch from insisting of the doctrine that had started the whole Pelagian controversy—that every human being is born with an original sin inherited from Adam, and so deserves eternal punishment. That God chooses to exempt some people from this eternal punishment is a sign of God's love and not of his cruelty.

Institutions and Organization

Original "Gifts" and Subsequent "Orders"

The word *apostle* is derived from the Greek verb *apostolein* meaning to "send out," and the word *missionary* is derived from the Latin word *mittere* meaning to "send out." The apostles were those first sent out by Christ and missionaries, but other functionaries were important in the days of the apostles and in the first generations following their mission. Paul, in his graded hierarchy of supernatural "gifts," lists also prophets, teachers, miracle-workers, healers, helpers, and administrators (1 Cor. 12:28). Apostles, prophets, and teachers, however, were the basic ministries of the earliest generations of Christianity. But within a hundred years, one saw no more of the apostles, prophets, and teachers; Christians were ministered to by a bishop, presbyters, and deacons. We do not know the exact history of this transition, nor do we know the exact functions that these types of ministers fulfilled.

Among the early Christian writers, Ignatius of Antioch (ca. 35–ca. 107) writes clearly about the three distinct ministries, describing a monarchical bishop assisted in some functions by presbyters and in others by deacons. Clement of Rome (fl. ca. 96), in one of his letters, implies the existence of two orders of ministry: bishops or presbyters (the titles are applied to the same people) and deacons. In some of the later writings of the New Testament there are references to bishops and deacons; the words *bishop* and *presbyter* are applied to the same person. It may be, then, that the churches established by the apostles and prophets were maintained by a local, stationary clergy subordinated to the traveling apostolic and prophetic authority. In the *Didache,* an early manual of morals and church practice, there are rules about hospitality to apostles and prophets with admonitions to appoint bishops and deacons, who should be "men of honor together with the prophets and teachers."

The earliest distinctions probably developed between the bishop-presbyters and the deacons. During the Eucharistic service (where the various functions were ceremonialized) the bishop-presbyter celebrated while the deacon assisted. Deacons, and a significant group of deaconesses (the only women who were part of the early organizational structure), helped the bishops in distributing charities and in looking after church properties. As congregations grew larger some of the deacons became men of considerable financial power. It was not long before the individual presiding bishops acquired authority over their fellow bishop-presbyters. The one in charge came to be called "bishop," while the subordinate colleagues came to be called "presbyter." When Latin became the principal language of the Christian Church, the word for "priest" (applied only to Christ, the "new high priest" in the New Testament) was used instead of the term *presbyter* (which in its Greek form means "elder").

Several factors contributed to the establishment of a hierarchy made up of a monarchical bishop and his assistant presbyters, or priests. First of all, the distinctive right assigned to the senior member of the presbyteral group was the power to ordain other presbyters. But then these senior members came to have other distinct functions: to carry on the correspondence between churches, to represent their church in the laying on of hands for the creation (ordination) of bishops and presbyters of other churches. And, generally speaking, it was very useful in times of confusion and disagreement to have a single person as the focus of authority. The monarchical episcopate appeared very early in the churches of Jerusalem and Antioch, and as time went on, perhaps because of the influence of these churches, assumed functions that at various times and places had been allowed to simple presbyters. There are records, for example, that presbyters in some churches may have consecrated their own bishop without calling on bishops from other churches.

As the organizational situation developed, the bishop inherited the roles of apostle and prophet as listed by Paul, and the presbyter inherited the role of teacher; and we recognize that in the early Church there were a variety of names and a variety of functions. Although the limits of the duties and prerogatives of each ministerial functionary varied somewhat from generation to generation and from place to place (there are even records of deacons presiding at eucharist on occasion), a number of structural patterns were established at the very beginning that have lasted until the present day in the majority of Christian Churches. The various Churches prefer to believe that the "gifts" that were given to the Christian Church at the beginning are still present among them and in their local churches; however, they name, depute, and divide the ministerial functions in different ways.

Monasticism

The worldliness of the church organization and the distractions of life in society, especially in the large cities, caused a number of Christians to live strictly and apart, to seek solitude and tranquillity where they could better appreciate the presence of God and the meaning of their lives. But different types of people were attracted to a solitary, self-disciplined life for different reasons. Admiration of both Jews and Christians for the martyr-personality and for martyrdom was the legacy of several centuries of sporadic persecution of Christians and many centuries of Jewish persecution before that. More intellectual persons taken with renewed emphasis on some areas of Plato's philosophy were attracted to an interior search: the Platonic "flight of the alone to the alone" became the search to find the Christ within. There were others who believed that all pleasure, especially sexual pleasure, was dangerous or inextricably bound up with sin, and so rejected marriage and the give-and-take of family life. Some were people of extreme gentleness and generosity, some were social and sexual misfits, but most felt called to a special search for truth and peace, whatever the personal characteristics.

The earliest ascetics were drawn to the deserts of Egypt, Syria, and Palestine, but it was Egypt that was the cradle of the monastic movement. In the fertile lands higher up the Nile valley two different modes of monastic life appeared—the life of the solitary or hermit, and the life of the member of a community. The models for these forms of life were provided by two Egyptian monks, Antony (250?–356) and Pachomius (ca. 290–346). Antony, whose life was made famous by Athanasius' biography of him, had retreated to the most inaccessible part of the desert and was a genuine pioneer of the life of spiritual isolation. He experienced all of the psychological dangers of this form of life, the discouragements, the hallucinations; everything became a form of

"temptation" that he could fight only by his prayer and perusal of the Christian tradition. Pachomius started a community of monks by the Nile at Tabennisi, where large numbers retreated to live a life of strict discipline and strenuous manual labor. Complete and military obedience was insisted on.

It was a difficult problem to keep the monks from passing completely out of the control of the local bishops, and some hermits and communities regarded sacramental prayer as secondary or a matter of indifference. Several great bishops, therefore, attempted to create monastic rules that would forestall the possible isolation from authority and orthodox teachings. Basil (ca. 330–79), the bishop of Caesarea, in the Eastern Church, and Augustine in North Africa, in the Western Church, both established rules for monks that were to anticipate later developments in Europe. Basil's rule in particular anticipated the spirit of the Benedictine rule to come. But bizarre forms of self-discipline developed among the monks of Syria and Mesopotamia. Many wore a heavy iron chain as a belt, and a few adopted an almost animal form of life, feeding on grass and living in the open air without shelter or clothing. The best remembered practice, though, was the experiment of St. Simeon Stylites (ca. 390–459) of living on top of a great column for many years. His perseverence gained him universal respect, and there were even some who tried to emulate his ways.

The main figure in the history of monasticism—that is, Western monasticism—was Benedict, born in the small Italian town of Nursia around 480 (d. ca. 550). Of an old Roman aristocratic family, he grew up in a society that had been considerably altered by the barbarian invasions, and he knew well the tensions between orthodox and Arian. As a young man he determined to live the life of a hermit, but after a period of isolation and severe self-discipline he gathered a small community around him. The *Rule* that he gave this community was a model of order and moderation: he prescribed a proper diet, a little wine, sufficient sleep, and decent sleeping conditions. In times of scarcity, though, he expected the monks to make do with what they had.

Benedict said that the monastic life was built on two basic foundations: stability and obedience. The monk practicing stability would remain for the rest of his life in the monastery he originally joined, unless he was ordered to go to some other place. The monk practicing obedience commits himself to the authority of the Rule as embodied in the authority of the Abbot. There could be deprivations and punishments for monks who committed themselves to the Rule and then failed to follow its stipulations. Physical labor was a fundamental activity of the monks with cooking and care of the sick among the most important tasks. The center of the monastic life was, of course, prayer. While time was allowed for private prayer, the community prayers took place in chapel, where the monks were to gather seven times during the day and once in the middle of the night. Although Benedict himself did not have much to say about study, this soon became one of the main preoccupations of the monks. To celebrate the prayer services (called the "Divine Office") books were needed, which before printing meant work for many copyists. By means of this manuscript work, the Bible and other writings, both religious and secular, were preserved for future generations.

The effect of the Benedictine monks on Western Christian culture and life has been incalculable. The monks preserved a heritage of religion and learning across the decades of devastation by warring barbarian tribes and, later, feudal lords. The Rule was soon followed by a large number of monks in the city of Rome, and was taken by missionary monks to the British isles (where it eventually replaced an indigenous form of monasticism that had developed in Ireland and parts of Scotland). Finally, the Benedictine Rule spread throughout the Western Church affecting the basic structure of Christian life during the Middle Ages and beyond.

Development of Papal Authority

Some sort of priority of the bishop of Rome over the other bishops of the Christian world was recognized practically from the beginning, but ever since the beginning there have been disagreements about the extent of his authority. The word *pope* is the English translation of the low Latin word *pappa,* which obviously means "father," and was used occasionally to refer to any important bishop. In the Western Church the title was gradually reserved for the bishop of Rome.

In the earliest centuries reference was made to the Pope of Rome as the successor of St. Peter, because it was believed that Peter had authority over the other apostles. Great stress was laid on the quotation from Matthew (16:19) where Christ is reported to have conferred important authority upon Peter. The words suggest, though not unequivocally, priority. It was the tradition of the Roman bishop from the beginning that Christ definitively gave superior authority to Peter (who was also presumed to have been head of the Church at Rome and to have been martyred in that city), and that his authority was definitely passed on to subsequent heads of the Church at Rome. There are documents that indicate that some of the early popes did try to intervene, or at least mediate, in the affairs of the churches of other cities, but the superior strength, numbers, and sophistication of other great bishops such as those at Antioch, Alexandria, and Nicomedia—and, of course, Jerusalem at the beginning—served as an effective brake to the growth of papal power.

The decline of the power of the Western Roman emperor, headquartered at Rome itself, was matched by the growth of the power of the Pope. The Eastern Roman emperor, headquartered at Constantinople, did not weaken in the same way. Politically and especially militarily the city of Rome and all of the Italian peninsula were no match for the armies of those peoples that came from the north and east: the barbarian tribes. On several dramatic occasions a pope was able to negotiate with the leaders of barbarian armies who had arrived at the gates of Rome. In 452, for example, Pope Leo I (d. 461) went out to meet the advancing armies of Attila the Hun and somehow convinced them to turn away from the city. Later popes were able to negotiate with the Lombards and the Ostrogoths. Pope Gregory the Great (ca. 540–604), who reigned at the end of the sixth century and into the early seventh century, found himself responsible for the care and protection of the city of Rome and the areas of Italy closest to it. His reorganization of government and armed forces, and his voluminous and influential writings are evidence of a fully consolidated papal authority. Leo, Gregory, and the intervening popes, in a period of about 150 years, laid the foundations for the papacy of the Middle Ages, a papacy that believed itself empowered with supreme spiritual authority over all Christianity, and with a legal/political authority that gave them the right to the last word over kings and emperors. But in Constantinople, the bishops and the emperor—to whom popes, including Gregory the Great, had submitted themselves—resented this inflation of authority. Eventually, Rome and Constantinople would go their own ways.

Branches, Divisions, and Groups

Earlier Divisions

Those who disagreed with the Councils of Nicaea and Chalcedon went their own way (we have already seen how Arians, Nestorians, and Monophysites formed their own Churches, with their own separate hierarchies and bodies of doctrine). The Monophysites, the group that we discussed the least, (only because their leaders were less famous than Arius and Nestorius), became the most widespread, and are still a force to be reckoned with today in Egypt, Ethiopia, Armenia, and Syria; the Nestorians and the once powerful Arians have virtually died out. As we look back on these Churches, we can see that there was a ''main'' or principal group from whom they separated themselves. As we study the history of Christianity we shall label the majority opinion ''mainline Christianity.'' We make no judgments about those who differed from mainline Christianity, but we must accept the evidence that the viewpoints of the Arians, Nestorians, and Monophysites (and for that matter, the views of the Ebionites, the Marcionites, the Gnostics, and the Montanists) did not become ''mainline,'' but rather they became separated from the larger group. The disputing Churches themselves would refer to their opponents as ''schismatics'' or ''heretics,'' depending upon whether or not the Church thus negatively labeled had simply cut itself off from Church authority (schismatics) or had denied some central teachings (heretics).

The major separation in Christianity, between the East and West, was the result of differences that had existed from the beginning. The centers of Eastern Christian thought and practice were the great cities of Asia Minor and eventually Constantinople (also called Byzantium and, in modern Turkey, Istanbul). The first centers of Western Christian thought were in Rome, but then also North Africa and Southern Gaul. Political and ethnic differences existed from the beginning, too, because the division of the Roman Empire into the Eastern Roman Empire and Western Roman Empire dated back to the days of Diocletian. Somewhat by happenstance Diocletian centralized his authority at Nicomedia, but it was not until many decades later that Constantine began the expansive development of the great city that bears his name. The Eastern Christian thinkers of Antioch, Nicomedia, Constantinople, and so on experienced life differently, used thought patterns and styles of logic based on the qualities of their own language; and the Western Christian thinkers of Rome, Milan, Alexandria, Carthage, Lyon, and so on were limited to their own experiences of land, people, and language.

Western Christianity evolved into what are today called the Roman Catholic and Protestant churches, and Eastern Christianity became the Orthodox Church. To tell the story of how this happened we must discuss the Eastern and Western Empires, the relations in the Middle Ages of the kingdom of Charlemagne, the old Empire of Byzantium, and the great new third force, exterior to the two Christianities and more powerful than either of them—Islam. Then, we shall deal in sequence with developments in the medieval Western Church and the Protestant Reformation. Finally, we shall present the progress of the Eastern Orthodox Church in Russia and Eastern Europe.

The Two Empires

To comprehend the broad picture we have to understand that, although the Roman Empire in the West declined to almost nothing in the fifth century, the Eastern Roman government survived without interruption until the thirteenth century. And it was not until the Ottoman Turks took over Constantine's old capital completely in 1453 that the supposed imperial successors to Constantine disappeared. Practically from the time of Constantine on, Greek culture, Greek thought, and Greek political science were more refined than the Latin or Western. The emperors residing at Constantinople (Byzantium) were better able to defend their city militarily because of its natural location and because of the persistence of a money economy, whereas in the West soldiers and officers were paid in grants of land or recruited from conquered territories. One of the greatest of the Byzantine emperors was even able to extend his power over to the West. In the sixth century, Emperor Justinian (483–565) was able to reconquer Italy, parts of North Africa, and southeastern

Spain, but of course, domination from distant Constantinople could not last. Not long afterward, the Arabs were galvanized into unity and action by the teachings of Muhammad, and within a short time were able to seize Syria, Palestine, Egypt, and part of Asia Minor from Byzantine control. This restricted the Byzantine Empire to western Asia Minor and the Balkan peninsula, which itself was eventually taken over by Slavic tribes.

The Eastern Christians evolved a distinctive style of art, and Justinian's great church of Hagia Sophia provided the model most often imitated in the construction of Eastern Christian church buildings. A distinctive liturgy based on Byzantine court ceremonial and with elaborations of Byzantine court dress was gradually developed. Many in the Byzantine church considered the theology and worship to be much more sophisticated, and believed the Western Church to be barbaric—with some justification, because the preponderance of Western Christians had been barbarians only several generations earlier. Eventually most of the Slavic peoples of the Balkan peninsula were converted to Eastern Christianity. The missionary enterprise was extended into Moravia. Liturgical and other books were translated from the Greek into what is now called Old Slavonic, and the greek alphabet was modified to fit the slavic tongues (this is the so-called Cyrillic alphabet used in present-day Russia).

In Rome, religious ways were different, but these differences need not have become anything more than irritants. The Romans reconciled penitents within the apse of the church, while the Greeks did not; the Greeks excommunicated those who failed to receive communion for three successive Sundays, but the Romans did not; Roman monks had slaves, whereas the Greeks did not; the Greeks accepted widows as nuns, whereas the Romans did not. All of these were minor differences, but ultimately there were so many of them that the differences became serious. Political problems consolidated the separation.

The relationship between the two empires, no matter who controlled them, was for centuries a function of the developing power of Islam. Undoubtedly the emperor of Byzantium was so concerned about his power struggle with the king of Persia that he could not have noticed the simple events taking place in Arabia, at Mecca and Medina, where a trader named Muhammad proclaimed

Mosaic of Christ, the Pantocrator ("All-Sovereign"). *From the former Church of Hagia Sophia ("Holy Wisdom") in Istanbul. When the 5th Century Church, a high point of Eastern Christian culture, was turned into a mosque, the mosaics were plastered over—only recently have they been uncovered.* (Courtesy of Hyla Converse)

a final revelation from the One, True God, and called on all people to believe him as the last messenger. But less than twenty years after the founding of Islam, the Arabs had taken all of Persia, Palestine, and Syria. Within a few years they had Egypt, and before a century had passed they had conquered and claimed for Islam an empire greater than the old Roman empire at its height. The presence of Islam had radical consequences on the territories that had formerly belonged to the two empires. The Eastern empire had been changed the most, because a much higher percentage of its territory came under Muslim control. The Western territories that had come under the control of the Franks proved to be too far away from the centers of Muslim power to be conquered. When the grandfather of Charlemagne, Charles Martel (ca. 690–741), had defeated an advance Islamic army at Poitiers, it became clear that the conquering of the

Frankish territories was beyond the abilities of even the immensely powerful Muslim forces.

It is not clear that the Byzantines understood the immense religious significance of Islam, because their theologians refused to consider it to be anything but a Christian heresy invented by a fanatic. But they were well aware that the Muslims who had conquered the old traditional rival empire in the East, the Persian, were far more sophisticated than the rough barbarians in the West. Although the Muslims had taken over a great deal of the Byzantine empire, they were unable to take over a large area that is now the Balkans, Greece, and the Western half of Turkey. And they were never able to conquer the city of Byzantium itself (this was accomplished by Turkish Muslims in the fifteenth century). Periodically, there would be minor attempts to conciliate, as when, for example, the following message was sent to a Muslim ruler in the tenth century by a Patriarch of Constantinople: "The two powers of the universe, Saracens and Romans, shine out like the two great luminaries of the firmament. So we must live together as brothers, although we differ in custom, manners, and religion." The Muslims and the Eastern Christians always felt that they had more in common than did Muslims and the small numbers of Western Christians who remained in those areas that had been taken over by the Muslims. The principal Christian challenge to Islamic power came from the Kingdom of the Franks.

Charlemagne and the Rise and Fall of Western Christendom

On Christmas day, 800, Charlemagne (ca. 742–814) knelt before Pope Leo III at St. Peter's Church in Rome and was crowned emperor of the Romans; he was understood to be the successor of Caesar, Augustus, and Constantine. It was the beginning of what was called "The Holy Roman Empire" in the Western world, centered not in the city of Rome, but in areas close to the modern-day border of France and Germany where Charlemagne established his court. Charlemagne set out to establish order and unity not only in the political realm but in the Church as well.

Standardization of Christian worship and Church organization were priorities for Charlemagne. Due to his efforts the ceremonial forms of worship used in Rome came to be the model for the whole western Church. When Charlemagne had his official liturgist, the British monk, Alcuin of York (ca. 735–804), send for copies of the Roman liturgical books, a process was begun whereby the beauty of the ancient ceremonies was enhanced, but spontaneity and local expression were taken away. Otherwise much of the early legislation of Charlemagne was concerned with the duties of bishops and the assurance of their authority. Bishops were required to be diligent in the performance of their duties; it was in the public interest that they did so. They were to stay in their own dioceses, examine the faith and learning of their clergy, see that their people knew at least the Lord's Prayer, and regulate contributions and the building of churches. More detailed directives came out in the decades after Charlemagne's death: bishops were required to be totally committed to the care of temporal and spiritual affairs of their dioceses, and were made chief agents in the royal government of the kingdom.

Monasticism was somewhat neglected in these reforms, had experienced a gradual weakening, and was in drastic need of reform. The combined efforts of a nobleman and a monk led to the establishment (927) of an independent monastery at Cluny in the Burgundy region of France. At first the monks of Cluny strove to have a place where they could follow the Rule of Benedict in its entirety, but then they set out to establish a network of other monasteries. The Abbot of Cluny was the ultimate authority, but the monasteries under Cluny had a reasonable measure of independence. At the height of the Cluniac reform, the monks, led by some of their most distinguished abbots, set about to reform the entire Western Church. It was the reform of Cluny that gave monasteries the reputation of being centers of learning and art. Cluny encouraged the nobles to learning and to war, the people to pilgrimage, the bishops to holiness, and other monks to poverty, chastity, obedience, and, in the beginning, to work. Under the influence of Cluny, monastic worship services became lengthy and lavish. Eventually the monks came to spend most of their time chanting the psalms at various hours of the day and night, celebrating elaborate Eucharists, and neglecting the physical labor that Benedict recommended as a counterbalance to the hours of prayer. Increased influence and power brought increased wealth. Cluny inherited vast lands from wealthy donors and used these resources to insure lavish art and architecture for the monasteries.

However, when the Cluniac reform lost its energy, there were other reformers, other monasteries founded where the Rule of Benedict could once again be carefully kept, and where the worldliness, that had in the end rendered Cluny ineffectual, could be kept out. The Cistercians are the principal successors to Cluny, but prayer and contemplation, as well as faithful adherence to a regime of work in the fields and at various crafts were the new emphases. Because they established their monasteries far from city centers, the Cistercians became an important economic force—they extended the boundaries of European civilization by the cultivation of new land. A Cistercian, Bernard of Clairvaux (1190–1153), became the most influential figure of his day, ensuring the dedication and spirituality of his own fellow monks, and preaching those great movements of kings, warriors, and merchants that so preoccupied medieval Europe, the Crusades.

In the early thirteenth century Dominicans and Franciscans were established: two religious orders whose purpose was also reform. Because of the progress made by groups considered to be heretical by the centralized Christian authorities, a group of preachers that would be more mobile and specifically trained in the task of combating heresy was required. The Spaniard, Dominic Guzmán (1170–1221), founded a group—named "Dominicans" after Dominic—who were specifically trained for, and dedicated themselves completely to, the preaching of orthodox Christianity. Francis of Assisi (1181/2–1226), born of a wealthy family, was a young man of generous and poetic temperament. He set out on spiritual quest for a life of simplicity and poverty that would be a perfect imitation of the life of Christ. By attempting to repeat in his own life the life of Christ, he so captured the imaginations of others that tens of thousands of men became "Franciscans" within several decades of his death. Although living in community—they called themselves "little brothers"—they renounced all personal property and clothing. Prayers of the day were much simpler than in the Benedictine tradition, and all hierarchical organization was avoided as much as possible. But it was not long before the pope and bishops—recognizing what a spiritual force they had at their disposal—required the Franciscans to adopt a more controlled and traditional monastic organization. One positive result of this was that the Franciscans as well as the Dominicans contributed to the flowering of the medieval Christian theology that we will now discuss.

Medieval Learning. The Dominican rule required that each friar work with three books: the Bible, the *Sentences* of Peter Lombard (ca. 1100–1160), the bishop of Paris, and a history of the world by Peter Comestor (d. ca. 1179). The first two books were the primary influences on medieval intellectual life. Thomas Aquinas, the greatest theologian of the Middle Ages, grew to intellectual maturity by commenting on Peter Lombard's work. In fact, Lombard's *Sentences* had an influence on medieval learning that can be compared to the powerful influence today of psychology and sociology in every area of life and learning: one could not be considered an intellectual if one did not comment on the great themes of Christian theology as presented by Lombard: (1) the Trinity; (2) the Creation and Sin; (3) the Incarnation and the Virtues; and (4) the Sacraments and the Four Last things. The work contained a rich collection of quotations from the great Latin Christian writers, especially St. Augustine, and from the Greek Fathers.

Thomas Aquinas (ca. 1225–1274). Born in Italy, as was Peter Lombard himself, Thomas Aquinas taught at the great medieval University of Paris. Among his early writings, the most important was his set of commentaries on the *Sentences;* and among his later writings, the most famous is the vast systematic composite of Christian theological teachings, the *Summa Theologica.* But Thomas' principal contribution to Christian theological history was his use of the philosophy of the great Aristotle to interpret the entire corpus of Christian Bible-based doctrine and the principal doctrinal interpretations of earlier Christian authors. Thomas' writing took on its characteristic qualities under the influence of the recently recovered metaphysical writings of Aristotle—due to Muslim philosophers and centers of learning the writings of the ancient and great Greek philosophers had been preserved. And while Plato had considerable influence across the centuries, Aristotle was not used seriously by Christian thinkers until the age of Thomas.

Fundamental in Thomas' teaching is his distinction between reason and faith. Even though reason is the primary faculty of the human being, many of the basic Christian truths—such as the Trinity, the Incarnation, original sin, resurrection—lie well beyond its limits. But while such doctrines cannot be established by reason, they cannot be considered contrary to reason, because reason can indicate their probability and refute arguments designed to overthrow them. On the other hand, Thomas thought that the existence of God, His eternity and simplicity, and His creative power and providence, can be discovered by the natural reason, quite apart from revelation.

The Incarnation of Christ and the meaning of the sacraments were of special interest to Thomas. He held that the Incarnation would not have taken place apart from the fall of Adam and that the Virgin Mary was not immaculately conceived. He thoroughly examined the conditions governing Christ's human knowledge, held that the sacraments were instituted by Christ, that Eucharist was the highest of them, and that the primary purpose in ordaining priests and bishops was for the sake of the Eucharist. Thomas elaborated a teaching about the presence of Christ in the Eucharist using several notions from Aristotle's theory of metaphysics.

Within Thomas' system are the Aristotelian notions of potency and act, matter and form, and substance and accidents—abstract notions that help put order into an all-encompassing interpretation of divine and human reality. Potency is pure potential and act is pure existence according to Aristotle: pure potential is not possible and only God is pure existence, while the human being is a combination of potency and act, said Thomas. Matter is the primary substance out of which everything is made, and form is the factor that causes the distinct species of beings that the universe is divided into. Thomas used these notions to deal with the specialized theological problems of the individuality of angels—since each angel cannot be individualized by matter, each angel is a distinct species. Substance is the underlying reality of every being and accidents are the secondary qualities that substance supports: a theory that explains the transubstantiation of the Eucharist bread and wine into Christ's body and blood, because the substance is changed from bread and wine into Christ's body and blood while the accidents of bread and wine remain.

To deal with all these and other questions, Thomas divided up his *Summa* into three sections and further subdivided the middle section. The first section, sometimes referred to as the *"Prima"* (the Latin adjectives for "first, second, third" are used even today when working with modern translations of Thomas) is concerned with God and Creation. The *"Secunda"* is concerned with the final end of humans and general moral virtues (*"Prima secundae"*) and the particular virtues and vices (*"Secunda secundae"*). And the *"Tertia"* is about Christ and the Sacraments.

Worship During the High Middle Ages. The organization of the prayer life of medieval Christians was based on the heritage of the monasteries, but the new centers of worship were the cathedrals. Since the power of the bishops and the pope was at its height, and since both could command attention from kings and peasants, the worship services and the buildings in which they took place had to be appropriate for the clergy, the nobles, and the common people. The vast and beautiful cathedrals, still in existence and actively used today, were the result, along with the great cathedral liturgies and the somewhat mysterious effect that these elaborate ceremonies had on everyone.

Belief in the presence of Christ in the bread and wine, though a tradition from the earliest days, received a new—at times magical—emphasis. With the bishop and his clergy presiding far away in the sanctuary of the cathedral, perhaps the king on his throne and the nobles close by, with light streaming through the stained-glass windows and incense smoke rising slowly in richly scented white clouds, a medieval man or woman would have a different idea of the meaning of Eucharist than would a second-century Christian standing close to a small altar or table in an oratory or private house. There Christ was present in order to be shared, whereas the impression conveyed by the cathedral ceremony was likely to be different: Christ there would seem to be an awesome presence to be safeguarded in splendid isolation. If Communion was distributed at all (to anyone other than the clergy) utmost care was used, and the wine was not distributed because of presumed dangers of irreverence due to spilling. This emphasis on the mystery and power of God's presence in the different sacraments was a valid one, but it became such a strong emphasis that Christians in later centuries would fight to diminish it.

Seven sacraments, or official worship services, were listed as normative. Previously, no special number had been absolutized. Everyone admitted that Christ had established Baptism and Eucharist. But the distinguishing of Confirmation from Baptism, the elaboration of an official ceremony for the reconciliation of sinners and the ordination of the clergy, the necessity of a specific church celebration of marriage, and formal prayers for the sick and dying—these sacramental activities had only gradually become universal throughout the Church. Peter Lombard was the first one to definitively list seven sacraments: Baptism, Confirmation, Eucharist, Penance, Holy Orders, Marriage, and Anointing of the Sick. Baptism (and the occasional isolation of some of the baptismal anointings into a distinct ceremony of Spirit conferral called Confirmation) and Eucharist have been discussed. Confirmation is conferred by the imposition of the bishop's hands and the anointing of the forehead of the candidate with a special oil called *chrism*. The sacrament of Penance involved a special acknowledgment of guilt by prayer, fasting, almsgiving, and as time went on, confession of specific sins to a member of the clergy—who then forgave and reconciled the sinner in the name of the Church. Ordination is the official conferral of sacramental powers on the bishop, priest (minister), or deacon; it is principally conferred by the laying on of hands, but is often surrounded by elaborate ceremonial. The sacrament of Marriage, or Matrimony, is the official Church witness to the marriage promises of the couple being married. (Often in Christian history this did not involve a special ceremony in Church, but could involve a familial or "civil" ceremony, with the promises consciously given a Christian sense by the man and wife, and the conscious witness by other Christians on behalf of the Church community.) Anointing, Unction, of the Sick is, as the name implies, a rubbing or anointing with oil in order to effect a spiritual and at times physical healing.

Peter Lombard's list became the norm for centuries to come—until the Reformation controversy as to which sacraments were instituted by Christ and which were developed by the Church.

Poetry and Prayer. Official liturgies impeded neither poetic inspiration nor interior reflection. The *Divine Comedy* of the great medieval Italian poet, Dante, was a

The Cathedral of Chartres. *With much of its sculpture and stained glass preserved, this structure dominates the town today as it did in the high Middle Ages. Connected to the cathedral was a school that made this small French town a center of learning that rivaled Paris.*

powerful intellectual and artistic synthesis of the medieval world-view, a combination of Greco-Roman mythology, the Christian Bible, and the politics of Dante's own era. And the writings of the great German mystic, Master Eckhart, represented the deepest currents of Christian (and non-Christian) mysticism.

Dante Alighieri (1265–1321) was not only the synthesizer of intellectual life of the thirteenth century, but he was also an initiator of a new literature. Writing in the vernacular instead of in Latin, he established his Florentine dialect as literary Italian, the standard for all subsequent writers. In his *Divine Comedy* he recounted his imaginary travels through Hell, Purgatory, and Heaven.

On his literary journey he encounters the leading figures of mythology and history, learning from them the supposed secrets of the universe. By imagined conversations with men of his own era, Dante gives voice to his views of society and events. By placing different figures in hell, purgatory, or heaven he ingeniously causes the punishment or reward to fit the nature of the bad or good behavior of those so placed. Corrupt leaders of his day, both political and religious, were not spared. The poem weaves Dante's own personal life with his discouragement, goals, and idealized love of the girl Beatrice into the fabric of his imagined universe. Although it is a more personal statement than Thomas Aquinas' theological synthesis, the *Divine Comedy* has been compared to the *Summa Theologica* as a summary of medieval faith and spirituality.

Eckhart von Hochheim (ca. 1260–1327), known as Master Eckhart, a contemporary of Dante's and a Dominican like Thomas Aquinas, placed in high relief the utter sublimity of the divine nature. Prayer, he believed, should be the quiet and interior contemplation of an Ineffable God beyond all images and words. One should guide one's imagination beyond all biblical stories, because God is not known by imagination or study or rational argument. God is much more unlike anything we can say about Him than he is like what we can say about Him. Unlike Francis of Assisi, Eckhart did not find his inspiration in the contemplation of Jesus as a historical human being; he was not interested in the history or geography of biblical events. Instead, Eckhart believed that God is known through mystical contemplation in which one is lost in the divine life. Eckhart was accused of pantheism—seeing people and the world as part of God—and of holding the similar belief that the soul was not created but eternal. Eckhart denied that he taught such doctrines, but it took many years and the influence of some of his more practical followers to ward off official condemnation of his writings.

Holy War. The so-called Crusades—the word is derived from the Latin "*crux*," because of the cross that Crusaders wore emblazoned on their outer garments—involved an ill-fated attempt on the part of European nobles and knights to take control of Jerusalem and other areas of Palestine that were the setting for the important moments of Jesus' life and ministry. Until 1071 C.E.

Muslim authorities had freely allowed both Christians and Jews to make pilgrimages to their holy places. But then the Seljuk Turks captured Jerusalem and closed it to all Christians in a holy "crusade" of their own. Christian authorities wished to reopen Jerusalem for pilgrimage, but it is unlikely that this is the real motive behind the major military campaigns that constituted the Crusades. Most likely economic, political, and military motives predominated. During the several Crusades, the armies on their way to "liberate" the Holy Land attacked and pillaged Christian peoples and cities. At first the Crusaders were able to occupy the city of Jerusalem, but were subsequently able to maintain only a small "Crusader kingdom" on the coast of Palestine, centering around the city of Acre.

The importance of the Crusades for medieval Christianity did not lie in religious achievements. Because of the Crusades, Christians came to idealize the notion of fighting for the cause of Christ and Christianity. A notion of "Holy War" was introduced that was foreign to the Christian tradition, although Christian teachers from Augustine on were quite willing to tolerate the waging of a "just" war.

The Crusades and the consolidation of the Holy Roman Empire constituted a significant chapter in the making of Europe. But the Holy Roman Empire itself did not essentially involve the production of Christian holiness, nor the preservation of an authentically Roman tradition, nor the establishment of a durable empire. And the Crusaders hardly were a serious tribute to the Christian reality of the cross. Rather, the heritage of Western Christianity passes from the monks, philosophers, and mystics of the medieval period to the Protestant and Catholic reformers of the next major era of European history.

The Protestant Reformation

So centralized was Church authority in the Middle Ages, and so closely intertwined were Church and State, that reformation was not possible without division. There were many attempts at reform across the centuries, the best known being the founding or reorganizing of the monastic orders, but the organization of Church and society had become so absolutized that general reform became at once more of a necessity and more of an impossibility. Neither General Councils of bishops nor spiritually powerful individual clergy were able to effectively combat official corruption. Although Christianity flourished in individual personalities, it did not flourish throughout societies.

In the Eastern Church corruption was far less dramatic because power was less centralized—virtually all of Eastern Christendom had come under the control of the Muslims. But in Western European society, centuries of papal centralization and political involvement had resulted in a status quo that could not be reformed by insiders. Reformers always came from inside the community of the Church, but for a variety of reasons they were not able to stay. Not until the advent of Martin Luther and John Calvin, however, was there a combination of individual charism and societal acceptance that led to the establishment of distinctly reformed Churches.

Attempts at Reform. General Councils consistently tried to combat the most obvious clerical corruption and moral evil in the Church of the late Middle Ages. For some decades the Pope lived outside of Rome (in southern France) causing confusion about his role as bishop of Rome, and at one point there were two rival popes. Several Councils tried to remedy the problems resulting from unclear procedures for electing a pope, but were notoriously unsuccessful; there even emerged a third claimant to the papal throne. Individual Councils sought the reunification of East and West, the reorganization of the Church hierarchy, and a return to genuinely Christian morality. In fact, just before the reforming activity of Martin Luther, a Council met at the Lateran palace in Rome to attempt a reform of the Church ''in its head and in its members.'' There were no significant or long-lasting results.

Individuals preached radical reform, but their efforts were isolated. Only later, when the actual Reformation had taken place, were they vindicated. The preaching and teaching of three priests—Wycliffe in England, Huss in Bohemia, and Savanarola in Italy—were directed toward a reform of Church and society that was only later realized by Luther and Calvin. John Wycliffe (ca. 1329–1384) was an English priest, educated at Oxford, who was especially disturbed by the spiritual damage caused by competing claimants to the papal throne. He said that legitimate authority comes only from God and is best exemplified by Christ who served rather than dominated. He began teaching that the true Church of Christ is not the pope and bishops but rather the invisible community of those who were in God's good grace—here Wycliffe drew his ideas from Augustine. He further insisted on the central authority of the Bible as interpreted by the Church. Consequently he believed the Bible should be translated from Latin so as to be accessible to all, and he organized preachers to go among the common people. Wycliffe rejected some of the detailed theological interpretation of Christian Eucharist known as transubstantiation—made normative by a Church Council and elaborated by Thomas Aquinas—but he maintained a belief in the real presence of Christ in communion.

Jan Huss (ca. 1369–1415) was a renowned preacher, scholar, and rector of the University of Prague at the beginning of the fifteenth century. He first came under scrutiny by the authorities because he championed not the ideas of Wycliffe—with whose heterodox views he disagreed—but the right of theologians to discuss the ideas of Wycliffe. Huss and other Czech scholars were opposed at Prague by a German contingent who felt that heresy was being cultivated there. As time went on, Huss continued to champion freedom within the Church. Believing in the authority of the pope, he nevertheless held that it could be rejected if not found in conformity with biblical teachings. Without entering into any controversy about Eucharist, he promoted the return of the cup to the people and criticized the medieval practice of distributing only the bread. Huss was finally brought before the Council of Constance, where his rather moderate views were taken to be heresy, and he was burned at the stake.

Girolamo Savanarola (1452–1498) was an Italian Dominican friar who made his reputation as a dramatic preacher in Florence. He preached against the evils of the time, and about the incompatibility of the true Christian life and the love of luxury—and by doing so he offended a number of powerful figures in the city. Savanarola reformed the Dominican community of which he was a member and later Prior. He believed that study should be at the center of reformation and accordingly had his friars learn languages useful in biblical scholarship. There was nothing offensive in the teachings of the saintly, learned, and severe Savanarola that should have aroused the antagonism of Rome, but the problem centered on politics. Savanarola had such influence in the city that his advice on military and political alliances was faithfully followed, advice that was disadvantageous to the pope and some of the Florentine authorities. Among the nobles, opposition to him grew, while the enthusiasm of his followers—looking for miracles and prophecy—waned. He was tortured and hanged, and then his body was burned and thrown into the Arno river—his message of simplicity and learning forgotten for the moment.

Followers of these three reformers never developed into large Church bodies, although the Wycliffe and Huss groups maintained an identity for many centuries. The followers of Wycliffe eventually came to be called "Lollards" and the followers of Huss split into various factions, some of which reacted strongly against any centralized authority. Although Hussites went through several phases, including one in which they were in communion with the Roman authorities and even managed to extract several privileges from them, they were more a presence among the Protestant communities after the Reformation, and came to be known as the "Moravian Brethren." The cause of Savanarola was not taken up by later Protestantism, but from his own day to the present there have been those in the Roman Catholic Church who have continued to believe that he was a saint.

Martin Luther. The German monk, Martin Luther (1483–1546), is credited with initiating a reform movement that grew into what is today called the Protestant Reformation. A man of great intelligence and profound emotions, Luther was born of a prosperous mining family, and joined a group of monks called the Augustinians. In his early years as a monk Luther made a pilgrimage to Rome, where he was scandalized by the immorality of the city and the worldliness of the clergy. This disappointment grew to disillusionment over the years, particularly when he saw worldliness and commercialism at the center of several preaching campaigns that were undertaken in some German regions close to his monastery. The papacy had crushing financial obligations, especially those deriving from the construction of St. Peter's Basilica in Rome, and required payments could not be made. Preachers were requested to secure donations from people in return for prayers and the remission of punishment due to sin. This granting of remission of punishment, called an "indulgence," was a custom that developed in the Middle Ages, presumably because of the Pope's

Martin Luther Posting His Theses. *Luther wrote 95 arguments (theses) against the practice of indulgences (remission of punishment due to sin) current in his day. He proposed his theses by posting them on the door of the University Church at Wittenberg.* (Religious News Service Photo)

special power to "bind" and to "loose," but the granting of an indulgence had been contingent upon the performance of a proper penance or at least the recitation of proper prayers. A receptive attitude and good will on the part of the one receiving the indulgence was also presumed. But added financial pressures on the papacy, and the advantage to local bishops resulted in a new and crude form of preaching indulgences. In particular, a Dominican, Friar Tetzel, preached a remission of punishment due to sin in return for a contribution of money.

In 1517 Luther responded to this situation by posting ninety-five theses, or propositions, about the problem of indulgences on the door of his university church. This was the customary way for a theologian and professor of the university to post a series of problems that he wished to propose for scholarly discussion. But this was the beginning of Luther's inexorable march to Church reform, even though he had no intention of undertaking a systematic review of all the medieval teachings that might be in need of correction.

Personally, Luther had been haunted for a long time by a sense of guilt and an inability to believe in God's love for him; he gradually began to come out of his haunted state by interpreting the Psalms in the light of Christ's experience. He saw Christ undergoing experiences similar to his own, but his consolation in Christ's sufferings was not sufficient to overcome his anguish. His great discovery came when he was reading the first chapter to the Epistle to the Romans. Challenged by the phrase, "justice of God," he hated it at first because he thought that God's justice would bring punishment on the sinner. Luther then realized that the justice is not a criterion that God uses to condemn by, but that His justice and righteousness are infused into those who open themselves up to it by faith. It is not given because people themselves are righteous—Luther was suffering precisely because he lacked any feeling of righteousness—but God comes to people. Luther saw at this point that both faith and justification are a free gift of God: "I felt that I had been born anew and that the gates of heaven had been opened. The whole of scripture gained a new meaning, and from that point on the phrase 'the justice of God' no longer filled me with hatred, but rather became unspeakably sweet by virtue of a great love."[10]

Although Luther's theses may have been undramatic in their initial appearance, they nevertheless attracted wide attention, probably because they had a direct affect on the hierarchy's financial situation. The Archbishop of Magdeburg who had supported Tetzel's preaching was offended, and quite quickly Pope Leo X (1475–1521) responded with concern, and directed that the Augustinian order itself discipline Luther. Luther began to fear being punished as a heretic, especially because the Dominicans who had taken up argument with him were attempting to turn his attack on indulgences into an attack on the Pope. He would probably have been silenced successfully were it not for the support of his local prince, Elector Frederick of Saxony. Frederick was proud of his University of Wittenberg, disliked the notion of Italians meddling in Saxon German affairs, rather enjoyed the discomfort of the Archbishop of Magdeburg, and trusted his own chaplain who was a friend of Luther. When Luther was summoned before the official ruling body of the Empire, the Diet, meeting under the jurisdiction of the Emperor Maximilian at Augsburg, Frederick obtained a guarantee of Luther's safety from the Emperor.

At the Diet of Augsburg Luther was forced to answer to the Pope's representative, Cardinal Cajetan. Cajetan, who had other missions to accomplish while in Germany, refused to discuss Luther's ideas and insisted that Luther renounce them. Neither side gained satisfaction, and a month later Luther wrote an account of his encounter with Cajetan and appended a commentary on the doctrinal

foundations of the papal claims to divine primacy and infallibility. His arguments were no different from those of a number of medieval theologians, but Luther was drawn the next year into a disputation with the brilliant Dominican theologian John Eck that took place at Leipzig. Since Eck's brilliance lay in debate, he was able to maneuver Luther into repudiating the infallibility of the Pope and of a General Council. Luther was shortly afterward persuaded by friends to write a letter to the Pope, submissive in tone and reverent, but not retracting anything.

Following the disputation in Leipzig, the Pope communicated a bulletin to Luther in which he declared that a wild boar had entered the Lord's vineyard, that all of Luther's books were to be burned, and that Luther himself had sixty days to submit to Roman authority or be excommunicated. When the bulletin finally reached Luther he burned it publicly, together with some other books that represented for him the worst of "popish doctrines." There remained only one more authority figure to challenge Luther, the Emperor. In 1521 the Diet was meeting at Worms, and there in the presence of the Emperor and German nobility Luther refused to take back anything that he had written. He said that some things had been said too harshly, perhaps, but that he could not deny their truth unless someone could convince him that he was in error. He concluded with the oft-quoted words: "I cannot and will not recant, for to disobey one's conscience is neither just nor safe. God help me. Amen."

Three famous treatises of Luther, his so-called *Reformation Treatises*, were written in the year before the Diet of Worms. The first, *To the Christian Nobility of the German Nation*, is the most revolutionary of his writings. In it he calls upon the rulers of Germany to reform the Church, because clergy were unable or unwilling to do so themselves. He says also that rulers and magistrates must abolish pardons, dispensations, the worldliness and secular rule of the popes, and the wealth of cardinals. The abuses of excommunications must be ended, the Roman curia curbed, celibacy de-emphasized, and control established over processions, pilgrimages, masses for the dead, begging friars. In the universities emphasis should be put on biblical studies and not on the scholastic philosophers. This treatise is viewed as Luther's manifesto for the Reformation, much more so than the ninety-five theses. The second treatise, *The*

Babylonish Captivity of the Church, is an attack on the medieval doctrine of seven sacraments (Luther wanted only those established by Christ), and the third treatise, *Of the Liberty of a Christian Man*, is a statement of the doctrine of justification by faith and its consequences for the moral life of the Christian. These three works, one a manifesto, the other a doctrinal study, and the third an essay in spirituality are vital to any understanding of the initial Protestant spirit of Luther.

The fundamental teachings of Luther can best be summarized as ''scripture alone,'' ''grace alone,'' ''faith alone.'' Of course, the three phrases belong together, revealing different facets of the same teaching. The scriptures are the sole role of faith because they are the Word of God; in them Jesus who is the Word of God comes to human beings. For Luther, then, the material words of scripture were not of primary importance, but rather the Word of God, and he was not fond of biblical books that did seem to him to facilitate his encounter with the Word (e.g., he referred to *the Epistle of James* as ''pure straw'' and he had problems with the Book of Revelation). To the argument that the early Christian communities—that is, the Church—had produced the Bible and determined its normative content, Luther said that the Church does not have authority over the Bible, nor the Bible over the Church; final authority lies in the message of Christ, who is the Word of God. Luther believed, however, that the actual written scriptural passages were a more trustworthy witness to the message of Christ than uncertain traditions and a corrupt Church. Grace and faith go together because grace, which is God's life, his righteousness and justice, within a person cannot be infused unless a person is willing to open up him or herself in faith. Faith was the fundamental stance that a person would take relative to God, and Luther exhorted people to acceptance, knowing that the power to accept God's grace, to open oneself up to it, also depended on God's power. But here Luther tried for no more precision than did Augustine; it remained for another reformer to strengthen the idea that the logical outcome of these beliefs was unqualified acceptance of an unqualified doctrine of predestination.

Gradually, Luther organized those who had with him repudiated their old ties to Rome. The University, and, in fact, the town of Wittenberg were reorganized: monastic customs were abolished, marriage of former monks was permitted and encouraged, and worship services were reformed. Here Luther allowed his people a great deal of freedom of choice, encouraging those who wished to, to retain a very traditional—even a Latin—form of Eucharist. He found a theological spokesman in the moderate and bright Philip Melancthon, under whose leadership a basic creed was formulated and published at Augsburg. Called the Augsburg Confession, it closely resembles the classical creeds of early Christian history, and gives no hint of attempting to establish a new and different Christian Church. Since the organization of Church life was haphazard under German princes, Luther asked the Elector to form consistories, or committees, that might coordinate Church life without returning to the styles of governance that characterized the medieval Church and the papacy.

The common people benefitted from Luther's pastoral concerns more than from his theology. He translated the Bible into German, thus rendering it, with the invention of printing, accessible to a great number of people. With the centrality of scripture to life and to worship, the vernacular Bible was Luther's first pastoral priority. His composition of hymns and promotion of the old chorale melodies enabled the people to take a part in the liturgy that had previously been reserved to clergy and monks. Finally, he produced catechisms that were understandable to children and the unlettered, thus reducing the vastness and richness of scripture to manageable units of learning.

Politics were always a problem for Luther, because by repudiating the authority of the Pope and bishops, he had to rely on the strength of princes. He encouraged authority to exercise authority, and on one occasion— the suppression of the peasants' revolt—he was embarrassed and shamed that his encouragement of suppression had been anticipated by the mindless savagery of murdering knights. When Luther was required to deal with the remarriage of one of his royal supporters, Philip of Hesse, he was forced to allow a marriage that in effect made Philip a bigamist. To Luther's advantage, a minority of German princes banded together after the Diet that was held at Speyer, and proclaimed their own unity and separation from the Roman Communion. They called themselves—and this is the first time the word was used— ''Protestants.'' Whatever their motives for supporting Luther across the years, the nobles who furthered the cause of his reform were the necessary condition for his success.

Luther's own personality was rough and simple, indicative of his peasant background. But he enjoyed laughter and beer and conversation among friends. He was an honest family man, having married a plain and good woman, Catherine Bora, the "Katie" that he could not do without and who was mother to his children. Luther's day-to-day recollections and conversation were taken down by friends who would gather around the dinner table with him and his family. This "table talk" reveals a man who was sometimes vulgar, but always big-hearted.

Luther and Zwingli. Ideas for reform of organization and teaching could be found in some of the major cities just outside of Germany—Strasbourg, Geneva, and Zurich. The strongest personality in any of these cities was Ulrich Zwingli (1484–1531), a priest of the city of Zurich. Zwingli was a humanist and a lover of order; he was less the passionate pastor of souls than was Luther, and less of a traditionalist. Although an admirer of Luther, he felt no qualms about radically changing the celebration of the Eucharist—where abuses had attracted his reforming zeal. Zwingli arranged a ceremony in which breads could be placed on a table in the center of the congregation, and then passed in silence to the participating members of the congregation. This approach to the Eucharist entailed an interpretation of Christ's physical presence in the bread and wine that brought Zwingli into conflict with Luther. Zwingli believed that something spiritual could not be communicated through the physical (the physical elements being only reminders of Christ's presence), while Luther upheld the notion of Christ's physical, or real, presence. It was in attempting a resolution of this conflict between Luther and Zwingli that other reformers, Martin Bucer, William Farel, and John Calvin—friends of one another—developed their ideas of Eucharist in particular and Church reform in general. By far the most influential was John Calvin.

John Calvin. His father a bishop's secretary, John Calvin was born in Noyon, France in 1509 (d. 1564) and brought up in an ecclesiastical environment. As a young man he studied theology at the University of Paris, only gradually coming to embrace the reform ideas of Luther and some other leaders. He switched to the study of Law for a while, but then gave himself over to work on a synthesis and interpretation of reformed theology—for this it was safer to work in Switzerland. In 1536, he published a work that he would revise and expand over the years, *The Institutes of Christian Religion*. At that time William Farel persuaded him to work for reform in the city of Geneva, where there was some hope of convincing the ruling class of the city to organize life according to the principles of the Reformation. Calvin pressed the city council too hard at first, so that he had to leave Geneva for several years, but when he returned he was able to organize the city in accordance with his own ideas of Church organization, which he understood to be, in turn, modeled on the organization of the "primitive" Church.

In a series of regulations, known as the *Ecclesiastical Ordinances,* Calvin set up a system whereby pastors chose pastors, although the city council could reject their choices. These clergy were to meet once a week for the common study of the Scriptures. They chose the teachers who would be responsible for the teaching of Scriptures and general education of the people. Calvin instituted the office of "Elder," perhaps believing it to be the office of "presbyter" (which, as we have seen, means "elder") in the primitive Church. But for Calvin, the Elders were disciplinary officials, and not pastors—that is, they were not priests or ministers—as they were in the early centuries. Elders were to watch over the morals of the congregations, ensure that obvious sinners did not receive Holy Communion, and made reports to the pastors, meeting them regularly in consistory. Over the years, in fact, the Elders warded off serious moral evil and obvious heresy, but were also unremitting in their war against miniature faults and superstitions. In Geneva, the Reformation appeared to be working: scripture was attended to and morals were at a reasonably high level.

Calvin was a private person who kept his own counsel and shared his personal feelings with no one—the direct opposite of Luther. He had an extremely sharp, well organized legal mind; there was no humor or vulgarity in his life. He quietly married a widow and lived happily with her until her death. Careful and severe in his administration of justice, he never became the tyrant of Geneva, because he continued to work out the running of the

John Calvin Speaking to a Crowd. *Calvin would often lecture on the Bible in the Geneva public hall to audiences of up to 1,000 people.* (Religious News Service Photo)

city with the city council. Although he supported the death sentence, he tried to eliminate any torture from the procedure. Before the end of his life he saw the establishment of a Genevan Academy, which attracted students and scholars from various places on the continent and in Britain, and prepared them to later propagate the Reform on their home territory. It was at Geneva that the most famous promoter of Calvinist reform in the English-speaking world, John Knox, prepared himself for his preaching and the establishment of the Presbyterian Church in Scotland. The full summa of Calvinist teaching was arranged by Calvin himself five years before his death in the 1559 edition of the *Institutes*.

For Calvin, there is an infinite abyss between God and human beings, which can be crossed over by means of the Scriptures: by the Scriptures and Scriptures alone, human beings can know the workings of the divine mind and will. The teachings of Calvin were based on faith in God's special providence, His mind and will guiding the events of the world. God by his personal decrees, directs all the events of nature, and guides the wills and inclinations of human beings to walk in the ways that He directs. For Calvin the ultimate response of the human being is "Thy will be done." Nothing happens by chance, and human beings can do nothing by their own will power. Accordingly, Calvin's teaching on predestination—the notion that God predestines human beings to heaven or hell—was in accordance with traditional Church teaching from the time of Augustine. But he insisted on emphasizing the difficulty of the teaching: it was a hard teaching, but people should accept it and place it at the center of their devotional lives. Calvin's logical mind pressed the doctrine of predestination to its ultimate conclusions, namely that God does not will all people to be saved, and that Christ died only for the just. Neither Augustine nor Luther had ever described predestination quite so strongly or logically. Consequently, his teaching on predestination has come to be known as "quintessential" Calvinist teaching. In his sermons and writing Calvin promoted these ideas, spelling out the results of predestination in people's lives. For his churches, Calvin naturally made the reading of scripture and preaching central, but he encouraged weekly Eucharist, believing, like Bucer, that Christ is present in the reception of Communion.

About a half a century after the death of John Calvin, leading Calvinists, at their Synod of Dort in Holland (1618–1619), spelled out in simple and direct formulae the basics of Calvin's teaching. "Unconditional election" meant that the God's choice of those predestined to heaven is based only on the unlimited, unscrutable will of God, and not on the foreknowledge of each person's response to the offer of salvation. "Limited atonement" meant that Christ died only for the elect. "Total depravity" meant that, although there is still in fallen human nature a vestige of natural light, that nature has been so corrupted that the light cannot be properly used. "Irresistible grace" and "perseverance of the saints" meant that the elect would persevere in grace and not fall from it, and that such perseverence is not the work of the believer but of God; it should serve to give humans trust in their own salvation and steadfastness in doing good, even though they see the power of sin still active in them. Succeeding generations of Calvinists, without mitigating the hard teachings about predestination, pointed out the somewhat comforting fact that one's ability to live according to the Gospels could be considered a sign of predestination, thus discouraging the idea that one's behavior did not matter if one's fate is predetermined. In fact, Calvinists gained reputations as austere, dedicated, and devout people of Scripture, and Calvinism has emerged as the most influential of all the traditions that date from the Protestant Reformation.

The Reformation in England. Against the crass political background of King Henry VIII's maneuverings to ensure a male heir to his throne, churchmen in England gradually effected a reform that combined the liturgical and most of the organizational way of the Roman Church with the scriptural and particular theological orientation of the reformers on the continent. Not only did Henry's wife not give him a male heir (important, because England for several generations had been wracked by wars of royal succession), but she was not at all romantically interesting. Henry (1491–1547) wanted an annulment of the marriage from the Pope, but for reasons both political and theological the Pope refused. With the help of his Chancellor, Cardinal Wolsey, Henry engineered a divorce and remarriage, finding it necessary to have himself recognized as a species of head of the Church in England. All legal rights and duties were transferred from the Pope to the Crown, and those who objected, such as Wolsey's successor and one of the leading bishops, were beheaded.

Appointed to the principal bishopric of England, Canterbury, was the quiet scholar, Thomas Cranmer (1489–1556). It was Cranmer who worked out the delicate compromise between Catholic sacramentality and Protestant biblicism that would characterize the Church of England down to the present day. Since Henry wanted only a reorganization of the Church and no changes in doctrine or liturgy, Cranmer recognized Henry's Catholic "Six Articles." On the other hand, Cranmer wrote a "Protestant" preface to the English Bible published at that time. When Henry's sickly young son, Edward VI, became king, the supporters of continental Protestantism became more numerous, enabling Cranmer to shape a Book of Common Prayer in accordance with his own canons of balance and beauty. He used traditional ceremonies and prayer formulae, but allowed for the possibility of liberal interpretations of their meaning. The 1549 Prayer Book replaced the Latin Mass with a Communion characterized by the beauty of its concepts and English language. The formal morning and evening prayers bore the influence of services that had been developed in Lutheran Germany. A later edition, however, seemed to encourage a more radical, Zwinglian interpretation of the meaning of Christ's presence in the Eucharist.

This rapid movement of the English Church toward Protestantism was completely reversed for a brief time by the uncompromisingly Catholic Mary Tudor, the daughter of Henry by his first wife, who came to the throne upon the death of Edward. She, in turn, was succeeded by Elizabeth (1533–1603), who was, so to speak, a Protestant of Catholic sentiments. She allowed further revisions of the Prayer Book, and appointed bishops who had little of the traditional anxieties about doctrinal or organizational continuities, especially in the complex area of apostolic succession—the notion that bishops across the centuries must be ordained in accordance with standardized formulae and that a succession be traceable back to the apostles. In fact, since the days of Elizabeth, the Church of England, often called the Anglican Church in England and the Episcopal Church in the United States, has enjoyed the benefits and suffered the consequences of this marriage of Catholicism and Protestantism: it can take the best of two worlds, but it must live with the tension of two tendencies that can easily be at odds with one another.

Radicals of the Reformation. During the early decades of the Reformation period, a loosely organized collection of groups formed on the continent of Europe—they were called the *Anabaptists*. In general, neither the controversies of Luther and Calvin nor the theological and political concerns of the churchmen of England were priorities for them. In fact, political involvement was of no concern because their priority was separation from such worldly activity; they looked to the end of time, to the destruction and transformation of the earth. For them life was a period of waiting, with total concentration on and commitment to the Second Coming of Christ. Such a commitment could only be realized, they thought, by baptism at its most serious: adult baptism by immersion. For the most part the groups had little organization, and met quietly to read and study the bible; their religious services and pious practices were quite diverse. The earliest attempt to gain some form of unity is represented by a document called the "Confession of Schleitheim" (1527), which not only insisted on adult baptism and separation from the world, but also proscribed all ceremonies and customs that harkened back to the ways of Rome—thus ensuring Reformation credentials. Separation from the world was further ensured by condemnation of the use of force, having recourse to the law courts, becoming a magistrate, or taking oaths.

By any standards of their day, the Anabaptists were a distinct group. On the one hand, there were communities where peace and mutual support were the foundation of life, and on the other, there was a lunatic fringe composed of self-styled prophets of the Second Coming. Two of them, the infamous Thomas Münzer and John of Leiden, their minds addled by wild prophecies of the imminent end of the world, attempted to establish the new Kingdom of God by force. John of Leiden took over one German city, was proclaimed King of New

Zion, wore a type of vestment as his kingly garb, and held court in the center of the city. He introduced community of goods and what he understood to be proper Old Testament polygamy. Fortunately, the Anabaptist groups that lasted down to the present day were those that lived by peace, brotherly love, and flight from the wickedness of the world. Well-known today by their old-fashioned life-styles and distinctive garb, the Hutterites can be found in rural areas of Canada and the United States. The Mennonites sometimes follow these distinctive ways (e.g., the Amish Mennonites), sometimes not; they are divided into strict and liberal groups depending upon their views on marriage (with non-Mennonites) and excommunication (whether or not it should involve social exclusion).

With the spread of Anabaptist-*like* ideas in England, a number of congregations separated themselves from the Church of England. They were called "Separatists," but their spiritual descendents are better known by the more specialized names of "Congregationalists" and "Baptists." For most of them the idea of *covenant* was fundamental: all members were to bind themselves by a solemn covenant with God to a holy life, and on the basis of this covenant they exercised a moral discipline upon one another. From this collection of "Separatists"—alternately, and even more vaguely, called "Puritans"—came the Pilgrims and Puritans who settled in New England and formed the core colonies of what eventually came to be the United States.

Methodism. In the eighteenth century another great reform of religious life took place in England under the leadership of the Anglican clergyman, John Wesley (1703–1791). Wesley experienced a profound and moving conversion of heart after he was ordained—that is, he completely rededicated himself to the person of Christ and the spreading of the Christian message. He attempted preaching methods and organized conferences that were not in the style of traditional Anglican churchmanship. His fellow clergy would often refuse to let him preach in their churches, with the consequence that his open-air style of preaching attracted crowds that would not "fit" within the traditional preaching framework. Given the nature of his sermons—closely reasoned and complex—it is remarkable that he attracted many people at all. His intensity and dedication, and his special concern for the needy and neglected were so apparent that he had outstanding success. People brutalized by the Industrial Revolution were changed by his challenges to moral perfection and by the small classes and the services he organized for them. And he encouraged them to joyous expression of their faith in the hymns he composed.

Wesley, the preacher who broke so many conventions, did not fit well into the Anglicanism of his day. English church life under the Hanoverian kings had become dull and lifeless. Wesley was a threat, and there was nothing he could do to reduce the antagonism between his group, called Methodists, and those safeguarding Anglican tradition. The situation was made worse, in fact, when Wesley ordained his own clergy and set up chapels outside the traditional parish structure. Although he himself never wanted to break with Anglicanism, and, in fact, never did, Methodists formed a separate religious body after Wesley's death. They today constitute one of the principal Protestant groups in the contemporary English-speaking world.

Roman Catholic Counter-Reformation

During the first decades of the Reformation period, it was often difficult to discern who was "Catholic" and who was "Protestant." Both words were used less frequently than they are today. "Catholic," meaning "Universal," was *one* of the adjectives used to describe the Christian Church in the early centuries, and even after the Reformation was not considered to be a quality possessed solely by the Bishop of Rome, the Pope, and those in communion with him. When the German princes at Speyer decided to use the term "Protestant" to describe those who adhered to the reform ideas of Luther, they did not assume that everyone who had severed connections with the Church of Rome would use the term. Furthermore, there were individual cases where someone still part of the Rome-connected Church government would actually embrace the Reformation. At one point, for example, it was not known whether the Bishop of Mainz in Germany was a Catholic or a Protestant. The simple solution to this problem in terminology is to call all those who are in official communion with the Pope "Catholic" and all others "Protestant," but in order to allow for Christians who consider their commitment to be Catholic, but are not in communion with Rome,

the term "Roman Catholic" has been used since the nineteenth century.

Catholicism as it is known today represents not only a core of teaching held in common with all Christians dating back to the time of Christ, not only a body of beliefs and customs dating back more than a thousand years; Roman Catholicism is very much the result of a Reformation that took place within the Rome-connected national Churches of Europe. Beginning with a Reformation of Catholicism in Spain that had little or nothing to do with the Reformation that separated itself from Rome in the rest of Europe, this Catholic Reformation developed in contradistinction to the major changes in Christian thought and practice represented by Luther, Calvin, the divines of the Church of England, and other reformers.

Before Luther's success in Germany, the efforts of a dynamic churchman and the development of a university in Spain produced great reforming results. The fight against the Muslims in Spain had already united the Spanish crown and the Spanish Church into a unified Crusade. Cardinal Ximenes (1436–1517), the leading Spanish Archbishop, conducted a reformation under the auspices of the crown: he enforced a poverty among the religious orders and dissolved the religious houses that failed to live up to his standards; he compelled bishops to reside in their dioceses, to preach the scriptures, and to educate children; and he created the University of Alcalá, where the study of the Hebrew and Greek languages could be encouraged and theologians could be trained. At Alcalá leading scholars welcomed the ideas of the leading Christian humanists such as Erasmus, and a polygot Bible in six volumes was produced—with Hebrew, Greek, and Latin texts, and a critical apparatus.

Out of Spain came new religious orders, including the primary Counter-Reformation force of Catholicism, the Jesuits, founded by the pious and determined ex-soldier, Ignatius of Loyola (1491 or 1495–1556). At a time when the Spanish Reformation was closing in on itself, and the University of Alcalá was being placed under restriction by heresy-hunting Spanish Church conservatives, Ignatius and a simple band of followers pronounced special vows of missionary dedication to the Roman Church. Although not specifically founded to combat the Protestant Reformation, the new religious order, called the "Society of Jesus" or "Jesuits," was transformed into a unit for the propagation and defense of the faith, which meant promotion of the specific approach to Christianity of the Roman Church. In the years after a major Council of the Catholic bishops, wherein a very detailed response to all of the reforming ideas and practices of Protestantism was worked out, the Jesuits led what is today called the "Counter-Reformation" or the "Catholic Reformation."

The Council of bishops, under the patronage of the Pope, met in 1545 in the small town of Trent, not far from the Austrian-Italian border. They met periodically until 1563, and when they had finished they had produced an enormous range of documents that would dictate Catholic belief and practice to the present day. To the reformers' teaching of justification by faith alone, they responded that faith alone is not sufficient for justification, but must be accompanied by hope and love. To the reformers' appeal to Scripture, they responded that unwritten traditions and Scripture are to be received with equal reverence. To the reformers' declaration that the sacraments of the Gospel were two or three in number, they responded that the sacraments are seven in number. Whereas the reformers wanted to put the Greek writings of the Old Testament to one side (as instructive but not part of the canon), the Council of Trent declared that the Latin Vulgate (which included the Greek texts) is the canonical text. Whereas the reformers preached that Christ's sacrifice on Calvary was not repeated at each Eucharist, the Council of Trent declared that each Eucharist is an atoning sacrifice of Christ. And whereas the reformers wanted the liturgical services to be in the language of the people, the Council of Trent declared that they should be in Latin.

After this Council there was little hope that there would be a meeting of minds of those Christians who called themselves Catholic and those who called themselves Protestant. There would be wars of religion for more than a hundred years, and there would be a cold war thereafter, until the middle of the twentieth century and the flourishing of the ecumenical movements.

The Holy Orthodox Church

From the time of Charlemagne's rule in the West through the time of the Reformation, Eastern Orthodox Christianity has had its own share of triumphs and trials. Before the final break with the Western Church in 1054—ultimately a disagreement about the relative powers of the Pope and the Archbishop of Constantinople—the great challenge to Orthodoxy was the power of Islam. Scarcely had the Church of Constantinople developed to the fullness of its powers when it was forced to maintain itself in the midst of the moral and military power of the Islamic kingdoms. The Byzantine Empire itself controlled independent territories until the fifteenth century, but other kingdoms, such as those of Moravia and Bulgaria and other parts of what is now Eastern Europe, came under Muslim domination.

In Russia, the Eastern Church had its greatest success. Conversion of the Russian rulers was accomplished in the tenth century by Germanic missionaries, but for reasons that are not clear—but that may have some relation with the appeal of the liturgical services—Byzantine Christianity was the form finally established. This form of Christianity became an important bond of unity for the peoples of Western Russia when the country was ruled by the Mongols for two centuries: a powerful hierarchy was developed, monastic life was firmly implanted, and specifically Russian forms of Christian prayer and theological reflection had their beginnings. When the invaders were finally driven off, and when Constantinople fell to Turkish Muslims, Russia possessed such a flourishing Christianity that some came to see Moscow as "the Third Rome," signaling that the center of Christianity,

St. Peter's Basilica in Rome. *This structure has come to be a symbol of Counter-Reformation and modern Catholicism with its emphasis on the primacy and (since 1870) personal infallibility of the Pope.* (Courtesy of Kyle Yates)

which had first been at Rome and then at Constantinople, was at long length Moscow.

Because Orthodoxy so often has had to maintain a "holding pattern," it is the branch of Christianity that has concerned itself most with the preservation and handing on of the traditions of the first seven Councils of the Church, including those all-important declarations of Nicaea, Constantinople, and Chalcedon. Orthodoxy preserves the earlier Christian beliefs in the holiness and ultimate infallibility of the Church, supports a hierarchy of bishops, priests, and deacons, and emphasizes seven sacraments. Orthodox Christians pray for the dead, as they pray for the living, without entering into the Catholic–Protestant argument over "purgatory" as a place of suffering where the dead expiate their sins before entering heaven. They have a Eucharistic celebration that is most elaborate in that there is extensive use of vestments, images of Christ and the saints (called "icons"), incense, and ornate chants; but there is an informality about the celebration also in that members of the congregation may move about during the service as they wish. There are numerous monasteries throughout Orthodox lands.

Orthodoxy is the form of Christianity practiced today in Greece, Russia, many countries of Eastern Europe, and in some areas of the Near East. In the West, many Protestant and Catholic Christians feel an affinity for Orthodoxy because it has well safeguarded the mainline Christian tradition. While Orthodoxy does have much to teach these two great divisions of Western Christianity, it is limited in its effectiveness by the very nationalism that enabled it to preserve its most sacred traditions against all incursions. Westerners consider it very "Eastern." But Orthodoxy, Eastern or not, may someday be a source of unity for the West, because it preserves all the beliefs and practices that Catholics consider important, and presents to Protestants a unified Tradition that is not bound to the authority structure of the Roman Church.

Religion and the Formation of Modern Society

All across the Reformation and Counter-Reformation period there was a growing functional distinction between religion and society. Whereas previously religion was part of society, it began to function separately when people of a given region could not express themselves in accord with their own religious beliefs. Rulers tried to force religious beliefs and practices on subjects who had opted for another religious way. Thus, Catholic rulers would force Protestant subjects into separation from the society that the ruler was trying to make completely Catholic, and Protestant rulers would attempt the same thing with the same results. With the Reformation came the experience of doing one's religion in isolation from surrounding society, making possible new forms of human thought and culture. Great intellectual-cultural movements gained momentum—before, during, and after the Reformation—and in interaction with religion fundamentally shaped Western thought as we know it today. These movements, often complex and representing great diversity, are well known by the labels of "Renaissance," "Enlightenment," and "Revolution" (in the sense of "Age of Revolution").

Reacting to changes in society, religious groups emphasized conversion (from erring ways) and revival (of weak faith). Individual religious leaders and thinkers helped their people meet the political, social, and intellectual challenges of new forms of government, transformation of social institutions, and the rapid advance of technology. The story of religion and the formation of society is, then, the story of great intellectual and political movements, far reaching religious revivals, and strong leaders in times of crises.

The Enlightenment and Its Renaissance Foundations

Well before the Reformation, the cities of Italy were the scene of a vigorous artistic and intellectual life. The recovery of the greatness of the classical world of Greece and Rome was believed to be a return to true civilization after a long period of societal darkness, characterized by wars, narrow superstition, and inbred philosophy. In Italy, the cultivation of a new art, sculpture, and literature in imitation of the classical models became a new way of social life for the great cities of Florence and Rome. Admiration for the works of pagan literature helped to alter the Christian faith of many humanists. Not only did some of them invoke the pagan gods in their writings, in imitation of Homer and Virgil, but some abandoned Christianity completely, criticizing the Church and its officials in bitter terms. Artists painted scenes inspired by pagan literature, and introduced a new sensuousness into all their portrayals of the human face and figure. In sculpture and architecture, imitation of Greek and Roman models was coupled with a disdain for anything that had been produced by the so-called Middle Ages (''gothic'' was a term of derision and meant ''barbarian'').

The Renaissance Ideal. If there can be anything called the ''Renaissance ideal'' it is perhaps best summed up in *The Courtier* by Baldassare Castiglione (1478–1529), a book of manners describing the talents and accomplishments a cultivated man should possess. Castiglione emphasized humanistic education, a ready wit, a strong and graceful body, and the cultivation of diplomacy—saying the right thing to the right person at the right time. There is no reference to the Bible, no deference to any ecclesiastical organization, and certainly no interest in religious reform. During the Renaissance purely human accomplishments and the powers of unaided reason were placed in high relief. At a more profound level the writings of Pico della Mirandola, Marsilio Ficino, and Lorenzo Valla analyze the qualities of the human being that should be the basis of the finished, exterior cultivation of the civilized life.

In general, it should be noted that the intellectuals and artists whose work predominated across the years of this period we call the Renaissance, did not set themselves at all to the rejection or destruction of the Church. In fact, the Catholic Church itself tried to adopt the results of the Italian Renaissance to its own needs, often patronizing this style of art, sculpture, and promoting literature, philosophy, and the new sciences. Certainly the humanism of Northern Europe provided some Reformation leaders with new means of Scripture translation and interpretation. The invention of printing may be as responsible for the success of the biblical reform at the center of Protestantism as are the efforts of Luther and Calvin. But the foundations were laid for modern secular society.

Enlightenment Thinkers. The growing prestige of the natural sciences highly influenced the philosophical outlooks of many intellectuals of seventeenth- and eighteenth-century Europe. The ability to place diverse natural phenomena under common laws caused many to believe that human reason would eventually gain intellectual and physical mastery over nature. Enlightened thinkers began to believe that human nature is fundamentally good and everywhere the same. Bad institutions and wicked leaders corrupt the natural goodness of people. But with the reorganization of some institutions (some thought of the absolutist governments) and the suppression of other institutions (some thought of the Church), the primitive good nature of the human being, and the society of human beings in relation to one another could flourish. State and Church as they existed—in France especially—should be changed or done away with. Life, liberty, and property were recognized as natural rights, and to this list many added equality.

John Locke in England, David Hume in Scotland, and Jean-Jacques Rousseau in France sought a new basis for sovereignty and political authority, and thereby undermined traditional religion. The notion here was that the creator of the universe is a master mathematician, who, having placed the sun and the stars in their orbits interferes no further in the working of the laws of nature which He had established. Accordingly, these philosophers denied the possibility of divine intervention in mundane affairs, and believed miracles to be the inventions of superstitious, self-interested clergy. The principal obstacles to the rule of reason were the remnants of the old days of superstition.

In his *Essay on Human Understanding,* John Locke (1632–1704) insists that all knowledge is derived from experience, the outer experience of the senses, the inner experience by which we know ourselves and the functioning of our minds, and the experience of God—whose existence is proven by the existence of the experiencing self. In his treatise, *The Reasonableness of Christianity,* Locke wrote that Christianity is the most reasonable of religions, because he believed that Christianity adds nothing of importance that is not known by the correct use of reason. This treatise did not please the pious because they did not believe that revelation should be reduced to an exalted form of reason. Nor did it please those who felt that the very notion of revelation is contrary to reason. However, Locke's views did please a wide variety of thinkers who were looking for an understanding of religion that went beyond narrow orthodoxy, and yet did not end in atheism or freethinking. Such thinkers called themselves "Deists," and believed that true religion must be natural to all humankind. It should not be based on particular revelations nor on historical events, but on natural human instincts. For the Deist, the basic truths of religion are these: the existence of God, the obligation to worship God, the ethical requirements of such worship, the need for repentance, and reward and punishment, both in this life and the one to follow.

Such confidence in human reason, however, was undermined by David Hume (1711–1776), who was most pessimistic about the powers of reason. He believed that what Locke and others believed to be the powers of reason are really the result of irrational mental habits, and that experience cannot be counted on at all. Hume's most famous attack on the powers of experience is his example of the "billiard ball." Presumably, our experience is that when one billiard ball strikes another it causes it to move, and when this happens the principle of cause and effect is at work. We say that the movement of the first ball caused the movement of the other one. Actually, says Hume, we have only developed the mental habit of referring to the "causality" of the striking billiard balls and other similar phenomena by seeing the movements repeated over and over again. Hume insists that we have not really experienced causality and have no right to appeal to experience as a guarantee of truth. That this argument strikes at the heart of the Deists' argument in favor of the reasonableness of religion is obvious: if one cannot know for sure the existence of cause and effect, one cannot hold that someone, God, must have caused this world. Other writings of Hume, such as his *Essay on Miracles* and *Natural History of Religion,* aroused the ire of churchmen in England and elsewhere, but his attack on reason and empirical knowledge, his carefully argued skepticism, has emerged as one of the greatest challenges of the Enlightenment—and of the entire history of thought—to natural and supernatural religious truth.

Jean-Jacques Rousseau (1712–1778), and French thinkers in general (we call them *philosophes,* simply using the French word for philosopher), could not stay with the abstract flights of Hume. In one of his letters to Voltaire, he said "All the subtleties of metaphysics will not make me doubt for a moment the immortality

of the soul or a beneficent Providence. I feel it, I believe it, I want it, I hope for it, and I shall defend it to my last breath." Rousseau concentrated more on the personal, political, and social implications of reason understood as common sense. For Rousseau, religion itself was a matter of common sense. He believed that the human being in the state of pure nature, undamaged by the decadence of human society as it had developed, is good and innocent. The exagerration of the social tendency toward organization and restraint that develops in society causes individuals to dominate one another and degrade themselves. All of these ideas were developed in great detail in his philosophical novels and in his best-known work, *The Social Contract.*

The philosophers of this so-called Enlightenment period, like the Renaissance leaders, felt a nostalgia for the great classical age of Greece and Rome, but the Enlightenment, of course, could also draw on the heritage of the Renaissance period. The common experience of the Enlightenment philosophers has been described by a modern scholar as an interplay of a number of features: appeal to the authority and culture of antiquity, tension with Christianity, and pursuit of modernity. He says,

This dialectic defines the philosophes and sets them apart from other enlightened men of their age: they, unlike the others, used their classical learning to free themselves from their Christian heritage, and then, having done with the ancients, turned their face toward a modern world view. The Enlightenment was a volatile mixture of classicism, impiety, and science; the philosophes, in a phrase, were modern pagans.[11]

A Christian response to these ideas was forthcoming in Germany primarily. Immanuel Kant (1724–1804), one of the greatest philosophical minds of his era and a practicing Lutheran, in answer to Hume's skepticism developed his own philosophy on the role of reason in the discovery of truth. In his *Critique of Pure Reason* Kant argues that reason does not discover laws and realities of the universe, but imposes categories within. We do not know things as they are but insofar as the mind is able to grasp them. And just as the mind imposes categories for understanding, so does moral obligation come from within: Kant said that each person should act in such a manner that the rule that governs the individual act could be made a universal rule. On the foundations of this philosophy of moral obligation, Kant constructed his system of teachings on God, freedom, and immortality. He wanted to provide a radical alternative to empiricism with its emphasis on the truth revealed in experience, believing that by doing so he could refute some of the major points of Hume's philosophy.

G. W. F. Hegel (1770–1831) promoted the supreme value of reason in another way. Hegel said that the mysteries of the universe cannot resist the powers of the intelligence. In fact, the intelligence—reason—should be identified with reality. Reality should not be considered as a disconnected series of things and events, but as a dynamic, living whole. And reason itself is dynamic, an extension of the absolute Idea or Spirit that is realizing itself in history by a process of thesis, antithesis, and synthesis (everything generates or encounters its opposite and resolves into a synthesis of the opposing thesis and antithesis). Hegel believed that this understanding of reality and reason is most clearly presented in Christianity, which he took to be the culmination of the entire process of human religious development: the Incarnation represents the full union of the divine and the human, and the Trinity is the union of eternal idea, creation, and the force that brings together heaven and earth. Hegel's powerful philosophy has a grandeur and subtlety that attracted many thinkers, mostly because it is a vast and integrated system of ideas.

Two Christian writers, also working on the borderline between philosophy and theology, did not wish to depend on the notion of reason as a defense against skepticism. Friedrich Schleiermacher (1768–1834)—of the Reform tradition but under pietist influence—had little interest in showing the rational value of Christianity. For him life and truth are matters of a profound feeling of dependence on the ultimate force which is God. Feeling in this sense is not mere sentiment or emotion, but a relational attitude at the deepest levels of one's personality. Schleiermacher said that the essence of Christ was his unique sense of his relationship to God, his God-consciousness. And the role of the Church that Christ founded is to communicate to people the experiences that generate the feeling of dependence. It was, then, the obligation of each Christian to explore the reality of this feeling in all areas of life: in the self, in the relationship to the world, and in the relationship to God. Many of today's liberal Christian theologians trace their spiritual ancestry to Schleiermacher.

Soren Kierkegaard (1813–1855), a Danish Lutheran, found reason unrewarding and emotions a cause of suffering. Against Schleiermacher and Hegel, he insisted that Christianity is a matter of faith. Kierkegaard did not define faith by a few glib words, however. He said that faith (true Christianity) is existence, not activity of the intellect, and existence is prior to any "essense" (the classical philosophical notion that the fundamental reality in everyone and everything is an essence, i.e., what the person or thing *is*). Existence is more fundamental than any abstract essence, because it is actual, painful, quite simply, "there." True Christianity is a leap of faith, not a feeling or a mighty philosophical system. Kierkegaard rejected the idea that faith should console people, should make their life easier, or should provide intellectual satisfaction. Although little known in his own day, he exerted such an influence on later theological thinking that he is considered to be the father of twentieth-century existentialism, a way of understanding life that can embrace all tragedy, all mystery—and still submit to the ultimate meaning of Christianity, whether taken figuratively or literally.

The Age of Revolution

There is a temptation at first to consider the French Revolution as the heritage of the Enlightenment; in fact, many of the rational and societal ideas of the philosophes motivated the actions of a number of revolutionary leaders. The French Revolution began without the antireligious bias of the philosophes, but within a few years went to extremes of antireligious violence and general terror that those redoubtable defenders of reason of a generation or two before would never have condoned. The Revolution, and other imitations of it in Europe, had its own bizarre and uneven life. Groups with widely different political loyalties arose, and civil wars were added to foreign. Opinions and political groupings shifted with astonishing speed. The radicals of one year became conservatives of the next. A Reign of Terror was introduced in the name of "liberty," "equality," and "fraternity," which brought political leaders and thousands of private citizens to the scaffold. From the fall of the Bastille in 1789 to the fall of Napoleon in 1814, the successive governments of France sought to reform, destroy, or use the Church in their midst.

The other great European revolution took place in our own century, in Russia, where the suppression of secularism in all its revolutionary manifestations was successful well beyond the first decade of our own century. The hostility that had been building up against the absolutist rule of the Czars and the Orthodox Church, which served at the beck and call of the government, broke loose. The new government was officially atheist—with none of the philosophical nostalgia for a universal God of reason that had characterized the political ideologies of the French revolutionaries.

Secularism. Between the French and Russian revolutions the general trend in Europe was for the most part toward emphatic secularization. Science was placed in increasingly open conflict with the Judeo–Christian scriptures, and historical scholarship resulted in a new view of the scriptures as a piecemeal collection of accounts and interpretations bearing all the defects of human documentation. Scholars denied that the gospels were eyewitness accounts and doubted whether Jesus had intended to found a new religion. One influential life of Jesus eliminated the supernatural element from his life. Then came the shock of Charles Darwin's *Origin of Species* (1859) with its teachings on "survival of the fittest" and the evolution of human beings from lower forms of life. By the mid-nineteenth century, Western Europe and the British Isles had reached a high point of secularizing enthusiasm, and thereafter alternated between post-revolutionary liberalism and conservative (and proreligious) reaction.

Today in virtually every nation where Christians represent a substantial part of the population, they are distinct (though not always totally distinct) from their governments. Relative to their governments they are special interest groups with lives of their own; at one and the same time they need the support of their governments and separation from them. Governments, in turn, have found that the Churches are powerful, and that they have to be treated as living, permanent social forces. They have discovered that the reform or suppression of the modern Christian Churches in the various modern nations must be left to the Churches themselves. The heritage of the Age of Revolution is the secularization of the State, and the separation of the Church from it.

In both the Protestant and Catholic traditions, leaders reacted pointedly to the secularization that occurred in the modern revolutionary age. Efforts were begun in the nineteenth century and were continued well in to the twentieth century to safeguard people's faith against the incursions of enlightenment and revolutionary thinking. Within Protestantism a split developed between liberals, who wanted to reinterpret traditional doctrines to make them relevant to modern needs, and fundamentalists, who based their understanding of contemporary life on a literal understanding of the Bible. For Roman Catholicism the problem was more political. From the middle of the nineteenth century, the Popes worked hard to form official responses to new political structures in Europe, particularly—in the twentieth century—fascism and communism. This is not to deny the political concerns of Protestant leaders or the biblical and doctrinal concerns of Catholic leaders, but to state the principal challenges facing each group.

The Protestant Response. Revival movements had enjoyed great success in America in the nineteenth century (although the American Protestant revival movement goes back much earlier). Presbyterian, Methodist, and Baptist preachers travelled throughout the southern United States gathering enthusiastic audiences for bible-based sermons. Listeners were encouraged to repent their evil ways, and to feel the presence of Christ within. Methodists and Baptists in particular were flexible enough in their organization to make use of "lay preachers," or men who were not trained members of the clergy, but who felt themselves called to the task of spreading the gospel message. By the middle of the nineteenth century, some forms of this religious enthusiasm led some members of these eminently successful denominations to form new groups, and thus were begun the Holiness, Pentecostal, and Adventist families of churches. But from the middle of the century on, there was also a growing anxiety about the inroads of secular life and thought. In 1895 there was in Niagara Falls a meeting of leading preachers, who wanted a forthright statement of what they called the "fundamentals" of the Christian faith. They were later called "fundamentalists."

Fundamentalists insist on the literal acceptance of the inerrancy of scripture, the divinity of Jesus, the Virgin Birth, Jesus' atoning death on the cross, and Jesus' physical resurrection and impending return. While these fundamentals, simply stated, would be accepted by the majority of Christians, many of those who called themselves fundamentalists evolved a distinctive style of interpreting scripture, treating all of the biblical stories as factual historical accounts, and treating every verse in scriptures like every other verse (instead of recognizing the varieties of literary forms used by the inspired authors). After World War I, American fundamentalists gained notoriety by their efforts to ban the teaching of evolutionary theory in the public schools, and the prohibition and sale of alcoholic drinks. Not all conservative biblical Christians consider themselves fundamentalist in this militant sense, however, and the term "evangelical Christian" has come to be used for those conservatives who do not have one systematized set of literal interpretations of Christian life, and who admit the goodness to be found even in those forms of Christianity they do not find congenial.

Liberals in Protestantism are harder to define, but from the last century on, those calling themselves liberals have found modern secularism a challenge rather than a threat. They place a high premium on personal and intellectual freedom, whether they believe in the fundamental goodness of human nature or not. The European Christian philosophers of the nineteenth century—Kant, Hegel, Schleiermacher, Kierkegaard—provided the intellectual foundations of twentieth-century Protestant liberalism. But the experience of the two great World Wars in Europe changed the orientation of many liberals. Human evil, social justice, and the role of the state were the profound concerns of many independent-thinking Christian leaders.

In the United States, the Baptist Walter Rauschenbusch (1861–1918) fought against the evils of unlimited capitalism. Preaching what he called the "Social Gospel," he campaigned to help the urban poor to rise out of their condition. Basically optimistic about human capabilities, he believed that control of capitalism would enable his people to live fulfilled Christian lives. Much less optimistic than Rauschenbusch, Reinhold Niebuhr (1894–1962), with his experience in a Detroit parish during the depression, also wished to control elements of the capitalist system. But he believed that he was dealing with what he called "immoral man" in an even more immoral society.

The rise of Naziism in Germany terrorized anew a Europe devasted less than twenty years before by World War I. At first, some liberal Christian leaders, because of their own belief in human perfectibility, were attracted by the Nazi emphasis on the construction of a superior society. Because of the attempt to establish a national Church, called the German Evangelical Church, Lutheran and Reformed Church leaders issued a formal statement of Christian theology called the Barmen Declaration (1934). They insisted that the Church was established by the Revelation of God in Christ, and was not the result of human striving toward perfection. In the formulation of this statement, the German pastors were much influenced by the theologian Karl Barth, whose experience of World War I had already taught him that the liberal message of rationality and development was unacceptable as the Christian message.

Neo-Orthodoxy, the name given to the systematic religious thought of Karl Barth (1886–1968) became the most influential Protestant theology of the twentieth century. Barth believed that in a world gone mad the Kingdom of God must be at the center of the Christian message; awareness of human sinfulness was the counterbalancing theme in what some have called his "crisis theology." As a young pastor, he began a *Commentary on Romans* that developed almost by happenstance into a major book. But his voluminous *Church Dogmatics,* an imposing intellectual monument, has had an enormous influence on the lives and ministries of many Protestant clergy. Barth belonged to the Calvinist tradition within Protestantism, but he was quite willing to reformulate Calvin's thought to eliminate what he believed to be some contradictions. He did not attack modern biblical criticism, nor did his reactions to the earlier liberalism of European Christian thinkers send him at all in the direction of fundamentalism.

World War II also provided the background for the experience and writings of the Lutheran pastor, Dietrich Bonhoeffer (1906–1945). While doing advanced studies in the United States, Bonhoeffer felt obliged to return to his native Germany to actively oppose Hitler. His reflections on the meaning of Christian discipleship and the failure of the organized churches to effectively oppose the ravages of Naziism led him to speak of a "religionless Christianity" that freed the bonds of formal organization and unchanging collective identity. He said that the world was "coming of age," and that God's presence in such a world is like that of a wise parent who recedes into the background as the child grows. Although he greatly admired Barth, his vision of the present meaning and future role of religion was based much less on revelation.

Biblical revelation also received radically new treatment from two other German Protestant thinkers, Rudolph Bultmann and Paul Tillich. Bultmann (1884–1976) taught that the message of the New Testament was expressed in myths in which God and other supernatural forces intervene, and in which the universe is pictured on three levels with heaven above and earth below. In the light of philosophical and scientific advances since the Renaissance, thinking people can no longer literally accept and graphically picture supernatural intervention and the three-tiered universe. Bultmann, accordingly, wanted to "demythologize" the New Testament so that its radical call to conversion and service could be followed. Efforts of faith should be concentrated on the reality of God and submission to Him; faith should not be wasted on attempts to take myths literally.

Paul Tillich (1886–1965) was the theologian who came to have an influence almost equal to Barth's, at least in America. Professor for years at Union Theological Seminary, then Harvard, and finally the University of Chicago, Tillich's ideas have had great influence on a generation of divinity students and philosophers of religion. Often Tillich's ideas are quoted without the awareness that they are his. Always on the boundary between philosophy and theology, Tillich formulated expressions and interpretations of God's existence that made him acceptable to those who were not orthodox Christian believers (and sometimes unacceptable to some who were). For Tillich, faith was "ultimate concern" for life, for the universe, for the mystery symbolized by revelation. God did not have to be pictured in a graphically personal way, but could be thought of as the "ground of our being." In his sermons, essays, and *Systematic Theology,* Tillich outlined an interpretation of Christianity that brought Protestant liberalism full circle: free to determine the meaning of Christianity outside the boundaries of Church authority, but without simplistic expectations of ultimate perfection in human life and thought.

The Roman Catholic Response. For the leaders of Roman Catholicism in the twentieth century, the crisis was one of authority more than of belief. But just as the Protestant reinterpretation of faith involved the changing politics of Europe and America, so the crisis of authority entailed new challenges to traditional Catholic faith. The Popes of this century maintained their independence of all political systems, in that they never became the pawns of any one government. But they were ineffectual in dealing with the breakdown of political relationships that resulted in the prolonged conflict of World War I. After trying to work out several agreements with Mussolini's and Hitler's fascism they turned against it—though maintaining an uneasy relationship with the rightest, but very Catholic, General Franco in Spain. Their opposition to Communism was unremitting. Conservative in their insistence on a fairly literal interpretation of scripture and continuity with religious statements of their predecessors, successive Popes gradually became more open in their political, economic, and ethical teachings—except in areas of sexuality and religious authority.

Pius XI, Pope from 1922–1939, was a scholar who had deep pastoral concerns, giving special attention to the Catholic mission to the Third World and special encouragement to more active participation of the lay people in a Church that had become too clericalized. Much more worried about Communism than Fascism, he signed an agreement with Mussolini in 1929, which gave Vatican City independent political status. After initial opposition to Hitler he signed a Concordat, or treaty, in the hopes of gaining a measure of security for German Catholicism. Finally, however, he issued two powerful encyclicals (letters containing formal papal teachings or admonitions), one against Fascism and one against Communism.

Pius XII, who was Pope until 1958, contributed much to the modern Catholic reverence of the papacy. Aristocratic, mystical, authoritarian, tireless, and a master diplomat, he was politically more conservative than his predecessor, and theologically more liberal. He entered into an alliance with Franco, but excommunicated all who would join the Communist party. While he was against innovations in theology on those questions that had to do with Counter-Reformation Catholic teachings, he allowed the use of modern historical and linguistic approaches in biblical research, encouraged reform in the liturgy, and could be "permissive" on selected moral issues—he did not insist that medical professionals make use of extraordinary technical means to preserve life, for example. Although he was much concerned about the plight of the poor in the Third World, he suppressed the French "priest-worker" movement (priests would literally become factory workers during the day) as it tried to reach the urban poor.

The supreme authority of the Pope was enhanced in the last decades of the nineteenth century and across the twentieth century by the official declaration at Vatican Council I in 1870 that the Pope must be considered infallible (and should always have been considered infallible) on matters of faith and morals when he invokes his extraordinary teaching authority. In actual fact, only one Pope on one occasion has made such an infallible pronouncement: in 1950 Pius XII declared that Mary must be believed to have been assumed, body and soul, into heaven. This was a highly spiritual teaching, a theological deduction based on the Christian belief in Mary's special privileges as the Mother of Jesus Christ. "Infallibity," then has had little effect on the content of Catholic teaching; but the teaching put such emphasis on the spiritual authority of the Pope, that it took another Council, almost a century later, to affirm the prerogatives of bishops, other clergy, and of all the Catholic people. The Second Vatican Council, which opened in 1962 under the leadership of Pius XII's genial and open successor, John XXIII, marked the beginning of an era where independent thought, creative spirituality, and human freedom have become more important to Catholics at large then papal infallibility.

Christian Missions and the Third World

In modern times, clergy, monks, and lay people traveled to parts of the world where Christianity is limited to very small areas or is not known at all. In the age of exploration and at the beginning of the period of European colonization the vast majority of the missionaries were Catholic, because they did not have family responsibilities and could easily go where they were sent. Catholic Spain sent a great number of missionaries to South America, not just to minister to Spanish immigrants, but to convert the indigenous peoples. Portugal sent missionaries to India, France sent missionaries to Canada, and so on. English, Dutch, German, and Scandinavian Protestant clergy were more rooted in the religious life of their homelands, and would move out to other parts of the world to minister to their own people, who were re-establishing their own kind of society in new lands.

By the nineteenth century, however, colonialism was a full-time occupation of European governments, and both Catholic and Protestant missionaries went out to all parts of the world, sometimes representing their governments more than their Christian communities, sometimes taking care of their own needs more than the needs of those they were preaching to, but primarily preaching that Christianity is truth and life for all peoples. Even the basic presentation of the Christian message was conditioned by the personalities and national backgrounds of the individual missionaries. In what is now India, Bangladesh, Pakistan, and Sri Lanka, a Western gospel was preached by Portuguese and British missionaries. In Indo-China the Christian religious influence was chiefly French, in China it was chiefly British, in Japan it was British and American, and in Indonesia, the influence was Dutch. By 1914 the entire African continent was divided up by the Portuguese, British, French, Spanish, Germans, Belgians, and Italians—the missionaries coming from the religions that predominated in those countries. Only two countries in Africa, Ethiopia and Liberia were not technically the colonies of some first-world power.

In many of these colonial areas a native Christianity developed over a number of generations, in spite of the strong European influence. In those areas where the indigenous religions were dependent on nature and magic, Christianity, with its powerful organization and sophisticated message, had a great deal of success; truths and rituals out of the Christian repertoire could be used to supplant those of the native religions. Elsewhere, the success of Christianity depended on the balance and depth of the world religion that had been established centuries before. If people's needs were fulfilled by Hinduism or Buddhism, there was much less call for Christianity. In other areas the competition was between Christian and Muslim missionaries, the Muslims also being somewhat latter-day arrivals in such areas as Indonesia.

Today, Christian leaders and thinkers place great importance on the success of the Christian implantations in the Third World. They are anxious lest Christianity be considered to be European, therefore white, and a first-world import. The old colonialism haunts Christian leaders in the Third-World countries, some of whom

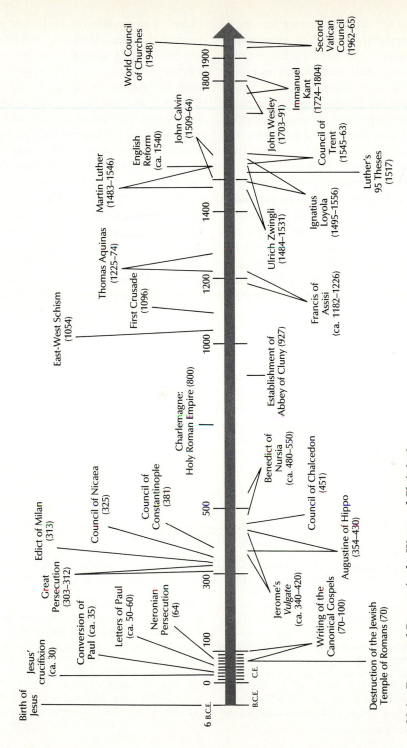

Major Events and Persons in the History of Christianity.

Birth of Jesus

Jesus' crucifixion (ca. 30)

Conversion of Paul (ca. 35)

Letters of Paul (ca. 50–60)

Neronian Persecution (64)

Great Persecution (303–312)

Edict of Milan (313)

Council of Nicaea (325)

Council of Constantinople (381)

East-West Schism (1054)

Thomas Aquinas (1225–74)

First Crusade (1096)

Martin Luther (1483–1546)

English Reform (ca. 1540)

John Calvin (1509–64)

World Council of Churches (1948)

John Wesley (1703–91)

Immanuel Kant (1724–1804)

Second Vatican Council (1962–65)

Council of Trent (1545–63)

Luther's 95 Theses (1517)

Ignatius Loyola (1495–1556)

Ulrich Zwingli (1484–1531)

Francis of Assisi (ca. 1182–1226)

Establishment of Abbey of Cluny (927)

Charlemagne: Holy Roman Empire (800)

Benedict of Nursia (ca. 480–550)

Council of Chalcedon (451)

Augustine of Hippo (354–430)

Jerome's Vulgate (ca. 340–420)

Writing of the Canonical Gospels (70–100)

Destruction of the Jewish Temple of Romans (70)

1800 1900

1400

1200

1000

500

300

100

0

6 B.C.E.

B.C.E.

C.E.

have become so thoroughly Europeanized that they themselves cannot fully empathize with their own people. Other Third-World leaders, after having adapted Christianity to their own backgrounds, find themselves at odds with the governing bodies of their Christian Churches. But the mainline Christian groups seem to be aware that their general failure to produce indigenous churches with indigenous leadership has to be repaired as well as possible. Christian communities founded in the Third World by European or American missionary efforts are considered to be Churches in their own right, not to be referred to as "the foreign missions." The expression "Younger Churches," coined at the Missionary Conference of Jerusalem in 1928, has come into general use. Africans, Indians, and Chinese are no longer viewed as objects for Western missionary work, but as partners in a common undertaking, the preaching of the message of Christ. Missionaries from the West are most often willing to work under native Church leaders.

Christian communities of the Third World may eventually become "missionaries" to the Churches of the First World. Catholic Sisters born and raised in Africa serve in hospitals and schools in France, Priests born in India serve in parishes in the United States, and Chinese Baptists and Methodists teach in North American Protestant seminaries—this comes at a time when there are few vocations to the Catholic Sisterhood in Europe and America, and less than five percent attendance at the "national" church services in former Christian countries such as Sweden, England, and France. Furthermore, the growth of Christian Churches in the Third World has brought home a very important object lesson to European and American Churches: that the first priority of Churches who believe themselves to possess a message of love and unity for all humankind must be unity within their own ranks. It became clear to the younger Churches that the old rivalries were ultimately destructive of Christianity itself. Cooperation of rival Christian denominations began in the Third World.

The World Council of Churches was founded in England as a forum for discussion and cooperation among all Christian groups. The Council has remained at the center of a developing movement for reconciliation—called the "ecumenical" ("worldwide") movement—although Catholicism has only token representation in the membership. However, the great Council of Catholic bishops, the Second Council of the Vatican, was a scene of significant reconciliation—though certainly not of reunion—of Catholicism with Protestantism and Eastern Orthodoxy.

The message of Christ is that the love of one person for another can bring about the presence of an all-good God and the perfection of the human race, which is to say the Kingdom of Heaven. Only when the Christian Churches are a living witness to love and unity will they fulfill the goals set for them by their founder.

NOTES

1. Paul Claudel, "Ma Conversion," quoted in Henri Guillemin, Le "Converti," Paul Claudel, étude (Paris: Gallimard, 1968), p. 15.
2. Augustine of Hippo, Confessions, 8:12, translated by Rex Warner (New York: New American Library, 1963), pp. 182–183.
3. C. H. Dodd, The Interpretation of the Fourth Gospel (Cambridge: Cambridge University Press, 1970), p. 8.
4. W. H. C. Frend, Martyrdom and Persecution in the Early Church (Grand Rapids: Baker, 1965), pp. 15–16.
5. Norman Perrin and Dennis Duling, The New Testament: An Introduction, 2d ed. (New York: Harcourt Brace Jovanovich, 1982), p. 43.
6. Ibid., p. 69.
7. Hippolytus, Apostolic Tradition, translated by Burton Scott Easton (Hamden, Conn.: Archon Books, 1962), pp. 35–36.
8. Eusebius of Caesarea, Epistle to the Caesareans, quoted in Justo L. González, The Story of Christianity, vol. 1 (New York: Harper & Row, 1984), p. 165.
9. Augustine of Hippo, The Spirit and the Letter, 27:48, translated by John Burnaby (Philadelphia: Westminster Press, 1940), p. 231.
10. Martin Luther, Preface to the Latin Writings, quoted in González, op. cit., vol. 2, pp. 19–20.
11. Peter Gay, The Enlightenment: An Interpretation, vol. 1: The Rise of Modern Paganism (New York: W. W. Norton, 1977), p. 8.

GLOSSARY

Abba Aramaic word for "Father," used by Christ and having special qualities of both reverence and familiarity.

Arianism doctrine in the early Church denying the true divinity of Christ.

Byzantium Greek city chosen by Constantine as the capital of the Eastern Roman Empire and center for the later development of Eastern Orthodox Christianity.

basilica early form of a building used for Christian worship, modeled on the Roman law-court and commercial exchange building of the same name.

canon list of inspired books that the Church regarded as composing the bible.

cathedral official church of a bishop of a specific region.

Christ title given to Jesus of Nazareth; greek translation of the Hebrew word for "Messiah."

Cluny monastery in Burgundy (France) that exercised decisive influence on the life of the Church in the eleventh and twelfth centuries.

confirmation a ritual whereby the grace of the Holy Spirit is conveyed in a new or fuller way to those who have already received it in baptism.

divine office obligatory vocal prayer of the Church, recited by clergy and monks, and others upon whom this duty is imposed.

dogma a religious truth established by divine revelation and defined by the Church.

eucharist the service of the Lord's Supper; from a greek word meaning "thanksgiving."

fundamentalist one who adheres to the literal inerrancy of scripture, and requires the same stance of other Christians and even of the State.

gentile the Jewish term for non-Jew, it later came to mean simply "foreigner."

gospel written book in which the Christian Gospel—or "Good News"—was set down.

Gnosticism a diversified group of religious movements putting emphasis on a special secret knowledge of the meaning of God and the universe.

grace a supernatural assistance of God, a sharing in the strength and life of God, for holiness and salvation.

Hellenistic world the Near Eastern culture that developed after the break-up of the empire of Alexander the Great.

heresy denial or doubt of any formal teaching of the Christian faith.

homoousios term used to indicate the relationship of the Son to the Father: "of one substance" with the Father.

incarnation teaching that the eternal Son of God took human flesh from his human mother.

Kingdom of God the sphere of God's influence: always present because God's power is unlimited, but belonging also to the future because it is not yet fully manifest.

liturgy an official prayer service of the Church.

logos a term that in ancient philosophy meant "reason," in Hellenistic philosophy signified an intermediary agent between God and the world, and in Christian theology was used of Christ as the Word of God.

Lord a title signifying kingship and divinity and attributed to Christ by the early Christians.

Manichaeism semi-Christian religion presupposing a primaeval conflict between Light and Darkness and requiring total self-discipline of its followers.

martyr a term meaning "witness," but gradually restricted to those who died because of their refusal to renounce Christianity.

monk member of a religious community for men, and living under vows of poverty, chastity, and obedience.

Monophysitism belief that in Christ there is a single, divine nature.

Nestorianism doctrine that there were two separate Persons in the Incarnate Christ, the one Divine, and the other Human.

ordination ceremony conferring powers of ministry.

orthodoxy right belief, as contrasted with heresy; a term formally adopted as the title of the Eastern Christian Church to distinguish it from the Nestorian and Monophysite Churches.

Pelagianism theological system that holds that humans take the initial and fundamental steps toward salvation by their own efforts.

pope title, meaning "Father," used of important bishops in the early Church; in the Western Church the use is restricted to the Bishop of Rome, spiritual leader of Roman Catholicism.

predestination belief that certain persons are infallibly guided to salvation by God; subject to a Christian controversy as to whether the divine decree of predestination is made with or without foreknowledge of an individual's behavior.

Protestant an adherent of one of the major Churches of the Reformation.

Reformation a term covering the activity of a number of reform movements in Christianity; in particular, the period of European reform deriving from the efforts of Martin Luther, Ulrich Zwingli, and John Calvin.

Roman Catholic a Christian whose faith and practice is in communion with the Bishop of Rome; used in particular of Catholicism as it has developed since the Reformation.

sacrament an official prayer service, said to be instituted by Christ; Christians differ on the number of sacraments.

Synoptic Gospels Gospels of Matthew, Mark, and Luke, which have large areas of subject matter in common, and can be consequently read together in parallel columns.

theology systematic, philosophical study of divinely revealed religious truths.

SUGGESTED READINGS

Primary Sources in Translation

The New English Bible, with Apocrypha. New York: Oxford University Press/Cambridge University Press, 1970.

ALAND, KURT. *Synopsis of the Four Gospels.* English ed. New York: United Bible Societies, 1982.

BETTENSON, HENRY, ed. *Documents of the Christian Church.* 2d ed. New York: Oxford University Press, 1963.

Secondary Sources

AHLSTROM, SYDNEY E. *A Religious History of the American People.* New Haven: Yale University Press, 1972.

AUNE, DAVID. *The New Testament in Its Literary Environment.* Philadelphia: Westminster Press, 1987.

BROWN, PETER. *Augustine of Hippo: A Biography.* Berkeley: University of California Press, 1967.

CHADWICK, HENRY. *The Early Church.* New York: Penguin Books, 1967.

CHADWICK, OWEN. *The Reformation.* New York: Penguin Books, 1972.

CRAGG, G. R. *The Church and the Age of Reason, 1648–1789.* New York: Penguin Books, 1967.

CROSS, F. L., and E. A. LIVINGSTON, eds. *Dictionary of the Christian Church.* 2d ed. Oxford: Oxford University Press, 1974.

DODD, C. H. *The Interpretation of the Fourth Gospel.* Cambridge: Cambridge University Press, 1970.

FITZMYER, JOSEPH A. "Pauline Theology," in *The Jerome Biblical Commentary,* edited by Raymond E. Brown, Joseph A. Fitzmyer, and Roland E. Murphy. Englewood Cliffs, N.J.: Prentice-Hall, 1968.

FOX, ROBIN LANE. *Pagans and Christians.* New York: Alfred A. Knopf, 1987.

FREND, W. H. C. *Martyrdom and Persecution in the Early Church.* Grand Rapids: Baker, 1981.

GERRISH, BRIAN, ed. *Reformers in Profile.* Philadelphia: Fortress Press, 1967.

GONZÁLEZ, JUSTO L. *The Story of Christianity.* 2 vols. New York: Harper & Row, 1984.

JEREMIAS, JOACHIM. *Jerusalem in the Time of Jesus.* Philadelphia: Fortress Press, 1969.

KELLY, J. N. D. *Early Christian Doctrines.* New York: Harper & Row, 1959.

OZMENT, STEVEN. *The Age of Reform, 1250–1550: An Intellectual and Religious History of Late Medieval and Reformation Europe.* New Haven: Yale University Press, 1980.

PERRIN, NORMAN, and DENNIS C. DULING. *The New Testament: An Introduction.* 2d ed. New York: Harcourt, Brace, Jovanovich, 1982.

VIDLER, ALEC R. *The Church in an Age of Revolution: 1789 to the Present Day.* New York: Penguin Books, 1971.

WARE, TIMOTHY. *The Orthodox Church.* New York: Penguin Books, 1964.

9

Islam

Translation of the Quranic basmalah: "In the name of God, Most Gracious, Most Merciful."

In relation to the other major religious traditions, Islam is relatively young. The year 1979 marked the beginning of the year 1400 according to the Muslim calendar. As Islam has spread from its beginnings in the Arabian peninsula, it has encompassed a wide variety of cultural and ethnic groups. The "World of Islam," as the area in which Muslims predominate has traditionally been called, thus represents a great deal of regional diversity. Yet a common pattern of religious and social life based on Islam has given this world a sense of unity that is reflected in the art, architecture, and urban life of major Muslim centers all over the world.

The encounter of the World of Islam with the growing military and economic power of European colonialism from the seventeenth to the twentieth centuries disrupted the character and patterns of life of most Muslim peoples, whose lives came to be governed or influenced by the policies of the respective colonial powers. Much of their recent history reflects the desire on the part of newly created Muslim nation-states to free themselves from dependence, and to gain greater control over their affairs. The pressures and challenges generated by global politics and nation-building have not always made the task easy. As a result, the effort to create modes of life that would reflect past values and provide a sense of continuity with the Muslim heritage is still fraught with tension. But most Muslims continue to perceive Islam as more than a mere source of religious values. In their view, it is still the basis for a whole way of life.

The followers of Islam, properly called *Muslims,* are expected to number over one billion by the end of the twentieth century. They are concentrated for the most part in the developing countries of Asia and Africa, stretching from as far east as the Phillipines and westwards to Morocco, including places such as western China, southern Russia, and Yugoslavia. Migration and conversion in more recent times has led to the emergence of a small but significant Muslim presence in western

Europe and North America. The accompanying map illustrates the extent to which Islam is practiced throughout the world.

Beginnings: Arabia Before Islam

The Arabian peninsula where Islam had its beginnings in the seventh century C.E. was mostly an arid region populated by nomadic tribesmen called Bedouins. To the north were Arab kingdoms that had contacts with the two major empires of the time, the Byzantine and the Persian Sassanian empires. In the south were other centers of ancient Arab civilization in Yemen. The peninsula was also dotted with growing urban centers and oases. Among these, the most important was the city of Mecca. It served as a center for the caravan trade routes that crisscrossed the peninsula. Besides its significance as an important trading center, Mecca had a religious sanctuary to which the Arabs were drawn for annual rites of pilgrimage, which also became an occasion for expressing a shared cultural and linguistic heritage.

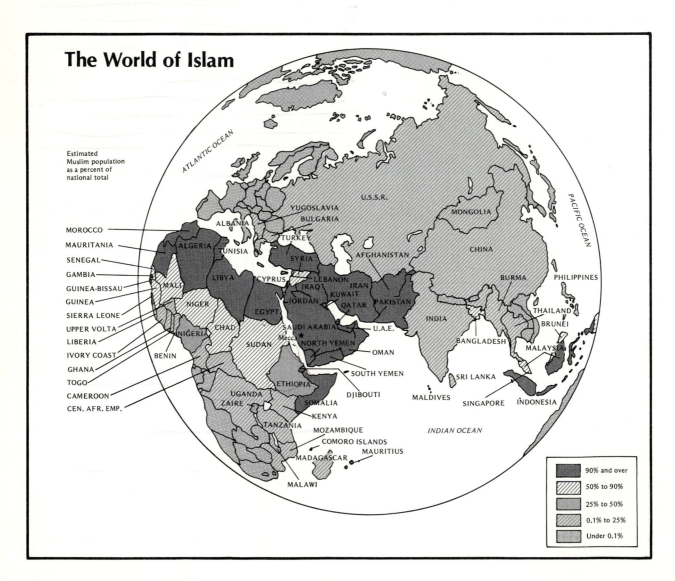

The World of Islam

Estimated Muslim population as a percent of national total

90% and over
50% to 90%
25% to 50%
0.1% to 25%
Under 0.1%

Prayer Scene. *These Mulsims are at prayer in a desert locale. Prayer carpets have been spread out and the worshipers are kneeling in the direction facing Mecca.* (Courtesy of Fred Denny)

Bedouin life was governed by tribal custom. Primary allegiance was to the tribe that formed the focal point of the nomadic existence. Economic life was based on the size of their camel herds, on occasional raiding of caravans, and on trading with settled city communities. In religious life, each tribe possessed certain deities that its members worshiped. The sanctuary of Mecca contained shrines of some important goddesses, in addition to a host of other divinities. An element of religious cosmopolitanism was also provided to the peninsula by the presence of small Jewish communities and to a lesser extent Christians.

The importance of trade and caravan routes across Arabia led to the growth of a merchant community in Mecca. The merchants had developed their own organiza-tions to control and consolidate their hold on the economy of Mecca, and they maintained the religious sanctuary to protect Mecca's importance as a pre-Islamic center of pilgrimage. Also in order to safeguard its trade, they established cordial relations with the Bedouins, so that they might not raid the caravans and thereby destroy the mainstay of Mecca's economy.

The Life of Muhammad

The Early Years in Mecca

It was in such a milieu that Muhammad, the Prophet of Islam, was born about 570 C.E. Muslim tradition provides a record of the major events of his life, furnishing us with a picture of the man, his mission, and the impact of his personality and life on the Arab society of his time. The first years of his life were marred by the deaths of both parents and the grandfather who had come to take care of him. He grew up in the home of his uncle, Abu Talib, a merchant in the city. Much of his early life was spent helping his uncle, but as a young man Muhammad also came to be admired by other Meccans for his trustworthiness and sincerity. His reputation and personal qualities led to his marriage at the age of twenty-five to Khadija, a widow whom he had assisted in business; henceforth, he became an important and trusted citizen of Mecca.

Although a prosperous and well-established merchant in his own right, Muhammad never felt fully content to be part of a society whose values he considered to be materialistic and devoid of true religious significance. He sought such a significance in his own life by spending long solitary hours in a cave on nearby Mount Hira. There were others in Arab society, referred to as *hanifs,* or the ''pure'' ones, who also devoted their lives to contemplation and asceticism. Muhammad, however did not choose to cut himself off from his family and society. Khadija gave birth to several children; two sons died in infancy, but four daughters survived, among whom the best known was the youngest, Fatima. Muhammad thus had ongoing responsibilities both as a father and as a citizen in Mecca's public life. His most profound moments, however, came through the acts of solitary meditation and self-contemplation on Mount Hira. Out of these experiences emerged the prophetic call that was to alter dramatically Arab and world history in time to come.

During one such evening in the cave, Muhammad heard a voice. The words he heard heralded a series of revelations that were to come to him for the rest of his life. They are recorded in the *Quran,* which is for Muslims a faithful recording of the entire revelation of God through Muhammad, his chosen Prophet to humankind. These first words called upon Muhammad to

Recite: In the name of your Lord who created—created Man from a clot [of blood].
Recite: Your Lord is Most Noble,

Who taught by the Pen,
taught Man what he did not know. (*Surah* 96:1–5)[*]

The initial effect of this experience was to plunge Muhammad into a state of anguish and fear. He hurried home to his wife, from whom he sought solace and help in understanding the significance of what had happened to him. These moments of anguish, plus the ambivalence he felt about the nature of the experience and his own uncertainty regarding the call, indicate that the role asked of him was not one he had consciously sought, nor one to which he was led by any self-seeking ambition. Into his human consciousness had erupted the full force of a revelatory experience. It was this reality that he gradually and steadily came to learn and believe, until he was at last driven to proclaim it as the truth. In addition, this comprehension of his role as a messenger of divine revelation helped him to understand his mission in the light of prophets and messengers who had come and gone in earlier times and places. Henceforth his work would represent a continuing link in the transmission of the message, which according to the Quran had begun ages ago and was being channelled through him to the society in which he lived, and beyond. At this time Muhammad was forty years old.

His first convert was Khadija, whose support and companionship provided necessary reassurance and strength. He also won the support of some close relatives and friends. Gradually he began to proclaim the message to others in Mecca. The Meccans responded initially with puzzlement and even amusement. It astonished them to see a trusted and respected citizen claiming to be the recipient of a divinely revealed message that told them to forsake their gods, laws, and customs. Some even pronounced him mad. Muhammad persisted, however, preaching openly with increasing fervor.

The style and poetic quality of the early message, as preserved in the Quran, conveys a powerful sense of this message.

In the name of God, most Gracious, most
    Merciful.
By the night as it enshrouds,

---

[*] Wherever the Quran is quoted in this chapter, the first Arabic numeral indicates the number of the *Surah* or chapter and the second set of numerals the number of the verses (*ayat*).

By the day as it illuminates,
by Him who created the male and the female
indeed your affairs lead to various ends.
For who gives [of himself] and acts righteously,
and conforms to goodness,
We will give him ease.
But as for him who is niggardly deeming himself
  self-sufficient and rejects goodness,
We will indeed ease his path to adversity.
Nor shall his wealth save him as he perishes,
for Guidance is from Us
and to Us belongs the Last and the First. (92:1–14)

The basic themes of the early message were the majesty of the One, unique God; the futility of idol worship; the threat of judgment; and the necessity of faith, compassion, and morality in human affairs. All of these themes represented an attack on the materialism and idolatry prevalent in Mecca and among the Bedouins.

These attacks resulted in mounting opposition from the tribe of Quraysh, which controlled Mecca. Since Muhammad was a member of the same tribe, they tried at first to exert pressure on Abu Talib to stop his nephew from preaching; they then tried to bribe Muhammad by offering him an important role in Meccan affairs, but to no avail. When these efforts failed, the merchants began persecuting Muhammad and his small band of followers. Some of the new converts had to leave their homes and seek refuge in Ethiopia in 615. Meanwhile Muhammad continued to face opposition and hostility, which eventually extended to a commercial and social boycott of his family. Khadija, who had been a devoted companion, and Abu Talib, his uncle, both died during this period of trial. Muhammad's attempts to seek converts outside the city of Mecca failed. Persecution often turned to violence, endangering the lives and families of the converts. This period was emotionally for Muhammad the lowest point in his mission. A chapter of the Quran captures the mood exquisitely as it seeks to give solace to the Prophet:

By the radiance of morning and the hush of night
Your Lord has neither forsaken you nor left you forlorn;
and the Last shall be better for you than the First.
Your Lord shall give and you shall be satisfied.
Did he not find you an orphan and shelter you?
Did he not find you erring, and guide you?
Did he not find you needy, and enrich you?

As for the orphan, do not oppress him
and as for the beggar, do not spurn him,
and as for your Lord's blessing, declare it openly. (93)

Muhammad also drew comfort from the knowledge revealed to him about other prophets such as Abraham, Joseph, and Moses, each of whom had been persecuted, tested, and challenged by seemingly invincible forces. Their eventual success testified to divine support and ultimate victory. Sustained by these beliefs, Muhammad's community continued to adhere to the message, worshiping together and drawing courage from his example and leadership.

Some distance north of Mecca lay the city of Medina, then called Yathrib. It was an agricultural community with differences among its major groups. There was also a Jewish community there, so that the Arabs of the city were conversant with monotheistic beliefs. Following a meeting of some of its inhabitants with Muhammad, they invited him to come to Yathrib to arbitrate some of the differences among the various factions. They also responded favorably to his teaching and pledged him their support. Meanwhile, the Quraysh were plotting to kill Muhammad. Before such a plan could be put into action, he asked his followers in Mecca to join those who had already left for Yathrib. Under the cover of darkness, he and his followers succeeded in eluding the pursuit of his enemies, arriving in the city that would henceforth carry his title—*Madinat al Nabi* (The City of the Prophet) or Medina, as it is generally known. This event in the year 622 is known as the *Hijrah*, or migration, the date from which the Islamic calendar would henceforth begin. The year of migration thus marks the first year of the new lunar calendar.

The Years in Medina

The city of Medina provided the first real opportunity for Muhammad and his followers to organize themselves into a community. The community included the Arab residents of Medina, some of whom had converted to the new teaching, and the Jews who lived there. The community was called the *Ummah*. Muhammad was recognized as its leader by virtue of his status as Allah's Prophet, and all the groups agreed to support each other in the event of Meccan opposition. The Jews were permitted to continue their way of life and recognized as "people of the Book" to whom God had revealed a message in the past through other prophets. But Muhammad also sought to attract them to the new faith.

The growth of the *Ummah* in Medina, and Muhammad's continuing efforts to spread the new faith further antagonized the Meccans. For the new Muslim *Ummah*, the effort to win converts and exercise control over their own destiny signified a *jihad*, a struggle in the way of God. The word *jihad* literally means "struggle" or "striving." In early Muslim history it signified the military struggles to establish and consolidate the *Ummah*, the task of spreading Islam through preaching and conversion, and the effort to establish a social and economic order based on the teachings of the Quran. This struggle for power resulted in a series of military battles. The first of these, the Battle of Badr, took place in 624. The battle pitted the smaller, somewhat apprehensive army of Muhammad against the Quraysh contingent, which far exceeded them in numbers and weapons. Muhammad led the Muslims, organizing them in battle. The Muslims, standing their ground, eventually forced the enemy to withdraw and finally to flee from the field of battle. The victory was a tremendous boost to the growing *Ummah*. It reinforced their faith and morale, and consolidated their belief in Muhammad's divine mission and leadership.

In subsequent battles, the Muslims became the dominant religious and political force in the region. It was then decided that those Muslims who had once been forced out of Mecca should now have an opportunity to visit it, and a truce was arranged. In a subsequent visit to Mecca in 629, Muhammad and his followers returned in triumph to take control of the city. The final victory was a peaceful one. To underline his ties with the city, Muhammad invited his enemies to embrace Islam, shun their past way of life, and become members of the *Ummah*.

In the next two years the new religion found many converts. Religious practices became established and a revealed "law" governed relationships within the *Ummah*, which now had its own distinctive Islamic identity. Muhammad sent emissaries to invite other Arab tribes to Islam, and also sent representatives to the rulers of surrounding states and to the emperors of Byzantium and Persia. It is clear that he envisaged his message as not being limited to the Arabs, but sought to spread the message of Islam beyond the borders of Arabia.

By 632 the *Ummah* embraced almost the whole of Arabia, its members bound together by the acceptance of the message and messenger of Allah. In the same year, Muhammad undertook his last visit to Mecca, a farewell pilgrimage to the sanctuary that had now become a symbol of Allah's revelation.

The Death and Significance of Muhammad

Muhammad died later in Medina on the twelfth day of *Rabi al Awwal*, the year 10 of the new Muslim era. It is said that many of his followers refused to accept his death. Then one of his trusted companions, Abu Bakr, reminded them of the Quranic verse that states:

Muhammad is but a messenger. Many messengers before him have come and gone. Were he to die or be killed, would you take to your heels? Those who turn back cause no loss to Allah and He will surely reward those who are grateful to Him. (3:144)

Within the Arabian setting, Muhammad gave an impetus to the lives of his followers that was to lead them to spread Islam far beyond the borders of Arabia. His mission encompassed several goals, but primary among these were the goals of creating a society cemented by loyalty to Islam rather than to tribe; linking his people to the worship of One God who had chosen to speak to them through one of their own in their own language; and providing a framework of values, actions, and institutions that would continue to bind them together so that, in the words of the Quran, they might become "an Ummah of the middle way and a witness to humanity as the Prophet was a witness to them" (2:143).

After the death of the Prophet, Muslim scholars set about collecting material on his life. These consisted of the *hadith*, a standardized report of things he did and said, transmitted by his companions or members of his family. These traditions were then passed on to succeeding generations. These *hadith* and the chain of transmitters were in turn submitted to a test of authentication to enable scholars to judge the relative validity of the accounts. The corpus of the Prophet's sayings and actions thus constitutes an important source of values in Islam. For Muslims, they are a model and represent an ideal pattern, referred to as the *Sunnah*, meaning custom or practice of the Prophet. The *Sunnah* provides Muslims with a pattern they can emulate. In so doing they look to Muhammad as an exemplary human being, who had realized in his own life the ideals of Islam revealed by God.

Muhammad's practice of prayer and devotion to God; his role as husband and parent; his example of humility, compassion, justice, and brotherhood; and his acts of kindness to children, orphans, the disadvantaged, and animals all serve as a model of proper conduct. It is this role of Muhammad envisioned as teacher, exemplar, and ideal that has the greatest impact on the ordinary lives of Muslims and is illustrated vividly in the *hadith* given below as they have come to be recorded and preserved. Generally, each *hadith* is preceded by the name of a transmitter or chain of narrators and then a report of what "The Messenger of God said: . . ."

To pursue knowledge is obligatory on every Muslim, man and woman.

The ink of the scholar is holier than the blood of martyrs.

Paradise lies at the feet of mothers.

None of you (truly) believes until he wishes for his brother what he wishes for himself.

Acting justly between two people is an act of charity, a good word is charity; and removing a harmful thing from the road is charity.

Let him who believes in God and the Day of Judgment refrain from harming his neighbor, let him honor his guest and either speak good or hold his tongue.

Those who do not show tenderness and love, cannot expect to have tenderness shown to them.

He who shows concern for the widows and the disadvantaged is like one who struggles in the way of God or fasts by day and rises at night for prayer.

Adore God as though you see Him; if you do not see Him, He none the less sees you.

God said "Heaven and earth cannot contain Me, but the heart of my devotee does contain Me."*

Imitation of the Prophet's behavior thus represents a goal of all Muslims. Although Muhammad is emulated and deeply loved as God's final messenger, he is not

* This last type of *hadith* is called *Hadith Qudsi* ("Holy Tradition") because according to tradition the Prophet quotes God directly.

the object of worship. His tomb in Medina is visited by Muslims and prayers are offered there; but no attempts have been made to convert the tomb into an object of undue veneration, and no images or likenesses of Muhammad are preserved. In fact, Muslim tradition has resisted any such attempts, to guard against possible deification of the person of the Prophet.

In their daily prayers, and whenever his name is mentioned, Muslims invoke blessings on Muhammad and his descendants as a continuing mark of remembrance and gratitude. In addition to being a model of piety and of continuing struggle at all levels of life against adversity, his life is also a paradigm or ideal model of spiritual life and love, of one who attained closeness and intimacy with God. Besides being the object of historical writing, his life has also been a rich source of poetry and folk literature written in praise and love of his work and example. Above all, for all Muslims he is the recipient of God's final message, enshrined for all time in the revelation contained in the Quran.

The Quran

For Muslims, the Quran is the faithful and complete recording of all revelation that came in the form of divine inspiration to Muhammad. The language of the revelation was Arabic, and the work of systematizing and organizing the text of the revelation is believed by Muslims to have been undertaken by Muhammad himself.

Revelation came to Muhammad over a period of twenty-two years. It came in powerful, jolting experiences. Often, as described by Muhammad to others, it was like the tolling of a bell, holding him in its grip until it was over, sometimes leaving him shivering and cold. To those who doubted that the revelation was genuine, the Quran had this to say:

By the stars as they retreat, your companion [i.e. Muhammad] is neither mistaken nor deceived. Nor is he speaking out of his own whims. Indeed his words are nothing but a genuine inspiration. He who is mighty in power, endowed with strength has taught him.
Erect, away in the far horizon, he stood, then came closer and descended until he was two bows-length away, drawing closer and revealed to His servant that which He revealed. The heart does not lie for he did have the vision. (53:1–11)

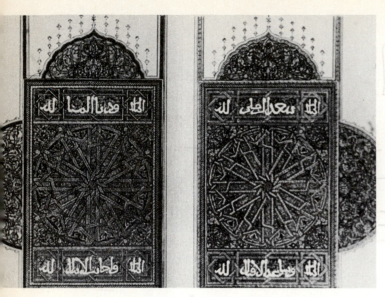

Quranic Calligraphy. *This is a page from an ancient copy of the Quran.* (Courtesy of Aramco Magazine)

The process of revelation thus involved vision as well as audition. Elsewhere the medium of revelation is described as the "Spirit of Holiness" (16:102), which brought the message to Muhammad. It is this cumulative process revealed at successive intervals that is described specifically as the "Quran" in 17:106. The word literally means "recitation," and it was in this recited form that Muhammad conveyed it to his followers.

During his lifetime, this continuous revelation provided Muhammad with the basis on which the religion developed. Whereas most of the revelations were memorized by the followers, Muhammad also had scribes put the revelation down in writing. Certain individuals in the growing Muslim community were noted for their powers of memorization and recitation, and they acted as teachers of the new converts.

By the time of Muhammad's death, the Quran existed in writing and had also been memorized by many of his followers. Soon after his death, attempts were made to establish a complete written text. The process was undertaken to eliminate any risk of violating the sacred text or of having differences regarding its contents. Since most of the transmission of the Quran among new converts was being done orally, it was also important to establish a fixed, written text. On the basis of Muham-

mad's own systematization and arrangement, a written text was compiled and copies sent to all areas of the new Islamic empire. For Muslims, therefore, the Quranic text has existed unchanged for fourteen centuries and is believed to contain the complete message revealed to Muhammad.

The Quran is divided into 114 chapters, each called a *surah*. The number of verses in each chapter varies greatly, each verse being referred to as an *ayah*. After a short opening *surah*, the chapters are arranged according to length, the longest ones coming first, followed successively by shorter ones. The chapters have titles, either indicating the main content or referring to a word or phrase from the text. All of the chapters, with the exception of *Surah* 9, begin with the formula, the *basmalah*, "In the name of God, most Gracious, most Merciful." Chapters are also identified as having been revealed in Mecca or Medina, or as having verses revealed in both places. Thus Muslims also recognize a chronological order of revelation.

The aspect of recitation is the key to understanding the impact of the Quran on its hearers. The Quran is meant to be recited, to be heard, and to be experienced. It is impossible to convey the majesty and power of the Arabic recitation in any other language in which the Quran may be rendered. The power of the "Word of God" for a Muslim lies not only on its impact on the mind, but also on the heart. One of the sciences developed to maintain this tradition is that of proper modes of recitation of the Quran. Muslims often gather in groups and listen to exponents of this art, and there is even today an international competition held every year to find the best reciters of the Quran.

The language of the Quran pervades all walks of Muslim life, influencing even the mode of writing Arabic and, subsequently, the other languages used by Muslims that adopted the Arabic script, such as Persian, Turkish, Urdu, Hausa, and Swahili. The art of calligraphy developed from the Quranic text represents much of the aesthetic impulse in Muslim art, and the written text is given the same devoted reverence as is the art of recitation. Calligraphy, in all its elaborate forms, is the means of providing an experience for the eye, as is the recited word for the ear. The art of calligraphy, coupled with illumination and coloring, has produced copies of the Quran that represent some of the most skilled creations

A Quran School. *A children's Quran school in Indonesia. Adjacent to a mosque, the school is where children learn to recite and memorize the Quran.* (Courtesy of Fred Denny)

of decorative art in Islam. Much of this calligraphic art influences the decoration of places of worship and the tradition of the arts in the Muslim world.

A variety of Quranic formulae, such as "in the name of God" (*"Bismillah"*), "If God wills" (*"Insha'llah"*), "Glory be to God" (*"Subhanallah"*), are an integral part of the daily life of Muslims. Even the physical presence of the Quran is considered a source of blessing. Verses are recited during moments of personal and family crisis, occasions of celebration and joy, and the moments of birth and death; a copy of the Quran is given an honored place in the house, where it is generally placed at a level higher than other belongings and furnishings. Muslims often carry a text from the Quran on their persons in a small ornamental amulet.

The Quran also became the starting point for the Muslim search for knowledge. It provided a new language, a new tool of inquiry, a new mode of expression, and a means to explore new vistas of knowledge. The effort to understand the Quranic message gave rise to the sciences related to linguistics and grammar, primarily of Arabic. Muslim scholars also devoted themselves to clarifying and explaining the Quran through works of exegesis known as *tafsir*. The study of the Quran has thus been at the heart of all Muslim scholarship and has given the intellectual and scientific endeavors of the Islamic world and a great sense of unity in the quest for new knowledge.

Quranic Teachings: Fundamental Beliefs

The greatest impact of the Quran from the earliest period of Islam has been the world-view it teaches and the guidelines for daily life it provides. These have served as the basis for Islamic beliefs and practices that have continued to remain normative for all Muslims to the present. Among the beliefs, there are certain basic concepts that are regarded as fundamental for all Muslims.

Tawhid, *the Unity of God*

The central concept around which all Quranic teaching revolves is that of *tawhid*, the unity or oneness of Allah, the Quranic name for God. Such a concept emphasizes a rigorous monotheism, stating Allah to be a unique absolute Reality. It is best expressed in a Quranic chapter said to be revealed in response to questions asked of Muhammed concerning the nature of God:

Say: He, Allah, is One, the Ultimate Source,
He does not give birth, nor was He born [of anyone]
and there is nothing comparable to Him. (112)

The unity of God is emphasized repeatedly in the Quran and echoed in other verses such as the following:

And your God is One God,
There is no God but Him,
the most Gracious, the most Merciful. (2:163)

In denying plurality, the Quran rejects all forms of idolatry, disallows any association of other divinities with God, and specifically denies all other definitions of God that might compromise unity, such as the Christian dogma of the Trinity. Thus, in Islam Allah is the sole reality on whom the existence of everything else depends.

One aspect of this oneness is expressed on God's creative power. The Quran also refers to God as *Rabb al Alameen*, the Lord of all creation (literally "the worlds"). The whole of the cosmos, nature as well as humanity, is created and sustained by God. This notion of God's sovereignty is expressed in the well-known "verse of the Throne":

Allah, there is no god but He,
the Living, the Eternal.
Neither slumber nor sleep seizes Him.
To Him belongs what is in
the heavens and in the earth.
Who can intercede with Him,
except by His permission?
He knows what lies before
them and after them
and they know nothing of his knowledge,

save such as He wills.
His throne encompasses the heavens and the earth
and He never wearies of preserving them.
He is Sublime, the Exalted. (2:255)

Although One, God is known by many names, which are referred to in the Quran as "the most beautiful names" (7:180). Muslim tradition has established a sequence of ninety-nine of these names of God, and the Muslim rosary contains a chain of ninety-nine beads, in a thrice thirty-three arrangement, so that the names may be recollected during prayer. These names are also a key to understanding God, because they focus on divine attributes such as the *Compassionate, Merciful, Just, Mighty, First, Last, Eternal, One whom no vision can grasp,* and yet *He who is ever near.* Among the images used to portray God's nature, none is perhaps as striking as that of "light":

Allah is the light of the heavens and of the earth
The symbol of his light is a niche,
within which there is a lamp,
the lamp enclosed in a glass,
the glass as though it were a shining star
which is lit from a blessed tree—
an olive neither of the East nor of the
West, whose oil gives forth light though
no fire touches it—light upon light—
Allah guides to His light whom He pleases
and He strikes parables for humankind and
of all things He is aware. (24:35)

Although transcendent in nature, God is still close to creation. He is viewed as being as close to human beings as their jugular vein, responsive to human appeals, and, above all, universal: "To Allah belong the East and the West: wherever you turn, there is His Face. He is all-present, all-knowing" (2:115).

Communication from God

Next to *tawhid* comes the concept of God's revelation to creation, primarily through messengers who have communicated His will. In Islam such communication is seen as a process that has accompanied human history from its beginnings. It establishes as the purpose of this history the constant interaction between God and human beings. Continuing communication has come either through messengers, some of whom are named and identified in the Quran, or through scriptures that have been revealed to the messengers for their peoples. The Quran states, ''To every people have we sent a messenger'' (16:36) and ''There is no people to whom a warner has not been sent'' (35:24).

Among the ones identified by the Quran and referred to repeatedly are biblical figures such as Noah, Abraham, Moses, and Jesus. All of them are seen as coming from the same One God:

We have inspired you [Muhammad] as We inspired Noah and the prophets after him, as We inspired Abraham, Ishmael, Issac, Jacob and the tribes; and Jesus, Job, Jonah, Aaron, and Solomon; as we gave to David the Psalms and Messengers of whom we have spoken to you and others that we have not mentioned. (4:163–164)

God eventually spoke to Muhammad, who is regarded as the ''Seal of the Prophets'' (33:40), with whom this process of communication through messengers reached its most perfect stage in the revelation that is the Quran. This final revelation completed the process of communication, while at the same time it supersedes all previous revelations.

Muhammad and all the biblical and other prophets, however, are to be considered as human beings through whom God has chosen to communicate. They may be offered great respect, but in the Quranic view they can never be the object of worship, which is due to God alone.

Creations of God

Nature and the Universe. Although the primary means through which God communicates are messengers and revelation, the universe as a whole is also a sign from God. The Quranic universe unfolds in a harmonious pattern, each element in balance with the others, and it is this sense of natural order and equilibrium that is pointed out as a sign of God's creative power and unity. His power extends also to other created things in nature that are endowed with qualities than enable them to function in an ordered way. A good example cited in the Quran is the bee:

And your Lord inspired the bee saying: ''Make your hives in the hills and the trees'' . . . there comes from them [bees] a

finely colored drink, with the power to heal. Indeed here is a sign for those who ponder. (16:68–69)

The whole of nature is created to conform to God's will. In this sense all of creation can be understood to be paying homage to and worshiping God:

The seven heavens and the earth and all that is in them glorify Him; there is nothing that does not praise Him but you do not understand their praise. (17:44)

Angels, **Jinn,** *and the Unseen.* Among God's other creations referred to in the Quran are spiritual beings such as angels, *jinn,* and those elements referred to as the ''unseen.'' The function of angels is to protect and pray for forgiveness for all on earth and to undertake errands on behalf of God. The *jinn,* in contrast, may be good or bad, and human beings can often fall prey to such spirits and may even falsely worship them. The ''unseen'' is that which human beings have no direct knowledge of and constitutes a realm that lies beyond human understanding. Among the angels, mention is also made of Satan, the symbol of disobedience to God whose function is to lead people astray (4:119–120).

Thus, besides the realms of the cosmos and the natural world, the Quran recognizes a variety of other creations that have their function in an ordered, created universe. Nevertheless, the Quran's central message is for those regarded as the most honored among God's creation, human beings.

Human Beings. Human beings have a special place within creation (95:4). They are special because in creating human beings, God endowed them with a capacity to know and respond to Him greater than that given to other creatures. They are also special because built into the human condition was the notion of choice, by which they could either fulfill their potential as the most honored among God's creation or sink to a level furthest away from God by disobeying or denying Him. This freedom of choice is best illustrated in the Quranic account of the creation of Adam. Having shaped Adam from clay, breathed into him His own spirit, and taught him the knowledge of all things, God asked the angels to bow down to Adam. One of the angels refused and thus became Iblis, or Satan, who henceforth would attempt to lead humans away from God. His first target was Adam, who succumbed, came to realize his error, was forgiven by God and returned to his original status. Adam is thus the symbol of two possibilities of human conduct. Those who accept the message of the Quran are addressed as follows:

O humankind! We have created you as male and female and have made you nations and peoples that you may come to know and understand one another. The noblest of you in the sight of Allah are the most pious. (49:13)

Those who choose not to accept this path are compared to those

Who are like those who light a fire
Which sheds a light all around
And Allah puts out the light, leaving them
in a state of darkness—deaf, dumb and blind. (2:17–18)

Ultimately, human conduct is subject to judgment, expressed in the Quran as a "Day of Resurrection." It is on this occasion that all individuals will realize the fruits of their actions:

And the fate of every one we have made the individual's own responsibility [literally: fastened to one's own neck] and We shall bring forth on the Day of Resurrection, a record that will reveal all. (17:13)

Both heaven and hell are depicted with dramatic vividness in the Quran. The reward of heaven is described as

Gardens of eternity which they will enter along with all of their ancestors, spouses and descendants who have acted righteously. From every gate will come angels greeting them "Peace be with you who persevered." Joyous will be the abode! (13:23)

Hell is portrayed as the antithesis of this, a place of suffering, punishment, and anguish, an inferno for the wretched.

Finally, when the Quran comes to define ideal human behavior, moral and spiritual perspectives ultimately determine whether one reflects Islamic goals or not:

By (the Token of) Time (through the Ages)
    Verily Man is in loss
Except such as have Faith
    and do righteous deeds
    and join together
    in the mutual teaching
    of Truth, and of
Patience and Constancy.
    (103, from the translation of Yusuf Ali, *The Holy Quran*)

A parallel is thus established between human beings, nature, and other creatures who submit to the will of God. In that sense all are *muslim* for they participate in a universal act of submission implied in the word *Islam*. However, it is only persons, because of their God-given capacity to know and respond to his message, who can attain through their own intelligence to the highest state of being *muslim*. This state implies both peace and fulfillment, since human action can discover and conform to the Divine Will, thus actualizing "Islam" as the harmonious, nondichotomous order that results when all creation works in harmony rather than conflict with divine purpose.

Ummah: *The Community in Islam*

The Quran regards individuals as part of a community in which the totality of Islamic values and goals can be expressed and realized. First accomplished in Medina, the setting and the context in which this is done is called *Ummah:*

You are the best Ummah ever brought forth
so that you might enjoin righteousness and forbid evil.
    (3:110)

The *Ummah* is thus the embodiment of the model behavior expected of society and individuals, and as such represents an example to other human societies. It also embraces the wider goal in the Quran of maintaining a balance between the material and spiritual aspects of life. It is significant that the *Hijrah* of the Prophet constitutes a major turning point for Muslim history, since it marks the transition of the early Muslims from a state where they could not give full expression in society to Islamic norms, to one where such norms could be given concrete expression in personal and social life. The implications of the *Ummah* as a basis of social, political, and moral order will be examined in greater detail later in this chapter.

Quranic Teachings: Major Practices

During the lifetime of the Prophet Muhammad, the Quranic teaching on the practice of the faith and the organization of the community came to be elaborated and certain basic ritual practices emerged. These are often termed *pillars,* and have come to be regarded as religious practices that anchor human relationships with God and with others within the *Ummah.*

Shahadah, *the Profession of Faith*

"There is no God but Allah, and Muhammad is His messenger" (*"La ilaha illa Allah, wa Muhammad rasul Allah"*) is the statement of Muslim acceptance of the basis of Islam. This profession is whispered at birth, at death, during daily prayers, and at virtually all other events of significance in individual and community life. For a new convert to Islam, it represents the initial act of commitment that henceforth leads to an acceptance of all other aspects of Islam. The profession is also a statement of faith, inasmuch as it comprises essential elements of belief. The first statement (*"la ilaha illa Allah"*) affirms acceptance of the absolute unity of God and the second statement (*"wa Muhammad rasul Allah"*) relates this unity to the medium through which the Absolute becomes manifested. This manifestation thus makes it possible for human beings to respond to God in this world. The *shahadah* thus links God, the Prophet, and the believers.

Salat, Dhikr, *and* Du'a: *Acts of Worship*

Three practices articulate the Quranic concept of worship. One, defined as *salat,* is the formal ritual prayer for which both patterns and times are indicated, and further elaborated, based on Prophetic practice and tradition. The others, referred to as *dhikr* and *du'a,* represent individual attempts to draw near to God in a more personal relationship. These aspects of worship are referred to in the Quran as follows:

Establish prayer [*salat*] at the two ends of the day and in the later part of night. Surely good deeds erase evil ones. This is a reminder [*dhikra*] for those who are mindful. (11:114)

Muslims may pray at any time, although the traditional times for ritual prayer are dawn, noon, afternoon, sunset, and late evening, some of which may be combined. When possible, Muslims are urged to join with others, particularly for the Friday congregational ritual prayer

at noon. *Salat* is preceded by an act of ablution in which Muslims purify themselves. The cleaning involves the hands and the arms, the mouth and the nostrils, and finally the feet to the ankles. Where running water is available, these parts are washed. All mosques provide facilities for this act of cleansing. Where water is unavailable, sand or a stone is used for a symbolic cleansing of the same parts of the body. This act of ablution links water as the symbol of purity to the idea of prayer as the means of purification of the soul. The ritual of cleansing is therefore inseparable from the ritual of prayer itself, reflecting a commitment to the total state of outer and inner purity.

Any clean place may be chosen for prayer, although when possible Muslims are encouraged to pray with others at a mosque. Prayers are customarily performed on prayer carpets where these are available. These carpets are intricately decorated, the pattern incorporating a niche with a lamp in it. The niche is the symbol of orientation to Mecca and the lamp signifies illumination, the light of understanding and faith that comes through prayer.

The *salat* begins with a call to prayer often recited from the *minarets* that adorn a mosque, inviting the believers to hasten to the virtuous act of prayer. An individual competent in performing the prayer acts as a leader called *Imam,* with the congregation gathered behind him in straight rows. All face in the direction of Mecca, which serves as a point of orientation referred to as the *qiblah.* The prayer consists of two to four units, depending on the time, and involves the recitation of the first Quranic chapter—*al Fatiha:*

In the name of Allah, most Gracious, most Merciful
All praise is due to Allah, the Lord of the Worlds
The most Gracious, the most Merciful.
Lord of the Day of Judgment.
You alone we worship
and from You alone we seek help
Guide us on the right path,
the path of those on whom you have bestowed grace,
not of those with whom you have been displeased,
nor those who have gone astray. (1:1–7)

In addition, other verses from the Quran are recited. The recitation is accompanied by bowing and prostration in a rhythmic cycle. Each complete ritual movement, known as *rak'ah,* follows a set pattern based on the example of Muhammad.

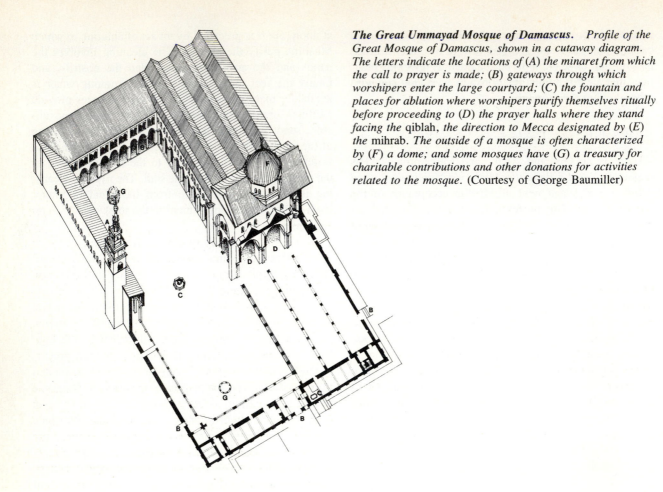

The Great Ummayad Mosque of Damascus. *Profile of the Great Mosque of Damascus, shown in a cutaway diagram. The letters indicate the locations of (A) the minaret from which the call to prayer is made; (B) gateways through which worshipers enter the large courtyard; (C) the fountain and places for ablution where worshipers purify themselves ritually before proceeding to (D) the prayer halls where they stand facing the* qiblah, *the direction to Mecca designated by (E) the* mihrab. *The outside of a mosque is often characterized by (F) a dome; and some mosques have (G) a treasury for charitable contributions and other donations for activities related to the mosque. (Courtesy of George Baumiller)*

The pattern of *salat* may be divided into seven steps:

1. The first step consists of facing the *qiblah* (Mecca), raising one's hands to the ears, and pronouncing the *takbir,* or recitation of praise: "God is Great" ("*Allahu Akbar*"). The worshiper remains silent, readying his attention for the performance of the prayer.

2. During the second step, known as the "standing," the chapter *al-Fatiha* is recited together with additional verses from the Quran.

3. With the recitation of another *takbir,* the worshiper bows, with his hands on his knees, and in this bent position, praises God.

4. After resuming the standing position, the worshiper prostrates with the forehead touching the ground, as a sign of humility and submission.

5. The fifth step involves raising oneself from prostration while reciting another *takbir* and remaining in a sitting position, praying.

6. There follows another act of prostration, when the praises of God are repeated.

7. The final step involves the sitting position and silent recitation of a personal prayer, after which the individual worshipers turn their faces to the right and the left to greet their neighbors. This greeting, or *salam,* concludes the prayer proper. However, it must be noted that where additional *rak'ahs* are to be said, the first six steps are always repeated.

In the prayer the words of supplication and praise, the postures of submission, and the acts of cleansing all come together to symbolize the meaning of true worship, integrating the Muslim into a rhythm of universal adoration. The parts of the prayer also remind them of their created state, the sense of direction in life symbolized by the *qiblah,* the goal of purification necessary for spiritual life, and the fellowship of the *Ummah,* through which they participate in the worship of God.

On Friday, Muslims are enjoined to take part in a congregational prayer at noon. The prayer has a special social significance in most Muslim countries, where Friday is a holiday, although Islam does not recognize the notion of a "Sabbath," or a day set aside for specifically spiritual activities. The times of prayer are meant to conform to the rhythm of the daily cycle of life so that the prayers complement other activities, rather than being an escape from the ordinary pattern of life.

The term *masjid,* "mosque," which refers to every place of prayer in Islam, literally means "a place of prostration." It is thus the place where the believer responds to God by paying Him homage in a state of purity, by bowing to the Divine Will in an act of prayer, and by submitting to God in a total act of prostration.

Most mosques share certain common features on the inside and on the outside. Within, the *qiblah,* or direction to Mecca, is signified by a niche, called *mihrab,* often adorned with Quranic writings and other designs. Next to it, there is a rostrum called the *minbar,* from which a preacher addresses the congregation. Such an address is an integral part of the congregational Friday prayer and is called a *khutba.* Outside the mosque, the features most easily noticeable are the *minaret* and the open courtyard. The *minaret* is the focus of the call to prayer. From here the caller, known as a *muezzin,* chants the words calling the faithful to worship. Within the courtyard, there is invariably a fountain and places where the worshipers may perform the acts of cleansing. The mosque, both in terms of its structure and function, symbolizes the aspect of unity in Islam more than any other physical structure in the Muslim world.

Dhikr, remembrance of God, and *du'a,* voluntary or private prayer, are the other forms of worship that complement the ritual prayer in Islam. They provide an opportunity for meditation and contemplation within the heart, and a way of drawing closer to God. The ritual act of prayer, with its formal aspects and physical orientation to Mecca, is complemented by remembrance, which draws the individual inwards, creating an inner sense of harmony and peace. The Quran emphasizes this aspect

Inside a Mosque. *Here we see the* mihrab *(niche) and the* minbar *(pulpit) inside the famous Sultan Hasan Mosque in Cairo.* (Courtesy of Fred Denny)

in the verse that states, "Surely in the remembrance of Allah, do hearts find peace" (13:28).

The essence of such prayers is devotion and adoration. Muslims consider Muhammad's vigils on Mount Hira and his profoundly moving experiences of revelation and closeness to God, as examples of such worship. Such devotion is also reflected in prayers preserved from the sayings of well-known devotees, such as a Muslim woman called Rabia, who lived in the eighth century:

My Lord, if I worship Thee from fear of Hell, burn me in Hell, and if I worship Thee from hope of Paradise, exclude me from Paradise, but if I worship Thee for Thine own sake, then withhold not from me Thine Eternal Beauty.[1]

These forms of worship, representing the devotional spirit in Islam, have the goal of bringing believers into daily communication with the Creator through public as well as personal and private actions.

Zakat, *Purification Through Sharing*

Many of the verses of the Quran that enjoin worship also make it obligatory on Muslims to pay a share of their wealth to the community. The word *zakat* means "purification," thus indicating that the act of sharing is a necessary prelude to making one's wealth and property pure. The amount varies according to the category of wealth or property, being calculated differently on agricultural products, cash, precious metals, and livestock.

The Quran also specifies the purposes for which dues from the *zakat* are to be used, including aid for the poor, the needy, and those heavily in debt who require assistance, as well as for education, health services, and facilities for travelers. The duty of *zakat* is coupled with that of charity, which may range from almsgiving to a kind act:

Those who share their wealth in Allah's way may be compared to a grain which grows seven ears, each with a hundred grains. Allah grants an increase to whom He will. (2:261)

A kind word of forgiveness is better than an act of charity followed by harm. (2:263)

Quranic injunctions, while condemning hoarding of wealth and economic injustice, also urged individuals and the community at large to act as trustees, through whose acts of sharing the moral and spiritual vision of a just society could be fulfilled. An equitable sharing of justly earned wealth, through *zakat*, was thus a key element in redressing imbalance and poverty.

Ramadan, the Month of Fasting

The Quran prescribes fasting for all able, adult Muslims for the period of the month of *Ramadan* (the ninth month of the Muslim calendar). Fasting begins at daybreak and ends after the setting of the sun. The spiritual, moral, and physical discipline observed during these hours included a more intensive commitment to the values and practices of Islam as well as refraining from food, drink, and sexual activity. The month of Ramadan is singled out because the Quran was first revealed during that month, the night of the first revelation being described as the "night of power." On this night Muslims stay up, praying, remembering God, and reading the Quran until daybreak.

The rhythm of abstinence and quietude during the daylight hours of Ramadan alternates with times of feasting and socializing throughout the evenings. When the time of sunset arrives, the fast is broken in the traditional manner of eating a few dates and having a refreshing drink. Prayers follow, and then part of the night is spent sharing a meal with family and friends. The evenings reflect an air of gaiety, with most of the cities and towns alive with people, mingled with a stronger sense of piety reflected in prayers and intense reading of the Quran. The spirit of joy and festivity reaches its climax after the last day of fasting. The following day is called *'Id al Fitr,* a time of celebration, feasting, and sharing; this day is one of the major festivals in the Muslim year.

Fasting has significance in Islam at several levels: it commemorates the experience of revelation that was granted to Muhammad; it singles out a month in the changing lunar calendar during which all adult Muslims practice a common act of discipline, self-denial, and self-examination; it enlarges their sympathy and compassion for persons deprived of the daily means of survival; and finally it establishes a continuity of practice with religions such as Judaism and Christianity, in which fasting is recognized as an important practice.

Hajj, the Pilgrimage

The ritual event that represents one of the peak experiences in the life of a Muslim is the *Hajj* or Pilgrimage to the sacred places of Islam in and around Mecca. This duty is prescribed for Muslims, if it does not become financially too burdensome or render the individual and the family destitute. The *Hajj* takes place in "The Month of Hajj" (*Dhu-l-Hijjah*), the last month of the Muslim year.

The event can best be understood by tracing the steps through which pilgrims pass and noting the significance of the places and objects they encounter during the *Hajj*. The occasion begins even before departure from home for Arabia, for the period before departure is spent readying oneself emotionally and spiritually.

When the pilgrims arrive in the vicinity of Mecca, they enter into a state called *ihram* or sacredness. This is done by putting on two seamless garments for the men, and a simple, modest gown and a headcovering for the women. In this state, the pilgrims refrain from shaving hair, cutting nails, and wearing jewelry or other adornments; they also abstain from any acts of violence, hunting, and sexual relations. It is in this purified state

The Ka'ba. *The Ka'ba during the Pilgrimage.* (Courtesy of the Ministry of Information: Kingdom of Saudi Arabia)

that the pilgrims make a commitment to fulfill the duties that are to follow.

The sequence of rituals that follow lead most pilgrims first to the sanctuary of the *Ka'ba*. Before the rise of Islam, this sanctuary was used by the Arabs for their own religious festivals and to house the images of their divinities. When the Prophet conquered Mecca, he cleansed it of all its idols. In the Quran the *Ka'ba* is referred to as the "Sacred House" (5:97) and the "sanctuary established for humanity" (2:125). In Islam, therefore, the significance of the *Ka'ba* lies in its being the symbol of the initial human attempt to express a relationship with God. The Quran also refers to it as the "place of Abraham" (2:125), which he and Ishmael, his son, sanctified for the worship of the One true God. It is

thus also the link between Islam and the tradition of Abraham.

The *Ka'ba* is not merely a structure signifying the physical axis of the Muslim world, the direction to which all Muslims turn in prayer. It also has a cosmic significance in Islam, for it is the symbol of the human encounter with the Divine for all times. As the symbolic center, it is the point toward which all Muslims converge daily for prayer and once during their lives, if possible, for pilgrimage.

The stone structure is located in the middle of the courtyard of Mecca's great mosque. It is about fifty feet high, cubical in shape, with its four corners aligned with the cardinal points of the compass. It is covered with a cloth, generally black in recent times, embroidered

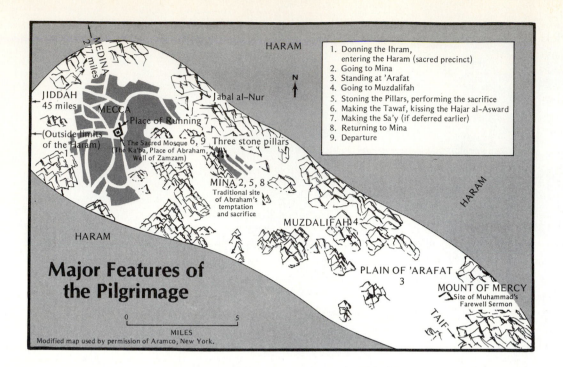

Major Features of the Pilgrimage

HARAM

1. Donning the Ihram, entering the Haram (sacred precinct)
2. Going to Mina
3. Standing at 'Arafat
4. Going to Muzdalifah
5. Stoning the Pillars, performing the sacrifice
6. Making the Tawaf, kissing the Hajar al-Asward
7. Making the Sa'y (if deferred earlier)
8. Returning to Mina
9. Departure

N

MEDINA 277 miles
JIDDAH 45 miles
MECCA
Jabal al–Nur
Place of Running 7
(Outside limits of the Haram) 1
The Sacred Mosque 6, 9
(The Ka'ba, Place of Abraham, Well of Zamzam)
Three stone pillars
MINA 2, 5, 8
Traditional site of Abraham's temptation and sacrifice
HARAM
MUZDALIFAH 4
HARAM
PLAIN OF 'ARAFAT 3
MOUNT OF MERCY
Site of Muhammad's Farewell Sermon
TAIF

0   5
MILES
Modified map used by permission of Aramco, New York.

in gold thread with verses from the Quran. In one corner of the *Ka'ba,* set within the wall, is the Black Stone, which Muslims, following the tradition of the Prophet while he was on Pilgrimage, kiss or touch. The stone is believed to be a relic that has survived from the time of Abraham.

Upon first entering Mecca, all pilgrims pay their respect to this central symbol of Islam. They perform the "circling" of the *Ka'ba,* going around it seven times in a counterclockwise direction. Having done this, the pilgrims embark on the *Hajj* proper. Moving away from the center, the pilgrims run between two spots called Safa and Marwa. This ritual (called *sa'y*) signifies the running of Hagar, Abraham's second wife, as she sought water for their son Ishmael. Islamic tradition states that when Abraham left Hagar and Ishmael there on his mission for God, he promised that God would not abandon them. When the small supply of dates and water ran out, Hagar ran between the two spots, searching desperately for water for her thirsty son. The spot during her quest when water miraculously sprang forth is called the Well of *Zam-Zam.* It is now enclosed in a marble

chamber, and pilgrims draw water from it to drink and take home to share wih others as a symbol of God's mercy and care.

The next ritual takes the pilgrims from Mecca to Mina, a few miles away. After spending the night there, they proceed to the plains of Arafat. There the whole day is spent in remembrance, meditation, and prayer, and the pilgrims remain standing for as long as they can. In fact, the ritual is called "the Standing," and the pilgrimage cannot be considered complete without its performance. Just before sunset, everyone proceeds to Muzdalifah, a place between Arafat and Mina, where they spend the night.

Before daybreak the next day, the pilgrims leave to return to Mina. There they participate in a ceremony of stoning three pillars. The pillars symbolize evil, and the stoning, an act of repudiation. Tradition also recounts that the stoning has its roots in Abraham's rejection of Satan, who tried to persuade him to disobey God's command to sacrifice his son.

After this event, the pilgrims prepare for the festival of *'Id al Aḍha,* the Festival of Sacrifice. In commemoration of Abraham's willingness to sacrifice his son, the pilgrims ritually slaughter a sheep, goat, or camel and give away a portion of the meat to the poor. Muslims all over the world celebrate the same event by performing an identical sacrifice, thus uniting in spirit to honor the end of the Pilgrimage. The pilgrims now gradually begin to resume their normal lives, but must await the final act of circling the *Ka'ba* seven times before they can no longer be considered in a state of *ihram*. After the circling, the pilgrims worship at a location called "the Place of Abraham" that is also within the courtyard of the mosque. The Pilgrimage is now completed and each pilgrim can be honored by the title of *hajji* for men and *hajjiyah* for women, a designation that brings much respect in the various communities to which the pilgrims now return.

The Pilgrimage is a dramatic re-enactment of the founding of Islam. Historically, these rituals were performed by the Prophet Muhammad. But the rituals also remind pilgrims of an earlier time, the founding of the *Ka'ba* by Abraham as a sanctuary in which to worship God. Thus, the pilgrims are taken further back into history, where the roots of Islam are traced in God's communication with Abraham. At the same time the state of *ihram* puts each pilgrim in a state of equality with all other pilgrims, affirming a sense of oneness and fellowship. Within the precincts of the *Ka'ba*, the pilgrims affirm the Quranic concepts of a God who has communicated with humans from time immemorial and of a community that is drawn from all over the world, of which each pilgrim is an integral part. The days of the *Hajj* mark a separation of the individuals from their daily lives to which they can now return with a renewed sense of commitment to God and to the *Ummah*, whose founding experiences they have witnessed and shared during the pilgrimage.

Other Significant Practices and Places

In addition to the practices of Islam mentioned above, there are several important days and places observed and honored by Muslims because they are referred to in the Quran and are linked to the Prophet's life.

Besides the *Ka'ba* and the sacred places around Mecca, importance is given to the cities of Medina and Jerusalem,

called *al-Quds*, "the Holy," in Arabic. Muslims revere Medina as the place that offered Muhammad safety and a home, as the city in which the *Ummah* was established, and as the site of the Prophet's mosque and tomb. Jerusalem is significant because it was the first point of orientation of prayer for the early Muslims. During Muhammad's early preaching in Mecca, the Quran enjoined Muslims to face in the direction of Jerusalem when praying. Later, the direction was changed to the *Ka'ba* in Mecca. The city is also associated with the "Farthest Mosque" referred to in connection with an event described in the Quran as the *miraj*, a journey into heaven by Muhammad (17:1). This night is commemorated by Muslims at special gatherings. Jerusalem is also the location of one of the earliest and best known sites in Islam, the Dome of the Rock. This site is sacred to Muslims because it recalls Abraham, David, Solomon, and Jesus, as well as being the place associated with Muhammad's *miraj*, thus establishing a point of continuity among the great prophets sent by God and relating Muslims to the "People of the Book."

Two major festivals have already been referred to in connection with the month of fasting and the pilgrimage. Muslims also celebrate the birthday of the Prophet with great rejoicing and prayers. See Table 9–1 for a more complete description of the Islamic calendar.

TABLE 9–1. *The Islamic Calendar**

Month		Special Days
Muharram	1	New Year
	10	'Āshūrā'
Safar		
Rabi al Awwal	12	Birthday of Muhammad
Rabbi al Thani		
Jumada al Awwal		
Jumada al Thani		
Rajab	27	The night of Mi'rāj
Shaban		
Ramadan		The month of fasting
Shawwal	1	'Īd al Fiṭr
Dhu-l-Qaddah		
Dhu-l-Hijjah	10	'Īd al Adḥā

* The Islamic year is a lunar year with twelve months, each calculated from new moon to new moon. Thus, it has no fixed relation to other calendars like that of the Common Era.

Life in the *Ummah*: Social, Political, and Moral Order

The *Ummah* provides the setting or context in which Muslims practice Islam. The practices described above are acts of individuals set in a context that enables each Muslim to interact with fellow Muslims. In addition to this interaction at the level of ritual observance, the Quranic and Islamic tradition also provide a framework within which other social and personal aspects of daily life are defined. It is in this sense that Islam can be said to address the totality of human life, so that the *Ummah* is not merely a religious community in the strictest sense of the word, but also a political, economic, moral, and social order. The word most often used in the Quran to define this totality of religious perspective is *din,* translated as "religion." This *din* as expressed in Islam consists of responding to God's will in all spheres of human life; its formal aspects are encompassed in a concept that reflects the idea of the "right path" that fulfills these comprehensive goals of organizing society. This concept is that of the *Shariah.*

The Shariah

The basis of political, moral, and social life in Islam is defined by the *Shariah,* often translated as "law" but having the connotation of the total sum of duties, obligations, and guidelines for the *Ummah.* Within a century of Muhammad's death, Islam spread very quickly outside Arabia; it is therefore necessary to understand the process of growth before looking in detail at how the concept of *Shariah* came to be developed in the Muslim community.

The Muslim Conquests. The conquests undertaken by Muslims after the death of the Prophet represent a spectacular military achievement. Within less than one hundred years, the area under Muslim rule stretched from the Atlantic to India, including most of what once was under Byzantine and Sassanian rule. The conquest of these territories carved out the central domain of what was to become the world of Islam. The initial period of conquest was followed by a long period during which Muslim rule was consolidated.

After the death of Muhammad, all territories were ruled from Medina by successors of Muhammad known as *Caliphs.* The early Muslim community believed that such leadership was necessary to ensure continuity, preservation, and spread of the Islamic message. After the death of the first four Caliphs, who are considered by most Muslims as model rulers, a series of Muslim dynasties came to rule the various conquered territories. During these conquests Muslims also attempted to spread their faith. Quranic and Prophetic practice required that the people of conquered territories be offered the option of converting to Islam or remaining true to their own traditions. If they chose to remain in their traditions, they became *Ahl al Dhimma* (people protected under Muslim rule), and were given the right to practice their own faith in exchange for paying a tax.

The actual process of Islamization of people in these conquered territories took a long time and was effected mostly through the work of Muslim preachers, traders, or rulers. On the whole the process of conversion to Islam was a peaceful one, although many earlier Western writers on Islam tried to portray conversion to Islam as having been undertaken by force. There were occasions when zealous Muslim rulers destroyed places of worship in certain areas and persecuted non-Muslims, but this was generally an exception rather than the rule. Most Muslims followed the Quranic injunction, "There is no compulsion in Religion" (2:256), and attempted to spread their faith more by example than by coercion.

The Formation of Islamic Institutions. As the territories under Muslim rule grew, it became necessary to organize a common pattern of institutions and rules that would govern the lives of the people. Much of this early systematization and organization was carried out by Muslim thinkers and administrators who attempted to work largely within the framework defined by the Quran and the *Sunnah.* It is the resulting framework that is generally referred to as the *Shariah,* judicial in basis, but having the wider connotation of a comprehensive system that regulated every aspect of life within the Muslim community and governed its relationship with non-Muslim subjects. At the political level the *Shariah* defined the nature of the Muslim state, the duties and responsibilities of the Caliphs, the organization of institutions that would assure the security and well-being of its inhabitants, and the nature of relationships with both Muslim and non-Muslim states. At the social and personal level, it provided for rules and regulations affecting economic, social, and family life. The *Shariah* also defined in detail the specifically religious duties incumbent on Muslims. For the *Shariah* to be implemented fully, the state had an organized system of courts and judges whose function it was to mediate disputes at all levels and to oversee the workings of the *Shariah* by administering justice through the courts. The individuals specializing in law were known as *fuqaha* or jurists (singular *faqih*), whose task was to define and systematize specific legal prescriptions within the *Shariah*.

The totality of political, moral, and social order in Islam was thus given specific definition. It was not meant, however, to be a fixed system of rigid rules and regulations. Within the *Shariah* there was always a wider purpose of *maslah* (the public good), which enabled Muslim scholars to interpret and apply the *Shariah* in relation to existing conditions and places. Several schools of thought developed in various parts of the Muslim world, which applied the *Shariah* differently in cases where human and geographical conditions varied. Some scholars tended to be stricter in their interpretations than others, but on the whole the *Shariah* continued to provide for the world of Islam, through its various schools, a common framework and code that gave that world much of its sense of unity until modern times.

The "Model" Muslim City

One way of attempting to understand the ways in which such an all-embracing system influenced the daily life within society is to study the traditional Muslim city. Urban evnironment in Islam has varied according to time, place, and human condition, but it is possible by looking at the city to isolate those common aspects that illustrate Islam's role at the social and human levels. Such environments, though undergoing erosion at present, may still be recognized in the older, traditional parts of Muslim cities.

The Muslim city is by definition a city of God. Its beginnings lay in the building of a place of worship, which would constitute its center. Within this mosque, the *qiblah* established the point of orientation—toward the *Ka'ba*, the heart of Islam. Each city thus in its initial state was an attempt to create an environment in which Muslims could put their faith into practice. The mosque was not just a place of worship; it became by extension a place of learning. Adjacent to most mosques were schools or, in the case of larger mosques, more elaborate centers of learning. Learning thus complemented worship, and encompassed a variety of disciplines. Some of these Muslim cities became seats of learning that attracted scholars from medieval European and Byzantine states. These institutions provided accommodation for the students and the teachers, both of whom were paid stipends. Students went through an organized program of study, which varied according to the subjects in which the institution specialized. The famous Al-Azhar mosque and university in Cairo, founded in the tenth century and still flourishing, offered a comprehensive curriculum and recognized students for their achievements by granting them titles. It has even been suggested that the system of gowns worn by teachers and students today in the West developed at this time.

Radiating from the mosque was a vast array of streets, which led to the commercial or market sector known as the *bazaar,* or branched off into dead-end streets that ended in houses. The *bazaar,* often covered, was organized in such a way that shops or boutiques dealing in common products were grouped together. Some commercial products, like meat, fish, or perishables, were kept as far from the center as possible to avoid an unpleasant environment around the mosque. Other products were not found in the *bazaar* because certain categories of food and drink are prohibited in the Quran; among these are pork, the meat of carrion, and all forms of alcoholic drink and intoxicants. The Quran also recommends that the name of God be pronounced when animals are being slaughtered for food.

Besides shops, there were also studios and workshops for artesans and craftsmen. Economic life was represented by the flow of human life, which was a dominant part of city life during the daytime. The rules and regulations governing commercial activity were also defined in the *Shariah* and implemented by officials whose function it was to see that rules were applied. Certain practices such as gambling and games of chance are prohibited in the Quran, and the function of such officials was to see that these prohibitions were followed. Offenders, if found guilty by the courts, were liable to punishment.

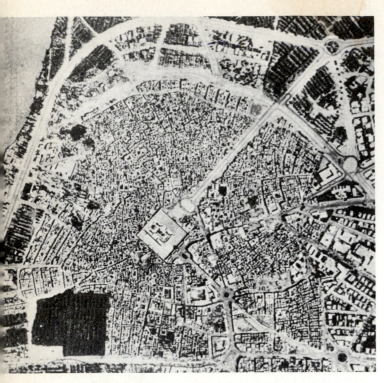

A Muslim Cityscape. *An aerial view of the traditional quarter in Baghdad known as Kadhimiyah, showing the traditional Muslim urban form with the mosque complex and the streets radiating from it as it was in the 1950s. Since then a great part of the urban pattern has been changed by modernization. The mosque complex, a Shi'ite sanctuary, contains the mausolea of two Ithna Ashari Imams.* (Courtesy of Andrzej Basista)

Family Life and Housing in the City

Family life is a vital part of the Muslim social order and, based on Quranic injunctions, the *Shariah* defines in great detail the rules affecting marriage, orphans, inheritance, and other aspects of family life.

One of the major changes brought about in the status of the family from pre-Islamic Arab times was the provision of legal rights and status for women; these rights were defined in the context of family life. The practices of female infanticide and unrestricted polygamy, practiced by certain pre-Islamic Bedouin tribes, were abolished.

The Quran permits a man to have a maximum of four wives at one time. However, equality in the treatment of wives is made a condition in such cases, as is a due recognition of each person's rights within a polygamous household (4:129). The Quran also recognizes the possibility of marriages breaking down, and allows for divorce after reasonable attempts have been made at reconciling the parties. Marriages are to be accompanied by the signing of contracts in which the husband is asked to specify the amount of settlement to be made to the wife in the event of a divorce. Divorced persons, widows, and widowers are also encouraged to remarry. Another area of family life touched upon in the Quran is that of inheritance.

From that left by parents and close relations, there is a share for the men and a share for the women. Each one has a designated share, whether it be small or great. (4:7)

A particular concern is expressed for orphans and the disadvantaged. The overriding factor at all levels of personal and social life is to be a strong sense of justice:

O you who believe
Be firm in justice and as witnesses
for God even though it be against
yourselves, your parents or those close to you—
rich or poor.
    (4:135)

It is the notion of intimacy and privacy, however, that dictates the way in which traditional Muslim dwellings are built and organized. Housing is set off from the commercial sector of the city. The concept of *haram* (and *harim*, meaning sanctuary), vulgarized in European literature as the "harem," is essentially a notion of protection because of the recognition that family life and personal life are private but vulnerable. The covering of the interior courtyards of traditional Muslim houses and the traditional clothing worn by Muslim men and women are means of protecting this vulnerability. In urban centers the system of *purdah* or veiling, a practice adapted by Muslims from cultures such as those of ancient Persia, affirmed this notion of privacy and anonymity.

Beyond the mosques, the places of learning, the *bazaar*, and the housing, there was fortification, which now has almost completely disappeared. Traditionally, the walls around cities acted as a layer of protection from outside attack and as a definition for those who lived within them. The city also maintained contact with the Bedouins, the farmers, and visitors through way-stations built especially to provide rest and refreshment for those from the outside. Nomadic life, fast disappearing in the contemporary world, was a significant part of traditional Muslim life. The city often provided a point of contact between the nomadic and urban lifestyles, enabling both to nourish and revitalize each other through a mutual exchange of ideas and energies.

Cemeteries generally fringe the edges of the city. At death, the body is carefully washed and wrapped in a seamless white shroud. The body is placed in a grave with its head facing Mecca and special prayers are said for the soul of the deceased.

Another distinguishing feature of the traditional Muslim city is the presence of nature in it. Most are endowed with gardens and fountains, which provide a welcome retreat in most arid climates as well as places for social gatherings and family strolls. This quality of the presence of nature also lends the city a certain serenity and a congruence with the natural environment. The city does not appear to dominate its surroundings; rather, it seems to blend into them. The city is also enlivened by the festivities celebrating Muslim holidays and the joyous gatherings that mark weddings, births, and the circumcision of male children, which is a required practice in Islam.

In ideal terms, the physical form of the city in Islam—including the places of worship, work, family habitation, and institutions serving the city—can be said to symbolize the vision of unity in Islam. The architecture and the design, the gardens and the parks all echo the promises of the hereafter described by the Quranic paradise. The physical structures in a Muslim city are therefore a reflection of the spiritual quality of life and the social and personal values enjoined by Islam.

The existence of such a heritage of organized daily life is, however, under constant pressure of erosion and even total destruction in modern times. It serves as a constant reminder and a challenge to present-day Muslim societies as they wrestle with the problem of maintaining and adapting this environment to their current needs and past traditions.

Groups in Islam

Over the passage of time, the Islamic *Ummah* came to be composed of a number of groups. Each of these represented a synthesis based on a response to the foundations laid down by the Quran and developed in the life of the Prophet. Although the groups reflect divergent views on certain matters of practice and doctrine, it is not proper, strictly speaking, to classify them as "sects" in Islam. The idea of "sects" implies a centrally established body of doctrines or authority from which departures take place. Since no such "centralization" exists in Islam, the various groups may more properly be defined as schools of thought and practice, with no divergence concerning the fundamentals. Rather, they represent differing views as to how these fundamentals can best be fulfilled in the practical life and organization of the *Ummah*.

After the death of Muhammad, the Muslims had to wrestle with the immediate problems of growth and organization. Differences arose over the question of authority in the community. Since there were to be no more prophets, the issue revolved around how best the community could continue to implement the teachings of the Quran and the ideals of the Prophet, and which person was most capable of leading such a community. Some Muslims felt that Abu Bakr, a respected early convert to Islam and father-in-law of the Prophet, was best suited to this task. Others favored Ali, the son-in-law and cousin of the Prophet. Eventually, Abu Bakr came to assume this task; no conflict erupted, and the unity of the community was maintained during that early period in spite of differences. Abu Bakr became known as *Caliph*, the term now used to designate the head of the Muslim *Ummah*. Before his death in 634, he nominated another respected Muslim leader, Umar, to succeed him. Umar in turn was succeeded by Uthman, a member of one of the leading families in Mecca. After the Caliphate of Uthman, Ali eventually became head of the Muslim community in 656.

This initial period of the history of Islam, together with the period of the Prophet, has come to be regarded retrospectivelly, as a "golden age." It has been felt that in spite of existing differences, these leaders and the Muslim community strove to remain united, maintained the high standards set by the Prophet, and sought to reflect these standards in their personal lives and in the life of the growing Muslim state.

During the Caliphates of Uthman and Ali, however, differences came to a head and eventually led to a civil war; and out of this conflict emerged the earliest groups in Islamic history. The basic issues in the conflict were those of authority and interpretation of the Quran.

The Kharijites (Khwarij)

The first of these groups is known as the *Kharijites*. Muawiyah, who had been appointed as governor of the newly conquered province of Syria by Uthman, revolted against Ali when the latter became Caliph. During a fruitless attempt at arbitration, Ali was assassinated and Muawiyah forcibly assumed the reigns of power, initiating the rule of a dynasty called the Ummayads, after his ancestors. The seat of this dynasty was in Damascus in Syria. Those Muslims who felt that arbitration should not have been attempted left the army of Ali and came to be called *Khwarij* (those who "left"). It was their contention that no arbitration should have taken place, since the Quran did not allow arbitration in cases where right was clearly distinguished from wrong. In their view, Ali, by agreeing to arbitration, had compromised himself. Their differences with the rest of the Muslims led to much violence and their history was beset with warfare until they eventually ceased to be a factor in Islam.

Only one minor group of *Khwarij* has survived. They continue to represent the tradition of close fidelity to the Quran in matters that pertain to administration and justice, but are not as exclusive as their early predecessors in their relations with others. They are represented today in North Africa, Oman, and Zanzibar on the East Coast of Africa and call themselves *Ibadi*.

Among the other groups that subsequently developed, the two largest and most important are the Shia and Sunni. They represent two parallel syntheses that have emerged to provide frameworks for realizing their respective visions of Islam.

The Shia

The death of Muhammad marked the end of his prophetic mission. In Muslim belief, he had been the last of the prophets, who had completed the divinely entrusted task of making known God's final revelation. In order to discharge his mission effectively, he had combined in his person religious, political, and military power.

After his death the early Muslim community was faced with the question of how to maintain the sovereignty of the Muslim state effectively and further the cause of Islam. The question involved them in a discussion and dispute regarding the position of head of the newly established Muslim state.

The Muslims who felt that Ali was best suited to assume leadership of the *Ummah* after the death of the Prophet eventually became known as the *Shia*. The word means "followers," and refers to those who gave their support to Ali. During the eighth century, these followers and others crystallized into a group with definite views about the question of authority, which they saw as being intimately linked to the issue of understanding and implementing Islam. They believed that the Prophet had specifically designated Ali as successor before his own death on the occasion of his "Farewell Pilgrimage," and that Ali was henceforth to represent a new institution called *Imamah* (from the Arabic word *imam*, meaning leader). Such an institution was meant to guarantee protection and continuing implementation of the Islamic message, and to assure that that message would continue to be interpreted for the *Ummah* by the person best suited to do so. The *Imamah* was to continue among the descendants of the Prophet, through Ali and Fatima, the daughter of the Prophet, in a direct succession. Each Imam would be specifically nominated by his predecessor to be responsible for the community after his death. The Shia, like other Muslims, continued nevertheless to affirm that there would be no more prophets after Muhammad.

This belief in the *Imamah* as an institution to complement and sustain the work of the Prophet Muhammad is integrated by the Shia in their profession of faith, embodied in the *shahadah*. In addition to professing belief in the Unity of God and the Prophethood of Muhammad, the Shia also profess that Ali, the commander of true believers, is the Friend (*Wali*) of God. Devotion to the Imams thus becomes a cardinal act of faith among the Shia. The Imam is believed also to possess divinely endowed knowledge and the capacity to provide spiritual guidance. This belief reflects the Shia view that in order to understand and implement the Quran and the *Sunnah*,

Shia Ritual. *This is a Shia gathering to commemorate Ashura in the city of Ray, Iran.* (Courtesy of Mohammed Torabi-Parizi)

it is necessary that the Imam be divinely inspired. He can thus provide both material and spiritual leadership, enabling Muslims to remain united both in affairs of state and those of faith. The Imams also act as intercessors, as does Muhammad, seeking forgiveness and welfare for persons who have sinned or are dead.

In time, Shia thought developed the view that a true understanding of the Quran was not limited merely to the literal aspects of revelation. There was also an inner dimension to the Quranic verses that could be grasped through the teachings of the Imams. The science of *tafsir,* consisting of the explanation of the outward significance and context of the Quran, was complemented among the Shia by the science of *tawil,* the analysis of the

inner dimension and deeper meanings of revelation. In this respect the Shia contributed greatly to the intellectual tradition in Islam and influenced the development of philosophical and mystical thought in Islam.

On the death of Ali in 661, the *Imamah* devolved to his eldest son Hasan and then to a younger son Husayn. The latter is one of the great tragic figures of early Islam. In order to combat the growing and oppressive rule of the Ummayads and to affirm his role as Imam, he refused to accept Yazid, Muawiyah's son and appointee, as the head of the Muslim community. Yazid sent troops to forestall any uprising, and in a brutal massacre Husayn and members of his family were put to death at Karbala in Iraq. This event shocked the Muslims, strengthened the opposition to the Ummayads, and rallied support to the cause of the Imams who succeeded Husayn.

These Imams, though constantly persecuted, maintained an active role in the religious life of the community. They contributed a great deal to the developing sciences of law, philosophy, and theology. In particular the sixth Imam, Jafar al Sadiq, played a key role in keeping alive the aspirations of the Shia. On his death the Shia split into two major divisions: one recognized the appointment of his son Ismail and continued to give allegiance to the successors of Ismail, while the other supported a younger son, Musa al Kazim. The former group is known as the *Ismailiyya* and the latter as *Ithna Ashariyya*. On occasions, because of the insistence on the rights of their Imams to head the Muslim community and the emphasis on certain esoteric aspects of faith, each of these Shia groups has suffered persecution and been accused by other Muslims of holding heretical beliefs.

Ithna Ashariyya. After the death of Jafar al Sadiq there were six more Imams. The twelfth and last of these was called Muhammad al-Mahdi; he is believed to have gone into *ghaybah,* a state where he is not perceived physically, a state of being hidden from the world. The *Mahdi,* or "messiah," will manifest himself when God wills and restore justice and peace on earth. In the meantime, he is in touch in a spiritual way with human beings, though they cannot physically perceive him. Since this group of the Shia believes in twelve Imams, it has come to be called *Ithna Ashari* ("Twelver").

In the physical absence of the Imam, the community is guided by individuals who strive to maintain and teach Islam. They are called *mujtahids,* or those who strive for knowledge. Those recognized for their additional knowledge and example are given additional titles, the highest among which is that of *ayatollah*. Although it is only on the return of the hidden Imam that the ideal society can be truly restored, the community, through the *mujtahids* and *ayatollahs* (who represent the hidden Imam), strives to preserve the principles and practice of faith. These leaders receive their training in centers of Shiite learning that are found in Iraq and Iran.

In addition to the various Islamic practices, this group emphasizes the traditions and teachings of the various Imams as supplements to the Quran. They attach impor-

tance to these traditions and incorporate them into the concept of *Sunnah,* which in their tradition includes the sayings and actions of the twelve Imams, in addition to the *Sunnah* of the Prophet. All of these constitute sources for the development of a specifically Ithna Ashari school of law. Acts of devotion to the Imams and visits to their tombs are also significant. Sanctuaries such as Najaf and Karbala in Iraq, Meshed and Qum in Iran, and others play a prominent part in their religious life.

The ritual practice that stands out most clearly, however, is the commemoration of the events leading to the martyrdom of Imam Husayn. During the month of *Muharram* this tragic event is depicted through sermons, recitations of poems, and a drama called *taziyah*—all of these practices being vivid reminders of the theme of good combating evil, the righteous sacrificing their lives in the cause of truth, and above all the passionate commitment in tribute to the figure of Husayn, who for the Shia is the embodiment of Islam's struggle for survival and triumph.

The Ithna Ashari School is the largest of the groups within the Shia. Although most of them are in Iran and Iraq, they are represented in other parts of the Muslim world.

Ismailiyya. As noted earlier, this group differs from the Ithna Ashari by recognizing the line of Imams descended from Ismail, the eldest son of Jafar al Sadiq. The line of Imams continued until 1094 when a further split developed, dividing the Ismailis into two subgroups: the *Nizari Ismailis* gave allegiance to Nizar, whom they believed to have been designed by his father; the other group followed another son Mustali, after whom they are known as *Mustali Ismailis*. It is the Mustali belief that after several successors, their last visible Imam has also gone into *ghaybah*. His successors, though hidden, are in touch with the community through a representative known as *dai*. This *dai* acts as head of the community until the appearance of an Imam, also called the *Mahdi*. The Mustali Ismailis live in the Indo–Pakistan subcontinent and Yemen, and are scattered in small communities in East Africa.

Meanwhile the Nizari Ismailis have continued giving allegiance to a line of Imams whom they believe to be in direct succession from the Prophet and Ali. The present Imam of the Ismailis, Shah Karim al Husayni, is well known as the Aga Khan. The Ismailis, like other Shia, emphasize the spiritual dimension of Islam; but for its understanding and for maintaining a balance between material and spiritual life, they consider that the Imam cannot disappear from the world and that his teachings and physical presence are necessary to ensure the implementation of Islam in the context of changing times and circumstances. The Nizari Ismailis are in Afghanistan, Iran, Pakistan, India, East Africa, Syria, and increasingly in the Western world, particularly in Britain, Canada, and the United States.

Zaydiyya. A final group among the Shia, the Zaydiyya, trace their origin to Zayd, one of the grandsons of Imam Husayn. His followers considered him an Imam, and gave allegiance to him and his successors as individuals descended from the Prophet, who could, by their example and military capability, establish a just state. Most Zaydis are to be found at present in Yemen.

The Sunnis

The Sunnis represent the majority of Muslims. As with other Muslims, the *Sunnah* has a central significance for them. But because of their particular emphasis on the role of the *Sunnah* in their tradition, they have been called *Ahl al Sunnah* or *Sunnis.* Conformity to past tradition and practice is thus the cornerstone of the Sunni intrepretation of Islam.

The position of Sunnism became defined as a response to questions concerning authority and practice that had also given rise to the Khwarij and the Shia. Much of the eventual content of Sunni thought developed as a result of its reactions to these other groups. In regard to practice, the Sunnis evolved a means of elaborating the *Shariah.* In addition to the Quran and the *Sunnah,* their scholars developed the concepts of *ijma,* consensus, and *qiyas,* analogy. According to *ijma,* a consensus of most scholars on the validity of a practice, followed by common agreement on it, was sufficient to establish the validity of the practice in *Shariah.* According to *qiyas,* the validity of a practice could be tested by scholars employing reasoning drawing analogies with other laws of the *Shariah.*

For instance, a parallel could be established between a case treated in the Quran or by the Prophet and newly arising issues. By considering the parallels, the jurists could then proceed to a logical deduction. A specific example of this relates to the Quranic command to put commercial transactions in writing to prevent fraud. By analogy, the Muslim jurists made it compulsory to register marriages officially, although the Quran makes no reference requiring this. The jurists, however, considered it to be a serious transaction of trust between two individuals to which the Quranic ruling ought also to apply. By thus checking agreement in the present and consistency with the past through *ijma* and *qiyas,* a flexibility was provided by which the scholars could accommodate practices not specifically referred to in the Quran and in the *Sunnah* but not contradictory to their spirit. The scholars and jurists thus acted as interpreters of Islam, assuming both universal application and a sense of continuity.

Nevertheless, certain minor areas of disagreement have led to variations in the interpretation of the *Shariah.* Four schools of law in Sunni Islam have developed, each named after the scholar responsible for defining its main features: they are Shafi'i, Maliki, Hanbali, and Hanafi. Each school, however, has recognized the right of the others to disagree on minor points of interpretation, and therefore all four are considered as normative in Sunni Islam. The attitude of some of these schools has not always been as tolerant toward other groups in Islam.

The scholars in the Sunni tradition, generally referred to as *ulama* in Arabic or *mullah* in other languages, have acted as learned experts and teachers of Islam. They have received their training in a variety of schools, specializing in Quranic and legal sciences. In Sunni Islam, they have played an important role as custodians of knowledge and protectors of the tradition.

Since the divine law was the basis on which a Muslim state was to be organized, the law in Sunni Islam also involved a definition of the nature of the state and politics. Like the Shia, the Sunni tradition accepted the necessity of having a head of the state generally referred to as *Khalifah* (Caliph). His role, as defined by jurists, was to act as the custodian of the state and the Shariah. Jurists developed elaborate theories that defined and circumscribed the conditions under which one could become a ruler and the duties and responsibilities that the ruler was to carry out.

Besides having its own specific systematization of mat-

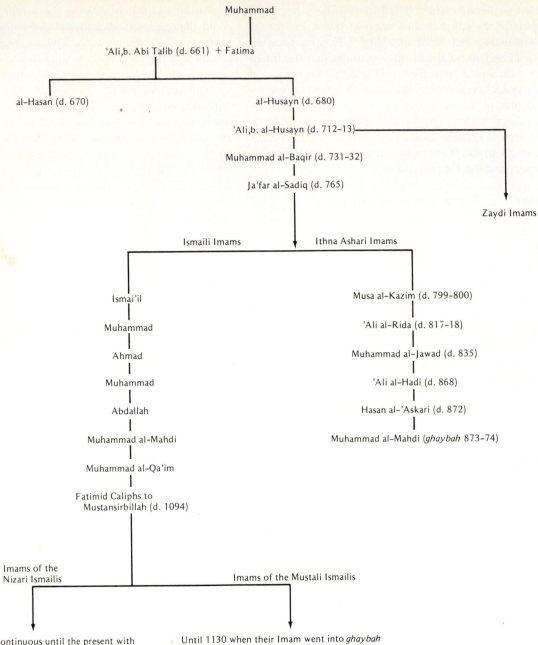

Muhammad

'Ali,b. Abi Talib (d. 661) + Fatima

al-Hasan (d. 670)

al-Husayn (d. 680)

'Ali,b. al-Husayn (d. 712–13)

Muhammad al-Baqir (d. 731–32)

Ja'far al-Sadiq (d. 765)

Zaydi Imams

Ismaili Imams | Ithna Ashari Imams

Ismai'il

Muhammad

Ahmad

Muhammad

Abdallah

Muhammad al-Mahdi

Muhammad al-Qa'im

Fatimid Caliphs to
Mustansirbillah (d. 1094)

Musa al-Kazim (d. 799–800)

'Ali al-Rida (d. 817–18)

Muhammad al-Jawad (d. 835)

'Ali al-Hadi (d. 868)

Hasan al-'Askari (d. 872)

Muhammad al-Mahdi (*ghaybah* 873–74)

Imams of the
Nizari Ismailis

Imams of the Mustali Ismailis

Line of Imams continuous until the present with
Shah Karim, Aga Khan as 49th living Imam.

Until 1130 when their Imam went into *ghaybah*

The Shia Imams.

ters related to the law and the state, Sunnism also defined itself in relation to the interpretation of doctrine. An interesting example of how this happened in early Islam is the controversy regarding Muslim attitudes to the "createdness" of the Quran. One group of Muslims, called Mutazilah, believed that the Quran, since it could be considered as the speech or word of God, should be regarded as created. This position was based on their view that the concept of the unity of God, *tawhid,* implied that God was pure Essence, and this belief would be violated if the Quran, the speech of God, were to be considered as uncreated and, therefore, part of this pure Essence. On this issue, the Mutazilah were supported by the Caliph in Baghdad, al Mamun (ruled 813–833), who set about imposing their view and persecuting those who rejected it. However, it was from their opponents, who could not accept the idea of the createdness of the Quran and who believed instead in its eternal nature, that the majority Sunni view came to be established and eventually accepted after al Mamun's death. Subsequent Sunni scholars, the main ones being al-Ashari (d. 935) and al-Maturidi (d. 944), used rational, theological tools to refute Mutazili arguments and defined Sunni theology regarding the nature of God and the Quran.

Sunnism continued to produce great scholars who sought to establish main doctrines and the practice of the majority against diverging points of view. One of the best known was al-Ghazali (d. 1111), who played a major role in establishing the validity of the Sunni position against the views of the philosopher and Shia groups like the Ismailis. Al-Ghazali's condemnation of certain views of the philosophers and Ismailis was aimed at discouraging departures from what he regarded as the established norms of Muslim belief and practice. In helping to consolidate the Sunni position, he also stimulated a greater concern for the dimension of religious experience as an integral part of acts of devotion and piety. His major work, entitled *Ihya Ulum al-Din (The Revitalization of Religious Sciences),* has had a major influence on all subsequent Sunni thought.

Another important theologian and legal scholar, was Ibn Taimiyah (d. 1328). His strong reaction to the growth of popular Sufism became the basis for much of the reform that developed in the Islamic world in the eighteenth and nineteenth centuries. Like al-Ghazali, he be-came a strong defender of the Sunni position. In particular, he directed his writings and arguments against persons whom he felt to be exercising undue restraint in applying reason to the interpretation of basic Islamic concepts. He argued for a more literal and strict adherence to the Quran and *Sunnah* in thought and practice, occasionally rejecting some of al-Ghazali's views as well. His works have had a great influence on subsequent Muslim thinkers, who have argued for a return to the basic ideas and practices of early Islam.

A Sunni thinker whose work went beyond theological concerns was Ibn Khaldun (d. 1406). He wrote a monumental work on history with a lengthy introduction on the nature and meaning of human history and social process, which has been considered as one of the most original works of the time—so much so that he has earned the title, in the opinion of some modern European scholars, of "father of sociology."

In addition to these major groups, there have been other Muslims who in the course of Islamic history developed specific approaches to the understanding and practice of Islam. Groups such as the philosophers and the Sufis (to be discussed shortly) did not consciously establish "schools" of their own, but some of their interpretations of Islam are sufficiently divergent from Sunnism, in particular, to warrant identification as major groups.

The Muslim Philosophers

As the Muslim empire expanded, it came into close contact with cultures that had long-established intellectual roots. The most important of these were in the Mediterranean world, Persia (Iran), and India. Under the patronage of various rulers, academies were set up in which translations were made of scientific and philosophic works from Greek, Pahlavi (the language of Iran), and Sanskrit. Thus, there developed within Islam an intellectual tradition that undertook a study of these sources and created a new synthesis that would incorporate, modify, and further develop this heritage. One direct result was the rise of Muslim philosophers who, like other groups in Islam, began to address themselves to the intellectual problems raised by the Muslim encounter with other religious and intellectual traditions. The Mutazilah, mentioned earlier, were the first along with the Shia to emphasize rational

Master and Pupil. *A teacher and student engaged in the study of the Quran.* (Courtesy of Fred Denny)

and intellectual tools as means of explaining Quranic principles. Both of these groups in turn influenced later thinkers.

Among early Muslim philosophers, the most important was al-Farabi (d. 950). He defined the goals of Muslim philosophy on questions of metaphysics, ethics, and politics, and the relationship of these goals to Islamic society. His main aim was to promote philosophical inquiry as a tool for interpreting and clarifying the basis of Islam in terms of doctrine and practice. His philosophical investigation led to a definition of the nature of a truly Islamic community. He also attempted to harmonize philosophy and religion by arguing that they were analogous, comparing the true prophet (Muhammad, in the case of Islam) to Plato's philosopher-king. He was also recognized for his commentaries and interpretations of the works of Plato and Aristotle, whose philosophies he attempted to reconcile with each other.

Another great figure in Islamic philosophy was Ibn Sina, known to the Latin West as Avicenna (d. 1061). His contributions to thought, medicine, and natural science have led to his recognition as one of the intellectual giants of the medieval period. Among the Muslim philosophers who followed, the best known are Ibn Rushd (d. 1198), known as Averroes, and Ibn Tufayl (d. 1186), both of whom lived and worked in Spain and North Africa during the twelfth century.

An excellent illustration of the attempts by Muslim philosophers to relate reason and revelation is the philosophical tale *Hayy bin Yaqzan,* written by Ibn Tufayl.[2] The story begins with the birth of a male child born through spontaneous generation out of natural elements. He is called Hayy bin Yaqzan, "Living, the son of Awake." The child, cared for by a deer, grows up on an island and, after learning to provide for himself, learns to explore, experiment, and eventually to speculate and philosophize. He becomes aware of his status as a rational being in the world and establishes a pattern of ethical behavior based on his perception of the living things around him and the movement of the planets. Ultimately, his consciousness develops to the point where philosophical abstraction leads him to meditation and ecstatic contemplation. The search for truth is expressed in terms of a rational process as well as profound religious experience. This stage of perfection is reached entirely through the use of his natural rational capacities.

In the story, Hayy is led to a nearby island where he encounters a human society bound by the norms that govern human life and regulated by rules derived from prophetic revelation. Although he recognizes the same truths expressed in the images of revelation that he has already arrived at through philosophy, he is unable to convince the people of the island of this link and thus to awaken in them an awareness of their full potentialities as rational beings. He leaves the island to return to his own secluded and blissful life.

The tale highlights some of the problems faced by philosophers as they attempted to reconcile the roles of reason and revelation in Muslim thought, both for themselves and for the larger community. It is in this wider context that the role of Muslim philosophers needs to be evaluated, as they attempted to bridge the claims of reason and revelation and inspire ways of philosophical thinking among Muslims.

The refutation of some of the views of Muslim philosophers by the Sunni theologian al-Ghazali—and his charge that some of their views were unacceptable—created an unfavorable climate for the development of philosophy in some parts of the Muslim world. The study and development of philosophy flourished, however, in other areas, such as Iran. During the seventeenth century, Islamic philosophy gave rise to major thinkers like Mir Damad and Mulla Sadra. In their thought, philosophy came to be closely linked with some of the basic ideas underlying Islamic mysticism, or more properly Sufism.

The Sufis

The Sufis are Muslims who seek to understand and experience the dimension of Islam that relates to the cultivation of an inner life in search of divine love and knowledge. The name *sufi* is derived from *tasawwuf:* the act of devoting oneself to a search for an inner life. Sufis are also referred to as *faqir* or *dervish,* both meaning ''poor'' (in spirit), words that have become part of the English language. The word ''sufi'' may in part also be attributed to the use of *suf,* woolen garments, such as some early Muslim mystics wore.

The roots of Sufism lay in some of the early Muslims' experience of the Quran and their desire to understand the nature of the Prophet's religious experience: ''From God we are and to Him is our return'' (2:156). Verses of the Quran like this constituted the basis of what became the Sufi understanding of spiritual life. Sufis themselves often employed vivid imagery to describe their quest for religious meaning. The poet Rumi (d. 1273), whose *Mathnawi* is considered one of the great classics of Sufi literature, began his work by citing the analogy of a flute, made out of reeds, playing soulfully:

Listen to the reed as it tells a tale, complaining of separation—, crying:

''Ever since I was torn from the reed-bed, my complaint has brought tears to man and woman. I seek a heart torn by separation, that I may reveal the yearning of love.''

All those torn asunder from their source, long for the day they were one with it.[3]

The central image of the flute or pipe, as it is used in this passage and elsewhere in Sufi literature, mirrors the yearning of the soul, which, like the reed out of which the flute is made, has been separated from its source, namely God.

Since the major concern of Sufism was to enable an individual Muslim to seek intimacy with god, it was felt that such seekers must embrace an inner life, a path of devotion and prayer that would lead to spiritual awakening. In Sufism, therefore, the *Shariah* (law) has had a counterpart called the *Tariqah* (way) that complements the observance of Islam. The *Tariqah* is the journey and the discipline undertaken by a Muslim in the quest for knowledge of God, which leads ultimately to an experiential understanding of the true meaning of *tawhid,* or divine unity.

From this early stage when Sufism was no more than a very intense and personal seeking of God on the part of certain Muslims, it developed into a system of mystical orders centering around the teachings of a leader. This gave rise to the establishment of several Sufi Orders in Islam, named after their founding teachers but also tracing their spiritual genealogy back to the teachings of the Prophet and Ali, whom they considered to have been endowed with the special mission of explaining the mystical dimension of Quranic teachings. By the thirteenth century these Orders had grown and spread all over the Muslim world. Muslims were attracted from all walks of life and from all groups in Islam, among them al-Ghazali and Ibn Sina. Later Jalal al-din Rumi, Ibn al Arabi (d. 1240), and many other important figures all over the Muslim world sought an experiential understanding of Islam through the Sufi path.

Within the Orders, the path or way began with the acceptance of a teacher as a guide. His teaching was aimed at enabling the disciple to develop discipline through strict, ascetic practices and by meditation on certain formulas, mostly attributes of God, from the Quran. Through acts of meditation, remembrance, and contemplation, the Sufi passed through several spiritual ''stations,'' each representing the development of inner life, until finally through the experience of ''annihilation'' (*fana*) the true meaning of spiritual union with God was realized. Sufism taught that at this point the Muslim devotee had reached a true understanding of Islam, having finished the *Tariqah,* or path of discipline built on the *Shariah.*

The Sufi quest is described by the poet Attar (d. 1229) in a famous mystical poem called *Mantiq al-Tayr* (''The Conference of the Birds'').[4] The poem depicts the quest of a large number of birds for the *Simurgh,* the mythic King of the birds. After many tribulations, and having crossed over seven valleys, thirty of the birds reach the end of their journey and come to the gate where the Supreme Majesty lived. The gatekeeper tests them and then opens the door. As they sit on the dais awaiting

A Sufi Mausoleum. *Here are the dome and minarets within the courtyard that contains the shrine of a famous Sufi leader, Shah Niamatullah. The shrine is in Mahan, Iran.* (Courtesy of Mohammed Torabi-Parizi)

the King, an inner glow awakens in all of them at the same moment and they realize that the *Simurgh* has been with them all along, guiding them from within. They realize further that the goal of their quest was ultimately the recognition that their inner selves, together, represent the *Simurgh* (the Persian words *si* and *murgh* mean "thirty" and "birds," respectively). The parable thus illustrates the Sufi concept of the return of the soul to its original source—God Almighty.

Much of the understanding and practice of Sufism has been based on Quranic formulations and on the model of Muhammad. For example, the Quranic admonition "and seek to remember Allah often" (62:10) contributed to the practice of meditation, and the Quranic statement that "In the messenger of God [Muhammad] you have a beautiful example of him whose hope is in God and the Last Day and who remembers God a great deal" (33:21) pointed to an appropriate model for the Sufi quest. In addition, Sufis have appealed to a saying attributed to Muhammad, "There is a means for polishing everything that removes rust; what polishes the heart is the remembrance of God." Nevertheless, certain Sufi observances, such as the use of music or dancing as aids to spiritual ecstasy and the veneration of Sufi leaders,

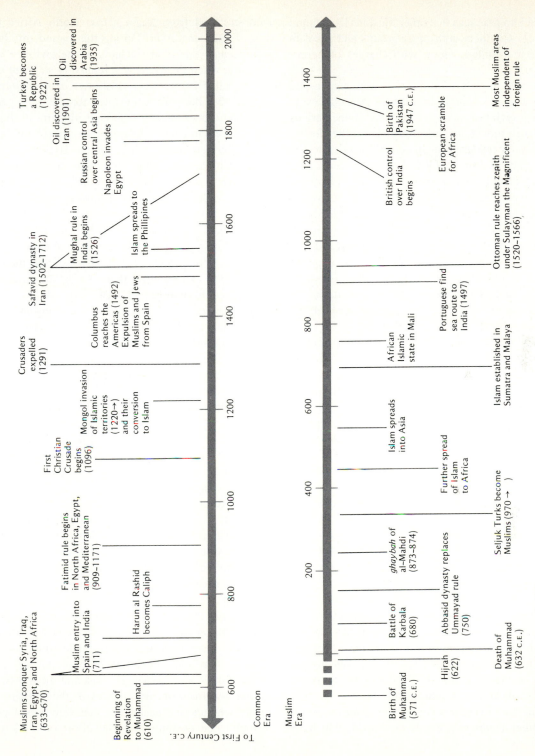

Historical Developments in Islam.

Timeline (Common Era):

Beginning of Revelation to Muhammad (610)

Muslims conquer Syria, Iraq, Iran, Egypt, and North Africa (633–670)

Muslim entry into Spain and India (711)

Harun al Rashid becomes Caliph

Fatimid rule begins in North Africa, Egypt, and Mediterranean (909–1171)

First Christian Crusade begins (1096)

Mongol invasion of Islamic territories (1220→) and their conversion to Islam

Crusaders expelled (1291)

Columbus reaches the Americas (1492) Expulsion of Muslims and Jews from Spain

Safavid dynasty in Iran (1502–1712)

Mughal rule in India begins (1526)

Islam spreads to the Phillipines

Napoleon invades Egypt

Russian control over central Asia begins

Oil discovered in Iran (1901)

Turkey becomes a Republic (1922)

Oil discovered in Arabia (1935)

Common Era

To First Century C.E.

Timeline (Muslim Era):

Muslim Era

Birth of Muhammad (571 C.E.)

Hijrah (622)

Death of Muhammad (632 C.E.)

Battle of Karbala (680)

Abbasid dynasty replaces Ummayad rule (750)

ghaybah of al-Mahdi (873–874)

Seljuk Turks become Muslims (970 →)

Islam spreads into Asia

Further spread of Islam to Africa

African Islamic state in Mali

Islam established in Sumatra and Malaya

Portuguese find sea route to India (1497)

Ottoman rule reaches zenith under Sulayman the Magnificent (1520–1566)

British control over India begins

European scramble for Africa

Birth of Pakistan (1947 C.E.)

Most Muslim areas independent of foreign rule

degenerated into practices that other Muslims have found unacceptable. Conflicts with other groups and scholars in Islam have resulted, along with charges of heresy and unbelief.

On the whole, however, Sufism has been responsible for creating a deeper awareness of the spiritual dimension of Islam. Through the education provided in the various Orders and their travels and preaching all over the Muslim world, the Sufis rendered an invaluable service to the spread of Islam in Africa, the Indian subcontinent, Indonesia, Malaysia, and southeast Asia. They influenced Muslim piety and created the means to express it through their writings and works of art. Sufi poetry and literature in Arabic, Bengali, Persian, Turkish, Urdu, Sindhi, Swahili, Hausa, and the languages of Indonesia and Malaysia did much to add to the culture of those peoples. Further, this literature provided them with a medium in their own language to express their particular sense of devotion and love for Islam and for the Prophet and to create a bridge for greater understanding of Islam among most non-Muslims in that area. On the other hand, a number of Muslims in the past, and even in the modern era, who have sought to restore Muslim practice to the norms of the Quran have accused Sufism of causing degeneration in Islam.

In addition to their contributions at the literary and cultural levels, some Sufi Orders have also acted as vehicles for political and social movements. To a significant extent, the national struggles in parts of the Muslim world in the nineteenth century derived their fervor from a common bond forged by allegiance to the Sufi Orders.

Islam in Contact and in Transition

Islam and the Medieval West

The interaction between the world of Islam and the West dates back to the seventh and eighth centuries C.E. At that time, the military expansion of Islam gave Muslims control of the Mediterranean and Spain, and even brought them for a short time beyond the Pyrenees into Southern France. Over the next six centuries this control was consolidated, and the area became culturally as well as politically an integral part of the Islamic world, which by then stretched from Spain across North Africa to the Middle East and Asia. During this period this Islamic area became one of the centers of the civilized world, at a time when the West was relatively stagnant during the so-called Dark Ages. Hostilities existed from time to time, but the period remained for the most part one of peaceful coexistence. Although Muslims at that time made efforts to acquire learning from other civilizations in the Mediterranean or Asia such as Byzantium, Persia (Iran), China, and India, they were indifferent to the West, from which in their view nothing useful was to be gained. In Western Christendom, which had been forced to come into contact with Islam, there was generally a negative attitude toward the religion that it saw as threatening its own existence and influence.

It was in the second major phase of the interaction between the two religions that coexistence gave way to military confrontation and, ironically, almost as a by-product, a more fruitful influence in learning and culture. The military confrontation was initiated in the First Crusade, launched in 1095 by European Christians to recapture Jerusalem. By this time, the city and the "Holy Land" had been part of the Muslim world for over four hundred years, although pilgrimages by devout Christians to Jerusalem had continued since the Muslim conquest. Leaders of Christianity, the rulers of Europe, and the Byzantine Emperor joined in support of this Crusade. The result was the capture of Jerusalem, as well as the major cities of Antioch, Edessa, and Tripoli, where the Crusaders established themselves. The Muslims were slow to respond, but in due course a concerted effort was made to recapture these cities. In 1187, the Muslim general Saladin recaptured Jerusalem. The Crusades continued intermittently through the thirteenth century. By 1291, the remaining areas in the hands of the Crusaders had been recaptured and the Crusader Kingdom finally put to an end.

Although the Crusades failed in their military purpose of recapturing the "Holy Land" from the Muslims, they did have other enduring results. The most significant of these were the stimulation of economic contact between Europe and the Middle East and the transmission of learning from the universities of the Muslim world to the scholars and academies that were developing in Europe. One example was the effort of Frederick II,

A Muslim Monument in Sarajevo, Yugoslavia. (Courtesy of Yugoslavia National Tourist Office)

ruler of Sicily from 1215–1250, to house and translate into Latin manuscripts on philosophy, mathematics, and science preserved in Muslim centers of learning. The most significant and fruitful cultural interaction, however, took place in Spain, where the Muslims settled and ruled for over seven centuries, until the fifteenth century. In its scale and importance, this legacy had a profound influence on Spain and medieval Western Europe.

One major feature of that Islamic presence was the cultural and linguistic Arabization of Spain. This was reflected in varied ways, ranging from agriculture to arts and crafts and from war to philosophy and science. The terminology and influence also spread to architecture, literature, and music. Another aspect of this cultural diffusion was the transmission of Muslim philosophy and science. As mentioned earlier, Muslim philosophers and scientists had sought to preserve and develop Greek learning. Indeed, many works of Aristotle and other classical Greek writers survived primarily through the efforts of these Muslim scholars. This heritage, in its classical form and in the developed form of Islamic philosophy and science (including mathematics, medicine, and astronomy), came to be transmitted through centers of Spanish Muslim learning in Cordova, Granada, and later in Seville and Barcelona. These centers attracted Jewish and Christian scholars from the Middle East, North Africa, and Europe, and provided the intellectual climate in which Jewish scholars such as Moses Maimonides produced their works. The philosophical commentaries and works of Averroes and the scientific and medical texts of Avicenna, among others, also played a role in stimulating the renewal of scientific and intellectual thought in Europe prior to the onset of the Renaissance. For instance, the works of Averroes exerted an influence on the famous medieval Christian theologian Thomas Aquinas.

Although "borrowing" is perhaps too simple a word to describe a process of cultural exchange, a large portion of this transmission continues to be reflected both in material culture and in the intellectual and cultural life of the West. Some examples of transmitted material culture are the Arabian horse, gum Arabic, tobacco, and muslin fabric; in mathematics, the most obvious are the Arabic numerals and the terms *algebra* and *algorithm;* in chemistry, terms such as *alcohol* and *alkali;* in astronomy, *zenith* and *nadir;* in military terminology, *admiral* and *arsenal;* and in agriculture and horticulture, there are a vast number of new plants, fruits, and vegetables that made their way into Europe and eventually to the Americas. All of this transmission suggests that a cosmopolitan culture was forged in medieval times by the interaction of Islam with the Mediterranean world and with Europe, and that much of this heritage came to be appropriated by and further elaborated in the West. In recent times migration from many parts of the Muslim world has led to the emergence of small Muslim communities in most of the larger cities of Western Europe and Britain, in addition to the already established Muslim communities of Eastern Europe, such as in Albania and Yugoslavia.

Islam, Africa, and Asia

Although the focus above has been primarily on the interaction that took place between Islam and the Mediterranean world and Europe, it must be remembered that a similar contact also took place between Islam and Africa and Asia. A major difference is that, while in most of Europe Muslim rule ended by the seventeenth and eighteenth centuries, much of Africa and Asia where Islam established roots retained its Muslim heritage. The confluence of Muslim and African cultures south of the Sahara led to a distinctive flowering of civilization. This change took place particularly during the thirteenth, fourteenth, and fifteenth centuries and is reflected in the rise of Muslim empires in West and Central Africa. Considerable assimilation of Islam and its culture took place, influencing in particular various African languages. The African Muslims were also stimulated to write their own languages in the Arabic script. Today, as Africa passes through an era of change, Islam continues to grow on that continent and retains strong roots in the areas where it had already established a strong presence.

In Central Asia, Islam had a series of confrontations that came in successive waves. The first were the Turks, followed by the Mongols, and then the Tatars who dealt a severe blow to the lands of Islam in the thirteenth and fourteenth centuries; but in time each of the three invading groups became Muslim and part of the Islamic world. After a long period of Mongol supremacy, Muslim rule in Central Asia was focused in small states, centered around major cities like Bukhara and Samarqand. In time these influences would give way to control by the rising power of Russia.

In India, the Muslims encountered an established religious and cultural tradition. Although this encounter often produced violence and led to intense mutual antipathy, the Indo–Muslim confluence produced a culture that is generally regarded as one of the finest that arose in the Muslim world. In the areas of mathematics, astronomy, music, and literature, the Muslims learned a great deal from the indigenous culture of India, which they built

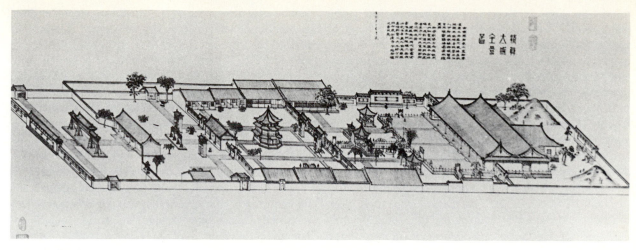

Islam in China. *This is a well-known complex, including "Great Mosque" in Xian, China.*
The architecture has been adapted to the style prevalent among Buddhist temples in the area.
(Courtesy of Mary Bush)

on and developed further in the course of their long rule. The dichotomy, however, that was part of Indo–Muslim culture eventually resulted in religious tensions and conflicts between Hindus and Muslims that could not be fully resolved and are dealt with later in this section.

In Indonesia, the situation developed somewhat differently. Wherever it spread in Indonesia and Malaysia, Islam interacted with the indigenous traditions to produce a synthesis of the two. As in Africa, south of the Sahara, Islam spread into southeast Asia through traders coming from the heartlands of Islam. International trade routes, until late medieval times, were dominated by Muslim merchants and seafarers, and provided a ready channel for the flow of Muslim ideas and influence. While it was the trading community that opened up these areas of Islam, the specific work of conversion was done by Sufi preachers. Further east, Muslim influences and conversion also took place, along trading routes leading into Western China.

The foregoing account traces the various contacts and influences resulting from Islam's interaction with various parts of the world from the ninth to the seventeenth centuries. By then Islam had attained its largest growth, and the territory of the world of Islam had tripled in size from the period of first expansion during the eighth century. At its peak, several major Muslim dynasties ruled this territory and the world of Islam at this time had achieved a high degree of cosmopolitanism in its culture and civilization.

The Period of the Great Empires

The largest of the Muslim states was the Ottoman Empire based in Turkey. During the sixteenth and seventeenth centuries, it extended over Central Asia, parts of Europe and the Mediterranean, and most of the Middle East. Other large Muslim states were represented by the Safavid dynasty, which ruled Iran, and the Mughals, who ruled the Indian Subcontinent. Smaller Muslim states were to be found in parts in Africa, Indonesia, Malaysia, and western China.

The three large empires were militarily powerful and had a strong established base of Islamic institutions at all levels of administration. Two events, however, that took place toward the end of the fifteenth century profoundly affected the subsequent history of the Muslims and ushered in an era of transition that has continued into the twentieth century. The first of these two events was the unexpected discovery of the New World by Columbus beginning in 1492. The second was the sea voyage of the Portuguese explorer, Vasco da Gamma, around the Cape of Good Hope to India in 1497. The subsequent colonization of the Americas, the onset of an age of European exploration and expansion in Asia and Africa, and the increase in material prosperity generated by the economic exploitation that followed, changed drastically the balance of political and economic power in favor of Europe. By the nineteenth century, all three Islamic empires were faced with disintegration in the wake of European expansion and military power.

Even before the actual loss of political power by the Muslim world, there had been an era of revivalism in certain areas, which had resulted in attempts to revitalize the faith of Muslims. One such movement took place in Arabia and was led by Muhammad ibn Abdul Wahhab (1703–1792). He launched a movement whose primary purpose was to make Muslims in Arabia aware of an internal decay in their lives, which in his view could only be put right by returning to the Islamic practice of the early period (i.e., the period of the Prophet and his immediate successors). His attack was primarily directed at practices that had developed among Sufi circles, involving visits to the tombs of saints. This attempt at reform was aided by a cooperative effort on the part of Abdul Wahhab and the head of the Sa'ud family, which subsequently gave Arabia its present name—Saudi Arabia.

Similar internal efforts at revitalization and reform also took place in India, where scholars like Shah Waliyullah (1703–1762) set about establishing schools of learning to stimulate greater thinking on the part of Muslims concerning their heritage. Their attempts at reform also influenced revival among Sufi orders in Africa. In the nineteenth century, several massive attempts were made to revitalize and unite Muslims in Central and West Africa by *jihad* movements. These *jihad* movements were military and educational efforts by leaders of Sufi Orders like Uthman Dan Fodio (d. 1817) in West Africa, Al-Hajj Umar (d. 1864) in what is now Senegal and Gambia, and Muhammad al Sanusi (d. 1859) in North Africa.

Developments under European Rule and Influence

By the end of the nineteenth century and the early part of the twentieth, European expansion and colonization had brought almost the entire Muslim world under direct European rule or influence. Britain controlled India, Malaysia, the Gulf area, Egypt, and portions of West, Central, and East Africa. France exercised power in North Africa and part of West Africa, as well as the Middle East. The Russians had overrun Central Asia, and after the revolution of 1917 several of the large Muslim areas there were incorporated into the newly formed Soviet Union. The Muslim population there numbers 50 million and is expected to constitute one-fifth of the total population of the Soviet Union by the end of the century.

The East Indies and parts of Asia and Africa came under the control of other European powers such as Holland, Italy, Spain, and Portugal. Those areas not directly colonized—such as Arabia, Turkey, Afghanistan, or Iran—were nonetheless regarded as spheres of Western influence, where power was exercised indirectly through diplomatic means. Thus, there was virtually no area of any significance in the Muslim world that had not been directly or indirectly affected by European power, or was not a target of the scramble for colonies. As in other colonized parts of the world, these Muslim regions faced a major disruption of their institutions and cultures during the colonial period. Their attempts to respond to this challenge at the intellectual and political levels underlie much of modern Muslim history until recent times.

The Intellectual Response. It was at the intellectual level that concerned Muslims were led to address the questions of an Islamic response to the influx of European ideas and institutions. Several individuals stood out by their efforts. In the Middle East, the key thinkers were Jamal al din Afghani (1830–1897) and Muhammad Abduh (1849–1905). Afghani was concerned primarily about the intellectual challenge posed by Western ideas of humanism and science. He argued that the basic principles of Islam were not incompatible with science, but that Muslim thought during this period had allowed itself to lapse into intellectual stagnation. He sought to arouse a new spirit of inquiry among Muslim scholars that would reconcile Islam with the needs of a changing world of ideas. In addition, he struggled during his travels through the Muslim world to arouse among Muslims a sense of unity to combat the rule of European powers. He urged a form of Pan-Islamic federation of states. Afghani's views were not supported in those areas where western influence came to predominate and whose rulers were more concerned with national goals, but he did influence individuals, among whom was an Egyptian scholar, Muhammad Abduh. Abduh, in his role as a leader of religious education and law, put many of these ideas into practice. The changes came to be reflected in interpretations of law and in the curriculum of the religious schools, particularly at the University of al-Azhar in Cairo, regarded at the time as a major center of Muslim learning.

In the Indian subcontinent similar attempts were made at reconciliation by scholars such as Sayyid Ahmad Khan (1817–1889), Sayyid Amir Ali (1849–1928), and Muhammad Iqbal (1876–1938), a poet and philosopher. The efforts of Sayyid Ahmad led to the establishment of what eventually came to be called the Aligarh Muslim University in Aligarh, India, where the curriculum reflected a desire to blend traditional Muslim studies with subjects dealing with the sciences of the day. Amir Ali also argued strongly for a reassessment of the social principles of the *Shariah* on the basis of a more contemporary interpretation of the Quran. Muhammad Iqbal tried in his works to fuse the concepts of faith and intuition. Basing his thought on that of the Muslim philosophers and the Sufis, as well as on contemporary Western philosophic thought, he tried to give a new direction to modern Muslim thinking by asserting that Quranic principles supported intellectual and spiritual life and that by reviving these principles Muslims could revitalize and reconstruct their contemporary social and community lives.

The views of some of these intellectuals did not necessarily reflect those of all Muslim thinkers of the time. It was among those who did not espouse this "modernist" approach that alternative approaches arose, which in turn gave rise to organized movements. One of these was the *Ikhwan al Muslimin* (Brotherhood of Muslims), which developed in Egypt primarily as a result of the work and teachings of two individuals: Hasan al Banna (d. 1949) and Sayyid Qutb (d. 1966). They believed that Islam, as a total way of life revealed by God, ought to be fully implemented uniformly in all Muslim countries. They regarded the emerging nationalism of various Muslim countries and the trend of Westernization as divisive elements. The truly Islamic state, if established, would embrace all Muslims, and its leaders would be elected and rule in consultation with the members of that state.

The movement organized itself in Egypt to spread its views, but its activities were considered a threat to the goals of nationalism by the Egyptian government and the movement was declared illegal; its leaders were often imprisoned and either assassinated or executed. It managed to continue its work in other parts of the Middle East, and has been permitted recently to play a public role in Egyptian political and social affairs once again.

A similar movement developed in India (and subsequently in Pakistan) called the *Jamat-i-Islami*. It was founded by Abu Ala Mawdudi (d. 1979) and sought to create an Islamic state based on the *Shariah;* it established itself as a political party to attain its goals. Although it never attained power, it continued to play a major role in determining the role of Islam in the life of Muslims of the Subcontinent. In general, such movements sought inspiration by relating their goals to the model of Muslim life and organization, which they believed had been attained in the beginnings of Islam, in the community founded by God through Muhammad.

The Political Response. All of these efforts were going on at the same time as the movement to regain independence from European rule, a movement that began to intensify in the Muslim world in the twentieth century. These movements eventually led to the establishment of a host of independent Muslim nation-states. One significant question in this process was that of political forms and models of development to be adopted by these countries.

An early example was Turkey. Under the leadership of Mustafa Kemal, known as Ataturk, the disintegrating Ottoman Empire was replaced in 1923 by a new secular state called Turkey. Ataturk believed that the influence of outmoded Muslim institutions and leaders had caused the Muslim peoples to fall behind Europe in progress and development. He therefore initiated a deliberate program of Westernization at all levels. This process limited the scope of the *Shariah* drastically. Government, education, and law were the areas most strongly affected. The position of the Caliph was abolished and replaced by a republican form of government with Ataturk as President. A system of education modeled on a European pattern was set up and the application of Islamic law was limited to personal matters. Ataturk also attempted to abolish traditional forms of dress, replaced the Arabic script with a Latin one, and encouraged the integration of women into the new educational institutions and the workforce of the country. Thus, a total revision of institutions took place—Islam continued to be a living force in the lives of most Turks, but it ceased to be a vehicle for transformation of traditional institutions into modern ones; Turkey had become a secular state.

At about the same time, Iran was also going through a phase of political change. The rule of the Safavids had been followed in the eighteenth and nineteenth centuries by that of shorter dynasties. By the beginning of the twentieth century, a movement for constitutional reform had begun and a new constitution providing for a modern state had been promulgated in 1906. But intense rivalries and European involvement did not allow this process to be continued. In 1921, power came into the hands of a colonel called Reza Khan who, after proclaiming himself a new "Shah" (the Persian title for Emperor), set about a policy of Westernization similar to that of Ataturk. In Iran, the problem was complicated by the fact that the religious scholars, or mullahs, had always played a decisive role in influencing the life of the state. The policies of Reza Shah were continued by his son Mohammed Reza Shah. His policies of modernization, fuelled to a large extent by growing revenues from oil exports, led to the increasing isolation of the mullahs from the political and economic life of the country. However, their close contacts with the people allowed the mullahs to build a network of opposition to what they regarded as alien, secular influences under the Shah. The more Western-educated desired to integrate contemporary developments with their Muslim heritage. A leading figure in this movement was Ali Shariati (d. 1977), who, in spite of continuing harassment by the state, was able to evoke a significant response among the students and the younger segment of the population, who perceived rampant but superficial technological modernization and Western influence in Iran as detrimental to religious values and cultural identity. All of these groups united in calling for a more Islamic society to be created in Iran. This opposition, in combination with other political and economic factors, eventually led to mass opposition to the Shah, followed by a revolution (led by Ayatollah Khomeini) that brought into existence the Islamic Republic of Iran in 1979.

Meanwhile, in British-ruled India, a movement had arisen among Muslims that led to the demand for an independent state. Their spokesmen, led by Muhammad Ali Jinnah, known as the founder of Pakistan, wished for the creation of a separate Islamic state. In 1947, the British partitioned what was then India, and, from the predominantly Muslim northwest and northeast areas, Pakistan was born, consisting of West and East Pakistan, separated by over one thousand miles and major ethnic and linguistic differences. In spite of these differences, the desire for a unified state for all Muslims of the Subcontinent had been an overwhelming force in the creation of the new Islamic state. The definition of this state, its form of government, the role of the *Shariah* in its legal system, and the diversity of its ethnic groups were all factors that eventually put great stress on the unity of Pakistan, and led to the eventual dissolution of the two-part state and the emergence of a new country, Bangladesh, which superseded East Pakistan in 1971. Today, Bangladesh, Pakistan, and India together are home to over 200 million Muslims.

In Indonesia, an independence movement that combined elements of nationalism and Islam led to the expulsion of the Dutch colonial power and to political independence in 1949. Under Sukarno, who became President of Indonesia, a policy of "Indonesian socialism" was implemented to create national and economic unity. His policies, however, were unsuccessful and led to internal conflict and the eventual establishment of military rule in Indonesia. Today, Islam continues to be a major force in Indonesia, which is recognized as the country with the largest population of Muslims in the world.

Muslim populations in North and West Africa also succeeded in their struggle for independence during this period. Some of these movements received their momentum and organization from allegiance to Muslim institutions such as Sufi Orders, or were organized by individuals who claimed leadership on the basis of leading Islamic movements. A good example of the latter was the revolt against the British led by the Mahdi of Sudan.

A whole series of nation states had thus emerged in the present century, most of whom at the time of attaining independence found themselves facing political, economic, and social challenges in many fundamental ways, far different from the experience of Muslims in the past.

Dar al Islam Complex. *The Muslim Presence in North America: The Dar al Islam Complex near Abiqui, New Mexico.* (Courtesy of The Dar al Islam Foundation. Photograph by Paul Logsdon)

It is fair to say, that for most of them the reference point and models of development were the examples of the West (including the Soviet Union) and that such a pattern led in time to a strong emphasis on western cultural and technological values that had already taken root in their societies.

Islam in North America

The first contact of Islam with the Americas probably dates back to the time of the Spanish voyages of exploration in the sixteenth century. It is uncertain whether there were many among the Spaniards who still retained their Moorish-Islamic heritage.

We can, however, be more certain about the fact that among the many blacks who were forced to come to America under the yoke of slavery, there were many Muslims from the Islamic regions of West Africa. Although the memory of Islam may have survived among the early generation of slaves, the inhuman conditions under which they served and the imposed standards of slavery all but eliminated any traces of their religious heritage.

It was not until the twentieth century that among some of the descendants of these involuntary immigrants a recovery of the awareness of an Islamic heritage began to develop. The figure responsible for this process was a black man who would eventually call himself Elijah

Muhammad. He learned about Islam from a somewhat mysterious figure, named Wali Farrad, who claimed to have come from Mecca to awaken among the black people of America an awareness of their lost Islamic heritage. The task of doing this was left to Elijah Muhammad, who was designated as "the messenger of Allah." He became a figure of great controversy, but it is clear that his primary motivation was to provide his followers with a sense of self-identity and dignity, long denied to them, based on the past link with Islam. The movement, which became known as the "Nation of Islam," found many converts, among whom were Malcolm X and Muhammad Ali.

After Elijah Muhammad's death in 1975, the role of leader was assumed by his son Warith Deen Muhammad (Wallace Muhammad). The name of the movement was changed to World Community of Islam and eventually to the American Muslim Mission. Under Warith Deen Muhammad, the movement has sought to receive recognition as a member of the worldwide Muslim community and attempted in its practice and philosophy to conform to standards generally common among all Muslims. He has tried to de-emphasize some aspects of legend and controversy associated with Elijah Muhammad, in particular the exclusively "black" nature of the movement and the definition of his role as messenger of Allah. Although the group is not without its internal differences, the American Muslim Mission now considers itself as representing the interests of Islam in North America; it counts among its goals the fostering of greater awareness of traditional Islam among its adherents. It has also recently sought to abolish its separate, organizational framework and to identify more fully with the larger Muslim community in America, while still continuing to promote economic and social development at the local level.

In addition to this group, there are now in North America other Muslims, descendants of immigrants from all parts of the Islamic world, who now attest to a strong Islamic presence. There are approximately 600 centers serving Muslims, and mosques in each of the major cities in the United States and Canada. There is also an active association of Muslim students of North America that serves the needs of many local as well as international Muslim students. Without question, the Muslim presence is now a visible part of the religious landscape of North America.

Islam in the Contemporary World

The new Muslim states and communities that constitute the world of Islam today, are expressing a need, in varying degrees, to relate their Islamic heritage to questions of national and cultural self-identification and development. This phenomenon, which has drawn worldwide attention, is however part of a global process affecting virtually all religions, and points to the continuing vitality and persistence of the religious dimension in contemporary life. In the Muslim World as elsewhere, its occurrence has in some cases become linked to domestic or international conflict, which has come to be expressed in religious terms, causing a great deal of misunderstanding and confusion regarding the role of Islam in contemporary Muslim societies.

Since the modern conception of religion familiar to most people in the West assumes a theoretical separation between religious and secular activity, the integration of these perspectives in Muslim discourse, particularly in political life, appears alarming and often retrogressive. Where the language of politics expressed in religious terms has in some cases become allied with radical change or violence, it has led to distorted conceptions of the relationship between Islamic values and change. In general, such perceptions have derived from experience with change in a small number of Muslim countries that have gained recognition because of the presence of important natural resources such as oil or because their geopolitical location is of strategic importance in international affairs. All of this has resulted in an unfortunate preoccupation with immediate and primarily political implications and dimensions of change and the overlooking of much of the larger process in which diverse Muslim societies, with differing backgrounds, ways of life, and economic experience, are dealing with the relationship between their Islamic heritage and their contemporary life.

It must be noted that the practice and influence of Islam in all these areas did not cease during the period of colonial rule, nor in the period immediately following the attainment of sovereign status. Rather, it was the traditional role of Islam in shaping political, social, and cultural life that had come to be undermined or curtailed. The recent emphasis and debate has been on reviving this role, which many Muslims believe was eclipsed, to the detriment of their societies. Further, the loss of economic and political power and the emphasis on nationalism as an ideology, was also believed to have affected Islam's role in assisting societies to adapt to changing conditions and to redress the balance against dominant, alien influences. This discussion about Islam's role in political and cultural life has become much more pronounced recently, and involves a definition of such issues in traditional religious terms. It is against this background and effort to create continuity with past values, based on the conception of Islam as a total way of life, that the general phenomenon, sometimes called the "resurgence" of Islam, can best be understood.

In the varied responses, no one trend can be identified as typical, for the influence of Islam in these diverse areas is neither monolithic nor homogeneous. Some of the responses have led to internal conflict and an increasingly aggressive stance against outside influences, often expressed in political action against the West and the Soviet Union. In most cases, however, there has been an increasing recognition of global interdependence, and the wider contacts possible among Muslims today has tended to shrink the divisive effects of national and ethnic boundaries. Various international organizations and activities now link Muslims with each other and with the rest of the world and have become vehicles for addressing common problems and needs. Education has led to greater self-awareness of how the Islamic heritage can be integrated within the framework of contemporary institutions and needs and this has led in most areas of the Muslim World to a greater interest in retaining and adapting, within the context of the Islamic heritage, institutions, laws, educational principles, modes of architecture, and patterns of urban, rural, and social life. Islam has just entered a new century: its fifteenth promises to be at least as dramatic as any that has preceded it.

NOTES

1. Margaret Smith, *Readings from the Mystics of Islam* (London: Luzac & Co., 1972), p. 11.
2. Ibn Tufayl, *Hayy Ibn Yaqzan,* trans. by L. E. Goodman (Boston: Twayne Publishers, 1972).
3. Jalal al-din Rumi, *Mathnawi* (London: Luzac, 1926), Part One, vss. 1–4.
4. Farid al-din Attar, *The Conference of the Birds,* trans. by C. S. Nott (Berkeley: Shambala Publications, 1971).

GLOSSARY

adhān (*uhd-haahn*)   the call to prayer made from a mosque, five times a day. The giver of *adhan* is known as a *muezzin* (*mu'adhdhin*).

Allāh (*uhl-laah*)   the Quranic term for the one true God.

dār al-Islām (*daahr-uhl-is-laahm*)   the World of Islam, the territory where Islam is most prevalent.

dhikr (*dhi-kruh*)   invocation or remembrance of the names of God, one of the mediative practices, particularly in Sufism.

dīn (*deen*)   the concept of religion in the Quran.

du'ā (*doo-aah; the apostrophe represents the Arabic glottal stop*)   voluntary prayer, in addition to *salat*.

al-Fātiḥah (*uhl-faah-ti-huh*)   the title of the opening *surah* of the Quran.

fiqh (*fik'-uh*)   literally "understanding"; the term applied to the science of Islamic law. The specialists or legalists are called *faqih* (pl. *fuqaha'*).

ḥadīth (*huh-deeth*)   a report recording a saying or action of the Prophet Muhammad.

Ḥajj (*huhjj*)   the pilgrimage to Mecca and its environs during the month of pilgrimage. When visited at other times during the year, the visit is called *'Umrah.*

Hijrah (*hij-ruh*)   the Prophet's emigration from Mecca to Medina in 622, the year from which the Muslim lunar calendar dates.

'Īd (*'eed*)   festival; there are two major *'Īd* in the Muslim year: The *'Īd al Adhā* (the Festival of Sacrifice), part of the concluding ceremonies of the pilgrimage; and *'Īd al Fiṭr* (the Festival ending the fast of Ramadan).

iḥrām (*ih-raahm*)   the state of sanctity and purity during the pilgrimage.

ijma *or* **ijmā'** (*ijj-maah*)   consensus of scholars reflecting their unanimous opinion at any given time.

ijtihād (*ij-ti-haahd*) literally "exerting oneself," the personal intellectual effort to understand Islam. One who exercises *Ijtihād* is called a *mujtahid*.

Imām (*i-maahm*) leader, generally referring to the person who leads others in prayer. In the past the term was used interchangeably with *Caliph*, for the head of the state and occasionally as an honorific title for very learned religious scholars. Among the Shi'a, the Imam is a divinely appointed leader, succeeding the Prophet. He possesses spiritual knowledge and guides Muslims to an understanding of the inner meaning of relevation as well as implementing Islamic values according to changing times and circumstances.

jihād (*jih-haahd*) struggle in the way of Islam; also applied to armed struggle for the cause of Islam. The one who fights is called *mujahid*.

jinn (*jin*) spirits and invisible beings referred to in the Quran.

Ka'ba (*kuh-buh*) the cubic structure in Mecca, the focal point of ceremonies of pilgrimage and the direction to which all Muslims turn for prayer.

Khalīfah (*khuh-lee-fuh*) Caliph, the title adopted by the rulers of the Muslim community after the death of Muhammad.

Khwārij (*or* **Kharijites**) (*khwaah-rij*) those among early Muslims who separated themselves from the rest of the community and established themselves as a distinct and often militant group.

Mahdī (*muh-dee*) the title given by the Shi'a to the hidden Imam whose return is awaited.

masjid (*muhs-jid*) mosque, the place of worship in Islam.

miḥrāb (*mih-raahb*) the niche in the mosque that marks the *qiblah*, the direction towards Mecca.

minbar (*min-buhr*) the pulpit in the mosque for preaching.

Miraj *or* **Mi'rāj** (*mih-raahj*) the event in the life of Muhammad when he experienced the **isra'** or "ascent" into heaven, the night commemorated by Muslims with special prayers and remembrance.

Muḥarram (*muh-huhr-rum*) the month of the Muslim year of special significance to the Shi'a, who commemorate the memory and martyrdom of their Imam Husayn during the first ten days of Muharram, the tenth day being known as *'Ashūra'* (*aah-shoo-raah*)

Qāḍī (*kaah-dhee*)glan official appointee of the state as judge to administer the *Shariah*.

qiblah (*kib-luh*) the direction of Mecca toward which Muslims turn in ritual prayer.

qiyās (*ki-yaahs*) analogy, a principle in law, enabling scholars to use analogous reasoning.

Quran *or* **Qur'ān** (*kur-aahn*) the revelation of God to Muhammad in its collected form.

rak'ah (*ruhk-uh*) the unit of ritual prayer, during which a Muslim performs the specific required actions.

Ramaḍān (*ruh-muh-dhaahn*) the month in which fasting is practised.

salām (*suh-laahm*) the greeting of peace exchanged by Muslims, more fully, *salam alaykum:* Peace be upon you!

ṣalāt (*suh-laaht*) the ritual prayer in Islam.

ṣawm (*sawm*) fasting, particularly during the month of Ramadan.

shahādah (*shuh-haah-duh*) the act of witnessing or attesting to the formula—"There is no god but Allah; Muhammad is the messenger of Allah." This formula is known as *kalima*.

Shariah *or* **Shari'ah** (*shuh-ree-yuh*) the concept of the right way, formalized as law and code of conduct.

Shia *or* **Shi'ah** (*shee-yuh*) the group of Muslims who initially supported the claims of 'Ali and his descendants to the headship of the Muslim community and subsequently developed into a distinctive religious group within Islam. Among the various subgroups the most important are the *Ithna 'Ash-ari*, the *Isma'ili*, and the *Zaydi*.

Ṣūfi (*soo-fee*) the Muslims who seek through the path of religious experience and spiritual discipline to acquire personal knowledge and intimacy with God.

Sunnah (*sun-nuh*) the custom or tradition of the Prophet that complements the Quran as a source for Muslim faith and practice.

Sunnī (*sun-nee*) the term used to designate the group in Islam called "ahl al Sunna wa'l Jama'a" (The People of the Tradition and the Majority).

Sūrah (*soo-ruh*) a chapter of the Quran.

tafsīr (*tuhf-seer*) explanation of the Quran with primary emphasis on the study of the context and meaning of revealed verses.

takbīr (*tuhk-beer*) the recitation of praise, "Allahu Akbar," which means "God is Great."

Ṭarīqah (*tuh-ree-kuh*) the path of discipline leading to knowledge of God, also a Sufi Order or group.

Tawhīd (*toh-heed*) the doctrine of Divine Unity.

ta'wīl (*taah-weel*) explanation and analysis of the inner meaning of Quranic verses.

Ulama *or* **'ulamā'** (*ul-luh-maah; the first "u" is as in "pull"*) plural of *'alim*, the learned scholars and custodians of religious knowledge. In Iran they are called *mullah* and also referred to with other titles, the highest among which is that of *ayatollah*, meaning "sign of God."

Ummah (*um-muh; the first "u" is as in "pull"*) "community," an inclusive concept signifying Muslims as well as those that are under Muslim protection.

wuḍū (*wu-dhoo; the first "u" is as in "pull"*) the act of ablution or cleansing prior to the performance of ritual prayer.

zakāt (*zuh-kaaht*) the act of almsgiving as a means of purification.

ziyārah (*zee-yaah-ruh*) (pl. *ziyārāt*) visits paid, particularly among the Shia and the Sufis to places where the Imams or other pious figures are buried.

SUGGESTED READINGS

Primary Sources in Translation

The Quran   There are several good translations available: *The Meaning of the Glorious Koran,* trans. by Mohammed Pickthall, New York, Mentor, 1953; *The Holy Qur'an,* trans. by Yusuf Ali, Lahore, Muhammad Ashraf, 1959; *The Koran Interpreted,* trans, by A. J. Arberry, New York, Macmillan, 1964; and M. Ayoub, *The Qur'ān and its Interpreters,* Vol. 1 Albany, State University of New York Press, 1984. For Quranic recitation, see K. Nelson *The Art of Reciting the Qur'an,* Austin, University of Texas Press, 1985.

Biographies of the Prophet   One of the earliest biographies is available in translation: Ibn Ishaq, *Life of Muhammad,* trans. by Alfred Guillaume, Oxford, Oxford University Press, 1955. An excellent synthesized, biographical rendering based on the traditional sources is, M. Lings, *Muhammad—His Life According to the Earliest Sources,* London, George Allen and Unwin, 1983.

The *Hadith*   Selections of *hadith* are available in translation. A good compendium is the *Mishkat al-Masabih,* 4 vols., trans. by J. Robson, Lahore, Muhammad Ashraf, 1956–65. Among the Sunni collections, the most famous, that of al-Bukhari, is now available in a translation: *Sahih al-Bukhari,* trans. by Muhammad Khan, revised edition, Ankara, 1976.

Shia materials   Passages from Shia collections of *hadith,* including the celebrated *Nahj al-Balagha* of Ali, are contained in *A Shi'ite Anthology,* ed. and trans. by W. C. Chittick, New York, State University of New York Press, 1980.

Sufi materials   *Mathnawi of Jalal al-din Rumi,* 3 vols., trans. by R. Nicholson, London, Luzac & Co., 1977; and Attar, *The Conference of the Birds,* trans. by C. S. Nott, Berkeley, Shambhala Publications, 1971.

Muslim philosophy and theology   Al-Farabi, *On the Perfect State,* trans. by R. Walzer, Oxford University Press, 1985; *Hayy Ibn Yaqzan,* trans. by L. Goodman, Boston, Twayne Publishing Company, 1972; Ibn Rushd (Averroes), *Agreement of Philosophy and Religion,* trans. by G. Hourani, London, Luzac & Co., 1961; al-Ghazali, *Deliverance from Error,* translated in W. M. Watt, *Faith and Practice of al-Ghazali,* London, George Allen and Unwin, 1953; and Ibn Khaldun, *The Muqaddimah: An Introduction to History,* trans. by F. Rosenthal, Princeton, Princeton University Press, 1958.

Secondary Sources

ABDALATI, H. *The Structure of Family Life in Islam.* Indianapolis: American Trust Publications, 1978.

ADAMS, CHARLES. "The Islamic Religious Tradition," in *Religion and Man.* Edited by W. R. Comstock. New York: Harper & Row, Publishers, 1971.

AHMAD, K., ed. *Islam: Its Meaning and Message.* London: Islamic Council of Europe, 1976.

AHMED, A. *Religion and Politics in Muslim Society.* Cambridge: Cambridge University Press, 1983.

BENNINGSEN, A., and S. E. WIMBUSH. *Muslims in the Soviet Empire.* Bloomington: Indiana University Press, 1986.

BURCKHART, TITUS. *Art of Islam.* London: World of Islam Festival Publications, 1976.

The Cambridge History of Islam. 2 vols. Edited by P. M. Holt, et al. Cambridge: Cambridge University Press, 1970.

CRAGG, K. *Islam from Within.* Belmont: Wadsworth Publishing Company, 1979.

DANIEL, N. *Islam and the West: The Making of an Image.* Edinburgh: the University Press, 1962.

DENNY, F. M. Islam: *An Introduction,* New York: Macmillan Publishing Co. 1985.

Encyclopaedia of Islam. Rev. ed. Leiden: E. J. Brill, 1960–.

Encyclopaedia of Religion. New York: Macmillan Publishing Co. 1986.

ESPOSITO, J. and DONAHUE J., eds. *Islam in Transition.* New York: Oxford University Press, 1982.

FAKHRY, M. *History of Islamic Philosophy.* New York: Columbia University Press, 1974.

FARUQI, I., AND L. FARUQI. *A Cultural Atlas of Islam.* New York: Macmillan Publishing Co., 1986.

GEERTZ, C. *Islam Observed.* Chicago: University of Chicago Press, 1971.

GIBB, H. *Mohammedanism.* Oxford: Oxford University Press, 1970.

HODGSON, MARSHALL. *The Venture of Islam.* 3 vols. Chicago: University of Chicago Press, 1974.

JAFRI, S. *The Origins and Development of the Shiah.* Beirut: Longman, 1979.

KELLY, M., ed. *Islam: The Religious and Political Life of a World Community.* New York: Praeger Publishers, 1984.

KRITZECK, J., ed. *Islam in Africa.* New York: Van Nostrand Reinhold Co., 1969.

LEWIS, BERNARD, ed. *Islam and the Arab World.* New York: Alfred A. Knopf, Inc., 1976.

LINGS, MARTIN. *What is Sufism?* London: George Allen and Unwin Ltd., 1975.

MALCOLM X. *The Autobiography of Malcolm X.* New York: Grove Press, Inc., 1964.

MARTIN, R. *Islam: A Cultural Perspective.* Englewood Cliffs, N.J.: Prentice-Hall, 1982.

MOMEN, M. *An Introduction to Shi'i Islam.* New Haven: Yale University Press, 1985.

MOTTAHEDEH, ROY. *The Mantle of the Prophet.* New York: Simon and Schuster, 1986.

NASR, SEYYED HOSSEIN. *Ideals and Realities of Islam*. Cambridge, Mass.: Beacon Press, 1972.

———, ed. *Ismaili Contributions to Islamic Culture*. Tehran: Iranian Academy of Philosophy, 1977.

QUTB, SAYYID. *Social Justice in Islam*. Washington: American Council of Learned Societies, 1953.

RAHMAN, FAZLUR. *Islam*. 2d ed. Chicago: University of Chicago Press, 1979.

———. *Major Themes in the Quran*. Minneapolis and Chicago: Bibliotheca Islamica, 1980.

———. *Islam and Modernity*. Chicago: University of Chicago Press, 1982.

RUTHVEN, M. *Islam in the World*. New York: Oxford University Press, 1984.

SAID, E. *Orientalism*. New York: Pantheon, 1978.

SAVOURY, R. *Islamic Civilization*. Cambridge: Cambridge University Press, 1977.

SCHACHT, J., ed. *The Legacy of Islam*. London: Oxford University Press, 1974.

SCHIMMEL, A. *Mystical Dimensions of Islam*. Chapel Hill: University of North Carolina Press, 1976.

———. *And Muhammad is His Messenger*. Chapel Hill: University of North Carolina Press, 1986.

SCHUON, F. *Understanding Islam*. Baltimore: Penguin, 1972.

Shorter Encyclopedia of Islam. Leiden: E. J. Brill, 1953.

SMITH, W. C. *Islam in Modern History*. Princeton: Princeton University Press, 1957.

TABATABAI, ALLAMAH SAYYID. *Shi'ite Islam*. Edited and translated by S. H. Nasr. New York: State University of New York Press, 1974.

WATT, W. *The Majesty That Was Islam*. Chicago Praeger Publishers, Inc., 1976.

———. *Muhammad, Prophet and Statesman*. Oxford: Oxford University Press, 1974.

WAUGH, E. et al., eds. *The Muslim Community in North America*. Edmonton: University of Alberta Press, 1982.

WILLIAMS, J. A. ed. *Islam*. New York: Mentor Books, Inc., 1961.

10

New Religions in America

Important religions have been founded on American soil. Some are worthy of attention because of the number of adherents they have attracted; three groups originating in the nineteenth century have millions of followers—the Mormons, Jehovah's Witnesses, and Christian Scientists. Other groups originating in the twentieth century have attracted the attention of the American news media and social scientists interested in group behavior, but the adherents of each group number in the several thousands. The two twentieth-century groups we shall look at closely—the International Society for Krishna Consciousness (better known as the Hare Krishnas) and the Unification Church (sometimes disparagingly called Moonies)—are well-known to the American public at large in spite of their smaller numbers.

These American religions are related to other great religions already dealt with in this book, but their beliefs and circumstances have changed so much that they are really *new* religions. Although *cult,* the word often used as a label for these groups, suggests secrecy and even perversion, we shall not discover secrets or perversions by studying these "new" American religions, but we shall learn something about the structures and dynamics of religious group life.

Fundamental Features of the New Religions

Besides *cult,* other labels may be applied to religious groups, namely *sect* and *church.* The clarification of the meaning of these labels is the first step toward understanding the new American religions. A church is the established religion of a nation or a clearly defined ethnic subgroup within a nation, and is completely integrated into the life of the nation or ethnic group wherein it is found.* Literally speaking, Roman Catholicism is a church in Italy. A sect is a group that has cut itself off from a church (the Latin word *secare* means to "cut away"). Sects separate themselves from the principal church in order to maintain the force and vigor of a reforming effort, which often entails opposition to standard national or ethnic morals and customs. Methodism was in late eighteenth- and early nineteenth-century England a sect of the Anglican Church, because it separated itself from the national Church of England. A cult is a form of religion that is new to a nation or ethnic group, and has nothing to do with earlier cultural and religious ways. The International Society for Krishna Consciousness must be considered a cult—although it represented one form of Krishna worship in India, it was a new way of worship for Protestant, Catholic, and Jewish young Americans.

Of course, we must change the labels of some groups across the decades or across the centuries: a group may loose the qualities that characterize a sect and take on the qualities that characterize a cult. To take an example from ancient and medieval history, Christianity began

---

* Note that when there are several churches fully established in an area like the United States, the term *denomination* is often used. In this chapter we use the terms *church* and *denomination* interchangeably; *denomination* is, however, a more sociologically neutral term, and is sometimes used to label sects and even cults.

in Jerusalem as a sect of Judaism, but when it was exported to other areas of the Roman Empire, it was, relative to Roman religion or various tribal religions, a cult. When Christianity came to be the predominant religion in the Empire after Constantine, it then became a church.[1]

Persons who are attracted or dedicated to a church are often pleased to have the familiar, natural cultural life consolidated by the church's beliefs and practices; persons who are members of a sect appreciate their own culture enough to want to reform it, and believe that regular church life holds them back—the only alternative is separation (with hope of absorption of the unreformed groups of brethren). Cult members often are opposed to the culture from which they come and so join radically innovative groups (cults) that have radically innovative interpretations of the meaning of life. While these basic characteristics do not hold true in every case, they give us some general ideas to work with as we begin the history of each religious group. We will study why the new American religions are considered cults, even though some of them have sect-like qualities. And we will indicate those that have become so well established in the United States that they may be considered churches.

Religion in America

Most of the religion in America in the nineteenth century was not new, and the same is true for most of the religion in twentieth-century America: the old faiths of Protestant and Catholic Christianity, and Judaism are the primary religious ways of the American people. But America is the "new world," a land of new challenges—the soil, the climate, the resources, and above all the simple open spaces and vast distances offered new challenges to the enterprise of old settlers and new immigrants. Those who came from the British Isles and Europe brought their religious ways and their clergy with them—Puritans (Congregationalists, Baptists, and Presbyterians) and later Anglicans and Methodists. Wherever the Spanish or French settled Roman Catholicism was the basic religious tradition. Successive waves of immigration brought other Christian groups, such as Lutherans from Germany and Orthodox from Eastern Europe. Although there were synagogues in America even in the days of the Revolu-

tion, the greatest immigration of Jews from Eastern Europe and Russia took place at the end of the nineteenth and beginning of the twentieth century.

Often it was necessary to meet the difficulties presented by the newness of America, and for some the "old ways" no longer worked. The Church of Jesus Christ of the Latter-Day Saints, often called the Mormons, is the best known example of a new response to the physical and psychological challenges of America from colonial days through the first part of the nineteenth century. Begun by the visionary in an area of New York state that was the setting for revivals and communes, the Mormons migrated in a group across America to what is now Utah—some settling in Missouri. Newness, migration across America, and a chosen land within America: these stereotypical features, as well as their basic beliefs and practices make the Mormons a fundamental new religion in America. We begin with them, then move to the Christian Scientists, and finally explore the nineteenth-century beginnings of the Jehovah's Witnesses.

Nineteenth-Century Foundations

Church of Jesus Christ of the Latter-Day Saints

Born in Vermont and raised near Palmyra, New York, Joseph Smith, Jr. (1805–1844) lived his early years in a region where religion was turned into a burning issue by itinerant preachers. Members of his family, in earlier generations, had been Methodist and Presbyterian, but Smith did not find any of the preaching that he heard satisfying. His indecision as to which group to join was resolved by a vision that he had in 1820.

When the light rested upon me I saw two personages, whose brightness and glory defy all description, standing above me in the air. One of them spake unto me, calling me by name, and said pointing to the other—"This is my beloved son, hear him." My object in going to inquire of the Lord was to know which of all the sects was right, that I might know which to join. No sooner, therefore, did I get possession of myself, so as to be able to speak, then I asked the personages who stood above me in the light, which of all the sects was right—and which I should join. I was answered that I must join none of them, for they were all wrong, and the personage who addressed me said that all their creeds were an abomination in His sight: that those professors were all corrupt; that "they draw near to me with their lips, but their hearts are far from me; they teach for doctrines the commandments of men: having a form of godliness, but they deny the power thereof." He again forbade me to join with any of them; and many other things did he say unto me, which I cannot write at this time.[2]

The appearance of Christ and the Father were followed by visions of John the Baptist and angelic beings. In 1823 Smith received a visitation from an angel named Moroni who told him of some gold plates—buried in the nearby hills—upon which were engraved what is now known as the *Book of Mormon*. Buried with the plates were two divining stones, the "Urim" and "Thummim" (referred to in the biblical book of Exodus 28:30). The angel revealed the exact location of the plates several years later, but in the meantime Smith had a vision of John the Baptist who, he believed, conferred on him and an acquaintance who was with him a restored Aaronic priesthood. With this priesthood came the authority to re-establish the true Church of Christ. In a second vision, Peter, James, and John gave them the higher priesthood of the Apostles, the priesthood of Melchisedeck.

Smith wrote other treatises that Mormons take to be inspired, but the most important, other than a version of the Bible itself (Mormons differ as to whether or not Smith produced an inspired translation) and the *Book of Mormon,* is a collection of revelations published now under the title *Doctrine and Covenants.* These revelations were first published a year after Smith officially formed a small group into the Church of Christ—a name soon changed to the fuller title the group has today. The new church attracted a following almost immediately, and in 1831 Smith moved the headquarters to Kirkland, Ohio, where the construction of a temple was begun. The group moved on in Ohio and Missouri and then to Nauvoo, Illinois, rendering the city, in a brief period of time, the largest city in the state. When the practice of polygamy was introduced there, the situation, already made tense by political differences with non-Mormons and among the Mormons themselves, exploded. After legal action, the opponents of Smith managed to have him jailed, and on June 27, 1844 a mob broke into the jail, murdering Smith and his brother, Hiram.

In the *Book of Mormon* a story is told of two groups of people, the Jehedites, who came to America directly after the attempt to build the Tower of Babel, and the Israelites, who came following the destruction of Jerusalem in the sixth century B.C.E. The Jehedites had been destroyed shortly before the arrival of the Israelites (themselves divided into two warring subgroups), and the Israelites were essentially destroyed in the fourth century C.E. The last of the prophets of the Israelites was commanded to write the history that was buried in New York, and the American Indians remained as the only remnant of this people. Central to the *Book of Mormon* is the story of Lehi, a Hebrew prophet, and his family. Lehi presumably fled Jerusalem around 600 B.C.E. to escape the Babylonians and the impending captivity of the Jews. Guided by God, he and those with him crossed the Arabian desert, built ships, and sailed to a new continent (later known as America). Here Lehi's descendants, supporting themselves by agriculture, built cities and temples. They obeyed the Law of Moses and kept to the prophetic tradition with its expectation of a Messiah. In time, Christ himself came to them, after his death and resurrection; he preached, performed miracles, and organized a Church—just as he had in Palestine. He ordained twelve disciples who were to preach the Gospel and establish the Church everywhere. Eventually the descendants of Lehi became corrupt, reviving a struggle that had taken place between two of Lehi's sons, Nephi and Laman. The Nephites, although representing a more advanced civilization, had become effete and materialistic; and the Lamanites, given over to hunting and war, had plunged further into barbarianism.

As the story goes, this early American religious culture in its original form disappeared: the Nephites were conquered by the more crude and powerful Lamanites, who lost track of their origins (the American Indians are their descendents). But the Nephites engraved a detailed history of their people on metal plates. Mormon, one of the last Nephite prophets and generals, basing himself on these records, wrote a brief historical account on gold plates, passed them on to his son Moroni, who buried them, both to prevent their seizure by the Lamanites and to allow for their future discovery by those who could restore the true Gospel in America. It was this same Moroni who, in a postmortal state as an "angel," led Smith to the Hill of Cumorah and the discovery of the plates.

Beliefs. That Moroni was once a human who then became an angel is one of a developed set of Mormon beliefs about the nature of God, the meaning of angels, and the relation of the human race to both. Smith taught that God and Christ were persons of flesh and bone, but not of blood. The Holy Spirit, although invisible to mortals, possessed a spiritual body that was, nevertheless, composed of a kind of matter; in other words, God was material. In the beginning God organized the earth out of already existing matter, and He did not establish the laws of nature but learned to understand and control them—He was a developing God.

If God undergoes stages of development, there was a time when He was less than He is now. It is conceivable, then, that at some future time humans might evolve to the stage where God is now: the famous Mormon phrase states, "As man is God once was; as God is man may become." This development is pictured as the onward march of the Supreme Being, with whom may be associated other intelligent beings: angels who have become Gods, humans who have become angels, and humans who have achieved a higher state of human postmortal existence. God, angels, and humans are all of the same species, one race and one family, widely diffused among the planetary systems as colonies and kingdoms. The only hierarchies of existence are those of intelligence and purity. Ultimately there can be said to be a plurality of Gods even though there is one Supreme Head.

In order to explain the fall of the human race and the role of Christ, Smith taught that before the creation of the earth humans had lived in the presence of God in a spiritual state. But in keeping with the eternal law of progress, it was necessary that they acquire mortal bodies and live on earth. In a great council in heaven, Lucifer, one of the great spirits of the "preexistence," presented the plan that after a no-risk sojourn on earth, where there would be no exercise of free will, all would return to the presence of the Father. Christ, however, presented a more daring plan that would lead to the greater good: only those who freely obeyed the commandments of the Father would be allowed to return to his presence. The majority accepted Christ's plan, while Lucifer rebelled and was cast out; those who did accept Christ's plan were allowed to move on to a higher state—mortality on earth. With foreknowledge of Adam's sin, God planned the mission of Christ to undo the consequences of the fall.

Since all humankind became capable of committing sin because of Adam, Mormons believe that the first step on the road back to God is faith in Christ; the second, repentence; the third, baptism by immersion for the remission of sins; and the fourth, laying on of hands for the gift of the Holy Ghost—all of which required an authority structure to ensure proper teaching and practice.

Organization and Practice. The Mormon Church is structured by the two priesthoods mentioned above. The Aaronic priesthood is the lesser order, and all adult males are members of it; from it are drawn deacons, teachers, and priests. The Melchizedeck priesthood is the higher order, and from it comes the church's leadership—the elders, the council of seventy, the high priests, and the presidency. Organizationally, the church is ruled by a series of councils. At the top of the hierarchy is the first presidency composed of three people, the president and two other high priests elected by the twelve apostles. When the office of the first presidency is filled, the council of twelve apostles operates under its direction as a traveling presiding council. Unanimous decision by the council of twelve has authority equal to the decisions of the first presidency. The presiding group of seventy and the presiding bishopric hold jurisdiction over the duties of other bishops in the Church and over the organization of the Aaronic priesthood.

Baptism with emphasis on personal repentance is required of all believers, and infant baptism is condemned. Baptism is necessary both as a witness to Church membership and for the remission of sins. In the Mormon baptismal teachings there is no implicit denial of the goodness of the human being. Rather, baptism seals the Mormon's basic covenant with God and participation in the salvation brought by Christ. A quite distinctive element of Mormon baptismal teaching is the promotion of baptism of the dead through the baptism of living persons who stand in for the dead; baptism by proxy, in other words. This enables the dead to progress in the afterlife, and ensures that those who would have otherwise existed in a state of eternal nonproductive suspension might be saved. In other words, those who came before the miraculous restoration of Mormon teachings have a chance to participate in the cosmic movement toward perfection. A Mormon is not only expected to be mindful of and serve as proxy for the baptism of his or her ancestors, but should also serve as proxy for all those whose names can be recovered from the annals of history. A consequence of this stand on baptism is the Mormon genealogical office in Utah. In a great, virtually indestructable, building implanted in a mountainside there is a collection of genealogical records that are being expanded until the ideal of completeness is realized. This means that the Mormons literally try to keep records of every person who has ever lived. These records are not only useful to Mormons in their attempts to baptize by proxy, but are helpful to all those who are trying to trace their family history. And the Mormons are willing to provide this genealogical service to anyone who desires it.

In addition to faith and baptism, Mormons are required to establish a new and everlasting covenant of marriage. They must be "sealed" by priestly authority to partners of the opposite sex for all time. Only Mormon temple marriages are valid for all eternity; otherwise, marriage is terminated by death. There are two important by-products of this belief: (1) emphasis on the temple marriage itself, because those who enter into such a marriage covenant will be able to achieve the highest state of progress in the world to come; and (2) encouragement to have large families and to practice polygamy (the latter was outlawed in 1890 because of pressure from the United States government). Progress in the next world is directly related to the number of children a person is able to engender, provided that the children are truly the fruit of a covenant marriage.

Most Mormons today may be divided into the Utah Mormons and the Missouri Mormons. Carrying on the main theological and ecclesiastical traditions of Smith is the Church of Jesus Christ of the Latter-Day Saints, with headquarters in Salt Lake City, Utah. Brigham Young, who had been president of the Council of Twelve Apostles in Smith's day, was elected president of the church. In 1847, the majority of Mormons who had fled Nauvoo, Illinois migrated with Young to and settled in the present city of Salt Lake City. Shortly after, they began their worldwide mission, concentrating on Western Europe and Scandinavia. In the twentieth century the Church has experienced phenomenal growth, spreading across the Rockies to Phoenix in the southwest and to the northwestern cities. The Missouri Mormons, with headquarters in Independence, Missouri, are known officially as the Reorganized Church of Jesus Christ of the Latter-Day Saints, which was formed in 1860 by groups in the east and the midwest. They believe that the headship of the Church is a hereditary prophetic office, to be held, therefore, by the descendents of Smith. Although they agree with the Utah Mormons on a number of important points, the Missouri Mormons reject the notions of the sealing of marriage for all eternity and marriage by proxy; they further reject the notion that "As man now is, God once was; as God now is man may become" as contradictory to the monotheism of the Bible.

Social Profile. In his report on his initial revelation, Smith was quite clear about rejecting all other religious groups. He had a radically new relevation into which the Judeo-Christian scriptures were subsumed. And he formed a new, separate group of people—early on, under his influence, they socially isolated themselves from their environment; then they physically moved on, first founding separate settlements in Ohio, Missouri, and Illinois, and later moving on to Utah. When they became involved in local politics, the results were disastrous, because of the radically different world-view they represented. In spite of the obvious predominance of Christian imagery, the Mormons cannot properly be called a sect; they do not even have sect-like qualities because they believe that all Christian groups propagate fundamental doctrinal errors. Smith made no attempt whatsoever to reform Christianity. In innovation and separation, Mormonism was a cult. And, even though Smith presented a revelation that was native to America and led his followers on a pioneering trek that was part of the great American frontier movement, the Mormons have never been considered "typically American." Mainline Protestant Christianity had become so well established that any group that did not have a relationship to it was doomed ahead of time— or so it would seem now.

Smith was not as fortunate as Muhammad, whose own new revelation galvanized into unity vast cultural areas that had not previously been given a centralizing set of beliefs and behaviors that could give meaning to a common effort. America already had a species of religious unity; many Americans already had a sense of destiny. Mainline Protestant Christianity had already provided the unity and strengthened the sense of destiny. The Church of Jesus Christ of the Latter-Day Saints was never to become *the* American Church. However,

An Artist's Concept of a Mormon Departure from Nauvoo, Illinois in Early Spring, 1846. Moving on to Salt Lake City under Brigham Young, the Mormons projected an image— that never really caught on—of basic American pioneer religion. (Religious News Service Photo)

the group is so extended now, constituting a large percentage of the population in Utah—with established congregations across the nation—that we should probably give the sociological label *church* (or *denomination*) to the Mormons. The Missouri Mormons in particular consider their beliefs to be similar to those of mainline Protestant Christians, and even encourage the reading of certain Protestant authors. Mormons take full part in American political life, and, although they promote a rigorous moral life, they have the same life-styles as other churchgoers. Mormonism is viewed a cult that is on the verge of becoming an American church.

Church of Christ, Scientist

The founder of the Church of Christ, Scientist—members are called Christian Scientists—was Mary Baker Eddy (1821–1910). She was born in New Hampshire, but most of her ministry was exercised in Boston. In 1866 Eddy suffered a serious fall, cured herself, and in so doing she discovered Christian Science, or the divine laws of life. On the way to a meeting, she fell on an

icy street, and was carried into a nearby house, apparently with severe injuries. Moved to her own home, she showed no improvement, but when she opened her Bible and read an account of some of Jesus' healings, she was filled with an overpowering sense that her life was of and in God. Healed instantly, she arose, dressed, and walked downstairs to the amazement of those who were keeping watch. This experience, she later explained, was her first clear understanding of the truth she called Christian Science.

Early in her career Eddy was associated with a famous practitioner of mesmerism and animal magnetism, P. P. Quimby. Although she later strongly rejected magnetism and mesmerism, vestiges of Quimby's ideas can be found in her own teaching. Quimby believed that the mind was the central agency of healing and that if the mind could be changed healing would occur. He followed in the footsteps of Anton Mesmer (from whose name we have the word "mesmerize"), who had taught that some persons have such magnetism that by the forces within them they can heal both themselves and others. Quimby combined Mesmer's approach with the study of philosophical questions dealing with ultimate reality. But Eddy centered these ideas around some traditional Christian beliefs: reliance on biblical revelation with emphasis on the life and work of Jesus Christ; belief in a God who is transcendent to mortal thought and distinct from mankind; insistence on the radical regeneration from the flesh of living persons.

Beliefs. Eddy believed that the true biblical Christianity was lost when the healing as practiced in the early Church was abandoned, and she believed that this happened when Christianity became the established religion of the Roman Empire. But Eddy believed that her teachings represented more than a simple return to biblical Christianity (which was the ideal of sixteenth-century Protestant reformers). According to her interpretation, Jesus had objectively accomplished everything for the salvation of humankind, but he did not try to elucidate the basis of the power of the Spirit—a power that was, nevertheless, fully present in him. The presentation and demonstration of the power of the Spirit, she believed, remained to be discovered in Christian Science. Jesus had prophesied the coming of Christian Science when he said, "The Comforter, who is the Holy Spirit, whom the Father will send in my name, he shall teach you all things, and bring all things to your remembrance, whatsoever I have said to you." For Eddy, Divine Science was the Holy Spirit, and Christian Science represented a humanly comprehensible statement of Divine Science.

Christian Science was presented by its founder as genuinely scientific, because it provided a method or rule for demonstrating the universal law of God. She used the word *science* in this context to indicate the certainty with which her method could be applied. She felt it to be infallible, absolute, and exact. Eddy's claim was that Christian Science was the product of revelation—not in the unique biblical sense, but because God's continuing divine action included revelation. But if not a new revelation in the biblical sense, Christian Science was a "discovery," and one vastly more important than the discovery of the natural sciences. The data always had been there: the power of the Holy Spirit always had been operative and it had been her role to discover it. Once discovered by her and presented in Christian Science, everyone could understand and demonstrate it. God had

appointed her and no one could take her place. She said, "It is not because I have been specially chosen to reveal this Science, but it is as if there were those standing near a window, and because I was nearest the pane, the light fell upon me."[3]

In 1875 the first edition of *Science and Health with Key to the Scriptures* appeared. In it Eddy described two major phases in the development of her teaching:

1. The discovery of this Divine Science of mind-healing, through a spiritual sense of the Scriptures and through the teachings of the Comforter, as promised by the Master.
2. The proof, by present demonstration, that the so-called miracles of Jesus did not specially belong to a dispensation now ended, but that they illustrated an ever-operative divine Principle. The operation of this Principle indicates the eternality of the scientific order and continuity of being.[4]

A Church was established in Boston of which the only "pastor" was to be the Bible. But as discoverer and founder of Christian Science, Eddy receives an allegience that is second only to God and to Jesus. In a book published by the movement in 1893, she is pictured hand in hand with Jesus with a tablet inscribed "Christian Science."

Eddy's understanding of God is similar to the concepts of Quimby and other teachers influenced by Quimby. God is mind, life principle, souls, and spirit. God is all in all, the only reality. Eddy rejected any personal categories for God. Her fundamental and most controversial view is the denial of matter (the opposite of Smith). She vigorously combatted the ideas current in her day that all is matter, that matter originates in mind, and is as real as mind. She maintained that the erroneous beliefs about mind and matter were the result of inferior human thinking. Mortal mind is the lower mind of the physical world and opposes a higher metaphysics—it is the source of erroneous thinking, of disease, of evil and sin. What it takes to be reality is not reality at all. Through study and practice of Christian Science, humankind could demonstrate with complete certainty the presence and power of Divine Science. Mortal mind convinces persons that they are sick, and for that reason they become sick. No techniques on mortal-mind levels could give more than temporary relief of symptoms. By reliance on the Divine Mind one directs oneself toward truth, love, and life, which is accomplished by Christian Science by a process of mental fermentation. Eddy put it this way:

Mortal mind will vanish in moral chemicalization. This mental fermentation has begun, and will continue until all errors of belief yield to understanding. Belief is changeable, but spiritual understanding is changeless. As this consummation draws nearer, he who has shaped his course in accordance with Divine Science will endure to the end. As material knowledge diminishes, and spiritual understanding increases, real objects will be apprehended mentally instead of materially.[5]

Organization and Practice. The "class" was established, beginning in 1875, as the basic structure in Christian Science. By means of the class practitioners were trained to know the truth, demonstrate it, and serve as a catalyst for the healing of patients. Students were attached to teachers in a permanent structure. With the passage of time the number of students and classes became limited, and a present rule limits each teacher annually to one class of no more than thirty students. There is a board of education that approves teachers and strictly regulates class content. The structure is so tightly knit that if a teacher loses his or her status, the students do also and must go through another class to regain it. Class lecture notes are carefully guarded to the extent that even notetaking is forbidden.

With the death of Eddy in 1910 the authorities of the Publishing Society, which she had established, and of the Mother Church in Boston had to be determined and placed in proper relationship to one another. Highest authority went to the Board of Directors of the Publishing Society, who today authorize all Christian Science teachers and have the power to remove practitioners or readers without question. Perhaps the best-known form of the promotion of Christian Science is the system of Christian Science reading rooms that are found across the nation. Within them one can find a selection of books by Eddy and other approved authors, a large number of pamphlets and booklets, and periodicals that provide a contact with Christian Science that is beyond the circle of members and institutions. In fact, *The Christian Science Monitor* has achieved an international reputation as a first-rate daily newspaper.

Social Profile. We cannot easily establish the social profile of Christian Scientists. Eddy's religious background was New England Congregationalist, a strong Calvinist Protestantism. She did not explicitly reject all existing forms of Christianity, as did Smith, nor did she claim to have a new revelation. Yet she set up an organization that was separate from the New England Christian churches of her day. Although Eddy believed that other Christian groups needed the reform that she was promoting, she was not advocating reform in either the Catholic or Protestant or Eastern Christian sense of reform: a return to the purity of the Gospel. She called it a "discovery," but it was *her own* discovery; it had not been explicitly articulated by Christ.

Many consider Eddy's discovery a radical innovation. Much more of an innovator than the previous so-called reformers of early and medieval Christian history and of the Protestant and Catholic reformations, Eddy was, nevertheless, not as strong an innovator as was Smith. Smith had new revelations: there were *new* scriptures in addition to the Judeo-Christian Bible, whereas Eddy provided only what she called a "key" to the scriptures. So we have a major obstacle to the categorization of the Church of Christ, Scientist as a sect. It did not break from any of the forms of American Protestantism—from which its founder and members came—with the idea of reform (the reform, let us say, of New England Congregationalism). With the much vaguer goal of reforming Christianity in general (really, Protestant Christianity, because Catholicism was for Eddy a basic corruption of Christianity). So, organizationally Christian Scientists were not a sect that had a relationship with a specific Christian group that needed reform. The "discovery" is an innovation vis-a-vis any existing form of Christianity. The history of the Church of Christ, Scientist is one of radical innovation and opposition to the American Protestant cultural setting in which it developed.

There is one principal area of opposition among Christian Scientists to the behavioral ways of American society—standard medical practice (although in dire circumstances Christian Scientists will accept the services of a medical doctor). Since modern medicine is an area of science that affects the lives of all people, Christian Scientists often appear to other Americans to be in radical opposition to standard behavior. Accordingly, we must label Christian Science a cult. Although it had sect-like qualities when it began, and has in its membership today adherents who do not wish to attract attention to the uniqueness of Christian Science (thereby allowing the group to move to church status) the Church of Christ, Scientist has the basic qualities of a cult.

Jehovah's Witnesses

One of the offspring of the so-called Adventist movement, the Jehovah's Witnesses can be traced back to 1881. The Adventist William Miller (1782–1849) had predicted the imminent return of Christ in 1843. After the failure of that prediction, the Adventists splintered into a number of factions. One faction continued to set dates for the Second Coming, and the Jehovah's Witnesses emerged from among this group. The history of the Witnesses is really a composite of the stories of the group's leaders and their beliefs.

Beliefs. Charles Taze Russell (1852–1916) was much influenced by an Adventist minister who had set a new date for the Second Coming, but Russell himself developed some idiosyncratic teachings about hell, redemption, and Trinity. He believed that hell meant annihilation and not eternal torment, that humanity had been ransomed from that annihilation and not from hellfire, and that there was no biblical basis for the doctrine of the Trinity. Most importantly, because Christ did not return on the date projected by the Adventists, he believed that Christ had returned as an invisible presence. Accordingly, the Greek word *parousia,* usually translated as "coming," meant instead "presence" to Russell.

Russell was born in Pittsburgh, Pennsylvania of Scottish-Irish presbyterians. He worked in his father's clothing store chain and became religiously involved while he was in his teens. The first issue of Russell's journal, *Zion's Watchtower,* appeared in 1879, and soon a group, called the "Millenial Dawn Bible Students," was formed to study the scriptures with the help of Russell's writings. In 1881 Zion's Watch Tower Tract Society was set up, and thus began the forerunner of today's Jehovah's Witnesses. Five years later volume 1 of Russell's major work, *The Divine Plan of the Ages,* was begun.

The most important feature of *The Plan* was a historical chronology with emphasis on the date 1914. Russell divided history into a series of eras: the period from Adam to the flood, the patriarchal age (up to the death of Jacob), the Jewish age (which lasted until Christ's death), the Gospel age (until 1874) and, finally, the millenial age. According to Russell, the first forty years of the millenial age would see the return of the Jews to Palestine and the gradual overthrow of the Gentile nations. But 1914 would be marked by the glorification of the saints, the establishment of God's direct rule on earth, and the restoration of humankind to perfection on earth. Russell's doctrine of the future church was bound up with the date 1914. He believed, on the strength of the biblical book of Revelation, chapter 7, that the Church consisted of 144,000 saints from the time of Christ to 1914. Those saints who came afterward would make up a class of heavenly servants called "the great company."

At the time of Russell's death in 1916 he had not appointed a successor, probably because he had directed his group in a personally charismatic fashion without establishing his own role as a permanent officer. The decade following was marked by controversy and factionalism. But the rise to power of J. F. Rutherford marked the beginning of a new era.

In 1931, Judge Joseph Franklin Rutherford (1869–1942) assumed a position of absolute authority in the group's affairs. At a meeting of Bible students connected with the Watch Tower Bible and Tract Society in 1931 at Columbus, Ohio, the name "Jehovah's Witnesses" was adopted and the authority of Rutherford was confirmed. For more than a decade he had molded the group according to his own views. He united the loosely organized group into a close-knit body, whose mission was to inform the world of Jehovah's reign. He said that since God had a name in Hebrew, Jehovah, God's people should be called by that name. Rutherford attacked the established structures of what he took to be Satan's world—the Church, particularly the Roman Catholic Church, and the government—and he mobilized members of the society to distribute the Watch Tower collection of books and pamphlets.

Gradually Rutherford's writings began to replace Russell's. In the twenty years before his death Rutherford wrote twenty books and numerous pamphlets, slowly revising the doctrine and structure left to him by Russell. He altered Russell's view of a final anarchistic battle (Armegeddon) between the good and evil to an all-encompassing universal war, and he emphasized ethics over eschatology. The life of Witnesses were henceforward to be centered around the Kingdom Halls, local churches that Rutherford established across the nation.

Organization and Practice

Organization and Practice. Today most of the Witnesses' time is spent in kingdom-hall activity. Witnesses must spend their time selling and distributing literature, and in door-to-door evangelization. Witnesses are encouraged not to socialize with non-Witnesses beyond presenting them with the truth. Witnesses are pacifist, tend to downgrade public education, and withdraw from political involvement. Unique special practices—refusal to salute the flag and to accept blood transfusion—are further indications of their rejection of social conventions and accepted scientific procedures.

Witnesses see their organization as ruled by Jehovah through Christ. Jehovah's authority on earth is revealed in the Jehovah's Witnesses organization, the Watch Tower Bible and Tract Society (and its affiliate corporations). Direct control of the Society and the entire organization is in the hands of the president and governing body of seventeen members. Literature is written and published at the international headquarters in Brooklyn and distributed through branch offices. Each branch is further divided into districts and each district into circuits. A circuit will have approximately twenty congregations. Both districts and circuits are headed by an overseer appointed by the governing body. Each congregation, although still the responsibility of the overseer, is headed by a presiding elder, who is joined by other elders in the distribution of literature to the public, in presiding at worship, and in the organization of training sessions.

Social Profile. Although Russell worked out his own ideas in conversation with Adventist preachers, he promoted a set of biblical interpretations that were very different from those of his interlocutors (there was such variety among the Adventists themselves that those in Russell's position would not know whether they were ''in'' or ''out'' of the basic group). When an ever-widening circle of sects develops, those on the outer edge cannot be clearly labeled because they have so little to do with the original group. However, with the formation of a group of followers around Russell, the beliefs that formed the basis of biblical interpretation were Russell's unique ideas. In other words, the Jehovah's Witnesses started as a cult (although if Russell had gathered a group of followers around him in his earliest years, he might have been said to have established a sect).

Witnesses seem to have accommodated themselves very little to American society because of several major antagonisms that developed across the decades: their pacifism during the World Wars, and their singular and occasionally fatal refusal of blood transfusions (even for young members of their families in death-threatening situations). Their early promotional style, a ''foot-in-the-door'' approach with an accompanying abrasive lecture, also contributed to the social distancing that occurred between themselves and other Americans. Like the Christian Scientists, the Jehovah's Witnesses' are considered to be a cult because of their innovative teaching and opposition to the rest of society. Unlike Christian Scientists, however, there are few Witnesses who promote a church-like acceptance of society. One reason for the difference might be that Witnesses do not promote higher education, and thus remove themselves from a level of social exchange where religious dialogue and mutual respect can flourish.

However, the Witnesses have grown from 142,000 members in 1945 to over 2 million today. While growth slowed during the 1970s in the United States, it accelerated in other areas such as Italy.

Twentieth-Century Foundations

International Society for Krishna Consciousness (ISKCON)

The founder of the International Society for Krishna Consciousness (ISKCON) was A. K. Bhaktivedanta Swami Prabhupada (1896–1977). Born Abhay Charan De, in India, he became a businessman, and was himself initiated into Krishna Consciousness only in middle age. For the next thirty years Prabhupada gave himself over to spiritual development. At the age of 59 he became part of an order of ascetics in India, and in 1965 he came to America to build a movement. Although the group exists elsewhere, it has found a home in America. As the movement spread it gained fame for its festivals and feasts, including a summer festival that features a mass parade and an open invitation to a vegetarian meal.

Weekly feasts that are open to the public are a feature of every temple. Prabhupada, or "His Divine Grace" as his followers call him, has produced lengthy and scholarly studies about Krishna worship. *The Bhagavad Gita as It Is* (1972) is his best-known work and has received praise from scholars of Hinduism. When Prabhupada died in 1977 the leadership of the society passed to a "governing body commission" of twenty-two members, taken from among the older devotees.

Beliefs. The Caitanya Krishnaite sect that Prabhupada represented might be considered a "fundamentalist" version of Krishna worship, in that it rejects other manifestations of Vishnu beyond Krishna and Rama, and believes that the Krishna stories are literally and historically true. The central teachings are based on the *Bhagavad Gita* in which Krishna is presented as the incarnation of the God *Vishnu* in human form (see Chapter 1). The group is an offshoot of the main body of orthodox Krishna worshippers and follows a devotional tradition that was taught by Caitanya in the early sixteenth century and then revived again in the nineteenth century. Worship consists principally in the practice of chanting a mantra:

Hare Krishna Hare Krishna
Hare Hare Krishna Krishna
Hare Rama Hare Rama
Hare Hare Rama Rama

This chanting is done to bring about a pure consciousness of God in his incarnations both as Krishna and as Rama, and to dispel the illusion of reality presented by the world. Krishna is the supreme personal Lord who dwells in a paradisal world. He came to earth 5,000 years ago, so that for a short time people on earth might experience and acquire a desire for heaven. The stories of Krishna as a child and as a young lover are evidence of the seductive and incomprehensible power of God. Members of ISKCON offer worship to the statues of the gods found in all Krishna temples, properly mark their bodies with clay pigment in twelve places with each place representing the name of a god, publicly chant and dance in honor of Krishna, and eat food offered to Krishna.

Organization and Practice. There are four fundamental rules of conduct that ISKCON members must follow:
1. No eating of meat, fish, or eggs.
2. No illicit sex.

Swami Prabhupada. *An Indian businessman, he became a spiritual leader only in middle age. Member of a Krishna-worshiping sect in India, he established his form of worship in the United States by founding the International Society for Krishna Consciousness.* (Religious News Service Photo)

3. No intoxicants.
4. No gambling.

In addition, they study traditional Hindu lore, the history of bhakti yoga, and the writings of the founder, Prabhupada.

The life-style and practices of ISKCON group members are designed to establish the divine mysteries and the divine presence in their consciousness and to give them hope for rebirth in a paradise of Krishna. Those who become part of the monastic organization (there are numerous associates) follow a schedule that begins at 3:45 A.M. and ends at 10 P.M. Courtship or dating among devotees is not ordinarily permitted, but those who wish to marry can be given permission to do so when the Guru (now the governing body) believes that they will advance the cause of Krishna. Overall, the group does strive to maintain a family atmosphere, and observers have found this to be genuine: there is play, child-like joy, genuine sharing, and a structured protective environment. Criticisms of the group center around the adults' lack of decision making and the highly stylized life that is forced on children who are born into the monastic community.

Social Profile. ISKCON is an example of a cult, completely new in every respect to American culture. More than eighty percent of those joining the group were twenty-five years old or younger, and more than one-half joined before their twenty-first birthday. ISKCON's U.S. membership consists of whites (eighty percent), blacks (six percent), hispanics (five percent), and other foreign-born persons (nine percent). The majority of members has completed high school, but less than one-fourth has received a college or graduate degree. However, over sixty percent of those who completed high school have attended at least one year of college. In fact, a substantial number of members had first contacted the group while at an educational institution. The majority come from middle- and upper-middle-class families, with over one-third indicating that their parents' combined incomes was $30,000 or more.[6]

The religious family backgrounds of the adherents has been of primary interest to students of religion and social science. With few exceptions ISKCON members came from families who attended mainline Christian churches or synagogues. More than one-half of the members say that their parents put emphasis on religious beliefs and practices for the family, and approximately one-half of the members attended religious services on a regular basis during their childhood. Of these only twelve percent were active in the faith in which they were raised at the time they were introduced to ISKCON, and forty percent practiced some sort of religion at the time of their introduction to the group. ISKCON members come from a variety of religious backgrounds: Protestant (thirty-five percent), Catholic (thirty-three percent), Jewish (fifteen percent), unspecified Christian (six percent), Hindu (five percent), and those who had no previous religious involvement (six percent). One researcher suggests that the foregoing figures on previous religious involvement suggest two distinct types of recruits: the unchurched, for whom conversion may mean the acceptance of and commitment to a religious world-view; and the churched, who are already committed to a religious

world-view, but alter or intensify it. The members gave the following primary reasons for joining ISKCON:

1. Philosophy of the movement (thirty-nine percent).
2. Warmth and friendliness of the devotees (sixteen percent).
3. Attraction to the guru, Prabhupada (twelve percent).
4. Attraction to a guru (*not* Prabhupada) (two percent).
5. "My life was going nowhere and I wanted to explore another life-style" (eight percent).
6. Participation in the kirtans with other devotees (two percent).
7. A more secure way of life (one percent).
8. Deity worship (one percent).
9. Other (seven percent).

The thirty-nine percent of members giving "philosophy of the movement" as their primary reason for entering ISKCON made statements such as the following:

I saw logically and scientifically that this philosophy explains the how and why of everything I saw in this world. I also saw that as in other religious philosophies that I approached there was no need for "blind faith," everything was provable logically and to a certain extent "scientifically."

I read every philosophy I could get my hands on but none of them offered a practical solution to social and personal problems. I immediately saw how this philosophy actually filled in the missing link, the center; there were no loopholes; all my questions were satisfied.

I sincerely wanted to serve God—know who I was, what my purpose was in life in relation to God. The Church was no longer able to answer my questions. I believed in one supreme Lord and was wanting that strict spiritual life that the movement offered. I could perceive that what I was looking for was in ISKCON from hearing about the Krishna-conscious philosophy! Certainly not what I was seeing externally. I didn't know what the deities were. Why did the people [devotees] dress like that . . .[9]

Sociologists have found that the social relationships of ISKCON members are more or less free of personal/social ties that might otherwise hinder their participation in the movement. A number were recently divorced or separated from their spouses at the time of entry into the movement. And others had already separated from their previous social ties just before entry: one-third said they were already "on the road" when they joined. A general conclusion is that while previously limited social ties facilitate the recruitment process, strong outside social ties will not unfailingly limit participation.

Unification Church

When Rev. Sun Myung Moon (b. 1920) was aged sixteen he had a vision of Jesus in which he was told to carry out Jesus' unfinished task of redemption—and his vision occurred at a time when Korean Pentecostal Christians were predicting a Korean messiah. Moon first tried to establish a community around him in his Native North Korea right after World War II, but was imprisoned by the new Communist government. Released after several years, he emigrated to South Korea and founded the Unification Church in 1954. In 1959 the message of Moon was brought to the United States by a Korean woman, Young Oon Kim, who produced an English translation of the basic scripture revealed to Moon, the *Divine Principle*.

Beliefs. The teachings of the *Divine Principle* are an original interpretation of the creation and fall of humankind. Adultery is the basic problem of humanity: Satan seduced Eve, who thereby became impure and passed on the impurity to Adam and their children. This adultery upset what Moon calls the "Four Base Relationships": all things come in pairs, and within the polarities of God/humankind, male/female, inward/outward there is a fourfold hierarchy. The hierarchy is arranged in the following way: (1) God, as Head; (2) male and (3) female, coequal in the middle; (4) child, on the bottom as New Life. The adultery, then, put Satan on top instead of God.

Jesus was sent to earth to redeem humankind, but although he accomplished spiritual redemption, he did not accomplish a full redemption. Jesus was killed before he could marry and father children, and so physical pollution was not overcome. Hope must therefore be placed in a third Adam, the Lord of the Second Advent. This Third Adam will be sent to marry a perfect woman, and their children will be the first of a new, redeemed race.

Although Moon himself does not unequivocally claim to be the Messiah but prefers to let others judge, it is obvious that functionally he exercises that role within the community. His marriage to his present wife is called the "marriage of the lamb," and when members of the Unification Church are married, the purity of Moon's own marriage is symbolically transferred to them. The new Messiah was supposed to appear in the East, especially in Korea; during the early days of the Unification Church Moon was identified as the New Messiah, but in more recent years the more equivocal stand has been taken: Moon may be the Lord, but that is a matter of individual interpretation.

Members are taught to regard themselves as models for the rest of mankind, since life in the movement is supposed to instruct members to live God-centered lives as individuals in God-centered families. This involves strict celibacy among members before marriage. It also means that Moon and his wife select individuals as mates for one another and preside at marriage ceremonies for the transferral of purity. Thus, the solution to the fall of humankind is the submission with filial piety to Moon the True Parent and founder of the "Perfect Family" on which all future relationships should be based. Transformation of the family will result in transformation of social institutions, and beyond them to the whole world.

Moon points out that there has been a surge of satanic power in this century, and such evil indicates that mankind has reached such a state that the time is ripe for a Messiah. During World War I Kaiser Wilhelm was the satanic imitation of Adam, and during World War II Hitler was the satanic imitation of Jesus. Now, Communism represents the full culmination of satan's powers. With the defeat of Communism, a new day of spiritual goodness and perfected physical familihood will dawn.

Organization and Practice. The daily schedule of many active members includes hours of both prayer and fund raising. On an average day one rises at 6 A.M., and a short period of physical exercise at 6:30 is followed by a prayer meeting composed of songs, prayers, and a spiritual message. The role of the prayer leader is rotated in order to cultivate responsibility and self-expression in individual members. Breakfast is at 7:30 and is often followed by an organizational meeting. The day's work begins at 9 A.M., when members are assigned to either a witnessing or a fund-raising team. Teams of about a half-dozen members are transported to particular

Reverend Sun Myung Moon. *Reverend Moon (right), founder of the Unification Church, and his wife officiating at a mass wedding of 2,200 couples in Madison Square Garden. Members believe that their marriage makes them an extension of the "Perfect Family" of Reverend Moon and his wife, thereby reversing the evils of the Fall of humankind.* (Religious News Service Photo)

areas for their work. Individual team members work by themselves until early afternoon when they get together for lunch. Following the half-hour lunch break, work is resumed until 7 P.M. Some members then return to the center on those days that guests are expected; otherwise, witnessing and fund-raising continues until late evening. Guests are given supper at about 9 P.M., after an hour or so of lecture and discussion, and a final prayer meeting for the community is held at 11 P.M. Seldom is there free time for relaxation, but periodically a group may take a day off for rest and recreation. When quotas are not met, groups will spend as many as eighteen to twenty-four hours per day working.[10]

Social Profile. Moonies are mostly unmarried and young; twenty-five percent have finished college, and more than fifty percent have begun. Research done on the Moonies has been on the individual and social psychological characteristics of individuals at the time of conversion. In a 1979 study of the emotional states of Moonies before and after conversion, a leading research psychiatrist and his aids found that the average convert appeared to experience emotional stress in the period before conversion that was higher than the period after conversion, and higher than for a comparison group of the same age.[11] Researchers judged that there was likelihood of a higher incidence of psychiatric illness because of the high percentage of those who had sought prior professional help and hospitalization for emotional problems.

Affiliation with the Unification Church apparently provided considerable and long-term relief from nervous distress. And a greater religious commitment was reported by those who indicated the most improvement. Transcendental experiences during the conversion period were reported by many—in terms of intensity or a presence or a different sense of time.

Continued membership provided a certain psychological stability, because after about three years most members who were questioned reported a lower level of stress. Increase in stress, however, was reported by those who experienced a decline in work satisfaction. In the long-term there was a general decrease in stress. Scores on questionnaires that assessed a general level of well-being were significantly lower than the average of a comparable group of their same age and sex categories.

A 1980 study of those who stayed with the Moonies after their initial contacts as over against those who departed (a further distinction is made between earlier and later dropouts) also yielded some interesting results.[12] The early dropouts were found to have weaker affiliative ties with the group and less acceptance of the group's religious beliefs. Later dropouts showed a high level of affiliativeness toward fellow workshop members, which was similar to those who ultimately stayed with the group; their commitment to the group's beliefs was also similar to those who ultimately joined. The principal difference between the late dropouts and those who finally joined was in affiliation with friends and relatives outside the group—they simply had stronger ties with the outside. This indicates that an important factor in joining the group is the presence of relatively weak ties to outsiders. The balance between affiliation to members in the group and to old associates—relatives and friends—is important. In this study there was no significant difference between the joiners and the dropouts regarding the presence or absence of real, existential meaning in their lives.

Significance of Twentieth-Century Cults

Cults have grown in membership and number since World War II. There are now five to six hundred cults in the United States. The older cults—the nineteenth-century groups—have memberships in the millions, while the cults established in this century rarely number over a few thousand and the vast majority must count their members in the hundreds. The author of the leading contemporary encyclopedia of American religious groups estimates that the total number of those who at one time or another have been members of the cults is probably around 150,000 to 200,000. A considerably larger number of persons have had close associations with cults or have spent some time as members.[13]

Growth in membership and number has not been striking: twentieth-century cults have not become major social, economic, or religious forces in the population. Whenever there has been a sudden increase in the number of cults in an area, however, or one group has rapidly gained members, the interest of social scientists has been aroused. Some of them have thought that the dynamics and structures of the new religions, and the developmental steps of their establishment would cast some light on the establishment of a number of religious groups across history. All of the major world religions were at one time innovations, cults, or sects that eventually became churches (in the social scientific sense; in religious discourse we generally restrict the application of the label to Christian groups). The problem is this: the sociological conditions favorable to the formation of a cult in the twentieth century might be different from those of a cult in the first century, and so the information we derive from contemporary social scientific studies of the 20th-century cults must not be applied indiscriminately. There are several reasons for the sudden flowering of new religions in the last few decades. Although there had been a tradition of interest in Eastern religion and the attempt to practice Hindu and Buddhist ways of meditation for well over one hundred years in the U.S., the transplanted Asian religions became much more visible and available in recent years. With the relaxation of immigration laws by President Johnson in 1965, Asians, whose immigration had heretofore been much more restricted than that of Europeans, arrived in the hundreds of thousands, bringing with them their religious beliefs. College and university students were interested in alternative branches of psychology, such as parapsychology and humanistic psychology, and in Eastern religions. They were attracted by opportunities to experiment with these ideas. Disgust with the interminable and failing war efforts of the American government in Viet Nam evolved into an attraction to the pacifism of some of the Buddhist groups and Hindu gurus (this also explains why Islam—never formally Pacifist—did not enjoy a similar popularity).

The American religions we have discussed have all been cults at one time. Some have become so implanted in American life that they are arriving at the sociological status of churches. In many different parts of the country one can see the individual church units of the Mormons, the Christian Scientists, and the Jehovah's Witnesses. They are achieving an acceptance by Protestant and Catholic Christians and by Jews that is equivalent to the way these groups accept one another. These great old cults are also more accepting of American society, of the mainline churches, and of Judaism (Jehovah's Witnesses, as we have said, trail far beyond the other two in this respect). But the cults of the past few decades have not established themselves in the same way. They do not even have the advantage—as have the older cults—of American origins (frontier and pioneer images, connection with American intellectual movements and fashions). Members are likely to be different from the rest of Americans. If one is alienated from society's public values, or has weak connections with family and friends, membership in a cult offers close affiliation with a particular, well-knit, family-like society. Whether that American society in general is worth conforming to is a personal judgment. Whether a particular society—the closed society of a cult—offers a fundamentally satisfying refuge and source of human companionship is a matter of personal need.

Other American Cultic Traditions

We have presented a sampling of American cults, choosing the nineteenth-century groups because of their size and influence and the twentieth-century groups because of their importance to contemporary researchers in psychology and sociology—and because they have achieved some degree of notoriety through the media. There were other groups in the nineteenth century that had connections with Christianity or the "Eastern" religions, Hinduism and Buddhism. Two of those groups, alive in twentieth-century America, have an Islamic connection:

the Black Muslims and the Baha'i Faith. Interestingly enough, the Black Muslims (see Chapter 9) began quite separately from official Islam, and have been moving toward greater orthodoxy in recent years, while the Baha'is were founded by Iranian Muslims who quickly led their followers away from Muslim orthodoxy.

The Baha'i World Faith began in the last century in Iran, at a time when both Sufism and the expectation of the coming of the Mahdi were strong influences on Iranian Shi'ite Muslim faith. A Sufi named Mirza Ali Muhammad said that he was the "Gate" ("Bab" in Iranian) through whom people would come to know a new Messenger of God. One of the followers of the Bab, while in prison (the Bab had been executed and a number of his followers imprisoned), came to believe that he was that Messenger. Accordingly, Mirza Husayn Ali Nuri took the name "Splendor of God" ("Baha'ullah" in Iranian) and set himself to the writing of a fundamental scripture of his faith, the "Most Holy Book." It declares that God is unknowable except through His "manifestations," the prophets, including Baha'Ullah himself, who, as "mirrors of God" are sent to the human race. It aims to establish a unity of the human race, of all religions, and of science, and advocates universal education, world peace through social equality, equal rights to the sexes, an international language, and an international tribunal. Work is viewed as a necessity for all and is taken to be a basic form of worship. In addition, regular weekly assemblies featuring prayers and readings from the sacred writings are held. There is a fasting period every year; eight holidays commemorate events in the lives of the founders. There are Baha'i temples at Wilmette, Illinois; Frankfort, Germany; Sydney, Australia; and Kampala, Uganda. The temples are designed in such a way as to emphasize the unity of the great world religions.

Other cults, too numerous to study individually here, may be grouped under the headings "Metaphysical," "Psychic," and "Magick."

The Metaphysical groups include the Christian Scientists, whom we have examined above, and a broad spectrum of communities we can describe as "New Thought" groups. Both independent centers and the larger denominations developed the loosely coordinated "International New Thought Alliance" in 1914. New Thought writers try to demonstrate what they take to be the deeper meaning of orthodox Christian terminology. For example, some say that a sense of the fatherhood of God refers to a feeling of security in the universe, and the image of the biblical figure Job represents the passage from self-righteousness to change of heart. The ultimate principle of intelligence, that is, Thought, or Mind, is God.

Psychic groups differ from New Thought groups in that they are more oriented toward mystical experience (New Thought is more oriented toward results and meaning). Nevertheless, psychics want scientific demonstration of the truth of their beliefs, and they depend to a certain extent on the development of the new division of psychology called "parapsychology," which studies telepathy, clairvoyance, and mental control of matter. They believe that they can establish the scientific basis of healing power and the arts of divination. By the end of the nineteenth century, various societies for psychical research had been established in England and America, but the most popular and best-known examples of the psychic groups are the Swedenborgians, the various Spiritualist and Theosophical societies, and the Rosicrucians. Some of them try to trace their spiritual ancestry back to earlier centuries, but virtually all come from the nineteenth and twentieth centuries.

The Magick groups believe in the control and manipulation of the fundamental forces in the universe. Such control is achieved by ritual and incantations, and the climax of the ritual is the invocation of the deity or spirit for some precise purpose. Special garb, sacred vessels and utensils, and secrecy all add to the drama of the rituals, and are instrumental in obtaining contact with and power over the fundamental forces. Groups practicing Witchcraft, Neo-Paganism, and Satanism are all part of the Magick family of cults. Naturally, they tend to have a "bad name," because of the countercultural labels and practices they promote. They have the common goal of promoting the primal life force in the universe, a force they believe to be embodied in all its reality and earthliness in the ancient religions of a Mother goddess, or in the pre-Christian nature religions of Europe, or in the vital power (named Satan)—represented by political forces and human sexuality—that is fundamentally good, but which because of Judeo-Christian prejudices has been taken to be fundamentally bad.

In the last analysis, the term *cult* cannot be used to indicate a negative value judgment. Rather, it should be used to indicate a certain kind of socioreligious reality that is not inferior to the more developed church or the more familiar sect. At their best the cults are centers of vitality, newness, and rebirth, and they provide social liberation and psychological outlet. At their worst they can induce extremely destructive behavior in people—as can all the varieties of human religious experience.

NOTES

1. This discussion is derived from Rodney Stark and William Sims Bainbridge, "Of Churches, Sects, and Cults: Preliminary Concepts for a Theory of Religious Movements," *Journal for the Scientific Study of Religion* 18 (1979): 117–131.

2. Joseph Smith, *History of the Church*, vol. 1 (Salt Lake City: Deseret Book Company, 1902), pp. 5–6.

3. Helen W. Bingham Reminiscences, Archives of the Mother Church, Boston, quoted in Stephen Gottschalk, *The Emergence of Christian Science in American Religious Life* (Berkeley: University of California Press, 1973), p. 29.

4. Mary Baker Eddy, *Science and Health with Key to the Scriptures* (Boston: Trustees under the Will of Mary Baker Eddy, 1906), p. 123.

5. *Ibid.*, p. 96.

6. E. Burke Rochford, *Hare Krishna in America* (Brunswick, N.J.: Rutgers University Press, 1985), pp. 148–49.

7. *Ibid.*, pp. 52–54.

8. *Ibid.*, p. 70.

9. *Ibid.*, pp. 69–71.

10. David G. Bromley and Anson D. Shupe, Jr., *"Moonies" in America: Cult, Church, and Crusade* (Beverly Hills: Sage Publications, 1979), pp. 181–182.

11. Marc Galanter et al., "The 'Moonies': A Psychological Study of Conversion and Membership in a Contemporary Religious Sect," *American Journal of Psychiatry* 136 (1979): 165–170.

12. Marc Galanter, "Psychological Induction into the Large Group: Findings from a Modern Religious Sect," *American Journal of Psychiatry* 137 (1980): 1574–1579.

13. J. Gordon Melton, *Encyclopedic Handbook of Cults in America* (New York: Garland, 1986), p. 9.

SUGGESTED READINGS

BECKFORD, JAMES. *The Trumpet of Prophecy: A Sociological Study of the Jehovah's Witnesses*. New York: John Wiley, 1975.

BROMLEY, DAVID G., and ANSON D. SHUPE. *"Moonies" in America: Cult, Church, and Crusade*. Foreword by John Lofland. Beverly Hills: Sage Publications, 1979.

ELLWOOD, ROBERT S., JR. *Religious and Spiritual Groups in Modern America*. Englewood Cliffs, N.J.: Prentice-Hall, 1973.

GOTTSCHALK, STEPHEN. *The Emergence of Christian Science in American Religious Life*. Berkeley: University of California Press, 1973.

HANSEN, KLAUS J. *Mormonism and the American Experience*. Chicago: University of Chicago Press, 1981.

JACKSON, CARL T. *The Oriental Religions and American Thought: Nineteenth-Century Explorations*. Westport, Conn.: Greenwood Press, 1981.

MARTY, MARTIN. *Pilgrims in their Own Land: 500 Years of Religion in America*. New York: Penguin Books, 1984.

MELTON, J. GORDON. *The Encyclopedia of American Religions*. 2d ed. Detroit: Gale, 1987.

MOORE, R. LAWRENCE. *Religious Outsiders and the Making of America*. New York: Oxford University Press, 1986.

ROCHFORD, E. BURKE, JR. *Hare Krishna in America*. New Brunswick, N.J.: Rutgers University Press, 1985.

STARK, RODNEY, and WILLIAM SIMS BAINBRIDGE. *The Future of Religion: Secularization, Revival and Cult Formation*. Berkeley: University of California Press, 1985.

11

Enduring Questions and Quests

The religious world combines the ancient and the new, the traditional and the experimental, the universal and the particular. Consequently, the religious world is characterized by a variety of questions and quests: some of them basic to human existence as such, some of them of particular importance to communities of faith in the world. The previous chapters contain descriptions and interpretations of a number of such questions and quests. All of the chapters depict individuals and groups (e.g., Native American tribes, African societies, the Indo–Aryans in India) who have understood their living situations to have religious significance, and have interpreted the religious import of their times and places through oral traditions, rituals, institutions, and written documents. Some chapters portray unusually thoughtful individuals (e.g., Gautama, Muhammad) who have had, by most standards of measurement, the necessary ingredients for happy lives, yet were driven to discover meaningful answers to the troubling questions they had about human existence and ultimate reality. Other chapters provide insight into the questions and quests of individuals (e.g., Nichiren, Martin Luther, Moses Mendelssohn) who have attempted to find and formulate new interpretations of the beliefs and practices of the religious traditions to which they belonged.

Human Questions and Quests

We hope that you have been engaged by the questions raised in the preceding chapters and have gained increased understanding of the communities of faith in the religious world. Now we want to raise some additional questions that extend beyond the boundaries of this book and indicate the ongoing nature of the study of religion. After presenting the questions, we will indicate how the world's religions deal with these enduring questions of human existence.

There is, we think, an interesting connection between asking fundamental questions and participating in quests to find the correct answers. The answers are not simple, and not everyone agrees as to which answers are the "correct" ones. Nevertheless, there are important questions about life—sometimes stemming from the intellect, other times arising from emotional experiences—that confront each of us and that are addressed by the world's religions.

To be human (and a person) is to question, and in response to engage in a variety of quests: for survival, for liberty, for truth, for happiness, and, in many cases, for some kind of meaning to life. At least six combinations of fundamental questions and resulting quests comprise human existence. They range from the very practical to the theoretical, as indicated by their order of presentation below.

Survival. Virtually all human beings, with the exceptions of infants who fail to thrive and persons who decide to commit suicide, address the problem of survival and respond by seeking the physical necessities of food, sleep, and shelter. When human life is lived at its extremes (e.g., the experiences of Jews in German concentration camps), thoughts and emotional responses commonly converge around one question: "What must I do to survive?" There are persons, however, who come up with a negative answer to the question of survival. In the United States each year, 27,000 persons (12.6 per 100,000) decide that death is preferable to life and end the normal human effort to survive with an act of self-destruction.

Security. Most persons seek a measure of security, in response to the questions "What can I hold on to?" and "In what or whom can I put my trust?" The precise forms that security may take vary greatly: stable interpersonal relationships, an income-producing job, sufficient money to pay the bills, familiar physical surroundings, a sound marriage, acceptance in a community, an important personal possession, consistent governmental activities, the absence of the threat of war, a predictable future. Although the definition of what makes life secure varies from person to person, and although that which makes life secure for one person may represent intolerable boredom for another, most persons nevertheless need something or someone to hold on to—or else their lives become chaotic.

Quality of Life. Most persons also pursue a certain quality of personal life, in response to questions like "How can I be happy?" and "How can I be the kind of person I want to be?" The precise definition of what the appropriate quality of personal life is ranges from egoism to altruism, from an independent to a submissive life-style, from pessimism to optimism, and from an attempt to collect and use up the materialistic things of life to an effort to do without these symbols of industrialized, technological life. However the quality of personal life is defined, the quest to realize that quality is reflected in an individual's work, expenditure of money, personal associations, family life, and use of leisure time.

Personal Identity. Another quest common to persons is that of personal identity: "Who am I?" Related to the quest for a certain quality of personal life, the quest for personal identity is the pursuit of an accurate self-understanding. Beginning at the age of conscious thought and continuing until serious mental illness, senility, or death makes self-understanding an impossibility, the quest to know oneself is a recurring feature of human existence. Serious attempts to gain this self-understanding require information regarding one's past ("What are my roots?"), an assessment of one's present ("What kind of person am I?"), and an analysis of one's probable future ("What are my goals, and which ones may I realistically hope to achieve?").

Transpersonal Goals. Many persons engage in quests to achieve certain goals that transcend personal concerns. The question "What are the really important goals in life?" has brought forth quests for truth, excellence, liberty, and justice in all periods of history. More than merely personal questions, the myriad attempts to discover the truth, to achieve excellence, to attain liberty, and to bring about justice have been made in the belief that the achievement of even close approximations of these goals stands to benefit the human community by making the world a better place to live. For the benefit of others, numerous writers, artists, philosophers, scientists, religious figures, and political leaders have devoted their careers and, in many cases, been willing to lose their lives—because the importance of one or more of these transpersonal goals was overriding.

Meaning. At some point along the way, many persons address, or at least wonder about, the ultimate question of human existence: "What is the meaning of life?" Depending upon the context in which it is raised, the question may actually be an inquiry regarding the significance of an individual's life ("Is there a purpose to my existence?") or an inquiry into the totality of reality ("Is there a purpose to it all?"). Often the question regarding life's meaning involves both of these subsidiary questions. Unless this ultimate question is immediately dismissed as being pointless or unanswerable, a quest frequently ensues to see if, as a matter of fact, there is some ultimate meaning of life (my own and/or life as such) that can be discovered and around which an individual's life can be focused.

Leo Tolstoy, the nineteenth-century Russian novelist, provides an illustrative example of this quest for meaning. At the age of fifty, Tolstoy was acknowledged as one of the great writers of the world. He had satisfactorily handled most of the important questions and quests of life, and had even wondered if he would become a more famous writer than Gogol, Pushkin, Shakespeare, or Molière had been. But at the height of his fame, he began to ask seriously about the meaning of life and, on more than one occasion, came close to committing suicide. Later, he reflected on this period of his life:

I had tasted of the seduction of authorship, of the seduction of enormous monetary remunerations and applauses for my insignificant labor, and so I submitted to it, as being a means for improving my material condition and for stifling in my soul all questions about the meaning of my life and life in general. . . . Thus I proceeded to live, but five years ago something very strange began to happen with me: I was overcome by minutes at first of perplexity and then of an arrest of life, as though I did not know how to live or what to do, and I lost myself and was dejected. But that passed, and I continued to live as before. But those minutes of perplexity were repeated oftener and oftener, and always in one and the same form. These arrests of life found their expression in ever the same questions: "Why? Well, and then?" . . . .

"But, perhaps I overlooked something, or did not understand something right?" I said to myself several times. "It is impossible that this condition of despair should be characteristic of men!" And I tried to find an explanation for these questions in all those branches of knowledge which men had acquired. I searched painfully and for a long time, and I searched not from idle curiosity, not in a limp manner, but painfully and stubbornly, day and night—I searched as a perishing man searches for his salvation—and I found nothing. . . .

My question, the one which led me, at fifty years, up to suicide, was the simplest kind of a question, and one which is lying in the soul of every man, from the silliest child to the wisest old man—that question without which life is impossible, as I have experienced it, in fact. The question is: "What will come of what I am doing today and shall do tomorrow? What will come of my whole life?"

Differently expressed, the question would stand like this: "Why live, wish for anything, why do anything?" The question may be expressed still differently: "Is there in my life a meaning which would not be destroyed by my inevitable, imminent death?"[1]

Religion and the Question(s) of Meaning

These sets of questions and quests are a perennial feature of human existence and, in many cases, these question-motivated quests can be satisfactorily completed. Many persons succeed in the quests for survival, security, and a satisfying quality of life; a smaller number of persons succeed in the quests for authentic self-understanding and the accomplishment of important transpersonal goals. But what about the quest for the meaning of life? Is this a continually elusive quest, or is it possible for Tolstoy and other persons to find that this quest can also be satisfactorily concluded?

Questions regarding the meaning of life have always been an integral part of the humanities, dating back at least to the times during which *The Epic of Gilgamesh* (c. 2300 B.C.E.) and Homer's *Iliad* and *Odyssey* (c. 850 B.C.E.) were written. Since the periods of these early literary pieces, numerous poets, dramatists, artists, novelists, composers, philosophers, theologians, and historians have addressed various aspects of the meaning of life. Along the way they have raised questions about the meaning of individual lives and of life as such: Why are we here? Why do people suffer? Why do people have to die? Is there a God? Why is there natural evil? Is there personal existence after death?

Among some contemporary philosophers, the question of life's meaning is itself questioned. To ask, "What is the meaning of life?" is sometimes regarded as nonsensical as to ask, "What is bigger than the largest thing in the world?"[2] Specific questions relating to the meaning of life (e.g., those dealing with suffering, death, and so on) may be addressed and wrestled with, but the comprehensive question is often dismissed as absurd, senseless, and, if addressed at all, subject to infinite regression.

Yet, as the philosopher John Wisdom points out, the question of life's meaning takes on meaning itself when life is compared to plays seen in a theater. If you, for example, see only a portion of a play, you might appropriately ask someone else who had seen the entire play, "What does it mean?" In this context, you would be inquiring into the specifics of the play (What happened at the beginning? What did the leading actors do in the play? How did the play end?). If, in contrast, you see an entire play which is unusually difficult to interpret (e.g., Samuel Beckett's *Waiting for Godot*), you could again ask, "What does it mean?" and be asking a very different kind of question. In this second context, the question, far from being nonsensical, is an inquiry into the significance and purpose of the entire play: Was it a satire, or was it intended as a serious statement? Did it have "a point" and, if so, what was it?

In a similar manner the question of life's meaning is

not senseless, and can be addressed by philosophers, religious thinkers, and other reflective persons. When philosophers address the question, two positions are commonly taken. The first position says that the answer to the question of the meaning of *life as such*—and possibly the answer to the question of the meaning of individual lives—is finally no answer or, at best, an elusive one. The universe is in this view unintelligible, unplanned, uncaring, and indifferent to the plight of human beings. The world in which we live is monstrous and savage, as indicated by countless instances of natural evil and human misery. The human condition is most accurately described by the ancient myth of Sisyphus, in which a man was condemned by the Greek gods to roll a large stone repeatedly up a tall mountain only to watch the stone roll back down the mountain of its own weight each time it neared the summit. Therefore, life as such appears to be meaningless, if not absurd. This position is best reflected in the words of the French existentialist philosopher Albert Camus: ''I don't know whether this world has a meaning that transcends it. But I know that I do not know that meaning and that it is impossible for me just now to know it.''[3]

The second, and more common philosophical position states that, whether or not life as such is meaningful, it is possible for *individuals* to have meaningful lives. Even in the face of what may be an unintelligible universe and a hostile world, it is possible for individual human lives to take on meaning. That meaning may be given by someone else through an important interpersonal relationship, and may take the form of being loved, needed, or wanted. Or, perhaps more often, that meaning may be realized through an individual's devotion to a task worth doing or a goal worth achieving for its own sake. That task or goal may, for some religious believers, be understood to be something like the expression of God's glory. For other persons, the task or goal that gives meaning to individual lives may be understood in terms of devotion to one's career, one's family, or the service of others.[4]

In contrast to these philosophical positions, most of the religions discussed in this book claim that both subsidiary questions regarding the meaning of life can be answered affirmatively: life as such has meaning and individual human lives can have meaning, especially as individuals discover the fundamental purposefulness of existence and apply that meaning to their own life situations. The religions do not agree on the precise way of interpreting the meaning of life as such, and often disagree on the specific ways in which individuals can discover religious meaning in their own lives. But most of the religions do agree that life is ultimately good, even though they cannot give that religious claim a factual basis; and they do agree that the individual lives of religious believers often take on a significance they would not otherwise have, even though it is sometimes difficult for these individuals to explain the sense of wholeness they feel in their lives as a result of their religious experiences.

Yet something important happens, and religious believers often claim to have an added dimension to their lives that other persons do not have. The chapters in this book reflect the fact that millions of persons in widely varying times and cultures have engaged in quests for the meaning of life, have discovered—either suddenly or gradually—that life is ultimately good and purposeful, and have then found their lives noticeably changed through that discovery.

Tolstoy again provides an illustrative example. After he had struggled for several years to discover the meaning of life, he stopped to reflect on his quest:

Then I looked at myself, at what was going on within me, and I recalled those deaths and revivals which had taken place within me hundreds of times. I remembered that I lived only when I believed in God. As it had been before, so it was even now: I needed only to know about God, and I lived; I needed to forget and not believe in him, and I died.

What, then, are these revivals and deaths? Certainly I do not live when I lose my faith in the existence of God; I should have killed myself long ago, if I had not had the dim hope of finding him. ''So what else am I looking for?'' a voice called out within me. ''Here he is. He is that without which one cannot live. To know God and live is one and the same thing. God is life.''

''Live searching after God, and then there will be no life without God.'' And stronger than ever all was lighted up within me and about me, and that light no longer abandoned me.[5]

Several twentieth-century studies of religion and psychology have confirmed that persons can, through authentic religious experience, discover an added dimension to their lives that gives them a sense of meaningfulness they would not otherwise have. At the beginning of the century, William James, the American philosopher and psychologist, described religious experience as a process of unification:

> To be converted, to be regenerated, to receive grace, to experience religion, to gain an assurance, are so many phrases which denote the process, gradual or sudden, by which a self hitherto divided, and consciously wrong, inferior and unhappy, becomes unified and consciously right, superior and happy, in consequence of its firmer hold upon religious realities.[6]

The Swiss psychologist Carl Jung later pointed to the important relationship between authentic religious experience and the discovery of life's meaning. He stated:

> Religious experience is absolute. It is indisputable. You can only say that you have never had such an experience, and your opponent will say: "Sorry, I have." And there your discussion will come to an end. No matter what the world thinks about religious experience, the one who has it possesses the great treasure of a thing that has provided him with a source of life, meaning and beauty and that has given a new splendor to the world and to mankind. He has *pistis* [faith] and peace. Where is the criterion by which you could say that such a life is not legitimate, that such experience is not valid and that such pistis is mere illusion? Is there, as a matter of fact, any better truth about ultimate things than the one that helps you to live?[7]

Gordon Allport, an American psychologist, has more recently pointed out the continuing importance of religious belief. The "ever-insistent truth" is, according to his research findings, that

> what a man believes to a large extent determines his mental and physical health. What he believes about his business, his associates, his wife, his immediate future, is important; even more so, what he believes about life in general, its purpose and design. Religious belief, simply because it deals with fundamentals, often turns out to be the most important belief of all.[8]

A Variety of Perspectives on Religious Meaning

Millions of Hindus, Buddhists, Jews, Christians, Muslims, and members of other religious traditions hold beliefs and engage in practices which, as these persons will often attest, give their lives a significance they would not otherwise have. There are serious differences, as well as similarities, among these religious traditions. Yet there is an intriguing consistency with which members of these religions experience, in a variety of ways, an important dimension of life through their religious beliefs and practices.

This extra dimension of life—religious meaning—can for our purposes be described in two ways. First, religious believers, having discovered a fundamental purposefulness to existence, generally find that their religious experiences provide satisfactory answers to most, if not all, of the major questions and quests of life. Second, religious believers often disagree about the precise formulation of life's meaning because they function in different religious and cultural contexts and because, even within the same religion, believers sometimes disagree about which specific aspects of their religion are most significant.

Life's Questions and Religious Meaning

The initial question of survival is addressed in two ways by all of the religions discussed in this book. First, some of the religions allow for cases of justifiable suicide, most notably Hinduism's justification of self-destruction by ascetics who passively accept death, and Buddhism's justification, especially in its Mahayana forms, of the self-destruction of an honorable person in the face of dishonor. Yet, even with exceptional cases such as these, all religions generally regard suicide as a wrongful act. Hinduism and Buddhism usually oppose suicide because it goes against *ahimsa,* the principle of noninjury; Judaism, Christianity, and Islam generally consider suicide wrong because it is an inappropriate way of exercising stewardship over God's gift of life.

Moreover, the survival question often applies in these religious contexts to some kind of personal survival of death, rather than to the more immediate issue of the threat of death imposed by famine, war, torture, or severe hardship. Precisely how religious believers, and possibly all humans, will survive death is open to debate: for Hindus, survival hangs on the continued existence of one's soul; for Buddhists, it depends on the ongoing process of rebirth; for Confucians and Taoists, it is understood in the context of ancestral spirits; and for many Jews, Christians, and Muslims, it involves the passage of one's soul or "spiritual body" to heaven. Even in the portions of the Jewish tradition that doubt the personal survival of death and reject the notion of heaven, there is still an emphasis on surviving death through the continued existence of the people of Israel. The practical result of these religious perspectives is that religious believers have reasons to find a greater depth of meaning in death than do persons who believe that death represents total annihilation.

The second question, that of security, is handled by all religions that postulate a transcendent realm of existence beyond this world. In addition to the stable relationships and societal contexts that normally offer a measure of security to persons, all major religious traditions, with the exception of Theravada Buddhism, offer another dimension of security through their doctrines regarding a force or power or presence ultimately in control of all reality. In contrast to the view that there can be no fundamental security because the world is absurd and the universe unintelligible, most religions put forth the claim that security is finally possible because there is an Ultimate Power—variously described as *Brahman-Atman,* Heaven, the *Tao,* the *kami,* Yahweh, God, or Allah—in which persons can trust and have confidence.

As to the third question, every religion offers the possibility of a certain quality of personal life not frequently found among nonreligious persons. The quality of life held up as normative by a particular religion may be described in terms of certain character traits, or virtues: devotion in Hinduism; compassion in Buddhism; filial piety in Chinese religions; justice in Judaism; faith, hope, and love in Christianity; and submission to God in Islam. The normative quality of life may also be interpreted in terms of certain kinds of conduct: nonharmful actions and disciplined meditation in Hinduism and Buddhism; the five relationships in Confucianism; nonaggressive behavior in Taoism; the five precepts in Buddhism; the ten commandments in Judaism and Christianity, supplemented by the two great commandments to love God and neighbor; and the various obligations (e.g., prayer, fasting) in Islam. When these character traits and modes of conduct are combined over a period of time—as illustrated in the lives of gurus, monks, nuns, priests, and the Confucian "superior man"—the result is an unusual quality of life in which devout religious believers experience a kind of joyous fulfillment and self-realization.

The fourth question, that of personal identity, has several aspects to it, and three of these are especially significant when the question is raised in a religious context. First, in most religions (exceptions are the religions of China and certain portions of Buddhism), the question and quest regarding personal identity take place in a life situation believed to be governed by one or more transcendent powers having certain personal attributes. When that is the case—whether the personal transcendent power is called Yahweh, God, Allah, or Shiva or Vishnu as manifestations of Brahman-Atman—the question takes on the meaning of "Whose am I?" as well as "Who am I?"

Then, too, the question of personal identity, when raised in a religious context, necessarily involves a critical assessment of the human condition and one's place in it. An accurate self-understanding is impossible unless there is awareness of the inherent limitations to human existence (described by various religions in terms of ignorance, suffering, or sinfulness) as well as the realizable possibilities of that existence (e.g., discipline, devotion, duty).

The question of personal identity as raised in the context of most religions also asks about the relation of the individual to the community. Most religions supplement the emphasis upon individual character and conduct with an emphasis upon life in community: a religious believer is not alone, but part of a larger collective body having an important history and future goals. In Buddhism, this emphasis upon life in community is seen in the Sangha; in Christianity, it is seen in the Church. In Judaism and Islam, as well as in Native American and African religions, an accurate self-understanding entails focusing upon one's place in the community of faith.

The fifth question, involving transpersonal goals, is addressed by all religions. The discovery of the truth, for example, has been the goal of countless persons before they arrived at a religious belief; once having discovered the truth for themselves, their urge to share that truth with others is sometimes virtually irrepressible. The importance of the truth in religion can be seen in that two of the world's religions, Buddhism and Christianity, sometimes refer to their founders as "the truth-finder" (the Buddha) and "the truth" (Jesus). The quest for excellence is also a consistent feature of the world's religions, with excellence being understood in terms of prolonged meditative efforts in Hinduism, the completion of the Eightfold Path in Buddhism, the realization of perfection or sanctification in Christianity, and the life of complete submission to Allah's will in Islam. The achievement of religious excellence is noted through the use of honorific titles: *arhat,* saint, Imam, and so forth. The quests for liberty and justice are also seen in most of the world's religions, with Judaism being the most notable example. Because of the exodus from Egypt, the resounding calls for liberty and justice by the Jewish prophets, and the experiences of bondage and persecution endured by Jews in many times and places, Judaism places an unusual emphasis upon liberty and justice.

In addition to addressing these five questions, the religions discussed in this book also provide insights regarding the fundamental question of life's meaning. Most of these religions, in their own ways, affirm the value of *life as such,* either because life is believed to have been created by a transcendent power or because there is a kind of awesome purposefulness and predictability to the ongoing process of life. Moreover, these religions hold out the possibility that *individual human lives can,* because of their functioning in particular religious contexts, *take on meaning* they would not otherwise have. Whether the religion is Hinduism, Buddhism, Taoism, Judaism, Christianity, Islam—or even quasi-religious ideologies such as nationalism or Marxism—the possibility of an individual's life taking on religious meaning depends upon that individual's finding a center of value around which life can be oriented and in devotion to which life can be lived to its fullest. To bring enduring meaning to life, and to give the individual a sense of wholeness, this center of value has to provide significant linkage with the past and with other persons holding the same value, and also provide a significant goal that extends into the future.

Religious Meaning in a Pluralistic Religious World

The world is unquestionably pluralistic in its religious traditions, as well as in its ethnic, racial, and political groups. In terms of the perennial quest for meaning, and the number of times this meaning is discovered in a religious context, this religious pluralism results in a variety of perspectives on what religious meaning is.

The particular religious beliefs and practices that make life authentic for one person or for members of one religion may not, and often do not, make life meaningful for another person or for members of another religion.

Why is this the case? The most obvious reason is that religions, as indicated in this book, disagree on many aspects of doctrine, practice, goals, or institutional life. As a result, the beliefs, practices, and related religious matters that make life meaningful for a Buddhist, precisely because they give the Buddhist a center of value and a sense of wholeness, simply cannot do the same thing for Jews or Muslims or members of other traditions because they do not share the same *center of value.* The beginnings, literature, doctrines, and institutions of Buddhism may be interesting, perhaps even fascinating, to a member of another religion, but they do not provide a framework of orientation and devotion. The words of the Buddha, to cite a specific example, may be interesting and worthwhile to a non-Buddhist, but they simply do not carry the same weight or represent the same kind of guidance as they do for a Buddhist.

Less obvious, perhaps, are the reasons why perspectives on religious meaning sometimes differ significantly within the same religious tradition. Nevertheless, perspectives do differ among Hindus, Christians, and members of other religions. One of the reasons for these diverse perspectives within particular religions is the fragmentation that has occurred in all major religions. As noted in earlier chapters, most Hindus are either Shaivites or Vaishnavites; Jews are generally either Orthodox, Reform, or Conservative in their beliefs and practices; Christians include Roman Catholics, Orthodox Christians, and Protestants; and Buddhists and Muslims have their own respective divisions and groups. These divisions within religions frequently represent long-standing and important differences, usually having to do with doctrine or practice, and sometimes represent more emotional areas of disagreement than do disagreements with other religions. The additional fragmentation of a religion into smaller groups means still other, more narrowly conceived perspectives on religious meaning within that particular religion.

Another reason for the differences within religious traditions is the frequent tendency of believers to give more weight to certain aspects of a religion than to others. Rather than having a holistic perspective in which all parts of a religion contribute to its being the center of value in a believer's life, some persons tend to place more weight on scripture than on ritual, on beginnings than on goals, or on institutions than on doctrines. The result is that some believers, to cite one example, find religious meaning primarily through long periods of studying scripture but find substantially less meaning in the rituals performed in an institutional setting. In some instances, this tendency to focus on only certain aspects of a religion gets to the point of making only one part of a religion absolutely important. When this happens, religious meaning is found exclusively through a religion's founder, or its scripture (and perhaps only one portion of scripture, or the scripture interpreted in only one way), or its institutions, and so forth. Thus, some believers end up with a limited perspective on religious meaning that is not shared by all persons in the same religion.

Perspectives on religious meaning also differ within traditions because people differ in their religious experiences and commitments. Not every religious experience has the depth and enduring quality of Tolstoy's. Not all people are equally committed to their respective traditions. In some instances, in fact, it is obvious that while a person claims to be a Buddhist, a Christian, or a Muslim, the person's center of value is actually found somewhere else: in a job, in a personal relationship, in a serious avocation. Whenever this happens, this person's perspective on religious meaning is significantly different from that of another Buddhist, Christian, or Muslim who has found in religion an added dimension to life that undergirds and strengthens the process of living.

The reasons for religious pluralism are thus multiple, and provide subject matter for debates among religious adherents and ongoing research by scholars in the study of religion. That the religious world is increasingly pluralistic, however, seems beyond serious challenge. In Western Europe and North America, for example, a reasonably small, but increasing number of persons find Buddhism and Islam to be preferable alternatives to Christianity and Judaism, the two religions traditionally strong in those parts of the world.

Even more striking is the emergence of religious pluralism in societies that have tried, in the name of atheism, to stamp out the practice of religion. For example, as indicated in Chapter 6, the People's Republic of China has begun to show toleration for a variety of religious practices in the years following the disastrous "Cultural Revolution" (1966–1976). The Chinese government, in its post-Mao phase under the leadership of Deng Xiaoping, has permitted a limited resurgence of Christianity and Islam as well as a revitalization of the traditional religions of China.

A parallel development has taken place in the Soviet Union. After decades of closing religious institutions and persecuting religious believers, the government of the U.S.S.R. under the leadership of Mikhail Gorbachev has recently begun to tolerate religious practices in a manner unprecedented in the years since the October, 1917 revolution. Although many Russian Orthodox churches have been turned into historical museums, an increasing number of Orthodox churches are now open for religious practice—and are filled by Orthodox Christians several times a week. Likewise, Protestant churches are opening in increasing numbers, and their members, although under frequent surveillance by governmental agents, number approximately one million. Perhaps even more notable, approximately twenty million Muslims carry out many of the practices of Islam in several of the Central Asian republics, even though the Soviet government has previously destroyed many mosques and still has apprehension about the fundamentalist and nationalist appeal of some Islamic leaders outside the U.S.S.R. Even Soviet Jews, many of whom have been denied exit visas from the country, seem to be experiencing a limited amount of religious freedom, especially when compared with their history of being discriminated against and persecuted in that country.

This pattern of religious pluralism, involving differences between religions and within religious traditions, will, we think, continue into the future. The present variety of perspectives on religious meaning is likely to become more complex and almost certainly will continue to spread geographically. The result will undoubtedly be new questions about and quests for religious meaning, and possibly the emergence of significant new perspectives on what religious meaning is. Perhaps some of you will be active participants in discovering or formulating these new perspectives on meaning in the religious world.

NOTES

1. Leo Tolstoy, *My Confession,* in *The Complete Works of Count Tolstoy,* trans. by Leo Wiener (New York, AMS Press, 1968), vol. 13, pp. 16, 25–26.
2. John Wisdom, "The Meanings of the Questions of Life," in *Paradox and Discovery* (Oxford: Basil Blackwell, 1965).
3. Albert Camus, *The Myth of Sisyphus and Other Essays,* trans. by Justin O'Brien (New York: Alfred A. Knopf, Inc., 1955), p. 51.
4. Karl Britton, *Philosophy and the Meaning of Life* (Cambridge: Cambridge University Press, 1969).
5. Tolstoy, *My Confession,* p. 69.
6. William James, *The Varieties of Religious Experience* (New York: New American Library, 1958 ed.), p. 157.
7. Carl Gustav Jung, *Psychology and Religion* (New Haven: Yale University Press, 1938), pp. 113–114.
8. Gordon W. Allport, *The Individual and His Religion* (New York: Macmillan Publishing Co., 1950), p. 89.

Index

Abhidhamma Pitaka, 117, 118, 131
Abraham, 213–14, 231–32
Africa
    Christianity in, 48–50
    Islam in, 34–48, 311, 346, 350
African religions, 32–50
  beliefs, 35–38
  contemporary, 49–50
  healing practices, 41–42
  initiation rites, 42–44
  missionaries, effect of, 33
  moral conduct, 47
  oral tradition, 33
  origins, 33–35
  prophetic movements, 40
  religious institutions, 38–40
  ritual, 42–46
  sacred literature, 3
  sacred places, 36–37
  symbols, 36–37
  tradition, 5, 33–35
  in transition, 48–50
Agni, 52, 57–58, 109
Agnihotra, 52, 57, 59–60, 109
Agricultural rituals, 21–22, 45–46
Ahimsa, 4, 67, 109
Ahl al Dhimma, 330
Ajiva, 65–66, 109, *see also* Jiva
Akan, 37, 47
Akbar, 96, 100
Akiba, 228, 230
Aksobhya, 134
Alberuni, 94–95
Alexander the Great, 224–25
Ali, 333, 334, 335, 341
Allport, Gordon, 379
Amaterasu, 200–201
Amitabha, 145, 147

Amos, 221, 243
Anabaptists, 296
Anatta, 119, 121
Ancestor worship
  African, 44, 45
  Chinese, 138–39, 172–73, 178–79, 181
  Confucian, 178, 179
Anglican Church, 295–96
Animal sacrifice, 44, 45, 91, 174, 235
Annals of Spring and Autumn (Ch'un Ch'iu), 177
Anointing of the Sick, 287
Antony, 280
Apaches, 28
Apostolic Tradition, 271–72
Apostle, 279
Arabia, pre-Islamic, 313
Aramaic, 229
Arapaho, 23, 28
Arhat, 135
Arianism, 274
Aristotle, 246, 286
Arjuna, 83–86
Ark of the Covenant, 220
Artha, 72, 76, 109
Arthashastra, 76
Arts
  African, 33, 45–47
  Buddhist, 153
  Hindu, 76
  Japanese, 155
  Native American, 22
  religion, relation to, 9, 205
Arya, 109
Aryans, 52–63, 109
Arya Samaj, 101–102, 103
Aryavarta, 57, 64, 109

Asceticism
  Buddhist, 69–70, 126
  Hindu, 72, 75, 77–78, 80, 104
  Jain, 66, 80
Ashanti, 46
Ashoka, 127, 133
Ashram, 109
Asia, Islam in, 93–99, 346, 347
Athanasuis, 269
Atharva-Veda, 60
Atheism, 67
Atisha, 161–62
Atman, 61–63, 69, 78, 119, 137
Augustine, 254–55, 276–79
Avatar, 77, 83, 87–88, 90, 109
Ayah, 318
Ayatollah, 336

Ba'al, 219–20, 242
Babalawo, 41
Baganda, 32, 38, 40, 43, 46
Bahai, World Faith, 372
Bambara, 42
Baptism, 270–71
Bar Mitzvah, 240–41
Barth, Karl, 304
Basilica, 272–73
Bas Mitzvah, 241
Benedict, 280–81
Benedictines, 280–81
Benin, 32
Bhagavad Gita, 83–86, 97, 105
Bhagavata Purana, 82–83, 87
Bhakti, 77, 82–83, 104, 136
Bhakti Sutras, 82–83, 86
Bhikkhunis, 129
Birth, rituals of, 18, 44
Bishop, 279

Blacks, *see also* Africa: African religions
    Islamic heritage, 346
Bodhisattva, 132–33, 135, 142
Bonhoeffer, Dietrich, 304
Book of Changes (I Ching), 175, 177, 178
Book of Songs, 172, 174, 177
Book of the Dead (Tibetan), 162
Brahma, 78–80, 88
Brahman, 61–62, 109
Brahmanas, 60–61, 80
Brahmins, 63, 72, 73, 74, 98, 109
Brihadaranyaka Upanishad, 61
Buddha (Gautama), 4, 9–10, 69, 132–33,
    142
    Buddhism, role in, 117
    death, 116
    early life, 114–115
    enlightment, 69, 115
    ministry, 115–116
Buddha-carita, 133
Buddhas, 134–35, 153
Buddhism, 69–71, 113–70
    branches, 5, 131–38, 143–45
    in Burma, 163–66
    in China, 138–49, 166–67
    Confucianism, relation to, 148–49
    contemporary, 7, 163–67
    doctrine, 3, 5, 10, 69–71, 119–23, 126–
        27, 134–38, 151–58
    Five Precepts, 125–26, 129, 130
    Four Noble Truths, 116, 119, 120–21
    Hinduism, relation to, 70–71, 76, 90, 99
    historical developments, 164–67
    historic sites, 141–42
    in India, 53, 56, 64, 69–71
    in Japan, 150–59
    in Korea, 150
    lairy, 129–30
    Mahayana, 5, 131–38, 141–42, 143–45,
        159, 161
    meditation, 4, 70, 125–26, 136, 143–44,
        152, 154–55
    Middle Path, 126–27
    Monasticism, 116, 118, 124, 127–29,
        138–39, 143, 145–47, 149, 150, 153,
        201, 202–203
    Noble Eightfold Path, 121
    origins, 114–16
    persecution, 148–49
    practice, 123–27, 151–57
    ritual, 123–27, 146
    sacred literature, 3, 117–19, 133–35, 139–
        41
    Sarvastivadins, 131
    Shinto, interaction with, 151, 202–205

Buddhism—*Continued*
    in Sri Lanka, 163–65
    in Thailand, 163–65, 167
    Theravada, 5, 131–32, 151, 163–66
    Three Refuges, 123, 130
    Three Treasures, 150
    in Tibet, 159–63
    Vedic religion, relation to, 64, 69–71
    in the West, 167
    White Lotus Societies, 193–94
    Zen, 136, 154–55
Bultman, Rudolph, 305
Burma, Buddhism in, 163–66

Calumet, 16–17
Calvin, John, 293–295
Calvinism, 293–295
Camus, Albert, 378
Canaanites, 219–20
Canonization, 227
Canon of the New Testament, 269
Castes, 71–73, 91, 93
Catholicism, 297–98
Ch'an, 144–45, 155
Chang Chiao, 187
Chang Tao-ling, 186
Charlemagne, 283–285
Ch'eng Huang, 180
Chen Yen, 152
Cherubim, 220
Cheyenne, 28
Chiang K'ai-shek, 196
Chih-i, 143
China
    ancient religions, 6
    Buddhism in, 138–49, 166–67
    Cultural Revolution, 166, 197, 176
Chinese Buddhist Association, 147
Chinese religions, 171–97
    ancestor worship, 178–79, 181
    animal sacrifice, 174
    chronology, 192
    contemporary, 196–97
    doctrine, 172–75
    folk, 189–93
    foreign religions in, 194–96
    gods, 190–93
    hero deification, 190–93
    origins, 171–77
    practice, 175, 177
    religio-political movements, 193–94,
        195–96
Ch'ing Tan, 186
Ching T'u Tsung, 144
Chippewa, 23

Christianity, 254–310
    in Africa, 33, 48–50
    branches, 5
    centers of, 259
    in China, 194–96
    contemporary, 7, 302–308
    doctrines, 4, 293–299
    hierarchy, 279–282
    Hinduism, relation to, 100, 102, 103
    in Japan, 204
    liberalism in, 304–05
    monasticism, 280–281
    Native American religions, interaction
        with, 26, 28–30
    organization, 279–280
    origins, 257–263
    practices, 269–273
    ritual, 270–272
    sacred literature, 265–69
    schism, 282
Christmas, 270
Chuang Tzu, 6, 182–84
Church, definition of, 357
Church of Christ Scientist, 362–65
    beliefs, 363–64
    organization and practice, 364
    social profile, 364–65
Church of Jesus Christ of Latter-day Saints,
        358–62
    beliefs, 359–360
    organization and practice, 360–61
    social profile, 361–62
Church Year, 269–70
Circumcision, 43, 240
City gods, 180, 190
Claudel, Paul, 254
Clitoridectomy, 43
Cluny, Order of, 284–285
Code of Hammurabi, 215
Color, religious significance, 37
Comanche, 28
Communism, religious aspect, 197
Confession, 287
Confirmation, 271–287
Confucianism, 139
    Buddhism, interaction with, 148–49
    as Chinese state religion, 180–81
    doctrines, 5, 178–80
    neo-, 149
    practice, 180–81
    sacred literature, 177–78
    sacrifice in, 180
    Shinto, interaction with, 202
Confucius, 151, 177, 178–79

Consciousness Only School (Yogacara), 137–38, 143, 151
Conservatism, 5–6
Councils
  of Chalcedon, 275–76
  of Constantinople, 275
  of Jabneh, 227, 229
  of Nicaea, 274–75
  of Trent, 298
  of World Buddhism, 164–65
Counter-Reformation, 297–98
Courtship, 18
Covenant, 215–16, 250
Cow, role in Hinduism, 62, 93, 102
Crammer, Thomas, 295
Creation myths, 2
  African, 35–36, 45
  Japanese, 198
  Judaic, 213, 232
  Native American, 13–15
Cremation, 25
Crow (Native American tribe), 13, 24
Crusades, 249, 288
Cults, definition, 357
Culture, religion in context of, 8–9
Cyril of Jerusalem, 271–72

Dalai Lama, 162
Dance
  Hindu, 72, 76, 89–90
  Native American, 15–17, 26, 29–30
Dante, 287–288
Dasas, 53, 57, 109
David, 218
Dayananda Sarasvati, 101–102
Deacon, 279
Dead Sea Scrolls, 230, 244
Death
  African concepts of, 36, 38, 40, 43
  Taoist concepts of, 183–84
  Vedic concepts of, 60
Death songs, 24–26
Deer dance, 15
Dependent origination, doctrine of, 121–22
Dervish, 341
Desire, 120
Deva, 109
Devadasis, 89–90
Devotion
  in Chinese folk religions, 190–91
  in Hinduism, 82–93
Dhammapada, 118
Dharma, 72, 75–76, 84–85, 101, 109, 116–17, 127, 134–35, 137–38, 145, 151
Dharma-kaya, 134

Dharmashastras, 71–72, 109
Dhikr, 323–325
Dhyana, 81, 109, 125
Didache, 279
Digambaras, 68
Diné, 23
Diocletian, 264
Divination
  in African religions, 41, 42
  in Chinese religions, 175, 177
  in Judaism, 243
Divorce
  in African religions, 44
  in Buddhism, 127
  in Hinduism, 74
  in Islam, 332, 333
Diwali, 105, 109
Doctrine, 3–4, see also under individual religions
Doctrine of the Mean, 178
Dogen, 155
Dominic, 285
Dominicans, 285
Donatism, 277–78
Dravidians, 53, 55, 109, see also Indus Valley
Du'a, 323, 325
Dualism, 68, 77, 268
Dura-Europos, 272
Durga, 90, 109

Earth, worship of, 174–75
Easter, 269
Eastern Orthodox Church, 282–84, 287, 298–299
Ebionites, 267–68
Eckhart, Meister, 288
Ecstasy, 221, 243
Eddy, Mary Baker, 362–63
Egwugwu, 45
Egypt, Islam in, 33
Elijah Muhammad, 351, 352
Enlightenment, 299–302
Equality, 99–100
Erasmus, 297
Eskimos
  arts, ritual expression, 22
  death, beliefs regarding, 25
  morality tales, 24
  sacred pipe ritual, 16–17
Essenes, 244, 256
Ethics
  in Jesus' teachings, 262
  Judaic, 241–242
  religion, relation to, 4

Ethiopia, Islam in, 33, 48
Eucharist, 270, 271–72
Europe, influence on Islam, 348–351
Existence, meaning of, 377–79
Exodus, 214–17, 231, 381

Family life
  African, 49
  Islamic, 332–33
Fasting, in Islam, 326
Fatherhood of God, 257–58
Fa Tsang, 143–44
Festivals
  Buddhist, 147
  Christian, 269–70
  Hindu, 83, 88, 91–93, 105
  Islamic, 326, 328–29
  Judaic, 237–241
  Shinto, 202
Filial piety, 178–79
Fire ritual, 52, 57–58, 109, 153
Five Classics (Confucian), 3, 177–78, 188–89
Folk religion, Chinese, 189–93
Four Books (Confucian), 178
Four Noble Truths (Buddhist), 116, 119, 120–21
Franciscans, 285
Francis of Assisi, 285
Fundamentalism, 303–304

Gandhi, 102–104
Ganesha, 91, 109
Gautama, see Buddha
Gelukpa, 162
Gemara, 229, 241
Ghost dance, 26–28
Gikuyu, 33–36, 38–43, 44, 45, 47
Gita Govinda, 83
Gnosticism, 268
Goals, transpersonal, 376–80
God
  African concept, 37–38
  Chinese concept, 173–74
  Hebrew names for, 214–216
  Islamic concept, 320, 321, 322
  Jesus' teachings about, 257–58
  Judaic concept, 216–17, 232
  Kingdom of, 257
  Native American concept, 12, 15, 16
Gods and goddesses, see individual names
Golden Rule, 178
Goma, 153
Gopi, 83, 109
Gospels, 259–260, 262–263

Gotama the Man (Rhys Davids), 117
Grace, 278–79
Great Learning (Confucian), 178
Gryha Sutras, 63
Guru, 74, 98, 109

Haggadah, 239
Hajj, 326–329
Hanukkah, 240
Hanuman, 87–88
Happiness
    Buddhist concept, 120
    Vedic concept, 58–59, 71, 105
Hasidism, 247
Hayy bin Yaqzan, 340
Healing rituals, 20–21, 41–42
Heaven, *see also* Life after death
    Chinese concept, 173–74
    Islamic concept, 321, 322
Hebrew language, 214
Hebrews
    Babylonian exile, 223–24
    early history, 214–215
Hegel, G. W. F., 302
Heresy, 282
Herod, 256
Heroes, as deities, 190–93
Heschel, Abraham, 223, 241
Heyoka, 19
Hijrah, 315, 319, 322
Hinayana, 131–32
Hinduism, 52–112, *see also* Vedic religion
    branches, 5, 83–93, 100–104, 105–106
    Buddhism, interaction with, 69–71, 74–
        76, 79, 99
    caste system, 71–73
    Christianity, interaction with, 100–102,
        103
    classical, 71–93
    contemporary, 104–105, 107
    doctrines, 61–63, 72, 77–82, 83–87, 106
    goals, 72, 75–93
    Islam, interaction with, 93–99, 344, 346,
        347
    Jainism, interaction with, 65–68, 71, 74,
        75, 76, 99
    monasticism, 72, 78–79, 90
    movements
        devotional, 83–93, 97–98
        modern, 100–104
    origins
        non-Vedic, 63–71, 105
        Vedic, 55–63, 105
    poetry, devotional, 82–83, 88, 96–98
    priesthood, 71, 72, 73

Hinduism—*Continued*
    as release from life, 72, 76–96
    as religious organization of life, 71–77
    sacred literature, 4, 56, 106
    Western influences, 99–105
Hippolytus, 271
History, Judaic view of, 233–34
Holi, 105
Holocaust, 249–50
Holy Law (Vedic), 59
Holy People (Navajo), 23–24
Holy Power (Vedic), 59
Honen, 153–54
Hope, as Buddhist concept, 121
Hopi, 26
Hosea, 221–22
Hosso (Yogacara), 151
Ho'zhq', 23–24
Hsün Tzu, 180
Hua Yen, 143–44, 151–52
Hui-yuan, 141
Human nature
    Buddhist concept of, 136
    Confucian concept of, 179–80
Humanism, 99–101, 103–104
Human sacrifice, 172
Hume, David, 301
Hunting rituals, 44
Husband, duties of, 74, 127
Huss, John, 289
Hymns, *see also* Songs
    Hindu, 82, 97
    Islamic, 96
    Vedic, 55–59, 60

Ibadi, 334
Ibn Khaldun, 339
Ibn Taimiyah, 339
Ibo, 37, 43, 45, 47
I Ching, 175, 177, 178
'Id al Adha, 328
Identity, personal, 376–80
Ignatius of Antioch, 279
Ignatius Loyola, 297–98
Image worship, 75–76, 82–83, 86–87, 93,
    94, 98, 101, 104
Imam, 334, 335, 336
Imamah, 334
India
    Buddhism, 69–71
    Hinduism, 71–93, 99–107
    Islam in, 93–99, 349–50
    Jainism, 64–68
    religious violence, 94, 98, 102, 103
    Sikhism, 98

Individual concepts of, 376–80
Individual freedom, 23
Indo-Aryans, *see* Aryans
Indra, 53, 58, 109
Indus Valley, 53–55
Inipi, 19
Initiation rituals, 12, 13, 18–20, 42–44
Inspiration, 226
Institutes of Christian Religion, 293
Interior Gods Hygiene School, 186
Iran, Islam in, 350
Isaiah, 221
Islam, 311–356
    African religions, interaction with,
        33
    beginnings, 312–13
    branches, 6, 333–44
    in China, 149, 347
    conquests, 330–31
    contemporary, 7, 352, 353
    doctrines, 3–4, 320–23
    empires, 347–48
    European influence, 348–51
    Hinduism, interaction with, 93–99
    historical development, 343
    institutions, 330–31
    medieval, 344–46
    mysticism, 340–44
    philosophers, 339–41
    practice, 322–29
    social structure, 331–33
    West, contacts with, 344–46
    Word of Witness, 4
    worship, 323–25
Islamic law, 330–31
Ismailiyya, 336–37
Israel, 249–50
Ithna Ashariyya, 336
Ittoeni, 207

Jainism, 65–68, 109
    branches, 67–68
    doctrine, 4, 65–68
    ethics, 67
    Hinduism, interaction with, 71, 74–76,
        99
    origins, 114
    reality, concepts of, 65–66
    rituals, 68
    suffering, concept of, 65–67
    world view, 65–68
James, William, 398
Japan
    Buddhism in, 150–59
    Christianity in, 206

Japan—*Continued*
  mythology, 198–200
  new religions, 205–208
Japanese religions, 198–209
  gods, 200–201
  modernity, response to, 208–209
  origins, 199
Jatis, 72–73
Jehovah's Witnesses, 365–66
  beliefs, 365–66
  organization and practice, 366
  social profile, 366
Jeremiah, 222
Jerome, 269
Jerusalem, 220, 223, 255–56, 329–30
Jesuits, 194, 297–98
Jesus Christ, 257–58
  doctrines pertaining to, 258–63
  life, 257
  teachings, 257–58
Jew, definition, 213
Jihad, 48, 316, 348
Jinn, 321
Jiva, 65–68, 109
Jnana, 77
Jodo Shu, 154
John, gospel of, 262, 263
John the Baptist, 257
Joshua, 218
Judaism, 213–53
  branches, 5, 235, 240–41, 242–50
  Conservative, 5, 240–41, 248–50
  development, 217–26
  doctrines, 230–34
  early groups, 242–44
  ethics, 241–42
  goals, 250–51
  Graeco-Roman, 224–26
  mosaic, 216–17
  movements
    medieval, 245–247
    modern, 247–50
    prophetic, 220–23, 243–44
  origin, 213–19
  Orthodox, 5, 234, 235, 247–48, 250
  patriarchal, 214
  practice, 235–41
  pre-exilic, 217–19
  Reform, 5, 235–36, 240–41, 247–48, 250
  rituals, 235–241
  sacred literature, 3, 226–230
  talmudic, 245–46
Jung, Carl, 379
Justin the Martyr, 270, 273–74

Ka'ba, 327–29, 331
Kabaka, 40
Kabbalah, 246–247
Kabir, 97–98
Kachina, 16, 21
Kafirs, 95–96
Kali, 91–92, 102, 109
Kalpas, 164
Kama, 72, 76, 109
Kamasutra, 76
Kami, 198, 200, 201
Kant, Immanuel, 301–02
Karaites, 246
Karma, 63–69, 71–73, 80, 82, 97, 98, 99–100, 109, 114–17, 121–22, 126, 146, 162–63
Karma-yoga, 84–86, 97, 102–03, 109
Karttikeya, 91
K'é, 23
Kegon (Hua Yen), 151
Kegyur, 160
Kethubim, 227
Khalifah, 337
Kharijites, 334
Khwariji, 334
Kierkegaard, Soren, 302
Kingdom of God, 257
Kings
  burial of, 173–74
  sacred, 40–41
Kinni-kinnik, 19
Kiowa, 28
Kiva, 16
Knowledge
  Hinduism, way of, 77–80
  Judaism, role in, 250
Knox, John, 294
Koan, 145, 155
Kohen, 243
Ko Hung, 185–86
Kojiki, 198, 199
Koran, *see Quran*
Korea, Buddhism in, 150
Krishna, 83–86, 109
Krishna Consciousness, International Society for, 366–69
  beliefs, 367
  organization and practice, 367–68
  social profile, 368–69
Kshatriya, 72, 73, 110
Kuan Kung, 190–191
Kuan Yin, 147–48, 190
Kukai, 152–53
Kumarajiva, 141

Laity
  Buddhist, 131–33, 147, 152, 163
  clergy, conflict with, 7
Lakshman, 87–88
Laliltavistara, 134
Lamaism, 131, 159–63
Lankavatara Sutra, 133
Lao Tzu, 181
Law
  Islamic, 316, 330, 331, 337
  Judaic, 215–16
Laws of Manu, 65, 73, 76, 104, 127
Legend, 2
Liberalism, 5, 304–305
Life, sanctity of, 126, 242
Life after death
  Judaic concept of, 250
  Native American concept, 26
  as religious goal, 6
  Vedic concept, 60–62, 63
Life cycle
  in African religions, 45
  in Hinduism, 74
  in Native American religions, 18–20
Lila, 79–80, 88, 110
Lingam, 54, 79, 88–89, 110
"Living dead," 36, 43
Locke, John, 300–01
Lodge society, 23
Lotus Sutra, 3, 132–33, 135, 143, 156–57
Love, as doctrine, 8
Luke, gospel of, 264–67
Luria, Isaac, 246–47
Luther, Martin, 290–293, 375
Luzzatto, Samuel David, 234
Lying, 24

Maccabees, 226, 230, 244, 245
Magic, 61
Magick cults, 373
Mahabharata, 82, 83, 122
Mahaparinirvana Sutra, 134
Mahavairocana Sutra, 134
Mahavira, 65, 114
Mahayana, 6, 132–38, 141–45, 159, 161, 166–67
Mahayana sraddhotpada, 133
Mahmud of Ghazni, 94–95
Maimonides, 234, 242, 246, 250
Maitreya, 142
Maji maji movement, 40
Majjhima Nikaya, 127
Malachi, 243

Male
    Chinese concept of, 174
    Shiva as symbol of, 88, 90
Mali, 35, 42–43, 48
Mana, 35, 36, 51
Mandala, 91, 153
Manichaeism, 149, 277
Mankind
    Islamic concept of, 321–22
    Judaic concept of, 232–33
Mantra, 91, 153, 163
Manu, Laws of, 65, 73, 76, 104, 127
Mao Tse-tung, 196–97
Mappo, 157
Marcionism, 268
Mark, gospel of, 264–67
Marpa, 161–62
Marriage, *see also* Husband; Wife
    in African religions, 43, 44
    in Hinduism, 74
    in Islam, 332–33
    in Native American religions, 18
    as sacrament, 287
Masai, 42
Masks, in African religions, 45–47
Masquerades, in African religions, 45–47
Matsu T'ien Hou, 191, 193
Matthew, gospel of, 264–67
Mecca, 312, 313–15, 324, 326–29
Medicine, folk practices, 20–21, 41–42
Medicine men, *see* Shamans
Medicine societies, 17
Medina, 315–16, 317, 329
Meditation
    in Buddhism, 4, 70, 125, 143, 145, 152, 154–55
    in Hinduism, 77–82
Mencius, 179–80, 182
Mendelssohn, Moses, 234, 247, 375
Messianic movements, 26–28
Metaphysical cults, 372–73
Methodism, 296–97
Micah, 222
Middle Path (Buddhist), 126–27
Midrash, 241
Mihrab, 325
Milarepa, 161–62
Minaret, 325
Mishnah, 228–9, 241, 245
Missionaries
    in Africa, 33
    in China, 194–95
    in India, 93, 102
Mi Tsung, 152
Mohenjodaro, 53, 54, 55

Moksha, 72, 77 ff.
Monarchians, 274
Monasticism
    Buddhist, 116, 118, 123–24, 127–29, 138–39, 143, 145–47, 149, 150, 153, 202–203
    Christian, 280–81
    Hindu, 72, 74–75, 79, 90
    Jain, 66–67
    Taoist, 188–89
Monolatry, 232
Monophysitism, 276
Monotheism, 232
Montanos, 268–69
Moon, Sun Myung, 369
Moral conduct
    Buddhist, 125–27
    Christian, 258–262
    Hindu, sva-dharma, 76, 110
    Islam, 322
    Jain, 67
    Native American, 22–24
    religion, relation to, 22–24, 47
    ritual, relation to, 4
Morality tales, 24
Moran, 42
Mormon, book of, 359
Moses, 214–16, 242
Mosque, 324, 325, 331
Mountains, as sacred places, 34, 37
Mount Sinai, 215–17
Mourning rituals, 24–25, 29
Mudra, 153, 159
Muezzin, 325
Muhammad
    life, 313–16
    significance, 316–17
Muhammed, Elijah, 351–52
Mujtahid, 336
Murder, 241–42
Music, *see also* Hymns; Songs
Muslim, meaning of, 322
Mutazilah, 337–39
Mysticism, 10
Mythology
    African, 34–37, 41
    creation myths, 2, 13–15, 34–37, 198, 213, 232
    Dogon, 35
    Japanese, 198–200
    Judaic, 213, 232
    Native American, 13–15

Nagarjuna, 136–37
Naming ceremonies, 17–18

Nanak, 97–98
Nandi, 42
Nan-in, 155
Nan-wu A-Mi-T'o-Fo, 144
Nation of Islam, 352–53
Native American Church, 28–29
Native American religions, *see also* names of Indian tribes
    agricultural rituals, 21
    arts, expression of, 22
    Christianity, interaction with, 25, 28–30
    costume, ceremonial, 21
    death, practices related to, 24–26
    doctrine, 12
    healing rituals, 20, 21
    initiation rituals, 12, 13
    location of tribes, 14, 27
    moral conduct, 22, 24
    movements
        messianic, 26–30
        prophetic, 26–30
    nature in, 15–16
    oral tradition, 12
    rituals, 12–13, 15, 16, 22, 24–26, 27–30
    sacred literature, 3
    sexual behavior, rules of, 22, 23, 24
    shaman, role of, 16, 19, 20
    societies, 16–19, 20, 21, 22, 23, 30
    supernatural, belief in, 15, 16
    tradition, 5
    transition, 26–30
    vision quest, 18–20
Nature
    African concepts of, 38
    Islamic concepts of, 321
    Native American concepts of, 13–15, 16
    Vedic concepts of, 57–63
Natyashastra, 76
Navajo, 22, 23–24
Nehru, Jawaharlal, 103–104
Nembutsu, 154
Neo-Platonism, 277
Nero, 263–64
Nestorian Christianity, 100, 149, 194, 275–76
New Testament, development of, 265–69
Nez Percé, 20
Nichiren, 155–59, 375
Nihongi, 198, 201
Nirvana, 7, 8, 70, 117–19, 122–23, 129, 132, 135, 136
Noble Eightfold Path (Buddhist), 120–21, 122
Nootka, 22

North America, Islam in, 351–52
Nuns
    Buddhist, 116, 118, 123, 129, 146–47
    Jain, 66

Ogun, 44–45
Ojibwa, 21
Omaha (Indian tribe), 18, 19, 24, 25
Om Mani-padme Om, 163
Omoto Group, 208
Oral tradition, 3, 5, 13, 33
Ordination, 7, 287
Origen, 274
Orisha, 34, 35
Osage, 13–15, 25
Outcastes, 63, 72, 73

Pachomius, 280
Paiute, 24, 28
Pali texts, 117, 139
Pao P'u Tzu, 185–86
Papago, 17, 21
Parajika, 128
Parinirvana, 123
Parshva, 65
Parvati, 90, 110
Passover, 238–39
Paul of Tarsus, 260–262
Pawnee, 17
Pelagianism, 277–78
Penance
    in Native American religions, 23–24
    as sacrament, 287
Pentateuch, 241
Personal identity, 376–80
Pesach, 238–39
Peter, 285–287
Peyote and peyotism, 28–29
Phallus, see also Lingam
    images of, 54, 88–89, 103
Pharisees, 244, 256
Pilgrimage
    Christian, 288
    Hindu, 82, 86, 88–90, 92, 104
    Islamic, 326–29
    Shinto, 199
Plains Indians
    burial rituals, 25
    courtship rituals, 18
    ghost dance, 26–28
    sacred pipe ritual, 16–17
Plato, 246, 274, 280
Pleasure
    Buddhist concept of, 120
    Hindu concept of, 72, 76

P. L. Kyodan, 207
Pluralism, 381–82
Poetry, devotional, 55–59, 84–85, 88, 97–98
Polygamy, 45, 332–33
Polytheism, 232
Pomca, 18
Pope, 281–82
Pope Gregory, the Great, 281–82
Pope Leo, the Great, 281–82
Pope Pius XI, 305
Pope Pius XII, 305–06
Powwows, 29–30
Prabhupada, Swami, 366–67
Prajna-paramita, 133
Prakriti, 77–78, 110
Pratimoksha, 128
Predestination, 278–79, 294–95
Presbyter, 279, 293
Priesthood
    Christian, 279–80, 287
    Hindu, 72, 73
    Judaic, 243
    Shinto, 201, 203–04
    Taoist, 187–89
Prophetic movements
    African, 37, 40, 41
    Judaic, 220–223, 243–244
    Native American, 26–28
Propriety, as virtue, 176, 196
Prostitution, sacred, 89, 90, 219–220
Protestantism, 5, 7, 290–297
Psychic cults, 373
Puberty rituals, 19
Pudgala, 131
Pudgalavadin, 131
Pueblo (Indian tribe), 16, 21
Puja, 88, 110, 123
Pure Land (Ching T'u Tsing), 144–45, 147, 153–54
Purim, 240
Purusha, 77–78, 106, 110
Pygmies, 36

Qiblah, 324, 325, 331
Quran, 3, 317–329

Radha, 83
Radical Christian Morality, 258
Raka'h, 324
Rama, 87–88, 110
Ramadan, 326
Ramakrishna, 102
Ram Mohan Roy, 100–101
Ramayana, 82, 87–88

Ratnasambhava, 134
Rauschenbush, Walter, 304
Reality
    Buddhist concept, 69–70
    Jainist concept, 65–67
    Vedic concept, 57–63
Rebirth, 69–70, 79
Record of Rites (Li Chi), 177
Reformation, 288–297
Reincarnation, see also Transmigration, Rebirth
    Buddhist, 69–70, 121–22
    Hindu, 71–72, 110
    Jain, 64, 66
    Judaism, 247
    of women, 66
Release, quest for, 66, 70, 72, 77 ff.
Religion, see also individual religions
    appreciation, 10
    arts, relation to, 9, 22
    branches, 5–6
    in contemporary society, 7–8
    criticism, 10
    cultural context, 8–9
    definition, 1–2
    ethics, relation to, 4
    goals, 6–7
    human needs and, 375–77
    moral conduct, relation to, 23–24, 47–48
    organization, 5, 7
    origins, 2–3
    role, 1
    social structure, role in, 5, 6, 7
    study of, 8–10
Religious experience, understanding of, 9–10
Renaissance, 299–300
Resurrection, 260
Revelation, 226
Revolution, Age of, 302–06
Righteousness, as doctrine, 178, 179
Rig-Veda, 53, 55–61, 80, 88, 90, 110
Rinzai, 155
Rissho Kosai Kai, 207
Ritual, 3, see also under individual religions
    agricultural, 21, 44–45
    arts expressed through, 22, 46–47, 155
    courtship, 17–18
    dance as, 15–17, 89–90
    healing, 20–21, 41–42
    hunting, 44–45
    moral conduct and, 4
Roman Catholicism, 297
Rosh Hashanah, 237
Rousseau, Jean Jacques, 301

Russell, Charles Taze, 365
Rutherford, Joseph Franklin, 365–66

Saadya ben Joseph, 246
Sabbath, 237
Sacraments, 270–72, 287
Sacred drinks, 58, 60
Sacred literature, 3, *see also* under individual
    religions; specific texts
    as literature, 8–9
Sacred pipe, 16–17
Sacred places, *see also* Pilgrimage, 36–37,
    92
Sacred Thread, 4, 74
Sacrifice
    in African religions, 44–45
    animal, 37, 44, 174, 235
    in Confucianism, 180
    in Hinduism, 91
    human, 172
    in Judaism, 214, 226, 235
Sadducees, 244, 246, 256
Sages, 244
Saicho, 152
Sakyamuni, *see* Gautama
Salat, 323, 324, 325
Salvation
    Buddhist concept, 144
    Christian concept, 261
Samadhi, 70, 80–81, 106, 110, 125
Sama-Veda, 60
Samkhya, 77–79
Samsara, 7, 122, 123, 136–37
Samuel, 221
Sand painting, 16, 20
Sangha, 127, 128, 131, 141
Sanhedrin, 244
Sannyasin, 74–75, 110
Sanron, 151
Sanskrit, 55, 63, 97, 110, 112, 117, 142–
    43
Sarvastivadins, 131
Satori, 155
Saul, 218, 221
Savanarola, 289
Savitar, 52, 57, 58, 59, 110
Schism, 282
Schleiermacher, Friedrich, 302
Schleitheim, Confession of, 296
Scripture, 226–28, *see also* specific texts
Seasons, rituals relating to, 237–41
Second Coming, 259–60
Sects, definition, 357
Secularism, 6–7, 303
Security, 376–80

Self
    Buddhist concept, 69–70, 119–20
    Hindu, 77–80
    Jain, 65–66
    Vedic concept, 61–63
Self-realization, 379
Seminole, 15, 22
Seneca, 15
Separation of church and state, 6
Septuagint, 227, 230
Sexual behavior
    in African society, 48
    in Native American society, 23
Sexual pleasure, 76
Shahadah, 323
Shah Jahan, 96, 100
Shaivism, 5, 79, 88–92, 102
Shakti, 90, 91, 110
Shaman, *see also* Witchdoctor
    in Chinese religions, 187
    as healer, 21
    in Native American religions, 16, 17, 20,
        31
Shankara, 79–80
Shariah, 330–32, 337, 341
Shavuoth, 239–40
She chi, 174
Shema, 230–31, 232
Shembe, Isaiah, 49–50
Shen Nung, 180, 190
Shia, 96, 334–36, 338
Shingon, 154
Shinran, 152–54
Shinto, 151, 198–205
    Buddhism, interaction with, 151, 202–204
    Confucianism, interaction with, 203
    doctrine, 4
    Emperor as deity, 204–205
    festivals, 202
    historical developments, 203–206
    practice, 201–205
    priesthood, 201, 203–205
    ritual, 201–202
    Taoism, interaction with, 203
Shiva, *see also* shaivism, 79, 88–92, 102,
    110
Shiva, family of, 88–92
Shivaratri, 91
Shoshone, 25
Shotoku, 150–51
Shrines
    Buddhist, 124
    Judaic, 235
    Shintoist, 201–202
Shudra, 72, 73, 74, 97, 110

Shunning, 23
Siddhartha, *see* Gautama
Sikhs, 98
Sila, 128
Sioux
    burial rituals, 24–25
    moral conduct, 23
    sacred pipe ritual, 16–17
    vision quest, 18–20
Sita, 87–88
Skandhas, 120, 121
Smith, Joseph Jr., 358–59
Social Gospel movement, 7, 304
Social responsibility, as Judaic concept, 242
Social structure, religion's role in, 5, 6–8,
    23–24, 40–42
Societies, ceremonial
    dance, 16, 21, 29–30
    lodge, 23
    medicine, 17
Soka Gakkai, 207–208
Solomon, 218, 220, 224
Soma, 58, 60, 110
Songhay, 34
Songs
    in agricultural rituals, 21–22
    death, 24–26
    initiation, 42
    Native American, 21, 23–26
Soto Zen, 155
Spirits
    in African religions, 36
    evil, 36
    images of, 22
    in Native American religions, 16
Spiritual intermediaries, 41–42
Spirit worship, 127, *see also* Ancestor wor-
    ship
Sri Lanka, 163–165
Srimala, 134
Stupa, 129
Suffering
    Buddhist concept, 69–71, 119–121
    Jain concept, 65–68, 71
Sufis, 93, 96–97, 98, 339, 341–44
Suicide, 66–67, 376
Sukhavati-vyuha, 133
Sukkoth, 237–38
Summa Theologica, 286
Sunday, 269–70
Sun gods, 52, 57, 58, 59, 110
Sunnah, 4, 317, 330–31, 337
Sunnis, 6, 95, 337, 339
Surah, 318
Sutra, 161

Sutras of the Perfection of Wisdom, 133
Suttanipata, 117–18
Sutta Pitaka, 117–19, 131
Sva-dharma, 76, 85, 102, 110
Synagogues, 223, 235–36, 239
Synod of Dort, 295
Synoptic problem, 264–67

Tafsir, 320, 335
T'ai Hsu, 166
Takbir, 325
Talmud, 3, 228–29, 245
Tangyur, 161
T'an-luan, 144
Tantra, 159–162
Tantrayana, 159–61
Tao, 8, 171–72, 181–182
Taoan, 141
Taoism, 6, 140, 181–89
    doctrine, 181–186
    monasticism, 188–89
    movements, 186–87
    practice, 186–89
    priesthood, 187–89
    ritual, 187
    sacred literature, 181–86
Tao Shih, 187, 188
Tao Te Ching, 181–82, 184, 186
Tao Tsang, 184
Tariqah, 341
Tattooing, 22
Tawhid, 320, 339, 341
Temple chariots, 93
Temple of Solomon, 220–21, 224, 235, 243
Temple prostitution, 89–90
Temples, *see also* Shrines
    Buddhist, 90, 148–49
    Confucian, 180–81
    Hindu, 82, 86, 88, 89–90
    Taoist, 187
Ten Commandments, 215, 216, 241–42, 243
Tendai, 151–52
Tenri-Kyo, 206–207
Tertullian, 269, 270, 273
Thailand, Buddhism in, 167
Theravada, 5, 130–32, 151, 163–66
Thomas Aquinas, 285–86
Three Refutes, 123, 130
Three Treasures, 150
Thunderbird, 29, 31
Tibet, Buddhism in, 159–63
T'ien, 174
T'ien T'ai, 143–44, 152
Tillich, Paul, 305
Tirthankara, 65

Tlingit, 22
Tolstoy, Leo, 376–78
Torah, 3, 215, 227, 228, 230–31, 234, 235, 237, 239, 244, 246, 250, 251
Tosefta, 229
Totem poles, 22
Tradition
    in African religions, 5, 35
    in Chinese religions, 196
    in Native American religions, 5
    social change and, 7
Transmigration, 110, *see also* Reincarnation, Rebirth
Transubstantiation, 286
Trees, as sacred beings, 36
Trikaya, 134
Trinity, concept of, 274–76
Tripitaka, 3, 117, 132
Tsawataineuk, 25
Tsongkhapa, 162
T'u Ti Kung, 174, 180

Uddalaka Aruni, 61–63, 79, 80, 110
Umma, 90, 110
Ummah, 316, 322, 330–33, 334
Unification Church, 369–71
    beliefs, 369
    organization and practice, 369–70
    social profile, 370–71
Upanishads, 61–63, 71, 78, 100–101, 110, 114

Vaishnavas, 83–88
Vaishnavite, 5, 83–88
Vaishya, 68, 72, 73, 110
Vajradhara, 134, 159
Vajrayana, 159
Varna, 57, 71, 110
Varuna, 58, 110
Vasubandhu, 137–38
Vatican, Second Council of the, 308
Vedanta, 77–80
Vedanta Sutra, 78
Vedic religion, 55–63
    Buddhism, interaction with, 64–65, 69–71
    doctrine, 55–63
    happiness, concept of, 52, 57–59, 61–62, 71
    Holy Law, 59
    hymns, 52, 53, 55–60
    Jainism, interaction with, 64–65, 71
    modern movements, 101–102
    nature in, 59
    rituals, 57–61

Vegetarianism, 130
Vimalakirti Sutra, 133
Vinaya, 148
Vinaya Pitaka, 117–18, 128
Vishnu, 58, 83–88
Vishnu, avatars of, 83–88
Visions, 18, 19–21, 25, 29
Vivekananda, Swami, 102
Vulgate, 169

Wakan Tanka, 20
Water, sacredness of, 36
Wesley, John, 9, 296–297
Western civilization
    Buddhism, interaction with, 164
    Hinduism, interaction with, 99–55
    Islam, interaction with, 344–46, 348–51
    religion, role in, 6
White Lotus Societies, 193–94
Widows, 74, 96, 101, 102
Wife, 74, 127
Wisdom, 179, 181
Wisdom, John, 377
Witchcraft, 42
Witchdoctor, 41–42
Women
    in Buddhist society, 127, 130, 146–48
    in Chinese society, 174
    in Hindu society, 74, 91, 101, 102
    in Islamic society, 332
    in Jain society, 66–68
    ordination, 8, 199
    reincarnation, 66
    in Shinto priesthood, 199
Woodland Indians, 17
Word of Witness (Islamic), 4
World, withdrawal from, 66–68, 69–70, 71, 77–93
World Council of Churches, 308
World view, *see also* Creation myths
    African, 37–38
    Buddhist, 69–71, 164
    Jain, 65–68, 71
    Native American, 19, 23
    Vedic, 55–63
Worship, *see also* Ritual
    ancestor, 36, 44, 138–39, 172–73, 178–79, 181
    Hindu, 52, 74, 82, 85–93, 101–105
Wu-wei, 182, 186
Wycliffe, John, 289

Ximenes, Cardinal, 297

Yajnavalkya, 61–63, 79, 110
Yajur-Veda, 60
Yin and Yang, 197
Yoga, 55, 70, 80–82, 90, 114, 125
    bhakti-, 81
    hatha-, 81
    jnana-, 82
    karma-, 82, 85–86, 97, 102–03, 109
    raja-, 70, 81
Yogacara, 137–38, 143, 151
Yoga Sutra, 70, 80, 81
Yogi, 110
Yogin, 55, 56, 90, 110

Yom Kippur, 237, 250, 251
Yoni, 54, 89, 110
Yoni parast, 91
Yoruba
    creation myths, 34
    divination practices, 41
    hunting rituals, 44–45
    proverbs, 47
    religious institutions, 38
Young, Brigham, 361

Zaddik, 247
Zakat, 325–26

Zaydiyya, 337
Zealots, 244–45, 256
Zen, 136, 154–55
    Rinzai, 155
    Soto, 155
Zimbabwe, 32
Zimmis, *see* Ahl al
    Dhimma
Zionism, 249–50
Zohar, 246
Zulus, 49
Zuni, 16, 22
Zwingli, Ulrich, 293